COMMONWEALTH PRINCIPLES

Republican Writing of the English Revolution

The republican writing of the English revolution has attracted a major scholarly literature. Yet there has been no single volume treatment of the subject, nor has it been adequately related to the larger upheaval from which it emerged, or to the larger body of radical thought of which it became the most influential component. *Commonwealth Principles* addresses these needs, and Jonathan Scott goes beyond existing accounts organised around a single key concept (whether constitutional, linguistic or moral) or author (usually James Harrington). Linking various social, political and intellectual agendas, Professor Scott explains why, when classical republicanism came to England, it did so in the moral service of a religious revolution. The resulting ideology hinged not upon political language, or constitutional form, but upon Christian humanist moral philosophy applied in the practical context of an attempted radical reformation of manners. This opposed not only private interest politics, embodied by monarchy or tyranny, on behalf of the publicly interested virtues of a self-governing civic community. It was part of a more general critique of private interest society: a republican attempt, from pride, greed, poverty and inequality, to go beyond the mere word 'commonwealth' and reconstitute what Milton called 'the solid thing'.

JONATHAN SCOTT is Carroll Amundson Professor of British History at the University of Pittsburgh and is now established as one of the most important historians of the seventeenth century writing today. This association of author and topic will render *Commonwealth Principles* essential reading for numerous scholars of British history, political theory and English literature.

COMMONWEALTH PRINCIPLES

PRINCIPLES

Republican Writing of the English Revolution

JONATHAN SCOTT

University of Pittsburgh

CAMBRIDGE
UNIVERSITY PRESS

PUBLISHED BY THE PRESS SYNDICATE OF THE UNIVERSITY OF CAMBRIDGE
The Pitt Building, Trumpington Street, Cambridge, United Kingdom

CAMBRIDGE UNIVERSITY PRESS
The Edinburgh Building, Cambridge, CB2 2RU, UK
40 West 20th Street, New York, NY 10011–4211, USA
477 Williamstown Road, Port Melbourne, VIC 3207, Australia
Ruiz de Alarcón 13, 28014 Madrid, Spain
Dock House, The Waterfront, Cape Town 8001, South Africa

http://www.cambridge.org

© Jonathan Scott 2004

First published 2004

Printed in the United Kingdom at the University Press, Cambridge

Typeface Adobe Garamond 11/12.5 pt.   *System* LATEX 2$_\varepsilon$ [TB]

A catalogue record for this book is available from the British Library

Library of Congress Cataloguing in Publication data
Scott, Jonathan, 1958–
Commonwealth principles : republican writing of the English revolution / Jonathan Scott.
p.   cm.
Includes bibliographical references (p.) and index.
ISBN 0 521 84375 8
1. Great Britain – History – Puritan Revolution, 1642–1660 – Historiography.   2. Great Britain –
History – Commonwealth and Protectorate, 1649–1660 – Historiography.   3. Great Britain –
History – Commonwealth and Protectorate, 1649–1660 – Sources.   4. English prose
literature – Early modern, 1500–1700 – History and criticism.   5. Politics and literature – Great
Britain – History – 17th century.   6. Great Britain – History – Puritan Revolution, 1642–1660 –
Sources.   7. Political science – Great Britain – History – 17th century.   8. Republicanism – Great
Britain – History – 17th century.   9. Radicalism – Great Britain – History – 17th century.   1. Title.
DA403.S36   2004
941.06′3 – dc22   2004045709

ISBN 0 521 84375 8 hardback

For J. C. (Colin) Davis

Contents

vii

Preface

My doctoral and subsequent work upon Algernon Sidney (1623–83) yielded three wider perspectives. One was an argument concerning 'the shape of the seventeenth century'.[1] Another was a view of the European context of that period of English history which placed emphasis upon the formative influence of the United Provinces.[2] The third was an account of English republican thought alternative to that usually arrived at through the study of James Harrington.[3] It is to this last that I turn here, partly on the grounds that there still exists no single book-length introduction to a subject of relatively recent, though now buoyant, historiographical coinage.[4]

Thus in the first place this book draws heavily upon, and attempts to assess, a still-developing historiography of remarkable richness.[5] This connects subjects ancient, early modern and modern; continental Europe, the British Isles and the Americas; and social, economic, religious, political and intellectual history. This reflects the intellectual content of a body of seventeenth-century writing which itself spanned Renaissance, Reformation and Enlightenment, and had a wide, indeed global, subsequent impact.

[1] Jonathan Scott, *England's Troubles: Seventeenth-Century English Political Instability in European Context* (Cambridge, 2000). See also Scott, 'Radicalism and Restoration: the Shape of the Stuart Experience', *Historical Journal* 31, 2 (1988); Scott, 'England's Troubles: Exhuming the Popish Plot', in Tim Harris, Paul Seaward and Mark Goldie (eds.), *The Politics of Religion in Restoration England* (Oxford, 1990).

[2] This theme of *England's Troubles* is further explored in Jonathan Scott, 'What the Dutch Taught Us: the Late Emergence of the Modern British State', *Times Literary Supplement* (16 March 2001); Scott, '"Good Night Amsterdam." Sir George Downing and Anglo-Dutch Statebuilding', *English Historical Review* 118, 476 (2003).

[3] J. G. A. Pocock, 'England's Cato: the Virtues and Fortunes of Algernon Sidney', *Historical Journal* 37, 4 (1994) esp. pp. 917–21; Jonathan Scott, 'Classical Republicanism in Seventeenth-Century England and the Netherlands', in Martin van Gelderen and Quentin Skinner (eds.), *Republicanism: a Shared European Heritage* (2 vols., Cambridge, 2002) vol. 1, pp. 61–81.

[4] The nearest we have to this are the four chapters by Blair Worden in David Wootton (ed.), *Republicanism, Liberty and Commercial Society 1649–1776* (Stanford, 1994). The present study precedes its own chronological account with contextual and textual analysis.

[5] Daniel Rodgers, 'Republicanism: the Career of a Concept', *Journal of American History* 79 (June 1992); James Hankins, 'Introduction', in Hankins (ed.), *Renaissance Civic Humanism: Reappraisals and Reflections* (Cambridge, 2000).

It did so partly because the republican writing of the English revolution constitutes one of the finest bodies of political literature in the English language.[6] In addition, in the course of a penetrating engagement with the failures as well as hopes of one past society in crisis, it aspired to universal observations concerning the human condition.

The specific objective of this study is to supplement the work of those who have given accounts of English republicanism by reference to a single key concept (constitutional, linguistic or moral), or author (usually Harrington), with an analysis of this body of writing as a whole.[7] This attempts to show that we are less likely to understand English republicanism through Harrington's *The Commonwealth of Oceana* (1656), than we are to understand *Oceana* by relating it to the context of the republican and other political writing from which it emerged. One result is the demonstration that Harrington's republicanism was highly atypical.[8] Another, restored to its religious as well as humanist context, will be a reconsidered account of classical republicanism in England. This hinged not upon political language, or constitutional form, but upon Christian humanist moral philosophy applied in the practical context of an attempted radical reformation of manners.[9]

To seek thus to restore the appropriate relationship of texts to context is no more than to follow the methodological injunctions made famous by that university (of Cambridge) where this book was begun. Yet within the history of political thought contextual methodology is a partially realised aspiration. As it remains common to characterise a tradition of thought by reference to one or a few paradigmatic texts, so where contextualisation occurs it is more likely to be intellectual than political. Republican political thought has not always been systematically related to the larger upheaval (England's troubles) from which it emerged. Nor has it been integrated with

---

[6] The predominant focus here is upon prose. For republicanism and poetry see David Norbrook, *Writing the English Republic: Poetry, Rhetoric and Politics 1627–1660* (Cambridge, 1999).

[7] For an analysis organised around one constitutional idea, see Zera S. Fink, *The Classical Republicans: an Essay in the Recovery of a Pattern of Thought in Seventeenth Century England* (Evanston, Ill., 1945). For republicanism as a language see J. G. A. Pocock, *The Machiavellian Moment: Florentine Political Thought and the Atlantic Republican Tradition* (Princeton, 1975). For a discussion devoted to the recovery of a moral concept see Quentin Skinner, *Liberty before Liberalism* (Cambridge, 1997); Skinner, 'Classical Liberty, Renaissance Translation and the English Civil War', in Skinner, *Visions of Politics. Volume II: Renaissance Virtues* (Cambridge, 2002). All take Harrington's thought to exemplify English republicanism as a whole, as does Worden in chapters 1–4 of Wootton, *Republicanism*. See my review of the latter in *Parliamentary History* 16, 2 (1997).

[8] Jonathan Scott, 'The Rapture of Motion: James Harrington's Republicanism', in Nicholas Phillipson and Quentin Skinner (eds.), *Political Discourse in Early Modern Britain* (Cambridge, 1993).

[9] Scott, *England's Troubles*, in particular Part II. For the role of Christian humanism see especially chapters 2–3 below. For moral philosophy see especially chapters 7–8.

the larger body of radical thought (the English revolution) of which it was the most influential component. Above all there has been a historiographical disassociation between that revolution's classically informed political republicanism and its religiously inspired social radicalism. One reason for this is that the major historians of classical republicanism have tended to treat it as a secular, or secularising, ideological force. Another is that the most important historian of that social radicalism, the late Christopher Hill, had ideological preoccupations which led him to be less interested in classical republicans than in plebeian sectaries. The eventual exception to this rule was Milton, portrayed by Hill as a plebeian 'heretic' rather than a Christian humanist.[10] In fact, just as the revolution may be seen as a single intellectual process, so republicanism combined radical protestantism and anti-monarchical humanism. We will not understand it until we reintegrate our examination of its religious, social and political agendas: until we combine the worlds of Pocock, Hill and others.

This study does not pretend to have identified, let alone adequately treated, all relevant contexts of the subject. It does, however, attempt to give equal weight to long- and short-term contexts, and to ideas and events, in relation to both of which it subjects a range of key texts (and others) to comparative analysis. This analysis is first thematic, and then chronological. The objective is to assess, within a body of writing united in the prosecution of a cause, the nature and extent of its shared concerns, its internal variety and its development over time. We will find in the process that English republicanism cannot be reduced to that anti-monarchical component which was a negative precondition for the achievement of positive objectives. Nor can it be associated with a single political language, or constitutional prescription, not only because there were many of each, but because these things were held by most republicans to be secondary forms, adaptable in relation to an unchanging moral substance.

The writing of this book was made possible by the award of a British Academy Research Readership. Although an academic appointment in the United States cut my tenure of that award from two years to one, I am deeply grateful to the Academy, and especially Dr Ken Emond, for making that possible. I am no less grateful to Downing College, Cambridge, for the same support, and much else besides, over a very happy period of eleven years. Nor have my colleagues and students at the University of Pittsburgh

---

[10] Christopher Hill, *Milton and the English Revolution* (1977). Although its anti-intellectual posturing is tiresome, and its anti-classicism leads to the neglect of much that was important to Milton himself, this is a deeply learned study, particularly of the religious content of the major poems.

given me reason to be anything other than delighted with a new job and phase of life in that beautiful city.

This book is dedicated to Colin Davis, with whom it was first discussed twenty-three years ago, and who has throughout the intervening period continued to teach me about much more than history. Not for the first time I am indebted to the friendship and scholarship of James Belich, Mike Braddick, Glenn Burgess, Patrick Collinson, Barry Everitt, Miles Fairburn, Andrew Fitzmaurice, Richard Greaves, Janelle Greenberg, Mark Greengrass, Germaine Greer, Tim Hochstrasser, Julian Hoppit, Adrian Johns, John Kerrigan, Mark Kishlansky, Melissa Lane, Paul McHugh, John Marshall, Paul Millett, Hiram Morgan, John Morrill, John Morrow, Eric Nelson, Markku Peltonen, Paul Rahe and Richard Smith. In addition I have drawn particular inspiration from the work of David Armitage, Sam Glover, Mark Goldie, Jonathan Israel, David Norbrook, John Pocock, Quentin Skinner, Nigel Smith, Blair Worden and Keith Wrightson. Special thanks are due to Leonidas Montes and Eric Nelson for reading several chapters of an early draft, and to Markku Peltonen as well as the two readers for Cambridge University Press for penetrating criticisms of the entire manuscript. I have benefited from many conversations about republicanism with Annamarie Apple, Tania Boster, John Donoghue, Michael McCoy, Chris Magra, Jill Martin and Hiro Takezawa. I am grateful to Jill Goodwin of the Alexander Turnbull Library, Wellington, for help furnishing seventeenth-century materials during a period of leave in New Zealand in 2001. Finally I am greatly indebted to the stimulus provided by the European Science Foundation workshop on 'Republicanism: a Shared European Heritage', organised by Martin van Gelderen and Quentin Skinner, which met at Gottingen, Wassenaar, Perugia, Bordeaux, and Siena between 1997 and 1999.

That commonwealth principles were a tall moral order, in the attempted application of which the risk of failure was high, was well understood by the writers examined in this study. For their presence in our own lives, Sophia, Thomas and I are entirely beholden to Anne.

Introduction: English republicanism

> . . . remembring, that we are now put into a better course, upon the *Declared Interest* of a *Free State* or *Common-weal*, I conceived nothing could more highly tend to the propogation of this *Interest*, and the honour of its Founders, then . . . that the People . . . may . . . understand what *Common-weal Principles* are, and thereby . . . learn to be true Common-wealth's men, and zealous against *Monarchick Interest*, in all its Appearances and Incroachments whatsoever.
>
> Marchamont Nedham, *Mercurius Politicus* no. 92, March 1652.[1]

HISTORIOGRAPHY

The historiography of English republicanism is largely a creation of the past half-century. Before Zera Fink's ground-breaking *The Classical Republicans* (1945), such a general phenomenon had scarcely been identified.[2] Attention to English republican thought was largely confined to James Harrington's *The Commonwealth of Oceana* (1656), a work intermittently famous since the year of its publication, and by 1950 at the centre of a renowned dispute about early modern English social development.[3] Against this background it is not surprising that the most powerful impact of Fink's work should have been to furnish the most fertile context to date for our understanding

---

[1] *Mercurius Politicus* no. 92, 4–11 March 1652, pp. 1457–8.

[2] Fink, *Classical Republicans*. When, in his Fellowship dissertation on *Political Philosophy in England*, F. W. Maitland discussed seventeenth-century ideas of liberty and equality, his reconstruction of contemporary partisanship ranged Milton, Harrington, Sidney and Locke against Filmer, Hobbes, Clarendon and Hume. While describing Harrington as a 'great commonwealthsman', and Milton and Sidney as 'puritans', Maitland found as much connecting these eight theorists as dividing them, and the notion of 'republicanism' played no part in his analysis. *The Collected Papers of Frederic William Maitland*, volume 1 ed. H. A. L. Fisher (Cambridge, 1911) pp. 4–30.

[3] John Toland, 'The Life of James Harrington', in *The Oceana of James Harrington . . . with An Exact Account of his Life* (1700); H. F. Russell Smith, *Harrington and his Oceana: a Study of a Seventeenth Century Utopia and its Influence in America* (New York, 1971); R. H. Tawney, 'Harrington's Interpretation of his Age', *Proceedings of the British Academy* 27 (1941); H. R. Trevor-Roper, 'The Gentry 1540–1640', *Economic History Review Supplements* no. 1 (Cambridge, 1953).

of Harrington. By 1977, in the hugely influential analysis of John Pocock, Harrington had become not only 'a classical republican', but 'England's premier civic humanist and Machiavellian'.[4]

Pocock's achievement drew upon other important work. This included the identification, by Hans Baron, of the concept of Florentine 'civic humanism', and the application to the history of political thought, by Quentin Skinner among others, of linguistic methodology.[5] To this investigation of early modern history Pocock linked a developing debate about the 'ideological origins of the American revolution'.[6] Putting all of this together with his own prior engagement with historical thought, *The Machiavellian Moment* connected to the Florentine recovery of a classical understanding of politics an 'Atlantic republican tradition' by which this was conveyed, via seventeenth- and eighteenth-century England, to colonial America.

Although every detail of Pocock's analysis has now been fiercely criticised, this has largely occurred within the contours of the intellectual geography thus created.[7] The notion of classical republicanism has become hotly disputed. There are the controversies surrounding the particular interpretations by Baron and Pocock of their chosen texts and periods.[8] There is the vigorously contested nature of classical republicanism itself: was it primarily Greek in origin, or Roman? Can it be understood as a language? Did it hinge upon the defence of a particular form of government (a constitutional prescription), a way of life (a moral philosophy) or a still more general view of the world (entailing a natural philosophy and/or metaphysics)? Was it philosophy at all, as opposed to a series of rhetorical or polemical postures? Finally, can any meaningful connection actually be established between the moral and political thought of ancient and modern times? Did early modern classical republicanism exist?[9]

Informed by these developments, wildly disparate readings of Harrington's *Oceana* have proliferated. By 1975 the analyst of contemporary

---

[4] Pocock, *Machiavellian Moment*; J. G. A. Pocock, 'Historical Introduction', in *The Political Works of James Harrington*, ed. Pocock (Cambridge, 1977) p. 15.

[5] Hans Baron, *The Crisis of the Early Italian Renaissance* (2 vols. Princeton, 1955); J. G. A Pocock, *Politics, Language and Time: Essays in Political Thought and History* (New York, 1971); Quentin Skinner, 'A Reply to My Critics', in James Tully (ed.), *Meaning and Context: Quentin Skinner and his Critics* (Princeton, 1988); Skinner, *Visions of Politics, Volume 1: Regarding Method* (Cambridge, 2002).

[6] Caroline Robbins, *The Eighteenth Century Commonwealthsman* (New Haven, Conn., 1959); Bernard Bailyn, *The Ideological Origins of the American Revolution* (Cambridge, Mass., 1971).

[7] However, for an explicit attempt to transcend this geography see van Gelderen and Skinner, *Republicanism*.

[8] Hankins, *Renaissance Civic Humanism*; Phillipson and Skinner, *Political Discourse*.

[9] For negative answers to this question, associated with the followers of Leo Strauss, see Paul Rahe, *Republics Ancient and Modern* (3 vols., Chapel Hill, N.C., 1994); Thomas Pangle, *The Spirit of Modern Republicanism* (Chicago, 1988).

economic and social change had become the author of a 'Machiavellian meditation upon feudalism'.[10] For many scholars Harrington remains the exemplar of an English classical republicanism which is, however, variously depicted as Platonic, Aristotelian, neo-Roman, 'Virgilianised', Machiavellian, or a synthesis of several of these elements mediated by Polybian constitutionalism.[11] For others Harrington's principal intellectual debt was to Hobbes, the nature of which engagement has been vigorously disputed together with its impact upon his claimed classical republicanism.[12] Still others have depicted Harrington as a Utopian, a Stoic, a natural philosopher, and the author of a civic religion.[13]

A third developing area of study has been investigation of the thought of English republicans other than Harrington. This has involved the extension of attention from John Milton's poetry to his overtly religiously and politically engaged prose.[14] It has built upon the work of Pocock to pay much more attention to the ideological influence of the notorious journalistic

[10] Pocock, *Machiavellian Moment* p. 385. The origin of this phrase, together with that of many other aspects of Pocock's understanding of Harrington as a historical thinker, is to be found in his *The Ancient Constitution and the Feudal Law: a Study of English Historical Thought in the Seventeenth Century* (Cambridge, 1958) p. 147.

[11] For Harrington's Platonism see Charles Blitzer, *An Immortal Commonwealth: the Political Thought of James Harrington* (New Haven, Conn., 1970); Eric Nelson, 'The Greek Tradition in Republican Thought', Cambridge Fellowship dissertation submitted to Trinity College, Cambridge, August. 2000 ch. 3; J. G. A. Pocock, 'Introduction' in James Harrington, *The Commonwealth of Oceana and A System of Politics*, ed. Pocock (Cambridge, 1992) pp. xx–xxiv. For his Aristotelianism see Pocock, *Machiavellian Moment* pp. 66–80; James Cotton, *James Harrington's Political Thought and its Context* (1991) ch. 2. For his Machiavellianism see Felix Raab, *The English Face of Machiavelli: a Changing Interpretation* (1964) ch. 6; Pocock, *Machiavellian Moment*. For the Polybian synthesis see Fink, *Classical Republicans* ch. 3; Pocock, *Machiavellian Moment*; Blair Worden, 'James Harrington and *The Commonwealth of Oceana*, 1656', in Wootton, *Republicanism*; Arihiro Fukuda, *Sovereignty and the Sword: Harrington, Hobbes, and Mixed Government in the English Civil Wars* (Oxford, 1997). For the neo-Roman Harrington see Skinner, *Liberty before Liberalism*; for his 'Virgilianised republicanism' see Norbrook, *Writing the English Republic* pp. 357–78.

[12] For Harrington and Hobbes see Raab, *Machiavelli* ch. 6; Cotton, *Harrington* ch. 4; Scott, 'The Rapture of Motion'; Scott, 'The Peace of Silence: Thucydides and the English Civil War', in Miles Fairburn and W. H. Oliver (eds.), *The Certainty of Doubt: Tributes to Peter Munz* (Wellington, 1996); Rahe, *Republics Ancient and Modern, Volume II: New Modes and Orders in Early Modern Political Thought* ch. 5; Glenn Burgess, 'Repacifying the Polity: the Responses of Hobbes and Harrington to the 'Crisis of the Common Law', in Ian Gentles, John Morrill and Blair Worden (eds.), *Soldiers, Writers and Statesmen of the English Revolution* (Cambridge, 1998). See also my review of Fukuda, *Sovereignty and the Sword* in the *English Historical Review* 115, 462 (2000) pp. 660–2.

[13] J. C. Davis, *Utopia and the Ideal Society: a Study of English Utopian Writing 1516–1700* (Cambridge, 1981) chs. 8–9; Alan Cromartie, 'Harringtonian Virtue: Harrington, Machiavelli, and the Method of the *Moment*', *Historical Journal* 41, 4 (1988); Scott, *England's Troubles* ch. 14; Mark Goldie, 'The Civil Religion of James Harrington', in Anthony Pagden (ed.), *The Languages of Political Theory in Early-Modern Europe* (Cambridge, 1987).

[14] Fink's *Classical Republicans*, the work of a Miltonist, was an early result of this process. Its most important monument is Milton's *Complete Prose Works*, gen. ed. D. M. Wolfe (8 vols. New Haven, Conn., 1953–82). See also Hill, *Milton*; Nicholas von Maltzahn, *Milton's History of Britain* (Oxford, 1991);

turncoat Marchamont Nedham.[15] It has seen republication of the major work by Harrington's friend Henry Neville, and new accounts of the life and thought of Neville's colleague and second cousin Algernon Sidney.[16] At the same time the spotlight continues to fall on a succession of other members of the republican literary canon. These include Sir Henry Vane Jr, John Streater, Edmund Ludlow and Slingsby Bethel.[17]

In the wake of this work have come several attempts to delineate the contours of English republicanism more generally. Recent writing has done much to excavate its contemporary social, political and intellectual contexts.[18] We have a magisterial treatment of its relationship to poetry, an analytically acute examination of its understanding of liberty, and a major attempt to establish its relationship to seventeenth-century politics.[19] This is a literature still in a rapid state of development. This development is

David Armitage, Armand Himy and Quentin Skinner (eds.), *Milton and Republicanism* (Cambridge, 1995). On the contemporary fame of Milton's prose see chapter 12 below.

[15] Pocock, 'Historical Introduction' pp. 33–7; Jonathan Scott, *Algernon Sidney and the English Republic 1623–1677* (Cambridge, 1998) pp. 110–12; Blair Worden, '"Wit in a Roundhead": the Dilemma of Marchamont Nedham', in Susan Amussen and Mark Kishlansky (eds.), *Political Culture and Cultural Politics in Early Modern England* (Manchester, 1995); Worden, 'Marchamont Nedham and the Beginnings of English Republicanism, 1649–1656', in Wootton, *Republicanism*.

[16] Caroline Robbins (ed.), *Two English Republican Tracts* (Cambridge, 1969); Robbins, 'Algernon Sidney's *Discourses Concerning Government*: Textbook of Revolution', *William and Mary Quarterly* 3rd ser., 4 (1947); Blair Worden, 'The Commonwealth Kidney of Algernon Sidney', *Journal of British Studies* 24 (January 1985); Scott, *Algernon Sidney and the English Republic*; Scott, *Algernon Sidney and the Restoration Crisis 1677–1683* (Cambridge, 1991); Paulette Carrive, *La pensée politique d'Algernon Sidney 1622–1683. La querelle de l'absolutisme* (Paris, 1989); Alan Craig Houston, *Algernon Sidney and the Republican Heritage in England and America* (Princeton, 1991); Scott Nelson, *The Discourses of Algernon Sidney* (1993); Pocock, 'England's Cato'.

[17] On Vane see Margaret Judson, *The Political Thought of Henry Vane the Younger* (Philadelphia, 1969). On Streater see Nigel Smith, 'Popular Republicanism in the 1650s: John Streater's "heroick mechanicks"', in Armitage, Himy and Skinner, *Milton*; Adrian Johns, *The Nature of the Book: Print and Knowledge in the Making* (Chicago, 1998) ch. 4. For Ludlow and Bethel see Blair Worden, 'Introduction,' in Edmund Ludlow, *A Voyce From the Watch Tower Part Five 1660–1662*, ed. A. B. Worden (London, 1978). For Bethel as an exponent of mercantile interest theory, see Scott, *Algernon Sidney and the English Republic* ch. 13; Steve Pincus, 'Neither Machiavellian Moment nor Possessive Individualism: Commercial Society and the Defenders of the English Commonwealth', *American Historical Review* (June 1998).

[18] Patrick Collinson, *De Republica Anglorum: Or, History with the Politics Put Back* (Cambridge, 1990); Mark Goldie, 'The Unacknowledged Republic: Officeholding in Early Modern England', in Tim Harris (ed.), *The Politics of the Excluded, c.1500–1850* (2001); Scott, *England's Troubles* chs. 2–6; Blair Worden, 'Classical Republicanism and the Puritan Revolution', in V. Pearl, H. Lloyd-Jones and B. Worden (eds.), *History and Imagination* (Oxford, 1981); Markku Peltonen, *Classical Humanism and Republicanism in English Political Thought 1570–1640* (Cambridge, 1995).

[19] Norbrook, *Writing the English Republic*; Skinner, *Liberty before Liberalism*; in addition to Worden's four chapters in Wootton, *Republicanism*, see his 'English Republicanism', in J. H. Burns and Mark Goldie (eds.), *The Cambridge History of Political Thought 1450–1700* (Cambridge, 1991); and 'The Revolution of 1688–9 and the English Republican Tradition', in Jonathan Israel (ed.), *The Anglo-Dutch Moment* (Cambridge, 1991). See also Scott, *England's Troubles* chs. 10–16.

multi-faceted, argumentative and notable for a tendency to draw in hitherto discrete aspects of early modern studies. There is now a need to draw
this literature together, and enter into its key debates, from the standpoint
of the broadest analysis of our subject. This is particularly important given
that, whatever their positions, few historians have questioned the practice,
for the purpose of generalising about English republicanism, of taking Harrington to be its exemplar. To this extent much of the wider debate may
turn out to have been sustained by the variety of possible readings of a
peculiarly complicated and hybrid text.

The second reason for a holistic approach is that English republican
writers were polemicists united, and divided, by their commitment to a
cause. Their manuscript or printed utterances were interventions in, and
attempts to influence, a struggle going on in practice. This political engagement is one reason for the eclecticism of this literature. Such polemic can
be made to yield the single concepts or languages of particular interest to
modern political philosophers. But it cannot be reduced to them, or to
one use or understanding of them, without diminishing our own grasp of
the rhetorical requirements of a rapidly developing practical situation.[20]
To understand republicanism as a whole, or even any one text, we need
to recover the constellation of ideas informing what came to be known as
the 'good old cause'. By what contexts, themes and events was this intellectual phenomenon united? What were the causes, extent and nature of
its internal variation?

LONG-TERM CONTEXTS: INTELLECTUAL AND PRACTICAL

The first task is to draw together evidence concerning the longer-term
contexts of English republicanism. We begin with those which have been
the primary focus for historians of ideas. Recent work on English classical republicanism has tended to distinguish Greek from Roman moral

---

[20] Quentin Skinner's *Liberty before Liberalism* is open to this criticism (see Worden's review in the
London Review of Books, 5 February 1998). However, in his subsequent 'Classical Liberty, Renaissance
Translation and the English Civil War', the argument that the parliamentarian use of Roman law
sources has been neglected by historians preoccupied by common law or natural law traditions avoids
the suggestion that these other ideas played no important role (in Skinner, *Visions of Politics*, Volume
II: *Renaissance Virtues* pp. 312, 335–9, 342). Similarly the former reconstruction in exclusively neo-
Roman terms faced the objection that Hobbes accused parliamentarians of drawing upon 'Greek,
and Latine Authors', in particular, '*Aristotle*' and '*Cicero*' (Hobbes, *Leviathan* (Cambridge, 1996)
pp. 149–50). The later article pays some attention to Aristotle, if only as an influence upon Cicero
(Skinner, 'Classical Liberty' pp. 315–6).

philosophy, and to emphasise its Roman rather than Greek character.[21] Yet from Milton's *A Defence of the People of England* (1651) and Harrington's *Oceana* (1656), to Neville's *Plato Redivivus* (1680) and Sidney's *Discourses* (1698), there are few key texts which do not attempt to combine the authority of Plato, Aristotle, Cicero, Livy and others. Similarly English republicanism combined a powerful debt to Machiavelli's *Discourses* with another to that Greek and Roman moral philosophy by which Machiavelli had himself ostentatiously refused to be bound.

In addition, English republicanism was influenced by other, often related languages of history, philosophy, politics and law, including ancient constitutionalism, natural law theory, natural philosophy, Stoicism and interest theory.[22] Most importantly, there is hardly a single important republican work which is not also fundamentally animated by religious considerations and principles. The greatest shortcoming of the existing literature on English republicanism has been its relative neglect of the religious dimension.[23] The consequent need is not simply to recover the radical protestant republican religious agenda. It is to explain why, when classical republicanism came to England, it did so in the moral service of a religious revolution.

Two sixteenth-century contexts for the answer lay in Christian humanism and radical protestant reformation.[24] Both informed the practical identity of the republican experiment as an attempted reformation of manners. So did the rational Greek moral philosophy, as indebted to Plato as to Aristotle, common to certain humanist and Christian political languages. Consequently, Levellers, Diggers, Quakers and republicans shared many aspects of a common political, religious and social agenda. All came to oppose not only tyranny but monarchy, agreeing upon a substantially

---

[21] Quentin Skinner, 'The Republican Ideal of Political Liberty', in Gisela Bock, Quentin Skinner and Maurizio Viroli (eds.), *Machiavelli and Republicanism* (Cambridge, 1990); Skinner, *Liberty before Liberalism*; Peltonen, *Classical Humanism*; Martin Dzelzainis, 'Milton's Classical Republicanism', in Armitage et al., *Milton*; Norbrook, *Writing the English Republic*; Andrew Fitzmaurice, *Humanism and America: an Intellectual History of English Colonisation 1500–1625* (Cambridge, 2003).

[22] Scott, *Algernon Sidney and the English Republic* chs. 2–3, 12–13; Richard Tuck, *Philosophy and Government 1572–1651* (Cambridge, 1993).

[23] A point noted by David Loewenstein, *Representing Revolution in Milton and his Contemporaries* (Cambridge, 1991) p. 4. Loewenstein's response is, however, to restore the missing component, rather than focus upon the relationship between Christian and classical. The most important exception to this generalisation is the work of Worden (see, for instance, 'Milton, *Samson Agonistes*, and the Restoration', in Gerald Maclean (ed.), *Culture and Society in the Stuart Restoration* (Cambridge, 1995); 'Classical Republicanism'. Yet even Worden has done more to distinguish the humanist and 'puritan' components of English republicanism than to integrate them. For an alternative emphasis prefiguring that developed here, see Scott, *Algernon Sidney and the English Republic*, ch. 2.

[24] Scott, *Algernon Sidney and the English Republic* pp. 17–30; Margo Todd, *Christian Humanism and the Puritan Social Order* (Cambridge, 1987), p. 21; Scott, *England's Troubles* ch. 11; Michael Baylor (ed.), *The Radical Reformation* (Cambridge, 1991).

shared definition of liberty. All did so in the church as well as the state (that is to say, all demanded liberty of conscience). It was the fact of a revolution within which liberty and virtue had powerful religious as well as political content which required these writers to connect a Graeco-Roman commitment to civic action to a Platonic epistemology and metaphysics. In the words of Sidney to Jean-Baptiste Lantin in Paris in 1677: 'après la Theologie, ou la connoisance de Dieu et de la Religion, il n'y avoit point de sciance qui fut plus digne de l'application d'un honneste homme, que la politique'.[25]

This is to emphasise the extent to which the intellectual and practical contexts of English republicanism were intertwined. The most important practical context was the military collapse of English monarchy. This had been prefigured by Stuart military impotence on the European stage between 1624 and 1629.[26] With rebellion in Scotland, and subsequently Ireland and England, it became politically immobilising. The English civil war was an unsuccessful attempt by the king to undo this disaster. In this respect Harrington correctly noted that '*the dissolution of this government caused the war, not the war the dissolution of this government*'.[27] Thus Marchamont Nedham spoke mockingly in 1645 of the need 'to fill up that *roome* in the *Monarchie*, which hath been too long *empty* . . . Where is King Charles? What's become of him? . . . it were best to send a *Hue and Cry* after him.'[28] As with the church, the drastic dimunition of monarchy as a practical force pre-dated by some years the constitutional 'settling of the government of this nation for the future in way of a Republic, without King or House of Lords'.[29]

This demise of the crown had not only religious and political, but economic and social contexts. Most important was a state of fiscal weakness with its roots in the Europe-wide social and economic changes of the period 1540–1640, including price inflation. They lay more particularly in the failure of Tudor and early Stuart monarchs to respond to these successfully.[30] Meanwhile, it was in the localities that social, economic and

---

[25] Paris, Bibliothèque Nationale, Fr. MS 23254, Jean-Baptiste Lantin, 'Lantiniana' p. 101. On this Platonism see Pocock, 'England's Cato' pp. 917–21.

[26] Scott, *England's Troubles* chs. 3–6.

[27] James Harrington, *The Commonwealth of Oceana*, in *The Political Works of James Harrington*, ed. J. G. A. Pocock (Cambridge, 1977) [hereafter *Oceana*, in *Political Works*].

[28] *Mercurius Britanicus* no. 72, 24 February–3 March 1645, pp 575–6; *Mercurius Britanicus* no. 92, 28 July–4 August 1645, p. 825.

[29] Quoted in Austin Woolrych, 'Dating Milton's *History of Britain*', *Historical Journal* 36, 4 (1993) p. 933.

[30] Scott, *England's Troubles* chs. 3 and 16; Scott, 'What the Dutch Taught Us' pp. 4–6.

religious changes had been grappled with most keenly.[31] Local government survived the upheavals of 1640–60 and republican writing paid significant attention to the local government dimension. Equally, many of its themes reflected the longstanding struggle by a traditional society to respond to unsettling forces of social and economic change.[32] Drawing upon all of these contexts, republican writers attempted to oppose not only private interest politics, embodied by monarchy or tyranny, on behalf of the publicly interested virtues of a self-governing civic community. This was part of a more general critique of private interest society; an attempt, from pride, greed, poverty and inequality, to go beyond the mere word 'commonwealth' and reconstitute what Milton called 'the solid thing'.[33] At the same time, following successful parliamentary statebuilding between 1642 and 1649, many republican writers became preoccupied with the themes of empire and trade.[34] It is the power actually wielded by the English republic which helps to explain the otherwise surprising conjunction in many writers of the formidable moral forces of Plato and Machiavelli.

INTELLECTUAL CONTENT: ENDS AND MEANS

It is the second purpose of this study to offer a comparative thematic analysis of republican writing. Existing treatments have noted certain preoccupations connecting the thought of Nedham and Harrington, Vane and Ludlow, or Milton and Sidney. Yet what are the principal distinguishing features of English republican thought? What were the points of similarity, and of difference? What is the intellectual framework within which these may be identified? It is in relation to these questions that we may note both the nature and extent of internal variety and, thereafter, of development over time.

One approach has been to study republican thought as language.[35] While descriptively useful, this is less satisfactory when deployed to include

---

[31] In addition to Collinson, *De Republica* and Goldie, 'Unacknowledged Republic', see Steve Hindle, *The State and Social Change in Early Modern England, c.1550–1640* (Basingstoke, 2000); Michael Braddick, *State Formation in Early Modern England c.1550–1700* (Cambridge, 2000); Keith Wrightson, *Earthly Necessities: Economic Lives in Early Modern Britain* (New Haven, Conn., 2000).

[32] Whitney R. D. Jones, *The Tudor Commonwealth 1529–1559* (London, 1970); Andrew McRae, *God Speed the Plough: the Representation of Agrarian England, 1500–1660* (Cambridge, 1996); Scott, *England's Troubles* chs. 10–12.

[33] John Milton, *Of Education* (1644) in *Complete Prose Works* vol. 1, pp. 407–8.

[34] Scott, '"Good Night Amsterdam"'; David Armitage, 'The Cromwellian Protectorate and the Languages of Empire', *Historical Journal* 35, 3 (1992) pp. 534–5; Pincus, 'Machiavellian Moment'.

[35] See, for instance, Pocock, *Politics, Language and Time*; Skinner, 'Sir Thomas More's Utopia and the Language of Renaissance Humanism', in Pagden, *The Languages of Political Theory*.

some writers in, and exclude others from, a linguistically defined canon. No seventeenth-century republican wrote in one political language only, and most combined several, spanning the intellectual terrains of human- ism, Christianity, science and law.[36] Moreover, to identify the terminology deployed by a writer is not thereby to determine the use to which it was being put. Many of the most important early modern writers (includ- ing Machiavelli, Hobbes and Harrington) put conventional contemporary political language to startlingly unconventional use.[37] To this extent, draw- ing a distinction beloved of seventeenth-century radicals themselves, lin- guistic analysis may tell us more about the form of a contemporary text than about its substance. If so, a history of politics as language may not be best equipped to analyse what was, among other things, an anti-formal revolution of manners. This was precisely Milton's point in putting classi- cal republican language into the mouth of the republican moral anti-type Satan in *Paradise Lost*.[38]

A second approach is to focus upon conceptual content. The two most important republican concepts were liberty and virtue (or the virtues). It has been one ('Greek') view that 'it is as a politics of virtue that [English] republicanism most clearly defines itself'.[39] It has been a contrasting ('neo- Roman') view that it is a shared 'analysis of civil liberty' which 'constitute[s] the core of what is distinctive . . . [and] marks the[se writers] out as the protagonists of a particular ideology, even as the members of a single school of thought'.[40] In either case at least as much rigour needs to be applied to distinguishing the moral philosophies of Machiavelli, Nedham, Milton, Harrington and Sidney as has been employed in linking them. Thus the shared championship of austerity, frugality and activity over luxury, effemi- nacy and sloth was common to much ancient morality from Plato onwards and does not encapsulate Machiavelli's shocking new conception of *virtu*. If all these writers shared an exclusively 'neo-Roman' understanding of liberty, it is difficult to understand the central use made by all of them of Greek sources and examples.[41]

---

[36] Scott, 'The Rapture of Motion' pp. 143–4; Scott, Review of Peltonen, *Classical Humanism*, Armitage et al. *Milton*, and Sidney, *Court Maxims*, in *English Historical Review* 62, 448 (1997); Conal Condren, *The Language of Politics in Seventeenth Century England* (Basingstoke, 1994).

[37] Scott, *England's Troubles* p. 326.

[38] J. C. Davis, 'Against Formality: One Aspect of the English Revolution', *Transactions of the Royal Historical Society*, 6th ser., 3, (1993). See chapter 8 below. Also see the different but not incompat- ible discussion of Milton's anti-formalism by William Walker in '*Paradise Lost* and the Forms of Government', *History of Political Thought* 22, 2 (2001).

[39] Worden, 'Marchamont Nedham' p. 46.   [40] Skinner, *Liberty before Liberalism* pp. 22–3.

[41] Worden, 'Marchamont Nedham' pp. 57–8, 70–1; Skinner, 'The Republican Ideal of Political Liberty' p. 306.

The range of English republican moral philosophy reflected not only the complexity of the classical republican heritage, but also the diversity of contemporary intellectual contexts. Adherents to the good old cause were more effectively united by its practical context than by its philosophical content. This is not to deny that we will discover very important shared characteristics of this moral philosophy as a whole. One is a relationship between liberty and the virtues (however understood) as one of means to ends. In the virtues we are considering the positive moral good which the republican experiment proposed to itself. To these virtues, liberty was the indispensable precondition.[42] For some writers particularly influenced by Roman sources and/or Machiavelli, those virtues had a further end in glory. According to Aristotle the life of virtue (*eudaimonia*, usually translated as 'happiness') was itself the end (*telos*) of human life.

For their political realisation liberty and virtue required a constitutional framework. The historiography of English republicanism has been dominated by constitutional analysis. This reflects the influence not only of Harrington's *Oceana* but of Fink's *The Classical Republicans*.[43] Yet for most English republicans, constitutional prescription, where it existed, was far less detailed than in Harrington and secondary to the enunciation of general moral principles. This reflected aspects of the classical, humanist and radical protestant content of this thought, and was both cause and consequence of the interregnum's constitutional instability. Yet even such anti-formalism, shared with Machiavelli, did not preclude constitutional generalisation. Moreover, between 1653 and 1660, as instability threatened the republic, a range of writers entered a debate concerning not simply the appropriate constitution, but the role to be played within republican politics by constitutional prescription.

In the *Discorsi* Machiavelli introduced a distinction between free states, not simply in terms of their constitutional composition, but (by distinguishing between two routes to *grandezza*) in relation to their ends. 'Either you have in mind a republic that looks to founding an empire, as Rome did; or one that is content to maintain the *status quo*. In the first case it is necessary to do in all things as Rome did. In the second case it is possible to imitate

---

[42] Scott, *England's Troubles* chs. 13–16.
[43] This is particularly evident in the work of Worden, for whom 'All ... [English republicans] saw republican architecture as the necessary precondition of the recovery of liberty and virtue' ('Marchamont Nedham' p. 46), and of Fukuda, for whom 'the essence of [Harrington's understanding of] ancient prudence is to be identified as the Polybian idea of mixed government' (*Sovereignty and the Sword* pp. 5–6).

Venice and Sparta.'[44] Sidney, mocking the 'ignorance' of those who failed to understand the variety of 'constitutions of commonwealths . . . according to the different temper of nations and times', repeated this distinction, while adding to it secondary subdivisions relating to trade and federated republics.[45] That most English republicans followed Machiavelli in choosing expansion over preservation distinguished English republicanism from its Dutch counterpart.[46] Yet at times all of these writers moderated this enthusiasm for empire in response to particular circumstances. Moreover, both Harrington and Neville made a more fundamental departure from Machiavelli by seeking to avoid altogether the choice between Roman external expansion and Venetian internal stability.[47]

Their reason for doing this related to the wider assumptions informing Machiavelli's insistence that such a choice was necessary. The first was that the Roman republic's internal 'tumults' had been essential to its expansion, and 'should, therefore, be looked upon as an inconvenience which it is necessary to put up with in order to arrive at the greatness of Rome'.[48] It was Machiavelli's view, according to Harrington, that 'if Rome had cut off the occasion of her tumults, she must have cut off the means of her increase, and by consequence of her greatness'.[49] Underlying this belief, in turn, was Machiavelli's key assumption that 'all human affairs are ever in a state of flux and cannot stand still'.[50] The basis of Harrington's insistence on nevertheless embracing Venice as his domestic model was his contrasting belief that such flux (and the related tumults) could be transcended by constitutional means: '[I]f there be a contradiction or inequality in your commonwealth, it must fall; but if it have neither of these, it hath no principle of mortality.' Attention to the causes, nature and inevitability of change is one of the most important features of republican writing.[51] In addition there were the historical examples, spanning ancient (in particular the commonwealths of Israel, Greece and Rome), medieval (including the history of England, or Britain) and early modern periods, of which this material was substantially composed.

[44] Niccolò Machiavelli, *The Discourses*, ed. Bernard Crick (Harmondsworth, 1985) p. 117.
[45] Algernon Sidney, *Discourses Concerning Government*, ed. T. West (Indianapolis, Ind., 1990) ch. 2, section 22: 'Commonwealths seek Peace or War according to the Variety of their Constitutions.'
[46] Scott, 'Classical Republicanism'.
[47] David Armitage, 'John Milton: Poet against Empire', in Armitage et al., *Milton*; Scott, *Algernon Sidney and the English Republic* p. 191; see chapter 10 below.
[48] Machiavelli, *Discourses* pp. 123–4. [49] Harrington, *Oceana*, in *Political Works* p. 273.
[50] Machiavelli, *Discourses* p. 123.
[51] Scott, *Algernon Sidney and the English Republic* pp. 30–5; Scott, *Algernon Sidney and the Restoration Crisis* pp. 254–7; Scott, *England's Troubles* pp. 234–6, 306–7.

Both Milton and Sidney built upon Machiavelli's praise of tumults a defence of rebellion in prosecution of 'just causes and complaints'.[52] This was a particularly important element in works which defended the regicide, opposed the Protectorate, or opposed the restoration.[53] Such arguments drew upon biblical and classical sources. In addition they were deeply indebted to the resistance writings of early modern protestants in England, Scotland, the Netherlands and France.[54]

IDEAS AND EVENTS: THE IMPACT OF THE REPUBLICAN EXPERIMENT IN PRACTICE

The final task of this study is to examine the development of republican thought over time. As directly politically engaged, this writing was powerfully shaped by events. In relation to these, however, there remains a striking disjuncture between the high profile of republicanism as a component of the history of ideas, and the historiographical place occupied by the republican experiment in practice.[55] This fact may have a simple explanation: that as intellectually English republicanism was glorious, so constitutionally it was a mess. Thus for Blair Worden the 'English republicanism of the 1650s had been a criticism, not an endorsement, of the English republic'.[56] Yet as the English revolution was not primarily a constitutional occurrence, and within most republican writing constitutional prescription played a secondary role, we should not mistake this history of constitutional failure for the history of republicanism as a whole.[57]

At various points during the struggle to establish a non-monarchical, non-dynastic government, most major republican writers engaged in both compliment and criticism. Noting Milton's excoriation of the Long Parliament and Nedham's interlinear constitutional criticisms of the Rump,

---

[52] John Milton, *Commonplace Book*, in *Complete Prose Works* vol. I, p. 505; Sidney, *Discourses*, ed. West pp. 259–60, 519–24, 545; Scott, *Restoration Crisis* pp. 238–41, 260–4.

[53] John Milton, *The Tenure of Kings and Magistrates* (1649), in *Complete Prose Works* vol. III; John Streater, *Observations Historical, Political and Philosophical, Upon Aristotles first Book of Political Government* no. 11, 27 June–4 July 1654; Algernon Sidney, *Court Maxims*, ed. Hans Blom, Eco Haitsma Mulier and Ronald Janse (Cambridge, 1996): Sidney, *Discourses*.

[54] Scott, *Algernon Sidney and the English Republic* chs. 2–3; Scott, 'The Law of War: Grotius, Sidney, Locke and the Political Theory of Rebellion', *History of Political Thought* 13, 4 (1992).

[55] See, however, Derek Hirst, *England in Conflict* (London, 1999); Hirst, 'Locating the 1650s in England's Seventeenth Century', *History* 81, 3 (1996).

[56] Blair Worden, '*Oceana*: Origins and Aftermath', in Wootton, *Republicanism* p. 138; Worden, 'Republicanism, Regicide and Republic: the English Experience', in van Gelderen and Skinner, *Republicanism* vol. I.

[57] Scott, *England's Troubles* pp. 33–9. 'The general record of seventeenth-century republicanism is, in an obvious sense, one of failure': Worden, 'Marchamont Nedham' p. 48.

Worden has much less to say about the public role of both in celebrating the achievements of a free state.[58] Discussing what he takes to be Harrington's savage criticism of Oliver Cromwell's Protectorate, his analysis does not consider the possibility that *Oceana* was primarily a work of counsel. Moreover, while Harrington's observations upon the Rump were entirely critical, for most other republicans it was, in some respects at least, deserving of extravagant praise. This concentrated upon, not its constitutional shortcomings (about which many writers were frank), but rather its claimed economic, political, moral and military achievements.[59] Although initially Cromwell too was flattered by both Milton and Nedham, both came to agree with the 'commonwealthsmen' that the Lord Protector's ambition had destroyed what had been a genuine republican work-in-progress. It was 'pride' and 'ambition' which had made his 'choice/To reign . . . though in hell:/Better to reign in hell, than serve in heaven'.[60] The resulting usurpation had wrecked that government in which, in practice, 'the Power, Vigour, and Excellency of a *Councel* of a *Free People*' had so spectacularly manifested itself'.[61] The white heat given off by this achievement would still be generating much of the force animating Sidney's *Discourses* in 1681–3.

That insufficient attention has been paid to the fact of an English republic also owes something to the long-term effort, inaugurated by the 'happy Act of Indemnity and Oblivion'(1660), to command public forgetfulness of the whole republican episode. This was accompanied by the 'statute of 12 Car II, c.11 declaring the events of 1641–60 to be a constitutional nullity'.[62] One result is the negative language of absence (Rump parliament, signifying the

---

[58] 'The republicanism of the 1650s was a protest against the English republic, not a celebration of it.' Worden takes Milton's *Digression* to be an attack on the Rump, rather than the pre-Purge Long Parliament, and concludes that to Milton, 'as to Harrington and Neville, the new regime was no proper republic'. To Worden's broader view that 'Milton's republicanism is not often apparent in his public writings' an alternative reading is offered here, particularly, but not only, of the *Defence* (1651) and *The Readie and Easie Way* (1660). This suggests that Milton's republicanism, preoccupied by reformation of manners rather than constitutional forms, is visible in almost everything he wrote. Worden, 'Marchamont Nedham' pp. 48, 58.

[59] This was an emphasis upon moral and political ends, rather than constitutional means, to be taken up by William Godwin's *History of the Commonwealth of England* (4 vols., 1824–8), informed by the author's reading of Milton, Nedham and Sidney (see John Morrow, 'Introduction' pp. xiii, xxi–xxv).

[60] John Milton, *Paradise Lost* Book 1, lines 261–3, in *John Milton: A Critical Edition of the Major Works*, ed. Stephen Orgel and Jonathan Goldberg (Oxford, 1991) p. 362.

[61] John Streater, *The Continuation of this Session of Parliament Justified; and the Action of the Army Touching that Affair Defended* (1659) p. 11. See also, for instance, Henry Vane, *A Healing Question propounded and resolved* (1656); Slingsby Bethel, *The World's Mistake in Oliver Cromwell; or, A short Political Discourse, shewing, That Cromwell's Mal-administration (during his Four Years, and Nine Moneths pretended Protectorship) layed the Foundation of Our present Condition, in the Decay of Trade* (London, 1668).

[62] Hirst, '1650s'; Norbrook, *Writing the English Republic* p. 1; Scott, *England's Troubles* pp. 389–97.

absence of full parliament; interregnum, denoting the absence of monarchy) which continues to dominate the political historiography. Yet any
satisfactory account even of the constitutional consequences of the English
revolution must embrace, not simply the interruption of the old, but the
arrival of something new. On 30 January 1649, after an unprecedented
trial by a group of his own subjects, King Charles I of England, Scotland
and Ireland was publicly beheaded. Seven weeks later the institution of
monarchy, having been found 'useless, burdensome and dangerous to the
people', was abolished. That same '*Power* and *Authority* which first erected
a *King* . . . for the common good, finding him perverted, to their Common
Calamity . . . [resolved] to *change* that *Government* for a *better*'.[63] This is
why such a key feature of republican writing from 1649 is an insistence
upon the '*Right inherent in every Nation, to alter their . . . Governments, as
often as they judge it necessary*'. Even to Harrington 'this under an old name
was a new thing'.[64]

A separate political conclusion will be that no easy equation can be made
between adherence to a cause and allegiance to a regime.[65] Milton militantly
defended, and at other times despaired of, every stage of the struggle. Henry
Vane, the most prominent opponent of the military coup by which the
Rump was ejected in 1653, became the most prominent collaborator with
that by which it was later ejected again. Sidney's violent excoriation of the
restored monarchy did not prevent him offering his services to it in 1672.[66]
Among our writers it was Marchamont Nedham who raised reversals of
allegiance to the status of a notorious art form.[67] No one looks at James
Harrington in a similar light. Yet it was Harrington, not Nedham, who
during the later 1640s served Charles I personally with 'untainted fidelity'.
It was Harrington who 'vindicated . . . his Majesty's Arguments against the
Parliament at *Newport* and . . . [according to Toland, seconded by Aubrey]
accompany'd him on the Scaffold'.[68] These facts are of great significance for
our understanding of Harrington's republicanism, but they do not make

[63] *A Declaration of the Parliament of England, Expressing the Grounds of their late Proceedings, And of
Setling the present Government In the way of A Free State* (22 March 1648 [1649]).

[64] Nedham, *Mercurius Politicus* no. 52, 29 May–5 June 1651, p. 831; Harrington, *Oceana*, in *Political Works*
p. 205.

[65] Scott, '"Good Night Amsterdam"'.   [66] Scott, *Algernon Sidney and the English Republic* p. 233.

[67] *The Character of Mercurius Politicus* (14 August 1650), p. 1: 'so many times has our Mercury been
metamorphos'd, that now you may, if you please, call him *Mercurius Trismegistus*.'

[68] Toland, 'The Life of James Harrington' pp. xvi–xvii. According to Aubrey, too, Harrington 'was on
the scaffold with the King when he was beheaded; and I have oftentimes heard him speake of King
Charles I with the greatest zeale and passion imaginable, and that his death gave him so great a griefe
that he contracted a Disease by it; that never any thing did goe so neer to him'. *Aubrey's Brief Lives*
ed. Oliver Lawson Dick (London, 1958) p. 124.

it insincere. Nedham's case, though different in detail, demands equally careful scrutiny.

Had Nedham really been simply a parliamentarian, then royalist, and finally republican (both pre- and post-Cromwellian), we might take this to constitute evidence of absence of principle. As it happens, however, before and alongside all of these alterations of allegiance, Nedham was a Machiavellian and Lilburne-associated Leveller. Nobody accuses Machiavelli of lacking sincerity, or stature in the history of ideas, because he wrote both the *Discourses* and *The Prince*. No one questions the sincerity of John Lilburne, who supported parliament in 1645, the army against parliament in 1647 and the king against the army in 1648, in defence of consistent general principles. As with Harrington it would be wrong to underestimate the contextual importance of these reversals of public allegiance, partly because they registered real exigencies in Nedham's personal life, and also because he revelled in them. Yet as we will see, Nedham was much more than an ordinary party hack.

PART I

Contexts

CHAPTER I

Classical republicanism

[T]here were an exceeding great number of men of the better sort, that had been so educated, as that in their youth having read the books written by famous men of the ancient Grecian and Roman commonwealths concerning their polity and great actions; in which books the popular government was extolled by the glorious name of liberty, and monarchy disgraced by the name of tyranny; they became thereby in love with their forms of government. And out of these men were chosen the greatest part of the House of Commons, or if they were not the greatest part, yet, by advantage of their eloquence, were always able to sway the rest.

Thomas Hobbes, *Behemoth; or, The Long Parliament*[1]

'CLASSICAL REPUBLICANISM'

The concept of 'classical republicanism' was developed to explain something about the relationship between seventeenth-century English literature and politics. Zera Fink's *The Classical Republicans* was the work of an American scholar of Wordsworth and Milton who came, through his interest in the latter, to identify a group of writers whose work was influenced by classical sources and political examples.[2] This may now seem unremarkable, amounting to little more than the claim that seventeenth-century English republicans were humanists. Yet, as we have needed recent reminders that the era of Reformation, and Counter-Reformation, did not end in the sixteenth century, so recent scholarship, not least of English literature, has returned to underline contemporary claims both that seventeenth-century England remained a renaissance culture, and that this fact had important political implications.[3]

---

[1] Thomas Hobbes, *Behemoth; or, The Long Parliament*, ed. Ferdinand Tonnies (Chicago, 1990) p. 3.
[2] Fink, *Classical Republicans*.
[3] Nicholas Tyacke (ed.), *England's Long Reformation 1500–1800* (London, 1998); Scott, *England's Troubles* chs. 3–5; Worden, 'Classical Republicanism'; Peltonen, *Classical Humanism*; Norbrook, *Writing the English Republic*; Quentin Skinner, *Reason and Rhetoric in the Philosophy of Hobbes* (Cambridge, 1996).

According to Fink, for certain politically engaged writers the invocation of classical sources was not simply literary window-dressing, but had a serious practical purpose. This was in effect to suggest that seventeenth-century republicans heeded Machiavelli when he wrote of his 'astonishment and grief' to see antiquity everywhere 'admired rather than imitated'.[4] When a later Milton scholar, Christopher Hill, declared war on the 'prevalent donnish assumption that ideas are transmitted principally by books', he called for the replacement of a critical obsession with 'the poet's . . . [relationship to] the Greek and Roman classics, [and] to the Church Fathers' with an alternative emphasis upon his relationship to the radical politics of his time.[5] Yet in pre-empting this false distinction Fink had already showed the extent to which each of these things moulded the other.

In thus relating this use of classical literature to its political context, Fink was also helping to re-establish the context within which historians could return to Hobbes' account of the ideological origins of England's troubles. It was the claim of *Behemoth*, written in about 1667, that these were both religious and political. Earlier, in *Leviathan* (1651), Hobbes had explained more specifically:

In these westerne parts of the world, we are made to receive our opinions concerning the Institution, and Rights of Common-wealths, from *Aristotle, Cicero,* and other men, Greeks and Romanes . . . And because the Athenians were taught . . . that they were Free-men, and all that lived under Monarchy were slaves; therefore *Aristotle* puts it down in his *Politiques (lib.6.cap.2) In democracy, Liberty is to be supposed: for 'tis commonly held, that no man is Free in any other Government* . . . And by reading of these Greek, and Latine Authors, men from their childhood have gotten a habit (under a falseshew of Liberty), of favouring tumults, and of licentious controlling the actions of their Soveraigns . . . with the effusion of so much blood; as I think I may truly say, there never was anything so deerly bought, as these Western parts have bought the learning of the Greek and Latine tongues.[6]

For the origins of this analysis, which was answered by both Harrington in *Oceana* and Sidney in the *Discourses*, we must look further back still, to the

---

[4] Machiavelli, *Discourses*, Preface to Book 1, pp. 97–8.

[5] Hill, *Milton* p. 5.

[6] Hobbes, *Leviathan* pp. 149–50. This passage is discussed by Worden, 'Classical Republicanism' pp. 182–3; Jonathan Scott, 'The Peace of Silence: Thucydides and the English Civil War'; amended version in G. A. J. Rogers and Tom Sorell (eds.), *Hobbes and History* (London, 2000) pp. 95–105; Skinner, 'Classical Liberty '. A similar passage of *Leviathan* was noted by Fink, *Classical Republicans* p. 1, note 1.

prefaces to Hobbes's translation of Thucydides' *History of the Peloponnesian War* (1629).[7] These explained:

[T]he principal and proper work of history being to instruct and enable men by the knowledge of actions past, to bear themselves prudently in the present and providently towards the future: there is not extant any other . . . that doth more naturally and fully perform it, than this of my author . . . the most politic historiographer that ever writ . . . Thucydides writeth one war; [of] which . . . he was able certainly to inform himself . . . [and] sheweth that it was a great war . . . and . . . not to be concealed from posterity, for the calamities that then fell upon the Grecians; but the rather to be truly delivered unto them.[8]

One cause of this conflict lay in 'those human passions, which either dissembled or not commonly discoursed of, do yet carry the greatest sway with men'. The other lay in that rhetoric – the 'deliberative orations' – which, by appealing to those passions, furnished the 'grounds and motives' for war. By 1629 in Charles I's parliaments, as previously in democratic Athens,

such men only swayed the assemblies, and were esteemed wise and good commonwealth's men, as did put them upon the most dangerous and desperate enterprizes. Wheras he that gave them temperate and discreet advice, was thought a coward, or not to understand, or else to malign their power . . . By this means it came to pass amongst the Athenians, who thought they were able to do anything, that wicked men and flatterers drave them headlong into those actions that were to ruin them; and the good men either durst not oppose, or if they did, undid themselves.[9]

In this context, not only did Thucydides' masterful recreation of Athenian oratory succeed in conveying to a contemporary English readership the true causes of 'the greatest disturbance in the history of the Hellenes'.[10] It did so in a way which invited the reader actually to experience the dangerous passions concerned. 'Thucydides aimeth always at this; to make his auditor a spectator, and to cast his reader into the same passions that they were in that were beholders.'[11] The result was not simply the relation of a tragedy, but the imaginative experience of it. In 1629 this was offered by Hobbes not only to warn against, but hopefully to substitute for, the re-enactment of a similar tragedy in Charles I's England.[12]

---

[7] Thomas Hobbes, 'To the Readers' and 'On the Life and History of Thucydides', in R. B. Schlatter (ed.), *Hobbes' Thucydides* (New Brunswick, N.J., 1975).
[8] Ibid. pp. 6, 7, 20.   [9] Ibid. pp. 12–13.   [10] Ibid. p. 35
[11] Ibid. p. 18. Hobbes was here quoting Plutarch.
[12] Clarendon was not the only one to miss this point when he responded to *Leviathan* that 'had Mr Hobbes bin of this opinion when he taught Thucydides to speak English, which Book contains more of the Science of Mutiny and Sedition, and teaches more of that Oratory that contributes

Thus we may justly see in Hobbes the first identifier of an English classical republicanism upon which the modern work of Fink and his successors offers a commentary. For this the key sources given in *Leviathan* are Aristotle and Cicero, but the offending understanding of '*Liberty*' is from 'Aristotle's *Politiques*', and this is in line with Hobbes' identification of Athens as the root source of a self-destructive rhetorical political culture. Elsewhere Hobbes declaimed against 'All the Philosophers, Plato, Aristotle, Cicero, Seneca, Plutarch, and the rest of the maintainers of the Greek, and Roman Anarchies'.[13] Also in the late 1620s Sir Robert Filmer drew upon Plato, Aristotle, Thucydides, Xenephon, Livy, Tacitus, Cicero, Sallust, Suetonius and Plutarch's *Life of Sulla* to offer a similarly hair-raising account of the 'popular politics' invented in Athens and perfected in Rome. 'The Athenians sold justice as they did other merchandise . . . The blood hath been sucked up in the market-place with sponges: the river Tiber hath been filled with the dead bodies of citizens.'[14] Of course such hostile commentary should not be accepted uncritically. Yet it is significant that most republicans defended precisely the same authorities. Thus Sidney, who mocked Hobbes' passage[15] and wrote an entire book refuting Filmer, praised 'Aristotle . . . Plato, Plutarch, Thucydides, Xenophon, Polybius, and all the ancient Grecians, Italians and others who asserted the natural freedom of mankind'.[16]

Fink identified a seventeenth-century republican canon, focused upon Milton, Harrington, Neville and Sidney. He related their thought to a series of key sources, and exemplar republics, ancient and contemporary. These latter included Athens, Sparta and Rome; Venice, Switzerland and the United Provinces. To these should be added the republic of Israel, with

thereunto, then all that Aristotle and Cicero have publish'd in all their writings, he would not have communicated such materials to his Country-men'. Edward Hyde, Earl of Clarendon, *A Brief View and Survey of the Dangerous and pernicious Errors to Church and State, in Mr Hobbes' Book, Entitled Leviathan* (London, 1676) pp. 84–5. According to Hobbes, neither such oratory nor such passions needed to be introduced to Caroline England. Given their presence, what needed to be 'communicated' was their likely consequences.

[13] Quoted by Paul Rahe, 'Antiquity Surpassed: the Repudiation of Classical Republicanism', in Wootton, *Republicanism* p. 252.

[14] Sir Robert Filmer, *Patriarcha*, in Johann Sommerville (ed.), *Sir Robert Filmer: Patriarcha and Other Writings* (Cambridge, 1991) pp. 27–8 (and more generally pp. 24–33); for the dating of *Patriarcha*'s composition see pp. xxxii–xxxiv.

[15] 'Hobbes indeed doth scurrilously deride Cicero, Plato and Aristotle, *caeterosque Romanae & Graecae anarchiae fautores*. But 'tis strange that this anarchy . . . that can have no strength and regular action, should overthrow all the monarchies that came within their reach.' Sidney, *Discourses*, ed. West pp. 49, 143–4.

[16] Algernon Sidney, *Discourses Concerning Government*, in *Sydney on Government: the Works of Algernon Sidney*, ed. J. Robertson (1772) p. 11.

God as lawgiver.[17] As Sidney remembered from his French exile, 'the design of the English had been, to make a republic on the model of that of the Hebrews, before they had their Kings, and on that of Sparta, of Rome, and of Venice, taking from each what was best, to make a perfect composition'.[18] Fink examined the antecedents of this classical republicanism in Tudor England, not least in More's *Utopia* and Sir Thomas Smith's *De Republica Anglorum*, to which recent scholars have returned.[19] He considered its post-seventeenth-century influence in a British imperial context, a subject pioneered in relation to Harrington by Russell Smith and again now newly fashionable.[20] Fink's most important theme, however, was to trace at the core of this 'pattern of thought' English adherence to a particular 'theory of mixed government'. The mixture concerned was of the three forms – monarchy, aristocracy and democracy (or polity) – described by Aristotle in *The Politics* in a discussion drawing upon Plato's *Laws*. In relation to this, he asserted

It was the Greek historian Polybius who, by bringing into conjunction the three ideas of divided power, balance, and permanence in government, and applying these principles specifically to the mixture of monarchy, aristocracy, and democracy, was mainly responsible for giving the theory of mixed government its characteristic form.[21]

Thus notwithstanding the range of Fink's study, its theoretical focus was highly specific. Concentrating upon the end of permanence, and this constitutional formula for achieving it, pre-eminence was accorded to one classical source (Polybius) and one model republic (Venice).[22] It is hardly surprising that this mode of thinking found its exemplar in Harrington's *Oceana* (1656). For Harrington's work was indeed an attempt to realise the ambition of 'immortal government' by explicitly Venetian constitutional

---

[17] See, for instance, James Harrington, *The Art of Lawgiving* (1659); and for the Dutch case, Lea Campos Boralevi, 'Classical Foundational Myths of European Republicanism: the Jewish Commonwealth', in van Gelderen and Skinner, *Republicanism* vol. 1.

[18] Lantin, 'Lantiniana' p. 99 (my translation).

[19] Fink, *Classical Republicans* pp. 21–4; Quentin Skinner, 'Sir Thomas More's *Utopia* and the Language of Renaissance Humanism', in Pagden, *The Languages of Political Theory*; Eric Nelson, 'Nonsense in More's *Utopia*', *Historical Journal* 44, 4 (2001); Collinson, *De Republica*.

[20] Russell Smith, *Harrington*; Robbins, *Eighteenth Century Commonwealthsman*; Pocock, *Machiavellian Moment* chs. 13–15; David Armitage, *The Ideological Origins of the British Empire* (Cambridge, 2000) esp. ch. 5.

[21] Fink, *Classical Republicans* p. 3.

[22] Ibid. chs. 1 ('Politiques Learned out of Historians and Declaimers') and 2 ('The Most Serene Republic').

means.[23] Indeed a recent study has argued that Harrington's entire understanding of what he called 'ancient prudence' consisted in an adherence to the Polybian doctrine of the mixed constitution.[24] Accordingly Fink's study fell considerably short of furnishing an adequate overall account of its subject. If Harrington's objective of constitutional permanence was shared, among republicans, only by Henry Neville (less single-mindedly), his belief in the possibility of constitutional immortality was unique. If constitutional models played a limited role within English republican writing, among these, as we will see, the mixed constitution arrived relatively late and was vigorously disputed. Among the sources for republican constitutional thought, even in Harrington, evidence of a direct debt to Polybius is limited, while evidence for that to Plato, Arisotle and Machiavelli is abundant.[25]

Similarly, there is no doubt of the importance to Harrington of Venice, with Contarini (*Of the Magistracy and Republic of Venice* (1543)) and Gianotti as his sources. In this respect it was his view that Machiavelli had 'saddled the wrong horse, for though Rome . . . in her military part could beat it better, beyond all comparison . . . Venice, for the civil, hath plainly had the wings of Pegasus'.[26] Yet, by contrast, most English republicans combined praise for the exemplary achievement of 'the *Romans* (who were the noblest of them all)' with anti-Venetian hostility.[27] Thus for Nedham, according to whom 'those that have in their hands the Government of a State, ought to increase the number of their free Subjects', the restricted citizen base of the serene republic rendered it 'rather a Junta, than a Commonwealth'.[28] For John Streater, Venice's failure in this respect followed from a demographic failure resulting from 'their tollerating of Adultery . . . in men . . . [and] Whoredom in women'.[29] For Sidney also the addiction of the Venetians to peace was 'a mortal error in their constitution'.[30] These stances accepted Machiavelli's devastating attack on the exemplary status of Venice in the

[23] Ibid. ch. 3 ('Immortal Government: Oceana'); Harrington, *Oceana*, in *Political Works* p. 244; Scott, *England's Troubles* pp. 327–41.

[24] Fukuda, *Sovereignty and the Sword* esp. chs. 1 and 5–7.

[25] Scott, Review of Fukuda in *English Historical Review* 115, 462 (June 2000) pp. 660–2; see chapter 6 below.

[26] Harrington, *Oceana*, in *Political Works* p. 277.

[27] Marchamont Nedham, *Mercurius Politicus* no. 112. p. 1754; David Wootton examines such hostility after Harrington in '"Ulysses Bound": Venice and the Idea of Liberty from Howell to Hume', in Wootton, *Republicanism*.

[28] [Marchamont Nedham] *Vox Plebis, or, The Peoples Out-cry Against Oppression, Injustice, and Tyranny* (1646) p. 67; Nedham, *The Excellencie of a Free-State* (1656) p. 63.

[29] Streater, *Observations* no. 3, 19–26 April 1654, p. 18.

[30] Sidney, *Discourses*, in *Sydney on Government* (1772) pp. 175, 178–9.

Discourses. Even in Neville's *Plato Redivivus* (1680), if for the recovery of English political health and harmony Venice 'is this day the only school of the world', so Rome is 'the best and most glorious government that ever the sun saw'.[31]

This makes more striking across the whole range of republican writing an engagement with Machiavelli which transcended these differences and others. Fink's neglect of Machiavelli began to be remedied by Felix Rabb in 1964.[32] However the study which Machiavellianised classical republicanism was Pocock's *The Machiavellian Moment* (1975). Harrington's *Oceana* 'mark[ed] a moment of paradigmatic breakthrough, a major revision of English political theory and history in the light of concepts drawn from civic humanism and Machiavellian republicanism'.[33] By Anglicising the paradigm, Harrington prepared it for a second, transposed (and adapted) life in eighteenth-century England and America. This connected the Florentine civic humanism recently excavated by Hans Baron to the anglophone origins of American republicanism investigated by Caroline Robbins and then Bernard Bailyn.[34] One side product was the addition to the canon of Marchamont Nedham, whose role as pioneer of the English use of Machiavelli's *Discorsi* continues to be excavated.[35]

In fact, as we have seen, according to Hobbes by 1656 Harrington was a relatively late contributor to an established genre. Equally it is clear that what appeared to Pocock and others to be the distinct political languages of classical republicanism and natural law theory were more often combined by early modern republicans than separated. In the words of one scholar, 'It is impossible to see the division between a juristic-liberal and a republican tradition as fundamental to post-Renaissance political thought . . . Natural law . . . was readily adapted by republicans.'[36] Far from being mutually exclusive, classical republicanism and natural law theory shared an appeal to the faculty of human reason which was Greek in origin, but frequently

---

[31] Henry Neville, *Plato Redivivus: or, A Dialogue Concerning Government*, in Robbins, *Two English Republican Tracts* pp. 82, 91.

[32] Raab, *Machiavelli*.

[33] Pocock, *Machiavellian Moment* p. 384; see also David Underdown, 'The Harringtonian Moment' –, *Journal of British Studies* 18.2 (1979) pp. 171–9.

[34] Baron, *The Crisis*; Robbins, *Eighteenth Century Commonwealthsman*; Robbins, 'Algernon Sidney's *Discourses*'; Bailyn, *Ideological Origins*.

[35] Pocock, 'Historical Introduction' pp. 33–7; Scott, *Algernon Sidney and the English Republic* pp. 110–12; Scott, 'English Republican Imagination', in J. S. Morrill (ed.), *Revolution and Restoration: England in the 1650s* (London, 1992); Worden, '"Wit in a Roundhead"'; Worden, 'Marchamont Nedham'. The key early work is the Leveller pamphlet *Vox Plebis* (1646), noticed by Raab, *Machiavelli* pp. 170–2. See chapter 3 below, in particular notes 102 and 107.

[36] Knud Haakonssen, 'Republicanism', in Robert Goodin and Philip Pettit (eds.), *A Companion to Contemporary Political Philosophy* (Oxford, 1993) pp. 570–1.

in the early modern period Christian in application. Thus in America, too, John Adams spoke of what he called 'revolution principles. They are the principles of Aristotle and Plato, of Livy and Cicero, and Sydney, Harrington and Locke. The principles of nature and eternal reason. The principles on which the whole government over us, now stands.'[37]

No less important to his engagement with Harrington was Pocock's prior interest in historical thought.[38] This paid attention to Hans Baron's revelation of the invention, in the works of Bruni, Salutati and others, of a classical republican history for Quattrocento Florence. In addition *The Machiavellian Moment* was driven by a thesis about classical republicanism as a mode of self-awareness in time. This was characterised by a secular, or pagan, consciousness of temporality distinct from the 'timeless hierarchic universe' of the 'scholastic customary framework'. This 'polis, or republic . . . had to be conceived of as finite and localised in time, and therefore as presenting all the problems of particularity'.[39] It was in relation to this conciousness that Pocock accepted Fink's thesis about the important role played by the stabilising properties of the Polybian mixed constitution. At the same time, alongside Fink's Polybian exemplar of Venice, Pocock's Machiavelli now added Rome.

Yet Pocock's most important contribution to the genre lay outside the field of constitutional thought. For the principal limitation of Fink's study was its relative neglect of moral philosophy. As for Baron, however, so for Pocock, classical republicanism, associated with civic humanism, was an attempt politically to realise ethical ends. Thus for both scholars, the focus of any discussion of means was not simply constitutional structures but (within those structures) the practice of self-governing citizenship. This emphasis upon civic practice subsequently helped to give rise, in the work of Quentin Skinner, to a focus upon Cicero as the pre-eminent source for republican moral philosophy. Skinner has identified as the basis for Italian (and, more recently, English) republicanism a Roman rhetorical and legal culture to be distinguished from Greek moral philosophy in general, and 'scholastic' Aristotelianism in particular.[40] This has been associated with a broader characterisation of humanism as deriving almost exclusively from

---

[37] Quoted by Annabel Patterson, *Early Modern Liberalism* (Cambridge, 1997) p. 279.

[38] J. G. A. Pocock, *The Ancient Constitution and the Feudal Law . . . Reissue with a Retrospect* (Cambridge, 1987) Part I, ch. 6.

[39] Pocock, *Machiavellian Moment* p. 54; Pocock, *Politics, Language and Time* p. 85.

[40] Quentin Skinner, *The Foundations of Modern Political Thought, Volume I: The Renaissance* (Cambridge, 1978) chs. 1–4 and 6; Skinner, 'The Republican Ideal of Political Liberty'; Skinner, *Liberty before Liberalism*.

Roman sources, and a juxtaposition of the influence of Cicero, as proponent of the active political life, to that of Plato especially, but also Aristotle.[41]

It is true that Greek and Roman political thought cannot be equated, and that the distinction between the contemplative and active civic life played an important role within humanist culture in both Italy and England.[42] Yet the distinction between philosophy and politics did not coincide with that between Greece and Rome, as between these there were also important continuities. Most historians understand humanism, and its relationship to rhetoric, to derive from an engagement with classical sources in general, rather than Roman ones in particular.[43] Leonardo Bruni was, among other things, a scholar of Plato, who absorbed style as well as content 'from Platonic and Ciceronian dialogues'.[44] In Baron's study the Florentine understanding of the benefits of civic self-government derived from sources both Greek (Plato, Aristotle, Pericles' funeral oration in Thucydides' *History*) and Roman (Cicero, Seneca, Livy).[45] That Hobbes believed the same was true in England is hardly surprising, given his translation into English of the same funeral oration, according to which:

Our constitution is called a democracy because power is in the hands not of a minority but of the whole people. When it is a question of settling private disputes, everyone is equal before the law; when it is a question of putting one person before another in positions of public responsibility, what counts is not membership of a particular class, but the actual ability which the man possesses . . . And, just as our political life is free and open, so . . . [are] our relations with each other . . . We

[41] Quentin Skinner, 'Introduction: the Reality of the Renaissance', in Skinner, *Visions of Politics, Volume II: Renaissance Virtues*. Thus in Skinner, 'Sir Thomas More's *Utopia* and the Language of Renaissance Humanism', 'the' language of Renaissance humanism is Ciceronian, Aristotle appears as a source for scholasticism (and the pre-humanist prejudices of the landed nobility), and this humanism is challenged by More with Platonism. An alternative way of presenting this argument would be to depict Plato, Aristotle and Cicero as informing a debate within English and European humanism.

[42] Skinner, 'Sir Thomas More's *Utopia*' (in which respect Paul Rahe, 'Situating Machiavelli', in Hankins, *Renaissance Civic Humanism*, would appear to overstate his case).

[43] Paul Kristeller, 'Humanism', in Charles B. Schmitt, Quentin Skinner and Eckhard Kessler (eds.), *The Cambridge History of Renaissance Philosophy* (Cambridge, 1988); Nicolai Rubenstein, 'Italian Political Thought 1450–1530', in J. H. Burns and Mark Goldie (eds.), *The Cambridge History of Political Thought 1450-1700* (Cambridge, 1991) p. 54; Anthony Grafton, 'Humanism and Political Theory', in Burns and Goldie, *Cambridge History of Political Thought* pp. 13–16; Alistair Fox, 'Facts and Fallacies: Interpreting English Humanism', in Alistair Fox and John Guy (eds.), *Reassessing the Henrician Age: Humanism, Politics and Reform 1500–1550* (Oxford, 1986). This last, in emphasising the diversity of Tudor humanism, touches on many of the themes of this study.

[44] Baron, *The Crisis* vol. 1, p. 194; James Hankins, *Plato in the Italian Renaissance* (2 vols., Leiden and New York, 1990) vol. 1, chs. 1–2.

[45] Baron, *The Crisis* vol. 1, pp. 56, 97, 194, 358–64, 374.

are free and tolerant in our private lives; but in public affairs we keep to the law . . . especially those which are for the protection of the oppressed.[46]

It was thus not without reason that Hobbes complained of the contemporary impact of an idea of 'Libertie, whereof there is so frequent, and honourable mention, in the Histories, and Philosophy of the Antient Greeks, and Romans . . . derived . . . not from the Principles of Nature, but . . . the Practise of their own Common-wealths'.[47]

In Pocock's account, as in that of Hobbes, the core moral philosophy informing this Graeco-Roman synthesis was Aristotelian. It was Aristotle who 'articulated the positive conception of liberty . . . a style of thought . . . in which . . . the development of the individual towards self-fulfillment is possible only when [he] . . . acts as a citizen . . . [in] a conscious and autonomous decision-taking political community'.[48] For Pocock, Harrington exhibited both 'the humanist mode of discourse' and the doctrine of 'mixed government'.[49] Most importantly, and partly through Machiavelli, *Oceana* brought Aristotelian moral and political philosophy ('ancient prudence') to bear upon the new material circumstances created by the collapse of English feudalism and monarchy ('modern prudence'). '*The Commonwealth of Oceana*, then, is both a civil history of the sword and a civil history of property. It offers to explain, first, how . . . England has become a commonwealth of independent freeholders . . . and second, how this commonwealth may be organised for government as a republic.' As Aristotle had emphasised the importance of material independence as a basis for political citizenship, so *Oceana* showed historically how England had acquired 'an autonomous citizenry capable of individual participation in their government'.[50]

As one should expect from both its scope and complexity, this argument has opened itself to many objections. Among these it is useful to distinguish between those who have opposed Pocock's account of Harrington and those who have opposed his larger thesis concerning classical republicanism. The vulnerabilities of the latter are primarily ones of scale. In fact, far from arguing for the unaltered transmission of a single language, constitutional

[46] Thucydides, *History of the Peloponnesian War*, ed. M. I. Finley, trans. Rex Warner (Harmondsworth, 1975) p. 145.

[47] Hobbes, *Leviathan* pp. 149–50.

[48] J. G. A. Pocock, *Virtue, Commerce and History: Essays on Political Thought and History, Chiefly in the Eighteenth Century* (Cambridge, 1985) p. 40.

[49] Pocock, 'Historical Introduction' p. 15; Pocock, 'Spinoza and Harrington: an Exercise in Comparison', *Bijdragen en Mededelingen Betreffende de Geschiedenis der Nederlanden* 102, 3 (1987) pp. 444–5.

[50] Pocock, 'Historical Introduction' pp. 43, 42.

formula and moral philosophy, Pocock's is an account of successive adaptations of classical republicanism to meet changing circumstances. What is nevertheless striking is the pivotal role as transmitters of a tradition ascribed by Pocock to the two Renaissance writers who broke most radically with the republican contexts upon which they drew.

For Machiavelli the most important aspect of this break concerned moral philosophy. As Quentin Skinner has put it, there is no 'even approximate equivalence between [Machiavelli's] *virtu* and the virtues' to which his Florentine republican contemporaries ascribed.[51] This is a sceptical break with rational classical moral philosophy more generally.[52] Indeed there are few classical ideas, including that of the Polybian mixed constitution, of which Machiavelli does not make self-conciously innovatory use. Thus for Paul Rahe, who accepts Pocock's identification of classical republicanism with rational Greek moral and political philosophy, in Machiavelli we find a point of, not transmission, but truncation. From Machiavelli onwards, Rahe has argued, we see the replacement of classical republicanism with new, modern, institutionally orientated 'modes and orders'.[53] These are exhibited most clearly by Harrington, whose conception of a 'perfectly equal commonwealth' appears to make claims of a new kind for institutional science.[54]

Of course there was nothing peculiarly modern about constitutional thought. In Plato's *Laws* and Aristotle's *Politics* it was the role of laws to give appropriate institutional shape to the rational ordering of human souls. Among English republicans this idea remained inspirational. Yet, as we will see, it is the function of *Oceana*'s 'orders' to supply not the public 'discipline' supporting potentially rational civic behaviour, but the public *reason* which cannot actually be expected from individual political choices.[55] Nor did Harrington share the Greek or Roman understandings of reason or liberty ('reason is nothing but interest'; 'Mr Hobbs treatises of liberty and necessity are . . . those which I have followed, and shall follow').[56] Harrington was explicit in underlining the innovative status of these claims,

[51] Skinner, *Foundations of Modern Political Thought* vol. I, p. 138.

[52] Scott, 'Classical Republicanism'.

[53] Rahe, *Republics Ancient and Modern, Volume I: The Ancien Regime in Cassical Greece; Volume II: New Modes and Orders in Early Modern Political Thought*.

[54] Scott, 'Classical Republicanism'; Scott, 'The Rapture of Motion'; Scott, *England's Troubles* ch. 14; Davis, *Utopia and the Ideal Society* chs. 7–8. See also Vickie Sullivan, 'The Civic Humanist Portrait of Machiavelli's English Successors', *History of Political Thought* 15, 1 (1994) pp. 86–7.

[55] It is *Oceana*'s orders, not its citizens, that are rational. It is by them that 'divers' self-interests ('private reason, which is the interest of a private man') are united in the public interest ('right reason, or the interest of the whole'). See Scott, 'Peace of Silence' pp. 108–9 and chapter 8 below.

[56] See chapters 7 and 8 below.

which were indeed the product of his immersion in 'the new science' (mechanical natural philosophy).[57]

Certainly, if classical republicanism was a language, Aristotle, Machiavelli and Harrington all used it in very different ways. By Machiavelli only is *virtu* pitted against *fortuna*; by Harrington fortune ('if there be any such thing') is dispensed with.[58] By Harrington also classical republicanism is combined with several other languages, including astronomical imagery shared with his fellow natural philosopher John Streater, and the Hobbesian terminology of art and nature. Most importantly, the search for an Aristotelian moral philosophy in either Machiavelli or Harrington faces substantial obstacles. Rahe's response to this situation is to abandon the search for an early modern classical republicanism altogether. Yet this is to ignore evidence of it, even as Pocock and Rahe understand it, in Machiavelli's and Harrington's more conventional republican contemporaries. It is also to ignore the real classical content of both Machiavelli's and Harrington's work. Although both used ancient sources in consciously innovative ways – Machiavelli claiming to 'enter upon a new way, as yet untrodden by anyone else', Harrington to 'go mine own way, and yet to follow the ancients' – in both cases this was in order to adapt to modern political conditions what they took to be the genuine lessons of classical experience.[59]

Thus a second approach is to abandon, not the idea of early modern classical republicanism, but Pocock's formulation of it. One solution, that of Fukuda, is to pull back to Fink's focus upon constitutional prescription. Yet here too Polybius, Machiavelli and Harrington all use the mixed constitution, and the associated idea of 'balance', in very different ways. Moreover Harrington is the only English republican whose thought may usefully be approached in these primarily constitutional terms. Thus a third solution is to accept Pocock's reorientation of the inquiry towards moral philosophy, but to redefine that philosophy. Thus for Quentin Skinner the moral philosophy at the heart of classical republicanism was not Greek but Roman; its focus was upon not participatory virtue, but liberty; and this liberty was, in Isaiah Berlin's terms, not positive but negative (liberty from any possibility of dependence upon a will other than one's own).[60] In some ways this reformulation does appear capable of reintegrating both Machiavelli and

[57] Harrington, *Oceana*, in *Political Works* p. 320.   [58] Ibid. p. 276.

[59] Machiavelli, *Discourses* Preface to Book 1, p. 97; Harrington, *Oceana*, in *Political Works* p. 163; Scott, 'Classical Republicanism' p. 66.

[60] Skinner, 'The Republican Ideal of Political Liberty'; Skinner, *Liberty before Liberalism*; Skinner, 'A Third Concept of Liberty', *London Review of Books* (4 April 2002).

Harrington with a republican moral philosophy with authentically classical roots.

There is no shortage of evidence concerning the impact upon Harrington and his republican contemporaries of Sallust, Cicero, Livy and Tacitus. Such sources, and the anxiety they focused upon the problem of dependence upon a will other than one's own, became highly politically relevant not only during the early Stuart period, but again after the restoration. In particular, across the seventeenth century republican writers had recourse to Cicero, Tacitus and Machiavelli in order to confront the contemporary problem of one-time monarchies turned to tyrannies. Before the foundation of the republic this was evident in the language not only of parliamentarians, but of Levellers, and ultimately of the New Model Army, by whom parliamentarian rhetoric was appropriated and radicalised.[61] In the words of William Walwyn, 'And no doubt many of you understood by the Liberties of the People, that they intended to free the Commons in Parliament the peoples Representative, from a Negative voice, in King, or Lords.'[62]

Yet not only is it clear that republicans did not see liberty exclusively in these terms. Even the features upon which Skinner has focused, far from emanating exclusively from Roman sources, were heavily indebted to an Aristotelian formulation itself deriving from Plato's *Laws*. As observed by Hobbes, on the subject of 'Libertie . . . as *Aristotle* . . . so *Cicero*'.[63] For the crucial idea that 'law ought to be the most powerful in the state', Milton referred to Plato's *Laws*, as well as to Aristotle and Cicero.[64] In both *Oceana* (1656) and *The Prerogative of Popular Government* (1658) Harrington attributed his definition of 'ancient prudence' as 'the empire of laws and not of men' to 'Aristotle and Livy'. When Sidney made the same idea central to the *Discourses* he did so with a quotation from Book 3 of Aristotle's *Politics* ('*Lex est mens sine affectu, & quasi Deus*') and another from Livy's *History*.[65] Even Cicero and Machiavelli, in eliminating what had been for Plato and Aristotle the crucial distinction between monarchy and tyranny, were indebted to Greek analyses of the latter.[66]

[61] See chapter 11 below; Skinner, 'Classical Liberty'.

[62] William Walwyn, *The Bloody Project* (1648), in Jack R. McMichael and Barbara Taft (eds.), *The Writings of William Walwyn* (Athens, Ga., 1989) p. 298.

[63] Hobbes, *Leviathan* pp. 149–50.   [64] Milton, *Defence* pp. 383, 438.

[65] Harrington, *Political Works*, ed. Pocock pp. 161, 401; Sidney, *Discourses*, ed. West pp. 17, 288; Sidney, *Court Maxims* p. 20; Aristotle, *The Politics*, ed. Stephen Everson (Cambridge, 1988), in particular Book 3; Scott, Review of Fukuda pp. 660–2.

[66] Cicero, *On the Commonwealth*, in *On the Commonwealth and On the Laws*, ed. James Zetzel (Cambridge, 1999) pp. 47–50 (discussing Plato); Machiavelli, *Discourses* p. 276 (referring the reader to Xenophon).

This brings us finally to the no less important thesis of Eric Nelson.[67] Like Skinner, Nelson argues against the idea of a Graeco-Roman synthesis, focusing upon two differences between Greek and Roman political thought: their informing moral philosophy, and their attitudes to property. In relation to moral philosophy he sides with Skinner, and against Pocock, in situating Aristotle alongside Plato as an enthusiast for contemplative virtue. Yet Nelson's second suggestion is that the Greek emphasis upon contemplation need not stand in the way of the notion of a Greek classical republicanism. Classical republicanism and civic humanism should not be conflated: the latter is only one type of the former. Nelson's account of an alternative 'Greek tradition' has two bases. The first is Platonic contemplative metaphysics (and in Aristotle's relegation here to the status of vehicle for the same, Pocock and Rahe's Graeco-Roman synthesis gives way to a Greek synthesis). The second is a Greek attitude to the material context for successful politics which emphasises the dangers posed by extremes of private wealth. This perspective on property is found, first, in Plato and Aristotle themselves. It is then recovered in Greek historians of Rome (Plutarch, Appian) whose attitude to the Roman agrarian laws is shown to contrast sharply with that of Roman historians of the same subject (Cicero, Livy).

The stage is then set for the examination of a series of early modern and modern figures who worked with these Greek perspectives, material and moral. The first is More, whose *Utopia* not only combines the metaphysics and community of property of Plato's *Republic*, but does so within a humanist context which is self-conciously anti-Roman. The second is More's contemporary, Machiavelli, subverting the Roman tradition from within in a way which, while it does not borrow from Greek sources, brings him to an attitude towards private wealth capable of making such sources interesting to his followers. This helps to explain Harrington's otherwise puzzling attempt to bring the Greek tradition and Machiavelli together. Nelson's examination of Harrington suggests that he derived his understanding of the importance of agrarian laws from Plutarch, the agrarian law of Oceana itself largely from Plato's *Laws*, and the moral philosophy informing *Oceana* from Plato's *Timaeus*.[68]

---

[67] Nelson, 'The Greek Tradition in Republican Thought'. I am very grateful to Dr Nelson for allowing me to discuss his thesis in manuscript form. His book under the same title has now been published by Cambridge University Press.

[68] As Nelson acknowledges, Harrington's debt to Plato, and to the *Laws* in particular, has previously been noticed in general terms (Blitzer, *Immortal Commonwealth*). The same is true of his association of the principles informing the agrarian with Aristotle, a subject most fully explored in Cotton's *Harrington* esp. ch. 2.

There were certainly distinct Greek and Roman attitudes to private property, the protection of which was, for Cicero, a primary purpose of the republic, but extremes of which, in the Greek tradition, posed a potentially mortal danger to virtue. This aspect of Greek moral philosophy was at work not only in More and Harrington, but in their fellow Platonists Milton and Sidney, who praised 'that honest poverty, which is the mother and nurse of modesty, sobriety and all manner of virtue' and condemned 'those vices that arise from the superfluity of riches'.[69] Yet alongside the important points of connection between Plato and Aristotle, and of distinction between Greek and Roman writers, the other side of each case must be put. Although in the *Nicomachean Ethics* Aristotle followed Plato in praising contemplation as the highest form of happiness,[70] his practical interest in the *Politics* was in the context for a happy (that is, moral) *way of life*, and not simply for individuals but communities.[71] For those capable of it this entailed not only contemplative, but also practical wisdom (*sophia* and *phronesis*), as well as the other cardinal virtues (justice, courage, temperance). It was the point of Aristotle's understanding of civic activity as by turns *ruling and being ruled* (another formula derived from Plato's *Laws*) that only by the combination of contemplation and action could man's moral potential be fully realised. When Cicero laid *entire* emphasis upon the greater moral importance of *negotium* over *otium* he was thus building upon Aristotle, as well as departing from him.[72]

It is true that More, Erasmus and others understood their humanism as Greek *rather than* Roman.[73] Even for these figures, however, there was a difference between asserting the superiority of Greek over Roman philosophy, and dignifying the latter with the status of an opposition. Thus for Richard Pace 'Whatever seems to have originated with the Romans . . . was all taken from the Greeks . . . Cicero called Plato . . . "divine" . . . and Aristotle . . . "most wise".'[74] Thomas Starkey's *A Dialogue between Pole and Lupset* strove to combine Platonic metaphysics with a commitment to the *vita activa*, on the grounds that 'arystotyl . . . shoyth . . . the perfectyon of man to stond joyntely in both, and nother in . . . bare contemplation and knolege of thyngys, seperat from al besynes of the world[,] nother [only] in

---

[69] Sidney, *Discourses*, ed. West p. 350.
[70] Aristotle, *Ethics,* ed. Jonathan Barnes (Harmondsworth, 1984) pp. 333–5.
[71] Ibid. pp. 337, 342; Aristotle, *The Politics*.
[72] For the influence of Aristotle on Cicero see James Zetzel, 'Introduction', in Cicero, *On the Commonwealth and On the Laws*.
[73] Nelson, 'Greek Nonsense'; Skinner, 'Sir Thomas More's Utopia'.
[74] Quoted by Nelson, 'Greek Nonsense' p. 898.

the admynystratyon of materys of the commyn wele'.[75] For Robert Boyle similarly, the interdependence of contemplation and action was such that 'it is almost impossible [for anyone] to contemplate wel, who has not first, by Active Virtue; subdu'd & rang'd his inordinate Passions, & lawless desires'.[76] For seventeenth-century republicans nothing was more characteristic than the attempt to combine public political participation with contemplative wisdom (within a framework of self-government through laws, and civic education).

COMMONWEALTH PRINCIPLES

In early modern anglophone political writing the word 'commonwealth' was ubiquitous. It was also, until the mid-seventeenth century, uncontroversial. Capable of referring to the public social or political community, or both, to invoke commonwealth principles was to subscribe to the Platonic and Aristotelian commonplace that, whatever its constitutional form, government must be directed to the public good. In a related sense 'commonwealth' was the English rendering of the Latin *res publica*, meaning 'public thing', and defined by Cicero as 'the concern of a people . . . associated with one another through agreement on law [in Augustine 'a common sense of right'] and community of interest'.[77] Most broadly *res publica* denoted less a specific form of government than 'that public realm of affairs which people had in common outside their familial lives . . . [their] *res privata*'.[78]

In his consideration of what the full title of *Utopia* called 'the Best State of a Commonwealth', Thomas More aligned himself with Plato's treatment of this question (in *The Republic*) against that of Cicero (in *De Republica*).[79] When Bodin's *Six Livres de la Republique* was translated into English in 1606 as *The Six Bookes of a Commonweale* it emphasised that its concern was to clarify not, with Plato and More, how commonwealths ought to be, but what they actually were, in which connection the efforts of Aristotle and

---

[75] Thomas Starkey, *A Dialogue between Pole and Lupset*, ed. T. F. Mayer (London, 1989) pp. 3–4; Thomas Mayer, *Thomas Starkey and the Commonweal: Humanist Politics and Religion in the Reign of Henry VIII* (Cambridge, 1988) pp. 151–2.

[76] Quoted in J. R. Jacob, *Robert Boyle and the English Revolution* (New York, 1977) p. 74.

[77] Cicero, *On the Commonwealth* p. 18; Augustine, *City of God*, ed. David Knowles (Harmondsworth, 1972) p. 73; W. K. Lacey and B. W. J. G. Wilson, *Res Publica: Roman Politics and Society According to Cicero* (Oxford, 1970) p. 1.

[78] Haakonssen, 'Republicanism', p. 569.

[79] Thomas More, *Utopia*, ed. George M. Logan and Robert M. Adams (Cambridge, 1989).

Cicero left room for improvement.[80] When Hobbes approached the same task in 1651, the book he described as his 'discourse of Common-wealth' began, as Bodin had, with his definition of 'a COMMON-WEALTH, or STATE (in latine CIVITAS) which is but an Artificiall Man'.[81] Thus when, a year after the publication of *Leviathan*, Marchamont Nedham associated England's new republican government with the championship of something called '*Common-weal Principles*', this was, etymologically at least, uncontroversial. Following a period of conflict during which the commonwealth had in fact been torn asunder, Nedham spoke for one of a variety of groups each claiming to stand for, or be solely capable of serving, the public interest. In this context his controversial claim consisted in the identification of that general moral, with a specific political interest – 'the *Declared Interest* of a *Free State* or *Common-weal*' – continuing:

[Now] that we are put into [that] better course . . . I conceived nothing could more highly tend to the propogation of this *Interest*, and the honour of its Founders, then . . . that the People . . . may . . . understand what *Common-weal Principles* are, and thereby . . . learn to be true Common-wealth's men, and zealous against *Monarchick Interest*, in all its Appearances and Incroachments whatsoever.[82]

Earlier insisting that without a '*due and orderly succession* of Power and Persons . . . it is impossible any Nation should long subsist in a State of Freedom', Nedham had described this as 'good *Common-wealth* Lan-guage'.[83] It was perhaps a measure of the success of mid-century republican writers in associating a terminology which had been universal with a par-ticular political position that, by 1681, Algernon Sidney and Sir William Jones were driven to express their indignation that to be reputed a 'com-monwealthsman' had become a brand of infamy. For

if Common-wealth signifies the common good, in which sense it hath in all ages been used . . . and which Bodin puts upon it when . . . he calls [France] a republic, no good man will be ashamed of it . . . It is strange how this word should so change its signification with us in the space of twenty years. All monarchies . . . that are not purely barbarous and tyrannical, have ever been called Common-wealths. Rome itself altered not that name, when it fell under the sword of the Caesars . . . And in our days, it doth not only belong to Venice, Genoa, Switzerland, and the United

[80] Jean Bodin, *The Six Bookes of a Commonweale* ed. Richard Knolles (1606), a facsimile reprint, ed. K. D. McRae (Cambridge, Mass., 1962) pp. 1–3.

[81] Hobbes, *Leviathan* pp. 1, 3, 9.

[82] Marchamont Nedham, *Mercurius Politicus* no. 92, 4–11 March, 1652, pp. 1457–8.

[83] Ibid. no. 79, p. 1257; no. 80.

Provinces . . . but to Germany, Spain, France, Sweden, Poland, and all the kingdoms of Europe.[84]

Thus to the extent to which we are to continue to be guided by linguistic methodology we must recognise, well before the publication of Harrington's *The Commonwealth of Oceana*, long-standing medieval as well as classical components of what Nedham called 'good *Common-wealth* Language'. Quentin Skinner has drawn attention to the influence of Roman law assumptions upon the work of Henry Bracton, Sir Thomas Littleton and Sir Thomas Smith, all authorities much cited by early seventeenth-century parliamentarians.[85] One could speak equally of the fundamental Aristotelianism of Smith, of many of his Elizabethan contemporaries (John Aylmer, William Cecil, Richard Hakluyt), and of that most-cited of all medieval legal authorities Chancellor Fortescue.[86]

In fact all of these writers drew upon Greek, Roman and Christian sources to explain that the kingdom was also a commonwealth. In the words of Patrick Collinson, among Elizabethan parliamentarians 'It became the weariest of all political commonplaces to repeat the Roman Cicero, himself following Plato. "We are not born for ourselves alone, but our country claims a share of our being."'[87] In particular, two principles informed this commonwealth discourse. The first was that whatever its constitutional form, government must be directed to the public good. The second was that it must be legal and constitutional (as Fortescue had put it, both *regale* and *politicum*), rather than the product of the will of a single person.[88] Both of these principles, articulated in Plato's *Republic* and *Laws*, were elaborated in Aristotle's *Politics*. In *The Republic* the extreme embodiment of self-interestedness, and therefore injustice and unhappiness, was the tyrannical man, a slave to his own lusts.[89] To these sources as well as others, writers as

---

[84] Algernon Sidney [and Sir William Jones], *A Just and Modest Vindication of the Proceedings of the Two last Parliaments* (1681) in *State Tracts of the Reign of Charles II* (1689) vol. IV, Appendix 15, pp. clxviii–clxix. For the authorship of this tract see Scott, *Algernon Sidney and the Restoration Crisis* ch. 10.

[85] Skinner, 'Classical Liberty' pp. 309–12.

[86] David Harris Sacks, 'The Prudence of Thrasymachus: Sir Thomas Smith and the Commonwealth of England', in Anthony Grafton and J. H. M. Salmon (eds.), *Historians and Ideologues* (Rochester, N.Y., 2001); Armitage, *Ideological Origins* pp. 72–4, 75–6; Stephen Alford, *The Early Elizabethan Polity: William Cecil and the British Succession Crisis, 1558–1569* (Cambridge, 1998) pp. 14–24, 33–7; H. G Koenigsberger, 'Dominium Regale or Dominium Politicum et Regale', in Koenigsberger (ed.), *Politicians and Virtuosi* (1986).

[87] Patrick Collinson, 'Conclusion', in Collinson (ed.), *The Sixteenth Century* (Oxford, 2002) p. 233.

[88] Maurizio Viroli, *From Politics to Reason of State: the Acquisition and Transformation of a Language of Politics 1250–1600* (Cambridge, 1992).

[89] Plato, *The Republic*, trans. H. D. P. Lee (Harmondsworth, 1959) pp. 350–69; Plato, *The Laws*, trans. Trevor J. Saunders (Harmondsworth, 1975) p. 174.

diverse as Cicero, Fortescue, Erasmus, More and Smith all acknowledged their debt.[90]

Of the English constitution, Fortescue had insisted: 'Nor can the king there, by himself or by his ministers, impose tallages, subsidies or any other burdens whatever on his subjects, nor change their laws, nor make new ones, without the concession . . . of his whole realm expressed in his parliament.'[91] Building upon the same assumptions, John Aylmer explained in 1559: 'The regiment of England is not a mere Monarchie . . . nor a meere Oligarchie nor Democracie, but a rule mixte of all these . . . to be sene in the parliament house.'[92] When Smith remarked in his *De Republica Anglorum* (1583) that the English commonwealth was 'a society or common doing of a multitude of free men collected together and united by common accord . . . among themselves as well in peace as in warre', he concluded similarly that 'The most high and absolute power of the realme of Englande, is in the Parliament.'[93] Thus, when considering the question of 'whether monarchy be a power absolute', Milton noted in his *Commonplace Book* Smith's answer that this was no more the case than 'the elements are pure in nature, or the . . . temperatures in a body but mixt with other', so that 'the act of a k. neither approved by the people, nor establisht by act of parliament' is 'taken for nothing either to bind the k., his successors, or his subjects'.[94] In his *Defence of the English People* he observed: 'Thus Fortescue says, *De Laud. Leg. Ang.* Chapter 9: "The king of England governs his people not by the power of an absolute king but by that of a civil government," for the people is ruled by those laws which they have themselves passed.'[95] At his trial for treason Henry Vane affirmed that his understanding of the popular authorship of civil society ('the act of a community . . . by the right dictates . . . of . . . this . . . law of nature . . . in their hearts') was nothing other than 'what chancellor Fortescue calls political power in England'.[96] For Sidney too, under 'our antient legal monarchy . . . the liberty and welfare of a great nation was of too much importance to be suffered to depend upon the will of one man'.

---

[90] In *The Education of a Christian Prince* (ed. Lisa Jardine (Cambridge, 1997)) Erasmus identifies Plato as the 'purer' source for many good things found in both Aristotle's *Politics* and Cicero's *Laws* (p. 62; see also pp. 1–18).

[91] Fortescue, *De Laudibus*, quoted in A. L. Brown, *The Governance of Late Medieval England 1272–1461* (London, 1989) p. 13.

[92] John Aylmer, *An harborowe for faithfull and trewe subjectes* (1559), quoted in Alford, *The Early Elizabethan Polity* pp. 34–5.

[93] Sir Thomas Smith, *De Republica Anglorum*, ed. Mary Dewar (Cambridge, 1982) p. 78.

[94] Milton, *Commonplace Book* p. 442.   [95] Milton, *Defence* p. 506.

[96] *State Trials* VI, p. 161, quoted in Judson, *Vane* p. 62.

[I]f they mean by these lovers of Common-wealth principles, men passionately devoted to the public good and to the common service of their country, who believe that kings were instituted for the good of the people, and government ordained for the sake of those that are to be governed . . . every wise and honest man will be proud to be ranked in that number.[97]

Before the seventeenth century most English defenders of common-wealth principles assumed their compatibility with monarchy. There was, that is to say, nothing about this moral philosophy, in its Erasmian rather than Machiavellian formulation, which demanded a republican constitution, though More's *Utopia* had demonstrated that potential. However it is no surprise that, amid the intellectual responses to the crisis of English monarchy, these principles should have taken predominant place. It was during the mid-century revolution that it became a key republican claim that the once free and legal monarchies of Europe had all in practice become tyrannies. Henceforth that public good which was the objective of any reputable political system could only be secured by a government of laws distinct from, and antithetical to, that of a single person. Depicting a fatal divergence between the 'interest' of English monarchy and that of the community, defenders of the newly established 'English Commonwealth' could claim that they had not, in this sense, deserted the ancient constitution. Thanks to the corrupting efforts of tyrants it had deserted them.

Such arguments used Greek sources to explain that the present-day monarchies defended by royalists were what Plato and Aristotle had called tyrannies. Thus Milton doubted that there was ever 'any one person besides Salmasius of so slavish a spirit as to assert the outrageous enormities of tyrants to be the rights of kings'.[98] For John Streater, '*Aristotle* averreth plainly . . . *That he which ruleth without Law, or that liveth without Law, is not a God, but a Tyrant, and a Beast.*' The writings of Cicero, Plutarch and Tacitus illustrated that 'He that is a plague to his Country, by tyrannizing or usurping, is of the devil, and is his servant.'[99] At the same time, in defences of the regicide and attacks upon the Protectorate and restored monarchy we see the elision of the distinction between monarchy and tyranny altogether.[100] Thus for Marchamont Nedham writing in 1651, 'there is no difference between king and tyrant'.[101] John Hall and

[97] Sidney [and Jones], *A Just and Modest Vindication* pp. clxviii–clxix.
[98] Milton, *Defence*, quoted in Scott, *England's Troubles* p. 301.
[99] Streater, *Observations* no. 10, pp. 74, 75, 78.
[100] Scott, *England's Troubles* ch. 13; Scott, 'Classical Republicanism'; see Part III below.
[101] Marchamont Nedham, *The Case of the Commonwealth of England Stated*, ed. P. A. Knachel (Charlottesville, Va., 1969) p. 127; Scott, 'Classical Republicanism'.

Algernon Sidney spoke similarly of the 'contrareity and antipathy' of interest between monarch and people, 'we seeing People languish when their Princes are fullest'.[102] The most important source for this position was Machiavelli, the Second Book of whose *Discourses* had used the words 'prince' and 'tyrant' interchangeably:

> [I]t is beyond question that it is only in republics that the common good is looked to properly . . . The opposite happens where there is a prince; for what he does in his own interests usually harms the city, and what is done in the interests of the city harms him. Consequently, as soon as tyranny replaces self-government [the city] . . . ceases to make progress and to grow in power and wealth: more often than not, nay always, what happens is that it declines.[103]

CONCLUSION

To this extent the evidence for something appropriately called classical republicanism in seventeenth-century England is overwhelming. This was characterised by the combination not only of Greek and Roman sources, but, more challengingly, of Plato and Machiavelli (both used by almost all the writers studied here). Universally present within this synthesis, and perhaps somehow anchoring it, was Aristotle. Even Harrington's *constitutional* (as opposed to moral) thought may have been Aristotelian, rather than Polybian. Nor was his opponent Matthew Wren the only reader who understood *Oceana* to be an attempt to seek admission to the great 'train' of 'authority' established by 'Aristotle, Machiavel and Sir Thomas More'.[104]

Moreover, although positive reference to Machiavelli's *Discourses* was equally universal among English republicans, superficially by Milton, more substantially by Nedham, Streater, Harrington, Neville and Sidney, none but Harrington accepted his break with rational classical moral philosophy.[105] On the contrary, by Milton, Nedham, Streater and Sidney in turn, the political philosophy of Plato and (above all) Aristotle was opposed to a modern 'policy', or 'art of policie' associated with Machiavelli, Tacitus and

---

[102] John Hall, *The Grounds and Reasons of Manarchy Considered* (London, 1651) pp. 40–1; Scott, *English Republic* ch. 12.

[103] Machiavelli, *Discourses* II.2, pp. 275–6. This position had been nearly, but not fully, anticipated by Cicero.

[104] Matthew Wren, *Monarchy Asserted, or The State of Monarchicall and Popular Government*, 2nd edn (1660). The Preface to the Reader.

[105] In relation to Nedham this is disputed by Paul Rahe, 'Marchamont Nedham and the Origins of Liberal Republicanism', paper delivered at the Annual Meeting of the American Political Science Association, Philadelphia, 31 August 2003. See below, chapter 8.

'reason of state'.[106] The republican debt to Machiavelli is discussed below, particularly in chapters 5, 9 and 10. That to Greek moral and constitutional philosophy is analysed in chapters 6 to 8. Meanwhile the role of the latter was far from being confined to political thought. This will be evident when, in the next two chapters, we turn to the religious and social content of commonwealth principles.

[106] John Milton, *Of Reformation Touching Church-Discipline in England* (1641), *Complete Prose Works* vol. 1 p. 573; Streater, *Observations* nos. 1–11; Sidney, *Court Maxims* p. 24. To such tyrannical principles Milton opposed 'the Bible . . . *Plato* and *Aristotle*' in general, and '*Aristotle*['s] ethicks, and politiks' in particular (pp. 572–3). The focus of Streater's defence was '*Aristotle*'s first Book of Political Government'; that of Sidney's, 'Aristotle, *Politics* Bk 3'.

CHAPTER 2

The cause of God

Shalt thou give law to God, shalt thou dispute
With him the points of liberty, who made
Thee what thou art?

> John Milton, *Paradise Lost* Book v, lines 823–5.

God is our . . . only lord, because he only hath created us. If any
other were equal to him in wisdom, power, goodness, and beneficence
to us, he might challenge the same duty from us. If growing out of
ourselves, receiving being from none, depending on no providence,
we were offered the protection of a wisdom subject to no error, a
goodness that could never fail, and a power that nothing could resist,
it were reasonable for us to . . . submit ourselves to him . . . But what
right can from hence accrue to a mortal creature like to one of us, from
whom we have received nothing, and who stands in need of help as
much as we?

> Algernon Sidney, *Discourses Concerning Government*[1]

INTRODUCTION

In England, as in the United Provinces, republicanism was one product of
a struggle for not only political, but religious freedoms.[2] Yet despite this
shared context in early modern Europe's wars of religion, and the actual
(if incomplete) achievement of Dutch liberty of conscience, the fundamental premises of the Dutch republican ideology of 'true liberty' were economic
rather than religious.[3] It is true that for Spinoza, as for most English republicans, 'Our supreme good and perfection is wholly dependent on our

---

[1] Sidney, *Discourses*, ed. West p. 131.   [2] Scott, *England's Troubles* chs. 2 and 4.
[3] Jonathan Israel, 'Toleration in Seventeenth-Century Dutch and English Thought', in Simon Groenveld and Michael Wintle (eds.), *Britain and the Netherlands* XI: *Religion, Scholarship and Art in
Anglo-Dutch Relations in the Seventeenth Century* (Zutphen, 1994); [Pieter de la Court], 'De Witt and
other Great Men in Holland' *The True Interest and Political Maxims of the Republic of Holland* (1702);
Scott, 'Classical Republicanism' pp. 67–71.

knowledge of God and the consequences of that knowledge.'[4] In England, however, almost all republican writing was overtly religiously engaged. The most powerful reason for laying earthly monarchy in the dust was to realise the monarchy of God. In the words of Sidney, 'God had delivered us from slavery and showed us that he would be our king.'[5] In those of Milton, after the restoration, the cause of 'all our woe' was a rebellion by 'pride . . . Against the throne and monarchy of God'.[6]

The republic founded in 1649 was one product of a military outcome widely attributed to the hand of God. To the abolition of 'the deepest *Root . . .* of all the People's *suffering,* even *Kingship . . . we* have been *led* by several steps by the *providence* of *God'*.[7] 'Monarchy shall fall, first in England, then in France, then in Spain, and after in all Christendom, and when Christ hath put down this power he himself will begin to reign.'[8] Traces of providential and apocalyptic language appeared in most republican writing, from Milton's *Tenure* and Harrington's *Oceana* to the restoration works of Sidney and Ludlow. Such millennialism was one characteristic of radical reformation. Another was the demand for liberty of conscience: '*Truth,* to say That LIBERTY, *civill, and spiritual,* were the GOOD *old cause.*'[9] In the words of Sidney, 'The Power of Princes [could] not be fully established unless they had a power over consciences . . . so I shall take my liberty to differ from them when I see them apt to fall into the lowest path of sin and darkness . . . wanting light and therefore subject to the same errours I am.'[10]

A third key feature of the same literature was an emphasis upon practical Christianity (reformation of manners). This was no less important to the practical realisation of the government of God on earth. In the words of Milton:

CHRISTIAN LIBERTY MEANS THAT CHRIST OUR LIBERATOR FREES US FROM THE SLAVERY OF SIN . . . AS IF WE WERE EMANCIPATED SLAVES. HE DOES THIS SO THAT, BEING MADE . . . GROWN MEN

---

4 Benedict de (Baruch) Spinoza, *The Political Works of Spinoza*, ed. A. G. Wernham (Oxford, 1958) p. 71; Scott, 'Classical Republicanism' pp. 77–80.

5 Sidney, *Court Maxims* p. 197.	6 Milton, *Paradise Lost* Book 1, lines 3, 36, 42.

7 *A Declaration of the Parliament of England, In Vindication of their Proceedings, And Discovering the Dangerous Practices of several Interests, Against the Present Government* (27 September 1649) p. 16.

8 *A Vision which one Mr Brayne had,* quoted in John Patrick Laydon, 'The Kingdom of Christ and the Princes of the Earth: the Political Uses of Apocalyptic and Millenarian Ideas in England 1648–1653', Ph.D. dissertation, Cambridge University, 1976 p. 204.

9 G. H. Williams, *The Radical Reformation* (1962) pp. 858–9; Henry Stubbe, *An Essay in Defence of the Good Old Cause* (1659), Preface.

10 Warwickshire Record Office, MS CR 1886, Algernon Sidney, 'Court Maxims Discussed and refelled', pp. 81, 83.

INSTEAD OF BOYS, WE MAY SERVE GOD IN CHARITY THROUGH THE GUIDANCE OF THE SPIRIT OF TRUTH. Gal.v.i: *stand fast, then, in the liberty by which Christ has freed us.*[11]

In association with this, in most republican writing we can discern an optimistic rational moral philosophy anchoring the achievement of virtue (moral excellence) in theology (knowledge of goodness, deriving from the knowledge of God). As observed by Blair Worden,

> Where there were common doctrinal sympathies between republicans and Puritans, the alliance was formed on the liberal wing of Puritan theology, which was Platonist or Arminian or Socinian . . . Though Harrington and Sidney and Milton knew that man is sinful and fallen, they were nonetheless impressed by the scope left by God to human virtue and reason and wisdom.[12]

Again it was characteristic of the European radical reformation to combine an emphasis upon works with a reaction against morally pessimistic predestinarian theology.[13] But a no less important context for both this Platonic rationalism and its associated insistence upon Christianity of conduct was Christian humanism. In the words of Ernst Cassirer:

> in the midst of the serious religious and sectarian disputes of the seventeenth century . . . the old humanistic ideal of religion reappears in all its purity and power. The language of the Cambridge Platonists . . . does not differ on this point from that of . . . Colet, Erasmus and Thomas More. Undisturbed by all suspicions of the sanctification of heathendom, they maintain that he who bears within him the true spirit of Christ, though he has never heard His name, deserves far more to be called a Christian than those who know and profess all the articles of faith in Christendom, and yet do not exemplify them in their lives.[14]

It was in 1981 that Worden drew attention to the apparently ironical 'existence, at the climax of the Puritan Revolution, of a group of able and influential politicians whose idealism was fuelled, and whose politics was influenced, by their interest in and admiration for classical antiquity'.[15] Part of the explanation for this appeared to be the involvement of a group

---

[11] John Milton, *Two Books of Investigations into Christian Doctrine Drawn From the Sacred Scriptures Alone*, in *Complete Prose Works* vol. vi p. 537; Scott, *England's Troubles* ch. 11.

[12] Worden, 'Marchamont Nedham and the Beginnings' p. 47; see also Worden, 'English Republicanism' p. 471.

[13] Williams, *The Radical Reformation* pp. 846, 861, 865; Baylor, *The Radical Reformation*; Robert Birmingham, 'Continental Resonances in Mid-Seventeenth Century English Radical Religious Ideas', M.Phil. thesis, Cambridge University, 1998; Irvin Horst, *The Radical Brethren: Anabaptism and the English Reformation to 1558* (Nieuwkoop, 1972) pp. 30, 36; Scott, *England's Troubles* ch. 11.

[14] Ernst Cassirer, *The Platonic Renaissance in England* (1953) pp. 34–5.

[15] Worden, 'Classical Republicanism' p. 200.

of non-puritans ('wits' like Neville, Marten, Nedham and Chaloner) with an admiration for Machiavelli, and a far less godly ideological agenda. Yet alongside its Graeco-Roman-Machiavellian synthesis, a no less general feature of English republican writing is its Christian-classical synthesis. As for Thomas More and his circle, so for Milton, Sidney and others the need was to show how 'true Philosophy is perfectly conformable, with what is taught us by those who were divinely inspired'.[16] The question is not simply, therefore, how did classical republicans find a place at the helm of a religious revolution? Rather, how was classical republicanism seen to offer reinforcement to its religious objectives? Our answer begins with that northern Renaissance within which, in the words of Cassirer again, 'the forces of humanism work for the sake of religion'.[17]

CHRISTIAN HUMANISM

Christian humanism denotes a movement for moral reform characterised by the deployment of classical sources for Christian ends. It is partly because English humanism was Christian humanism that 'commonwealth principles' contained the recipe for not only a classical, but a Christian commonwealth. Thus More's *Utopia* opposed to the self-interest held responsible for the desperate ills of contemporary society not a formula for the rejuvenation of religious worship, nor merely the advocacy of moral re-education, of either the people or prince.[18] Since 'Pride is too deeply fixed in human nature to be easily plucked out' nothing less would do than the removal of that institution by which it had been allowed to govern society as a whole. '[E]asily might men get the necessities of life if that cursed money, which is supposed to provide access to them, were not in fact the only barrier to our getting what we need to live.' In arriving at this conclusion More was impressed, as were the radical protestants of the 1520s, by the example of Christ and his apostles.[19] At the same time he found his most important classical inspiration in Plato's *Republic* and *Laws*. Following 'Plato . . . I am wholly convinced that unless private property is entirely abolished, there can be no fair or just distribution of goods, nor can mankind be happily

---

[16] Sidney, comparing Plato with *Ecclesiastes* 10.6, in the *Discourses*, in *Sydney on Government* p. 65.
[17] Cassirer, *The Platonic Renaissance* pp. 12–13; for differences of emphasis, however, between More, Colet and Erasmus see Fox, 'Facts and Fallacies' pp. 18–22.
[18] J. H. Hexter, 'Introduction', in *The Complete Works of St Thomas More* vol. IV, ed. Edward Surtz and J. H. Hexter (New Haven, Conn., 1965).
[19] More, *Utopia* p. 96: the Utopians 'were . . . much influenced by the fact that Christ encouraged his disciples to practice community of goods, and that among the truest groups of Christians, the practice still prevails'.

governed. As long as private property remains, by far the largest and best part of mankind will be oppressed by a heavy and inescapable burden of poverty and anxieties.'[20]

This Platonism had a larger context in More's participation (with Colet, Linacre, Pace and other friends of Erasmus) in the English 'Greek revival'.[21] In common with other members of this circle, it was by his Christian moral preoccupations that More's engagement with Greek ethics in general, and those of Plato in particular, were driven. Plato had opposed to sceptical self-interest (embodied by the sophist Thrasymachus) a defence of common good. Its metaphysical basis lay in those unities called the forms by which Plato claimed that the imperfect world of sense experience was actually ordered. This metaphysics in turn underpinned a rational philosophy of virtue. The early impact of Plato's writings upon Christian thought was manifest in the gospel of St Paul and the writings of St Augustine. John Colet 'began his teaching . . . with a lecture on the Pauline Epistles . . . treated . . . as the expression of a single fundamental religious attitude . . . designed . . . to effect a reformation and revival of life'.[22] When Augustine, upon whom More lectured, descibed the Platonists as (like the pagan Utopians) 'representing the closest approximation to our Christian position', he continued: 'Plato defined the Sovereign Good as the life in accordance with virtue; and he declared that this was possible only for one who had the knowledge of God and who strove to imitate him.'[23] This was an assertion to be repeated by Milton and Sidney, both of whom used Augustine as well as Plato, despite the appeal of the former to their more morally pessimistic political opponents (including Filmer and Hobbes).

That despite its emphasis upon conduct this Platonism survived to inform protestantism is not surprising. Luther was an Augustinian; as Christian humanists had anticipated some protestant calls for reform, not least by translation of the Greek New Testament, so a copy of Erasmus' *Paraphrases* accompanied John Foxe's *Acts and Monuments* in most Elizabethan parish

[20] Ibid. p. 39.

[21] John Guy, *Thomas More* (2000) pp. 23–9; Nelson, 'Greek Nonsense'; Skinner, 'Sir Thomas More's *Utopia*'.

[22] Mayer, *Thomas Starkey* p. 217 and ch. 6 in general. Starkey combined the Platonism of Colet with the gospel of St Paul to derive an emphasis on faith working in harmony with reason.

[23] Augustine, *City of God* pp. 311, 310 (see also 304–5); Thomas White, 'Pride and the Public Good: Thomas More's Use of Plato in *Utopia*', *Journal of the History of Philosophy* 20, 4 (1982); Brendan Bradshaw, 'More on Utopia', *The Historical Journal* 24, 1 (1981) pp. 19–23. It seems to me possible to accept both Hexter's claim concerning the moral achievement of the Utopians in Christian terms, and Bradshaw's claim that nevertheless they remain pagans. It was part of More's intention to show the relevance of pagan philosophy (and that of Plato in particular) to Christian concerns.

churches. Milton's *Christian Doctrine* was heavily dependent upon Erasmus' biblical scholarship.[24] For Sir Philip Sidney, as for Edmund Spenser, it was 'Plato . . . whom I must confess, of all philosophers I have ever esteemed most worthy of reverence'.[25] In the *Defence of Poesy* Sidney's defence of Plato for banishing poets from his *Republic* was that he had been animated by not a hatred of poetry, but a love of true religion.[26] Sir Philip translated into English his Huguenot friend Philippe du Plessis Mornay's *The Trewnesse of the Christian Religion*, its theology 'suffused with platonic epistemology'[27]. Later Robert Boyle, like Milton an associate of the Hartlib circle, identified du Plessis Mornay and Sidney as 'the 2 greatest Favorites the two last Ages have afforded me'.[28] Sidney's companion and biographer Fulke Greville, Lord Brooke, was father of the Platonist writer and parliamentarian peer Robert, Lord Brooke. Greville's *Life of Sidney*, published under the English republic in 1652, placed appropriate emphasis upon the religious context of Sidney's life and heroic death. For Sir Philip, the war in the Netherlands was merely part of a global struggle against Spanish popery, cruelty and tyranny: 'I see the great work indeed in hand against the abusers of the world.'[29]

Links between the Elizabethan Platonist Sidney/Spenser circle and that majority of English republicans influenced by Plato included not only such family ties but relationships of patronage.[30] Henry Neville, author of *Plato Redivivus*, was Algernon Sidney's second cousin. During the 1630s Robert Sidney, second Earl of Leicester, sent either Algernon or his brother Philip to study at the Huguenot academy founded by du Plessis Mornay at Saumur. During the 1630s when Leicester was ambassador in Paris, the whole family attended services at the Huguenot church at Charenton where the minister was Mornay's protégée Jean Daillé.[31] On the eve of the civil

---

[24] Milton, *Christian Doctrine* pp. 127, 412, 589.

[25] Sir Philip Sidney, *The Defence of Poesy*, in *Sir Philip Sidney: Selected Writings*, ed. Richard Dutton (1987) p. 134.

[26] Ibid. pp. 135–6: 'Plato found fault that the poets of his time filled the world with wrong opinions of the gods, making light tales of that unspotted essence . . . So . . . Plato, banishing the abuse, not the thing . . . shall be our patron and not our adversary . . . especially since he attributeth unto Poesy . . . a very inspiring of a divine force, far above man's wit.'

[27] F. G. Robinson, *The Shape of Things Known* (Cambridge, Mass., 1922) pp. 102–3; Scott, *Algernon Sidney and the English Republic* pp. 22–7.

[28] Quoted in Jacob, *Robert Boyle* p. 27.

[29] Grevil[le], Sir Fulke, Lord Brooke, *The Life of the Renowned Sir Philip Sidney* (1652) pp. 117–18; J. H. M. Salmon, *The French Religious Wars in English Political Thought* (Cambridge, 1959).

[30] Worden, 'Classical Republicanism'; Scott, *Algernon Sidney and the English Republic* chs. 2–3.

[31] Kent Archives Office, Maidstone, De Lisle MSS U1475 C97/1, C124/2; *Historical Manuscript Commission Report, De Lisle and Dudley MSS*, vol. VI pp. xxii, 554; Scott, *Algernon Sidney and the English Republic* p. 53.

war the Cambridge Platonist Peter Sterry was chaplain to Robert, Lord Brooke. Thereafter he became closely associated with Sir Henry Vane Jr, religious and political mentor to Milton, Algernon Sidney and others. By the mid-1650s Sterry was chaplain to Sidney's brother Philip, Lord Lisle.[32] In 1633 Henry Hammond became chaplain to the Sidney family household at Penshurst Place in Kent. His scholarly speciality was Greek, his theology Platonic, and his two favourite modern authorities du Plessis Mornay and Hugo Grotius, the latter in many ways Erasmus's successor in matters both of theology and of biblical philology.[33] The importance of Grotius to republican writing is discussed particularly in chapter 5. Many of these sources would remain central to the rational 'Arminian' (and in some cases Socinian) theology of a group of early Enlightenment protestant exiles, including John Locke, who came together in the United Provinces during the 1680s.[34]

Part of the attraction of Platonic metaphysics to early modern protestantism lay in its emphasis on the directness of the individual's path to God's truth: the way, as du Plessis Mornay put it, to 'be lincked most straightly to Him'.[35] External clerical and state interference in this represented, in Platonic terms, the intrusion of obstacles from the fallible world of particulars onto the path to the forms; in protestant terms, the idolatrous substitution of a humane particular as the object for reverence in the place of God. Such a conception readily extended itself, when impelled by a political emergency, to the conception of 'divine right' monarchy also. Milton was not the only one to look back to 'those illustrious Greeks and Romans' among whom 'Not yet had tyrants, suddenly become viceroys, indeed, and vicars of Christ . . . Nor yet had the common people, maddened by priestly machinations, sunk to a barbarism fouler than that which stains the Indians.'[36]

No less importantly Platonic morality provided powerful reinforcement to the protestant campaign for reformation of manners. Like Sidney,

[32] A. Lichtenstein, *Henry More* (Cambridge, 1962) p. 17; V. De Sola Pinto, *Peter Sterry, Platonist and Puritan 1613–1672* (1934) pp. 3, 11; F. J. Powicke, *The Cambridge Platonists* (1926) pp. 175–6.

[33] Henry Hammond, *The Workes of the Reverend and Learned Henry Hammond*, ed. John Fell (1674) pp. 3–4, 191–2; Hammond, *A Defence of the Learned Hugo Grotius* (1655); J. W. Packer, *The Transformation of Anglicanism* (1969) pp. 64–70, 89–94, 189; Scott, *Algernon Sidney and the English Republic* pp. 27–8.

[34] John Marshall, *John Locke: Resistance, Religion and Responsibility* (Cambridge, 1994) chs. 4–5, 8; Sami-Juhani Savonius, 'John Locke and the Civil Philosophy of the *Bibliothecaires* circa 1688–circa 1702', Ph.D. thesis, Cambridge University 2002.

[35] Quoted in Robinson, *The Shape of Things Known* pp. 102–3.

[36] John Milton, *Second Defence of the English People* (1654), in Milton, *Complete Prose Works* vol. IV, pp. 550–1; see Sidney, *Discourses*, in *Sydney on Government* p. 483.

Milton and Vane, Plato condemned the servility and flattery of 'the tyrant [who] . . . is the real slave'. Like them he opposed temperance and self-discipline to gluttony, avarice, 'lusts . . . clouds of incense and perfumes and garlands and wines and all the pleasures of a dissolute life'.[37] Like them he looked to state-imposed education and literally Spartan discipline to redeem mankind from their 'lawless wild-beast nature' through the restraint of appetite and the training of reason. Platonic republican conceptions of not only education, but magistracy, placed key emphasis upon the 'vigour or slackness of discipline'. As Milton put it: 'Nor is there any sociable perfection in this life, civil or sacred, that can be above discipline . . . Discipline is . . . the very visible shape and image of virtue.'[38] For Sidney, too, 'The fierce barbarity of a loose multitude, bound by no law, and regulated by no discipline, is wholly repugnant to [good].' In particular, in words highly reminiscent of More:

> Daily experience too plainly shews, with what rage avarice usually fills the hearts of men. There are not many destructive villanies committed in the world, that do not proceed from it . . . Solomon warns us to beware of such as make haste to grow rich, and says, they shall not be innocent . . . Plato, Socrates, Epictetus, and others, made it their business to abate men's lusts, by shewing the folly of seeking vain honours, useless riches, or unsatisfying pleasures; and those who were like to them, if they were raised to supreme magistracies, have endeavoured by the severest punishments to restrain men from committing the crimes by which riches are most commonly gained.[39]

Within Elizabethan and early Stuart Christian humanism, this Platonism existed alongside Aristotelianism (both humanist and scholastic),[40] a growing interest in Roman sources, and the powerful influence of a neo-Stoicism associated with the Tacitean scholar Justus Lipsius.[41] Thus Sir Thomas Smith evoked 'the Greeks and Romans' among whom 'learning

---

[37] *Plato, Republic*, in *The Portable Plato*, ed. Scott Buchanan (Harmondsworth, 1982) Book 9 pp. 627, 637; for Milton on temperence, sobriety, frugality and industry, versus drunkenness, gluttony, avarice and luxury, see *Christian Doctrine* pp. 724–33.

[38] Plato, *Republic* Book 9 p. 626; Sidney quoted in Scott, *Algernon Sidney and the English Republic* p. 24; Milton quoted in Hill, *Milton* p. 253; for Milton on Christian magistracy see *Christian Doctrine* pp. 794–9.

[39] Sidney, *Discourses*, ed. West p. 67.

[40] John Coffey, *Politics, Religion and the British Revolutions: the Mind of Samuel Rutherford* (Cambridge, 1997) pp. 66–7.

[41] G. Oestreich, *Neostoicism and the Early Modern State* (Cambridge, 1982); Peter Burke, 'Tacitism', in T. A. Dorey (ed.), *Tacitus* (1969); Scott, *Algernon Sidney and the English Republic* p. 18; Tuck, *Philosophy and Governmment* (Cambridge, 1993) ch. 2; Geoffrey Baldwin, 'The Self and the State 1580–1651', Ph.d. thesis, Cambridge University 1998, pp. 4–5, chs. 1–2. Like Plato, Stoicism emphasised the necessary sovereignty of reason within the individual soul. The Roman Stoic hero Cato spent the evening before his suicide reading Plato's *Phaedo*.

and wisdom was most esteemed'.[42] Sir Philip Sidney asserted the fundamental continuity of thought of 'they that did imitate the inconceivable excellencies of God . . . David in his Psalms; Solomon in his Song of Songs, in his Ecclesiastes, and Proverbs . . . [with] many other, both Greeks and Romans' (including Homer, Solon, Plato, Aristotle, Plutarch, Cato, Livy, Virgil, Lucan and Tacitus).[43] In the same spirit, during the 1620s Thomas Scott praised not only the manifest lessons of scripture but 'the wisest amongst the *Grecians* or *Romans*'.[44]

ANTI-POPERY, ANTI-CLERICALISM, LIBERTY OF CONSCIENCE

For some of the same and other features of republican thought a no less important context was radical protestantism.[45] Crucial to the English development of this was the transposition of that anti-popery which had been a mainstream component of Elizabethan and early Stuart protestantism from the external struggle against European Counter-Reformation to an internal struggle against royal and clerical tyranny. The first step towards this came with Jacobean fraternisation with the Spanish enemy combined with inexcusable military inaction following the outbreak of the Thirty Years War.[46] In the words of Thomas Scott:

This Ship is the Church, is the State: the Windes, the Waves, the Rockes, the Sands, and . . . profest Pirates assault it. It concernes us all to looke about us, even from the Master to the Ship-boy. Nor shall it (I hope) be a capitall crime in me to awake the Supreme Governor, the *Defender of the Faith*, with the peoples voyce, *Master, carest thou not that we perish?*[47]

The next step, from 1624–5, was repeated military failure in Europe leading to dangerous ideological polarisation at home. As Milton recalled in *Eikonoklastes*: 'no man less belov'd, no man more generally condemn'd then was the King; from the time that it became his custom to break Parlaments at home, and either wilfully or weakly to betray Protestants abroad . . . All men inveigh'd against him.'[48] Directed against opponents informed by both anti-monarchical 'puritanism' and humanism, the objective of the

---

[42] Sir Thomas Smith, *A Discourse of the Commonweal of This Realm of England*, ed. Mary Dewar (Charlottesville, Va. 1969) pp. 13, 24–5.

[43] Sidney, *Defence of Poesy* pp. 108–9.

[44] Thomas Scott, *The Belgicke Pismire* (1623) p. 22; and see chapter 11 below.

[45] Scott, *England's Troubles* ch. 11; and see chapter 3 below.

[46] Scott, *England's Troubles* ch. 4; Kenneth Fincham and Peter Lake, 'The Ecclesiastical Policy of King James I', *Journal of British Studies* vol. 24, 2, 1985.

[47] Thomas Scott, *Vox Regis* (1625) p. 24.

[48] John Milton, *Eikonoklastes* (1649), in *Complete Prose Works* vol. III, p. 344.

king's subsequent clerically led attempt at confessional statebuilding was the reconstruction of a culture of monarchical obedience in England.[49] For many this amounted not only to a comprehensive assault upon protestantism, but to the erection of a clerical, as well as political tyranny. According to the *Grand Remonstrance* (1641) the chief actors in this plot were 'The Jesuited papists . . . The bishops . . . who cherish formality and superstition as the natural effects and more probable supports of their own ecclesiastical tyranny and usurpation [and] . . . Such councillors . . . as for private ends have engaged themselves to further the interests of some foreign princes.'[50]

As Milton observed in his *Commonplace Book*: '[T]he clergie [are] commonly the corrupters of kingly authority turning it to tyrannie by thire wicked flatteries even in the pulpit.'[51] Harrington remembered that Charles I 'received that unhappy encouragement from his clergy which became his utter ruin; while, trusting more unto their logic than the rough philosophy of his parliament, it came unto an irreparable breach.'[52] When during the 1670s England faced an apparent revival of the same policies, Henry Neville attributed it to the machinations of a clergy who had, since the Reformation, little justification remaining for their power.[53] When in the same context Sidney and Locke came to respond to Filmer's newly published *Patriarcha* (1680) both contextualised it as the resurrected political 'Doctrine' of Laudian clericalism.[54]

One response to Laudian/Caroline religious policies was flight abroad, to the Netherlands and/or New England. As the Dutch had already succeeded in sweeping away not only monarchy but 'all Bishops and ecclesiastical hierarchies', the United Provinces became a haven for English anti-episcopal opposition. In thus receiving English and Scots protestant exiles, as it had in the mid-sixteenth century and would again following the restoration, the Netherlands was reciprocating for the settlement of thousands of Dutch refugees, particularly in East Anglia.[55] In the United Provinces in turn

---

[49] Scott, *England's Troubles* chs. 4–5.
[50] J. P. Kenyon, *The Stuart Constitution: Documents and Commentary*, 2nd edn (Cambridge, 1986) p. 210.
[51] Milton, *Commonplace Book* p. 439.   [52] Harrington, *Oceana*, in *Political Works* p. 198.
[53] 'I cannot sufficiently admire why our clergy, who very justly refuse to believe the miracle which is pretended to be wrought in transubstantiation . . . yet will believe, that the same kind of spell or charm in ordination can have the efficacy to metamorphose a poor lay-idiot, into a heavenly creature: notwithstanding that we find in them the same human nature . . . to which they were subject before such transformation.' Neville, *Plato Redivivus* p. 118.
[54] Sidney, *Discourses*, in *Sydney on Government* pp. 4–5; John Locke, *Two Treatises of Government*, ed. Peter Laslett, 2nd edn (Cambridge, 1967) pp. 160–1.
[55] Ole Peter Grell, *Calvinist Exiles in Tudor and Stuart England* (Aldershot, 1996); H. Scherpbier, *Milton in Holland: a Study in the Literary Relations of England and Holland before 1730* (Amsterdam 1969)

thousands of English exiles experienced some modicum of liberty of conscience. From there poured publications in which 'bishops are dragged
forth as thieves and murderers, vermin . . . spiritual wolves, prelatical dogs,
crocodiles, asses, dunghill worms, locusts, venomous snakes and Amalekites
to be put to the sword'.[56] From Leiden, Rotterdam and Amsterdam came
many future leaders of English independency and republicanism (including
John Lilburne, John Goodwin and Hugh Peter) as well as some of the most
important English expeditions to America.[57] English peers involved with
the settlement at Massachusetts Bay included Lords Brooke, Pembroke,
Bedford, and Saye and Sele. Inhabitants of the colony included future
republicans Hugh Peter, George Downing, William Aspinwall and Sir
Henry Vane jr, whose governorship between 1636 and 1637 was ended by his
unpopular support for the prophetess Anne Hutchinson.[58] In his *Character*
of Vane, Sidney described New England as 'a place that then flourisht by
reason of its good order and discipline: he was there created Governor of
these colonies and performed his Office with great vigilance and honesty'.[59]

Thus in relation to radical reformation, as to Christian humanism, and
subsequently Enlightenment, Anglo-Dutch connections were crucial.[60]
This remained the case until the Dutch invasion of 1688–9 made possible
an English Act for Toleration.[61] It was during his association with Benjamin
Furly in Rotterdam that Sidney described what he called the '*Seventh Court
Maxim: Bishops are to be kept up in the height of their power and riches.*' These
were 'they who said it was better all the streets in England and Scotland
should run with blood than the power of the clergy be diminished'.[62] As
the church of Rome was 'an obscene spirituall adultress living in errors

p. 25; Charles Wilson, *Anglo-Dutch Commerce and Finance in the Eighteenth Century* (Cambridge, 1941, repr. 1966).

[56] K. H. D. Haley, *The British and the Dutch: Political and Cultural Relations through the Ages* (1988) p. 74.

[57] Scott, *England's Troubles* ch. 4; Haley, *The British and the Dutch* pp. 32, 48, 69–74.

[58] Scott, '"Good Night Amsterdam"'; T. H. Breen, *The Character of the Good Ruler: a Study of Puritan Political Ideas in New England 1630–1730* (New Haven, Conn., 1970) pp. 54–7; John Donoghue, '"Soldiers in the Army of the Lord": Thomas Venner, Impressment, and Radical Republicanism in the Atlantic World 1636–1657', unpublished essay, University of Pittsburgh, 2003.

[59] Algernon Sidney, *The Character of Henry Vane Jnr*, in V. Rowe, *Sir Henry Vane the Younger* (1970), Appendix F, p. 279; Scott, '"Good Night Amsterdam"'.

[60] Horst, *The Radical Brethren* pp. 30, 36.

[61] Grell, O., J. Israel, and N. Tyacke (eds.), *From Persecution to Toleration: the Glorious Revolution and Religion in England* (1991).

[62] Sidney, *Court Maxims* pp. 87, 103; spying for the English government in 1665, Aphra Behn reported Sidney to be 'often in Consultation with Benjamin Turly [*sic*] the quaker, being resolved to shape som designe for Ingland', and 'at present writinge a Treatise in defence of a Republique, and agst Monarchy, and designes it soone or late for ye presse'. W. J. Cameron, *New Light on Aphra Behn* (Auckland, 1961) pp. 47, 73.

and idolatry', so 'our mitre-bearing parasites' with '[t]heir wild howlings in churches, joined with the amazing sound of organs and brass instruments', were 'apes of Rome'. The new persecutions of 1662–5 were comparable to the 'fury of Francis I and Henry II of France . . . the blood shed by the duke of Alva and others in the Low Countries . . . their cruel thirst after the blood of innocents does in barbarity excel the bloody altars of Diana, Mars, or Pluto'.[63] Milton's entry onto the public stage of the revolution took the form of an attack upon the 'Church-tyranny' of 'prelaty'. This 'misgovernment of the Church . . . which persues and warres with all good Christians under the name of schismaticks, but maintains and fosters all Papists and Idolators', was to blame for 'tumult, and civill warres' in general, and the 'bloody . . . cruelties' and 'murdrous . . . rage' of the Irish in particular.[64]

The achievement of protestant liberty of conscience in 1649 did not unite republicans on the question of church government. One position was that radical independency which attacked both clerical and Erastian pretensions to government of conscience. Within the republic the lead in this direction was taken by Vane. This was celebrated by Milton in 1652 with his sonnet to

> Vane, young in years, but in sage counsel old
> than whom a better senator ne'er held
> The helm of Rome
> . . . to know
> Both spiritual power and civil, what each means,
> What severs each, thou hast learned which few have done.
> The bounds of either sword to thee we owe;
> Therefore on thy firm hand Religion leans
> In peace, and reckons thee her eldest son.[65]

For Vane the 'mystery of iniquity' and 'throne of the beast' was the mixing of religious (spiritual) with temporal authority. Those guilty of a 'furious imposing of their religion upon others' were not only the clergy, but those political authorities which had, since the Henrician Reformation, presumed to appoint them. 'Hence', explained Sidney in the *Court Maxims*,

grew the necessity of acknowledging the power of the civil magistrate in spiritual things, ridiculously setting a temporal head upon a spiritual body . . . the pure and undefiled spouse of Christ . . . Unto this body they give the head of a filthy

[63] Ibid. pp. 99–105.
[64] John Milton, *The Reason of Church-governement Urg'd against Prelaty* (1641), in *Complete Prose Works* vol. I, p. 798.
[65] Quoted in W. R. Parker, *Milton*, vol. I (Oxford, 1968) p. 414.

devouring fish or a savage wolf. Hence spiritual men in spiritual things are forced to receive law from worldly and carnal magistrates. Nothing can be imagined more directly opposite to right order than that princes that for the most part are utterly ignorant of spiritual things should impose rules in them to be followed by those to whom God has given the true light of his spirit to see their own way . . . Does God stand in need of acts of parliament to teach men to worship him?[66]

This was a stance shared not only by most republicans, but by most of the independent alliance by which the revolution had been made. By contrast, although Henry Neville opposed 'the empire which the ecclesiastics pretend to over the consciences and persons of men', he differed from the independents in equally resenting their claimed 'exemption from all secular power'.[67] Neville shared his position, combining a defence of liberty of conscience with an Erastian view of church government, with Harrington. Harrington's *Oceana* furnished the first English republican prescription for a civil religion.[68] This followed Hobbes in combining absolute power in the state with tolerant Erastianism in ecclesiastical government.[69] Thus although Harrington's system protected liberty of conscience, it did so in the context of greatly reinforced civil authority, presiding over a voluntary 'national conscience'. In erecting this he took square aim at the Vanist and godly project for separating civil and spiritual authority.

The religion of Lacedaemon was governed by the kings, who were also high priests and officiated at the sacrifice . . . And the ecclesiastical part of the commonwealth of Rome was governed by the *pontifex maximus*, the *rex sacrificulus* and the *flamines*, all ordained or elected by the people . . . ancient prudence is as well a rule in divine as human things; nay, and such an one as the apostles themselves, ordaining elders by the holding up of hands in every congregation, have exactly followed . . . [wherefore] I wonder whence it is men, quite contrary unto the universal proof of these examples, will have ecclesiastical government to be necessarily distinct from civil power.[70]

Harrington was similarly unimpressed by Vane's insistence, in *A Healing Question* (1656) and *A Needful Correction* (1659), on the restriction of republican citizenship to a spiritually equipped elite. In *A Discourse Showing That the Spirit of Parliaments, With a Council in the Intervals, Is not to be trusted for a Settlement* (21 July 1659) Harrington claimed that '1. Where there is no

---

[66] Sidney, *Court Maxims* pp. 95–6. In the last line I have corrected 'me' to 'men' by reference to the manuscript (f. 82).

[67] Neville, *Plato Redivivus* p. 119.   [68] Goldie, 'The Civil Religion of James Harrington'.

[69] Fukuda, *Sovereignty and the Sword*; Pocock, 'Historical Introduction' ch. 5; Richard Tuck, 'The Civil Religion of Thomas Hobbes', in Phillipson and Skinner, *Political Discourse*.

[70] Harrington, *Oceana*, in *Political Works* pp. 307–8.

public endowment of a ministry, there can be no national religion. 2. Where there is no national religion, there can neither be any government nor any liberty of conscience.'[71] This latter claim became the target of Milton's *The Likeliest Means to Remove Hirelings from the Church* (August 1659), dedicated to 'the Parlament of the Commonwealth of England', restored after its 'short but scandalous night of interruption'. Harrington responded in *Aphorisms Political* (31 August 1659), that on the contrary 'To hold that hirelings . . . or an endowed Ministry, ought to be removed out of the Church, is inconsistent with a commonwealth'.[72]

REFORMATION OF MANNERS

In *The Reason of Church-governement* Milton also attacked the 'autoriz-[ation] . . . a while since . . . of our publick sports, and festival pastimes . . . that they might be . . . the provocations of drunkennesse and lust'.[73] Similarly in the *Discourses*, Sidney remembered that

By the advice and instigation of these men, from about the year 1630, to 1640, sports and revelings, which ended for the most part in drunkenness and lewdnesse, were not only permitted on that day, but enjoined. And tho this did advance human authority in derogation to the divine, to a degree that may please . . . [Filmer], yet others resolving rather to obey the laws of God than the commands of men, could not be brought to pass the Lord's day in that manner.

'I may be told', Sidney explained, that such sensitivity to the sabbath 'savours too much of Puritanism and Calvinism. But I shall take the reproach, till some better patrons than Laud and his creatures may be found for the other opinion.'[74] As such perjorative polemical labels were

---

[71] James Harrington, *A Discourse Showing That the Spirit of Parliaments, With a Council in the Intervals, Is not to be trusted for a Settlement* (21 July 1659) in *Political Works* p. 752.

[72] James Harrington, *Aphorisms Political*, in *Political Works* p. 765; Austin Woolrych, 'Historical Introduction', in Milton *Complete Prose Works, Volume VII : 1659–1660*, rev. edn (New Haven, Conn, 1980) pp. 82, 84. Milton's arguments in this had been anticipated by several works by Vane's protégé Henry Stubbe.

[73] Milton, *The Reason of Church-governement* pp. 798, 819, 823. Milton's objection was to this immorality, rather than to the profanation of the sabbath: see *Christian Doctrine* pp. 708–9, 714–15.

[74] Sidney, *Discourses*, ed. West p. 437. In a bitter account in 1651 of the Stuart 'plot . . . to wipe out the Reformed religion', Samuel Hartlib drew a direct line from the 'first . . . public proclamation [which] authorized assemblies at the beginning of the Lord's Day for lawful sports, games, dancing', through the introduction of 'clerical vestments and habits, feast of saints, and external ceremonies', to 'The massacre in Ireland . . . in 1641 . . . [of] over 200,000 persons . . . if not by the order of the king, then by his conniving.' Quoted in Leo Miller, *John Milton and the Oldenburg Safeguard* (New York, 1985) p. 46. All of these accusations were repeated by Sidney, particularly in the *Court Maxims*.

not used with much precision this does not constitute evidence for clas-
sifying Sidney as a Calvinist. According to Burnet, Sidney 'hated all sorts
of church-men, and so he never joyn'd himself to any, but to ye Independents . . . he seem'd in discourse with me to believe ye truth of Christianity
very firmly, yet he thought devotions . . . were but slight things, and yt
good Morality was all yt was necessary'.[75] What we can say is that Sidney
and Milton, with Vane and others, were puritans on this point of manners.
'What chiefly constitutes the true worship of God', explained Milton, 'is
eagerness to do good works . . . These are called VIRTUES, and in them
is comprised the whole sum of our duty both towards God and towards
man.'[76] 'That faith alone which acts is counted as living . . . A true and
living faith cannot exist without works.'[77] Thus a very large proportion of
Milton's, as of Sidney's political writing, consisted in a juxtaposition of the
manners of commonwealths with those of courts. When Milton invoked
the moral superiority of republics in *The Readie and Easie Way*, he certainly
had the United Provinces, and perhaps also England in mind. In

a free Commonwealth . . . held by wisest men in all ages the noblest, the manliest,
the equallest, the justest government . . . civil, and Christian, most cherishing to
vertue and true religion . . . wherin they who are greatest, are perpetual servants
and drudges to the public at thir own cost and charges . . . yet are not elevated
above thir brethren; live soberly in thir families, walk the streets as other men, may
be spoken to freely, familiarly . . . without adoration. Wheras a king must be ador'd
like a Demigod, with a dissolute and haughtie court about him, of vast expence
and luxurie, masks and revels, to the debaushing of our prime gentry both male
and female . . . to the multiplying of a servile crew, not of servants only, but of
nobility and gentry, bred up then to the hopes not of public, but of court offices;
to be stewards, chamberlains, ushers, grooms, even of the close-stool.[78]

Here as elsewhere Christian and classical morality were combined. There
were many more such passages in Sidney's *Court Maxims* and *Discourses*
('Tho I should fill a volume with examples of this kind'). While republics

[75] British Library, London Add MS 63,057 Gilbert Burnet, manuscript transcript of 'History of My
Own Time' vol. II, pp. 137–8.
[76] Milton, *Christian Doctrine* pp. 474–6.   [77] Quoted in Hill, *Milton* p. 276.
[78] Milton, *The Readie and Easie Way* pp. 424–5. In *Observations Upon the United Provinces*, (1673)
William Temple remarked upon 'the simplicity and modesty of their Magistrates in their way of
living . . . I never saw . . . Vice-Admiral *De Ruiter* . . . in Clothes better than the commonest
Sea-Captain . . . Pensioner *De Wit* . . . was seen usually in the streets on foot and alone, like
the commonest Burger of the Town' (pp. 112–13). In 1651 Master of Ceremonies Oliver Fleming
claimed that in the English republic also 'no attention was paid to outward display; that men in
Parliament with incomes of 60, 70 and more thousands of pounds sterling who maintain whole
manors nowadays often go on foot, without servants, let themselves be served a wretched dinner
(*those were his words*) and so go on'. Herman Mylius quoted in Miller, *Oldenburg Safeguard* p. 37.

might lapse into corruption, monarchies were rooted in it. Those who doubted this might ask themselves 'whether bawds, whores, thieves, buffoons, parasites, and such vile wretches as are naturally mercenary, have not more power at Whitehall, Versailles, the Vatican, and the Escurial, than Venice, Amsterdam, and Switzerland.'[79] If a personal adherence to moral self-discipline was not universal among republicans, even Marchamont Nedham could talk the talk: '*Free-States must needs be more pleasing to God than any other Form, because in them . . . men are . . . much more zealous in the love of Religion.*'[80] That 'Free-States' were less given to 'the baits and snares of luxury' than monarchies, and more devoted to 'Temperance, Vertue, and Freedom', was evident not only in Athens and Rome, but in '*Milan, Florence, Siena . . . Luca . . . Switzerland* [and] the *United Provinces*'.[81] As for the English republic,

being supported by counselors, grave, serious, abstemious, and vigilant, and by a soldiery whose valiant commanders are severe and strict in discipline, both moral and military, when I consider this with the many other advantages which their enemies have not, their foundation seems to me impregnable and prompts me to this omen, that being every way qualified like those Roman spirits of old, they will be courted and confirmed by the Roman fortune.[82]

Nor did the witty style of Harrington's *Oceana* disguise its intended contributions to the interregnum reformation of manners. One was the government of the passions by the 'Reason' of Harrington's orders, in particular their institutional separation of debating and resolving. Another was an agrarian law intended to ameliorate not only the particular injustice of primogeniture inheritance, but the anti-Christian social consequences of inequality and greed. The basis of this was 'ancient prudence, first discovered unto mankind by God himself in the fabric of the commonwealth of Israel, and afterward picked out of his footsteps in nature and unanimously followed by the Greeks and Romans'.[83] The result would establish 'the throne of a commonwealth' in a way 'consonant unto the holy

[79] Sidney, *Discourses*, ed. West p. 258.
[80] Nedham, *Excellencie* pp. 19–20 (based on *Mercurius Politicus* no. 68, 18–25 September 1651).
[81] Ibid. no. 84, pp. 1333–37.
[82] Nedham, *Case of the Commonwealth* pp. 114–15. Harrington likened primogeniture to the drowning of younger puppies in a litter, 'nay yet worse, for . . . the children are left perpetually drowning'.
[83] Harrington, *Oceana*, in *Political Works* pp. 161, 174 (and see chapter 13 below); on the commonwealth of Israel see also Milton, *Defence* p. 344; Harrington, *The Art of Lawgiving*, The Second Book, Containing the Commonwealth of the Hebrews; J. W. Gough, 'Harrington and Contemporary Thought', *Political Science Quarterly* 45, 3, (1930) p. 398: 'it is noteworthy that he invariably makes the practice of the Jewish Commonwealth the first support of every theory he brings forward, while examples from secular history come second'.

Scriptures'.[84] 'If our religion be anything else but a vain boast, scratching and defacing human nature or reason, which, being the image of God, makes it a kind of murder, here is that empire whence *justice shall run down like a river, and judgement like a mighty stream.*'[85]

Henry Neville, having observed the 'debauch, profaneness, ignorance, and disability to preach the gospel' of those 'ordination-mongers . . . our clergy', described scripture as his 'only rule of faith, worship and manners'. Like Neville, Sidney thought 'that the fanatics are persecuted principally for reading the Bible, and doing what they learn in it'.[86] One prominent Restoration opponent of such persecution was William Penn, who signed a pamphlet written on behalf of a parliamentary election attempt by Sidney: '*Amicus Plato, Amicus Aristoteles, sed magis Amica Veritas*'. This counselled

> The sincere Promotion *of general and practical* Religion; by which I mean the *Ten Commandments, or moral Law, and Christ's Sermon upon the Mount,* with other Heavenly Sayings . . . True and Requisite *Religion,* in the Apostle *James's* Definition is, *To visit the Widow and Fatherless, and to keep our selves,* through the Universal Grace, *unspotted of the World* . . . 'Tis want of *Practice,* and too much *Prate,* that hath made Way for all the *Incharity* and *ill Living* that is in the World.[87]

An insistence upon the sufficiency for a Christian life of 'that which is clearly commanded in scripture', free of abstruse clerical (or scholastic) accretions, had been equally characteristic of Erasmian humanism. Following Erasmus, Milton's *Christian Doctrine* explained that 'We must look for . . . [Christian] doctrine not among philosophizing academics, and not among the laws of men, but in the Holy Scriptures alone and with the Holy Spirit as guide.'[88] A large proportion of all republican writing consisted in scriptural citation. For Vane and Ludlow in particular, both the history of God's chosen people and the life of '*Christ* the *Mediator*' furnished crucial guidance concerning that 'Tryal' between the 'Spirit of righteousness' and the 'kingdom of Darkness' which decided the destiny of every human life.[89] Neville's religion, like Harrington's, partook of a consciously non-enthusiastic rationalism. Sidney, however, followed Milton

---

[84] Harrington, *Oceana,* in *Political Works* p. 322.   [85] Ibid. p. 333.

[86] Neville, *Plato Redivivus* p. 118; Sidney, *Court Maxims* p. 112.

[87] William Penn, *One Project for the Good of England* (1679) and *England's Present Interest Considered* (1675), in *The Political Writings of William Penn,* ed. Andrew Murphy (Indianapolis, Ind., 2002) pp. 69–70, 136.

[88] Erasmus, letter to Johannis Slechta, 1 November 1519, quoted in Cassirer, *The Platonic Renaissance* p. 21; Milton, *Christian Doctrine* p. 668: 'internal worship, provided that it is sincere, is acceptable to God, even if the external forms are not strictly observed'.

[89] Henry Vane, *An Epistle General to the Mystical Body of Christ on Earth, the Church Universal in Babylon* (1662) pp. 11, 16.

and Ludlow in their commitment to the godly republicanism exemplified by Vane: 'It is from God, not the prince or hangman, that we must learn religion. His spirit discovers truth unto us by the wings of love and faith.'[90]

They that depend upon him fall not into impatience for the delay of his coming, nor are affrighted at the boasting of his and their enemies. They live in and by faith, they see things that to other eyes are invisible. That spirit that has planted faith in their hearts doth perpetually bring forth fruits of hope and joy. They have resigned themselves and all they have and are into God's hands as willing sacrifices.[91]

THEOLOGY

It may be because of the republican insistence upon the sufficiency of the Bible and reformation of manners that some historians have discerned in their writings 'a retreat from theology'.[92] In matters of doctrine, as well as discipline, there was no uniform position. For Ludlow, a doctrinal predestinarian, 'Christ rule[d] . . . alone by his Spirit in the hearts of his People', dividing the world between 'evill men', who trust in 'the flesh . . . the worlds goods . . . [and] their Lusts', and 'those that are good . . . the saints in God . . . choosing rather to Obey God then men . . . [who] prefer his Love before the favour of the World . . . resigne their Wills to the will of God, and yield up their Passions to Reason as regulated by the word of God'.[93] By contrast Milton's *Christian Doctrine* explained that 'God has clearly and frequently declared . . . that he desires the salvation of all and the death of none, that he hates nothing he has made, and has ommitted nothing which might provide salvation for everyone . . . scripture offers salvation and eternal life to all equally, on condition of obedience to the Old Testament and faith in the New.'[94] For Vane too, despite his emphasis upon human fallibility, 'the Choice God had given unto man' before the fall, 'either to trust his own guidance for the ordering of his steps', or to make an 'absolute . . . resignation of his will . . . into the Will of his Sovereign . . . for his good', remained true in every lifetime. It was the purpose of '*God's sending his Son in the likeness of sinful flesh, who by the*

[90] Sidney, *Court Maxims* p. 98.
[91] Sidney, 'Court Maxims' f. 78. Sidney returns to this language in his *Apology* and *Last Paper*.
[92] Worden, 'English Republicanism' p. 474; Worden, 'The Question of Secularization', in Alan Craig Houston and Steven Pincus (eds.), *A Nation Transformed* (Cambridge, 2001) p. 38.
[93] Bodleian Library, Oxford, MS Eng. Hist c.487, Edmund Ludlow, 'A Voyce from the Watchtower' f. 325.
[94] Milton, *Christian Doctrine* pp. 174–5, 176–7.

sacrificing of himself, condemned sin in the flesh, that the Righteousness of the Law might be fulfilled in all such, as walk, not after the flesh, but after the Spirit.' By the

Redemption which is wrought for *all men*, and *forgiveness of sins through the Blood of Christ* . . . an *Act of Oblivion* freely . . . hath been passed, the benefit whereof is conditionally extended unto all. Hence it is, that the Office of giving and putting in execution the Law of God . . . is committed by the Father unto Christ, as he is the Son of Man; First to *dispence Judgement with Mercy, great patience* and *long-suffering*; and afterwards *without Mercy*, as that *fiery Indignation*, which is reserved for *wilful* and *hardned sinners*.[95]

More generally the definition given by Sidney of 'Theology' as that 'Science' which concerned 'la connoisance de Dieu et de la Religion'[96] put the emphasis upon epistemology. This might be, as it was for Harrington, knowledge of God through his material creation: 'Human prudence, in the first cause, is a creature of God, and in the second as ancient as human nature . . . A commonwealth for the matter makes herself . . . Or, to speak more properly . . . a commonwealth is not made by men but by God; and they who resist his holy will are weapons that cannot prosper.'[97] It is in *Oceana* that we find the strongest early grounds for identifying what historians of 'radical enlightenment' have described as a conjunction of republican politics and the new 'mechanical' science, with important religious implications.[98] In this respect Margaret Jacob's flawed account of Harrington's political philosophy may have led her to understate her own case. Harrington's political actors were not 'rational', 'non-dependent' or 'free'. Rather they were the morally flawed beneficiaries of a constitutional rationality deriving from the successful 'imitation' of nature. This was not a secular vision. It was an attempt to realise God's moral purposes for man (especially peace and justice) by bypassing the flawed rationality of individuals in favour of the structures inherent within God's perfect creation.

For Ludlow, more conventionally, 'that worke . . . ye Lord hath on ye wheele' was to be known by 'his providence . . . his word . . . [and] that light he hath ingrafted in every man by Nature'.[99] Similarly for Sidney:

[95] Vane, *An Epistle General* pp. 11–12; David Parnham, *Sir Henry Vane, Theologian: a Study in Seventeenth-Century Religious and Political Discourse* (1997).
[96] 'Lantiniana' p. 101.   [97] Harrington, *The Art of Lawgiving* pp. 616, 704.
[98] Margaret C. Jacob, *The Radical Enlightenment: Pantheists, Freemasons and Republicans* (1981) pp. 77–80; Jonathan Israel, *Radical Enlightenment: Philosophy and the Making of Modernity, 1650–1750* (Oxford, 2001).
[99] Ludlow, 'A Voyce from the Watchtower' ff. 183, 323, 327, 335.

'we have but three ways of distinguishing between good and evil. 1. When God by his word reveals it to us. 2. When by his deeds he declares it; because that which he does is good, as that which he says is true. 3. By the light of reason, which is good, inasmuch as it is from God.'[100] The pursuit of virtue entailed, as Augustine had explained, that knowledge of God and his goodness which was the highest attainment of human rationality, accompanied by the attempt to be like him.[101] In English republicanism, as in its Platonic and Stoic parent-philosophies, the achievement of virtue in practice depended upon the rational knowledge of truth and goodness.[102] In the words of Sidney, echoing those of Milton,

> Plato . . . says . . . 'tis impossible for any man to perform the part of a good magistrate, unless he have the knowledge of God; or to bring a people to justice, unless he bring them to the knowledge of God, who is the root of all justice and goodness . . . The misery of man proceeds from his being separated from God: This separation is wrought by corruption; his restitution therefore to felicity and integrity, can only be brought about by his reunion to the good from which he is fallen . . . If Plato therefore deserve credit, he only can duly perform the part of a good magistrate, whose moral virtues are ripened and heightened by a superinduction of divine knowledge.[103]

'Virtue is the dictate of reason, or the remains of divine light, by which men are made benevolent and beneficial to each other.'[104] To replace kingship, and with it dependence upon the will of fallen man, by the self-government of God-given reason, was the nearest mankind could come to the government of God. At the same time it gave political expression to an assumption at the heart of all Christian theology: the acknowledgement of dependence, and the obligation to service. It was Filmer's greatest error in *Patriarcha* to assign to kings and fathers a relationship of subjection which belonged only to their genuine creator, God. Thus C. S. Lewis, discussing *Paradise Lost*, speaks of 'the heresy at the root of [Satan's] . . . whole predicament – the doctrine that he is a self-existent being, not a derived being, a creature'.[105]

---

[100] Sidney, *Discourses*, in *Sydney on Government* p. 27.
[101] See chapter 9. On knowledge of God as the key to virtuous behaviour see Milton, *Christian Doctrine* pp. 128–33 and Book One in general; as within Cambridge Platonism, 'Appeals to the Holy Scriptures and to Plato's doctrine of knowledge and to Neo-platonic metaphysics stand indiscriminately side by side.' Cassirer, *The Platonic Renaissance* p. 25.
[102] G. Lesses, 'Virtue and the Goods of Fortune in Stoic Moral Theory', *Oxford Studies in Ancient Philosophy* 7 (1989) pp. 96, 121.
[103] Sidney, *Discourses*, ed. West pp. 82–3.
[104] Sidney, *Discourses* in *Sydney on Government: the Works of Algernon Sydney*, ed. J. Robertson (1772) p. 229.
[105] C. S. Lewis, *A Preface to Paradise Lost* (Oxford, 1942) p. 95.

ENLIGHTENMENT

With its anti-clericalism, emphasis upon manners and predominantly rational theology, it is not surprising that republican writing greatly influenced thinkers of the early Enlightenment. This influence did not incorporate the mystical spirituality of Vane, so that prior to publication Ludlow's *A Voyce from the Watchtower* was radically rewritten by its editor John Toland.[106] It is correspondingly suspicious that the spiritual enthusiasm of Sidney's *Court Maxims* and his *Last Paper* is absent from his *Discourses*, probably also published by Toland, for which no manuscript has survived. It was the purpose of Toland's *Christianity not Mysterious* (1696) to show not only 'That there is nothing in the Gospel Contrary to Reason, Nor Above it', but 'that no Christian Doctrine can be properly call'd A MYSTERY'.[107] Even so, the impact upon later dissenting theology of all aspects of radical protestantism, including providentialism and millennialism, ought not to be underestimated.

One aspect of the religious impact of republicanism involved the Erastianism, civil religion and natural philosophy of Harrington as well as Hobbes. Toland was right to understand the religious significance of Harrington's metaphysics as hinging upon his interpretation of nature as a work of divine authorship.[108] Yet since, far from being '[the] founder of seventeenth-century Republicanism'[109] Harrington had been a minority voice within it, his was far from the only, or even the primary Enlightenment legacy. Another focused more conventionally upon the divine authorship of rational human nature. This entailed an anti-Erastian emphasis upon liberty of conscience, often expressed in the language of natural law, and common not only to Milton, Vane and Sidney, but to John Locke.[110] When Locke defended religious toleration he did so, like Sidney, on the grounds not only that 'No way that I walk in against my conscience will ever lead me to the mansions of the blessed', but that

He who wishes to enlist under the banner of Christ must first of all declare war upon his own vices, his own pride and lusts; otherwise, without holiness of life, purity of manners, benignity and meekness of spirit, it is in vain for him to seek

---

[106] Blair Worden, 'Introduction,' in Edmund Ludlow, *A Voyce from the Watch Tower*.

[107] [John Toland], *Christianity not Mysterious* (1696), Title page.

[108] Jacob, *The Radical Enlightenment* p. 80; J. A. I. Champion, *The Pillars of Priestcraft Shaken: the Church of England and its Enemies, 1660–1730* (Cambridge, 1992) pp. 133–7, 170–222.

[109] Ibid. p. 186.

[110] This position, 'a toleration rooted in the Dutch Arminians – Episcopus, Limborch, Le Clerc – and, following them, John Locke', Jonathan Israel associates with the 'moderate' Enlightenment, to be distinguished from the deistic or atheistic 'radical'. Israel, *Radical Enlightenment* p. 265.

the name of Christian . . . For if the Gospel and the Apostles are to be believed, no man can be a Christian without charity, and without the faith which worketh, not by force, but by love.[111]

Sidney and Locke shared not only this Erasmian language in religion and Grotian language in politics, but participation in the same English cause, interspersed with Dutch exile. During the 1660s Sidney anticipated by two decades Locke's formative friendship with Benjamin Furly.[112] In the same period he remembered those 'cautions in reading of [the Church Fathers] . . . learnt . . . from Monsieur Daillé, that excellent and learnd preacher of the Gospell in Charenton'.[113] During the 1680s a group of protestant exiles, including Locke, Furly, Jean Le Clerc and Charles Le Cene, gathered in Amsterdam to publish the *Bibliotheque Universelle*.[114] Le Cene, who praised the ancient Greeks for their concern for the poor and social justice, had like Daillé earlier been a minister at Charenton.[115] Like Sidney, Le Clerc attended the academy at Saumur, and praised both Daillé and 'the incomparable Grotius'. Le Clerc translated Henry Hammond on the New Testament, as Hammond had earlier defended Grotius upon that same subject. As a whole this group drew upon classical (in particular, Greek) and Christian sources in support of a programme for the rational reform of religious, political and social life echoing many of the themes discussed here.[116]

[111] John Locke, *A Letter on Toleration*, trans. J. W. Gough (Oxford, 1968) pp. 59, 99.
[112] Scott, *Algernon Sidney and the English Republic* ch. 13; Scott, 'Law of War'.
[113] Sidney, 'Court Maxims' f. 96; Scott, *Algernon Sidney and the English Republic* p. 53; Daillé's *A Treatise Concerning the Right Use of the Fathers* was translated under the republic in 1651.
[114] *Historical Manuscripts Commission Report, De Lisle MSS* vol. VI, pp. xxii, 554.
[115] Savonius, 'John Locke and the Civil Philosophy of the *Bibliothecaires*' p. 26. I am very grateful to Dr Savonius for allowing me to draw upon his unpublished work.
[116] Ibid.; Savonius, 'Jean Le Clerc's and John Locke's *Kulturkampf* against Authoritarianism, 1688–1702', seminar paper given at Trinity Hall, Cambridge, 27 February 2002; Scott, *Algernon Sidney and the English Republic* ch. 13; Israel, *Radical Enlightenment*.

CHAPTER 3

Discourses of a commonwealth

[In the] Times of our *Monarchs* . . . *Injustice, Oppression* and *Slavery*
were the [lot of] the *Common people* . . . [It] was intended for the *fate*
of *England,* had our *Monarch* prevailed over us . . . That [we would
be] . . . *contented with Canvas clothing, and Wooden shoes, and look more
like Ghosts then men* . . . To bring this to pass, their Beasts of Forrests
must grow fat, by devouring the poor man's corn . . . A *Tradesman*
furnishing *a great man* with most part of his *Stock* . . . and expecting
due . . . payment, is answered with *ill words,* or *blows,* and the dear-
bought Learning, That *Lords and Kings servants are priviledged from
Arrests and Process of Law* . . . A poor *Waterman* . . . a poor *Countreyman* . . . must *serve* the *King* for . . . not enough to finde themselves
bread, when their *wives* and *children* have nothing . . . [alongside the]
luxury and *intemperance,* the *corrupt* . . . *maners* . . . of . . . the *noblest
Families.*

A Declaration of the Parliament (March 1649)[1]

THE ENGLISH COMMONWEALTH

In Harrington's *The Commonwealth of Oceana* (1656) the collapse of monarchy in England is explained almost entirely in economic and social terms.[2]
In its place, Harrington's proposed new 'orders of a Commonwealth' are
supported by a regulated economic and social foundation, secured by an
agrarian law. His republican reconfiguration of English government attends
not only to the centre, but to the elaborate framework of local office-holding
through which most seventeenth-century political tasks were actually performed. This is to remind us that commonwealth principles had social as
well as political content. It is equally to redirect our attention towards the

[1] *A Declaration of the Parliament* (March 1689) pp. 17–19. The position of the words 'was intended for
the *fate* of *England,* had our *Monarch* prevailed over us' has been moved within this quotation.
[2] A fact discussed by Keith Wrightson, *Earthly Necessities* p. 4.

decentralised social state (or commonwealth) responsible for the day-to-day government of what Fortescue called 'the whole realm'.[3]

Even at the centre this government was, as it had been in the fourteenth century, 'both royal and conciliar at every level. The king had great but not independent power, and the English had a tradition of calling over-mighty kings to account.'[4] At the level of town, village and parish this political nation traversed a much broader range of social status than we used to think.[5] It was in this context that Patrick Collinson reminded us of a level of collective self-government, in the localities and at the centre, which might even warrant the label 'monarchical republic'.[6] Subsequently Markku Peltonen has examined the extent to which Elizabethan inhabitants of 'the Citties and cheefe Townes' considered it compatible with their duty as subjects to study 'the calling of a Cittizen' in its classical republican sense.[7] Steve Hindle and Michael Braddick have emphasised the participatory nature of early modern local office-holding, and Mark Goldie has called for a revision of our assumptions about what constituted political self-government in early modern England. During the seventeenth century, Goldie has estimated, the number of local office-holders may have totalled 50,000: one-twentieth of the adult male population in any given year.[8]

As monarchy functioned through these structures, so they furnish a vital context for understanding its collapse. Even before the troubles, the government of the English commonwealth had been struggling to come to grips with pressing economic and social, as well as religious, political and military problems. Following the abolition of monarchy many essential governmental offices continued to function. At the centre, such a monarchical 'interregnum' had been anticipated by William Cecil in January 1585 when drawing up a plan for 'The governement of the realme' to 'contynew in all respects' should the queen meet a sudden death with the succession contested.[9] Following the reigns, since 1537, of one minor and two women, it was 'implicit in much of Elizabethan politics' that 'Privy Councillors and

---

[3] The important theoretical analysis of the English state in these terms is Braddick, *State Formation*.

[4] Brown, *The Governance of Late Medieval England* pp. 12–13; Scott, *England's Troubles* ch. 3.

[5] A point emphasised by Hindle, *The State and Social Change*. See the review of Braddick and Hindle by Jonathan Scott in *The English Historical Review* 116, 469 (Nov 2001), pp. 1225–7.

[6] Patrick Collinson, 'The Monarchical Republic of Elizabeth I', *Bulletin of the John Rylands Library* 69 (1987); Collinson, *De Republica*.

[7] Markku Peltonen, 'Citizenship and Republicanism in Elizabethan England', in van Gelderen and Skinner, *Republicanism* vol. 1; see also Fitzmaurice, *Humanism and America*.

[8] Goldie, 'Unacknowledged Republic' p. 161.

[9] Patrick Collinson, '"The State as Monarchical Commonwealth": "Tudor" England', *Journal of Historical Sociology* 15, 1 March (2002) p. 89.

other public men bore a relation to the commonwealth and to God which might transcend their subservience to the [individual] monarch'.[10]

Since Lawrence Stone's *The Causes of the English Revolution* (1972) the economic and social contexts of that event have not been the focus of attention.[11] This reflected a revisionist reaction against the idea of long-term causes in general, as well as against the economic determinism of Marxist analyses in particular. Over the same generation, however, among economic and social historians, an understanding of the early modern period as one of decisive transformation (economic, social and cultural) has been greatly clarified.[12] The most important changes included population increase, price inflation, the commercialisation of agriculture and the economy, an increase in poverty and the consolidation of a self-consciously 'middling sort', and modernisation of the political economy of the state. Considering the political consequences of these developments, historians have described two distinct processes. In relation to the military-fiscal state they have used the deliberative word 'statebuilding', since the measures concerned were frequently the result of imperatives felt, and decisions taken, at the political centre.[13] By contrast, social historians have discerned in 'state formation' an incremental process whereby local office-holders deployed powers conferred by the state not only to underline their status, but to respond to a variety of urgent local problems.[14] Underlying both developments, however, was one social change and its effects. This was a more than doubling of the English population between 1524 and 1656.[15]

THE MILITARY-FISCAL STATE

This population increase was European in scope. For the military-fiscal state its most important impact was price inflation. Between 1540 and 1640 prices in England increased five-fold: 'In an age of inflation, rulers had to increase revenues . . . simply to stand still. A five-fold increase in revenues in the sixteenth century would still barely keep up with rising living costs.'[16]

---

[10] Collinson, 'Conclusion' p. 235.

[11] See however Anne Hughes, *The Causes of the English Civil War*, 2nd edn (Basingstoke, 1998) chs. 2–3, and the references there given.

[12] Wrightson, *Earthly Necessities*.

[13] John Brewer, *Sinews of Power: War, Money and the English State 1688–1783* (1989); Wolfgang Reinhard (ed.), *Power Elites and State Building* (Oxford, 1996); Charles Tilly (ed.), *The Formation of Nation States in Western Europe* (Princeton, 1975).

[14] Mike Braddick, *State Formation*; Braddick, *The Nerves of State: Taxation and the Financing of the English State, 1558–1714* (Manchester, 1996).

[15] Hindle, *The State and Social Change*.

[16] Richard Bonney, *The European Dynastic States 1494–1660* (Oxford, 1991) p. 354.

The political impact of this was serious in an age when innovation was unacceptable and inflation was not understood. This impact was, however, greatly exacerbated by two other factors. The first was the 'military revolution' which increased ten-fold the size of the largest armies in Europe between 1500 and 1700.[17] This added to the pressure for money a sharp cutting edge: states had to respond or risk being wiped out. The second exacerbating factor was the religious disintegration of Christendom. This fuelled the tendency towards war, both between states and within them. At the same time it contributed to such conflicts a dangerous ideological dimension. Would-be centralising governments were much more likely to face war; in the worst case this might be against a domestic rebellion sanctioned by religious ideology. In the period 1550–1650 rulers of the Holy Roman Empire, France, Spain and Stuart Britain all became embroiled in such conflicts.[18]

In this context, the first specific English factor was the near absence of effective Tudor statebuilding. Between 1529 and 1536 there occurred a jurisdictional revolution which dramatically augmented the responsibilities of the crown. These now included, in a religiously divided nation, the care not only of bodies but of souls. They included, in a religiously polarised Europe, the role of defender of the faith. By the seventeenth century the Stuarts were responsible for three kingdoms, and three churches. The only thing they had not acquired was any of the resources necessary to perform these functions.[19] The spoil from the monasteries was quickly squandered. Until 1558 there was at least a continuation of the incremental fiscal reform of the late medieval period. Under Elizabeth, however, with conservatism elaborated to the point of torpor, even this ended: 'The Tudors had never succeeded in putting the crown's finances on a strong long-term basis. Instead they lived off occasional windfalls – monastery land, chantries, debasement, bishops' lands . . . The crunch was bound to come.'[20] Revenue at the end of Elizabeth's reign (1603) was 40 per cent less in real terms than it had been in 1509. One response, particularly during the Elizabethan military struggle against Spain, was the sale of crown land. This was made the basis of political capital; in the words of Robert Cecil, 'She selleth her land to defend us'. As the Earl of Clarendon later put it, it was 'the popular axiom of Queen Elizabeth, that as her greatest treasure was in the hearts of

[17] Geoffrey Parker, *The Military Revolution: Military Innovation and the Rise of the West*, 2nd edn (Cambridge, 1996).

[18] Koenigsberger '*Dominium Regale*' pp. 17–20, 73–4; Scott, *England's Troubles* pp. 80–5.

[19] Scott, 'What the Dutch Taught Us'; Scott, *England's Troubles* pp. 72–3.

[20] Jennifer Loach, *Parliament under the Tudors* (Oxford, 1991) p. 160.

her people, so she had rather her money should be in their purses than in her Exchequer.'[21] Accordingly the Stuarts inherited a political context that was 'popular', and an exchequer which was empty.[22]

Though it would have been unfortunate at any time, it was the European situation which made this legacy fatal. During the Thirty Years War, with the nation's religious and dynastic interests vitally engaged, both early Stuart monarchs faced a deafening demand for military involvement accompanied by a complete absence of the material resources, and expertise, necessary to make this successful.[23] It was military failure on the Continent, and then later in Scotland, Ireland and finally England, which destroyed the monarchy. In Harrington's analysis,

Of the king's success with his arms it is not necessary to give any further account, than that they proved as ineffectual as his nobility. But without a nobility or an army (as hath been shown) there can be no monarchy. Wherefore what is there in nature that can arise but a popular government, or a new monarchy to be erected by the victorious army?[24]

When it came, from 1642, and most decisively from 1689, successful English statebuilding would be not monarchical but parliamentary, and not simply English but Anglo-Dutch.[25] The first English government to inherit the resulting transformation of military power was the republic of 1649–53. The spectacular military successes of this regime, in Ireland, Scotland and finally against the Dutch themselves, had a decisive impact upon the development of republican ideology.[26] When English republicanism emerged, it did so as (among other things) the ideology of the first fiscally and militarily modernised English and British state. This helps to explain the deep and developing interest of republican writers in the economic, social, maritime and military bases of modern state power. Its

---

[21] S. R. Gardiner, *History of England from the Accession of James I to the Outbreak of the Civil War 1603–1642* (10 vols., 1895) vol. I, p. 293; Conrad Russell, 'Parliaments and the English State at the end of the Sixteenth Century', first Trevelyan Lecture given at the University of Cambridge, 1995; Edward Hyde, Earl of Clarendon *The History of the Rebellion and Civil Wars in England*, ed. W. D. Macray (6 vol., Oxford, 1888; repr. 1958) vol. I, p. 98, note 1.

[22] Popular not, of course, in the sense of being democratic, but in the sensitivity of the crown to public opinion. This helps to contextualise James I's complaint about some JPs' 'puritanical itching after popularity' (see chapter II note 2).

[23] Conrad Russell, *Parliaments and English Politics 1621–1629* (Oxford, 1979); Kevin Sharpe, *The Personal Rule of Charles I* (New Haven, Conn., 1992) ch. 1; John Reeve, *Charles I and the Road to Personal Rule* (Cambridge, 1989); N. A. M. Rodger, *The Safeguard of the Sea* (New York, 1997) pp. 24–5; Scott, *England's Troubles* ch. 4.

[24] Harrington, *Oceana*, in *Political Works* p. 198.

[25] Scott, *England's Troubles* Part III, esp. ch. 21; see also below chapter 4, pp. 102–5; Scott, '"Good Night Amsterdam"'; Scott, 'What the Dutch Taught Us'.

[26] Scott, *Algernon Sidney and the English Republic* ch. 6; Scott, 'The English Republican Imagination'.

most important fiscal foundation was the monthly assessment, a land tax administered by those County Committees attacked by the Levellers as '*Horse-leeches of the Common-wealth*'.[27] Almost as important, and equally unpopular, was the Dutch-inspired excise on staple commodities introduced by John Pym in 1643.[28] In addition, throughout the century, an increasingly vital proportion of state income was provided by customs revenues on European and colonial trade. An advisory Council of Trade was established in 1650 and an executive Board of Trade during the 1690s.

From its inception, a striking feature of the English republic's record in practice was the vigour with which it pursued the nation's maritime and commercial interests. As Henry Stubbe later put it, 'Those Subtle men who ruled in the Council of State . . . esteemed nothing more beneficial, just and generous . . . than to assert the Dominion of the Seas, the Rights of the Fishery, and to vindicate the English commerce through all parts of the world. They did rightly apprehend that the strength of this nation consisted in Naval forces; and the life thereof was commerce.'[29] It was a key claim of the regime's *Declaration . . . Expressing the Grounds of their . . . Setling the present Government In the way of A Free State* (1649) that

the *scituation* and *advantages* of this *Land*, both for *Trade* abroad, and *Manufactures* at home, will be better understood, when . . . *Projects, Monopolies*, and *obstructions* thereof, are together with the *Court*, the *Fountain of them*, removed; and a *Free Trade, with incouragement of Manufacturies*, and *provision* for *poor*, be setled by the *Common-wealth*, whereunto the same is most agreeable.[30]

Crucial measures included a major investment in the navy (busy from 1649 pursuing royalists in the North Sea, the Irish Sea, the Mediterranean and the Caribbean), the 'nationalisation' of English European and colonial trade by the Navigation Act of 1651, and the aggressive military enforcement of these and other pretensions in the war against the United Provinces begun in 1652.[31] In mid-1651 a Venetian observer reported:

[27] *[Nedham] Vox Plebis* p. 61; *The humble petition of well-affected persons* (11 September 1648), in J. P. Kenyon (ed.), *The Stuart Constitution*, 2nd edn (Cambridge, 1986) p. 279 no. 11 (this also attacked the excise).

[28] Marjolein 'T Hart, '"The Devil or the Dutch"': Holland's Impact on the Financial Revolution in England, 1643–1694', *Parliaments, Estates and Representation* 11, 1 (1991).

[29] Henry Stubbe, *A Further Justification of the Present War Against the United Netherlands* (1673) 'To the Reader' p. 1.

[30] *A Declaration of the Parliament* (March 1649) p. 19.

[31] Bernard Capp, *Cromwell's Navy: the Fleet and the English Revolution 1648–1660* (Oxford, 1989); Hilary Beckles, 'The "Hub of Empire": the Caribbean and Britain in the Seventeenth Century', in Nicholas Canny (ed.), *The Oxford History of the British Empire, Volume I. The Origins of Empire: British Overseas Enterprise to the Close of the Seventeenth Century* (Oxford, 1998) p. 236; J. R. Jones, *The Anglo-Dutch Wars of the Seventeenth Century* (1996).

Owing to the care of parliament they have 80 men of war, which are certainly the finest now afloat, whether for construction, armament, or crews. They can increase these numbers with incredible facility to 150, 200 or more sail . . . [In addition] trade . . . has made great strides for some time past, and is now improved by the protection it receives from parliament, the government of the commonwealth and that of its trade being exercised by the same individuals.[32]

Many of these policies were inspired by the Dutch republic, within which politics and trade exhibited a similar interdependence, and the economic miracle of which underpinned the outstanding contemporary example of successful republican statebuilding.[33] Like many others John Dury, lobbying the government in 1652, took Dutch prosperity, by contrast with the poverty of Spain, as clinching evidence that 'the stren[g]th and foundation of commonwealths is commerce and Trade.'[34] The Anglo-Dutch war of 1652–4 involved less a rejection of the Dutch way of commerce than a determination that it no longer be pursued at England's expense. As Francis Bacon had strikingly suggested a generation earlier, 'To be master of the sea is [itself] an abridgement of a monarchy.'[35] Throughout the early Stuart period thousands of English and Scots soldiers, religious exiles and travellers had directly witnessed life in the Dutch republic.[36] In addition English republican policies had longer-term roots in an anti-Spanish protestant imperial ambition entailing a strong emphasis, in alliance with the Dutch, upon naval and commercial considerations. Thus in the Preface to his translation of John Selden, *Of the Dominion, Or, Ownership of the Sea* (1652), Marchamont Nedham recalled Elizabeth 'that excellent Ladie, who . . . was both Mother and Nurs of their ungrateful Republick . . . Had the *Netherlanders* been content to keep within their proper Bounds it had been still our Interest (as of old) to have had Peace with them above other Nations.' The reverse being the case, there was little doubt '*That the old English bloud and sens of honor, runs still in the veins of your Sea-men.*'[37] Nedham's translation, 'Published by Special Command

---

[32] *Calendar of State Papers and Manuscripts relating to English Affairs existing in the archives and collections of Venice*, vol. xxviii (1927) pp. 187–8.

[33] Jonathan Israel, *The Dutch Republic: Its Rise, Greatness and Fall 1477–1806* (Oxford 1995) chs. 13–14, 29; David Ormrod, *The Rise of Commercial Empires: England and the Netherlands in the Age of Mercantilism, 1650–1770* (Cambridge, 2003) ch. 2.

[34] *Hartlib Papers*, Electronic Edition, John Dury, 'Memo on Protestant Exiles and Commonwealth Trade', 53/6A; William Temple made the same point in *Observations* pp. 189–90.

[35] Francis Bacon, 'Of the True Greatness of Kingdoms and Estates', in *Bacon's Essays*, ed. Edwin A. Abbott (2 vols., 1889) vol. I, p. 110.

[36] Scherpbier, *Milton in Holland* p. 25.

[37] Marchamont Nedham, Epistle Dedicatorie, in John Selden, *Of the Dominion, Or, Ownership of the Sea* (1652).

[of] the Council of State', appears to have 'faln under . . . [the] noble Patronage . . . of [these] . . . heroick Patriots, who . . . are resolved to see our Sea-Territorie . . . bravely maintained by the Sword'.[38]

What interrupted this project was dissolution of the Rump by Oliver Cromwell in March 1653. This was probably partly motivated by disapproval of these policies, as well as by the rapidly developing naval site of military prestige, alternative to that of the New Model Army and encroaching upon its fiscal base. It was followed by an Anglo-Dutch peace accused by Bethel, Streater and others of throwing away all the remarkable gains of the previous war. Accordingly it was Cromwell who 'layed the Foundation of Our present Condition, in the Decay of TRADE':

When this late Tyrant, or Protector (as some calls him) turned out the Long Parliament, the Kingdome was arrived at the highest pitch of Trade, Wealth, and Honour, that it, in any Age, ever yet knew. The trade appeared, by the great Sums offered then for the Customes and Excise . . . The Riches of the Nation . . . in the high value, that Land, and all our Native Commodities bore . . . Our Honour, was made known to all the world, by a Conquering Navie, which had brought the proud *Hollanders* upon their Knees, to begg peace of us, upon our own Conditions, keeping all other Nations in awe.[39]

On the eve of restoration Marchamont Nedham predicted that 'as to . . . your *Trade*, it is easie to guess what will become of that, when it shall be counted Reason of State to keep you poor and low',[40] a theme amplified by Sidney's *Court Maxims*. In fact, between 1660 and 1675 the most important author of the new Navigation Act and associated legislation governing European and colonial shipping was the republican veteran and Dutch envoy Sir George Downing.[41] However in 1665–7, and again in 1672–3, Charles II was to find the associated military success and 'Honour' elusive. As Sidney observed caustically, 'The terror that the city of London was possessed with . . . when a few Dutch ships came to Chatham, shews that no numbers of men, tho naturally valiant, are able to defend themselves, unless they be well arm'd, disciplin'd and conducted.'[42]

---

[38] Ibid.   [39] Bethel, *The World's Mistake in Oliver Cromwell* p. 3.

[40] Merchamont Nedham, *Interest will not Lie: Or, A View of England's True Interest* (12 August 1659) pp. 45–6.

[41] Charles Wilson, *Profit and Power: a Study of England and the Dutch Wars* (1957) pp. 102–3; Henry Roseveare, 'Prejudice and Policy: Sir George Downing as Parliamentary Entrepreneur', in D. C. Coleman and Peter Mathias (eds.), *Enterprise and History: Essays in Honour of Charles Wilson* (Cambridge, 1986); Scott, '"Good Night Amsterdam"' pp. 350–3.

[42] Sidney, *Discourses*, in *Sydney on Government* p. 209.

THE SOCIAL STATE

Population growth had not only fiscal and military, but economic, social and cultural consequences. Describing these, historians have focused less upon central government as an institution, than upon local governance as a process.[43] They have emphasised the social range of local office-holding, embracing at parish and vestry level the yeomanry and 'respectable' middling sort. In the words of John Streater, 'It is the interest of a wise Prince to own the authority of the officers of the Commonwealth, the Constable in *England* hath been ever of great repute, it is a great Trust, he is intrusted with the Peace of the Nation.'[44] They have emphasised, secondly, the centrality of such office-holding to early modern English political participation, both in rural or village communities and in towns.[45] Thus although historians have spent a great deal of time debating the social extent of participation in the parliamentary franchise, it has recently been asserted that 'in early modern England the holding of the parliamentary franchise was not regarded as the pre-eminent criterion of citizenship'.[46] It is of course true that the parliamentary franchise was the subject of a famous day of debate between army leaders and Levellers at Putney church in October 1647, during which at least two speakers explicitly advocated universal manhood suffrage. It is equally clear that this advocacy occurred in defence of a document, the first *Agreement of the People*, the primary concern of which was the radical decentralisation of political (in particular parliamentary) power.[47]

As increased poverty, and market opportunity, fed a deepening process of social stratification, the importance of local office-holding increased not only as a means of solving problems (social amelioration, the maintenance of 'order'), but also as a mechanism through which social elites distinguished themselves, as part of the solution, from those problems, however personified (the idle poor, vagrants, criminals or papists). The resources deployed

---

[43] Hindle, *The State and Social Change*; Braddick, *State Formation*; Goldie, 'Unacknowledged Republic'.

[44] Streater, *Observations* no. 5, p. 37.

[45] Hindle, *The State and Social Change*; Paul Halliday, *Dismembering the Body Politic: Partisan Politics in England's Towns 1650–1730* (Cambridge, 1998).

[46] Goldie, 'Unacknowledged Republic' p. 153; Derek Hirst, *The Representative of the People? Voters and Voting in England under the Early Stuarts* (Cambridge, 1975); Mark Kishlansky, *Parliamentary Selection: Social and Political Choice in Early Modern England* (Cambridge, 1986).

[47] *The Agreement of the People* (1647), in Kenyon, *Stuart Constitution* pp. 274–6; C. H. Firth (ed.), *The Clarke Papers* (4 vols., 1899–1965) vol. I, pp. 280–363 (the two individuals were Rainsborough and Wildman); J. C. Davis, 'The Levellers and Democracy', *Past and Present* 40 (1968); Keith Thomas, 'The Levellers and the Franchise', in G. E. Aylmer (ed.), *The Interregnum: the Quest for Settlement 1646–1660* (1972); Scott, *England's Troubles* pp. 277–83.

for this purpose, often with severity, were both broadly political (the poor laws, the criminal law) and cultural (the Reformation, reformation of manners).[48] From this process in the localities, as well as among members of parliament who drew up the requisite legislation, emerged the rhetoric (and practice) of puritan magistracy. This was an important aspect of republican writing, as well as of actual government during the 1650s. Cromwell's Major Generals, though imposed in response to a military emergency, were charged with oversight of a moral reformation which had in fact already been pursued by the minority of godly JPs and parish officers since at least the Elizabethan period. Thus in his speech to parliament of 11 September 1654, which furnishes as we will see an important context for understanding Harrington's *Oceana*, Cromwell claimed a commission not only from 'Providence, in the sight of God', but from the entire community of local office-holders.[49]

Recent studies have highlighted the paradox of a social state at once fragile in terms of its capacity to impose its authority without continual negotiation, yet sufficiently durable to outlive the temporary collapse of central authority altogether during the 1640s. This is partly because in times of public anxiety about government policy a strong social state built upon local mediation and resources of social and cultural legitimation might become a force for resistance, rather than assistance, to fiscal-military statebuilding.[50] When it emerged, the military-fiscal state would be constructed by different means, cutting across local and customary arrangements by force if necessary. Meanwhile, during the early to mid-1640s, in the context of a military dispute for control of central political authority, local civic self-government became a newly dominant reality.

The most important example of this was the government of the City of London, described by Milton in 1644 as 'this vast . . . City of refuge, the mansion house of liberty', whose 'Free Citizens' were assiduously courted by leaders of the Commons and Lords alike.[51] As the war progressed and imposed new financial burdens, however, such citizenship came to feel to some of its victims more like slavery. If the project of the Levellers was to oppose 'tyranny and oppression . . . under what name or title soever', such complaints on behalf of 'an inslaved perishing people' were directed

---

[48] Hindle guesses that 'some 75,000 felons went to the gallows in the century before 1630': *The State and Social Change* p. 119.

[49] *Oliver Cromwell's Letters and Speeches*, ed. Thomas Carlyle (3 vols., 1857) vol. III, pp. 50–1.

[50] Braddick, *State Formation*.

[51] John Milton, *Areopagitica: A Speech of Mr John Milton for the Liberty of Unlicenc'd Printing* (1644), in *Complete Prose Works* vol. II, p. 553; *England's Memorable Accidents* (24–31 October 1642) p. 1.

as much against the outrages perpetrated by County Committees and the City as against 'King, Parliament, [or] Council of State'.[52] Indeed because

the miseries wherewith a Tyrant loadeth his people, cannot be so heavy as the burthens imposed by a cruell City . . . all free Cities . . . lest . . . their Governours . . . should, through ambition and misgovernment . . . take liberty to oppresse and inslave the people to their lusts and wils; have in their first Constitutions provided, that all their Officers and Magistrates should be elective *By Votes and Approbation* of the free people of each City; and no longer to continue then a yeare (as the *Annuall Consuls in Rome*).[53]

From the early 1640s until the Glorious Revolution (and beyond) the electoral accountability of the City government was a crucial issue. Thus in 1682, amid 'great Heats and Animosities . . . among the Citizens, concerning the manner of Chusing their Chief Officers', the advice of John Wildman, first published in 1650, was republished. This was that 'it was the ancient undoubted right of the citizens of *London* by themselves or their deputies, to make their election of their Mayor and Sheriffs, and other chief Officers of the City'.[54] The Levellers paid close attention to issues of participation, representation and accountability, both local and central. This helps to explain the increasingly elaborate arrangements of the *Agreements* both for making central authorities accountable, and for reorganising the basis for election of representatives within all 'Counties, Cities, or Borroughs'.[55] A demand for further decentralisation was expressed rhetorically in appeals *from* tyrannical authorities '*to the Representative Body of the People*'. 'If I prove a forfeiture of the people's trust in the prevalent party at Westminster . . . then an appeale from them to the people is not . . . anti-magisterial; not *from* that sovereign power but *to* that sovereign power.'[56] It was expressed in practice in those clauses of the *Agreements of the People* which sought to

---

[52] Quoted in John Sanderson, '*But the People's Creatures': the Philosophical Basis of the English Civil War* (Manchester, 1989) p. 102; *The Petition of January 1648*, in D. Wolfe (ed.), *Leveller Manifestoes of the Puritan Revolution* (New York, 1967) p. 264; *Petition of 11 September 1648*, in Wolfe, *Leveller Manifestoes* pp. 287–9.

[53] John Lilburne, *London's Liberty in Chains discovered* (1646) p. 2.

[54] *London's Liberties* (1682) Preface and p. 13; *London's Liberties; or a Learned Argument of Law and Reason Upon Saturday, December 14 1650. Before the Lord Mayor, Court of Aldermen, and Common Councell at Guild Hall, LONDON, Between Mr Maynard Mr Hales and Mr Wilde Of Councell for the Companies of London And Major John Wildman and Mr John Price Of Councell for the Freemen of London* (1650) p. 12; see also Gary De Krey, 'Revolution *Redivivus*: 1688–1689 and the Radical Tradition in Seventeenth-Century London Politics', in L. Schwoerer (ed.), *The Revolution of 1688–1689* (Cambridge, 1992).

[55] See, for instance, *Foundations of Freedom; or an Agreement of the People: Proposed as a Rule for future Government in the Establishment of a firm and lasting Peace* (1648) pp. 4–15.

[56] A point emphasised by John Morrill in 'The Army Revolt of 1647', in Morrill, *The Nature of the English Revolution* (1993); Richard Overton, *An Appeal from the Degenerate House of Commons* (1647),

reduce the extent, as well as duration, of central power, both by formally subordinating the representatives to the represented, and by withholding major areas of political jurisdiction from central government altogether.[57]

The relationship between this thrust of the Leveller campaign and republican ideology was complicated. Immediately upon its establishment, Leveller polemic was directed against the republic, and defenders of the regime like Nedham, himself previously a Leveller, felt it necessary to ridicule Leveller as well as royalist and presbyterian pretensions. In *The Second Part of England's New-Chaines Discovered* (1649) Lilburne and others measured the government against its own ideology, concluding its members, in their 'unjust, covetous, or ambitious practises . . . to degenerate so soon into the grossest Principles and practises of . . . long settled Tyrannies'.[58] Yet for all its new-found military prowess, accompanied by a powerful rhetoric of Machiavellian statebuilding and puritan moral reformation, the republic, like the monarchy, still had to function through local government. It may have been partly for this reason that, for all his anti-Leveller posturing, Nedham's own ideology took far more from the Levellers than it rejected. Most importantly, there was one republican writer who yielded nothing to Lilburne in the ferocity of his criticism of the Rump, though for entirely different reasons.[59] This was James Harrington.

On the face of it, Harrington's position on this question was opposite to that of the Levellers. In *The Art of Lawgiving* (1659) Harrington attacked the second *Agreement of the People* (1648) as a recipe for 'downright anarchy'. In fact

Where the sovereign power is not as entire and absolute as in monarchy itself, there can be no government at all. It is not the limitation of sovereign power that is the cause of a commonwealth, but such a *libration or poise of orders, that there can be in the same no number of men, having the interest, that can have the power, nor any number of men, having the power, that can have the interest, to invade or disturb the government.*[60]

Yet it was by the power of his absolute constitution that Harrington also proposed to limit that of *Oceana's* representatives, officers and citizens. '[S]overeign power . . . is a necessary but a formidable creature . . . tell us whether our rivers do not enjoy a more secure and fruitful reign within their

   in A. S. P. Woodhouse (ed.), *Puritanism and Liberty: Being the Army Debates (1647–9) from the Clarke Manuscripts with Supplementary Documents* (1951) p. 327.

[57] Scott, *England's Troubles* pp. 281–3.

[58] John Lilburne, Richard Overton and Thomas Prince, *The Second Part of England's New-Chaines Discovered* (1649) p. 2.

[59] Harrington, *Oceana*, in *Political Works* p. 206.   [60] Harrington, *Political Works* pp. 657–8.

proper banks, than if it were lawful for them, in ravishing our harvests, to spill themselves? . . . The virtue of the loadstone is not impaired or limited, but receiveth strength and nourishment, by being bound in iron.'[61] This constitution regulated election (by secret ballot), the functions of representatives (by the separation of debate from resolution) and office-holding, both central and local (by rotation). Moreover the entire constitutional superstructure was anchored in a foundation which limited discrepencies of individual wealth. These themes, both of social amelioration and the reform of local office-holding, were taken up by the author of *Chaos* (1659), which spent far more time on local ('provincial, sub-provincial and parish') office-holding than on central government.[62] In the aftermath of *Oceana* even Milton turned his mind to a configuration of local magistracy whereby 'every countie in the land' was to be made 'a kind of subordinate Commonaltie or Commonwealth'. As

in all things of civil government . . . they shall [also] have justice in thir own hands, law executed fully and finally in thir own counties and precincts, long wish'd, and spoken of, but never yet obtaind; they shall have none then to blame but themselves, if it be not well administer'd . . . They should have heer also schools and academies at thir own choice, wherin thir children may be bred up in thir own sight to all learning and noble education.[63]

Milton's preparedness, however, to pander to the mania for decentralisation, and the public loathing of interregnum central authority, was limited. Thus under its perpetual council Milton's republic would not be, as in the United Provinces, 'many Sovranties united in one Commonwealth, but many Commonwealths under one united and entrusted Sovrantie'.[64]

DISCOURSES OF A COMMONWEALTH

One response to contemporary economic and social change was the body of social legislation relating to enclosures, rents, the prices of staple commodities, unemployment, vagrancy and other manifestations of growing inequality and poverty.[65] Another was the genre of 'commonwealth literature' giving voice to contemporary complaint and canvassing sometimes

---

[61] Harrington, *Oceana* pp. 229–30.
[62] *Chaos: Or, A Discourse Wherin is presented to the view of the Magistrate . . . a Frame of Government by way of a Republique* (1659) pp. 5, 7–24.
[63] Milton, *The Readie and Easie Way* pp. 458–60.   [64] Ibid. p. 461.
[65] Wrightson, *Earthly Necessities* pp. 202–26; Hindle, *The State and Social Change*. Another analysis of the social and cultural consequences of economic change with important implications for political thought is Craig Muldrew, *The Economy of Obligation: the Culture of Credit and Social Relations in Early Modern England* (Basingstoke, 1998).

sweeping solutions.[66] Both diagnoses and solutions were couched in the language (classical and Christian) of vice and virtue. All changes associated with the commercialisation of agriculture, enclosure, and growing social inequality and want, appeared to accentuate the already painful discrepancy between Christian ethics and contemporary social and political practice. Against the vices pre-eminently identified as responsible (pride and greed, or covetousness) were promoted values (charity, thrift, neighbourliness, and doing unto others as we would be done by) held to be capable of upholding a genuine commonwealth.

Thus More's *Utopia* produced a devastating indictment of the 'social evils' of a so-called 'commonwealth' where 'money is the measure of all things . . . where all the best things in life are held by the worst citizens . . . where property is limited to a few – where even those few are always uneasy, and where the many are utterly wretched'.[67] Such a system rewarded 'greed' and 'insatiable gluttony' with a 'wanton luxury' which 'exists side by side . . . [with] hideous poverty'.[68] While 'a great many noblemen . . . live idly like drones off the labour of others,' the poor, deprived even of the opportunity to labour, are driven either 'to wander and beg' (in which case they are jailed as vagrants) or 'to the awful necessity of stealing and then dying for it'.[69]

For More, as for Plato and Aristotle, the aim of a commonwealth was that its members should enjoy 'happiness and justice'. To this interest of the commonwealth he juxtaposed the counsel of a tyrant that 'The king should leave his subjects as little as possible, because his own safety depends on keeping them from growing insolent with wealth and freedom.' In truth 'A king has no dignity when he exercises authority over beggars, only when he rules over prosperous and happy subjects . . . A solitary ruler who enjoys a life of pleasure while all about him are grieving and groaning is acting like a jailer, not a king . . . Such a king openly confesses his incapacity to rule free men.'[70] In a work published in 1652 Fulke Greville would depict Sir Philip Sidney as having devoted his life to opposing the Spanish and papal design 'to bring all the earth under one man's tyranny'. In France this had already deprived a 'once well-formed Monarchy' of 'her ancient, and reverend pillars (I mean Parliaments, Lawes, and Customes) . . . [and] transformed her Gentry into Peasants, her Peasants into slaves, Magistracy into Sale works, Crown-revenue into Impositions'.[71]

---

[66] Jones, *The Tudor Commonwealth*; McRae, *God Speed the Plough*. [67] More, *Utopia* pp. 38–9.
[68] Ibid. p. 20. [69] Ibid. pp. 16, 19. [70] Ibid. pp. 33, 34.
[71] Grevil[le], *Life of Sidney* p. 98; this work was quoted by Marchamont Nedham in *Mercurius Politicus* no. 84, 8–15 January 1652 pp. 1336–7.

In 1665 Sir Philip's grand-nephew Algernon's Platonic *Court Maxims*, which employed the dialogue form of *Utopia*, defended a similar account of the purposes of *politea* ('societies are constituted that men in them may live happily'). Since it was a maxim of the restored Stuart court that 'as long as the people continue strong, numerous, and rich, the king can never be happy . . . nothing has been more industriously sought by us . . . than that the number, strength and riches of the people of England must be abated'. For this 'work of impoverishing and bringing the people low . . . The court and . . . new-made nobility are fit [instruments] . . . their delight in vanity and sensuality . . . Their insatiable avarice . . . gives them a furious desire to get money . . . and the more oppressive such ways are to the people, the better we like it.'[72] On the scaffold twenty years later, Sidney invoked as a witness to the justice of his cause James VI and I, who had cited Plato, Aristotle, Xenophon, Cicero and Tacitus to explain that whereas 'a good King (after a happie and famous reigne) dieth in peace, lamented by his subjects . . . a Tyrannes miserable and infamous life, armeth in the end his owne Subjects'.[73]

A good King . . . emploieth all his studie and paines, to procure and maintaine . . . the well-fare and peace of his people . . . thinketh his greatest contentment standeth in their prosperitie, and his greatest suretie in having their hearts, subjecting his own private affections and appetites to the weale . . . of his Subjects . . . where by the contrarie, an usurping Tyran . . . thinketh never himself sure, but by the dissention and factions among his people . . . building his suretie upon his peoples miserie: and in the end . . . upon the ruines of the Republike.[74]

Following Machiavelli, however, it was an important claim by Sidney in the *Court Maxims* that not only tyranny, but monarchy was inherently self-interested. To replace pride, luxury, avarice and misery with a government devoted to the public interest, it was necessary to dispense with monarchy altogether. More's *Utopia*, too, was a republic. For it to be, however, a commonwealth not only in name but substance, a more radical reform was necessary.

When I run over in my mind the various commonwealths flourishing today, so help me God, I can see in them nothing but a conspiracy of the rich, who are fattening up their own interests under the name and title of the commonwealth . . . And yet

[72] Sidney *Court Maxims* pp. 71–3.
[73] Sidney, *The Very Copy of a Paper Delivered to the Sherriffs* (1683), in 'Memoir of Algernon Sidney', *Sydney on Government* pp. 39–40; James VI and I, *Basilikon Doron. Or His Majesties Instructions to His Dearest Sonne, Henry The Prince*, in *The Workes of the Most High and Mighty Prince, James* (1616) pp. 138, 155–6.
[74] Ibid. pp. 155–6.

when these insatiably greedy and evil men have divided among themselves goods which would have sufficed for the entire people, how far they remain from the happiness of the Utopian Republic, which has abolished not only money but with it greed! . . . Even poverty . . . would vanish if money were entirely done away with.[75]

In the following reign a more moderate diagnosis of the same problems, also 'made by way of dialogue', came in Sir Thomas Smith, *A Discourse of the Commonweal of This Realm* (written in 1549 and published 1581). In this a knight, a merchant, a husbandman, a craftsman and a doctor discussed enclosure, price inflation, and other symptoms of the contemporary economic and social malady. The diagnostic role was performed by the doctor, who 'perceive[d] by you all there is none . . . but have just cause of complaint'. His subsequent analysis drew upon the 'wisdom and policy' of 'the Greeks and Romans', in particular 'Aristotle . . . the sharpest philosopher . . . that ever was . . . [and] that other great philosopher . . . for his excellent wisdom . . . called Divine Plato'.[76] Formally at least this discussion was to have its echo over a century later in Henry Neville's *Plato Redivivus* (1680) which, like Smith's *Discourse*, comprised a Preface and Three Dialogues. These featured an English gentleman, a noble Venetian and a doctor. Once again, drawing upon 'Aristotle, Plato, or Cicero', the doctor took the lead in diagnosing a malady, the primary symptom of which was a fundamental 'division' of the commonwealth by which England had been plagued since Smith's day.[77] For Neville too this 'breach and ruin of our government: which having been decaying for near two hundred years, is in our age brought so near to expiration, that it lies agonizing; and can no longer . . . carry on the work of ordering and preserving mankind' had an economic and social foundation.[78]

None of the seventeenth-century classical republicans took up More's prescription of the abolition of private property. That more broadly, however, within the literature of the English revolution the idea was common reflected the impact of radical reformation. Inspired by an apostolic example which had also been noticed by More, pamphleteers during the German peasants revolt of the 1520s had emphasised the social obligations of practical Christianity.[79] '[A]s the Christians in the time of the apostles held all in

[75] More, *Utopia* pp. 108–9.   [76] Smith, *A Discourse of the Commonweal* pp. 13, 24–5, 106–7.

[77] In being structured around a dominant speaker, and as its title suggests, Neville's work, like More's *Utopia*, Smith's *Discourse* and Sidney's *Maxims*, deploys a Platonic (or Socratic) rather than Ciceronian dialogue form. Jennifer Richards, *Rhetoric and Courtliness in Early Modern Literature* (Cambridge, 2003) pp. 25–6, 91.

[78] Neville, *Plato Redivivus* p. 81.

[79] See chapter 2, note 19; Baylor, *The Radical Reformation*; Williams, *The Radical Reformation*.

common, and especially stored up a common fund, from which aid can be given to the poor', so the articles of the Swiss Brethren (1527) bound them to do the same.[80] Over a century later the Leveller William Walwyn wrote:

Consider our Saviour saith, He that hath this worlds goods, and seeth his brother lack, how dwelleth the love of God in him? . . . Looke about you and you will finde in these woefull dayes thousands of miserable, distressed, starved, imprisoned Christians . . . then walke abroad, and observe the generall plenty of all necessaries . . . What is here aimed at? . . . would you have all things common? for love seeketh not her owne good, but the good of others. You say very true, it is the Apostle's doctrine: and you may remember the multitude of beleevers had all things common . . . feare it not: nor flye the truth because it suites not with your corrupt opinions or courses.[81]

In the similar words of the pamphlet *Tyranipocrit* (Rotterdam 1649):

In the primitive Church the Christians had their goods in Common . . . If you should make and maintain an equality of goods and lands . . . as God and nature would have, as justice and reason doth crave . . . then mankind might live in love and concord as brethren should doe . . . then tyranny and oppression would cease and the Kingdome of Christ would flourish.[82]

In *Gangreana* (1646) Thomas Edwards claimed to be in possession of information about schemes whereby 'there ought to be a community of goods, and the saints should share in the lands and estates of gentlemen and rich men'. In October 1647 soldiers were reputedly demanding a restriction upon individual property holdings of two thousand pounds per year.[83] When Henry Ireton argued at Putney that to extend the parliamentary franchise to the property-less was to imperil the civil institution of property itself, Thomas Rainsborough responded: 'Sir I see, that itt is impossible to have liberty butt all propertie must be taken away . . . I would faine know what the souldier hath fought for all this while? He hath fought to inslave himself, to give power to men of riches, men of estates, to make him a perpetual slave.'[84]

---

[80] Quoted by James Stayer, *The German Peasants War and Anabaptist Community of Goods* (Montreal, 1991) p. 96. In the words of Hans Hubmaier: 'Concerning community of goods, I have always said that everyone should be concerned about the needs of others, so that the hungry might be fed, the thirsty given to drink, and the naked clothed. For we are not lords of our possessions, but stewards and distributors.' Quoted by P. J. Klassen, *The Economics of Anabaptism 1525–1560* (The Hague, 1964) p. 32.

[81] William Walwyn, *The Power of Love* (1643), in Jack R. McMichael and Barbara Taft (eds.), *The Writings of William Walwyn* (Athens, Ca., 1989) pp. 79–80.

[82] Quoted in W. Schenck, *The Concern for Social Justice in the Puritan Revolution* (1948) pp. 151–2.

[83] Christopher Hill, *The World Turned Upside Down: Radical Ideas during the English Revolution* (1991) p. 115.

[84] Firth, *The Clarke Papers* vol. I, p. 325.

For the most famous seventeenth-century English communist, the 'Digger' Gerrard Winstanley, at the root of the 'bondage . . . of monarchy or kingly government' was the 'inward bondage' wrought by 'covetousness'. 'True commonwealth's freedom' accordingly 'lay in the free enjoyment of the earth'.[85] For the so-called Ranter Abiezer Coppe, similarly, 'else my religion is in vain, I own for dealing bread to the hungry, for cloathing the naked . . . for letting of the oppressed go free . . . And as for Community, I own none but the Apostolical . . . spoken of in the Scriptures.'[86] All republican writing, drawing upon classical as well as Christian sources, shared this broader commitment to greater economic equality and social justice. For Thomas Scott, writing in 1623, it was the achievement of the Dutch republic to have solved the key problem identified by More: that 'effect of privacie, whilst every man cares onely for himself, and neglects the Common-wealth', so that the rich would 'rather let the poore sterve [*sic*], let the Common-wealth . . . runne to ruine, then they reforme any of their sinnes, or forbeare any of their superfluities'.[87] For the Aristotelian John Streater, in 1654: 'Another Rule to judge of the fitness of a person of pub-like . . . Trust, is *Whether doth he regard the Poor, or no; or the Rich more than the Poor*'. 'In this' the just magistrate 'imitateth God, who is no respecter of persons, indeed the end of Government is to protect and defend the poor'.[88] Thus returning to the republic's own official *Declaration* of March 1649, justifying the abolition of monarchy, we find a radicalism of social content which could easily have been lifted from a Leveller pamphlet, or from More's *Utopia*. It had been

intended for the *fate* of *England*, had our *Monarch* prevailed over us . . . That [we would be] *contented with Canvas clothing, and Wooden shoes, and look more like Ghosts then men* . . . To bring this to pass, their Beasts of Forrests must grow fat, by devouring the poor man's corn . . . A *Tradesman* furnishing a *great man* with most part of his *Stock* . . . and expecting due . . . payment, is answered with *ill words*, or *blows*, and the dear-bought Learning, That *Lords and Kings servants are priviledged from Arrests and Process of Law* . . . A poor *Waterman* . . . a poor *Countreyman* . . . must *serve* the *King* for . . . not enough to finde themselves *bread*, when their *wives* and *children* have nothing . . . [alongside the] *luxury* and *intemperance*, the *corrupt* . . . *maners* . . . of . . . the *noblest Families*.[89]

[85] Gerrard Winstanley, *The Law of Freedom in a Platform* (1651), in Christopher Hill (ed.), *The Law of Freedom and Other Writings* (Harmondsworth, 1973) p. 295.

[86] Abiezer Coppe, *A Remonstrance of the Sincere and Zealous Protestation of Abiezer Coppe Against the Blasphemous and Execrable Opinions recited in the Act of Aug. 10 1650* (1650), in Nigel Smith, *A Collection of Ranter Writings* (London, 1983) pp. 120–2.

[87] Scott, *Belgicke Pismire* p. 36.   [88] Streater, *Observations* no. 2 p. 13.

[89] *A Declaration of the Parliament* (March 1649) pp. 17–19. See chapter 3, note 1 above.

In '*Commonwealths*' by contrast, the people 'finde *Justice* duly administered, the great Ones not able to oppresse the poorer, the Poor sufficiently provided for, and . . . the *scituation* and *advantages* of this *Land*, both for *Trade* abroad, and *Manufactures* at home . . . better understood'.[90]

The most famous republican social proposal of the period was James Harrington's 'Agrarian Law'.[91] 'In giving encouragement unto industry', Harrington warned, 'we [must] also remember that covetousness is the root of all evil.' Accordingly,

> your commonwealth is founded upon an equal agrarian; and if the earth be given unto the sons of men, this balance is the balance of justice, such an one as, in having due regard unto the different industry of different men, yet *faithfully judgeth the poor. And the king that faithfully judgeth the poor, his throne shall be established forever* [*Proverbs* 29:14] Much more the commonwealth; seeing that equality, which is the necessary dissolution of monarchy, is the generation, the very life and soul of a commonwealth.[92]

Drawing upon both Plato and More, Bodin too had remarked that 'Among all the causes of seditions and changes of Commonweales there is none greater than the excessive wealth of some fewe subjects, and the extreme povertie of the greatest part.'[93] The classical sources for Harrington's agrarian (especially Plato's *Laws*) have been discussed by Nelson.[94] Yet within English republicanism the idea has been treated by historians, as it was by contemporaries, as spectacularly original. In 1641 Gabriel Plattes, an associate of Samuel Hartlib, proposed in his utopia of *Macaria* a husbandry law punishing the holding by any individual of 'more land than he is able to improve to the utmost . . . till his lands be forfeited, and he banished . . . as an enemy to the commonwealth'.[95] Although this did not establish a universal limit on property ownership, Oceana would contain other echoes of this work, including an 'academy of provosts' like *Macaria*'s 'Office of Addresses'.[96] In 1656, six months before the publication of *Oceana*, there appeared R.G.'s *A Copy of a Letter from an Officer in Ireland* (1656), which

[90] Ibid.

[91] In the 1656 edition of *Oceana* printed by Streater, Harrington (or his printer) always uses capitals for 'Agrarian Law' and frequently italics also (see for instance pp. 22–23, 257). In the *Works* edited by Pocock both are rendered in roman lower case. For the interpretative significance of these and other alterations of a work whose meaning is conveyed as much by its form as by its content see chapter 15, pp. 287–8 below.

[92] Harrington, *Oceana*, in *Political Works* pp. 239, 322.   [93] Bodin, *Sixe Bookes* Book 5, ch. 2, p. 569.

[94] Nelson, 'Greek Tradition in Republican Thought' ch. 3.

[95] [Gabriel Plattes], *A Description of the Famous Kingdome of Macaria* (1641) p. 4; W. Schenck, *Social Justice in the Puritan Revolution* p. 148. For Plattes's authorship see Jacob, *Robert Boyle* p. 17.

[96] Harrington, *Political Works* pp. 251–2; Scott, 'The Rapture of Motion' note 57. I am grateful to Eric Nelson for discussion of this point.

discussed agrarian laws in ancient Greece and Rome in the course of an anticipation of Harrington's broader economic analysis of the collapse of the monarchy.[97] Most importantly, however, attention should be paid to a chapter in Nedham's *The Case of the Commonwealth of England, Stated* (1650), wherein the author attacked both the Levellers and the Diggers. Not only was it the case, Nedham claimed, that in their third *Agreement of the People* 'all persons have an equality of right to choose and be chosen without respect of birth, quality or wealth . . . therefore the promoters of this way are not improperly called "Levellers"'. Moreover 'this term of leveling is equivalent with Aristotle's . . . *aequalitas juris*, the "equality of right" . . . mentioned [in *The Politics* Book 6]. And the same author saith, this plea for "equality of right" in government at length introduceth a claim for "equality of estates," and the making of such laws as the agrarian laws enacted by the popular boutefeus in Rome whereby it was made criminal for any man to grow richer than ordinary.'[98]

[A]nd from plundering they proceed to that flat leveling of estates as is evident by those Licinian and agrarian laws made by the populacy of Rome whereby it was provided that no man should grow too rich nor be master of above fifty acres of land. And touching this, there is an insolent passage recorded by Livy how that when the Senate seemed unwilling to permit the division of certain lands among the common sort, the tribunes, or ringleaders of the people, asked the Senators 'how they durst possess more than fifty acres apiece yet find fault with a division made of two apiece to the people! . . . Lastly, from leveling they proceed to . . . an absolute community. And though neither the Athenian nor Roman levelers ever arrived to this high pitch of madness, yet we see there is a new faction started up out of ours known by the name of Diggers.[99]

In fact the limit proposed by the Tribunes Sextius and Licinius had been five hundred 'jugera'.[100] As far as I am aware these claims, concerning a Leveller plot to introduce an agrarian law, have not been taken seriously by historians.[101] That perhaps they should be is suggested by an anonymous Leveller pamphlet, *Vox Plebis, or, The People's Out-cry Against Oppression,*

---

[97] R. G., *A Copy of a Letter from an Officer of the Army In Ireland, to His Highness the Lord Protector* (1656) pp. 4, 5.

[98] Nedham, *Case of the Commonwealth* p. 98.   [99] Ibid. p. 109.

[100] Livy, *The History of Rome by Titus Livius* (6 vols., 1926) vol. II, pp. 43–4 (Book 6, xxxv).

[101] Nigel Smith, *Literature and Revolution in England 1640–1660* (New Haven, Conn., 1994) pp. 150, 183–4, relates Nedham's attack on the Levellers in *The Case* to the genuine classical content of some Leveller writing, including *Vox Plebis*. He does not, however, focus upon the proposal for an agrarian law, which seems to me the key issue connecting these texts, furnishing a context for Harrington's *Oceana*. Glover, who does discuss this issue, does not connect *Vox Plebis* to Nedham, and therefore to *The Case*. Glover, 'The Putney Debates: Popular versus Elitist Republicanism', *Past and Present* 164 (1999).

Injustice, and Tyranny (1646).[102] The most significant feature of this tract, noticed by Felix Raab and Samuel Glover, is to have made the first systematic English public use of Machiavelli's *Discourses*. No less striking, from page one, was the interchangeable use of the words 'State', 'Common-wealth' and 'Republique'. In particular *Vox Plebis* referred to 'the case of the *Romane* State, when the *Romanes* having freed themselves of the government of the *Tarquins* their hereditary Kings; the Nobility began . . . the exercise of the like or greater tyrany the[n] the *Tarquins* had done; [accordingly] the people . . . created *Tribunes*, as *Guardians* of the publick liberty'.[103] It was the function of such tribunes to defend the people against the 'Avarice, Pride, and Cruelty' of its 'Governours', by whose 'greed . . . covetousness . . . and violence' they had been brought to 'poverty'.

As explained by 'Sir *Walter Rawleigh*', following Livy, the solution was provided by '*Caius Flaminius*' who, '*understanding the Majesty of Rome to be wholly in the people, and no otherwise in the Senate, then by way of delegacy, or grand Commission . . . [taught] the Multitude . . . to know and use their power . . . in . . . vindicating the publike liberty of his Countrey*'.[104] According to Livy it was the distinction of Caius Flaminius as tribune to succeed where his predecessor Licinius had failed, in carrying an agrarian bill 'into a law', despite 'the resentment and terrible threatenings of the whole body of the senate'.[105] *Vox Plebis's* praise of 'C. *Flaminius*' had already appeared in the same words in another Leveller pamphlet a year earlier, giving as its source not Ralegh but his authority '*Titus Livius* an unreproveable author'.[106] Meanwhile it is passages taken from Machiavelli's *Discourses* which allow us

---

[102] It seems likely that *Vox Plebis* had more than one author. Authorship has been attributed by Samuel Glover to John Wildman ('The Putney Debates', pp. 70–1), by R. B. Seaberg and others to Richard Overton ('The Norman Conquest and the Common Law: the Levellers and the Argument from Continuity', *Historical Journal* 24, 4 (1981) pp. 798–9, note. 18) and by Blair Worden to Nedham ('"Wit in a Roundhead"'). My case for Nedham's involvement hinges specifically upon the reappearance of passages adapted from Machiavelli's *Discourses* in his *The Case of the Commonwealth of England, Stated* (1650) (see note 107 below). No less important is the thematic connection between certain Leveller and Nedham's later republican works (see chapters 7 and 11–13). This anti-senatorial Roman populism, informed by Livy and Machiavelli and focused upon the office of tribune, is Nedham's most consistent theme.

[103] Nedham, *Vox Plebis* pp. 1, 3.

[104] Ibid. pp. 61–2, 64, 68; Sir Walter Ralegh, *The History of The World. In Five Bookes* (1621) p. 357. *Vox Plebis* follows Ralegh's wording closely. Glover, 'The Putney Debates' p. 65.

[105] Livy, *the Roman History by Titus Livius of Padua with the Entire Supplement of John Freinsheim* vol. III, (1744) pp. 437–8 (Book xx ch. xviii).

[106] *England's Miserie and Remedie in a Judicious Letter . . . concerning Leiutenant Col. Lilburn's Imprisonment in Newgate* (14 September 1645) p. 4. As in *Vox Plebis* the wording is almost identical to Ralegh (p. 357). This and the vagueness of the reference to Livy ('*Decad.5.* of his History') suggests that the author of *England's Miserie* may also have been using Ralegh.

to identify as one probable author of *Vox Plebis* Nedham himself.[107] When Nedham attacked the Levellers for seeking to introduce an agrarian law he apparently did so with the full authority of an author of that campaign.

Nedham is known to historians of republicanism as the editor of the republic's weekly newspaper *Mercurius Politicus*, whose pioneering use of Machiavelli's *Discourses* deeply influenced English classical republicanism. Traces of Nedham's other maxims, concerning for instance the importance of rotation, of a citizen militia, of the separation of powers, and of the propensity of '*Free-States*' to '*put . . . limitations to the wealth of the Senators, that none of them grow over-rich*', are visible throughout *Oceana*.[108] Having achieved fame in Harrington's *Oceana*, the device of an agrarian law was taken up by the Harringtonian literature of 1659–60, not least by the pamphlet *Chaos*, which offered an analysis of the economic and social basis of England's political disorder in some ways more thoroughgoing than Harrington's own.[109]

---

[107] Thus we read in *Vox Plebis* p. 60: '*Manlius Capitolinus*, notwithstanding that hee had valiantly defended the *Capitoll of Rome* against the invading *Gaules*, and by his virtue delivered the Citie of *Rome* from imminent danger; was, notwithstanding his good deserts, for a sedition he endeavoured to raise in *Rome* through envie to *Furius Camillus*, thrown headlong down from that *Capitoll*, which he to his great renown had formerly defended.' Nedham's *The Case of the Commonwealth* pp. 112–13 has: 'So the famous Manlius likewise, to whom Rome owed both herself and liberty, being by him preserved against the Gauls in the greatest extremity, was notwithstanding, upon a discovery of his afterintent to surprise their liberty, thrown headlong down the Tarpeian Rock within view of the Capitol which he had so nobly defended.' The common source is *Machiavels Discourses. upon the first Decade of T. Livius translated out of the Italian* by E. D[acre] 2nd edn (1636) p. 113 (Book One, ch. 24). *Vox Plebis* follows Dacre more closely, but makes several departures (including the substitution of 'Gaules' for 'French', of 'notwithstanding' for 'without any regard', and of 'defended' for 'deliver'd') all of which are followed by *The Case*. This and other passages were subsequently reused by Nedham in *Mercurius Politicus* and *The Excellencie of a Free State* (1656).

[108] *Mercurius Politicus* no. 101, 6–13 May, 1652, pp. 1585, 1587; Scott, 'The Rapture of Motion' p. 147.

[109] *Chaos*, Preface and pp. 1–54 (see chapter 14 below).

CHAPTER 4

Old worlds and new

Livy . . . tells us so many quarrels and tumults arose about division
of lands that the Senate knew not which way to prevent them till
they disburdened the commonwealth by sending forth colonies and
satisfying them with lands in the remote parts of Italy and other places.
Marchamont Nedham, *The Case of the Commonwealth* (1650)[1]

To Martiall men he opened wide the door of sea and land, for fame
and conquest. To the nobly ambitious, the far stage of America, to
win honor in. To the Religious divines . . . a calling of the last heathen
to the Christian faith . . . [and] a large field of poor Christians, misled
by the Idolatry of *Rome* . . . To the ingenuously industrious . . . new
mysteries, and manufactures . . . To the Merchant . . . a fertile, and
unexhausted earth. To the fortune-bound, liberty. To the Curious, a
fruitfull womb of innovation.
Fulke Greville, *Sir Philip Sidney* (1652)[2]

INTRODUCTION: THE QUESTION OF MODERNITY

Revolutions are harbingers of modernity. England's mid-seventeenth-
century upheaval is frequently understood as the first revolution of the
modern West. Yet at its ideological core we discover a humanist preoccupation with history in general and antiquity in particular; a protestant
commitment to restoration of the purity of the primitive Christian religion; and a vigorous defence of classical and medieval commonwealth
values against the ravages of contemporary economic, social and political
change. As we have seen, this ideological fusion had its origins in the first
part of the sixteenth century, or earlier. We have noted the debt of More's
Utopia to the thought of Plato, and to Christian values of apostolic community exhibited in practice in medieval monasteries. Yet even More's *Utopia*

---

[1] Nedham, *Case of the Commonwealth* p. 109.   [2] Greville *Life of Sidney* (Oxford, 1907) p. 119.

has been diagnosed as the work of 'a modern radical,' helping, as it may have done, to lay the moral foundations of the Enlightenment.[3]

After a brief absence, the question of the modernity of England's revolution has recently returned to the historical agenda.[4] As in relation to so many issues, we are now presented with a choice of allegiance between the 'revisionist' denial that any such revolution in fact took place, and the once Whig and Marxist opposite view that with the fall of the monarchy in 1649 came also the decisive fall of an *ancien régime*.[5] As a body of ideas standing at the heart of these events, republican writing furnishes an opportunity to call into question both of these polarities, conceived of as mutually exclusive. The English revolution occurred, to borrow the title of a recent study, 'between the ancients and the moderns'.[6] Thus parliament's *Declaration* of 1649 defending its settlement of 'the present Government In the way of a Free State' took comfort from the ancient prosperity of the Romans, the early modern success of the Venetians and Swiss, and the 'wonderful increase' attending the more recent 'change' in the United Provinces.[7] In fact English republicanism presents a case study in the paradoxes, and complexities, of early modernity.

THE CONTEXT OF TIME

First, as we will see in chapter 9, this was true of the republican politics of time. Like most humanist writing, republican polemic made extensive use of historical examples. Those references, drawn from Greek, Roman and Jewish experience and from the medieval and more recent past, furnished abundant evidence of that 'veneration of antiquity' which 'was a central feature of the ecclesiastical and political debates of the early modern era'. This was still vigorously on display, if equally vigorously contested, in the 'battle of the books' during the 1690s.[8] In addition, almost all republican

---

[3] J. H. Hexter, 'Thomas More: On the Margins of Modernity', *Journal of British Studies* 1, 1 (November 1961) pp. 35–7; D. B. Fenlon, 'England and Europe: *Utopia* and its Aftermath', *Transactions of the Royal Historical Society* (1974) pp. 116–17.

[4] Houston and Pincus, *A Nation Transformed?*; Roy Porter, *The Creation of the Modern World: the Untold Story of the British Enlightenment* (New York, 2000); Jacob, *The Radical Enlightenment*; Israel, *Radical Enlightenment*.

[5] Ronald Hutton's review of Houston and Pincus, *A Nation Transformed?*, in *English Historical Review* (2001) sees in the volume a surprising revival of Whig history.

[6] Joseph Levine, *Between the Ancients and the Moderns: Baroque Culture in Restoration England* (New Haven, Conn., 1999).

[7] *A Declaration of the Parliament* (March 1649) p. 16.

[8] D. R. Woolf, 'In Praise of Older Things: Notions of Age and Antiquity in Early Modern England', in Anthony Grafton and J. H. M. Salmon (eds.), *Historians and Ideologues* (Rochester, N.Y., 2001) pp. 123, 134; Joseph Levine, *The Battle of the Books: History and Literature in the Augustan Age* (Ithaca, N.Y., 1991).

writers deployed a mode of ancient constitutionalism indebted to English and other European legal thinkers, in the process making extensive use of medieval authorities. One predominant purpose of this republican historical analysis was to appropriate the rhetoric of tradition and condemn innovative contemporary royal policies.

By comparison to Sidney's *Discourses*, Locke's *Two Treatises* displays both a relative independence from historical sources and a determined lack of interest in the historical claims being made by Sir Robert Filmer. This looks both more modern and more characteristic of the Enlightenment. In fact, however, the contrast is far from complete, and not only because Locke's language and argument, which draws heavily upon the Leveller-republican ideology of the 'good old cause', is historically contextualised by its assertion (seconded by Sidney) that Filmer's ideology is a Caroline and Laudian innovation.[9] If Locke does not deploy the full historical paraphernalia of classical republicanism, he does use the natural law language employed by Milton, Streater and Sidney, all of whom assert that prescription alone carries no moral or political weight, and defend their use of classical and other authorities on the ground not that they are old, but that they are correct.[10]

The other most important feature of English republican historical thought was a startling preparedness to accept not only the inevitability, but under appropriate circumstances the desirability of political change. The broadest intellectual context for both aspects of this view of history is to be found in that late, and especially northern humanism with a strongly developed sense of temporal as well as spatial perspective. This was post-Machiavellian in that it accepted not only the continuing importance and relevance of classical example, but also the distance separating classical from contemporary societies and conditions. One example is Bodin's *Six Books of a Republic* which tried to systematise and explain variety in space as well as change in time.[11]

This relativism was fed by the European discoveries in the new world. Although classical civilisations had known about and colonised Africa and Asia, the discovery of America appeared to turn a new page in time, as well as space. In the words of John Elliott, 'The almost miraculous sequence of events which led to the discovery, conquest and conversion of the New World did much to reinforce the linear and progressive, as against the cyclical, interpretation of the historical process in sixteenth century

---

[9] Locke, *Two Treatises* pp. 160–1; Sidney, *Discourses,* in *Sydney on Government* pp. 4–5. See pp. 124–5 below.

[10] See p. XXX below.   [11] Bodin, *Six Bookes* Book IV and Book V, chs. 1–2.

thought.'[12] It was in line with this characteristic of northern humanism that for almost all English republicans 'The reason why God did not universally by his law tye all the world to one forme of Government, is, because the difference of persons, times, places, neighbours, etc, may make one forme best to one people, and at one time and place, that is worst to another.'[13] Indeed the variety of forms of government in the world was evidence of the God-given 'rights' of peoples 'in several nations and ages' to frame such governments 'according to the variety of circumstances . . . as best pleased themselves'.[14] As in space, so in time,

[N]o right judgement can be given of human things, without a particular regard to the time in which they passed. We esteem Scipio, Hannibal . . . Alexander, Epaminondas . . . to have been admirable commanders in war . . . and yet . . . if the most skilful of them could be raised from the grave . . . and placed upon the frontiers of France or Flanders, he would not know how to advance or retreat, nor by what means to take any of the places in those parts, as they are now fortified and defended.[15]

For Henry Vane as for other republicans 'no human ordinances or outward laws must expect to be perpetual and exempt from change . . . Ancient foundations, whence once [they] . . . prove hindrances, to the good and enjoyment of humane societies, are for their sakes, and upon the same reasons to be altered, for which they were first laid.'[16]

Such perspectives were capable of linking with both protestant anti-formalism and Platonism. They exhibited, that is to say, a scepticism about the durability of 'human things . . . human ordinances', rather than about the existence of permanent higher truths.[17] One writer invoked Augustine in support of the observation that 'That which in the present time appears new to us, is not new with him who appointed that time, and who before the time, comprehends those things which he attributes to every particular time, *according to its variety and change*. So that we may conclude with *Seneca* . . . Things do not suddenly and newly happen, as we conceive, but come in their due and appointed course.'[18] Yet English republicans were also highly receptive to Machiavelli's sceptical politics of change, along with useful derivations from the neo-Stoicism and sceptical reason of state

[12] J. H. Elliott, *The Old World and the New 1492–1650* (Cambridge, 1992) pp. 10, 51–2; see also Anthony Grafton, *New Worlds, Ancient Texts: the Power of Tradition and the Shock of Discovery* (Cambridge, Mass., 1992).

[13] Henry Stubbe, *An Essay in Defence of the Good Old Cause* p. 22.

[14] Sidney, *Discourses*, ed. West p. 99.

[15] Sidney, *Discourses*, in *Sydney on Government* p. 463; Sidney, *Discourses*, ed. West p. 525.

[16] Quoted in Judson, *Vane* pp. 19–21, 30, 56, 67.

[17] D. R. Woolf, *The Idea of History in Early Stuart England* (Toronto, 1990) pp. 4–10.

[18] *A Commonwealth, and Commonwealths-men, Asserted and Vindicated* (1659) p. 3.

associated with Lipsius and Tacitus (the tract above, quoting Seneca, took its frontispiece from Tacitus). These included humanist and republican analyses of monarchical statecraft, both Cromwellian and (in particular later) Stuart,[19] together with the republican interest theory of Marchamont Nedham in the 1640s and most English republican writing from 1649.[20] In the Dutch-influenced works of Sidney and Bethel this entailed a republican appropriation of the language of reason of state.[21] Yet in the hands of English writers even this republican interest theory opposed a modern monarchical 'policy' associated with Tacitus and Machiavelli, and antithetical to Greek moral philosophy. More generally recent work has questioned the completeness of the English transition from the Graeco-Roman Christian humanism of the sixteenth century to the sceptical humanism of the seventeenth.[22]

Both Aristotelian and Stoic influences help to account for the characteristic republican combination of classical republicanism and natural law theory. Although its origins lay in Roman Stoicism, the early modern revival of natural law language was primarily the work of the sixteenth-century Spanish followers of St Thomas Aquinas.[23] As James VI and I had before him, Sir Robert Filmer made much polemical mileage of the popish pedigree of this seditious opinion of the 'natural liberty of the people'.[24] This did not deter Milton, who accompanied his Erasmian campaign for humane classical education against the syllogistic pedantry of 'grammarians' with denunciations of 'the schoolmen'. From Sidney it drew the response that:

Thus did Euclid lay down certain axioms, which none could deny that did not renounce common sense . . . and they may with as much reason be accused of paganism, who say that a whole is greater than a part, that two halfs make the whole, or that a straight line is the shortest way from point to point, as to say, that they who in politicks lay such foundations, as have been taken up by Schoolmen and others as undeniable truths, do therefore follow them, or have any regard to their authority.[25]

[19] Burke, 'Tacitism'; Blair Worden, 'Ben Jonson among the Historians', in Peter Lake and Kevin Sharpe (eds.), *Political Culture in Early Stuart England* (Basingstoke, 1994); Tuck, *Philosophy and Government* chs. 2–3; Streater's critique of Cromwellian usurpation and Sidney's of later Stuart tyranny were both heavily indebted to Tacitus.

[20] See, for instance [Henry Ireton], *Humble Remonstrance of His Excellency the Lord General Fairfax* (16th November 1648); Hall, *The Grounds and Reasons of Monarchy*; and chapters 11–12 below.

[21] Scott, *English Republic* chs. 12–13.

[22] Baldwin, 'The self and the state'. Certainly it was characteristic of English republican writing to combine Plato and Aristotle with neo-Stoic sources (including Seneca and Tacitus).

[23] Richard Tuck, *Natural Rights Theories* (Cambridge, 1979); Skinner, *Foundations of Modern Political Thought*. vol. II; A S Brett, *Liberty, Right and Nature: Individual Rights in Later Scholastic Thought* (Cambridge, 1997).

[24] Filmer, *Patriarcha* pp. 15–24.

[25] Milton, *Of Education*; *Defence*; *The Readie and Easie Way*; Sidney, *Discourses*, ed. West p. 8.

What is clear is the debt owed by all English republicans to those early modern French and Dutch writers who appropriated this 'popish' language to construct a protestant resistance theory.[26]

Almost equally important to English republicanism was that natural philosophy marginally evident in the work of Nedham, Hall and Stubbe, and fundamentally so in Streater, Harrington and others. Natural philosophy informed the activities of the Hartlib circle, which received official patronage from the Long Parliament and republic and had many contacts with individual republicans (including Milton, Nedham and Neville).[27] The most important promoter of seventeenth-century English natural philosophy was Sir Francis Bacon. Evidence concerning the impact of Bacon upon Milton, Harrington and others is clear. This is one context within which Christopher Hill emphasised the 'progressive' puritanism of Milton and others.[28] Yet the modernity of early seventeenth-century natural philosophy is itself a complex matter.[29] The boldest recent thesis is that of Jonathan Israel, who associates 'Early Enlightenment' with a 'new mechanical philosophy' incorporating 'immense reverence for science, and for mathematical logic'. 'From its origins in the 1650s and 1660s' a radical subsection of this combined 'with . . . non-providential deism, if not outright materialism and atheism along with unmistakeably republican, even democratic tendencies'.[30] To Israel, however, the place of English republicanism within this European development is far from clear:

What has been termed the 'Anglicization of the republic' produced certain specific features – an emphasis on land as the basis of political influence and an orientation towards the outlook and needs of the English gentry – which render this corpus of thought appreciably different from the alternative republican tradition, essentially urban and commercial, originating in the work of such writers as Johan and Pieter de la Court, and Spinoza's Latin Master, Franciscus van den Enden, with its uncompromising anti-monarchism and egalitarian tendency, a tradition which sprang up on the continent and leads in a direct line of descent to the revolutionary rhetoric of Robespierre and the French Jacobins.[31]

---

[26] Scott, 'Law of War'; and see chapter 6 below.

[27] Mark Greengrass, Michael Leslie and Timothy Raylor (eds.), *Samuel Hartlib and Universal Reformation: Studies in Intellectual Communication* (Cambridge, 1994); Charles Webster, *The Great Instauration: Science, Medicine and Reform, 1626–1660* (1975); Michael Hunter, *Science and Society in Restoration England* (Cambridge, 1981) ch. 1.

[28] Christopher Hill, *Intellectual Origins of the English Revolution* (Oxford, 1965).

[29] For contrasting emphases see Webster, *The Great Instauration*; Johns, *The Nature of the Book*; see also the debate between Christopher Hill, Hugh Kearney and Theodore Rabb published as 'Science, Religion and Society in the Sixteenth and Seventeenth Centuries', *Past and Present* 31 (1965).

[30] Israel, *Radical Enlightenment* p. 12.   [31] Ibid. p. 22.

Yet this is an account of English republicanism deriving from one interpretation (that of Pocock) of the work of one atypical writer. Even in relation to Harrington there is no mention here of that material philosophy of nature which makes him the strongest English candidate for admission to the radical enlightenment so defined. More importantly, Harrington's emphasis upon the role of the gentry, and the agrarian basis of their wealth, was accompanied by an association with moderate royalism, and a commitment to healing and settling, unique among republicans. More characteristic (in the work, for instance, of Nedham and Streater) was an 'uncompromising anti-monarchism and egalitarian tendency' very like that of the brothers de la Court. Within English republican writing in general, as within Dutch, this anti-monarchism was Machiavellian, and this egalitarianism informed by a Christian humanist heritage common to England and the United Provinces.[32] Moreover, in practice what 'The Anglicization of the republic' really involved was the replacement of an agrarian monarchy with the London-dominated government form of a city-state. For this the most important model, and upon its policies the most important influence, was the urban and maritime United Provinces. Upon the work of Sidney and Bethel the direct influence of Dutch republicanism seems clear.[33] Finally English republican rhetoric itself directly influenced 'Robespierre and the French Jacobins'.[34] Thus the reintegration of Harrington within an account of English republican writing as a whole is essential to an understanding of the Enlightenment as 'an essentially European phenomenon'.[35]

For many historians, among the primary symptoms of modernity has been secularity. Yet as there has been widespread acknowledgement of the religious content of early modern natural philosophy, so there are important alternatives to such secularising accounts, even of Enlightenment itself.[36]

[32] Scott, 'Classical Republicanism'. [33] Scott, *Algernon Sidney and the English Republic* chs. 12–13.
[34] A. Aulard, *The French Revolution 1789–1804* (2 vols., 1910) vol. 1 p. 111; *Lettre de félicitation de Milord Sidney aux Parisiens et a la Nation Francoise, ou resurrection de Milord Sidney* (Paris, 1789); Rachel Hammersley, 'Camille Desmoulins's *Le Vieux Cordelier*: a Link between English and French Republicanism', *History of European Ideas* 27 (2001) pp. 115–32; Scott, *Algernon Sidney and the English Republic* pp. 5–6. Keith Michael Baker associates Robespierre and Rousseau with a genuine classical republicanism deriving from ancient as well as English sources (including Nedham and Sidney), to be distinguished from a 'modern' rights-based republicanism of the Enlightenment expressed by Condorcet and Paine. In the heat of the revolutionary moment these two understandings of liberty became dangerously 'combined'. Yet of the English revolution such a combination had been characteristic. Baker, 'Transformations of Classical Republicanism in Eighteenth Century France', *The Journal of Modern History* 73 (March 2001) pp. 32–5, 53.
[35] Israel, *Radical Enlightenment* p. 22. We may accept Israel's amendment to the more Anglocentric account of Margaret Jacob (*The Radical Enlightenment*) while resisting the impulse to understate England's actual role.
[36] Webster, *The Great Instauration*; the secularising tendency of Jacob's argument is moderated by her debt to Hill's thesis concerning the conjunction of 'puritanism', radicalism and science. It is the

Although the accusation of atheism was frequently levelled, often by natural philosophers themselves, such claims often reveal more about their constructive purposes than their ostensible subjects.[37] For most republicans, as for Robert Boyle, there was no tension between 'the doctrine of the gospel' and 'the light of nature (which it excludes not, but rather supposes)'.[38] Even during the Restoration period English republicans were much less likely to be associated with atheism than with 'fanaticism'. Certainly it was Harrington's desire, not to strike a blow in England's wars of religion, but to end them.[39] During the Restoration crisis Neville inveighed equally against the 'two infamous factions, the courtiers and the madmen of the people . . . the first would like to introduce tyranny, the other anarchy and confusion'.[40] Blair Worden has written that republicans participated in a 'transforming tendency evident within orthodox Christianity across the post-Restoration period: the shift of emphasis from faith to conduct'.[41] Yet, as we have seen, an emphasis upon conduct was as old as Erasmian humanism, and a defining feature of radical reformation. Moreover Harrington's project of healing and settling, no less than Sidney's of renewed and justified civil war, was given extensive religious justification.

   Probably the best-known English remark concerning the extent of contemporary change was Bacon's observation of the transforming effects of the compass, printing and gunpowder (adapted by Abraham Cowley to 'Printing, Guns, [and] *America*').[42] This may be compared with the earlier statement by Louis Le Roy in Paris in 1579 that 'the invention of the printing press and the discovery of the new world . . . [were] two things which I always thought could be compared . . . to Antiquity', and the later decisively modern claim of Adam Smith that 'the discovery of America, and that of a passage to the East Indies by the Cape of Good Hope, are the two greatest and most important events recorded in the history of

   conclusion of Michael Hunter that 'What is most striking about the religious and political affiliations of those devoted to the new science . . . is their heterogeneity.' Hunter, *Science and Society* p. 115. Emphasising the importance of religious assumptions within Enlightenment thought is Richard Drayton, *Nature's Government: Science, Imperial Britain and the 'Improvement' of the World* (New Haven, Conn., 2000).

37 Michael Hunter, 'Science and Heterodoxy: an Early Modern Problem Reconsidered', in Hunter, *Science and the Shape of Orthodoxy: Intellectual Change in Late Seventeenth-Century Britain* (Woodbridge, 1995); the classic demonstration of this truth is J. C. Davis, *Fear, Myth and History: the Ranters and the Historians* (Cambridge, 1986).

38 Jacob, *Robert Boyle* p. 119.

39 James Harrington, *The Common-Wealth of Oceana* (1656), printed by J. Streater, for Livewell Chapman [hereafter *Oceana* (1656)], pp. 46–8.

40 Quoted by Caroline Robbins, 'Henry Neville, 1620–94', in Robbins, *Two English Republican Tracts* pp. 16–17.

41 Worden, 'The Question of Secularization' p. 40.   42 Johns, *The Nature of the Book* pp. 49, 480.

mankind'.[43] The intellectual context of Bacon's own political thought was late humanist and Machiavellian.[44] His pre-eminent emphasis upon the moral rather than material basis of the greatness of states had much in common not only with Machiavelli, but with Sir Philip Sidney, John Milton and Algernon Sidney. Algernon Sidney was close to Bacon in asking

> if it be lawful for us . . . to build houses, ships and forts better than our ancestors, to make such arms as are most fit for our defence, and to invent printing, with an infinite number of other arts beneficial to mankind, why have we not the same right in matters of government, upon which all others do almost absolutely depend?[45]

By contrast Harrington identified Bacon with Machiavelli as a writer who had not properly understood the philosophical basis of his own political wisdom ('*Verulamius* (as Machiavill hath done before him) harps much upon a string which he hath not perfectly tuned, and that is the *balance of Dominion*').[46] Even for Harrington, however, one purpose of his republican co-option of Hobbes's natural philosophy was to show the author of *Leviathan* how wrong he had been to dismiss the political wisdom of the ancients. As Hobbes's own revolt against Greek political philosophy had been deeply informed by Thucydides and other classical sources, so in his mature work modern reason proved no entire substitute for rhetoric.[47]

POLITICAL ECONOMY

A related feature of republican thought which has recently been examined for symptoms of modernity is political economy. As we have seen, it was a feature of much English republican writing and practice to take a keen interest in the maritime (naval and commercial) bases of modern state power. Yet generalising from the case of Harrington, John Pocock saw a fundamental tension between a post-feudal English classical republicanism, within which territorial freeholds supplied a foundation for political virtue, and a less stable and independent commercial economy. This perception

---

[43] The latter from *Wealth of Nations* (1776). Both quoted in J. H. Elliott, *The Old World and the New* pp. 1, 10.

[44] Thus for Bacon, as for Machiavelli, mercenary forces were disastrous; money as the sinews of war does not compare to 'the sinews of men's arms'; states aiming at greatness must prevent the proliferation of nobility; 'above all' such a nation must 'profess arms as their principal honour, study, and occupation'. Bacon, 'Of the True Greatness of Kingdoms and Estates' pp. 104–8; Peltonen, *Classical Humanism* ch. 4.

[45] Sidney, *Discourses*, in *Sydney on Government* pp. 304–5; Sidney, *Discourses*, ed. West pp. 357–8.

[46] Harrington, *Oceana* (1656), The Introduction or Order of the Work, p. 1.

[47] Scott, 'Peace of Silence'; David Johnston, *The Rhetoric of Leviathan* (Princeton, 1996); Skinner, *Reason and Rhetoric*.

also built upon Machiavelli's deep suspicion, grounded in Florentine experience, of the potential corrupting influence of private wealth. According to Pocock, the citizen 'required the autonomy of real property . . . without being involved in dependence and corruption. The ideals of virtue and commerce could not therefore be reconciled to each other.'[48]

Responding to this thesis, Steve Pincus has divided English republicans into two groups.[49] The first were ancient 'Spartans' (Milton and Harrington) whose anti-commercial ethics (combining in this the influences of Plato and Machiavelli) praised rurality, austerity and frugality as the basis for republican virtue. The others were 'self-conciously modern' defenders of the new mercantile economy (including Nedham and Bethel) and adherents to the sceptical political language of 'interest'. Pincus's attribution of this modernisation of republicanism to English writers has subsequently been challenged. Mark Jurdjevic argues that it is no sounder to generalise about Florentine republicanism from the case of Machiavelli than about English republicanism from the example of Harrington. In general, 'Florentine humanists of the Renaissance had carefully and deliberately welded the private pursuit of wealth with civic virtue.' This was a 'bold and necessary innovation if republicanism, originally articulated in the agrarian, slave-based economies of classical Athens and Rome, was to survive in the modern world. This innovation, however, was a product of the Italian rather than English renaissance.'[50]

As Jurdjevic correctly identifies Bruni's positive appraisal of the role of wealth, so Pocock is right (up to a point) about Harrington, and Pincus about Bethel. It is equally true that both Machiavelli and Harrington were innovators in relation to their contemporary republican contexts. This should reinforce our hesitation about generalising from such particular examples. Moreover all three of these larger arguments share the assumption that there is a fundamental distinction to be made between the 'agrarian, slave based' political economies of the ancient world and the commercial ones of the modern. To recover the perspective of English republicans themselves our starting point must be to challenge this asserted bifurcation. Neither commercial society nor colonial expansion is exclusively modern. Classical civilisation was a culture of cities and colonies, and the relationship between republicanism, money and trade is as old as Athens and

---

[48] Pocock, *Virtue, Commerce and History* p. 48.   [49] Pincus, 'Machiavellian Moment'.
[50] Mark Jurdjevic, 'Virtue, Commerce, and the Enduring Florentine Republican Moment: Reintegrating Italy into the Atlantic Republican Debate', *Journal of the History of Ideas* 62, 4 (2001) p. 743.

Carthage.[51] Not only was the Athenian empire maritime and commercial, but during the great war for its survival the city accepted the advice of Pericles to abandon territorial Attica to annual Spartan invasion and concentrate upon maintaining itself by sea.[52] Money and commerce permeated the early modern republican experience in Florence, Venice, Genoa and the Netherlands. The global mercantile economies of the seventeenth century continued, as in the ancient world, to co-exist with an agrarian sector. Moreover, as in the ancient world these early modern economies, whether of the republican Netherlands or Britain, were also slave economies. Indeed the simultaneous burgeoning of the West Indies slave trade, the selling of military (especially Irish) prisoners, and declaration in England of a free state, caused 'the trade of buying and selling men' to become a political issue. In particular, in 1659 the claim that under the Protectorate 'threescore and ten . . . Free-born *English*-men' had been 'sold (uncondemned) into slavery' led to a vigorous defence by Henry Vane and other republicans of 'the liberty of the free born people of England'. '[W]e have a sense and loathing of the tyranny of the late King, and of all that tread in his steps, to impose on liberty and property.' 'Slavery is slavery, as well in a Commonwealth as under another form.'[53]

If there was nothing peculiarly modern about trade, so neither did an emphasis upon the agrarian economy, or critiques of luxury, necessarily denote Spartan (or any other type of bloody-minded) pre-modernity. It was from the standpoint of his unique preoccupation with the basis for stability, as 'the least subject unto innovation or turbulency', that Harrington invoked the example of Rome and the advice of Aristotle in favour of 'the Country way of life, though of a grosser spinning, as the best stuffe of a Common-wealth . . . Wheras Common-wealths, upon which the City life hath had the stronger influence, as *Athens*, have seldome or never been quiet.'[54] This may also have reflected Harrington's gentlemanly, and part-royalist, personal background. Unlike most other republican writers,

---

[51] A point made by Temple in *Observations* p. 189, who listed '*Tyre, Carthage, Athens, Syracuse, Agrigentum, Rhodes, Venice, Holland* . . . all . . . Commonwealths'.

[52] Thucydides, *The Peloponnesian War*. 160–1: 'The whole world before our eyes can be divided into two parts, the land and the sea . . . Of the whole of one of these parts you are in control – not only of the area at present in your power, but elsewhere too, if you want to go further.' In this speech Pericles associates the land with unnecessary luxury (gardens and other elegances that go with wealth) and the sea with what is necessary for the defence of 'our freedom' and 'our empire' from 'slavery'.

[53] Marcellus Rivers and Oxenbridge Foyle, *England's Slavery or Barbados Merchandize; Represented In a Petition to the High and Honourable Court of Parliament* (1659); Thomas Burton, *Diary of Thomas Burton*, ed. J. T. Rutt (4 vols., 1828) vol. IV, pp. 263, 264, 268.

[54] Harrington, *Oceana* (1656) p. 2. For the literal meaning of this 'quiet' (Athens being 'the most prating of those dames') see Scott, 'Peace of Silence'.

Harrington was not concerned with defending the existing English republic, or promoting its economic or military fortunes. It was from these perspectives that *Oceana* delivered unusually sharp, indeed contemptuous, criticisms of Athens and the United Provinces, to say nothing of the Rump parliament itself.

Yet even Harrington's preference for land over trade as the basis for Oceanic 'dominion' did not prevent him making the trading city of Venice ('of all others the most quiet, so the most equal commonwealth') his constitutional exemplar.[55] Indeed given the serenity of that republic, and the no less famous tumults of Rome, these agrarian prejudices were by no means easy to maintain. However since *Oceana* was to be a republic both for expansion and preservation, Harrington wished to combine features of Roman and Venetian organisation ('the Tillage bringing up a good Souldiery, bringeth up a good Common-wealth'), trusting to his agrarian law and the 'equality' of his orders to avert Rome's fate. Moreover an agrarian economy was not the only important feature of a country called *Oceana*, the maritime setting of which recalled not Sparta but Venice ('The Sea giveth law unto the growth of *Venice*, but the growth of *Oceana* giveth law unto the Sea').[56]

Milton, who did defend the existing republic, followed Bacon by recording that 'against riches Machiavelli argues rightly that "riches are not the nerves of war as is generally believed"'.[57] His praise of an austere and 'manly' virtue resorted to flourishes against uneducated block-headed shop-keepers and underhand 'merchant-like dealings'. Yet unlike Harrington, Milton also warmly praised both Athens and the United Provinces. Both furnished models of sophisticated societies which, having outgrown kingship (degenerated into tyranny), had found the valour to vindicate their liberty.[58] The sources of Milton's writing were largely generated by the classical culture of Athens and the protestant culture successfully defended by the Dutch. Most English republican writing combined, in varying proportions, a deep interest in classical precedent with close attention to the rapidly developing contemporary political economy. Both were considered crucial to the fortunes of the English republican experiment.

One example is John Streater who combined strictly traditional Aristotelian politics, and an explicitly Machiavellian defence of 'Frugality', with an early modern, moderately wacky, spiritual mechanics. Inspired

[55] Harrington, *Oceana*, in *Political Works* p. 276.   [56] Harrington, *Oceana* (1656) Introduction, p. 4.
[57] Milton, *Commonplace Book* pp. 414–15.
[58] Milton, *A Defence*, in Milton, *Political Writings*, ed. Martin Dzelzainis (Cambridge, 1991) pp. 88, 155; Milton, *The Readie and Easie Way*.

equally by classical and modern example, he was concerned with the promotion not only of all 'Arts and Sciences', but of manufactures, colonies and trade. '*Societies* or *Cities* were not only ordained for government and defence; but also for Trade and Commerce: the which I shall treat upon . . . with Rules for increasing of Trade more effectually than yet hath been written by any.'[59] 'Trade . . . is a great Mystery, of which most States-men are as ignorant, as Moles are blind.' That 'sociability' shown by Aristotle to be natural to man was exercised not only in the 'Senate-house or Town-house' but also 'the Market, Burses, or Exchange to trade'.[60] Having invoked Plato, Aristotle and God in support of the assertion that 'Increase is natural', Streater proceeded to the Machiavellian proposition that it was necessary 'to provide for increasing to prevent decreasing'. A prudent state would provide for this increase

either by sending of Colonies abroad as the Romans and other Cities did formerly, and now as we may do to *Virginia* and other parts of *America*, the planting of which places will bring great Riches into this Commonwealth, or else by increasing and incouraging of Artificers: and that may be done by not suffering of Staple Commodities to be transported before they be full wrought, as our Lead and Tin . . . Wools . . . and many other commodities . . . [and] by this means infinite numbers of people shall be provided for.[61]

Another example is Sidney, whose Graeco-Roman politics and frugal, Platonic philosophy of virtue are indistinguishable from Milton's. For Sidney, as for Milton, the key to liberty was its moral, rather than material foundation. Yet like Milton, Sidney's admiration of Sparta did not prevent him praising Athens, or deepening a relationship with the United Provinces begun by his great-uncle Sir Philip. Sidney's Platonic *Court Maxims*, written in the Netherlands in pursuit of an Anglo-Dutch republican alliance, anticipates and echoes much of the writing of his friend and collegue Bethel. It praises the wealth of free cities in general, the superior economic management of the States-General in particular, and furnishes a comprehensive English republican interest analysis.[62] The wealth of kings is another matter, because unrestrained by law. Thus courts are particularly prone to 'those vices that arise from the superfluity of riches'. If there must be kings, they should be made to partake of 'that honest poverty, which is the mother and nurse of modesty, sobriety, and all manner of virtue'.[63] This does not mean that Sidney approved, or disapproved, of wealth

[59] Streater, *Observations* no. 1, p. 6.   [60] Ibid. no. 7, pp. 50–1.   [61] Ibid. no. 4, pp 20–1.
[62] Sidney, *Court Maxims* pp. 71–8, 162; Scott, *Algernon Sidney and the English Republic* chs. 12–13.
[63] Sidney, *Discourses*, ed. West p. 350.

or poverty. Rather he approved of commonwealths, and disapproved of kings.

In general Sidney's *Discourses* exhibited an austere classical republican moral philosophy, fundamentally Greek, but capable of acquiring Machiavellian reinforcement. Like Machiavelli, it is anti-Venetian, on the grounds not that Venice was addicted to money but that it was unprepared for war. By contrast it praises martial republics, whether or not engaged in trade. Among these were

The Athenians . . . not less inclined [than the Romans] to war, but applied themselves to trade, as subservient to that end, by increasing the number of the people, and furnishing them with the means of carrying it on with more vigour and power. The Phoenician cities, of which Carthage was the most eminent, followed the same method; but knowing that riches do not defend themselves, or scorning slothfully to enjoy what was obtained by commerce, they so far applied themselves to war, that they grew to a power, which Rome only was able to overthrow.

On the other side the Spartans . . . framed a most severe discipline . . . banished all those curious arts, that are useful to trade; prohibited the importation of gold and silver . . . and educated their youth in such exercises only as prepared them for war. I will not take upon me to judge whether this proceeded from such a moderation of spirit, as placed felicity rather in the fullness and stability of liberty, integrity, virtue, and the enjoyment of their own, than in riches, power, and dominion over others; nor which of these two methods deserves most to be commended: But certain it is that both succeeded according to the intention of the founders.[64]

THE CONTEXT OF SPACE

Just as ancient literature appeared to offer the solution to many pressing contemporary problems, so the process of European discovery furnished new contexts within which those problems could be addressed. That the new world furnished a vantage point from which to identify European barbarism masquerading as civilisation is a well-known feature of Enlightenment culture from Le Clerc to Rousseau. But the early English classic of this genre is again More's *Utopia*. More's work is set outside England in more ways than one. It was written in Latin and the conversation it records took place in Antwerp. Its principal protagonist, Raphael Hythloday, accompanies a Florentine explorer, Amerigo Vespucci, working for the King of Portugal. On 'the farthest point' of the third such voyage Hythloday successfully begs to be 'marooned . . . as he was more eager to pursue his travels than afraid of death. He would often say, '"The man who has no

---

[64] Ibid. pp. 203–4.

grave is covered by the sky."' His further travels take him to what appears to be a temperate part of the southern hemisphere: the very other side of the world.[65]

Here, in Utopia, he finds in many respects an inverse image of his own corrupt society. Yet that non-European, pagan community exhibits the essence of the two European cultural forces that offer the cure for England's condition. One of these is Christianity in practice, rather than simply empty profession. The other is the distillation of that 'Greek philosophy' which is Raphael's 'main interest'. While lacking Europe's formal and historical connections to both of these cultures, the Utopians exhibit an openness to such truth standing in sharp contrast to Europe's proud ignorance. In Book 2 Raphael describes 'that new world' as 'distanced from ours not so much by geography as by customs and manners'.[66] Raphael accordingly returns to Antwerp, to a conversation in the cave, as someone who has seen Plato's sun. As we would expect, because they are contrary to 'corrupt custom' his ideas are dismissed by the character More and others as not only 'absurd' but 'outlandish'.[67]

Thus for authors preoccupied with the need for reform the geographical distance between old world and new could equate to the distance between ancient and contemporary culture, or between contemporary problems and their solutions.[68] Few authors exhibited these distances in More's extreme terms and More later regretted having done so. There is nevertheless abundant evidence of the interest taken in More's text by English explorers in the new world, and at least two attempts at practical application, leading Plymouth Governor William Bradford to conclude that

The experience that was had in this common course and condition, tried sundry years and that amongst godly and sober men, may well evince the vanity of that conceit of Plato's and other ancients applauded by some of later times; that the taking away of property and bringing in community into a commonwealth would make them happy and flourishing . . . For this community . . . was found to breed much confusion and discontent and retard much employment that would have been to their benefit and comfort . . . [so that those concerned] deemed it a kind of slavery.[69]

---

[65] More, *Utopia* pp. 10–11; Susan Brigden, *New Worlds, Lost Worlds: The Rule of the Tudors 1485–1603* (Harmondsworth, 2000) Prologue.

[66] More, *Utopia* p. 86.   [67] Ibid. p. 10; Nelson, 'Greek Nonsense' pp. 890, 892.

[68] A. A. Cave, 'Thomas More and the New World', *Albion* 23 (1991), explains that *Utopia* owes much more to the idea of the 'New World . . . [as] a metaphor for both the absence of [contemporary] civilization and the promise of a new beginning', than to what Europeans actually knew about the 'savages' of America (p. 229).

[69] Quoted in Stephen Innes, *Creating the Commonwealth: the Economic Culture of Puritan New England* (1995) p. 213.

More generally the most powerful intellectual forces informing English republicanism also underpinned the process of discovery and colonisation in Ireland, America and elsewhere. Thus one of the most common reasons given for English participation in European colonisation was as a response to the economic and social problems identified in commonwealth literature. When Streater argued for colonisation in America as necessary to provide for population 'increase', he was following, among others, Richard Hakluyt, who wrote in 1584:

[W]ee are growen more populous than ever heretofore: So that nowe there are . . . many thousandes of idle persons . . . wch having no way to be sett on worke be either mutinous and seeke alteration in the state, or . . . pitifully pyne awaye, or els at lengthe are miserbly hanged . . . wheras . . . yf this voyadge were put in execution . . . all sortes and states of men . . . women, and younge children by many meanes . . . shalbe kepte from idleness, and be made able by their owne honest and easie labour to finde themselves wthoute surchardginge others . . . [And] the honr and strengthe of a Prince consisteth in the multitude of the people.[70]

Thomas Scott noted similarly in 1622 that '[England's] West indian voyages . . . serve for draines to unloade [its] . . . populous State, which else would overflow its own bancks by continuance of peace, and . . . make a body fit for any rebellion'.[71] When the population of More's Utopia increased beyond a certain point, 'they enrol citizens out of every city and plant a colony under their own laws on the mainland near them, wherever the natives have plenty of unoccupied and uncultivated land'.[72] That other prominent commonwealth writer Sir Thomas Smith sent three expeditions to Northern Ireland to establish colonies between 1572 and 1575.[73]

In relation to colonisation's religious purpose the distinction between barbarism and civility was applied in England's favour and coincided with that between protestantism and Counter-Reformation. This religious struggle was, moreover, being waged on many fronts. It was thus Sir Henry Sidney, leader in the military subjugation of Ireland, 'who made the military arrangements for English intervention' in support of the protestants in France. It was Sir Henry's son Sir Philip Sidney, author of an 'heroical . . . enterprise of Planting upon the Main of America', who having failed to join Drake's 1585 voyage to the West Indies, travelled to fight

---

[70] Richard Hakluyt, *Discourse of Western Planting* (1584), in E. G. R. Taylor (ed.), *The Original Writings and Correspondence of the Two Richard Hakluyts* vol. II (1935) pp. 234, 236, 238.
[71] Thomas Scott, *Vox Populi. Or News from Spayne* (1622) no page number.
[72] More, *Utopia* p. 56.
[73] Hiram Morgan, 'The Colonial Venture of Sir Thomas Smith in Ulster, 1571–1575', *The Historical Journal* 28 (1985); Armitage, *Ideological Origins* p. 49.

and die at Zutphen in the United Provinces instead.[74] Hakluyt's *Discourse* explained the 'great bridle . . . this voyage will be . . . to the Indies of the kinge of Spaine', in all of whose 'Domynions' currently 'our men are dryven to flinge their Bibles and prayer Bokes into the sea, and to forsweare and renownce their relligion and conscience and consequently theyr obedience to her Ma[jesty]'.[75] In Thomas Scott it was a principal ambition of Spain's diplomatic relationship with James VI and I to 'cross [England's] West indian voyages . . . because . . . as they . . . may in tyme there perhaps raise an other Englan[d] to withstand our new Spaine in America, as this old England opposeth our present State, and clouds the glorious exte[nt] therof in Europ'.[76] By 1572, according to the Spanish ambassador, there were 20,000 Dutch and French protestant refugees in England. By 1620 most continental news came to England via the United Provinces, and the works of Hakluyt, Scott and most of those labelled 'puritan' by the Caroline regime display a deep conciousness of the interdependence of the Dutch and English struggles.[77]

The third element of the colonising mentality was classical. The impact of the discoveries was absorbed through humanistic lenses and both Greek and Roman literature contained a rich treasury for discussion of the theme of empire.[78] Smith's *Discourse of the Commonweal* explained that 'nations . . . that be politic and civil do master the rest . . . The empires of the Greeks and Romans do that declare, amongst whom, like as learning and wisdom was most esteemed, so their empires were spread widest and longest did continue.'[79] If the most important classical influence upon More, Sidney and Spenser was Plato, and upon Smith, Hakluyt and Scott, Aristotle, most also quoted Roman sources, and recent scholarship has drawn attention to the importance of expansionist Rome as a practical model, as well as of the Roman political ends of honour and glory (rather

---

[74] Grevil[le], *Life of Sidney* pp. 117–18 (Sidney's project for a 'plantation' would be 'as an emporium for the confluence of all nations that love or profess any kind of virtue or commerce'); Salmon, *The French Religious Wars* pp. 154–5; Brigden, *New Worlds* pp. 282, 286; Scott, *Algernon Sidney and the English Republic* pp. 50–1; Blair Worden, *The Sound of Virtue: Philip Sidney's Arcadia and Elizabethan Politics* (New Haven, Conn., 1996) ch. 3.

[75] Hakluyt, *Discourse* p. 211; David Harris Sacks, 'Discourses of Western Planting: Richard Hakluyt, European Wars of Religion and the Beginnings of the British Empire', seminar paper given at Trinity Hall, Cambridge, 21 November 2001.

[76] Thomas Scott, *Vox Populi* no page number.

[77] Grevil[le], *Life of Sidney* p. 118; Scott, *England's Troubles* ch. 4; Haley, *The British and the Dutch* pp. 32, 48, 69–74.

[78] Elliott, *The Old World and the New*; Anthony Pagden, *Lords of All the World: Ideologies of Empire in Spain, Britain and France c.1500–c.1800* (New Haven, Conn., 1995); Armitage, *Ideological Origins*; Grafton, *New Worlds, Ancient Texts*.

[79] Smith, *A Discourse of the Commonweal* p. 25.

than simply happiness, peace or safety).[80] This was underlined by the work
of Machiavelli in backing the ambition of Roman expansion over Venetian
preservation. This Machiavellian prescription was systematically applied
by Richard Beacon in 1594 to the problem of the 'universall reformation
of . . . Ireland', and explored in the following decades by Bacon among
others.[81]

In English republican writing reform of the commonwealth, defence of
the Reformation and classical republicanism all came together. Moreover
from the moment of its birth the English republic was 'a commonwealth
for expansion'. Following hard upon the victory in England, the first work
of the republic's army in 1649 was the bloody conquest, expropriation and
subjugation of Ireland. By the time of the Rump's dissolution in 1653, the
planting of Ireland was reaching a legislative climax under the leadership
of Sir Henry Sidney's great-grandson Algernon.[82] The next conquest, in
1650–1, was of Scotland. The committee established to draw up legislation
'in order to the Uniting of Scotland into one Commonwealth with England'
was led by Sir Henry Vane, and contained both Sidney and Henry Neville.
Neville explained later, 'The Union of that nation was then calculated for a
Commonwealth, and not for a Monarchy. England was then, by the blessing
of God, governed by its own representatives . . . You promised it to them,
to take them into your bosoms and make them one with you. The Romans
never did well till they did so.'[83] Both of these conquests were completed
as measures crucial for the defence of English protestantism and liberty.
The other political union remarkably proposed at this time, for the same
reason, was with the Dutch.[84] When the Long Parliament had demanded,
in its *Nineteen Propositions* (1642), 'that your Majesty will be pleased to
enter into a more strict alliance with the States of the United Provinces',
its envoy for this purpose in November of that year had been William
Strickland.[85] In 1651 Strickland returned to The Hague with Oliver St John
to request a 'comprehensive and permanent alliance' between the two states
for the mutual defence of their 'protestant religion and republican liberties'.

---

[80] Peltonen, *Classical Humanism*; Andrew Fitzmaurice, 'The Civic Solution to the Crisis of English
Colonization', *Historical Journal* 42, 1 (1999); Fitzmaurice, *Humanism and America*.

[81] Beacon, *Solon his follie: or a politique discourse, touching the reformation of common-weales conquered,
declined or corrupted*, discussed in Peltonen, *Classical Humanism* pp. 74–102.

[82] *Commons Journals* vol. 7, pp. 241, 242, 271, 278; Scott, *Algernon Sidney and the English Republic*
p. 101.

[83] *Diary of Thomas Burton* vol. IV, pp. 179, 183, 188, 190; Scott, *Algernon Sidney and the English Republic*
pp. 100–1.

[84] A point noted by Israel, *Dutch Republic* p. 714: 'A political union between England and the United
Provinces was proposed of the sort which Parliament had recently imposed, by force, on Scotland.'

[85] Haley, *The British and the Dutch* p. 76.

When the Dutch replied affirming the 'ancient friendship' between the two nations, the English countered by demanding 'a nearer union than formerly hath been . . . with all speed'.[86]

The reasons for Dutch hesitation at such a proposal can readily be imagined. Historians of the Netherlands have emphasised the damage such a union would have caused to Dutch primacy in world trade.[87] Historians of English politics have emphasised that the United Provinces was not simply a sympathetic republic, but contained a large constituency of pro-royal Orangists (to say nothing of exiled English royalists) who vilified the regicide English republic, and screamed abuse at their 1651 delegation.[88] To explain Dutch hesitation, however, it merely needs to be remembered that the Dutch had, only three years earlier, won an eighty-year struggle for their liberty. As prospective junior partner in the proposed coalition, could they really have been expected to hand over in friendship what they had only just purchased so dearly by the sword? In the not-disinterested words of Edward Hyde, St John returned from The Hague with 'extreme indignation . . . which he manifested as soon as he returned to the Parliament; who, disdaining likewise to find themselves undervalued (that is, not valued above all the world besides,) presently entered upon counsels how they might discountenance and control the trade of Holland, and increase their own'.[89] The English republic had been the result of a no less remarkable war. This had swept away not only the opposing armies but monarchy itself, and with monarchy English military impotence. In 1651–2 the republic was militarily triumphant, and determined to cement its own security. For that security, an end both to the Dutch haven enjoyed by English royalists and to the liberties taken by Dutch traders was necessary.

Thus if the Dutch would not recognise the benefits of peaceful union, they would be made to experience the consequences of independent English power. There followed the Navigation Act of 1651, which posed a severe challenge to Dutch colonial trade and the final draft of which was written by St John. This was described by John Streater as 'that Act for Trade, that never to be forgotten Act . . . the Glory and Top of their great Advice . . . which

---

[86] Jones, *Anglo-Dutch Wars* pp. 107–9.

[87] Jonathan Israel, 'England, the Dutch Republic, and Europe in the Seventeenth Century', *The Historical Journal* 40, 4 (1997) pp. 1117–21.

[88] Jones, *Anglo-Dutch Wars* pp. 18, 107; Steven Pincus, *Protestantism and Patriotism: Ideologies and the Making of English Foreign Policy 1650–1668* (Cambridge, 1996) pp. 35, 75 (and elsewhere). The apparent assumption of the latter study that because the war had political causes it could not also have had economic causes remains puzzling.

[89] Quoted in Pincus, *Protestantism and Patriotism* p. 44.

occasioneth a Chargeable and Dangerous War with *Holland*'.[90] It was, however, one aspect of a broader tightening of control over England's maritime and trading empire which had been in progress since 1649. This had resulted in a Plantation Act of 3 October 1650 vowing to 'reduce all . . . parts and places [in America] belonging to the Commonwealth of England' (Virginia, Maryland, Antigua, Barbados and Bermuda had declared for Charles II).[91] The Anglo-Dutch war was also the culmination of a build-up and projection of naval power which had been vigorously pursued since 1649. In his *The Case Stated* Nedham warned the Dutch that under a republican government England's interests would identified and defended. The Navigation Act had been long overdue to rectify the 'negligence of former Kings and the corruption of their Ministers of State' in relation to matters of 'Trade . . . Navigation and Maritin Defence'.[92]

Thus the frontispiece of Nedham's edition of Selden's *Dominion of the Sea* (1652) 'showed the English republic ("Angliae Respub.") as Minerva/Britannia, the emblems of the three kingdoms held under . . . her feet, with Neptune exhorting her to extend her *imperium*, "For Sea-Dominion may as well bee gain'd,/By new acquests as by descent maintain'd"'.[93] The Preface explained: '[Since before] the old *Roman* Invasion . . . the Soveraigntie of the Seas flowing about this Island . . . has . . . been held . . . as an inseperable appendant of the British Empire.'[94] The military triumphs which followed were celebrated amid invocations of the 'days of worthy Hawkins and Drake'.[95] Published under a government containing two members of its subject's family, Greville's *Life of the Renowned Sir Philip Sidney* (1652) contained an appropriately maritime, imperial and protestant account of 'The True Interest of *England*, as it then stood in relation to all Forraign Princes . . . Together with . . . the Maximes and Policies used by Queen *Elizabeth* in her Government.' The country's new-found military prowess would allow Algernon Sidney to ask Hobbes, with characteristic indignation,

Whether it were an easy work to conquer Switzerland: Whether the Hollanders are of greater strength since the recovery of their liberty, or when they groaned under

[90] Quoted in ibid. pp. 11–12.
[91] Robert Bliss, *Revolution and Empire: English Politics and the American Colonies in the Seventeenth Century* (Manchester, 1990) pp. 45–61.
[92] [Marchamont Nedham], *The Case Stated Between England and the United Provinces, In this present Juncture* (1652) p. 13.
[93] Armitage, 'The Cromwellian Protectorate' p. 534.
[94] Marchamont Nedham, Epistle Dedicatorie, in Selden, *Of the Dominion, Or, Ownership of the Sea* (1652).
[95] Worden, 'Classical Republicanism'.

the yoke of Spain: And lastly, whether the entire conquest of Scotland and Ireland, the victories obtained against the Hollanders when they were in the height of their power, and the reputation to which England did rise in less than five years after 1648, be good marks of the instability, disorder and weakness of free nations?[96]

Finally, in the actual conduct of the 1652–4 war there are strong indications of an attempt to pursue the Anglo-Dutch union scheme by military means. In 1659 Thomas Scot claimed: '[W]e intended to have gone off with a good savour and provided for a succession of Parliaments, but we stayed to end the Dutch war. We might have brought them to a oneness with us. Their Ambassadors did desire a coalition. This we might have done in four or five months.'[97] The most important manager of the war, Sir Henry Vane, was described by his Council of State colleague Algernon Sidney as 'an absolute Master of the Naval affairs' who 'zealously promoted the peace with Holland, and helpt to carry on vigorously whatever War was begun by any other Nation'.[98] Certainly those in receipt of Cromwell's ire on the day of dissolution of the Rump included Vane (in particular) and Sidney.

It was in 1655 that this republican imperial assertiveness suffered its first sharp reverse with the defeat of the Cromwellian expedition to Hispaniola. Cromwell's spiritual crisis was not eased by Vane's diagnosis in *A Healing Question propounded* (1656) that the reason for this rebuke from God was that '[t]he root and bottome on which [the expedition] stood, was not publique interest, but the private lust and will of the Conqueror'. Harrington's *Oceana* attempted to respond to the same crisis, laying out the prescription for Oceana as a 'Common-wealth for increase', the mission of which blended classical, protestant and commonwealth agendas.[99] Nor did this setback significantly undermine the perception by other European countries of the first exhibition of that British maritime military and imperial potential to be realised during the eighteenth century. This was demonstrated not only by growing assertiveness in the Atlantic, Mediterranean and Caribbean, and naval superiority against the Dutch, but also by the capture of Jamaica in 1655 and Dunkirk in 1658, and the receipt from Portugal in 1661 of Tangier and Bombay.[100]

---

[96] Sidney, *Discourses*, ed. West, pp. 143–4. [97] *Diary of Thomas Burton* vol. III, pp. III–12.
[98] Sidney, *Character of Henry Vane* p. 279.
[99] Vane, *A Healing Question* p. 4; Armitage, 'The Cromwellian Protectorate' pp. 544–52.
[100] Jonathan Israel, 'The Emerging Empire: the Continental Perspective 1650–1713', in Canny (ed.), *The Origins of Empire* p. 423.

PART II

Analysis

CHAPTER 5

The political theory of rebellion

Against a bad ruler there is no other remedy than the sword. 'To cure the ills of the people, words suffice, and against those of the prince the sword is necessary. Macchiavel. discors. c 58. Book 1.

> John Milton, *Commonplace Book* entry 1651–2[1]

[H]ands and swords were given to men, that they only may be slaves who have no courage.

> Algernon Sidney, *Discourses Concerning Government*[2]

INTRODUCTION: THE LAW OF WAR

That republicanism has not usually been seen as furnishing a resistance theory owes something to the historiographical disassociation of classical republicanism from natural law theory. It also relates to the perception of republicanism as a theory of government, rather than against it. In fact as republican writers combined these languages, and others, so republican government was both preceded and succeeded by armed resistance. Within the historiography of resistance theory attention has focused predominantly upon natural law arguments and sources. While these were also crucial in the English case, so were classical anatomists of tyranny, both Greek and Roman, and early modern humanists including Machiavelli.

The justification of armed resistance against tyranny was a major component of English republicanism. The republic emerged from a war against Stuart 'popery and arbitrary government' sharing many characteristics with earlier protestant rebellions in France, Scotland and the United Provinces.[3] As resistance theory had been among the most important ideological products of these earlier struggles, so those theories were revived, augmented

---

[1] Milton, *Commonplace Book* p. 456.   [2] Sidney, *Discourses,* ed. West p. 523.
[3] Scott, *England's Troubles* chs. 3–6.

and adapted to English needs.[4] By the time the country acquired a republican government, 'liberty' had been defended by word and sword for the best part of a decade. As George Wither indignantly demanded of the government's opponents in 1650, what was wrong with

a Reformation gained, and maintained by the Sword in *England* [?] . . . These Objectors themselves would account that man a Papist, or Popishly affected, who should thus reproach the Protestants in *Bohemia, Germany, Switzerland, France, the United Provinces,* and *Scotland,* yet did these maintain their Religion, and gain their Liberties by the sword, by this the Switzers cantoniz'd themselves, and the *Dutch* became a Free-state; by this the Protestant Religion was defended, and the Presbyterian Government first setled in Scotland, their Queen being deposed, and forced to flie to save her Head, for opposing it.[5]

Thereafter republican resistance theory was further developed under the Cromwellian usurpation of 1653–9, and following the Restoration of monarchy in 1660. To these generalisations the most important exception was James Harrington, seconded more equivocally by Henry Neville.

Writing between 1628 and 1640 Sir Robert Filmer identified three contemporary ways of speaking about politics which supported what he called 'the whole Fabrick of this vast Engine of Popular sedition'.[6] The first was ancient constitutionalism, which Filmer associated with Sir Edward Coke and claims for the antiquity of parliaments.[7] The second was natural law theory, which he associated with Suarez, Bellarmine and Hugo Grotius.[8] The third was classical republicanism, which he associated with the bloody politics of ancient Athens and Rome, and the latter's defender Machiavelli.[9] English republicanism combined all of these sources and languages, and together with arguments from a specifically religious standpoint, they account for most of the content of English republican resistance theory.

Among all of these sources the two which must be singled out are Machiavelli and Grotius. Both had confronted the key political problem of the age in endemic war.[10] Among modern sources Machiavelli's impact upon English republican theory was pre-eminent. It was, however, Hugo Grotius's *The Law of War and Peace* (1625) that was identified by Sidney as one of the two 'Livres il estimoit le plus pour se perfectionner dans la

---

4 Skinner, *Foundations of Modern Political Thought* vol. II; Salmon, *The French Religious Wars*; Martin van Gelderen, *The Political Thought of the Dutch Revolt 1555–1590* (Cambridge, 1993); Scott, 'Law of War'.
5 G[eorge] W[ither], *Respublica Anglicana or the Historie of the Parliament* (1650) p. 43.
6 Filmer, *Patriarcha* p. 4.   7 Ibid. pp. 89–92.   8 Ibid. pp. 5–22, 64–5, 208–34.
9 Ibid. pp. 24–31, 134, 288.   10 Scott, 'Law of War' pp. 116–18.

politique'.[11] This was not because it was an incendiary invocation of resistance. On the contrary, it was in part its qualities of religious and political moderation (Grotius being, as Sidney put it, 'a gentle spirited man'[12]) which helped to make it useful in this context. Thus Richard Baxter recorded that when, at the outset of the English civil war, English parliamentarians defended themselves by reference to 'the French, Dutch and German Protestants' wars',

> They alleged Barclay, Grotius and other Defenders of Monarchy, especially that passage of Grotius *De Jure Belli* where he saith, That if several Persons have a part in the *Summa Potestas* (of which he maketh Legislation a chief Act), each part hath naturally the power of defending its own Interest in the Soveraignty against the other part if they invade it. And he addeth over boldly, That if in such a War they conquer, the conquered party loseth to them his share.[13]

During the Restoration crisis Sidney would return to this passage of *De Jure Belli* (Book 1, ch. 4, para. 13) repeatedly, as would speakers in the Convention elected in January 1689.[14] Far, however, from being a personal 'Defender of Monarchy' Grotius had been closely involved with the Dutch republican cause until the fall of Oldenbarneveldt. In its support his scholarship brought together ancient constitutionalist, humanist and natural law arguments.[15] In some of his work at least 'princedoms and liberty are incompatible . . . As . . . personal Liberty excludes the Dominion of a Master, so does civil Liberty exclude Royalty.'[16]

When Machiavelli wrote, the scourge of war appeared to be destroying Italy. By 1625 it was ravaging much of Europe. 'I have had many and weighty reasons', explained Grotius, 'for undertaking to write upon this subject. Throughout the Christian world I observed a lack of restraint in

---

[11] 'Lantiniana' p. 101; the other was 'le Livre Espagnol intitule *el governador Christiano*' by Juan Marquez (Salamanca, 1621), another work of natural law theory.

[12] Sidney, *Court Maxims* p. 101.

[13] Richard Baxter, *Reliquiae Baxterianae: or, Mr Richard Baxter's Narrative of the most Memorable Passages of his Life and Times* (1696) p. 38.

[14] '[T]he right to war may be conceded against a King who, posssessing only part of the sovereign power, seeks to possess himself of the part that does not belong to him . . . whoever possesses a part of the sovereign power must . . . possess the right to defend [it] . . . in [this] case . . . the king may even lose his part of the sovereign power by right of war.' Hugo Grotius, *De Jure Belli ac Pacis Libri Tres* vol. II, trans. F. W. Kelsey (Oxford, 1925) The Translation, Book 1, p. 158; Sidney, *Discourses*, in *Sydney on Government* pp. 190, 280, 256.

[15] Martin van Gelderen, 'The Machiavellian Moment and the Dutch Revolt: the Rise of Neostoicism and Dutch Republicanism', in Gisela Bock, Quentin Skinner and Maurizio Viroli (eds.) *Machiavelli and Republicanism* (Cambridge, 1990) p. 215; Richard Tuck, 'Grotius and Selden', in Burns and Goldie, *The Cambridge History of Political Thought* pp. 499–509; Annabel Brett, 'Natural Right and Civil Community: the Civil Philosophy of Hugo Grotius', *Historical Journal* 45, 1 March (2002).

[16] Quoted by Tuck, *Philosophy and Government* p. 193.

relation to war, such as even barbarous races should be ashamed of . . . and that when arms have once been taken up there is no longer any respect for law, divine or human.'[17] Grotius's response was not what that of his fellow-countryman Erasmus had been, namely, to seek peace. That was to react from the insupportable to the unattainable. Grotius sought 'a middle way': to civilise war by uniting it with law. 'Nothing is more common', he wrote, 'than the assertion of antagonism between law and arms . . . this very serious error must be refuted . . . There is a law of war, as well as of peace.'[18] In Grotius's study, accordingly, war became a judicial instrument. It is 'the duty of the Christian soldier' to fight 'on behalf of justice . . . on behalf of the safety of the innocent . . . It is in the love of innocent men that both capital punishment and just wars have their origin.' Such wars appealed to the divinely authored law of nature, a law 'of perpetual validity and suited to all times', for 'War is directed at those who cannot be held in check by judicial processes.'[19] During England's troubles this argument was reapplied from the case of international wars to that of armed domestic self-defence.

In the words of John Streater, who called Grotius '*th[e] great Oracle of the Civil Law*', 'There is not a person under Heaven but will say, That the Warr that is made in defence of a people's Liberty, is a just War.'[20] More extensively, from Sidney:

And when the Protestants of the Low-Countries were so grievously oppressed by the power of Spain . . . why should they not make use of all the means that God had put into their hands for their deliverance? . . . by resisting they laid the foundation of . . . a most glorious and happy Commonwealth, that hath been, since its first beginning, the strongest pillar of the Protestant Cause now in the world, and a place of refuge unto those who in all parts of Europe have been oppressed for the name of Christ . . . wheras they had slavishly . . . suffered themselves to be butchered, if they had left those empty provinces under the power of Antichrist.[21]

In defence of such war both Levellers and republicans (including Milton, Nedham, Lilburne and Sidney) drew upon not only Grotius but Buchanan.[22] For the latter also,

---

[17] Grotius, *De Jure Belli* Prolegomena, p. 20.   [18] Ibid. pp. 3, 20, 33.
[19] Ibid. pp. 19, 21, 33, 90, 91.   [20] Streater, *The Continuation* pp. 4, 10.
[21] Sidney, extract from the *Discourses* read at *The Trial of A Sydney*, in Sidney, *Discourses Concerning Government . . . with His Letters Trial Apology and Some Memoirs of His Life* (1763) pp. 127–8.
[22] See also *The People's Right Briefly Asserted. Printed for the Information of the Commonality of England, France, and all other neighbour Nations, that groan under the oppression of Tyrannical Government* (1649), invoking Aristotle, Buchanan, the author of *Vindiciae Contra Tyrannos*, and the English examples of Edward II and Richard II.

if a king do those things which are directly for the dissolution of society, for the continuance whereof he was created, how do we call him? A Tyrant . . . Now a Tyrant hath not only no just authority over a people, but is also their enemy . . . Is there not a just and Lawfull war with an enemy for grievous and intolerable injuries . . . It is forrsooth a just war . . . and . . . Lawfull not only for the whole people to kill that enemy, but for every one of them.[23]

Such resistance was authorised, firstly, by the right possessed by all rational beings to institute and alter their governments. So in 1646 William Ball defended the right of a 'Nation or People . . . to make use of their first primitive power, to dispose . . . themselves at their pleasure, or as they shall think good . . . as is sufficiently discerned by the severall Alterations of Government in Athens, Rome, Geneva, Switzerland, Holland'. For 'the Cantons of *Switzerland*, the Provinces of *Holland, Zeland* etc' to 'have regained their Freedome . . . by plain defiance and Arms . . . is lawfull . . . there need no speciall Warrant from God for anything that they shall do agreeable to their Naturall, or Human Reason'.[24] It was more specifically confirmed by the authority conferred by the law of nature upon God's creatures to defend themselves against molestation. Thus in 1647 the Leveller Richard Overton reminded his readers of the

firme Law and radicall principle in Nature, engraven in the tables of the heart by the finger of God . . . for every living, moving thing . . . to defend, preserve . . . and deliver it selfe from all things hurtfull [and] destructive . . . from hence . . . [by] the law of nature . . . and of Religion too . . . is conveyed to all men . . . an undoubted principle of reason . . . to defend and deliver himselfe from all oppression, violence and cruelty . . . Upon this *Principle* the *Netherlanders* made a . . . defence and resistance against the King of *Spaine* . . . and upon the same *point* rose the *Scotch* up in Armes, and entred this Kingdome . . . and even this Parliament upon the same principle, took up armes against the King. And now (*right worthy patriots of the Army*) you yourselves upon the *same principle*, for *recovery of common right* and *freedome,* have entred upon this your present honourable and *Solemne Engagement,* against the oppressing party at *Westminster*.[25]

MILTON AND NEDHAM

In the late 1630s and early 1640s Milton made a series of entries in his *Commonplace Book* in support of the contention that 'subjects are at liberty

---

[23] George Buchanan (trans.) 'Philalethes', *De Jure Regni apud Scotos* (1680) p. 127; J. H. M. Salmon *Renaissance and Revolt* (Cambridge, 1987) pp. 142–3.

[24] William Ball of Barkham, Esquire, *Constitutio Liberi Populi. OR, The Rule of a Free-born People* (1646) pp. 4, 6, 14.

[25] Overton, *An Appeale from the Degenerate House of Commons*, in D. M. Wolfe (ed.), *Leveller Manifestoes* pp. 159–60.

to ward off by force a force advanced against them contrary to the law, even by the magistrates'.[26] This was shown in France by Hotman's *Francogallia*; in the Netherlands by the achievement of 'The Estates General of Holland [in] tak[ing] away Philip's power'; and in Scotland by the example of 'The Scottish nobles' in driving 'Mary . . . from the kingdom'.[27] Many of these examples reappeared in *The Tenure of Kings and Magistrates* (1649), written in part to discomfort presbyterian opponents of the regicide. The most important feature of *The Tenure* in this respect was its appeal to 'reason' against the 'tyrannie, of Custom'. Within a present Christian framework such custom might be overriden either by the 'authorite and power of self-defence and preservation' in God-given natural law, or by a more particular 'Sword of God, superior to all mortal things, in whose hand soever by apparent signes his testified will is to put it'.[28]

God's abhorrence of tyranny was evident from scripture.[29] Among the rational ancient Greeks and Romans the right of resistance against tyranny was taken for granted and frequently exercised.[30] Finally, Milton's rhetoric against custom notwithstanding, the existence of this right was affirmed by English history and law since the time of St Edward,[31] as well as by early modern example, not only in England but Scotland (invoking Buchanan and Knox), the Holy Roman Empire, Holland and France.[32] The tract ended with supporting extracts from Luther, Calvin, Zwingli, Bucer and Christopher Goodman.

Most of Milton's authorities in *The Tenure* reappeared in *The Defence* (1651). The latter made, however, more use of both ancient constitutionalist and classical sources. At the same time, entries in his *Commonplace Book* dated to 1651–2 show Milton finding in Machiavelli two arguments for resistance. 'Against a bad ruler there is no other remedy than the sword. "To cure the ills of the people, words suffice, and against those of the prince the sword is necessary." Macchiavel. discors. c 58. Book 1.'[33] In a less straightforward case, however, Milton converted Machiavelli's praise of the benefits of 'tumults' within a republican state into a defence of 'rebellion':

The rebellion of a people has often been the means of their regaining their freedom, and therefore they should not be blamed, because very often they act from just causes and complaints. Witness Machiavelli: 'I say that those who condemn the riots between the nobles and the common people thereby, in my estimation, blame

---

[26] Milton, *Commonplace Book* pp. 455, 501.   [27] Ibid. p. 445.
[28] Milton, *Tenure* pp. 190, 193, 196, 198–9.   [29] Ibid. pp. 206–13, 216–17.
[30] Ibid. pp. 202–9, 212–13.   [31] Ibid. pp. 201, 218–22.   [32] Ibid. pp. 222–7.
[33] Milton, *Commonplace Book* p. 456.

those things that were the principal means of keeping Rome free.' For good laws were derived from those disturbances, etc, discors. Book 1 c 4.[34]

In fact the pioneer of this line of argument had been Nedham, with whom Milton was closely associated at this time. In *England's Miserie and Remedie* (1645) and *Vox Plebis* (1646) Nedham had explained that the tyranny of a senatorial nobility was not fundamentally different from the tyranny of a king. It was the Roman plebs who had found the solution to this problem, in taking up arms in defence of their liberty and rights. As he later put it in *The Excellencie of a Free State*: '[The people] resolved to be ridden no longer under fair shews of Liberty. They raised a Tumult under the conduct of their Tribune *Canuteius*; nor could they by any perswasion be induced to lay down Arms, till they were put in possession of their Rights and Priviledges.'[35] Between 1651 and 1652 this anti-senatorial line of argument reappeared in Nedham's *Mercurius Politicus*. Previously, however, his earliest defences of the republic had asserted a *de facto* right of conquest. Yet this was quickly underpinned by a claim to legal '*Right of war*' derived from Grotius's *De Jure Belli*, and in particular the key passage in Book 1, chapter 4, paragraph 13. If 'after the miserable Confusions of a *civill warr* . . . the *Conquerors* . . . may . . . erect such a Form as They themselves conceive most convenient for their own preservation' this followed from the opinion of 'the *Learned*... that... in, or after a *Civill warr*, the *written Laws*... are of no Force, but only those which are *non-written*, that is, which are agreeable to the *Dictates of Nature*, or the *Law and Custom of Nations*'. Further, these same learned persons

affirm . . . that if the Authority be divided betwixt a *King* and his people in *Parliament*, so that the *King* hath one part, the *people* another; the *King* offering to incroach upon that part which is none of his, the *People* may lawfully oppose him by force of Arms, because he exceeds the Bounds of his Authority: And not only so, but he may lose his own part likewise by the *Law of Arms* . . . [Therefore] if *a King* may thus by *Right of warr*, lose his Share and Interest in Authority and Power . . . the *whole* must needs reside in that part of the *people* which prevailed over him . . . [then] what Government soever it pleases them to erect, is . . . valid *de Jure*.[36]

Against the objection of 'many, That perhaps this Transmission of Title by *Right of warr* may hold good, when Nation is engaged against Nation, but in a single Nation within itselfe they suppose it cannot', Nedham responded with the view

---

[34] Ibid. p. 505.   [35] Nedham, *Excellencie* p. 12.
[36] *Mercurius Politicus* no. 17, 26 September–3 October 1650, pp. 277–8.

of a late learned *Royallist*, by name *Grotius*, who affirms; That *in a divided State, one Nation, during the time of it's Nationall Divisions, is esteemed as two Nations; so that what Preeminence Nation may gain over Nation by Right of* forein warre, *the same may be obtained likewise by one part of a Nation against the other, by Right of* Civill warr.[37]

STREATER AND SEXBY

With the dissolution of the Rump by Oliver Cromwell in 1653 a new context was created for republican resistance theory. As John Streater put it, 'Did not he Intend, what at last did notoriously appear in his making himself a Monarch, Exercising a more absolute power then any Kings that went before; nay more than the late King, whom he, amongst divers, Condemned to be beheaded for a Tyrant?'[38] It was Streater's *Observations* which, in 1654, picked up Nedham's line of argument about the beneficial effect of tumults, with explicit acknowledgement of '*Machiavel* upon *Livy. lib.2.chap.*58'. Thus 'as . . . the People of *Rome* after the death of *Virginia* chose 20 Tribunes from amongst themselves . . . thus many people have been forced to associate themselves, and repair to arms to cut off the Tyrants that tyrannized over them'.[39] Streater's anatomy of tyranny drew upon Aristotle, Cicero, Tacitus, Machiavelli and Plutarch's life of *Dionisius*, tyrant of Syracuse, to illustrate the case of one 'who rules by his own will, not . . . by reason . . . and the Law of society . . . he I say is a beast and not a man, and his subjects are worse than beasts . . . by making himself an absolute Lord, and a lawlesse person . . . he needs arms . . . Castles, Guards, and Strengths . . . being afraid of every ones hand, to be the Executioner of that which justly he had deserved'.[40]

For Streater the people's right to act in defence of their lives and liberties was established by an 'eternall . . . Morall . . . Law of Nature' which had proved a sufficient juridical basis against 'the tyrannical pride of *Tarquin* . . . to revenge a modest *Lucretia*'.[41] Streater's periodical suffered permanent interruption after issue 11, of 27 June to 4 July 1654, which discussed the question of what 'a people . . . according to the Law of Nature, which intendeth nothing but harmony, sweetness and mildness' may do to 'attempt the freeing of themselves from the servitude of a domineering,

[37] Ibid. no. 21, p. 342.
[38] John Streater, *Secret Reasons of State In Reference To the Affairs of these Nations, At the Interruption of this present Parliament Anno 1653* (23 May 1659) p. 3.
[39] Streater, *Observations* no. 7, pp. 52–3.   [40] Ibid. no. 7, pp. 53–4; no 8, pp. 51–8.
[41] Ibid. no. 8, p. 9.

usurping, insulting, mad Tyrant (he that ruleth by Force is little better)'.[42] In fact, since 'Those that rule by force, are mad; they have lost the Reason of true and just Policie . . . A People may as lawfully by force seize upon a Tyrant, as four or five (or more) servants may take their Master, and binde him hand and foot, in case he play the mad-man, in attempting to kill them.'[43]

The most sustained application of such arguments came in the 1657 pamphlet *Killing Noe Murder*, usually attributed to Edward Sexby.[44] This had many similarities to the work of Streater, as well as of Nedham, and Milton's *Tenure*, which also defended tyrannicide with many of the same sources. Now, as by Streater, the fundamental accusation made against the Lord Protector was of betrayal of the army's cause:

> Could ever England have thought to have seen that army, that was never mentioned without the titles of religious, zealous, faithful, courageous, the fence of her liberty at home, the terror of her enemies abroad, become her gaolers? Not her guard, but her oppressors? Not her soldiers, but a tyrants executioners, drawing to blocks and gibbets all that dare be honester than themselves.[45]

The pamphlet exhibited a Platonic anti-formalism reminiscent of Milton's *Tenure*, observing the tendency of 'the vulgar' to 'judge of things . . . by their exterior appearances . . . without penetrating at all into their causes and natures . . . their essences'.[46] In addition to the testimony of scripture,[47] it deployed the staple classical republican sources, Greek, Roman and Italian, in particular 'Plato, Aristotle . . . Plutarch . . . Tacitus, and his Highness' own Evangelist, Machiavelli'. Like Streater, as well as Milton and Sidney, Sexby begins with an Aristotelian account of 'the end for which men enter into society . . . not barely to live . . . but . . . live happily, and a life answerable to the dignity of their kind'. It is on this basis that both Plato and Aristotle defined tyranny as a phenomenon antithetical to civil society ('to be under a tyrant is not to be a commonwealth, but a great family, consisting of master and slaves'), as Tacitus and Machiavelli recounted the fraudulent maxims of tyrants in practice.[48]

---

[42] Ibid. no. 11, p. 85.   [43] Ibid.

[44] During the debates at Putney church on 29 October 1647 Sexby had incurred harsh personal criticism from Cromwell: 'I confesse I was most dissatisfied with that I heard Mr Sexby speake of any man here, because itt did savour soe much of will.' Firth, *The Clarke Papers* vol. 1, p. 328. This is the charge which is reciprocated in *Killing Noe Murder*.

[45] William Allen [i.e. Edward Sexby], *Killing Noe Murder. Briefly Discourst in Three Quaestions* (1657), in D. Wootton (ed.), *Divine Right and Democracy: an Anthology of Political Writing in Stuart England* (Harmondsworth, 1986) p. 362.

[46] Ibid. pp. 364, 367.   [47] Ibid. pp. 377–80.   [48] Ibid. pp. 367, 372, 381–3.

To these sources were added that theory according to which 'a tyrant, over whom every man is naturally a judge and an executioner . . . the laws of God, of nature, and of nations expose, like beasts of prey, to be destroyed as they are met'.[49] The association of this with a doctrine of just war ('*Bellum est in eos qui judiciis coerceri non possunt* . . . we have war with those against whom we can have no law') was attributed not only to 'the learned Grotius' but to Cicero, one of Grotius's own key sources.[50] Thus according to Grotius, 'everything is lawful against' a tyrant 'that is lawful against an open enemy, whom every private man has a right to kill'. For Tertullian similarly, against 'those that are traitors to the commonwealth, every man is a soldier'. It was on this basis that Cicero said that 'all good men . . . as much as in them lay, killed Caesar'. 'By these laws, and innumerable testimonies of authors, it appears that the Romans, with the rest of their philosophy, had learned from the Grecians what was the natural remedy against a tyrant.'[51] Among modern sources, in addition to Machiavelli and Grotius, particular mention was made of Sir Francis Bacon and 'the learned Milton'.[52]

HARRINGTON AND NEVILLE

As we should expect, a different attitude to resistance is encountered in Harrington's *Oceana* (1656). It was the purpose of this work, not to encourage tumults but to end them. In relation to the Protectorate it was Harrington's strategy not to argue for insurrection, but on the contrary to offer the Lord Protector a formula for the permanent achievement of his own ambition of 'healing and settling'. Accordingly not only did *Oceana* make no provision for legitimate resistance. It was a key feature of Harrington's constitution to render any such 'sedition' unnecessary, unlikely and futile.

It was unnecessary because the security of a regime depended upon its capacity to 'taketh in all *interests*'. The foundation of those interests was material: the balance of dominion (see chapter 7). Thus disaffection ('*corruption of Manners*') arose with 'the *Balance* altering a *People* as to the foregoing *Government*', as for instance with 'the *Ballance* swaying from *Monarchical* unto *Popular*'.[53] Thus the most important defence from

---

[49] Ibid. pp. 367, 364.
[50] Ibid. pp. 372–6: Grotius, *De Jure Belli* Book 1, pp. 10, 19, 21, 51; Scott, *Algernon Sidney and the English Republic* p. 19.
[51] Allen, *Killing Noe Murder* pp. 375–6.   [52] Ibid. pp. 380, 382.
[53] Harrington, *Oceana* (1656) pp. 45–6.

rebellion was to frame a governmental superstructure appropriate to the known foundation (in this case popular), and to prevent that balance from altering in the future (with an agrarian law). '[T]he greatest . . . fixation or security of a government . . . consist[s] . . . in an agrarian . . . our agrarian can never be the cause of . . . seditions . . . but is the proper cure of them'.[54] Both rebellions and tumults were symptoms of the imperfection or ill-ness of governments, particularly in the Gothic world, for which governors themselves were primarily responsible, and for which the establishment of a perfectly 'equal commonwealth' was the only genuine cure.

At the same time, however, Harrington took good care to design super-structures which were themselves proof against sedition. This was achieved by elaborate controls upon participation (including the secret and silent ballot, the segregation of debate from voting, and rotation) which radically limited the damage any disaffected private individuals could cause. Thus 'the nature of orders in a *Commonwealth* rightly instituted . . . [are] void of all Jealousie, because let the parties which she imbraceth be what they will, her orders are such, as they neither would resist if they could, nor could if they would'.[55]

And as man, seeing the world is perfect, can never commit any such sin as can render it imperfect or bring it unto a natural dissolution, so the citizen, where the commonwealth is perfect, can never commit any such crime as can render it imperfect or bring it unto a natural dissolution . . . If a commonwealth be a contradiction she must needs destroy herself; and if she be unequal, it tends to strife, and strife to ruin . . . but if it have neither of these, it hath no principle of mortality.[56]

The most important elements of this Harringtonian anatomy of rebellion survived into the Restoration work of Henry Neville. For Neville, too, rebellion was an evil signifying an illness of the body politic for which bad governments themselves were largely responsible. Thus,

Rebellion, which I believe to be not only a rising in Arms against any Government we live under, but . . . all clandestine Conspiracies too, by which the peace and quiet of any Country may be interrupted . . . I hold to be the greatest crime that can be committed amongst men, both against Policy [and] Morality . . . but . . . it is an offence which will be committed whilst the world lasts, as often as Princes tyranize, and by enslaving and oppressing their Subjects make Magistracy, which was intended for the benefit of mankind, prove a Plague and Destruction to it . . . If *Princes* will seriously consider this matter, I make no question but they will rule with Clemency and Moderation, and return to that excellent Maxim of the Ancients

---

[54] Harrington, *Oceana*, in *Works* pp. 235, 239.   [55] Ibid. p. 46.   [56] Ibid. pp. 320–1.

(almost exploded in this Age) that the interest of *Kings*, and of their people is the same.[57]

Significantly, however, at least in *Plato Redivivus* (1680), while continuing to abhor rebellion and civil war, Neville had recourse to the usual two modern authorities in support of the contention that even such acts might be consonant with justice:

> This is certain, that wherever any two coordinate powers do differ, and there be no power on earth to reconcile them otherwise, nor any umpire; they will, in fact, fall together by the ears. What can be done in this case justly, look into . . . Machiavel, and into Grotius; who in his book *De Jure Belli ac Pacis*, treated of such matters long before our wars. As for the ancient politicians, they must needs be silent in the point, as having no mixed governments amongst them; and as for me, I will not rest myself in so slippery a place.[58]

This was significant not only as a departure from Harrington, but because within this same political context Grotius would stand at the heart of the resistance theories of Locke and Sidney, with the addition of Machiavelli in the case of the latter.[59] This underlines the debt of Locke's *Two Treatises* to republican traditions of argument. As John Streater explained in 1659:

> The *Good Old Cause* was comprehended in these three particulars, *viz.* Security of *Life*, *Liberty*, and *Estate*. The *Laws of this Nation* speak no other *Language*. Contrary to which the *People* were invaded in the most miserable sort by the late K . . . [yet] the *Prince's* Authority is created upon no other ground, than the Consent of the *People*, to the End and Intent that the *People* should be preserved in their due and just Rights and Priviledges; the which being Invaded, the *People* may justly take up Arms to Defend . . . If a General of an Army shall Turn his Ordnance upon his Army, shall not it be Legal for them to oppose, nay destroy that General? . . . *Grotius* in his book *De Jure Belli* Part 1, *Sect.* 68, saith, *It is lawfull for the people to defend themselves by Arms, against the Illegal Cruelties of their Princes.*[60]

RESTORATION, 1660–1680

Sidney's *Court Maxims*, equally indebted to Grotius, anticipated Locke (as well as his own later *Discourses*) even more comprehensively. It was

---

57 [Henry Neville], *Nicholas Machiavel's Letter to Zanobius Buondelmontius in Vindication of Himself and His Writings* (1675), in *The Works of the Famous Nicholas Machiavel* (1675).

58 Neville, *Plato Redivivus* pp. 148–9.

59 In Sidney's *Discourses Concerning Government* (1698) and Locke's *Two Treatises of Government* (1689), both probably written between 1681 and 1683. See Scott, 'Law of War'.

60 Streater, *The Continuation* pp. 3–6.

not, however, the first work of the 1660s to argue for armed resistance against the restored monarchy. Moreover, unlike the *Maxims*, *A Treatise of the Execution of Justice* (1660) and *Mene Tekel; or, The Downfal of Tyranny* (1663) were both published, resulting in the execution of the printer of the latter. Both were grounded primarily in scripture, calling upon the 'Saints' to 'hear the Sighs and Groans of the Oppressed in every corner of the Land . . . in the day of [their] calamity . . . and deliver them'.[61] *A Treatise of Justice* argued that in commanding 'the People to Execute his Judgements upon the Transgressors of his Law', the Lord required 'that they ought to Execute Judgement upon the magistrate as well as any other'. Nor should the opprobrious word rebellion be applied to 'Just and Righteous Action[s], agreeable to the Law of Nature and Word of God'.[62] In particular, in insisting that '*it be the duty of the People to execute the Law of God upon Wicked Kings*', the *Treatise* took aim at quietist tendencies among the godly. In the face of a regime 'compelling the Nation to false worship, and [which] hath murdered hundreds of Saints in stinking Prisons for worshiping God according to his Word . . . We are not bound to suffer patiently . . . for there would be no living in the world, if we were bound to stand still and let any man that would, rob, wound or kill us.'[63] This was affirmed by 'many Presidents of those famous and faithfull Witnesses of Christ the *Waldenses*, the *Hollanders, Scots, French Protestants* . . . and our own Country-men, who have executed Justice upon their Kings'.[64]

Many of these themes were taken up by the more explicitly republican *Mene Tekel*, which took broader aim at the social, religious and political consequences of restored 'Tyranny . . . both in Church and State'. This was illustrated by examples not only biblical but Roman (in particular Nero), and with the help of sources and arguments which had previously appeared both in Milton's *Tenure* and in *Killing Noe Murder*. Like *A Treatise of Justice*, *Mene Tekel* addressed itself to the problem of the 'slavish spirit . . . upon *England* at this day! That we should suffer our enemies to domineer over us, and give them such excessive wages for keeping us in slavery.'[65] To the now newly reiterated text of Romans 13, *Mene Tekel* had the same response as that deployed by parliamentary resistance theorists at the outset of the civil war:

The Power the Apostle forbids us to resist, is a Power that if we do well, we shall have praise of the same, *Rom.*13.3. but an oppressing unrighteous Power, doth

[61] *A Treatise of the Execution of Justice, wherein it is clearly proved, that the Execution of Judgement and Justice, is as well the Peoples as the Magistrates Duty* (1660) p. 7
[62] Ibid. pp. 8–9, 12.   [63] Ibid. pp. 22, 26.   [64] Ibid. p. 31.
[65] *Mene Tekel; or, The Downfal of Tyranny* (1663) pp. 37, 41, 43.

not praise us when we do well, therefore we may resist that . . . Tyrants and
Oppressors . . . which are not God's but the Devil's Vicegerents . . . have been
often resisted by the Lord's People, as . . . the *French, Bohemians, Scots*, and most,
if not all the Protestant Nations.[66]

A parliamentary colonel wounded in action at Marston Moor, in 1659
Sidney had defended the regicide as 'the justest and bravest action that ever
was done in England, or anywhere'.[67] He was, according to Burnet, 'such
an enemy to every thing that looked like a monarchy, that he set himself in high opposition against Cromwell when he was made Protector'.[68]
During the writing of the *Court Maxims* (1665–6), Sidney was negotiating
with Dutch and French governments for support for a republican invasion
of England.[69] During the writing of the *Discourses*, he lectured his hesitant colleagues concerning 'the necessity we were reduced to, of taking up
arms . . . and . . . the lawfulness of it', and assured them that 'the oppressions . . . in Scotland . . . were so grievous, that (as he was inform'd) the
hearts of all the common people were set upon an insurrection to shake off
their yokes'.[70] In both cases, as befitted a descendant of Sir Philip Sidney,
Sidney's understanding of the issues at stake centred upon religion. As he
wrote to his fellow conspirator John Hampden Jr from his cell in the Tower
in October 1683:

Noblemen, Cittyes, Commonaltyes have often taken armes . . . to defend themselves, when they weare prosecuted upon the acount of religion . . . Somme may
say the protestants of Holland, France, or the valleys of Piedmont, weare guilty of
treason, in bearing armes against their princes, but [this] . . . is ridiculous . . . when
it is certaine, they sought noe more then the security of their owne lives.[71]

Like its 1660s predecessors, Sidney's *Court Maxims* began with the
assertion that the restored monarchy was a tyranny against which resistance was not only permissable but essential. This was underpinned by
a broader republican argument in support of the claim that in modern

---

[66] Ibid. p. 72 (the phrase order within this quote has been slightly altered); *Scripture and reason pleaded
   for defensive arms* (1643), quoted in Andrew Sharp (ed.), *Political Ideas of the English Civil Wars
   1641–1649* (1983) pp. 62–5.
[67] Scott, *Algernon Sidney and the English Republic* pp. 92–3.
[68] British Library, Add MS 63,057. Burnets' 'History of My Own Time', p. 341.
[69] Scott, *Algernon Sidney and the English Republic* ch. 11.
[70] Ford, Lord Grey, *The Secret History of the Rye House Plot* (1754) p. 51; Scott, *Algernon Sidney and the
   Restoration Crisis* ch. 12.
[71] East Sussex Record Office, Lewes, Glynde Place Archives no. 794, Letter from Algernon Sidney,
   probably to John Hampden Jr., 6 October 1683.

Europe monarchy and tyranny were indistinguishable.[72] In addition Sidney's response to the religious persecution of this period was to oppose the renunciation of that force which offered the only means of self-defence: 'At this day we find none to espouse these opinions but our Quakers, some few Anabaptists in Holland and Germany, and some of the Socinians in Poland. It is most generally known all christian churches have rejected the opinion of those that thought no use of the sword lawful, having made use of it against such princes and their ministers as have governed contrary to law.'[73] Later the *Discourses* would reiterate that 'Christians used prayers and tears only . . . whilst they had no other arms.'[74] Renunciation of force was not possible while the bishops themselves behaved like 'most savage wolves'. 'Those that by violence are brought to the hard necessity of sinning against God or suffering their families to be ruined and persons perpetually imprisoned, banished or murdered, may seem enough to justify those who by force seek to repel such violence.'[75] The bishops

preach patience that people may submit to their tyranny, as the thief persuades the traveller to go unarmed that he may safely rob and kill him . . . Who will endure that bishops, the greatest incendiaries in the whole world, should now preach the highest meekness? They who said . . . it is better England should be dispeopled, the best men in the nation banished and destroyed, than that their lusts should be resisted . . . No impudence is greater than that of those who preach doctrine so contrary to their practice.[76]

Christian pacifism under these circumstances made society ungovernable: it was 'disallowing the use of force, without which innocency could not be protected, nor society manintain'd'. That is why even Grotius considered resistance to authority justified in cases 'of the extremest injury', because such a transgressor 'breaks the common pact by which humane society is established . . . [and in doing so] renders himself a delinquent'. 'Whence I infer that, no man having a just power over my conscience, whoever offers violence to it, or to me for it, injures me in what is most dear unto me, [and] gives me a right in self-defence of repelling the injury.' The authority of Grotius on this point was seconded by that of Livy.[77]

As the most substantial early construction of the case for armed self-defence against restoration, particularly in its religious manifestation, it is not surprising that the *Maxims* anticipates much of Sidney's and

---

[72] Thus, although Sidney says in the last chapter, following Aristotle, 'I dare not say all monarchy is absolutely unlawful' (p. 200), in fact the tract as a whole is directed against not simply tyranny but monarchy. See Scott, *England's Troubles* pp. 299–305.
[73] Sidney, *Court Maxims* pp. 101–3.   [74] Sidney, *Discourses*, ed. West, p. 358.
[75] Sidney, *Court Maxims* p. 102.   [76] Ibid. p. 103.   [77] Ibid. pp. 101–2.

Locke's later classic treatments of the same subject. The option of force was particularly important to Sidney because the restored monarchy 'so well remember[s] the temper of [our subject's] swords, that we avoid all disputes that are determined that way'.[78]

SIDNEY'S *DISCOURSES*

That Locke's and Sidney's works shared the common ground of Grotian natural law theory is partly explicable on polemical grounds. Filmer had written to attack that doctrine of 'the natural freedom of mankind' and Grotius's *De Jure Belli* in particular. Tyrell's *Patriarcha Non Monarcha* showed an even greater preoccupation with the defence of Grotius against Filmer.[79] For Locke and Sidney, however, the shared refutation of Filmer was the preliminary to a practical end. This was to relay the basis for that very 'Popular sedition' against which Filmer had written. When Locke spoke '*Of the Dissolution of Government*' he referred in general to 'Miscarriages of those in Authority' which contradicted 'the ends for which Government is instituted' and by which, accordingly, that authority 'is forfeited'.[80] More specifically, 'As Usurpation is the exercise of Power, which another hath a Right to; so *Tyranny* is *the exercise of Power beyond Right*, which no Body can have a Right to.'[81] In his turn Sidney detailed the measures necessary 'against an usurping tyrant, or the perfidiousness of a lawfully created magistrate, who adds the crimes of ingratitude and treachery to usurpation'.[82] 'Why should . . . kings not be deposed, if they set up an interest in their own persons inconsistent with the publick good, for the promoting of which they were erected?'[83]

Both men identified Filmer as a modern ideological innovator who had destroyed political peace. 'In this last age', wrote Locke, 'a generation of men has sprung up . . . As if they had designed to make War upon all Government.' Filmer, repeats Sidney, 'seems to denounce war against mankind, endeavouring to overthrow the principle in which God created us'.[84] Both then go on to identify this 'generation of men' identically. They are those who believe that, in Locke's words, 'all Government is absolute Monarchy'; in Sidney's, that 'there is but one government in the world'.

---

[78] Ibid. p. 118.
[79] Filmer, *Patriarcha* p. 4; [James Tyrell], *Patriarcha Non Monarcha* (1681) pp. 10, 18–19, 20, 97–126.
[80] John Locke, *Two Treatises of Government*, ed. Peter Laslett 2nd edn (Cambridge, 1967) ch. 19 esp. pp. 424, 446.
[81] Locke, *Two Treatises* II, para. 199.
[82] Sidney, *Discourses*, in *Sydney on Government* pp. 193–4.
[83] Sidney, *Discourses*, ed. West, pp. 53, 226, 392.
[84] Locke, *Two Treatises* I, para. 3; Sidney, *Discourses*, in *Sydney on Government* p. 3.

According to Sidney, 'no-one had impudence enough . . . to publish [such] doctrines . . . till these times. The production of Laud, Manwaring, Sibthorp, Hobbes, Filmer, and Heylin, seems to have been reserved . . . to complete the shame and misery of our age and country.' Locke agreed: 'By whom this Doctrine came at first to be broach'd, and brought in fashion amongst us, and what sad Effects it gave rise to, I leave to *Historians* to relate, or to the Memory of those who were Contemporaries with *Sibthorp* and *Manwaring* to recollect.'[85]

What was contained within these observations was a threat. Filmer's ideology was a declaration of war, associated with those held responsible for creating the conditions for the last civil war. This threat had been made earlier in the same year by *A Just and Modest Vindication of the Proceedings of the Two last Parliaments* (1681). Replying to Charles II's *Declaration*, justifying the dissolution of his two last parliaments, the *Vindication* had observed:

The first Declaration of this sort which I ever met with, being that which was published in the year 1628[9] . . . was so far from answering the ends of its coming out, that it filled the whole kingdom with jealousies, and was one of the first sad causes of the ensuing unhappy war.[86]

Richard Ashcraft believed that the *Vindication* was written by Robert Ferguson, like Locke a client of the Earl of Shaftesbury. In fact it was written, as Burnet tells us, by Algernon Sidney, with his friend the Attorney General Sir William Jones.[87] For opponents of crown policy, the principal political issue after April 1681 was the indefinite suspension of parliaments. The obstruction of parliaments had been the major political issue throughout this crisis, as under Charles I. By 1683 Sidney was attempting to organise a repetition of the events of the year 1640. This would have seen a Scots rebellion forcing the summoning of parliament upon a popish and arbitrary monarch.[88]

Yet if suspension of parliaments was the major issue, it was not from 1681 the most pressing practical problem. It was the loyalist reaction, both political and religious, which forced the crown's opponents into armed self-defence. Specifically it was the loss of control of the government of the City of London that lay at the heart of the practical emergency of mid-1682. For it was by this event that the judicial powers of a murderously politicised

[85] Locke, *Two Treatises* I, para. 2, and pp. 160–1; Sidney, *Discourses*, in *Sydney on Government* pp. 1, 4–5.
[86] Sidney [and Jones], *A Just and Modest Vindication* p. cxxxvi.
[87] Richard Ashcraft, *Revolutionary Politics and John Locke's Two Treatises of Government* (Princeton, 1986) pp. 317–18; Scott *Algernon Sidney and the Restoration Crisis* pp. 186–7.
[88] Ibid. chs. 10, 12.

shrievalty were wrested back for use against its opponents by the crown.[89] This involved the overturning by force of a legitimate vote, taken by over a thousand people. A riot ensued, during which the ejected sheriff Slingsby Bethel and his patron Sidney were both arrested for incitement.[90] The agent of this coup was the loyalist Lord Mayor, Sir John Moore, who followed his instructions in claiming the right to impose new sheriffs. Bethel later claimed:

Sir John More . . . overthrew all the Rights of the City relating to the Choice of officers, and thereby laid us open to a Deluge of Misery and Blood . . . the Right of Electing Sheriffs belongs to the Freemen, so our Ancestors have been in nothing more careful than that all Elections should be managed with Freedom, without Fraud [or] force . . . [The Mayor's crime is great to] make the King lose the love and confidence of five parts in six of the whole City . . . [and] to engage the King in a visible Contest with a Great People, in a point that they will not part with, and which his Majesty cannot wrest from them, without declining from the course of the Law, which both his Justice and his Oath oblige him against.[91]

Locke subsequently listed three of the four principal ways by which governments are dissolved from within:

when [the] . . . Prince sets up his own Arbitrary Will in place of the Laws . . . declared by the Legislative . . . When the Prince hinders the Legislative from assembling in its due time, or from acting freely . . . [and] When by the Arbitrary Power of the Prince, the Electors, or ways of Election are altered, without the Consent, and contrary to the common Interest of the People.[92]

The final cause of political dissolution, explained Locke, was when the prince violently 'invade[s] the Property of the Subject . . . to make [himself] . . . Arbitrary disposer of the Lives, Liberties or Fortunes of the People'. What defence could there be now that the laws themselves had become instruments of political vengeance? In the words placed by Dryden into the mouth of Charles II:

> Why am I forc'd, like Heav'n, against my mind,
> To make Examples of another kind?
> Must I at length the Sword of justice draw?
> Oh Cursed Effects of necessary Law![93]

---

[89] Ibid.; Scott, 'Law of War'.
[90] *An Impartial Account of the Proceedings of the Common Hall of the City of London at Guildhal* (24 June 1682); Scott, *Algernon Sidney and the Restoration Crisis* pp. 272–4.
[91] [Slingsby Bethel], *The Right of Chusing Sheriffs* (1689) pp. 2–3.
[92] Locke, *Two Treatises* 11, paras. 214–16.
[93] John Dryden, *Absalom and Achitophel*, 5th edn, revised (1682) p. 30.

The king having informed Barillon that he would have to 'cutt off a few heads' to restore order, a series of executions followed.[94] The relevance of Grotius in this situation is not difficult to see. With the king's 'Arbitrary will in place of the Law' there was not only no tribunal of municipal law binding the king to his opponents. With the civil war being refought through the courts, there was no law in England now but the law of war.

Under these circumstances both men echoed Nedham on Grotius in insisting that rights of international war also applied domestically. According to Locke,

That *Subjects*, or *Foreigners* attempting by force on the Properties of any People, may be *resisted* with force, is agreed on all hands. But that *Magistrates* doing the same thing, may be *resisted*, hath of late been denied . . . Wheras their Offence . . . is greater . . . as being ungrateful, for the [power] . . . they have by the Law.[95]

Sidney repeated:

[as the sword of war was given by God] to protect the people against the violence of foreigners . . . [so] the sword of justice is put into the[ir] hands for protection against internal injury . . . The people think it the greatest of crimes to convert that power to their hurt which was instituted for their good . . . [and] that the injustice is aggravated by ingratitude.

'Nor let anyone think', said Locke, 'that this lays a perpetual foundation for Disorder: for this operates not, till the Inconvenience is so great, that the Majority feel it . . . and find a necessity to have it amended.' 'If it be said', echoes Sidney,

that this may sometimes cause disorders, I acknowledge it; but no human condition being perfect, such a one is to be chosen, which carries with it the most tolerable inconveniences . . . it being much better that the . . . excesses of a prince should be restrained or suppressed, than that whole nations should perish by them . . . no nation having been so happy, as not sometimes to produce such princes as Edward and Richard the second.[96]

Of these two statements, of course, the political implications were very different. One involved the inflection of Grotius towards the querulous Puffendorf; the other towards the warlike Machiavelli.[97] Locke was not, like Sidney, a 'Christian soldier', but a lifetime advocate of peace. For him

---

[94] Leopold von Ranke, *A History of England Principally in the Seventeenth Century* (6 vols. Oxford, 1875) vol. IV, p. 188.

[95] Locke, *Two Treatises* II, para. 231.   [96] Ibid. para. 224; Sidney, *Discourses*, ed. West, pp. 523–4.

[97] Sidney was here glossing Machiavelli's *Discourses* p. 121: 'So in all human affairs one notices . . . that it is impossible to remove one inconvenience without another emerging . . . Hence in all discussions one should consider which alternative involves fewer inconveniences.'

accordingly, the 'right of war', however presently necessary, was antithetical to the normal functioning of political society. If the intrusion of royal force made peace impossible, the right of war which resulted was not a fact of political relations but a consequence of their dissolution. That is why, although Locke shared with Sidney Grotius's preoccupation with war as an instrument of justice, unlike him he followed Puffendorf in carefully restricting its scope. According to Puffendorf, 'the Right of War, which always attends all Men in the State of Nature, is taken from private persons in Commonwealths . . . and Civil States . . . no private subject hath a Right of War'. Grotius, by contrast, had opposed the view that 'since the establishment of public tribunals, all rights to private war cease'. They 'still hold good . . . where judicial procedure ceases to be available . . . or where those . . . administering the law refuse to take cognizance'.[98] This was Sidney's view. But for Locke, as for Puffendorf, this 'Right' was applicable only in a state of nature, where there was no 'common establish'd Law and Judicature to appeal to'. In this case what Locke called his 'strange doctrine' of the 'Executive Power of the Law of Nature' gave people a 'Right of War'. '[F]orce . . . where there is no common Superior on Earth to appeal to . . . *is the State of War* . . . 'tis the want of such an appeal gives a man the Right of War . . . against an *agressor*.'[99]

For Locke, then, the right to resist was not a political but a natural right. It arose only after the dissolution of government, and responsibility for this desperate state of affairs rested with the monarch. It was arbitrary governors who, by invading their subjects' property, contradicted the end of their own institution and so laid 'a Foundation for perpetual Disorder . . . Tumult, Sedition and Rebellion'. Specifically they 'introduce[d] a state of War' where previously there had been peace. It was therefore such *monarchs* who were '*Rebels . . . Rebellare* [being] . . . to bring back again [a] state of War'.[100] Sidney's contextualisation of the right of war, though closely related to Locke's, was crucially different. When Sidney made the same etymological point about 'rebellion', perhaps informed by his or his father's reading of Livy,[101] his purpose was not to redirect the odium of it onto the government, but to defend it, both word and thing. Thus 'rebellion is not always evil':

---

[98] Samuel von Puffendorf, *The Law of Nature and Nations* (1749), Book 8, ch. 6, 'Of the Right of War', para. 8; Grotius, *De Jure Belli*, Book 1, ch. 3, para. 2.

[99] Locke, *Two Treatises* p. 298.

[100] Ibid. II, para. 226.

[101] In 1652 Sidney's father, the 2nd Earl of Leicester, recorded in his Commonplace Book: 'though Livy use the word Rebellare, that seems to be the makin warr again; rather than to imply subjection . . . Rebellare is used frequently in Livy.' Kent Archives Office, Maidstone, De Lisle MS, U1475 Z1/9, Commonplace Book of Robert Sidney, 2nd Earl of Leicester, loose pages, fourth item, f.2.

That this may appear, it will not be amiss to consider the word . . . [which] is taken from the Latin *rebellare*, which signifies no more than to renew a war . . . Rebellion, being nothing but a renewed war . . . of itself is neither good nor evil, more than any other war; but is just or unjust according to the cause or manner of it.[102]

No less remarkably, Sidney went on to justify the very 'seditions, tumults and wars' from which Locke had just dissociated himself. Here, as in relation to change, Sidney took from Machiavelli an inspiration precisely opposite to that of Harrington. The political provocation involved was not lessened by his insertion of the word 'civil' before 'wars': 'It is vain to seek a government in all points free from a possibility of civil wars, tumults and seditions: that is a blessing denied to this life, and reserved to complete the felicity of the next.' What must be asked, therefore, is not whether they ought to occur, but whether they are just or unjust:

It may seem strange to some that I mention seditions, tumults and wars, upon just occasions; but I can find no reason to retract the term . . . the law that forbids injuries, were of no use, if no penalty, might be inflicted on those that will not obey it. If injustice therefore be evil, and injuries forbidden, they are also to be punished; and the law instituted for their prevention, must necessarily intend the avenging of such as cannot be prevented.[103]

Thus a 'tumult' was simply the 'trial by force, to which men come, when other ways are ineffectual'. One possible result was the 'vengeance' for which Sidney had been calling since the execution of Sir Henry Vane in 1662, and which Milton praised in *Samson Agonistes* ('O dearly-bought revenge, yet glorious!'[104]).

The ways of . . . punishing injuries, are judicial or extrajudicial. Judicial proceedings are of force against those who submit or may be brought to trial; but are of no effect against those who resist, and are of such power that they cannot be constrained. It were absurd . . . and impious to think that he who has added treachery to his other crimes, and usurped a power above the law, should be protected by the enormity of his wickedness. Legal proceedings therefore are to be used when the delinquent submits to the law; and all are just, when he will not.[105]

Under such circumstances, indeed, 'Extrajudicial proceedings, by sedition, tumult or war, must take place', and 'whosoever condemns all seditions, tumults and wars raised against such princes, must say, that none . . . seek the ruin of their people, which is absurd, for Caligula wish'd the people

---

[102] Sidney, *Discourses*, ed. West, pp. 519–22.   [103] Ibid. p. 219.
[104] John Milton, *Samson Agonistes* (1671), in *John Milton: a Critical Edition of Major Works*, ed. Stephen Orgel and Jonathan Goldberg (Oxford, 1991) line 1660, p. 713.
[105] Sidney, *Discourses*, ed. West, p. 220.

had but one neck, that he might cut it off at a blow: Nero set the city on fire, and we have known such as have been worse than either of them'.[106] It was thus hardly surprising, if also a legal scandal, that in 1683 Sidney's manuscript would be used to convict its author of 'levying war against the king',[107] leaving him time to record in his *Apology* (1683), 'as I had from my youth endeavoured to uphold the Common rights of mankind, the lawes of this land, and the true Protestant religion, against corrupt principles, arbitrary power, and Popery, I doe now willingly lay down my life for the same'.[108]

---

[106] Ibid. p. 226.   [107] Scott, *Algernon Sidney and the Restoration Crisis* chs. 13–14.
[108] Algernon Sidney, *The Apology of Algernon Sydney, in the Day of his Death*, in *Sydney on Government*; Scott, *Algernon Sidney and the Restoration Crisis* pp. 336–8.

CHAPTER 6

Constitutions

All . . . things [which] depend on the person of a man . . . must . . . necessarily be perpetually wavering and uncertain, according to the life of him that gives the impulse unto them. But in commonwealths it is not men but laws, maxims, interests, and constitutions that govern: men die or change, but these remain unalterable. A senate or assembly . . . may be capable of some passions and be deceived. But their passions are not so easily moved when composed of many men of the greatest experience and choicest parts, nor are they so easily deceived as one man, who, perhaps, has small parts, little experience, and is informed by none but those who endeavour to deceive him.

Algernon Sidney, *Court Maxims* (1665)[1]

INTRODUCTION: THE EMPIRE OF LAWS AND NOT OF MEN

One essential means to the achievement of republican objectives was an appropriate constitutional framework. The constitution held liberty in its hand and enabled it to transcend not only the temporal but moral fragility of particular persons. The superiority of republican government over that of princes was partly a product of these and other aspects of the 'empire of laws and not of men'.[2] Nevertheless, in relation to the absolute moral ends of self-government, constitutions were themselves particular, and adaptable. Constitutions, 'depending upon future Contingents . . . must be alterable according to circumstances and accidents'. 'It is not so much the form of the administration as the thing administered, wherein the good or evil of government doth consist.'[3]

Thus when Algernon Sidney described constitutions as 'unalterable' he meant so only relatively:

---

[1] Sidney, *Court Maxims* pp. 27–8.   [2] Harrington, *Oceana*, in *Political Works* p. 161.
[3] Dzelzainis, 'Milton's Classical Republicanism' pp. 19–20; Nedham, *Mercurius Politicus* no. 354, 19–26 March 1657, p. 7675; Vane, quoted in Scott, 'The English Republican Imagination' pp. 40–5.

131

As there may be some universal rules in physic, architecture, and military discipline, from which men ought never to depart, so there are some in politics also which ought always to be observed; and wise legislators, adhering to them only, will be ready to change all others, as occasion may require, in order to the public good. This we may learn from Moses, who laying the foundation of the law . . . in that justice, charity and truth, which having its root in God is subject to no change, left them the liberty of [ordering all other things] . . . as best pleased themselves.[4]

This was in line with the general 'characteristic of humanist political thought', that it was 'concerned less with the fabric of institutions' than with 'the spirit and outlook of the men who run them'.[5] Alongside humanist relativism it was equally characteristic of radical protestant anti-formalism that 'Wise and prudent men are to consider what is profitable and fit for a people in general [only]; for it is very certain that the same sort of government is not equally convenient for all nations, nor for the same nation at all times.'[6] Thus although it was essential that liberty achieve stable constitutional expression to result in virtue, the value of constitutions themselves was purely instrumental. Particular laws were subject, from the standpoint of obedience as well as of moral truth, to the 'universall' and 'eternall . . . Law of God and Nature'.[7] 'Whatsoever written Law contradicteth the Law of God, nature and reason, is *ipso facto* void.'[8] 'That which is not just is not Law, and that which is not Law ought not to be obeyed.'[9] Nor was stability itself always accorded pre-eminent status within the republican hierarchy of values. For these and other reasons many of the most important republican writers remained relatively uninterested in constitutional details. Nor, since constitutions were contingent and mutable, do we find within English republicanism any universal constitutional prescription. Not even James Harrington claimed to have deduced a constitutional model suitable for all places and all times. Harrington's 'Principles of Government' identified by *Oceana*'s two great discoveries (the 'balance of dominion' and 'dividing and choosing') were universal truths founded upon God's 'footsteps in nature'.[10] Their constitutional implications in any given situation were, however, contingent upon the particularities of that place and time. What distinguished Harrington were two further beliefs emanating from his natural philosophy. The first was that the basis of these principles was material

---

[4] Sidney. *Discourses*, in *Sydney on Government* pp. 144, 404.
[5] Skinner, *Foundations of Modern Political Thought* vol. 1, p. 46.   [6] Milton, *Defence* p. 79.
[7] Streater, *A Glympse* p. 9; Streater, *A Continuation* p. 4; Streater, *Observations* no. 1, p. 3.
[8] Wither, *Respublica Anglicana* p. 36. See also Milton, *Defence* p. 169: '[I]f any law or custom be contrary to the law of God, of nature, or of reason, it ought to be looked upon as null and void.'
[9] Sidney, *Discourses* Chapter 3, Section 11 title.
[10] Harrington, *Oceana*, in *Political Works* pp. 161, 163, 172.

(they identified God's footsteps, not simply within created man, but within nature). For this reason, secondly, if embodied appropriately such a constitution (an 'equal commonwealth') might transcend its particularity in time. It was on the basis of these assumptions that the elaboration of Harrington's thirty orders, in his 'The Model of the Commonwealth', accounted for the bulk of *Oceana*'s length, dwarfing his account of 'The Principles of Government' in 'The First Preliminary'.

Yet if constitutional thought did not stand at the heart of republican writing as a whole, and if there was no single constitutional prescription, it does not follow that it was insignificant. If the level of constitutional specificity in Harrington's *Oceana* was exceptional, the invocation of exemplar states, and constitutional prescriptions at a higher level of generality, were common. They were also an important indicator of development over time. For in this area, more than most, positions were adopted, contested and abandoned in response not simply to the sources informing the republican tradition, but to public political developments and debates.

At the highest level of generality, the constitutional formula to which all republicans subscribed was that the government of a commonwealth consisted in the rule of laws, rather than of men. As Plato had explained in *The Laws*: 'Where the law is subject to some other authority and has none of its own, the collapse of the state . . . is not far off; but if the law is the master of the government and the government is its slave, then the situation is full of promise.'[11] This insight was developed in Aristotle's *Politics*, along with an account of the moral purpose of political association to which English republican writing was equally deeply indebted. Collective self-government by law ('written reason') was superior to the government of a single man, because it strengthened the rational against the passionate part of the soul. It did this by deploying a constitutional framework which functioned as an institutional expression of collective rationality.

From the same Greek sources, and others, English republicans derived a shared constitutional language, which spoke of government by the one, the few or the many.[12] This terminology was subsequently used by Polybius, Cicero and Machiavelli to argue that these forms should in some way be combined.[13] At the heart of classical republicanism a series of historians have discerned what they have described as the Polybian notion of the mixed constitution. According to John Pocock, and more recently Arihiro

---

[11] Plato, *The Laws* p. 174.

[12] Aristotle's point of departure for the constitutional analysis of *The Politics* (pp. 20–33) is a critical discussion of Plato's *Republic* and *Laws*.

[13] Machiavelli, *Discourses* pp. 109–24.

Fukuda, this first burst onto the English scene in King Charles I's *Answer to the Nineteen Propositions* (1642).[14] Yet far from marking the arrival of a new, specifically republican perception, the publication of a mixed constitution analysis by the king's moderate advisers more plausibly demonstrates that this analysis transcended the divide between republican (or parliamentarian) and royalist. It was, that is to say, contested real estate within a struggle for the status of legitimate guardian of the ancient constitution.

Moreover, throughout the late medieval and early modern periods this language had been deployed by writers as various as Fortescue, Erasmus and Francois Hotman to argue the case for legal, bounded or 'political' monarchy. However, by the mid-seventeenth century, the subsequent republican argument ran, government which was moderate, mixed and dedicated to the public good could no longer be provided by the rule of a single person (see chapter 1). One of Harrington's accomplishments in this context was to reconfigure this Aristotelian constitutionalism from its defunct mixed monarchy framework as the shape of a now materially essential English republic. This was an attempt, in a Protectoral context, to acclimatise English republicanism by giving it a more traditional, and mixed, constitutional form. Within republicanism adherence to the doctrine of a mixed constitution was limited before 1653, and fiercely disputed between 1653 and 1660. Among republicans by far the most important such adherent was Harrington, whose associates during the 1640s were not other republicans, but moderate royalists (like those who had penned the *Answer*) and the king himself.[15] Further, even by Harrington (and other republicans) the invocation of Polybius was rare, and that of Plato, Aristotle and Cicero ubiquitous. Finally, as actually developed in *Oceana*, Harrington's doctrine of 'the balance' was not Polybian. In Polybius this had referred to (in Harrington's terms) a balance within the tripartite constitutional superstructure. In *Oceana* it became 'the balance of dominion', denoting the predominant ownership of property within a material 'foundation' upon which the whole superstructure would stand.

Thus there are many obstacles to the argument that the classic English republican constitutional prescription was the Polybian mixed constitution. The idea was developed late, partly from moderate royalist thought, to

---

[14] Fink, *Classical Republicans*; Pocock, *Machiavellian Moment* pp. 361–6; Michael Mendle, *Dangerous Positions: Mixed Government, the Estates of the Realm, and the Making of the Answer to the XIX Propositions* (Birmingham, Ala., 1985); Fukuda, *Sovereignty and the Sword* chs. 1–2; Scott, Review of Fukuda pp. 660–2.

[15] Burgess, 'Repacifying the Polity' relates the thought of both Harrington and Hobbes to this intellectual background of 'constitutional royalism'.

counter the extremes advocated by Hobbes on the one hand, and partisan commonwealthsmen on the other. When it was so, it is not clear that Polybius was the source (Machiavelli is more likely, as Fukuda concedes). By 1656, however, amid the contested interregnum search for settlement, the issue of the appropriate constitutional form had been placed on the agenda with new centrality.

POPULAR UNICAMERALISM, 1623–1654

The first important seventeenth-century exemplar republic was neither Venice nor Rome, but the United Provinces. In the remarkable words of Thomas Scott, an inhabitant of Norwich where Dutch influence was pronounced: 'what need wee seeke for *Plato his communitie*, or Sir *Thomas More* his *Utopia*, when the realitie of their wishes and best conceptions are brought into action; and the best of whatever they fancied . . . is heere seene truly to bee, after a most exact and corrected Copie?'[16] Or in those later given by Sidney to his courtier Philalethes:

[Concerning] the United Provinces . . . we . . . look on their power and riches, the security, happiness, and prosperity they enjoy in a commonwealth, as a most pernicious example to England. Others leave their native countries . . . to seek new seats in Holland, of all Europe the most unwholesome, unpleasant, unprovided, of all things requisite to the life of man; yet through good government and liberty of traffic so rich, powerful and prosperous that no state in Europe dares singly contest with it. This example is so full and clear in our sight, that all our arguments for the splendour of a court and glory of a king . . . are destroyed, and the people naturally inclined to liberty.[17]

Yet the exemplar status of the United Provinces was attained despite, rather than because of, its constitution. It stood for liberty, both religious and political; good government, commercial prosperity, and successful war against Spain; and for a stern, and frugal, integrity of manners (both protestant and republican). As we have seen, when Milton celebrated the superior political manners of republics he had the United Provinces in mind.[18] Harrington, by contrast, emphasised the distance of the constitution of Oceana from such a federation as the United Provinces (or Switzerland), which 'tendeth . . . towards division'.[19] Sidney, too, admitted that federated republics 'composed of many cities associated together . . . every one retaining and exercising a sovereign power within itself . . . are more hardly preserved in

---

[16] Scott, *Belgicke Pismire* p. 90.   [17] Sidney, *Court Maxims* pp. 161–2.   [18] See pp. 55–6 above.
[19] Harrington, *The Art of Lawgiving* pp. 696–7; Harrington, *Aphorisms Political* p. 767.

peace'. Yet republics possessed sufficient other advantages to compensate for this problem: 'the cities of the United Provinces . . . still continuing in their union in spite of all the endeavours that have been used to divide them, give us an example of such steadiness in practice and principle, as is hardly to be parallel'd in the world, and that undeniably prove a temper in their constitutions directly opposite to that which our author [Filmer] imputes to all popular governments'.[20]

Nowhere before *The Readie and Easie Way* (1660) does Milton advocate a specific constitution. Until 1649 his celebration of English liberty is of a reviving moral and religious force; his savage criticism of the Long Parliament focuses not upon the manifest constitutional inadequacies of that body, but upon its members' deplorable moral and intellectual failures. Similarly, between 1649 and 1654, his writings are notable for their lack of interest in the constitutional niceties which gave other republicans pause. In *The Tenure* a military coup is rigorously justified, though without precedent, and by 'a few', because it was necessary for the survival of the cause. In the *Defence* (1651):

Our form of government is such as our circumstances and schisms permit; it is not the most desirable, but only as good as the stubborn struggles of the wicked citizens allow it to be. If, however, a country harassed by faction and protecting herself by arms regards only the sound and upright side, passing over or shutting out the others . . . she maintains justice well enough, and this too even though she has learned by her own woes to suffer no longer a king or his lords.[21]

This latitude even extended to Cromwell's dissolution of the Rump in April 1653, at least until those who 'wish to be free . . . recover your senses . . . learn to obey right reason, to master yourselves'. Cromwell is, at least, 'Commander over himself; victor over himself.'[22] A republican constitution exists to give public expression to that reason, liberty and virtues which are qualities of soul. This is 'true and substantial liberty, which must be sought, not without, but within, and which is best achieved, not by the sword, but by a life rightly undertaken and rightly conducted'.[23]

The case was otherwise for Marchamont Nedham, whose less severe approach to matters of personal morality was accompanied by a far more developed interest in constitutions. It is another irony in the career of a writer infamous for reputed lack of scruple that the genesis of Nedham's highly consistent line in these matters may be detected as early as 1645. Both *England's Miserie and Remedie* and *Mercurius Britanicus* invoked the

---

[20] Sidney, *Discourses*, ed. West pp. 206–7.   [21] Milton, *Defence* pp. 316–17.
[22] Milton, *Second Defence* pp. 668, 684.   [23] Ibid. p. 624.

example of '*Rome* (which remaineth a patterne and example to all Ages both for civill and Military government)'.[24] The following year *Vox Plebis* used Machiavelli's *Discourses* and Livy's *History* to develop this Roman example on behalf of the Leveller campaign. It was the lesson of Roman history that 'this Commonwealth ever thriv'd best, when the People had most power'.[25] The key constitutional development was the establishment of the tribunes. 'Now, and never till now, cou'd they be called a Free State, and Commonwealth . . . [for] not onely the Name of King, but the Thing King (whether in the hands of one or of many) was pluck'd up root and branch, before ever the Romans could attain to a full Establishment in their Rights and Freedoms.'[26]

This constitutional hostility to 'the few' was influenced by Machiavelli. For Machiavelli, however, what was important was that the few remain subordinate to the many, within an internally dynamic mixed constitution. Although in *Vox Plebis* Nedham quoted this passage of the *Discourses* approvingly, his own more extreme position was already manifest, and became constitutionally explicit in subsequent editorials of *Mercurius Politicus*. Sharing Machiavelli's belief that 'the People are the best *Keepers of Liberty*',[27] *Mercurius* followed him in rejecting Venice as a constitutional model. Nedham's anti-Venetian posture was, however, more extreme: the 'serene republic' was 'rather a *Juncta* then a *Common-weal*', whose 'subjects' preferred the '*Pagan Tyranny*' of the '*Turk*' to their own government.[28] More remarkable still was Nedham's other constitutional exemplar. Left to one side by Machiavelli because it did not have a mixed constitution, and later ridiculed by Harrington (following Hobbes) as a hotbed of demagoguery, this was democratic Athens.

Thus Nedham's celebrated Lawgiver was not Harrington's beloved Lycurgus, but Solon:

When the *Senators* of *Rome*, in their publick Decrees and Orations began to comply with and Court the *People*, calling them *Lords of the World*, how easie a matter was it then for *Gracchus* to perswade them to un-lord the *Senate*! In like manner, when *Athens* was quitted of *Kings*, the power was no sooner declared to be in the People, but immediately they took it, and made sure of it in their own hands, by the advice of *Solon*, that excellent Lawgiver.[29]

So excellent was Solon's work, in 'avoiding *Kingly Tyranny* on the one side, and *Senatoriall encroachments* on the other, hee is celebrated by all

---

[24] *England's Miserie* pp. 3–4.   [25] Nedham, *Excellencie* pp. 15–17.   [26] Ibid. pp. 12–13.
[27] Nedham, *Mercurius Politicus* no. 77, p. 1222.   [28] Ibid. no. 86, p. 1368.
[29] Ibid. no. 71, pp. 1125–6.

Posterity, as the man that hath left the only Patern of a *free state*, fit for all the world to follow'.[30] This admiration of Athens would find an echo in the Restoration writings of both Neville and Sidney.[31] For Nedham the histories of Athens, Argos, Corcyra, Rome and Florence all illustrated the importance of allowing no particular citizen to '*grow over-rich*' or achieve an 'overgrowth of *Grandeur*', and of permitting no '*Ranke*, or *Order* of Men, to assume unto themselves the State and Title of *Nobility*'.[32] Athens' aristocratic rival, Sparta, was also criticised, but less severely than Venice.[33]

In Nedham's subsequent constitutional guidelines for the maintenance of liberty, the overlap of Leveller and republican thought is most explicit.[34] Radical popular sovereignty was a matter, not simply of principle, but practice. Thus 'No Laws . . . whatsoever should be made, but by the Peoples consent and Election.' Such elections must result in 'a due and orderly succession of the Supreme Authority in the hands of the People's Representatives'.[35] Preservation of the people's liberties against faction, self-interest, overmighty grandees and 'upstart Tyrants' required not only the regular succession of legislative 'Supreme Assemblies', but equally rotation of executive magistracy ('succession of Powers and Persons').[36] During the interregnum, this anti-aristocratic Machiavellian populism was taken up by John Streater among others. Thus Streater emphasised, following Nedham, that one mark of a 'Free-people . . . is Elections annual . . . [whereby] Fools ordinarily are shut out, that may possibly come to lay claim to Government . . . by a right of Succession'.[37] Issue 5 of his *Observations* (1654) declared:

Machivil after a great deal of pro and con, ingeniously confesseth that a people are the best guard of those in power, and the best guardians of their own liberty . . . Read all Histories in the world, it shall be found that those who made the people their Sanctuary, have stood upon strong basis and have been durable, those that have made the Nobility their Sanctuary, have often, and do most commonly miscarry, the same may be said of an Army as of the Nobility, but this by the way.[38]

For a smaller number of republicans the best form of government was an 'elective Aristocracy', and Venice a powerful example in its support.[39]

---

[30] Ibid. no. 73 p. 1158.   [31] Neville, *Plato Redivivus* pp. 95–6.
[32] *Mercurius Politicus* no. 88, p. 1396; no. 89, p. 1406.   [33] Ibid. no. 90, p. 1434.
[34] A point made in relation to Nedham by Worden, 'Marchamont Nedham', and to Streater by Smith, 'Popular Republicanism'.
[35] Nedham, *Excellencie*, 'To the Reader'.   [36] Ibid. pp. 62–3.
[37] Streater, *Observations* no. 2 pp. 10–11.   [38] Ibid. no. 5, p. 35.
[39] *A Short Discourse between Monarchical and Aristocratical Government* (1649) pp. 11–16; John Cook, *Monarchy No Creature of God's Making* (1651) Dedication, p. 3; *A Perswasive to Mutuall Compliance under the Present Government. Together with A Plea for a Free State Compared with Monarchy* (18 February 1651) pp. 23–5.

What appears clear is that until the dissolution of the Rump, advocacy of one type or another of unicameral constitution was the dominant position among leaders of a single-chamber republic erected from a remnant of the House of Commons. Nor was this an issue animating the dissolution itself, which led to the replacement of one single-chamber assembly by another. It was, however, in the period 1654–6 that this position came to be challenged, from more than one direction. This was the same period which saw

England's transition from a republic, dedicated to the proposition that all just power derives from the people and that their representatives must therefore be sovereign, to a mixed government based on the principle of balance, not so much between the conventional elements of monarchy, aristocracy, and democracy as between the legisative, executive, and judicial powers in the state.[40]

THE MIXED CONSTITUTION, 1653–1658

To this extent it should not surprise us that the first important republican voice making the case for the superiority of a mixed constitution came from an apologist for the new *Instrument of Government*. Should it surprise us, at this stage in our study, that its author was none other than Marchamont Nedham? In his *A True State of the Case of the Commonwealth* (1654) Nedham explained that what had been established in the Protectorate was not a quasi-monarchy, but a constitutionally superior republic, in which the single person was 'not to exercise his Power by a Claim of Inheritance', but 'is *elective*, and that Election must take its rise originally and virtually from the People'.[41] The same person shared his power both with a council and with parliaments. Those parliaments were also elective, through a reformed constitution freer and fairer than under the previous monarchy, the exclusion of royalists notwithstanding. Finally this tripartite constitution, allowing for parliaments which were not perpetual, was proof against the tyranny of a single assembly. Thus 'though the *Common-wealth* may now appear with a new face in the outward Form, yet it remains still the same in Substance, and is of a better complexion and constitution then heretofore'. The *Instrument of Government* had at last established a stable defence of the people's 'plenary . . . Liberty as Christians . . . against Anarchie and Tyranny', by bringing together 'the Unitive vertue (but nothing else) of *Monarchy* . . . the admireable Counsel of *Aristocracie* . . . the industry and courage of *Democracie*'.[42]

[40] Austin Woolrych, *Commonwealth to Protectorate* (Oxford, 1982) p. 3.
[41] [Marchamont Nedham], *A True State of the Case of the Commonwealth* (1654) pp. 28–9.
[42] Ibid. pp. 52–3.

This was not Nedham's first visitation of the theme of separation of powers, which he had broached in *Mercurius Politicus* when discussing both
the ancient and present constitutions. *A True State* quoted directly from
Mercurius no. 109 of 1–8 July 1652, in which this position was made compatible with Nedham's Leveller/republican advocacy of Athenian/Roman
democracy by the specification that 'By the *Executive Power* we mean that
Power which is derived from the other', a capacity for 'the administration
of Government in the execution of those Laws', not for sharing in their
authorship.[43] On this occasion, however, Nedham made the same doctrine
into the basis for advocacy of a tripartite mixed constitution. Perhaps he
was serving the Protectorate by diluting his own unicameral commonwealth
principles with the constitutional thought of moderate royalism (especially
as deployed by the *Answer to the Nineteen Propositions*).

A second step away from a unicameral republican constitution came from
the ranks of the Lord Protector's most determined opponents. While most
'commonwealthsmen', among them Rump leaders Sir Arthur Haselrig and
Thomas Scot, continued to defend the undiluted sovereignty of a single
elected chamber, by 1656 Sir Henry Vane had published other ideas.[44]
This was a result of Vane's concern, allied to that of Milton, to protect
civil and spiritual liberty not only from those incapable of them, but from
those actively hostile. Here as elsewhere constitutional arrangements had
to be subservient to the pre-eminent value of principles emanating from
God. It was in this service that Vane's *A Healing Question* (1656) called
for 'a supream Judicature [to] be set up' only by those who 'have shewed
themselves, upon all occasions, desirers and lovers of true freedom, either
in civils, or in spirituals . . . by way of distinction from all Neuters, close and
open Enemies, and deceitful friends and Apostates'.[45] This should oversee
the establishment of

a standing Council of State setled for life . . . under the inspection and oversight
of the Supreme Judicature . . . [whose] orders were binding, in the intervals of
Supreme National Assemblies . . . [Neither] would there be any just exception to
be taken, if . . . it should be agreed . . . to place that branch of Soveraignty which
chiefly respects the execution of the Lawes, in a distinct office from that of the

---

[43] '*A Fifth* Error in Policy . . . hath been . . . *a permitting the Legislative and Executive Powers of a State
or Kingdom, to rest in one and the same hands and Persons* . . . In the keeping of these *two Powers*
distinct, flowing in distinct Channels, so that they may never meet in one . . . there lies a grand
Secret of *Liberty* and good Government' (pp. 1705–6).

[44] Barbara Taft's 'That Lusty Puss, the Good Old Cause', *History of Political Thought* 5, 3 (1984) furnishes
a useful history of the commonwealthsmen, though more attention is necessary to tensions and
differences between Rumpers, Vanists and Harringtonians, both in 1656 and 1659–60.

[45] Vane, *A Healing Question* pp. 9, 17.

legislative power (and yet subordinate to them and to the Lawes) . . . in the hands of one single person . . . or in a greater number, as the legislative power should think fit.[46]

The most significant constitutional intervention of this year was Harrington's *The Commonwealth of Oceana* (1656). Harrington's political purpose is discussed in chapter 13. What must be noted here is the way in which he drew upon all the elements of this debate to arrive at an independent constitutional position. In so doing one of his targets was that 'government of Oceana . . . consisting of one single council of the people, to the exclusion of the king and of the lords . . . invested with the whole power of government, without any covenants, conditions, or orders whatsoever. So new a thing that neither ancient nor modern prudence can show any avowed example of the like.'[47] In place of this boorish Gothic oligarchy, *Oceana* ransacked the archives of ancient prudence (Jewish, Spartan, Roman and Venetian) to arrive at the formula for a properly mixed and balanced commonwealth. On the other side, Harrington equally opposed those trying to complete the Protectorate's constitutional journey back towards monarchy. Unlike the *Instrument*, *Oceana* was a genuinely republican formulation which, in addition to separating the assemblies for debating and voting, replaced the government of a single person with a properly dispersed, and rotating, executive magistracy. Harrington's general target was all those 'parties into which this nation was divided . . . temporal or spiritual', who wished, like Vane, to exclude from the constitutional settlement all those unlike themselves: 'To the *Common-wealths-man* I have no more to say, but that if he exclude any party, he is not truly such; nor shall ever found a *Commonwealth* upon the natural principle of the same, which is *Justice*.'[48] Whereas for Milton and Vane, the success or failure of a republic depended upon the moral qualities of its citizens, for Harrington these were irrelevant. 'Give us good men, and they will make us good laws, is the maxim of a demagog, and is . . . exceeding fallible. But give us good orders, and they will make us good men, is the maxim of a legislator, and the most infallible in the politics.'[49]

In elaborating *Oceana*'s orders, Harrington insisted, against Hobbes, that these must be not monarchical but popular. In arriving at the constitutional formula for a commonwealth which was popular, however, he insisted, in sharp contrast to the anti-aristocratic rhetoric of Nedham and Streater, that such a constitution must be mixed. Here Harrington's insistence upon the

---

[46] Ibid. p. 18.   [47] Harrington, *Oceana, in Political Works* p. 205   [48] Ibid. p. 203.
[49] Quoted in Davis, *Utopia and the Ideal Society* p. 123 (and see the discussion pp. 206–40).

political importance of the gentry set him apart not only from such contemporaries, but from their shared sources. This is the more notable in that
Machiavelli's preference for social 'equality' had been one of his few points
of agreement with Thomas More.[50] This was the point that 'Machiavel
hath missed . . . very narrowly and more dangerously . . . [when] he speaks
of the gentry as hostile to popular governments, and of popular governments as hostile to the gentry'. The cause of this error was Machiavelli's
ignorance of the doctrine of the balance, and so of the fact that, the balance
being popular, the gentry were no more a danger to the security of the
commonwealth than citizens who had been royalists. On the contrary, 'a
nobility or gentry in a popular government, not overbalancing it, is the
very life and soul of it'.[51]

Accordingly, where Machiavelli had insisted, in contravention of the
Polybian doctrine of balance, that a republican mixed constitution must
place the 'guardianship of liberty' in the hands of either the few or the
many, Harrington disagreed, proposing a perfect equilibrium between
them. Where Machiavelli had juxtaposed stable Venice to expansionist
Rome, before choosing the latter as his exemplar, Harrington again made
great rhetorical play of refusing this choice, and disputing the necessity for
it, making Venice his political, and Rome his military model. Those tumults
and that capacity for internal mutation which Machiavelli had identified as
essential to Rome's mastery of *fortuna* were for Harrington the causes of its
collapse. This was because those changes Machiavelli ignorantly attributed
to fortune were in fact solely the outcome of constitutional imperfection.
Thus as 'Rome was crooked in her birth . . . [and] no man shall show me
a commonwealth born crooked that ever became straight', so

there never happened unto any other commonwealth, so undisturbed and constant
a tranquility and peace in herself, as in that of Venice, [in which respect] . . . If
Machiavel, averse from doing this commonwealth right, had considered her orders
(as his reader shall easily perceive he never did), he must have been so far from
attributing the prudence of them unto chance that he would have touched up his
admirable work unto that perfection which, as to the civil part, hath no pattern in
the universal world but this of Venice.[52]

---

[50] Machiavelli, *Discourses* pp. 245–7: 'those states where political life survives uncorrupted, do not
permit any of their citizens to live after the fashion of the gentry. On the contrary, they maintain
there perfect equality . . . where the gentry are numerous, no one who proposes to set up a republic
can succeed unless he first gets rid of the lot.'

[51] James Harrington, *The Commonwealth of Oceana and A System of Politics*, ed. J. G. A. Pocock
(Cambridge, 1992) p. 15.

[52] Harrington, *Oceana*, in *Political Works* p. 276.

Harrington's project, then, within a constitutional context contested by royalists, Protectoral apologists, and commonwealthsmen divided among themselves, was not to align himself with any of these positions against another. It was to draw upon all of them in a holistic opposition to disunity itself. In proposing to heal these divisions, the true basis of Harrington's proposed solution was not that constitutional complex which he called the 'superstructure', but the identification and 'fixing' of the 'balance of dominion' in the 'foundation'. It is by attending to this that Harrington described a history of political instability, and a formula for stability (in the Agrarian Law) permitting the commonwealth of Oceana to admit all 'parties'.

It was having determined this that Harrington turned from the material basis of 'empire' to the moral content of 'authority'. Here, no less strikingly, behind familiar constitutional language we find a formula which is entirely new. This is the second of Harrington's great 'discoveries . . . That which great philosophers are disputing upon in vain is brought into light by two silly girls: even the whole mystery of a commonwealth, which lies only in dividing and choosing.'[53] Within the constitution itself, a division of power which had in Polybius been tripartite becomes in *Oceana*, bipolar. The mechanism at the heart of Harrington's constitution is the distinction between debate and resolution ('dividing and choosing').

In seeking to make a decisive political intervention, Harrington was relying upon *Oceana*'s capacity to reach across party lines, and also its extraordinary claims to constitutional perfection, and so longevity. Yet within a highly contested landscape, in the aftermath of a civil war, these theoretical assets were also practical obstacles. The scope of *Oceana*'s intellectual synthesis, combining the Old Testament, Plato, Aristotle, Livy, Machiavelli, Bacon and Hobbes, attracted immediate attention but created its own problems of reception. Following the collapse of the Protectorate in 1659 Harrington succeeded in simplifying and reiterating his key positions. Predictably, however, and despite the work of key allies within the government, he was far less able to contribute to the kind of political compromise which might have yielded practical results.

THE MARINERS AND THE SHIP, 1659–1660

Harrington's summary of the arguments of *Oceana* was *The Art of Lawgiving* (20 February 1659). Its analysis of the contemporary economic and political

---

[53] Harrington, *Oceana*, in *Political Works* p. 172.

situation was supported in Richard Cromwell's parliament, and within the restored Rump, by Henry Neville among others. Neville was a co-author of *The Armies Dutie* (1659), which reiterated that 'it is essentially necessary to the securitie of freedome, that the same assemblie should never have the debating and finally resolving power in them, least it suddenly degenerates into an Oligarchie or Tyrannie of some few . . . as . . . in the long Parliament, who exercising both the debating and determining power, were strongly tempted to have made themselves perpetually legislators'.[54] By contrast, in support of the restored Rump, John Streater revived the pre-Harringtonian position concerning 'a due Succession of their Supream Assemblies, and exact Rules to the People, to choose such persons as are capable of such trust', rotation of office, and the interdependence of ruling and being ruled.[55] Meanwhile on 13 May the Rump received a *Humble Petition and Address of the Officers of the Army*, requesting that the government 'may be in a Representative of the People, consisting of a House successively chosen by the People in such a way . . . as this Parliament shall judge meet, and of a select Senate, Co-ordinate in Power, of able and faithful persons, eminent for Godliness, and such as continue adhering to this Cause'.[56] In advancing this proposal the officers' most important ally was Vane (supported by Milton). Three days later the *Humble Petition* was attacked by Harrington in *A Discourse upon this saying: The Spirit of the Nation is not yet to be trusted with Liberty; lest it introduce Monarchy, or invade the Liberty of Conscience* (16 May 1659). The officers were instructed to 'Detest the base itch of a narrow oligarchy. If your commonwealth be rightly instituted, seven years will not pass ere your clusters of parties, civil and religious, vanish.' This would follow both from the balance of dominion, established by God, and from 'the frame of your commonwealth'. 'The mariner trusteth not unto the sea, but to his ship. The spirit of the people is no wise to be trusted with their liberty, but by stated laws or orders; so the trust is not in the spirit of the people, but in the frame of those orders, which, as they are tight or leaky, are the ship out of which the people, being once embarked, cannot stir, and without which they can have no motion.'[57]

For Harrington's claim that 'the people, being once embarked, cannot stir', we must refer to his explanation elsewhere in the same tract:

at Rome I saw [a cage] which represented a kitchen . . . The cooks were all cats and kitlings, set in such frames, so tied and so ordered, that the poor creatures could

---

[54] H. M[arten], H. N[eville], I. W[ildman], I. I. and S. M., *The Armies Dutie* (May 1659) p. 25.
[55] Streater, *The Continuation* p. 15.   [56] Woolrych, 'Historical Introduction' p. 72
[57] Harrington, *A Discourse upon this Saying . . .* (1659), in *Political Works* pp. 737–8.

make no motion to get loose, but the same caused one to turn the spit, another to baste the meat, a third to skim the pot and a fourth to make green sauce. If the frame of your commonwealth be not such as *causeth* everyone to perform his certain function as *necessarily* as this . . . it is not right.[58]

It is equally worth pausing to consider the no less remarkable claim that Oceana's orders 'are the ship . . . without which the people can have no motion' (meaning motion across the sea). From Plato onwards a series of writers had used the metaphor of the mariners and the ship to make an opposite point: that for the ship of state there could be no safe motion without an adequately trained crew. In Plato's *Republic* this entailed many years of 'studying the seasons of the year, sky, stars, and winds, and all that belongs to . . . the science of navigation'.[59] In *Utopia*, More appealed to Raphael: 'Don't give up the ship in a storm because you cannot direct the winds.'[60] For Milton, defending his proposal for a perpetual council, 'The ship of the Common-wealth is alwaies under sail; they sit at the stern; and if they stear well, what need is ther to change them; it being rather dangerous?'[61] Later Algernon Sidney named Plato as his source for the view that as 'magistrates are chosen by societies, seeking their own good . . . the best men ought to be chosen for the attaining of it'. Accordingly it was 'a most desperate and mischievous madness, for a company going to the Indies, to give the guidance of their ship to the son of the best pilot in the world'.[62] Moreover, 'Who will wear a shoe that hurts him, because the shoe-maker tells him 'tis well made? Or who will live in a house that yields no defence against the extremities of weather, because the mason or carpenter assures him it is a very good house?'[63] For Harrington, however, in a new scientific era of shipbuilding the contribution of the crew − or the passengers − was greatly overrated. 'To say that a man may not write of government except he be a magistrate, is as absurd as to say that a man may not make a sea-card unless he be a pilot. It is known that Christopher Columbus made a card in his cabinet that found out the Indies.'[64]

Thus most fundamentally at issue in the three-way dispute between unicameral commonwealthsmen, Vanists and Harringtonians was more than simply the shape of the constitution. It was what, in this moment of supreme danger, was to be entrusted to constitutional politics itself. This

---

[58] Ibid. p. 744 (my emphases). Harrington's appropriation of the Hobbesian language of causation and necessity is discussed in chapters 7–8 and 13–14.

[59] Plato, *The Republic of Plato*, ed. F. M. Cornford (Oxford, 1941) p. 191.   [60] More, *Utopia* p. 36.

[61] Milton, *The Readie and Easie Way* pp. 433–4.

[62] Sidney, *Discourses*, in *Sydney on Government* pp. 61–2.   [63] Sidney, *Discourses*, ed. West p. 13.

[64] Harrington, *The Prerogative of Popular Government* (1658), in *Political Works* p. 395.

was clarified by Milton's *The Readie and Easie Way* (1660). Although it contained Milton's most substantial constitutional proposal, as usual this was not, primarily, a constitutional document. Its much-derided 'Grand or General Councel' was only part of a plan which attended to local as well as central government. Although consistent with Milton's earlier writings, including very recent ones, it was also an attempt to respond to the present extreme emergency. After a decade of 'disturbances, interruptions and dissolutions', in order to salvage the ends of the cause, Milton's was an attempt to shelve the question of means altogether. When the ship was sinking it was utterly perverse for the crew to continue their argument about future arrangements for the structure of command. For the immediate defence of unchanging principles, both the 'transitorie Parlaments' demanded by most commonwealthsmen and the rotation of office demanded by the Harringtonians 'are much likelier continually to unsettle rather then to settle a free government . . . having too much affinitie with the wheel of fortune'.[65] As 'Militarie men hold it dangerous to change the form of battel in view of an enemie', so it was 'Safest . . . to deferr the changing or circumscribing of our Senat . . . till the Commonwealth be thoroughly setl'd in peace and safetie'.[66]

For Harrington, by contrast, the only foundation of 'peace and safetie' was an adequate constitutional settlement. 'A commonwealth . . . swerveth not from her principles, but by and through her institution . . . a commonwealth that is rightly instituted can never swerve.'[67] Thus amid the present storm what was needed was not expert seamanship (or military strategy) but the launching of a vessel so technically sophisticated as to be capable of securing its own course.[68] A century later this innovation was recognised by David Hume, who compared the question of whether 'one form of government must be allowed more perfect than another, independent of the manners and humors of particular men' to the discussion among 'The mathematicians in EUROPE . . . concerning that figure of a ship, which is the most commodious for sailing.' In relation to which, 'All plans of government, which suppose great reformation in the manners of mankind, are plainly imaginary. Of this nature, are the *Republic* of PLATO, and the *Utopia* of Sir THOMAS MORE. The OCEANA is the only valuable model of a commonwealth, that has as yet been offered to the public.'[69]

---

[65] Milton, *The Readie and Easie Way* pp. 434–5.   [66] Ibid. pp. 441–2.

[67] Harrington, *Oceana*, in *Political Works* p. 321.

[68] 'But . . . if it be discovered once unto common understanding that monarchy is impracticable, then in cometh the commonwealth, not by halves, but with all her tackling, full sail, in her streamers, and with top and top-gallant.' Harrington, *The Art of Lawgiving* p. 700.

[69] David Hume, *Political Essays*, ed. Knud Haakonssen (Cambridge, 1994), 'Essay Twenty-Seven: Idea of a Perfect Commonwealth', pp. 221–2.

RESTORATION

Aside from its ferocious anti-monarchism, Sidney's *Court Maxims* offers no precise constitutional prescription. Yet it does mention, and emphasise, the several species of government ('call it aristocracy, democracy, or what you will'). Sidney draws upon Machiavelli's *Discourses* to describe 'The several constitutions of' commonwealths in relation to their 'ends', whether founded for 'the enlargement of dominion' (Rome) or 'maintaining liberty against foreign invasion or domestic conspiracy' (Sparta, Venice, Switzerland).[70] In addition, his Platonic account of the 'work of a prudent lawgiver' specifies Harringtonian ends, if not means:

[T]hat tune in music is well framed in which the sharpness of one tone is sweetened by the gravity of another; and the perfection of the harmony consists in the due proportion of one unto the other. So in civil societies those deserve praise that make such laws as conduce to a civil harmony wherein the several humors, natures, and conditions of men may have such parts and places assigned to them, that none may so abound as to oppress the other to the dissolution of the whole . . . But everyone, in his own way and degree, may act in order to the public good and the composing of that civil harmony in which our happiness in this world does chiefly consist.[71]

All of these themes were revisited, at greater length, in the *Discourses*, which opposed the outlandish suggestion by Filmer that there was only 'one form of government . . . prescribed to us by God and nature'. Sidney insisted, on the contrary, that 'we are left according to our own understanding, to constitute such as seem best to ourselves'. If 'there never was a good government in the world, that did not consist of the three simple species of monarchy, aristocracy and democracy', the myriad ways in which they could be combined made 'the variety of forms between mere democracy and absolute monarchy . . . almost infinite'.[72] We may take this, as Fink did, as Sidney's first endorsement of the doctrine of the mixed constitution. It is offered, however, as an empirical claim, rather than a constitutional prescription. It cannot be such a prescription because Sidney does not say what kind of mixture he prefers, either in general or for England in particular. His point is rather to insist upon the infinite variety of governments as evidence for his fundamental argument that nations are equipped by God-given reason

to institute such, as in relation to the forces, manners, nature, religion or interests of a people and their neighbours, are suitable and adequate to what is seen, or apprehended to be seen: And he who would oblige all nations at all times to take

---

[70] Sidney, *Court Maxims* pp. 15–17.   [71] Ibid. p. 23   [72] Sidney, *Discourses*, ed. West p. 166.

the same course, would prove as foolish as a physician who should apply the same medicine to all distempers, or an architect that would build the same kind of house for all persons, without considering their estates, dignities, the number of their children or servants, the time or climate in which they live.[73]

Within the context of this foundational point, however, Sidney does go on to make certain more specific observations. The first sounds like a criticism, or revision, of Machiavelli (and Nedham):

> If it be said, that those governments in which the democratical part governs most, do more frequently err in the choice of men or the means of preserving that purity of manners which is required for the well-being of a people, than those wherein aristocracy prevails; I confess it, and that in Rome and Athens the best and wisest men did for the most part incline to aristocracy. Xenophon, Plato, Aristotle, Thucydides, Livy, Tacitus, Cicero and others, were of this sort.[74]

A few pages later, however, Sidney returns to the 'various constitutions of commonwealths . . . according to the different temper of nations and times . . . some constituted for war, others . . . peace; and many having taken the middle . . . way . . . and kept in a perpetual readiness to make war when there was occasion'. This lengthy discussion expands Machiavelli's typology considerably, introducing subcategories, discussing mercantile republics, and considering other contemporary constitutional types (including federated commonwealths). In the process constitutionally unmixed Athens is praised equally alongside Sparta and Rome for its virtue, patriotism and military valour. The only republic singled out for criticism is Venice.[75] By contrast, the 'discipline' of Rome is identified as having been 'more perfect, better observed, and to have produc'd a virtue that surpassed all others'.[76] It is in line with all of these observations that in his general conclusion Sidney falls in line with, while also augmenting, Machiavelli:

> [T]he best judges of these matters have always given the preference to those constitutions that principally intend war . . . and think it better to aim at conquest, rather than simply to stand upon their own defence . . . These opinions are confirmed by the examples of the Romans, who prosper'd much more than the Spartans: And the Carthaginians, who made use of trade as a help to war, raised their city to be one of the most potent that ever was in the world: Wheras the Venetians having relied on trade and mercenary soldiers, are always forced too much to depend upon foreign potentates; very often to buy peace with ignominious and prejudicial conditions; and sometimes to fear the infidelity of their own commanders . . . But that which ought to be valued above all in point of wisdom as well as justice, is, the government given by God to the Hebrews, which chiefly fitted them for war, and to make conquests.[77]

[73] Ibid. p. 173.   [74] Ibid. p. 191.   [75] Ibid. p. 206.   [76] Ibid. p. 201.   [77] Ibid. p. 205.

Thus, although Sidney was clearly more amenable than Nedham both to aristocracy and to mixed constitutions, his praise for Athens shows that neither was a necessary qualification for a constitution to be admired. Elsewhere his comment upon democracy was not that it was good or bad, but that 'it can suit only with the convenience of a small town, accompanied with such circumstances as are seldom found'.[78] Secondly, Sidney's criticism of Venice and praise of Rome aligned him with Machiavelli and Nedham, and against Harrington. What explains all these preferences is that Sidney's criteria for allocating value are not constitutional. They are 'love to their country', virtue, vigour and valour. 'In this variety of constitutions and effects proceeding from them' they are ends rather than means.[79]

Despite his Harringtonianism, and in line with his other allegiance as translator of Machiavelli's *Works* (1675), Neville shared Sidney's admiration for Athens, as well as Rome, and his hesitations about Venice. It was 'By virtue of . . . [the] model of government . . . suitable to a democracy' drawn up by Solon, 'that [Athens] . . . grew and continued long the greatest, justest, the most virtuous, learned and renowned, of all in that age: drove the Persians afterwards out of Greece; defeated them both by sea and land, with a quarter of their number of ships and men; and produced the greatest wits and philosophers that ever lived upon earth'.[80] In a bogus *Letter* published with his translation, Neville has Machiavelli say,

[If from] my discourses upon *Livy* . . . men will conclude . . . that the excellency of those Counsels and Atchievements, and the improvement which mankind, and . . . humane nature it self obtained amongst the *Romans*, did proceed naturally from their Government, and was but a plain . . . consequence of the perfection of their Common-wealth . . . those who [disagree must] . . . shew the world to what other causes we may impute those admirable effects, those Heroick qualities and performances, that integrity and purity of manners, that scorning of riches and life it self, when the publick was concerned.[81]

In *Plato Redivivus* (1680) too, Rome is identified as 'the best and most glorious government that ever the sun saw'. Neville's grounds for this judgement, though expressed in Harringtonian constitutional language, are purely Machiavellian. Rome, which, although mixed, Neville calls a 'democracy',

is a government where the chief part of the sovereign power, and the exercise of it, resides in the people . . . And it does consist of three fundamental orders; the senate

---

[78] Ibid. p. 166.   [79] Ibid. p. 205.
[80] Neville, *Plato Redivivus* p. 96. Nevertheless, for Neville, as for Harrington, it is Lycurgus, not Solon, who is 'the greatest politician that ever founded any government' (p. 95).
[81] [Neville], *Nicholas Machiavel's Letter* p. 3.

proposing, the people resolving, and the magistrates executing. This government is much more powerful than aristocracy; because the latter cannot arm the people, for fear they should seize upon the government; and therefore are fain to make use of none but strangers and mercenaries for soldiers: which, as the divine Machiavel says, has hindered your commonwealth of Venice from mounting up to heaven.[82]

Thus Neville's preference was, like Sidney's, for Machiavellian popularity. While such 'democracy' may have been perfected in practice by the Romans, its theoretical (or rhetorical) foundations were laid earlier, as Hobbes had pointed out.

Why should I be condemned . . . for preferring a *Common-wealth* before a *Monarchy*? . . . [having] concluded that a *Democracy* founded upon good orders is the . . . most excellent Government . . . none . . . would oppose me, [but] such as will wrest *Aristotle*, and even *Plato* himself, and make them write for *Monarchy*.[83]

[82] Neville, *Plato Redivivus* pp. 91–2.   [83] [Neville], *Nicholas Machiavel's Letter* p. 4.

CHAPTER 7

Liberty

[T]he cause for which you were trusted was to defend and maintain
the peoples right to make laws for themselves, and thereby provide
for their own welfare and safety, by such persons as they should chuse,
and that without the negative controule of the King; and also to defend
the freedome of their consciences, persons, and estates, in being over
the only government[*sic*] of their own laws, without subjection to the
will or mercie of any man.

The Armies Dutie (May 1659)[1]

INTRODUCTION

English republicanism defined itself primarily in relation, not to constitutional structures, but moral principles. It was of these which Milton spoke
when he praised 'fortitude and love of freedom . . . wisdom . . . valour, justice
[and] constancy', and Vane when he wrote to Harrington 'joyning in witness with you . . . unto those principles of common right and freedome, that
must be provided for, in whatsoever frame of Government it be'.[2] These
constituted the moral philosophy of English republicanism: the positive
moral good it proposed to itself.

One aspect of this moral philosophy concerned means. Whatever its
constitutional form, the citizens of a republic were free. This freedom was,
in the words of Milton, 'the only school of virtue'.[3] Recently Quentin
Skinner has identified within these English writings a 'third theory of liberty', distinct from both the Greek positive liberty identified by Pocock and
the negative liberty associated with natural law language (liberalism).[4] In
fact, just as English republicans drew upon Greek, Roman and Christian

---

[1] H. M[arten] and others, *The Armies Dutie* p. 12.
[2] Milton, Eikonoklastes pp. 344, 346; Henry Vane, *A Needful Corrective or Ballance in Popular Government expressed in a Letter to James Harrington, Esquire* (1659) p. 3.
[3] Milton, *Second Defence*, p. 294.   [4] Skinner, 'A Third Concept of Liberty'.

sources, so they did so in support of a complex of ideas about liberty possessing both positive and negative attributes. This insisted, on the one hand, upon an exemption from obedience to all laws to which a people had not given their assent. It entailed, on the other, all the moral burdens, and benefits, of collective self-government. In the words of John Streater, 'The right knowledge of commanding and obeying are of necessity to be inseperable . . . It was the *Basis* of the Government of the State of *Lacedemon*, that all should be free, that all should be able to govern.'[5] This was the error identified by Charles I on the scaffold: 'liberty and freedom consists in having . . . laws by which their life and goods may be most their own. It is not for having a share in government, Sir, that is nothing pertaining to them. A subject and a sovereign are clear different things.'[6] This judgement was repeated during the trial of the regicides.[7]

Politically, as we have seen, this understanding incorporated an idea of constitutional government attributed by Milton to Aristotle and Cicero; and by both Harrington and Sidney to Aristotle and Livy. Morally it centred upon an idea of rational self-government, within the commonwealth and the soul, present from Plato to Sallust, Cicero, and Tacitus. This was combined by English writers with a Christian natural law language with its own emphasis upon the moral implications of human rationality, and its own Greek (Aristotelian) and Roman (Stoic) sources. Thus Levellers as well as republicans juxtaposed the 'Lusts and wills of tyrants' imposing 'insufferable bondage and slavery', to the 'originall reason' of government by 'Law'.[8] For Colonel Thomas Rainsborough it was because

the maine cause why Almighty God gave men reason . . . was, that they should make use of this reason, and that they should improve itt for that end and purpose that God gave itt them . . . that every man born in England cannot, ought nott, neither by the law of God nor the law of nature, to bee exempted from the choice of those who are to make lawes, for him to live under.

The present constitution 'which inslaves the people of England that they should bee bound by lawes in which they have noe voice att all' is 'I thinke . . . the most tyrannical law under heaven'.[9] John Wildman agreed:

---

[5] Streater, *Observations* no. 1, p. 4.

[6] Quoted in C. V. Wedgwood, *The Trial of Charles I* (1964) p. 191.

[7] 'It is not the sharing of Government, that is for the Libertie, and Benefit, of the People: but it is, how they may have their Lives, and Liberties, and Estates, safely secured under Government.' [Henry Finch], *An Exact and most Impartial Accompt of the Indictment, Arraignment, Trial, and Judgement (according to Law) of nine and twenty Regicides* (1660) p. 13.

[8] John Lilburne and Richard Overton, *The out-cryes of oppressed commons* (1647) title page; Richard Overton, *The Commoners Complaint* [n.d.] title page, p. 9.

[9] C. H. Firth (ed.), *The Clarke Papers* 4 vols. (1899–1965) vol. 1, pp. 304, 305, 311.

'Wee are now engaged for our freedome . . . Every person in England hath as cleere a right to Elect his Representative as the greatest person in England. I conceive that's the undeniable maxime of Governement: that all governement is in the free consent of the people.'[10] For Wildman's later associate Sidney, similarly, 'it is the fundamental right of every nation to be governed by such laws, in such manner, and by such persons, as they think most conducing to their own good'.[11]

MILTON

England's struggle for liberty was the central theme of Milton's writing. This liberty was juxtaposed to slavery and servility, both as political states and states of soul.[12] It was a key feature of Milton's writing, as it was of his most important classical sources, to insist upon the interdependence of self-government in the city and the soul. It was equally crucial to an intended revolution of manners that a prerequisite of public citizenship was private government of the self. '[R]eal and substantial liberty . . . within . . . [as] without . . . depends . . . on sobriety of conduct and integrity of life.' It was a violation of justice and nature that one who 'is incapable of governing himself, should . . . be committed to the government of another'.[13]

Among all Milton's sources on this subject – Greek (Plato, Aristotle), Italian (Dante, Machiavelli), patristic (Tertullian, Augustine), protestant (Hotman, Buchanan), and biblical (Samuel, Deuteronomy, Ecclesiastes) – his *Defence of the People of England* (1651) emphasised 'Aristotle and Cicero, who are surely our most reliable authorities'.[14] Hobbes's focus upon the same two authorities, in the same year, reflected a more widely shared classical republican determination to unite in the service of liberty 'All the history of Greece and Rome'.[15] Like most republicans Milton applied these examples to a political situation charged with religious significance:

I was born at a time in the history of my country when her citizens, with pre-eminent virtue and a nobility and steadfastness surpassing all the glory of their ancestors, invoked the Lord, followed his manifest guidance, and . . . freed the state

[10] Ibid. p. 318 Part of this passage appears (apparently inaccurately) in Maurice Ashley, *John Wildman: Plotter and Postmaster* (1947) p. 30.

[11] Sidney, *Discourses*, in *Sydney on Government* p. 462.

[12] For example Milton, *Defence* pp. 341, 343.   [13] Milton, *Second Defence* pp. 258, 299.

[14] Milton, *Defence* p. 343; Milton's combination of these two authorities is rightly emphasised by Dzelzainis, 'Milton's Classical Republicanism' pp. 12–19. 'For what lawyers declare concerning liberty and slavery' Milton's *Commonplace Book* also refers to the Institutes of Justinian, Book 1: *Commonplace Book* pp. 410, 470–1.

[15] Milton, *Defence* p. 360.

from grievous tyranny and the church from unworthy servitude . . . In the belief that such great blessings came from on high and . . . out of gratitude to God . . . I held that they should be reverently proclaimed . . . thus those illustrious Greeks and Romans whom we particularly admire expelled the tyrants from their cities without other virtues than the zeal for freedom, accompanied by ready weapons and eager hands.[16]

In addition to his decisive patronage of the present struggle, God was the general author of political freedom. This was shown historically by the Old Testament: 'A republican form of government . . . seemed to God more advantageous for his chosen people; he set up a republic for them and granted their request for a monarchy only after long reluctance . . . [in order to] bear witness to the right possessed by . . . all peoples and nations of enjoying whatever form of government they wish.'[17] More importantly, and above the claims of historical precedent, God created liberty with human reason. 'No man who knows ought, can be so stupid to deny that all men naturally were born free, being the image and resemblance of God himself . . . by priviledge above all the creatures born to command and not to obey.'[18]

It is the implication of Milton's analysis of the case of Israel that the natural gift of liberty entailed the right to renounce that political opportunity in practice. Within the spectrum of seventeenth-century natural law theory, this placed him closer to Grotius than to Overton or Locke, for whom such God-given properties were inalienable. 'When God gave . . . *Adam* reason, he gave him freedom to choose, for reason is but choosing.'[19] '[W]hat wisdome can there be to choose . . . without the knowledge of evil? . . . He that can apprehend . . . vice with all her baits and seeming pleasures, and yet abstain . . . and yet prefer that which is truly better, he is the true warfaring Christian . . . that which purifies us is triall, and triall is by what is contrary.'[20] Liberty was, accordingly, a fragile and demanding moral state, given sustained political expression with great difficulty. Thus, on the one hand, Milton described the virtues necessary 'to defend our Religion and our Liberties . . . against tyranny'.[21] On the other, in *The History of Britain* he recalled the disaster of 'som secretly aspiring to rule, others adoring the name of liberty, yet so soon as they felt by proof the weight of what it was to govern well themselves, and what was wanting within them . . . the wisdom, the virtue, the labour, to use and maintain true libertie, they

---

[16] Milton, *Second Defence* pp. 549–50.   [17] Milton, *Defence* p. 344   [18] Milton, *Tenure* pp. 198–9.
[19] Milton, *Areopagitica* p. 527.   [20] Ibid. pp. 514–15.   [21] Milton *Eikonoklastes* p. 346.

soon . . . shrunk more wretchedly under the burden of thir own libertie, than before under a foren yoke'.[22] In *The Readie and Easie Way*, invoking the account in Aristotle's *Politics* of the Greek 'people soon deposing thir tyrants, bet[aking] themselves . . . to the form of a free Commonwealth', he asked:

Can the folly be paralleld, to adore and be the slaves of a single person for doing that which . . . ten thousand to one . . . we without him might do more easily, more effectually, more laudibly our selves? Shall we never grow old anough to be wise to make seasonable use of gravest autorities, experiences, examples? Is it such an unspeakable joy to serve, such felicitie to wear a yoke? to clink our shackles, lockt on by pretended law of subjection more intolerable and hopeless to be ever shaken off[?][23]

Finally Milton explained, in *Paradise Lost*:

> I made him just and right,
> Sufficient to have stood, though free to fall . . .
> Not free, what proof could they have given sincere
> Of true allegiance, constant faith or love . . .
> What pleasure I from such obedience paid,
> When will and reason (reason also is choice)
> Useless and vain, of freedom both despoiled,
> Made passive both, had served necessity,
> Not me.[24]

Hence the poet's rejection of Harrington's *Oceana* which accepted Hobbes's 'treatises of human nature, and of liberty and necessity, they are the greatest new lights, and those which I have followed, and shall follow . . . as is admirably observed by Mr Hobbs . . . the will is *caus'd*, and being caused is *necessitated*'.[25] This was 'As if predestination overruled/Their will'. In fact God's creatures were

> authors to themselves in all
> Both what they judge and what they choose; for so
> I formed them free, and free they must remain,
> Till they enthrall themselves.[26]

---

[22] Milton, *The History of Britain* Book 3, in *Complete Prose Works* vol. VI, p. 131.

[23] Milton, *The Readie and Easie Way* pp. 448–9.

[24] Milton, *Paradise Lost* Book 3, lines 98–100, 103–11, pp. 404–5.

[25] Harrington, *The Prerogative of Popular Government* p. 423; see also James Cotton, 'James Harrington and Thomas Hobbes', *Journal of the History of Ideas* 42 (1981) pp. 416–17.

[26] Milton, *Paradise Lost* Book 3, lines 122–5.

NEDHAM

According to Marchamont Nedham's *The Excellencie of a Free-State* (1656) liberty was 'the most precious Jewel under the sun . . . of more worth than your Estates, or your lives'.[27] Like other features of Nedham's writing, this terminology had been anticipated by certain Leveller pamphlets, in the authorship of which he may have been involved. Thus in *London's Liberty in Chains discovered* (1646) 'Freedome and Liberty' are praised as 'the onely Jewels in esteem with the Commonalty, as a thing most pretious unto them, and meriting that men should expose themselves to all danger, for the . . . defence thereof against all tyranny and oppression of what nature and condition soever'.[28] Drawing upon 'the Monuments of the *Grecian* and *Romane* Freedom' as well as the experience of Italy and the Netherlands, Nedham was more interested in practical examples of such freedom and its benefits than the principles by which it was informed. Where Milton's humanism was Christian, Nedham's Christianity was lightly worn. Whereas Milton's classical republicanism had a Greek philosophical core, more of Nedham's examples were Roman.

Moreover, whereas in Milton the value of liberty was always related to its moral prerequisite (reason) and consequences (virtue), it was Nedham's pre-eminent preoccupation in its own right. This reflected partly a greater intensity of involvement in the practical defence of this fragile acquisition, and partly the impact of Machiavellian scepticism. Thus from Nedham we hear less about the universal moral obligations of reason (deriving from God) and more about the 'interest' and 'policy' of 'free states'. '*Children should bee educated and instructed in the Principles of Freedom*' not simply because of the inherent superiority of such principles, but because this was essential for the survival of a republic. '*Aristotle* speaks plainly to this purpose, saying, *that the Institution of youth should be accommodated to that Form of Government under which they live; forasmuch as it makes exceedingly for a preservation of the present Government, whatsoever it be.*'[29] Nedham also differed from Milton in abandoning, even in theory, Aristotle's moral distinction between kingship and tyranny.[30] In this he was seconded by his fellow interest theorist John Hall, for whom 'my natural Liberty' was

---

[27] Nedham, *Excellencie* p. 78.
[28] John Lilburne, *London's Liberty In Chains discovered. And, Published by Lieutenant Colonell John Lilburn, Prisoner in the Tower of London, Octob. 1646* p. 1.
[29] *Mercurius Politicus* no. 104, 27 May–3 June 1652, p. 1.
[30] Machiavelli, *Discourses* II.2, pp. 275–6; Nedham, *Case of the Commonwealth* p. 127; Scott, *England's Troubles* pp. 300–1.

the freedom 'to make my Life as justly happy and advantageous to me as I may'.[31]

As we have seen, the liberty Nedham defended was not only Roman but anti-aristocratic: not the senatorial morality of Cicero, or the mixed state of Polybius, but the hard-won and fragile popular liberty associated with the 'Tribunes of the People, preservators of the Common-wealth, and chief Guardians of our Laws and Liberties'.[32] In most of these respects Nedham aligned himself not only with Machiavelli, but with a sceptical reason of state more characteristic of seventeenth-century Dutch than English republicanism. A close interest in the Dutch republic is a constant feature of Nedham's writings, of both the 1640s and the 1650s.[33]

All of this helps to contextualise Nedham's most sustained treatment of liberty, in the Introduction to *The Excellencie* (1656). Although most of the body of the text had been composed earlier, that the act of publication was one of opposition to the Protectorate is something which the Introduction deeply underlined. Thus 'It is a pity, that the people of *England*, being born as free as any people in the World, should be of such a supple humor and inclination, to bow under the ignoble pressures of an Arbitrary Tyranny, and so unapt to learn what true Freedom is.' To be free was to acquire the capacity in practice to exercise a 'Right'. This entailed the popular 'power of calling and dissolving the Supreme assemblies . . . altering Government and Governours upon occasion . . . enacting and repealing laws'.[34] Once again this position had been anticipated by *London's Liberty in Chains*, which had advocated placing in

the Commonalty, the sole Power and Government . . . changing and altering your Lawes and Customes at their pleasure . . . [whereby] Senators . . . be chosen by the generall and free voyce of all, and not of a few . . . which being conceived to be the best forme of Government, and so hath been found to be by approved experience? For, did *Rome* ever so flourish, as when, not any thing was done but by the Senate and People there?[35]

This tract's successor deepened this commitment to radical popular sovereignty with a vision of a commonwealth 'In which the poorest that lives, hath as true a right to give a vote, as well as the richest and greatest'.[36] This is, of course, a precise anticipation of Colonel Rainsborough's defence of this position at Putney ten months later.

[31] Hall, *The Grounds and Reasons of Monarchy* p. 10.   [32] [Nedham], *Vox Plebis* p. 59.
[33] [Nedham], *The Case Stated*; Scott, 'Classical Republicanism'.
[34] Nedham, *Excellencie* pp. 1–2, 4–6.   [35] Lilburne, *London's Liberty In Chains* pp. 2, 5, 7.
[36] John Lilburne, *The Charters of London: The Second Part of London's Liberties in Chaines Discovered* (18 December 1646) p. 4.

Thus, when the power of the Roman republic was

> in the hands of the Senate, the Nation was accounted Free, because not subjected
> to the will of any single person: But afterwards they were Free indeed, when no
> Laws could be imposed upon them, without a consent first had in the Peoples
> Assemblies . . . Wheras, when the Senate afterwards worm'd the People out of
> Power, as that design went on by degrees, so *Rome* lost her Liberty.[37]

By 1656 Nedham had, like Milton, established a record of worrying in public about the 'unaptness' of the English to exercise that liberty that was theirs by right. Like Milton, he distinguished between the name or appearance of liberty and its substance. For Milton, however, the acquisition of this substance hinged upon the fulfilment, in private and public, of the taxing associated moral demands. For Nedham, by contrast, although the exercise of genuine liberty had moral and other consequences, its acquisition was first and foremost a practical and constitutional matter. When the Plebs

> were made capable of Offices of the Government, even to the Dictatorship; had
> Officers of their own, called Tribunes, who were held sacred and inviolable, as
> *Protectors* of the Commons, and retained a power of meeting and acting with all
> Freedom in their great Assemblies . . . Now, and never till now, cou'd they be called
> a Free State, and Commonwealth.[38]

STREATER AND VANE

Within a week of Cromwell's dissolution of the Rump, John Streater published *A Glympse of that Jewel, Judicial, Just, Preserving Libertie* (1653).[39] From April to July of the following year, he followed in Nedham's footsteps as the author of a weekly periodical: *Observations Historical, Political, and Philosophical, Upon Aristotles first Book of Political Government: Together, With a Narrative of State-Affaires in England, Scotland, and Ireland: As also from other Parts beyond the Seas.* One concern of both was vindication of 'the common Liberty' against 'oppression' by 'the rich and mighty'. As with Nedham one of the most effective means for its preservation from 'that yoak, Monarchie . . . [was] the yearly election of all Officers . . . both Military and Civil . . . for by this means they . . . [are] prevented of . . . making themselves Masters'.[40] Again this was illustrated by the example of a

---

[37] Nedham, *Excellencie* pp. 15–17.   [38] Ibid. pp. 12–13.
[39] For Streater's account of the dissolution see *Secret Reasons of State*.
[40] Streater, *A Glympse of that Jewel, Judicial, Just, Preserving Libertie* (1653) p. 1.

'Commonwealth of Rome', which 'began to decline, when the power and secret reasons of State were assumed by few, or one person'.[41]

As the title of his periodical might suggest, however, Streater made more use than Nedham of Greek examples and sources (Athens and Pericles; Sparta and Lycurgus; Plato, Aristotle, Plutarch, Thucydides). In addition, for Streater as for Milton, politics was governed by 'an eternal morall Law of Nature'. The existance of this had been proved against the sophists by Plato and then Aristotle. From the same authorities Streater derived the association of liberty with the government of laws. Here he had recourse to a counter-example in Turkey soon also to be deployed by Harrington:

it is more worthy to assume Supream Power to knock off Chaines, and leave a people free, then it is to usurp it to make people slaves . . . Riches is not a sign of freedom, though it be so that most States that are free are rich. There was rich Bondmen amongst the *Romans*: there are rich slaves under the *Turks; but it is their slavery that they cannot defend their Riches, as a Free-people do by their Laws.*[42]

Beyond the preservative of elections, liberty entailed broader participation in civic self-government. 'By this means . . . every one of the Commonwealth that affected Government, had hope of having share of the Government; therefore they endeavoured to improve themselves so, as to become capable of such and such trusts . . . so that almost everyone was an able defendant of their Libertie and Countrie.'[43] It was emphasised by Aristotle that 'He is a Governor of a Commonwealth that commandeth and obeyeth by turns . . . [I]t is agreeable to the Law of Nature . . . which maketh sweet harmony upon often touching on this string (*Do as you would be done to*) be contented to be governed, as well as to govern.'[44] Before such magistrates are '*elected* to the greatest Trusts, they ought to pass through most of the lesser Trusts in the Common-wealth, in which they must give a Testimony both of their abilities and fidelity'. No less essential to such participation was effective government of the self. In respect of this 'one speaking to *Cato* in praise of *Alexanders* . . . conquering the world: saith *Cato*, his Conquest was nothing since he did not overcome himself, and indeed *Alexander* lost himself, and that great . . . Empire . . . fell to nothing'.[45]

When Algernon Sidney wrote a 'Character' of Sir Henry Vane Jr, it emphasised these Stoic qualities of self-government. Vane

always preserved the same steady resolution of mind, without ever being transported with joy or ruffled and disturbed with Anger; and fearless and unmov'd in danger, so that by obeying reason, he at once seem'd to renounce all kind of

---

[41] Ibid.   [42] Streater, *Observations* no. 2, p. 10.   [43] Streater, *A Glympse*, p. 1.
[44] Streater, *Observations* no. 1, p. 3.   [45] Ibid. no. 2, p. 13.

unbecoming passions and affections: nay, such was his Magnanimity, that if the frame of the whole world had been dissolv'd and gon to rack about his ears, he would have remained undaunted in the midst of its ruins.[46]

Vane was, for Sidney as for Milton, the personal archetype of the godly republican magistrate. For Vane, as for Plato and for Thomas More, the basis of tyranny, the opposite of liberty, was selfishness, 'the mystery of iniquity, that great principle of self-interest in the heart of man'. This consequence of sin was 'no other than the spirit of man, lusting after the doing of his own will and procuring his own glory more than God's', the prototype for Satan in Milton's *Paradise Lost*.[47] For Vane, therefore, as for Milton, the military conquest of monarchy was only the beginning. To be genuinely free was to overcome this spirit within, and so become capable of public liberty and its desired moral consequences. For fallen man, however, this road was hard: 'Man, at his best, stands in need of the ballancing and ruling motion of God's Spirit to keep him stedfast . . . not only to heal and restore what is lost, but to add, by way of supply, that more grace that may preserve from the danger of future relapse.'[48] It was the moral imperfection of man which made monarchy as a political form so dangerous: 'For a rational man to give up his reason and will unto the judgement and will of another . . . whose judgement and will is not perfectly and unchangeably good and right is unwise and unsafe, and by the law of nature, forbidden.'[49] The only will upon which it was safe to depend was that of God.

The resulting government by reason, assisted by God's spirit, was again an empire of laws. Its basis was

the . . . consent and free gift by the common vote of the whole Body, which is the right door to enter into the exercise of supreme Power, and is . . . consonant to those pure Principles of mans nature, wherein he was at first created, and does declare the governed to be in the state of free Citizens, who as Brethren partaking of the Spirit of right reason, common to them as men made in the Image of God . . . agree to be subject and yield obedience to the Laws, that are . . . made amongst them by their own free . . . consent . . . So as this sort of Empire or Government is that of Laws, and not of Men, and is of a nature better agreeing with the many then the few, and least of all with the single person.[50]

These words, written to James Harrington, state the republican principles which Vane believed he shared with Harrington and other republicans. The

---

[46] Sidney, 'Character of Henry Vane' p. 278.

[47] Henry Vane, *The Retired Man's Meditations* (1655), quoted in Judson, *Vane* p. 19. Judson's definitive study appropriately emphasises Vane's Platonism, shared with his friend Peter Sterry (p. 56).

[48] Vane, *Needful Corrective* pp. 6–7.   [49] Vane, *The People's Case*, quoted in Judson, *Vane* p. 33.

[50] Vane, *Needful Corrective* pp. 3–4.

basis of these principles, in Vane as in Milton and Sidney, was a Platonist theology (and Sidney's *Court Maxims* were replete with Vanist spiritual politics). Within a historiography dominated by the paradigm of classical republicanism Vane has proved an awkward member of the pantheon. Because his writings are difficult, and because he made limited reference to classical sources, he is usually omitted from such discussions altogether. One response might be to accept that not all English republicanism was classical republicanism; that the contextual net must be flung more widely, in particular to embrace religious and biblical dimensions.[51] At one level this is clearly true. Yet it remains necessary to explain the contexts connecting Vane to other republicans, both practical and intellectual. One key to doing so is to emphasise that as most English humanism was Christian humanism, so English classical republicanism was a religious project with a shared theological, as well as confessional political, context. To this Vane's, and perhaps Harrington's, Platonism clearly belongs. The importance of such connections is underlined by the fact that Vane's principal purpose in writing to Harrington was to disagree with him in relation to fundamentals of both religion and politics.

For Vane, as for most republicans, it was crucial that individuals entrusted with citizenship possessed the appropriate moral qualifications. Thus it was vital

that in the time of the Common-wealths constituting, and in a Nation much divided in affection and interest about their own Government, none be admitted to the exercise of the right and priviledge of a free Citizen, for a season, but either such as are free born, in respect of their holy and righteous principles, flowing from the birth of the Spirit of God in them . . . or else who, by their tryed good affection and faithfulness to common right and publick freedome, have deserved to be trusted with the keeping or bearing their own Armes in the publick defence.[52]

Yet as we have seen Harrington's own approach to the nation's 'divisions in affection and interest' was altogether different. Thus for many republicans one of the most alarming features of *Oceana* was that it proposed to admit royalists to full citizenship:

the *Royalist* for having opposed a *Common-wealth* in *Oceana* (where the *Lawes* were so ambiguous, that they might be eternally disputed, and never reconciled) can neither be *justly*, for that cause, excluded from his full and equall share in the *Government*; nor *prudently*, for this, that a *Common-wealth* consisting of a party

[51] See Worden, 'Milton, *Samson Agonistes*'; Ludlow, *A Voyce*, ed. Worden; Worden, *Roundhead Reputations: the English Civil Wars and the Passions of Posterity* (2001).
[52] Vane, *Needful Corrective* pp. 7–8.

will be in perpetuall labour of her own destruction . . . [whereas] Men that have equall possessions, and the same security of their estates and of their liberties that you have, have the same cause with you to defend.[53]

HARRINGTON

Thus informing Harrington's proposal to admit all parties to citizenship was his belief that the basis of political interest, and moral philosophy, was material. 'Corruption . . . in manners' had a material foundation: it was 'from the *Balance* [of dominion]'. Given the current 'popular Balance', all that was now necessary for both stability and liberty was a legislator equipped with the 'skill of raising such *Superstructures of Government*, as are natural to the known *Foundations*'.[54] It was in turning from the '*Foundations*' to 'such *Superstructures*' that Harrington came to what he called the 'principles of authority', of which liberty was one. Here we encounter some familiar classical language, both Greek and Roman:

if the liberty of a man consist in the empire of his reason, the absence whereof would betray him into the bondage of his passions; then the liberty of a commonwealth consisteth in the empire of her laws, the absence whereof would betray her unto the lusts of tyrants; and these I conceive to be the principles upon which Aristotle and Livy (injuriously accused by Leviathan for not writing out of nature) have grounded their assertion that a commonwealth is an empire of laws and not of men.[55]

This claim Harrington then defended against Hobbes, who had ridiculed the pretensions of Lucca to that 'LIBERTAS . . . written on the turrets of the city' on the grounds that 'Whether a commonwealth be monarchical or popular, the freedom is the same.' Harrington's response, reminiscent of the earlier passage in Streater, was that whereas in Turkey 'the greatest bashaw is a tenant, as well of his head as his estate, at the will of his lord, the meanest Lucchese that hath land is a freeholder of both, and not to be controlled but by the law; and that framed by every private man unto no other end . . . than to protect the liberty of every private man, which by that means comes to be the liberty of the commonwealth'.[56] Quentin Skinner has drawn attention to this image of the Turkish tenancy of one's head, as illustrating the emphasis placed by the neo-Roman understanding of liberty upon independence from government by a will other than one's

---

[53] Harrington, *Oceana* (1656) p. 46.   [54] Ibid. p. 44.
[55] Harrington, *Oceana*, in *Political Works* p. 170.   [56] Ibid. pp. 170–1.

own. Yet here Harrington speaks of the ownership, rather than tenancy, of not only one's head, but one's 'estate'. As the basis of 'empire' lies in 'the goods of fortune', so it is the purpose of the republican empire of laws 'to protect the liberty of every private man . . . [even] the meanest Lucchese *that hath land*'. It is the sum of these 'private' liberties which 'comes to be the liberty of the commonwealth'. In short, for Harrington the foundation of liberty lay not in the soul but in 'riches', upon which men 'are hung, as by the teeth'; in an ownership of property widely enjoyed in Lucca, but not enjoyed by the greatest bashaw in Turkey. Thus *Oceana* dates 'The generation of the Common-wealth' to the early sixteenth century because not since then had the material basis for a viable English monarchy existed ('wherefore the dissolution of the government caused the war'). This meant that *Leviathan's* monarchical politics, far from offering a prescription for settlement, were instead a backward-looking recipe for perpetual future strife.

Earlier in Harrington's discussion of the principles of empire, Hobbes was congratulated for at least understanding the material basis of government ('But Leviathan, although he seems to skew at antiquity, following his furious master Carneades, hath caught hold of the public sword, unto which he reduceth all manner and matter of government').[57] Moreover the reason why Harrington found the suggestion in *Leviathan* that Aristotle and Livy did *not* 'write . . . out of nature' an 'injurious accusation', is that Harrington shared this Hobbesian methodological ambition. 'Policy is an art. Art is the observation or imitation of nature . . . by observation of the face of nature a politician limns his commonwealth.'[58] Thus when Matthew Wren observed that 'though Mr Harrington professes a great Enmity to Mr Hobs in his politiques, notwithstanding he . . . does silently swallow down such Notions as Mr Hobs hath chewed for him', Harrington replied candidly: 'It is true I have opposed the politics of Mr Hobbes, to show him what he taught me . . . I firmly believe that Mr Hobbes is, and will in future ages be accounted, the best writer at this day in the world.'[59]

Harrington did indeed write *Oceana*, opposing *Leviathan's* monarchical politics, to show Hobbes what he had taught him. This was that any art of a commonwealth capable of bringing settlement to England

---

[57] Ibid. pp. 165, 174; for a broader context for the following discussion see Scott, 'The Rapture of Motion'.

[58] Harrington, *Oceana*, in *Political Works* p. 417.

[59] Matthew Wren, *Considerations upon Mr Harrington's Oceana* (1657) p. 41; Harrington, *The Prerogative of Popular Government* p. 423.

had to be correctly informed by Hobbes' own natural philosophy. Nature was, according to Hobbes, material in perpetual linear motion: 'When a thing is in motion, it will eternally be in motion, unless somewhat els stay it.' Most politically important were those '*Voluntary Motions*' or species of 'Endeavour' called the passions: 'This Endeavour, when it is toward something which causes it, is called APPETITE, or DESIRE . . . And when . . . fromward something . . . AVERSION.'[60] All passions were aspects of desire and aversion and upon them depended individual moral judgements. In line with this analysis Hobbes redefined liberty not, as Aristotle had claimed, as collective civic participation, but as the absence of constraints upon individual action (material in motion):

> of *voluntary* actions the *will* is the *necessary* cause, and [as] . . . the *will* is also *caused* by other things whereof it disposeth not, it followeth, that *voluntary* actions have all of them *necessary* causes, and therefore are necessitated . . . [therefore] I conceive *liberty* to be rightly defined in this manner: Liberty is the absence of all the impediments to action that are not contained in the nature and intrinsical quality of the agent.[61]

As we have seen, about his agreement with these 'greatest new lights' Harrington was explicit. But his criticisms of *Leviathan*'s politics were accordingly severe. It was Hobbes's error to have failed to pursue this natural philosophy to its correct conclusion by identifying the material 'foundation' of English politics. Instead, *Leviathan*'s politics of the sword hung in the air 'as if by geometry', entirely forgetting that 'this sword . . . without an hand . . . is but cold iron . . . The hand which holdeth this sword is the militia of a nation . . . an army is a beast that hath a great belly and must be fed; wherefore . . . without . . . the balance of property . . . the public sword is but a name or mere spitfrog.'[62] By contrast Harrington, having successfully located the balance of dominion, explained how it might furnish the foundation for a republican superstructure offering not only stability, but liberty. Stability was achieved by 'fixing' motion in the foundation with an agrarian law. Liberty was given dramatic and perpetual expression by mechanisms of election and magisterial rotation (annual, biennial and triennial).

Thus Harrington's final revision of Hobbes, in relation to a liberty understood as the absence of constraints upon motion, concerned that motion's

---

[60] Hobbes, *Leviathan* pp. 37–46.
[61] Thomas Hobbes, *Of Liberty and Necessity: A Treatise* (1654), in Sir William Molesworth (ed.), *The English Works of Thomas Hobbes*, vol. VI (1840) pp. 273–4.
[62] Harrington, *Oceana*, in *Political Works* p. 165.

constitutional shape. The 'form of the commonwealth is motion . . . In motion consisteth life . . . [and] the motion of a Commonwealth will never be current, unless it be circular.'[63] Accordingly 'the motions of *Oceana* are spherical'. Order by order, the 'materials' of *Oceana* are pitched into perpetual circulation, 'the parishes annually pour themselves into hundreds, the hundreds into tribes, the tribes into galaxies'.[64] Like *Leviathan's* 'Artificial Man' this is also a giant imitation of the human body anatomised by Harvey, 'so the parliament is the heart which, consisting of two ventricles, the one greater and replenished with a grosser store, the other less and full of a purer, sucketh in and gusheth forth the life blood of *Oceana* by a perpetual circulation'.[65]

The most important reason for what Harrington took to be Hobbes's failure to draw the appropriate republican conclusions from his natural philosophy was his misguided dismissal of 'ancient prudence'. To dismiss the prudence (defined by Hobbes as experience) of the ancients on the grounds that 'the Greeks and Romans . . . derived . . . [politics] not from the principles of nature but . . . the [particular] practice of their own commonwealths' was as misguided 'as if a man should tell famous Harvey that he transcribed the circulation of blood not out of the principles of nature, but out of the anatomy of this or that body'.[66] In fact 'the opinion that riches are power is as ancient as the first book of Thucydides or the *Politics* of Aristotle, and not omitted by Mr Hobbes [in his translation] or any other politician'.[67] Had Hobbes paid as much attention to studying Aristotle as to refuting him, he would have found the doctrine of the balance 'in divers places, especially where he says that immoderate wealth . . . [is] where one man or a few have greater possessions than the . . . frame of the commonwealth will bear'. Had he studied Plato, Plutarch, Cicero and Livy, he would have been repeatedly reminded of the importance of such a material context for politics, and the calamitous consequences for the Roman republic of neglecting it. Had he consulted any authority on ancient republican citizenship, he would have been reminded of the importance,

---

[63] Ibid. pp. 212, 248. Harrington's opposition of circular to Hobbes's linear motion has a political context. It may also reflect the distinction of Harrington's astronomical from Hobbes's human political model. In addition, however, the two writers may have been drawing upon alternative physics. As far as I am aware no comparison has been made of this aspect of their natural philosophy.

[64] Ibid. p. 245.

[65] Ibid. p. 287. Note Wren's remark that 'this libration is of the same nature with a perpetual motion in the mechanics'. *Considerations* p. 67.

[66] Ibid. pp. 162, 178; Scott, 'The Rapture of Motion' p. 157.

[67] Harrington, *The Prerogative of Popular Government* p. 412.

in this context, of civic election and rotation. All of these principles had been discussed with reference to ancient authorities by a three-issue run of Nedham's *Mercurius Politicus* in May 1652.[68]

It is startling within a discussion of largely Christian humanist understandings of liberty to find that of the most important English republican author informed by a materialist natural philosophy and metaphysics. It is even more so to find Harrington using this natural philosophy to put to Hobbes, in Hobbesian language, the case for classical republicanism.

SIDNEY

Turning finally to Sidney we return to notably Miltonic ground, with Machiavellian additions.[69] From the scaffold in December 1683 Sidney issued a defiant *Last Paper* giving 'the scope of the whole treatise' later published as *Discourses Concerning Government*.

If [Filmer] might publish to the world his opinion, That all men are born under a necessity . . . to submit to an absolute kingly government . . . restrained by no law . . . and none must oppose his will . . . I know not why I might not have published my opinion to the contrary . . . that God had left nations to the liberty of setting up such governments as best pleased themselves . . . That magistrates were set up for the good of nations; not nations for the honour or glory of magistrates . . . That the right and power of magistrates in every country was that which the laws of that country made it to be. That those laws . . . and oaths . . . having the force of a contract between magistrate and people, could not be violated without danger of dissolving the whole fabric.[70]

As in Milton and the Levellers, as well as in Locke, much of what Sidney says about liberty is in the language of natural law. Thus the *Discourses* begin by defending

the principle of liberty in which God created us, and which includes the chief advantages of the life we enjoy, as well as the greatest helps towards the felicity, that is the end of our hopes in the other . . . . man is naturally free . . . he cannot justly be deprived of that liberty without cause, and . . . he doth not resign it, or any part of it, unless it be in consideration of a greater good, which he proposes to himself.[71]

---

[68] *Mercurius Politicus* no. 101–3, 6–27 May 1652. See Scott, 'The Rapture of Motion' pp. 146–7.
[69] Scott, *Algernon Sidney and the Restoration Crisis* ch. 10; Worden, 'Republicanism and the Restoration' pp. 172–4; Nicholas von Maltzhan, 'The Whig Milton, 1667–1700', in Armitage et al., *Milton* pp. 239–40.
[70] Sidney, *Last Paper*, in *Discourses* (1763) pp. 37–8.   [71] Sidney, *Discourses*, ed. West p. 8.

As for Locke, replying to the same section of Filmer, this liberty 'is not a licentiousness of doing what is pleasing to everyone against the command of God; but an exemption from all human laws, to which they have not given their assent'. At the same time, in line with this 'consideration of a greater good', the 'principle in which the Grecians, Italians, Spaniards, Gauls, Germans, and Britains, and all other generous nations ever lived' is defined in positive Aristotelian terms, 'insomuch that the . . . Asiaticks and Africans, for being . . . unable to govern themselves, were by Aristotle . . . called *slaves by nature*'. A few pages later, as Quentin Skinner has noticed, the point is elaborated with reference to Roman authorities:

For as liberty solely consists in an independency upon the will of another, and by the name of slave we understand a man, who can neither dispose of his person nor goods, but enjoys all at the will of his master . . . the Grecians, Italians, Gauls, Germans, Spaniards and Carthaginians, as long as they had any strength, virtue or courage amongst them, were esteemed free nations, because they abhorred such a subjection. They were, and would be governed only by laws of their own making: *Potentiora erant legum quam hominum imperia* [The rule of laws was more powerful than that of men].[72]

The source for this quote is Book 2 of Livy. Elsewhere on the political government of law, as we have seen, Sidney quotes from Book 3 of Aristotle's *Politics*. It is surely significant that in defending this formulation both Harrington and Sidney use the same pair of classical authorities.[73] It is equally significant that this defence occurs in Sidney's text against an assertion by Filmer ('that *the greatest liberty in the world is for a people to live under a monarch*') very like the Hobbesian defence of monarchical liberty to which we have seen Harrington responding. Like Harrington, Sidney counters by juxtaposing self-government by law to that of the 'Medes, Arabs, Egyptians and Turks . . . If it be liberty to live under such a government, I desire to know what is slavery.'[74] Upon the liberty of the Romans, as described by Livy, depended everything that was great about that state, or worthy of imitation:

That people which in magnanimity surpassed all that have been known in the world; who never found any enterprize above their spirit to undertake, and power to accomplish, with their liberty lost all their vigour and virtue. They who by their votes had disposed of kingdoms and provinces, fell to desire nothing but to live and see plays . . . which is enough to shew, that the strength, virtue, glory, wealth, power and happiness of Rome proceeding from liberty, did rise, grow, and perish with it.[75]

---

[72] Ibid. p. 17.   [73] Ibid. p. 288; Harrington, *Political Works* p. 401.
[74] Sidney, *Discourses*, ed. West p. 288.   [75] Ibid. pp. 147, 149.

More generally, in the *Discourses* as in *Oceana*, Aristotle and Livy are among the most frequently cited authorities. Elsewhere, like Milton Sidney speaks of 'Plato, Aristotle, Cicero and the best human authors'.[76] Equally Miltonic, the chapter defending the proposition 'That 'tis natural for Nations to govern [themselves], or to chuse Governors; and that Virtue only gives . . . reason why one should be chosen rather than another' contains the most important statement of Sidney's moral philosophy, and is based almost entirely on Aristotle and Plato (especially Plato's *Laws*).[77] Both Plutarch (*Life of Themistocles*) and Tacitus (*Annals*) are invoked in support of the view that

we have no other way of distinguishing between free nations and such as are not so, than that the free are governed by their own laws and magistrates . . . and the others . . . have subjected themselves . . . The same distinction holds in relation to particular persons. He is a free man who lives . . . under laws made by his own consent; and the name of a slave can belong to no man, unless to him who . . . subjects himself to the will of another.[78]

Much of the *Discourses* is spent defending not only the rights but superior accomplishments of free nations, with Machiavelli as guide. It also dwells at length upon the history, and parliamentary embodiment, of English freedom. Speaking of this history, Sidney invokes the same Livian formula:

the actions of our ancestors resemble those of the ancient rather than the later Romans: tho our government be not the same with theirs in form, yet it is in principle; and if we are not degenerated, we shall rather desire to imitate the Romans in the time of their virtue, glory, power and felicity . . . when *the laws were more powerful than the commands of men* . . . than what they were, in that of their slavery, vice, shame and misery.[79]

Presently in English parliaments lay not only 'the power of making, changing, and repealing laws', but 'whatever lay within the reach of human power', including 'the power of making kings'.[80] Finally, like Milton, Sidney makes extensive use of scripture and other Christian authorities, including the church fathers. Thus Tertullian is cited in support of the assertion that

liberty being only an exemption from the dominion of another, the question ought not to be, how a nation can come to be free, but how a man comes to have

---

[76] Ibid. p. 70.   [77] Ibid. pp. 77–87.   [78] Ibid. pp. 440–1.
[79] Ibid. p. 472. The italicised phrase has been moved from the end to the middle of this quotation.
[80] Ibid. pp. 416, 440.

a dominion over it; for till the right of dominion be proved and justified, liberty subsists as arising from the nature and being of a man . . . God only who confers this right upon us, can deprive us of it: and we can no way understand that he does so, unless he had so declared by express revelation, or had set some distinguishing marks of dominion and subjection upon men; and, as an ingenious person not long since said, caused some to be born with crowns upon their heads, and all others with saddles upon their backs.[81]

[81] Ibid. pp. 510–11.

CHAPTER 8

Virtue

Of all things transitory and vain, when sin
With vanity had filled the works of men:
Both all things vain, and all who in vain things
Built their fond hopes of glory or lasting fame,
Or happiness in this or the other life;
All who have their reward on earth, the fruits
Of painful superstition and blind zeal,
Nought seeking but the praise of men, here find
Fit retribution, empty as their deeds.

John Milton, *Paradise Lost*[1]

MILTON AND PLATO

In virtue we consider the most important consequence of liberty. In the words of one pamphlet of 1659, 'And doubtlesse the defence of these Liberties is essentially necessary to the well being of any Nation, and to the being of publick morall righteousness amongst men.'[2] This was, for most of our writers, the principal end at which the republican experiment aimed. That Milton's republicanism hinged upon a politics of virtue is well understood.[3] For Milton, as for most other republicans, this was the highest personal and political value, not only embodying as it did the moral life enjoined by God, but hinging upon the knowledge of God himself.

Virtues praised by Milton included wisdom, courage, justice, temperance, fortitude, magnanimity, piety, godliness and chastity. In what he took to be the broad agreement on this point of Greek, Roman and Christian authorities, his understanding of all virtue hinged upon 'self-discipline . . . an ordering of the self in accordance with . . . reason, which,

---

[1] Milton, *Paradise Lost* p. 413.   [2] H.M[arten] and others, *The Armies Dutie*, p. 12.
[3] See for instance Worden, 'Marchamont Nedham' pp. 52, 57; Dzelzainis, 'Milton's Classical Republicanism'; Perez Zagorin, *Milton: Aristocrat and Rebel: the Poet and his Politics* (Rochester, N.Y., 1992) pp. 153–4.

by subjecting unruly passions, gave priority to its highest moral capacities'.[4] One context for this lay in the Platonic metaphysics by which Aristotle, Cicero, and both early and later Christian sources were all to different degrees influenced.

The deep importance of Plato to Milton's writing has long been understood.[5] However far more attention has been paid to the implications of this fact for his poetry than for his republican politics. In fact not only the moral politics but epistemology and theology informing Milton's understanding of virtue were all Platonic. Thus not only were Plato's cardinal virtues central to Milton's writing. Not only was their achievement, in the soul and the commonwealth, interdependent. Such self-government (over the passions) hinged ultimately upon that achievement of real moral knowledge (of unalterable truth, rather than fluctuating opinion) that was the highest virtue of which reason was capable. In the *Republic* Plato set this wisdom, and the philosophical love of wisdom, against not only gratification of the senses but also a love of honour and reputation to which later Roman writers were to accord much more respect.[6]

Thus for Milton, as for many other English republicans, the highest of the virtues was wisdom. The highest form of wisdom was knowledge of God, the only source of goodness. To throw off the government of will, sin and passion, and be governed by that reason which was a fragment of the divine nature remaining in man, was to achieve that moral good of which man remained capable in this life. 'The end then of learning is to repair the ruins of our first parents by regaining to know God aright, and out of that knowledge to love him, to imitate him, to be like him, as we may the neerest by possessing our souls of true vertue, which being united to the heavenly grace of faith make up the highest perfection.'[7]

From his earliest prose writings Milton insisted upon the distinction between those who 'live . . . by faith and certain knowledge', whose 'vertue is of an unchangeable graine', and those misguided by 'credulity and prevailing opinion'. Whereas the former possessed 'fortitude and undaunted constancy', as well as 'goodnesse and magnanimity', of the latter it had to be said that 'vertue that wavers is not vertue'.[8] '[T]he only high valuable wisdom' depended upon the capacity 'to know any thing distinctly of God . . . and [so] what is infallibly good and happy in the state of

---

[4] Zagorin, *Milton* p. 154.
[5] See for instance Irene Samuel, *Plato and Milton* (Ithaca, N.Y., 1947); Arnold Stein, *Heroic Knowledge* (Minneapolis, Minn., 1957) ch. 2.
[6] Plato, *The Republic*, ed. Cornford pp. 177–8 and Part III (Books V–VII) in general.
[7] Milton, *Of Education* pp. 366–7.   [8] Milton, *The Reason of Church-governement* pp. 794–5.

man's life.'⁹ Elsewhere Milton explained that 'the ceaselesse round of study and reading led me to the shady spaces of philosophy, but chiefly to the divine volumes of *Plato*, and his equall *Xenophon*. Where . . . I learnt, of chastity and love, I meane that which is truly so . . . and how the first and chiefest office of love, begins and ends in the soule, producing those happy twins of her divine generation knowledge and vertue.'¹⁰ More generally Milton underlined the attraction of Greek practice in general, and Platonic injunction in particular, to puritan morality:

it were happy for the Commonwealth, if our Magistrates, as in those famous governments of old, would take into their care, not only the deciding of our contentous Law cases . . . but the managing of our publick sports, and festival pastimes, that they might be, not such as were autoriz'd a while since, the provocations of drunkennesse and lust, but such as may inure and harden our bodies by martial exercises to all warlike skil and performance, and may civilize, adorn and make discreet our minds by the learned and affable meeting of frequent Academies . . . sweetned with eloquent and graceful inticements to the love and practice of justice, temperance and fortitude, instructing and bettering the Nation at all opportunities, that the call of wisdom and vertu may be heard every where.¹¹

This reminds us not only of Sidney's similar denunciation of the Book of Sports, but of his boast to Lantin in Paris in 1677 that

*Que tandis l'armee du parlement avait ete sur pied on n'avoit veu un soldat jurer Dieu; qu'on n'y souffrait point de cartes, ni de des, ni de putains; que chaque soldat portrait a sa poche une Bible on anglais; que tous s'exercaient a la lutte ou a des jeux utiles et propres a fortifier le corps.*¹²

Both quotes anticipate Milton's memory in the *Second Defence* that during the civil war he had believed his countrymen 'were making the most direct progress towards the liberation of all human life from slavery – provided that the discipline arising from religion should overflow into the morals and institutions of the state'.¹³ In *Of Education* (1644), dedicated to Samuel Hartlib, Milton offered a prescription for such an academy capable of directing scholars' 'studies, their exercise, and their diet'. In many

---

⁹ Ibid. p. 801.
¹⁰ John Milton, *An Apology Against a Pamphlet Call'd A Modest Confutation of the Animadversions upon the Remonstrant against Smectymnuus* (1642), in *Complete Prose Works*, vol. 1 pp. 891–2.
¹¹ Milton, *The Reason of Church-governement* pp. 818–19. Annotations in the Yale edition pay appropriate attention to the Platonic content of this passage.
¹² 'Lantiniana' p. 100. 'That in the parliamentary army one never saw a soldier curse God; that no cards were suffered, or dice, or women [here in the manuscript the word 'filles' is crossed out and replaced by 'putains']; that each soldier carried in his pocket a Bible in English; that all exercised themselves at wrestling or other games useful to strengthen the body.'
¹³ Milton, *Second Defence* p. 622.

practical details this displayed the influence of Plato's *Laws*. More generally it followed the *Phaedo* in describing the necessary progression of the
'understanding' from 'conning over the visible and inferior . . . sensible
things' to 'arrive . . . to the knowledge of God and things invisible'.[14] The
chief objective of 'a compleat and generous education' (avoiding 'untutor'd
Anglicisms . . . the Scholastick grosnesse of barbarous ages . . . pure trifling
at Grammar and *Sophistry* . . . court shifts and tyrannous aphorismes') was
to 'fit . . . a man to perform justly, skilfully and magnanimously all the
offices both private and publike of peace and war'.[15] The means thereby
was to 'win them early to the love of vertue and true labour . . . in willing obedience, enflam'd with the study of learning, and the admiration of
vertue: stirr'd up with high hopes of living to be brave men, and worthy
patriots, dear to God, and famous to all ages'. A first step to the production of such ardour might be the eloquence of 'some easie and delightfull
book of Education . . . whereof the Greeks have store as . . . *Plutarch*, and
other Socratic discourses . . . [and] the first books of *Quintilian*'. Thereafter the study of agriculture, physiology, natural philosophy, mathematics
and arithmetic, drama and poetry was to be accompanied, as prescribed by
Plato, by strenuous physical training attended by 'the solemn and divine
harmonies of musick . . . to smooth and make them gentle from rustick
harshnesse and distemper'd passions'.[16]

Students were to be taught '*Politics*; to know the beginning, end and
reasons of politicall societies', and 'the grounds of . . . legall justice; deliver'd
first and with best warrant by *Moses*; and as farre as humane prudence can
be trusted, in those extoll'd remains of Grecian Law-givers, *Lycurgus, Solon,
Zaleucus, Charondas*, and thence to all the Romane *Edicts* and tables with
their *Justinian*; and so down to the *Saxon* and common laws of England,
and the Statutes'. They were also to learn 'Rhetorick . . . out of the rule
of *Plato, Aristotle, Phalereus, Cicero, Hermogenes, Longinus*'. Eventually they
would become capable of

that act of reason which in *Ethics* is call'd *Proairesis* [choice, discussed by Aristotle
in *Nicomachean Ethics*]: that they may with some judgement contemplat upon
morall good and evill. Then will be requir'd . . . instructing them more amply
in the knowledge of vertue and the hatred of vice . . . through all the morall
works of *Plato, Xenophon, Cicero, Plutarch, Laertius*, and those *Locrian* remnants
[*On the Soul of the World and Nature*, based on Plato's *Timaeus*]; but still to be
rduc't . . . under the determinat sentence of *David*, or *Salomon*, or the Evangels
and *Apostolic* scriptures.

---

[14] Milton, *Of Education* pp. 368–9.   [15] Ibid. pp. 373–9.   [16] Ibid. pp. 409–11.

The result, Milton hoped, would be the full acquisition of 'that knowledge that belongs to good men or good governours'. All of this amounted, he hoped, to a programme

likest to those ancient and famous schools of *Pythagoras*, *Plato*, *Isocrates*, *Aristotle* and such others, out of which were bred up such a number of renowned Philosophers, orators, Historians, Poets and Princes all over *Greece*, *Italy* and *Asia*, besides the flourishing studies of *Cyrene* and *Alexandria*. But herein it shall exceed them, and supply a defect as great as that which *Plato* noted [in the *Laws*] in the Commonwealth of *Sparta*; wheras that City train'd up their youth most for warre, and these in their Academies and *Lycaeum*, all for the gown, this institution of breeding . . . shall be equally good both for Peace and warre.[17]

Thus as the purpose of liberty was the acquisition of virtue, so that virtue, or the disposition towards it, was capable of being learned. Indeed for Milton and other English republicans, as for their classical sources, such education was essential to successful republican citizenship. Milton's recurring pessimism about the 'aptness' of the English for liberty, influenced by Bodin's analysis of the effects of latitude, was a doubt about their capacity for the learned higher virtues:

For Britain (to speake a truth not oft spok'n) as it is a land fruitful enough of men stout and couragious in warr, so it is naturallie not over fertil of men able to govern justlie and prudently in peace; trusting onelie in thir Mother-witt . . . and consider[ing] not that civilitie, prudence, love of the public more then of money or vaine honour are to this soile in a manner outlandish; grow not here but in minds well implanted with solid and elaborate breeding.[18]

Given that Milton's virtue hinged upon a knowledge of moral absolutes anchored in God, it is not surprising that his eventual analysis of the fall of the republic should focus upon this most fundamental failure. According to the famous dictum of John Pocock, 'republicanism in England was a language, not a programme'. However, according to Milton 'language is but the instrument convaying to us things usefull to be known . . . [so] though a linguist should pride himselfe to have all the tongues *Babel* cleft the world into, yet, if he have not studied the solid things in them as well as the words . . . he were nothing . . . to be esteem'd a learned man'.[19] For the republican writers of the English revolution, the value of their

---

[17] Ibid. pp. 407–8.

[18] John Milton, MS Digression to the *History of Britain*, in *Complete Prose Works*, vol. VI, p. 451.

[19] Pocock, 'Introduction' p. 15; Milton, *Of Education* pp. 369–70; note Locke's comparable warning in his own *On Education* against 'preferring the Languages of the Ancient Greeks and Romans, to that which made them such brave men' [i.e. the moral substance of their philosophy]; quoted by Savonius, 'John Locke and the Civil Philosophy of the Bibliothecaires' p. 318.

(frequently glorious) words hinged entirely upon the practical realization of the 'solid things in them'. For them, that is to say, there was indeed a programme, without enactment of which the language would be no more than an embarrassing monument to a failed cause.

In *Paradise Lost*, this and other aspects of the republic's moral failure are enacted by Satan, who as many commentators have noticed therefore deploys Milton's own republican language.[20] This is, however, in Milton's Platonic terms, mere words, empty of the solid things. The besetting sin of Satan is pride. The calamity to which this has led him is to choose to serve self, rather than God, and so to deny himself the purpose of liberty. His republican rhetoric and that of his accomplices in Pandemonium is accordingly empty because cut off from the only source of real virtue in God. 'Of good and evil much they argued then/Of happiness and final misery/Passion and apathy, and glory and shame/Vain wisdom all, and false philosophy.'[21] Though accorded by the fallen the 'awful reverence' due to virtue, in fact Satan possesses only 'monarchical pride . . . close ambition varnished o'er with zeal'. Belial also 'clothed in reason's garb . . . seemed/For dignity composed and high exploit:/But all was false and hollow'.[22] In the words of C. S. Lewis, discussing this moral 'blindness . . . What we see in Satan is the horrible co-existence of a subtle and incessant intellectual activity with an incapacity to understand anything. This doom he has brought upon himself; in order to avoid seeing one thing [his dependence upon God] he has, almost voluntarily, incapacitated himself from seeing at all.'[23]

Thus the tormented inhabitants of Milton's Hell are also the denizens of Plato's cave. Barred from 'celestial light . . . cloud instead, and ever-during dark/Surrounds . . . /Cut off, and for the book of knowledge fair/Presented with a universal blank'.[24] Moreover this separation from God, the most dramatic consequence of the Fall, was merely a physical

---

[20] A point discussed by Blair Worden, 'Milton's Republicanism and the Tyranny of Heaven', in Gisela Bock, Quentin Skinner and Maurizio Viroli (eds.), *Machiavelli and Republicanism* (Cambridge, 1990). In my view, however, this does not signify Milton's personal retreat from republican language, or any other aspect of the cause. Nor, although I agree with much of what he says about the poem, am I persuaded by David Loewenstein (*Representing Revolution* p. 205) that 'We need to be alert to the mercurial qualities of Satan's political language.' Satan's *language* is consistently republican. His disposition of soul and his actions are tyrannical. The point thus being made was by this time of long standing in Milton's writing, and older still within the Christian humanist tradition (it is no accident that the besetting sin of Satan – pride – is also that which preoccupied More). This was that a cause consisting merely of words, contradicted by the appropriate 'solid things', was a hypocritical abomination.
[21] Milton, *Paradise Lost* p. 389. [22] Ibid. pp. 378, 381.
[23] Lewis, *A Preface to Paradise Lost* p. 96. [24] Milton, *Paradise Lost* p. 403.

manifestation of its cause. Real liberty (from human will) entailed subjection (to God).[25] Laborious adherence to real virtue amounted to, and entailed, service to God (and reason, and the laws). The promise of republican liberty was the promise of subjection to none but a God whose goodness would never fail. Spurning this 'glorious' opportunity

> pride and worse ambition threw me down
> Warring in heaven against heaven's matchless king;
> Ah wherefore! He deserved no such return
> From me, whom he created what I was
> In that bright eminence, and with his good
> Upbraided none; nor was his service hard . . .
> Yet all his good proved ill in me
> And wrought but malice; lifted up so high
> I 'sdained subjection, and thought one step higher
> Would set me highest.[26]

It was the fatal folly of sinful man not only to prefer the empty rhetoric of virtue to its laboriously acquired substance, but to believe that rhetoric to the effect that man was the author of his own moral worth and destiny. This was to love, not God, but self. It was the penalty of such pride to be exiled from the source of goodness and of life to a world of death in which 'all good to me is lost;/Evil be thou my good':

> Of all things transitory and vain, when sin
> With vanity had filled the works of men:
> Both all things vain, and all who in vain things
> Built their fond hopes of glory or lasting fame,
> Or happiness in this or the other life;
> All who have their reward on earth, the fruits
> Of painful superstition and blind zeal,
> Nought seeking but the praise of men, here find
> Fit retribution, empty as their deeds.[27]

Nigel Smith has noted the operation within the poem of what he calls this 'principle of reversal', but not what the principle is. Rather than a 'veering between monarchical and republican colourings . . . meant to perplex the reader', we may rather discern a consistent distinction between the bogus rhetorical liberty and virtue attending a tyrannical soul, and

---

[25] Colin Davis, 'Religion and the Struggle for Freedom in the English Revolution', *Historical Journal* 35, 3 (1992).
[26] Milton, *Paradise Lost* p. 422.   [27] Ibid. p. 413.

the genuine substance of those qualities to be realized only by voluntary rational submission to the monarchy of God.[28]

By comparison to Milton, as we have seen, Marchamont Nedham placed less emphasis upon virtue and the moral consequences of liberty than upon the importance of achieving that political state and retaining it. Nevertheless for Nedham too, virtue and 'manners' were important themes and his treatment of them is very similar. Also for Nedham, because virtue was rational knowledge, education was crucial. The greatest danger to a free state was a people 'educated under monarchy . . . because they know not how to value or use their liberty'. Accordingly from 1650 *Mercurius Politicus* applied itself to the herculean task of the republican re-education of England. The authorities to which it turned included those most prized by Milton: Plato, Aristotle, Isocrates and Cicero. The examples which it gave included Athens and, pre-eminently, Rome. 'When Rome was in its pure estate, virtue begat a desire of liberty, and this desire begat in them an extraordinary courage and resolution to defend it; which three walked a long time hand in hand together . . . the ancient virtue which purchased their liberty and an empire over the world.'[29]

However, while clearly associating the moral and political benefits of self-government, what impressed Nedham most was territorial expansion of dominion. In celebrating this he drew upon Sallust and Guicciardini, but above all Machiavelli:

Nor is it . . . a meer Gallantry of spirit that excites men to the love of Freedom; but experience assures it to be the most . . . profitable way of Government, conducing every way to the enlarging a people in Wealth and Dominion . . . Nor do these things happen without special reason; it being usual in Free-States to be more tender of the Publick . . . than of particular Interests; wheras the case is otherwise in a Monarchy, because in this Form the Princes pleasure weighs down all Considerations of the Common good.[30]

This last passage paraphrases the interest theory established by the *Discorsi* Book 2, chapter 1. Moreover Machiavellian interest analysis is a more or less consistent feature of Nedham's writing from 1645 to 1660. It is therefore important to note that, anticipating Sidney's *Court Maxims*, even Nedham

---

[28] Nigel Smith, '*Paradise Lost* from Civil War to Restoration', in N. H. Keeble (ed.), *Writing of the English Revolution* (Cambridge, 2001) p. 255.

[29] Nedham, *Case of the Commonwealth* p. 113. See also pp. 114–15 (and chapter 12 below).

[30] Nedham, *Excellencie* pp. 18–20; based on *Mercurius Politicus* no. 68, 18–25 September 1651.

feels it necessary to distinguish his position from the modern reason of state most

> fully express'd in *Machiavel*; who as he hath left many noble Principles and observations upon record, in defence of the liberty of the people, so we find in some of his Books many pernitious sprinklings, unworthy of the light . . . the vile reason [for] which he gives . . . is this . . . *He which endeavours to approve himself an honest man to all parties, must of necessity miscarry among so many that are not honest.* Because some men are wicked and perfidious, therefore I must be so too. This is a sad inference, and fit onely for the practice of *Italy* where he wrot it: The ancient Heathens would have loathed this; and the *Romans* (who were the noblest of them all) did in all their actions detest it, reckoning plain honesty to have been the onely *policy*, and the foundation of their greatness . . . *The people of Rome attained to so great a height, by observing Faith and Piety.*[31]

While noticing this and associated defences of human political rationality, it is the view of Paul Rahe that they constitute 'passing rhetorical flourishes' at odds with Nedham's deeper commitment to Machiavelli's scepticism.[32] Yet the basis for attributing to one aspect of Nedham's rhetoric greater significance than another remains unclear. In his praise of the achievements of the Roman people, Nedham's words are not 'Honour, dominion, glory and renown' (Rahe's summary) but 'knowledge, valour, and virtuous poverty'.[33] It is this combination of Aristotle and Machiavelli, equally characteristic of Streater's *Observations*, Harrington's *Oceana* and Sidney's *Discourses*, which needs to be explained. This is not to dispute either the importance of Nedham's engagement with Machiavelli or its probable impact upon these later works.

STREATER AND ARISTOTLE

As we might expect, John Streater's understanding of virtue was deeply Aristotelian (with the component of Platonism which that involved). This Greek allegiance was underlined by the invocation of Erasmus's opinion of Aristotle as 'the Prince and perfecter of Philosophers; and a golden river . . . of wisdom'.[34] Moreover this Greek teleology was combined with elements of natural philosophy capable of yielding strikingly Harringtonian results.[35] It was the purpose of freedom to allow the 'Nature' of 'every

---

[31] *Mercurius Politicus* no. 112, 22–29 July 1652, pp. 1753–4.
[32] Rahe, 'Marchamont Nedham' pp. 5, 10.   [33] Quoted in ibid. p. 9.
[34] Streater, *Observations* no. 10, p. 73.
[35] For Streater's Aristotelianism see Smith, '*Popular Republicanism*'; for his natural philosophy, and relationship to Harrington, Johns, *The Nature of the Book* pp. 266–323.

Being' to realise 'it self'. 'All Essence bubbles out, flows forth.'[36] 'Man is an understanding creature, and therefore a sociable creature, whose property it is to meet and assemble together in Schools, to learn the Sciences, in the Market, Burses, or Exchange, to trade; and also in their Senate-house . . . to treat of their affairs: the which Meetings are the Priviledges and Rights by Nature that belong to . . . so noble a creature as Man is.'[37] Bees are also sociable, and organised, but man 'is the only Creature enjoying speech . . . to signifie what is profitable and . . . unprofitable . . . just and unjust'.[38] Thus, *'[E]very City or Commonwealth is . . . ordained for some good (for all men attempt and do all things for the end and purpose which in their opinion is good).'* Later Sidney would repeat in the *Discourses*: all men 'seek their own good; for the will is ever drawn by some real good, or the appearance of it . . . This is that which man seeks by all the . . . motions of his mind. Reason and passion, vice and virtue do herein concur, though they differ vastly in the objects in which each of them think this good to consist.'[39]

In prosecution of this end, 'The supreme Councel of the people should be free from force and over-awing . . . to set on foot debates of what is profitable and what is not profitable to the Commonwealth; of what is just, and what is unjust: They should rather sacrifice their lives, then condescend to anything that is not for the good of the publike.' Moreover *'such as are to command, are onely [to be] esteemed as they are either vertuous, wise or valiant'*.[40] 'Such was *Moses, Wisdom is to have the fear of God; and to fear God, is to do justly.* Wisdom and Valour mixed, maketh true Fortitude . . . Such was *Furius Camillus the Romane.'* Further (reflecting the profound influence upon Streater of Machiavelli, as well as of his Greek sources) such wisdom and valour had to be protected by frugality. Thus *'Herodotus . . .* saith that *Demaratus* told *Xerxes . . .* that the Greeks had entertained *Poverty*, and harboured *Virtue*, brought in by *Wisdom . . .* [thus] signifying . . . there was much difficulty of overcoming . . . such people.'[41]

As for other writers, education was crucial and 'Men until 25 years ought to be exercised in Arts and Sciences, in Merchandise or other professions.' More generally, as Aristotle explained, 'a Commonwealth is to be accounted perfect or imperfect' not only 'as the several Members thereof are either perfect or imperfect', but 'as they are arightly proportioned' for the end in view. As 'the whole is before the parts; then it may safely be concluded, that the publick should be before the private'. Concerning this 'whole', Streater

---

[36] Streater, *Observations* no. 1, p. 3.   [37] Ibid. no. 7, p. 51.   [38] Ibid. no. 8, p. 58.
[39] Sidney, *Discourses*, in *Sydney on Government* p. 37; Scott, *Algernon Sidney and the Restoration Crisis* p. 218.
[40] Streater, *Observations* no. 2, pp. 5, 7.   [41] Ibid. no. 3, pp. 12, 13.

explained, in a passage standing strikingly between Hobbes and Harrington, although human immortality was not possible, 'for that the Arteries, Veins, Sinews and Flesh could not be free from corruption', nevertheless as

in the body of a Commonwealth, the ministers of State and the Magistrates may be likened to the veins and sinews in the body of a man, the veins do serve for the conveying of the bloud and spirits, the sinews are for the actuating of the body, for the staying and putting forth of the joints . . . so should I say all ministers of State, and Magistrates are to convey justice and vertue to every part of the body, and be as staies and helps to the motion of the Commonwealth: and as in the natural body . . . Government should be so composed, that the [corrupt] humors in any part may be expelled, otherwise there cannot be continuance in the most perfect . . . form under heaven.[42]

Three years earlier Hobbes's *Leviathan* had asked: 'For what is the *Heart*, but a *Spring*: and the *Nerves*, but so many *Strings*; and the *Joynts*, but so many *Wheeles*, giving motion to the whole Body? . . . [so] a COMMON-WEALTH . . . is but an Artificiall Man . . . in which, the *Soveraignty* is an Artificiall *Soul* . . . The *Magistrates*, and other *Officers* of Judicature and Execution, artificiall *Joynts*', and so on.[43] In *The Art of Lawgiving* (1659) Harrington explained 'that the delivery of a model of government . . . is no less than political anatomy', and as we have seen *Oceana*'s bicameral constitution was a representation of the human body anatomised by Harvey.[44] According to Streater, in Aristotelian language again anticipating Harrington: '*Rome . . . flourished when the Spirits of men and women desired the goods of the minde, as their only honor and reputation . . . every man was careful to procure the common good, not his own; and chose rather to live poor in a rich Commonwealth, then rich in a poor City; they would not seek to purchase that by money or favour, which was onely due to vertue.*'[45] As in Harrington, moreover, this whole moral philosophy existed within the framework of a '*Natural Philosophy*' whereby

God in the infinite conception of his minde gave the form of the whole universe, all the things, causes and accidents . . . before he came to the parts . . . and . . . having perfected them, he saw them to be good; and since the creation, his power hath been still working in perfecting the whole by parts, as we see by the production of nature in new creatures, and innumerable [number] of new insects, as various forms of flyes . . . as well as plants; likewise the increase of mankinde; so that of late yeers many unknown countries to former ages, have been peopled with the late increase of mankinde.[46]

---

[42] Ibid. no. 4, p. 22.   [43] Hobbes, *Leviathan* p. 9.
[44] Harrington, *Oceana*, in *Political Works* p. 287; Harrington, *The Art of Lawgiving* p. 656.
[45] Streater, *Observations* no. 9, p. 67.   [46] Ibid. p. 66.

It is within this divinely created universe evolving towards its own completion that Streater set his understanding of man. 'He is a divine living thing . . . compounded . . . after the image of God . . . a partaker of Reason':

> Man is indued with a divine Understanding, to observe the order of the Celestial bodies, and to rule and govern the Terrestrial; in which every man according to nature, should have a share . . . He onely hath the knowledge of the Creator, God . . . The inquisition and search of truth doth belong properly to man, who hath power to contemplate upon the heaven, stars, earth, water . . . and the nature of all things. He, by serving God uprightly, obtaineth life eternal. By Man, Laws . . . were appointed, Equity justly prescribed, that the better and more happily we might conduct our lives . . . Mans spirit is more pure and divine then the elements, answering proportionably to the heavens, and coupling (as *Aristotle* saith) the soul to the body: which spirit is full of Reason, and Divine Understanding: it is bodiless, passionless, and immortal . . . Man being good and vertuous . . . he being indued with all these favours enjoyeth all things comprised within the circle of the world; which are innumerable in number, and wonderful in beauty.[47]

This was why 'It is profitable in a Commonwealth that every one seek after . . . excellency in Government, in the arts and sciences . . . in the professions of all Artificers, in husbandry and all things else.' As '*Aristotle* saith that *Man in perfection is the best of all living creatures.* It is to be granted he is so, when he maketh his perserverence in vertue all his life-time.'[48]

HARRINGTON

Oceana, too, is a work of Aristotelian political anatomy, set within the framework of a natural philosophy, accompanied by celestial imagery. This has been interpreted as being guided by a neo-Platonist spiritual mechanics similar to Streater's own.[49] Yet Harrington's natural philosophy, and the political philosophy which it sustained, does not serve as a framework for the moral completion of rational man. On the contrary, while not making this impossible it also renders it unnecessary. What is Aristotelian about *Oceana*'s 'government of laws and not men', though only up to a point, is its constitutional prescription rather than its moral philosophy.

In *Oceana* these moral 'goods of the mind' are secondary, as 'principles of authority', to the material foundation of 'empire'. Whereas liberty and virtue will be provided for only in certain types of superstructure, there are no exceptions to the Harringtonian law that 'empire' is determined by

---

[47] Ibid. no. 10, pp. 74–5.   [48] Ibid. p. 74.
[49] Craig Diamond, 'Natural Philosophy in Harrington's Political Thought', *Journal of the History of Philosophy*, 16, 4 (1978) pp. 387–98.

'the balance of dominion'. For Oceana to function successfully its citizens, to whom Harrington refers as 'the materials of the commonwealth', do not require that 'understanding' so emphasised by Streater. 'It is not possible for the people, if they can but draw the balls, though they understand nothing at all of the ballot, to be out.'[50] Rather what is crucial is the overall relationship of Harrington's political 'art' to his interpretation of nature. 'A man is sinful, yet the world is perfect, so may the citizens be sinful, and yet the commonwealth be perfect.' Like Streater's, this natural philosophy is an interpretation of the work of God. In a world of material in perpetual motion, the basis for stability in the foundation is the identification of the balance of dominion, and the prevention of its further motion (alteration) by an agrarian law. In the superstructure, in the case of a popular balance of dominion, it is the establishment of mechanisms of rotation allowing for perpetual circular motion. Thus 'the equality of a commonwealth consist in the equality first of the agrarian, and next of the rotation'.[51]

It is within this context that we must also understand Harrington's account of virtue. One recent interpretation of *Oceana* has attributed much of Harrington's celestial imagery, and his broader metaphysics, to Plato's *Timaeus*.[52] About the Platonic content of the celestial imagery of Milton there is little doubt. Neither is there any question that Harrington was deeply influenced by Plato, as well as by Hobbes. Thus in a reworking of *Leviathan*'s introduction, Harrington's lawgiver

conceived such a delight within him, as God is described by Plato to have done, when he had finished the creation of the world, and saw his own orbs move below him. For in the art of man, being the imitation of nature which is the art of God, there is nothing so like the first call of beautiful order out of chaos and confusion as the architecture of a well-ordered commonwealth. Wherefore Lycurgus, seeing . . . that his orders were good, fell into deep contemplation how he might render them . . . unalterable and immortal.[53]

Yet Plato was no materialist. Perfection and (therefore) immortality were properties only of forms standing outside the material world of sense. Thus although political constitutions could be rendered more or less stable (and stability was a major concern of the *Laws*), this was to be achieved by adherence to those moral truths, and could not be everlasting. Nevertheless it is significant that, as Harrington's account of liberty began by invoking Aristotle and Livy, so that of virtue begins in language which is perceptibly Platonic. Thus

---

[50] Harrington, *Oceana*, in *Political Works* pp. 320, 222.   [51] Ibid. p. 184.
[52] Nelson, 'The Greek Tradition in Republican Thought'.
[53] Harrington, *Oceana*, in *Political Works* p. 341.

The soul of man (whose life or motion is perpetual contemplation . . .) is the mistress of two potent rivals . . . reason . . . [and] passion . . . whatever was passion in the contemplation of a man, being brought forth by his will into action, is vice and the bondage of sin; so whatever was reason in the contemplation of a man, being brought forth by his will into action, is virtue and the freedom of soul . . . Now government is no other than the soul of a nation or city; wherefore that which was reason in the debate of a commonwealth, being brought forth by the result, must be virtue; and for as much as the soul of a city or nation is the sovereign power, her virtue must be law.[54]

How is the triumph of reason over passion to be secured in that government which is the 'soul' of *Oceana*? According to Milton and other classical republicans the first need was for a rigorous moral education to fit citizens for a liberty which consisted in choice (of good over evil, and public over private interest). In Sidney's formulation 'the chief and necessary duty of a governor is to divest himself of those interests and passions which sway with men intent on their private interests, so as to apply himself wholly to promote the public welfare'.[55] The second step was the reinforcement of that choice by the government of rational laws (which these citizens have chosen) rather than by the unregulated will of man. As Plato said in the *Republic*, 'For good nurture and education implant good constitutions, and these constitutions taking root in good education improve more and more.'[56] In both respects, a good and just city needed good and just men; it had nowhere else from which to obtain its moral character. Yet by Harrington even sceptical Machiavelli is reproved for this outmoded view.[57]

It is thus perhaps not surprising that the 'bringing forth into action' of 'whatever was reason in the contemplation of a man' is in Oceana an institutional rather than a personal achievement. It occurs as a consequence, not of choice within the 'soul of man', but of a constitutional mechanism within that 'government' which is the 'soul of a nation'. This is informed by what Harrington calls the second of his 'great discoveries . . . That which great philosophers are disputing upon in vain is brought into light by two silly girls: even the whole mystery of a commonwealth, which lies only in dividing and choosing.'[58] If one girl divides a cake, he explained, and the other chooses, the shares will always be equal. This disposition of equal shares is 'right reason', or 'the interest of the whole'. Yet this outcome depended upon Harrington's assumption of self-interested behaviour in both parties; should altruism occur the mechanism would break down.

---

[54] Ibid. pp. 169–70.   [55] Sidney, *Court Maxims* pp. 137–8.   [56] Plato, *Republic* Book 4.   [57] Harrington, *Oceana*, in *Political Works* p. 320–2.   [58] Ibid. p. 172.

Thus not only did *Oceana* not depend upon public-spirited virtue, in the conventional sense, it assumed its absence. In place of the Platonic and Aristotelian fantasy that public interest hinged upon individual rational choice, Harrington enunciated the maxim that as 'reason is nothing but interest, as there be divers interests . . . so divers reasons'. In this sceptical universe the transition from 'private reason, which is the interest of a private man' to 'that reason which is the interest of the whole' was a matter not of moral choice but of mathematical (or mechanical) computation. Here the material image of the cake is important because what Harrington was doing, as in his treatment of liberty, is 'mak[ing] a virtue of necessity'. And thus the virtue of *Oceana*, the 'bringing forth into action' the 'reason . . . of the whole' is the accomplishment not of its citizens, but of its orders. In the subsequent 'Model of the Commonwealth' Harrington's public 'orator' is charged with 'informing the people of the reason' of these orders.

As in Harrington's account of liberty, this reworking of virtue made substantial use of classical republican authorities. These included Machiavelli, but the most important was Plato. Yet here, as elsewhere, Harrington appears to have used Hobbesian natural philosophy to update his classical authorities and furnish their insights with what he took to be their necessary material foundation. This was again to show Hobbes how unwise he had been to allow the tragedy recounted by Thucydides to turn him away from classical political philosophy altogether.

'CLEAVE, SAW AND CUT': SIDNEY, VANE AND THE RHETORIC OF PURITAN MAGISTRACY

To turn finally to Sidney and Vane is to underline the debt of English republican moral philosophy to Plato, as well as to Aristotle. For by far the most striking feature of Sidney's philosophy of virtue is a Christian Platonic epistemology identical to Milton's. For Sidney, as for Milton, because the 'light of nature and reason in man . . . ha[d] its beginning in God', there was no contradiction between the teachings of 'Plato and other great masters of human reason' on the one hand, and 'Scripture . . . the reason and wisdom of the father' on the other. 'The essence of the law . . . consists solely in the justice of it . . . For the understanding of this Law we should not need to study Littleton and Coke, but Plato and Aristotle . . . above all the Scripture . . . being the dictate of God's own spirit.'[59] In this context Sidney

---

[59] Sidney, *Court Maxims* pp. 122–3.

was in the habit of referring to 'Aristotle, and his master Plato', as well as to 'Plato, and his scholar Aristotle'. In Sidney's *Court Maxims*, despite its own clear debt to Machiavelli's *Discourses*, we find a defence of Aristotle's *Politics* against Machiavellian 'policy' highly reminiscent of Milton, Nedham and Streater. Thus

> *Polis* signifies a city, and *politeia* is nothing but the art . . . of governing cities or civil societies . . . that men in them may live happily. We need seek no other definition of a happy human life in relation to this world than that set down by Aristotle as the end of civil societies . . . (Aristotle, *Politics* bk III). For as there is no happiness without liberty, and no man more a slave than he that is overmastered by vicious passions, there is neither liberty, nor happiness, where there is not virtue . . . By this you may see whether the name of policy be fitly given to that wicked malicious craft, exercised with perfidy and cruelty, accompanied with all manner of lust and vice, directly and irreconcileably contrary to virtue and piety, honesty or humanity, which is taught by Machiavelli and others.[60]

For Sidney, as for Milton, the loss of English liberty is the result of moral failure; of wickedness and vice; above all of ignorance. This signalled the failure of the republican educational project; of the attempt to instil the public preference for substance over appearance, for virtue over vice; to equip a people for self-governing rationality. The English people had failed 'to have bin taught by experience .. the mistress even of fools. Burnt children dread the fire, but we more childish than children, tho oft scorch'd and burnt, do agen cast ourselves into the fire, like moths and gnats, delighting in the flame that consumes us.'[61] This fire is again that in Plato's cave, a flickering of illusion, to be contrasted with the sun of truth: 'He is not happy that has what he desires, but desires what is good and enjoys it.' Like those deceived by Milton's Satan, 'The people of England, deceived by . . . [the] fraud of the courtiers and priests . . . grew to that height of madness as to seek servitude rather than liberty.' Their reward is a form of government which not only cannot produce virtue: rooted in evil, and specifically self-interest, it is dedicated to its eradication.

> [That] your court fears and hates all good and virtuous men . . . shows the evil of your government . . . An evil tree cannot bring forth good fruit, nor a good ill, so you may judge rightly of the tree by the fruit. Acts of justice, virtue, goodness proceed from good principles. The exercise of frauds, rapine, perfidy, and cruelty comes from a corrupt root . . . The utter contrariety between good and evil causes an irreconcileable enmity between the followers of each.[62]

---

[60] Ibid. p. 24. [61] Ibid., quoted in Scott, *Algernon Sidney and the English Republic* p. 186.
[62] Sidney, *Court Maxims* p. 188.

When, however, the English people 'discover their misery and folly in the emptiness of that enjoyment which they thought would make them happy . . . nothing is more reasonable than that they should repent of their choice *and endeavour to unmake what they have made*'.[63] It is on the basis of this hope that the *Maxims* returns to the republican educational project:

Magistrates ought so to exercise their power, as that under them we may live in all godliness and honesty, says the apostle. The like is said by all philosophers who deserve to be hearkened to. Aristotle says the end of civil society is *vita beata secundum virtutem*, Socrates and Plato say the perfection of action and contemplation, and others the attaining of justice in order to arrive at that perfection in action and contemplation . . . We may truly say that all rational men . . . have agreed in showing this to be the end of government:[64]

With this rational politics the hereditary principle was incompatible:

Man is by nature a rational creature. Everything that is irrational, is contrary to man's nature . . . We all breathe the same air, are composed of the same materials . . . and though they or their flatterers sometimes say they are Gods, they shall die like men. They are naturally no more than men and justly pretend to no more than others . . . This may show you whether . . . a thing so unreasonable, so unnatural as . . . hereditary monarchy . . . can be good for the people or not.[65]

In a rational political order, 'As equality is just among equals, it is unjust to reward equally those who in themselves are unequal.'

All inequality is natural or artificial; that preference which can be challenged by a natural inequality is reasonable, if the nature of it suits with the thing in question, and the proportion will bear. A wise man has naturally that advantage over a fool that his counsel ought to be hearkened to more than the other. He that excels in fidelity, valour, experience, and all military virtues has a juster pretence to the command of an army than one who has none of those qualities . . . To know what inequality gives preference to any man in point of government, we must see what the ends of government are and what qualities are required in those that govern conducing to those ends . . . Wisdom is the power in man of judging what is good or evil, of knowing the ways of attaining good and directing all . . . actions to the attaining of it . . . Wisdom only knows the end to which . . . [civil societies] are directed and how to find and use the means of attaining to it.[66]

Here two differences between Sidney's and Milton's careers had a considerable impact upon Sidney's exposition. Sidney had been a soldier, and for him the first institution through which superior moral discipline had come to have a decisive impact upon the revolution was parliament's army. Secondly, while Milton celebrated the power of a free people, served it and

[63] Ibid. pp. 4–7.   [64] Ibid. p. 127.   [65] Ibid. pp. 36–7.   [66] Ibid. pp. 34–5.

defended it, Sidney had also wielded it. It is from the standpoint of his personal participation in republican magistracy that both the *Court Maxims* and the *Discourses* returned to the moral philosophy elaborated by Milton and Streater. For Sidney, as for Milton, and in contrast to Harrington, the purpose of government was to 'make men better'. For Sidney too education was one key to this: men were capable of 'learning to be virtuous'. But what both the *Maxims* and the *Discourses* emphasised was the crucial role to be played in such education by good government (the government of laws) itself. This was, in the first place, a necessary consequence of human frailty:

Laws are made and governments constituted as remedies to human frailty and depravity. Those laws only are good which lead to and encourage virtue, and punish vice. Whoever is composed of flesh and blood . . . cannot always resist temptations to evil. In a commonwealth, therefore, well-constituted laws govern, not men. Though the magistrate be wicked, the constitution is to be such that his exorbitant lusts may be retrained and his crimes punished.[67]

The *Discourses* agreed:

[T]he fancy of . . . man . . . always fluctuates, and every passion that arises in his mind . . . disorders him. The good of a people ought to be established upon a more solid foundation. For this reason, the law is established, which no passion can disturb. 'Tis void of desire and fear, lust and anger.'Tis . . . written reason, retaining some measure of the divine perfection. It does not enjoin that which pleases a weak, frail man, but . . . commands that which is good, and punishes evil in all, whether rich or poor, high or low.[68]

Nor was this role of law simply negative. Rather it was the function of just law, by restraining the passions, to open the way for an accumulation of the benefits of reason:

The melioration of the law strengthens that which is good in the government, and still adds something better than what was before. Where things are in this right order, there is a perpetual advance in all that is good, until such nation attains unto the political perfection of liberty, security, and happiness, which were the ends for which government was constituted. As the rectitude of the will is wrought by the illumination of the understanding, the understanding advances in the discovery and knowledge of truth through the rectitude of the will.[69]

It was for this reason that, according to the *Discourses*:'The Grecians, amongst others who followed the light of reason, knew no other original title to the government of a nation, than that wisdom, valour and justice, which was beneficial to the people . . . if governments . . . are instituted

[67] Ibid. p. 196.   [68] Sidney, *Discourses*, ed. West pp. 400–1.   [69] Sidney, *Court Maxims* p. 132.

by men according to their own inclinations, they did therein seek their own good.'[70] In this respect 'Such only deserved to be called good men, who endeavoured to be good to mankind . . . and in as much as that good consists in a felicity of estate, and perfection of person, they highly valued such as had endeavoured to make men better, wiser, and happier. This they understood to be the end for which men enter'd into societies.'[71]

The other morally formative factor was a virtuous magistracy. Here, with his invocation of political architecture, and the clear shared debt to Plato's *Laws*, Sidney sounds like Harrington. This is not, however, the constitutional architecture of a lawgiver, but the moral impact sought by active participants in the kind of puritan magistracy from which Harrington dissociated himself ('My Lord, there is not any public person, not any magistrate, that has written in politics worth a button'[72]). For Sidney, as for Milton, the key word was 'discipline'. Vane had spoken similarly of the need to 'use [all] ordinary means, daily afforded by God's providence, that are most conducing to guide and regulate the will of the people, unto the making of good choice'.[73] For Sidney,

The weakness in which we are born, renders us unable to attain this good of ourselves; we want help in all things, especially in the greatest . . . The first step towards the cure of this pestilent evil, is for many to join in one body, that everyone may be protected by the united force of all; and the various talents that men possess, may by good discipline be rendered useful to the whole; as the meanest piece of wood or stone being placed by a wise architect, conduces to the beauty of the most glorious building . . . [Men] are rough pieces of timber or stone, which 'tis necessary to cleave, saw or cut: This is the work of a skillful builder, and he only is capable of erecting a great fabrick, who is so. Magistrates are political architects.[74]

Vane spoke of magistracy as deriving from the people's 'freedome . . . to set up meet persons in the place of Supreme Judicature . . . whereby they may have the . . . benefit of the choicest light and wisdom of the nation that they are capable to call forth, for the Rule and Government under which they will live; and through the orderly exercise of such . . . wisdom . . . to shape and forme all subordinate actings and administrations'.[75] Such 'Magistrates are to fear and forebear intermedling with . . . matters of Faith and Conscience.' Otherwise, however, 'They are . . . ordained of God to be his Minister unto men for good . . . [or] that which is good in the sight of men . . . and

---

[70] Sidney, *Discourses*, ed. West pp. 47, 49.   [71] Ibid. p. 6.
[72] James Harrington, *The Examination of James Harrington*, in *Political Works* p. 858.
[73] Quoted in Judson, *Vane* p. 51.   [74] Sidney, *Discourses*, ed. West p. 83.
[75] Vane, *A Healing Question* p. 4.

a Minister of terrour . . . to those that doe evill in matters of outward practice . . . and dealings in the things of this life.'[76] Thus this discipline was both negative (the restraint of sin or passion) and positive: a matter of harnessing the human potential for good in God-given reason. So crucial was this moral function of law and magistracy that for Sidney the rectitude or 'pravity' of government was the principal determinant of human progress, or decline.[77]

All men follow that which seems advantageous to themselves. Such as are bred under a good discipline, and see that all benefits procured to their country by virtuous actions, redound to the honour and advantage of themselves . . . contract from their infancy a love to the publick, and look upon the common concernments as their own. When they have learnt to be virtuous, and see that virtue is in esteem, they seek no other preferments than such as may be obtained that way; and no country ever wanted great numbers of excellent men, where this method was established. On the other side, when 'tis evident that the best are despised, hated, or mark'd out for destruction; all things calculated to the humour or advantage of one man, who is often the worst . . . and his favour gained only by a most obsequious respect, or . . . servile obedience . . . all application to virtuous actions will cease.[78]

Those who doubted this might look at history, as when 'the desire of that praise which is the reward of virtue, raised the Romans above the rest of mankind', or 'When Xerxes invaded Greece, [and] there was not a citizen of Athens able to bear arms, who did not leave his wife and children to shift for themselves in the neighbouring cities, and their houses to be burnt when they embarked with Themistocles; and never thought of either till they had defeated the barbarians at Salamis by sea, and Plataea by land.'[79] Finally, for proof of this, it was not necessary (though it was safer) to rely upon ancient examples.

---

[76] Ibid. p. 6.

[77] Vickie Sullivan argues that the *Discourses* displays a move away from the moral philosophy of Aristotle (with its championship of reason) towards that of Machiavelli (cultivating the passions): Sullivan, 'Algernon Sidney: Machiavellian Republican and Ambivalent Liberal', paper given at the Annual Meeting of the American Political Science Association: Philadelphia, 31 August 2003. Yet Sidney himself never repudiates reason, or endorses the passions (as distinct from 'the spirits of men') which on the contrary the *Discourses* frequently denounces. Moreover at no point does Sidney's engagement with Machiavelli, brilliantly analysed by Sullivan and at its deepest in chapter 2, actually displace Aristotle, who remains a fundamental source throughout chapter 3. This suggests that he did not see the contradiction discerned by some modern commentators. For him, as for Nathaniel Lee (also influenced by Machiavelli, see chapter 15 below), there did not appear any tension between pursuit of the rational political ideals prescribed by antiquity and the sometimes savage measures necessary for their defence.

[78] Sidney, *Discourses*, ed. West p. 274 (and see pp. 253, 272–3).   [79] Ibid. pp. 199, 201.

The same order that made men valiant and industrious in the service of their country during the first ages, would have the same effect, if it were now in being: Men would have the same love to the publick as the Spartans and Romans had, if there was the same reason for it. We need no other proof of this than what we have seen in our own country, where, in a few years good discipline, and a just encouragement given to those who did well, produced more examples of pure, compleat, incorruptible, and invincible virtue than Rome or Greece could ever boast; or if more be wanting, they may easily be found among the Switzers, Hollanders and others; but 'tis not necessary to light a candle to the sun.[80]

This moral polemic was to be powerfully influential over the following two centuries, in Britain, continental Europe and America. Thus Trenchard and Gordon's *Cato's Letters*, which quoted extensively from the *Discourses*, summarised the argument in 1721:

Ill governments, subsisting by vice and rapine, are jealous of private virtue . . . nor are they secure while any thing good or valuable is secure. Hence it is, that to drain, worry, and debauch their subjects, are the steady maxims of their politicks . . . There will be but little industry where property is precarious; small honesty where virtue is dangerous . . . Good government does, on the contrary, produce great virtue, much happiness, and many people. Greece and Italy, while they continued free, were each of them, for the number of inhabitants, like one continued city; for virtue, knowledge, and great men, they were the standards of the world; and that age and country that could come nearest to them, has ever since been reckoned the happiest. Their government, their free government, was the root of all of these advantages, and of all this felicity and renown.[81]

---

[80] Ibid. p. 216.
[81] John Trenchard and Thomas Gordon, *Cato's Letters*, ed. Ronald Hamowy (2 vols., Indianapolis, Ind., 1995) vol. I, p. 270 (22 July 1721).

CHAPTER 9

The politics of time

When the Father who had generated this saw here an image of the
Eternal Gods, he rejoiced, and in his joy sought to make the world still
more like to its model. And as the model is an Eternal Living Thing,
he sought to make the universe like unto it, as far as may be. But the
nature of that Living Model was eternal, and it was not possible to
give this character fully to a generated thing. Therefore he devised a
moving image of that fixed eternity: he made the heavens to be, by
their structure . . . a likeness of that eternity which is fixed and one;
and this we call *Time*.

Plato, *The Timaeus*[1]

THE POLITICS OF THE ANCIENT CONSTITUTION

Like most humanist writing, English republican argument was grounded
in an appeal to historical sources. In the words of John Hall, 'And truly I
conceive reading of History to be the most rational Course to set any judgement right, because it instructs by Experience and Effects, and grounds
the Judgement upon material Observations, and not blindly gropes after
Notions and Causes.'[2] Our specific concern in this chapter, in relation to
this historical frame of reference, is with republican arguments concerning
continuity and change.

One aspect of such argument was ancient constitutionalism. This co-
opted an account of ancient national laws and liberties, developed between
the twelfth and fourteenth centuries, and exploited by Tudor authorities
to establish the case for national independence from the church of Rome.[3]
From the beginning of the seventeenth century these sources were deployed

[1] Plato, *The Timaeus*, in William Whewell, *The Platonic Dialogues For English Readers*, vol. III
(Cambridge, 1861) p. 367.
[2] Hall, *The Grounds and Reasons of Monarchy* (1651) p. 7.
[3] Janelle Greenberg, *The Radical Face of the Ancient Constitution: St Edward's 'Laws' in Early Modern
Political Thought.* (Cambridge, 2001) chs. 1–3.

by English parliamentarians and common lawyers to oppose, first, the Jacobean project of Anglo-Scots union, and then other perceived aspects of early Stuart monarchical absolutism.[4] Such innovations, the argument ran, trespassed against laws and liberties either British or Saxon in origin, which had existed since before the date of legal memory, and which had not been interrupted by the Norman invasion. This account had many European parallels. Among those developed by protestant humanists, the most important for English republicans were the Scottish history by George Buchanan, Francois Hotman's *Francogallia* and Hugo Grotius's *Treatise of the antiquity of the Batavian now Hollandish Republic*, translated into English in 1649.[5]

All of these writers had enlisted a historical argument not only to oppose monarchical innovation, but to justify armed resistance to it. It is accordingly not surprising that during England's own civil wars ancient constitutionalist arguments played an important role.[6] Thereafter republican ancient constitutionalists deployed the full range of English and continental authorities, with some classical sources like Tacitus' *Germania*. The result was the defence of an ancient, free European 'Gothic polity', Germanic in origin, against early modern tyranny.[7] As Milton put it, 'Neither is it any new project of the Monarchs, and their Courtiers in these dayes, though Christians they would be thought, to endeavour the introducing of a plain Turkish Tyranny. Witness that Consultation had in the Court of *France* under *Charles* the ninth at *Blois*.'[8]

Yet in at least one respect the existence of republican ancient constitutionalism is an oddity. This is because a strenuous defence of the right of rational humankind to effect political innovation was one of the most striking features of this literature. The deployment in support of this claim of both natural law and classical republican political language would appear to have been in tension with the ancient constitutionalist defence of custom. In fact the extent to which this was the case should not be overstated. Glenn Burgess has stressed the capacity of the common lawyers' understanding of customary law as rational to embrace the notion of incremental change. Janelle Greenberg insists that appeals to the ancient constitution did not

[4] Ibid. ch 4; Glenn Burgess, *The Politics of the Ancient Constitution* (Basingstoke, 1992); Pocock, *The Ancient Constitution and the Feudal Law*.

[5] George Buchanan, *De Jure Regni apud Scotos*, trans. 'Philalethes' (1680); Francois Hotman, *Francogallia*, ed. R. E. Giesey, trans. J. H. M. Salmon (Cambridge, 1972); van Gelderen, 'The Machiavellian Moment' p. 215; Burgess, *Ancient Constitution* pp. 14–16.

[6] Greenberg, *Radical Face* ch. 5.   [7] Salmon, *The French Religious Wars*.

[8] John Milton, *Observations upon the Articles of Peace* (1649), in *Complete Prose Works* vol. III, p. 313.

simply, or necessarily, involve adherence to 'a static and immutable constitution'.[9] The medieval documents upon which she focuses were frequently
invoked in defence, not of conformity in detail to an ancient state of government, but rather of the general exercise of a rational popular sovereignty,
ennobled by precedent and prescription, but carrying with it the authority
for continuing change in the present. It is in just this sense that Algernon
Sidney explained:

the authority of a magistracy proceeds not from the number of years that it has
continued, but the rectitude of the institution . . . [Nevertheless] if that liberty
in which God created man, can receive any strength from continuance, and the
rights of Englishmen can be render'd more unquestionable by prescription, I say
that the nations whose rights we inherit, have ever enjoy'd the liberties we claim,
and always exercised them in governing themselves . . . from the time they were
first known in the world.[10]

To be thus informed by the past, and even anchored in it, was not
necessarily to be imprisoned by it. To believe otherwise may be an Enlightenment, or post-Enlightenment illusion. It may also, however, be the case
that the presence within republican argument of ancient constitutionalist
language owed more to its indespensability in a traditional society, and to
the polemical exigencies of answering authors like Salmasius and Filmer,
than to its conformity to other aspects of republican writing.[11]

Thus the most important republican treatment of the pre-Norman
national polity was Milton's *History of Britain* (commenced in 1649, though
not published until 1670).[12] This arrived at the depressing conclusion, in
sharp contrast to that of Hotman concerning the Franks, that both the
Britons and Saxons had been hopeless squanderers of their opportunities
for freedom. The main reason for this was that they suffered, perhaps incur-
ably, from 'two and fifty degrees of northern latitude' (see chapter 11). Again
in contrast to Hotman, it was Milton's view in *Areopagitica* that the fact
that 'we are not yet *Gothes* and *Jutlanders*' was owing entirely to the Roman
occupation of Britain, through which contact was first established with
'polite wisdom and letters' and 'the old and elegant humanity of Greece'.[13]
This was very like the view of Harrington in *Oceana* that 'if we have given
over running up and down naked and with dappled hides, learned to write
and read, to be instructed with good arts, for all these we are beholding
to the Romans . . . by whose means we are as it were of beasts become

---

[9] Greenberg, *Radical Face* pp. 294–5.   [10] Sidney, *Discourses*, ed. West pp. 478–9.
[11] For this fact in relation to the Levellers see Scott, *England's Troubles* pp. 284–5.
[12] Milton, *Complete Prose Works* vol. v, Part 1; von Maltzhan, *Milton's History of Britain*.
[13] Milton, *Areopagitica* p. 489.

men, and by whose means we might yet of obscure and ignorant men (if we thought not so well of ourselves) become a wise and a great people'.[14]

Yet needs must, and so at the climax of the revolution none of this stopped Milton publicly, in his *Defence of the English People*, voicing his

pride in our fathers who, in establishing this state, displayed a wisdom and a sense of freedom equal to that of the ancient Romans or the most illustrious Greeks; and these . . . fathers . . . cannot but rejoice in their sons who, when they had well-nigh been made slaves, did with such courage and good sense save that state . . . founded on liberty, from the unbridled tyranny of a king.[15]

In *The Tenure* he asserted the ancient freedom of all 'the Christian Empires in Europe, the Greek and German . . . French, Italian, Arragonian, English . . . and Scottish', adding the well-worn claim that '*William* the Norman . . . was compell'd the second time to take oath at S. *Albanes*, ere the people would be brought to yeild obedience.'[16] Like Sidney later he used '*Matthew Paris*, the best of our Historians' to prove the unbroken subjection of 'our Monarchs' to the Saxon laws 'of St. *Edward*'.[17] The lawfulness of resistance to tyrants was illustrated not only from scripture, from ancient Greece and Rome, and from the history of England, but from the works of Buchanan, Grotius and Hotman. The repetition and considerable amplification of these claims by the *Defence* occurred in response to arguments by Salmasius to the contrary ('Under the old Anglo-Saxon kings . . . it was never the custom to summon the populace to the national assemblies').[18] In response Milton insisted that both Britons and Saxons had always governed themselves, with or without kings; that in the assemblies deployed for this purpose under various names (including the Saxon '*Wittena-gemots*') lay the origin of those parliaments which remained the supreme English authority deriving from this popular sovereignty; and that when so elected ancient kings and their successors had always been liable to punishment or deposition for misgovernment. Thus what governed in ancient England, a Germanic society, as in contemporary England, was not the will of monarchs but the law. To prove these points Milton amplified the range of his English and other authorities (Tacitus, Matthew Paris, the *Mirror of Justices*, 'the laws of St Edward', Fortescue, Bracton). Goodman, Buchanan, Hotman and Philip de Comines underpinned the case against once-legitimate early modern monarchies which had degenerated into tyrannies.[19]

[14] Harrington, *Oceana*, in *Political Works* p. 192.
[15] Milton, *Defence* pp. 494–5; Greenberg, *Radical Face* pp. 240–1.   [16] Milton, *Tenure* p. 201.
[17] Ibid. pp. 218–19; on Matthew Paris see Greenberg, *Radical Face* pp. 47–53.
[18] Quoted by Milton, *Defence* p. 474.   [19] Ibid. pp. 474–507.

Another sustained ancient constitutionalist defence of the new republic was Rump MP Nathaniel Bacon's *An historicall discourse of the uniformity of the government of England* (1647–51). This also used Tacitus, Hotman and others to arrive at an account of the Germanic origins of English liberties.[20] Bacon concluded that 'as I found this nation a commonwealth, so I leave it, and so may it be forever; so will it be, if we may attain the happiness of our forefathers' ancient Saxons'. As 'a Saxon king was no other than a *primum mobile* set in a regular motion, by laws established by the whole body of the kingdom', so William I never shook 'off the clog of Saxon law' or 'raised the title of conquest'. On the contrary, the law by which he ruled was 'not the law of the conquerors own will, nor the law that suits with his desire; but the ancient law of the kingdom'.[21]

Although Marchamont Nedham in *Mercurius Politicus* mentioned the extinction of 'the good old *English* Lawes and Liberties' by that '*Norman Bastard*', he did not dwell upon the Saxon state.[22] For his overriding theme, in 1650–1 in particular, was the foundation of all government in the '*Power of the Sword*'. 'The *Sword* is the great *Engin*, used by the hand of God, in erecting, altering and establishing all Frames of Government in the world . . . [if it] was . . . the *Sword* . . . that did thus enslave us . . . shall we not free ourselves now we have the *Sword* in our own hands?'[23] In 1652, however, Nedham traced the progress of modern monarchical tyranny, from '*Lewis the eleventh*' in France, who established a 'patern . . . followed close by the late Tyrant in *England*'.[24] This development was accompanied by modern '*Raggione di Stato*', most completely exemplified by Machiavelli's *Prince*.[25] In this account, prefiguring his later defence of the Protectorate, Nedham found the key to the freedom of 'the old Constitution of the Commonweals and kingdoms of Europ' in their separation of '*Legislative* and *Executive* Power'. This had been true of Spain, France, Poland and Bohemia, and would be so again in France if the Bordelais rebels 'have but so much manhood as to reduce the *two Powers* into their antient, or into better Channels'.[26]

The most important subsequent republican analysis of the ancient constitution came from Harrington. In this, characteristically, the author of *Oceana* radically adapted the established mythology, so that what had been

---

[20] See also Nathaniel Bacon, *A historical and political discourse of the laws and government of England* (1682) p. 2; Scott, *Algernon Sidney and the Restoration Crisis* p. 246.

[21] Quoted in Greenberg, *Radical Face* pp. 224–6.

[22] Nedham, *Mercurius Politicus* no. 64, 21–28 August 1651, p. 1014.

[23] Ibid. no. 52, 29 May–5 June 1651, pp. 858–9 (misnumbered 855); see also no. 65 (and others).

[24] Ibid. no. 105, p. 1709.   [25] Ibid. no. 108, p. 1691; nos. 112–13.   [26] Ibid. no. 105, pp. 1708–9.

a subject for celebration became instead the focus of a savage critique. According to this, in matters of civil government the nearest kin of the Saxons were not the Greeks and Romans, but the Huns and Vandals. '[A]ncient prudence' had provided for 'the empire of laws and not of men'. By contrast, that 'modern prudence . . . beginning with the arms of Caesar' and followed by 'those inundations of Huns, Goths, Vandals, Lombards, Saxons which, breaking the Roman Empire, deformed the whole face of the world . . . [was] an art whereby some man, or some few men, subject a city or nation, and rule it according unto his or their private interest'.[27] In *Oceana* not only was the latter system unfree, it was unstable. That limited monarchy which had, according to Milton, provided for liberty, or to Sidney for military success, was for Harrington not the political solution, but the problem. 'By which means this government, being indeed the masterpiece of modern prudence, hath been cried up to the skies as the only invention whereby at once to maintain the sovereignty of a prince and the liberty of the people, wheras indeed it hath been no other than a wrestling match.'[28]

It followed from this analysis that the early modern instability culminating in England's troubles had been caused not simply by the monarchical subversion of the ancient constitution, but by the inherent flaws of that constitution itself. Accordingly the early Tudor '*dissolution of this government*', though disastrous for the monarchy, at least furnished the opportunity for the replacement of modern prudence altogether. Nor did Harrington ever accuse his friend Charles I of tyranny. On the contrary, he had lacked the real power even of a monarch. 'Nor was there anything now wanting unto the destruction of the throne but that the people, not apt to see their own strength, should be put to feel it, when a prince, as stiff in disputes as the nerve of the monarchy was grown slack, received that unhappy encouragement from his clergy which became his utter ruin.'[29]

Following the Restoration, however, Algernon Sidney returned to, and further developed, the ancient constitutionalist arguments already deployed by Bacon and Milton. In the process he developed an account of the Gothic polity which made him the nearest English equivalent to Hotman himself.[30] Like Hotman's, Sidney's history was a humanist one in which Gothic liberty was traced from classical times. Unlike Hotman's, however, Sidney's

[27] Harrington, *Oceana*, in *Political Works* p. 161.   [28] Ibid. p. 196.   [29] Ibid. p. 198.
[30] In *The French Religious Wars* (p. 60) Salmon describes Sidney as 'one of the first Englishmen to express the legend of the Gothic constitution'.

version was an aggressively republican one in which, in noticeable contrast to Harrington, the principles informing ancient and Gothic government are closely associated.

Like Milton's, Sidney's ancient constitutionalism was developed in response to royalist arguments to the contrary. In the *Court Maxims* it was Philalethes the courtier who asked, 'what think you of the right of conquest by which many kings hold their crowns, and particularly ours from William the Conqueror?' To this Sidney responded, first, that no conquest gave a right unless in prosecution of a just war, and that in such a case the right belonged not only to the leader of that war, but to all who fought in it. Secondly, William was falsely surnamed the conqueror: 'A good part of the nobles and commons of England did from the first make him their head and leader. Harold was never king but a pretender to the crown.'[31] Accordingly 'all since William the first can pretend to what they enjoyed only by election'. More generally, the English Gothic polity shared in the history

of those who have abhorred even the name of kings. While the vicious cowardly Asiatics chose that slavery which suited with their spirits, all those nations which deserve to be imitated were governed by their own laws, according to their several constituted commonwealths. The name of king was not known to the Greeks, Italians, Germans, Gauls, and Spaniards but as the object of their hatred. And that part of Africa which was not barbarous did flourish under the Carthaginian government.[32]

Similarly Sidney set his account of the transition of once vigorous medieval English kingship into effeminate, parasitic tyranny in its European context.[33] 'Our boisterous fighting kings of the Plantagenet race . . . content with a limited power at home' and assisted by 'a powerful, gallant nobility' (Sidney's own Percy ancestors among the most powerful) were characteristic of 'those old-fashioned monarchies which were in most parts of Europe till within the last hundred years'.[34] These were monarchical commonwealths, sharing many of the military virtues of earlier republics. '[T]hese princes understood not the refined policy of the latter age. They exposed

---

[31] Sidney, *Court Maxims* pp. 13–14.   [32] Ibid. p. 13.

[33] In *British Identities before Nationalism: Ethnicity and Nationhood in the Atlantic World, 1600–1800* (Cambridge, 1999) ch. 9, Colin Kidd rightly emphasises the European, rather than simply national, framework of Sidney's Gothicism.

[34] Sidney, *Court Maxims* p. 67; for the impact upon his thought of Sidney's Percy ancestry see Scott, *Algernon Sidney and the English Republic* pp. 43–8.

themselves to infinite troubles and dangers for a little glory. They passed more nights in the camp than in their palaces. Their soldiers were crushed with the weight of their arms.' By contrast it was the 'policy' of modern absolute monarchies not only that 'the nobility be suppressed, effeminated, and corrupted' but the kingdom as a whole 'brought to beggary'. This degradation was both moral and material, achieving the replacement of that wisdom, valour and prosperity which was dangerous to such princes with 'shameful practices . . . vile spirits . . . loss of reputation' as well as poverty which created an 'absolute dependence' upon the court.[35] Ultimately this process was self-defeating, making the prince, and his ravaged kingdom, easy prey to an invader.

This account of the 'corruption' of once moderate monarchies by 'modern despotical powers . . . careless . . . of the public good' was repeated by Henry Neville in *Plato Redivivus*.[36] Although Neville's analysis of the destruction of the power of the ancient nobility was directly indebted to Harrington, his reconstruction of its prehistory was not. Far from being neo-Harringtonian, Neville's praise of Saxon liberty, like Sidney's, resurrected the Gothic ancient constitutionalism against which Harrington had rebelled. Thus for Neville too, William I 'coming in by treaty . . . there was no conquest on any but Harold'. This, 'though it made in this kingdom a mixture between Normans and Saxons, yet produced no change or innovation in the government; the Norman peers being as tenacious of their liberties, and as active in the recovery of them to the full, as the Saxon families were'.[37] Who 'can imagine that' subsequently 'such brisk assertors of their rights could have acquiesced in . . . [the] ruin . . . of the government?' Like Sidney, Neville described the general 'debauchery of manners' which came with this ruin. But following Harrington, he recounted at greater length its economic basis, both in England and France. As a result, not only had the English nobility lost their previous 'great priviledges and jurisdictions' as well as their 'very considerable revenues . . . in demesnes', but 'two parts in ten of all those vast estates . . . by the luxury and folly of the owners, have been within these two hundred years purchased by the lesser gentry and the commons; which has been so far from advantaging the crown, that it has made the country scarce governable by monarchy'.[38] Sidney was in the *Discourses* to echo this conclusion more pointedly.

---

[35] Sidney, *Court Maxims* pp. 67–9 (and see the following Sixth Dialogue).
[36] Neville, *Plato Redivivus* pp. 86–7.   [37] Ibid. p. 121.   [38] Ibid. p. 88.

Almost all of the historical arguments of the *Maxims* Sidney repeated, and amplified, in the *Discourses*. Like those of Milton and Bacon, his account of 'All the kingdoms peopled from the north' was informed, for France, by 'Hottoman, a lawyer of that time and nation, famous for his learning, integrity and judgement, having diligently examined the antient law and histories of that kingdom'; by Philip de Comines; by Buchanan for Scotland; and by Hotman's own key classical source, Tacitus (*Germania, Agricola*).[39] Thus this theory of the Gothic polity, to be developed from Sidney by Molesworth's *Account of Denmark* and other later works, was fundamentally Tacitean in origin. The *Discourses* were indebted to Tacitus for an account of 'the German liberty' far more extensive than in the *Maxims*, and particularly that of 'the Saxons . . . from whom we descend . . . whose power, virtue, and love to liberty the abovementioned historian so highly extols'.[40] In 'all the legal kingdoms of the North', including 'Spain, Germany, France, Poland, Denmark, Sweden, Scotland, and England . . . the strength of the government has always been placed in the nobility'. These nobility, however, were no more than those 'ennobled' by military service; that is to say, all free men:

If any man ask how the nobility came to be so numerous; I answer, that the Northern nations, who were perpetually in arms, put a high esteem upon military valour; sought by conquest to acquire better countries than their own; valu'd themselves according to the numbers of men they could bring into the field; and to distinguish them from villains, called those noblemen, who nobly defended and enlarged their dominions by war; and for a reward of their services . . . distributed to them freeholds, under the obligation of continuing the same service.[41]

If England was 'anciently divided only into freemen or noblemen (who were the same) and villains . . . [who] were little better than slaves', then 'the name of noblemen' properly belonged not to 'court-creatures . . . preferr'd for servile and sometimes impure services render'd to the person that reigns'[42], but rather to 'such gentlemen and lords of manors, as we now call commoners, together with the freeholders, and such as in war were found most able to be their leaders. Of these the micklegemotes, witenagemotes, and other publick assemblies did consist', which 'William of Malmesbury calls . . . *the general senate and assembly of the people*'.[43] Thus lurking behind this use of the word 'nobility' was not an aristocratic

---

[39] Sidney, *Discourses*, in *Sydney on Government* pp. 252–3; Scott, *Algernon Sidney and the Restoration Crisis* pp. 245–6.
[40] Sidney, *Discourses*, ed. West pp. 480–1.   [41] Ibid. p. 487.
[42] Ibid. pp. 490, 492.   [43] Ibid. p. 497.

republic in classical terms. As the model was not Venice but Rome, so it is a popular Machiavellian commonwealth for expansion.[44]

In response to Filmer's claim that monarchy was the first form of government in the world, Sidney's initial response is that, even if this were true, 'it were nothing to the question; for no man or number of men was ever obliged to continue in the errors of his predecessors. The authority of custom as well as of law . . . consists only in its rectitude . . . We are not therefore so much to inquire after that which is most ancient, as that which is best, and most conducing to the good ends to which it was directed.' Nevertheless

We have already mentioned the histories of the Saxons, Danes and Normans, from which nations, together with the Britains [*sic*], we are descended, and finding that they were severe assertors of their liberties, acknowledged no human laws but their own, received no kings but such as swore to observe them, and deposed those who did not well perform their oaths and duty, 'tis evident that their kings were made by the people according to the law.[45]

Sidney's final addition to this historical account in the *Discourses* was the republican claim, probably influenced by Harrington, and following (while sharpening) Neville, that, once destroyed, this Gothic monarchy could no longer be recovered. 'The balance by which it subsisted was broken; and it is as impossible to restore it, as for most of those who at this day go under the name of noblemen, to perform the duties required from the antient nobility of England.' This was, most importantly, because the economic and social basis of the ancient constitution had gone. Even if their moral corruption could be repaired, the nobility

have neither the interest nor the estates required for so great a work. Those who have estates at a rack rent, have no dependents. Their tenants, when they have paid what is agreed, owe them nothing . . . This dependence being lost, the lords have . . . no command of men: and can therefore neither protect the weak, nor curb the insolent. By this means all things have been brought into the hands of the king and the commoners, and there is nothing left to cement them, and to maintain the union . . . all the disorders that we see or fear, are the effects of this rupture. These things are not to be imputed to our original constitutions, but to those who have subverted them . . . and if they perish, their destruction is from themselves.[46]

Accordingly a monarchical republic was no longer possible. For the defence of commonwealth values, of liberty against tyranny, the only modern option was the abolition of kingship altogether:

---

[44] Ibid. p. 492; Scott, *Algernon Sidney and the Restoration Crisis* pp. 257–60.
[45] Sidney, *Discourses*, ed. West pp. 458–9.   [46] Ibid. pp. 526–7.

While the ancient constitutions of our northern kingdoms remained entire, such as contested with their princes sought only to reform their governments . . . But they may not be so modest, when they see the very nature of their government changed, and the foundations overthrown . . . [I]t is not improbable, but that when men see there is no medium between tyranny and popularity, they who would have been contented with the reformation of their government may proceed farther.[47]

Thus if Harrington and Sidney disagreed about the merits of the Gothic constitution, they agreed in their perception of irrevocable contemporary change. This brings us to another still more important aspect of the republican politics of time.

THE POLITICS OF CHANGE

Thus one mode of republican argument was to observe (whether or not regretfully) that historical change had occurred, and that a resulting political change was now necessary. Such arguments featured particularly among *de facto* defences of the republic in 1650 and 1651, and also in Harrington's *Oceana*. Another approach was to liberate political argument, openly and aggressively, from the realm of custom and prescription altogether. The attempt to do this was a feature both of civil war radicalism in general, and of English republicanism in particular.[48]

In the stunning words of Richard Overton in 1646: 'whatever our fore-fathers were, or whatever they did or suffered or were enforced to yield unto, we are men of the present age and ought to be free'.[49] As early as 1644 Milton defended religious change, explaining that this was only bad 'if the Religion which a man changeth be the truth'. If not then '*not* to change Religion is evil'. The adherents of custom 'cry down the industry of free-reasoning, under the term . . . of innovation; as if the womb of teeming Truth were to be clos'd up, if shee . . . bring forth ought, that sorts not with their unchew'd suppositions'.[50] Milton's *Tenure of Kings and Magistrates* is an invective against that majority who are governed not 'by reason', but rather by 'a double tyrannie, of Custom from without, and blind affections within'. Milton's particular target is the superstitious popular 'feare of change', and the irrational addiction to 'customs, forms, and that old entanglement of Iniquity, thir gibrish Lawes, though the badge of thir

---

[47] Sidney, *Discourses*, in *Sydney on Government* p. 262.
[48] Scott, *England's Troubles* chs. 1, 10 and 13.
[49] [Richard Overton and William Walwyn], *A remonstrance of many thousand citizens . . . to their House of Commons* (1646), in Andrew Sharp (ed.), *Political Ideas of the English Civil Wars 1641–1649* (1983) pp. 181–2.
[50] Milton, *Areopagitica*, quoted in N. H. Keeble, *The Literary Culture of Nonconformity in Later Seventeenth-Century England* (Athens, Ga., 1987) p. 13.

ancient slavery'.[51] At any 'great actions, above the form of Law or Custom' many will 'swerve, and almost shiver . . . disputing presidents, forms and circumstances'. Against this faintheartedness, Milton writes on behalf of that 'Victory' given by 'God and a good cause' which 'inevitably draws after it the alteration of Lawes, change of Gover[n]ment, downfal of Princes'.[52] Most strikingly, he declares that 'if the Parlament and Military Councel doe what they doe without precedent, if it appeare thir duty, it argues the more wisdom, vertue, and magnanimity, that they know themselves able to be a precedent to others'.[53]

As we have seen, the innovatory status of the republic was hard to ignore. As parliament's *Declaration* of March 1649 defended the people's right to change their old form of government for a better, even the limited *de facto* theory of Nedham or Ascham began from the assertion that change was inevitable: 'Nature . . . can find rest in no posture'; 'There is, saith Tacitus . . . a wheeling of all things.'[54] When the bestselling *Eikon Basilike* (1649) claimed that it was 'no newes to have all innovations usherd in with the name of Reformation', Milton replied characteristically: 'sure it is less news to have all reformation censur'd and oppos'd under the name of innovation; by those who being exalted in high place above their merit, fear all change though of things never so ill or so unwisely settl'd'.[55] To abolish a hereditary monarchy, with its House of Lords, in favour of a system appealing to the rational recognition of merit was not simply to exchange the old form of government for something different. It was a declaration of independence from prescription.

In the words of Nedham's *Mercurius Politicus*: 'What if *England* will change yet seven times more? What is that to Scotland? It being a *Right inherent in every Nation, to alter their particular Governments, as often as they judge it necessary for the publick weal and safety*.'[56] When, on these grounds, Henry Vane Jr objected to Henry Marten's description of the new government's '*restor[ation] to it's auncient Government of a Commonwealth*', Marten 'meekly replied that *there was a Text had much troubled his spirit for severall dayes and nights of the man that was blind from his mother's womb whose sight was restored at last*'.[57] Indeed the government's defence of its own innovatory status exposed it to the criticism that the changes which had been effected had not gone far enough:

---

[51] Milton, *Tenure* pp. 193, 194.   [52] Ibid. pp. 192, 194.   [53] Ibid. p. 237.
[54] Anthony Ascham, *Of the Confusions and Revolutions of Governments* (1649) and Nedham, *Case of the Commonwealth* (1650), both quoted in Scott, 'The English Republican Imagination' pp. 39–40.
[55] Milton, *Eikonoklastes* p. 503.   [56] *Mercurius Politicus* no. 52, 29 May–5 June 1651, p. 831
[57] Aubrey, *Aubrey's Brief Lives* (1958) p. 194.

hetherto in the chandge of our Government nothing materiall as yet hath bin done, but a takinge of the head of monarchy and placing uppon the body or trunck of it, the name or title of a Commonwealth, a name aplicable to all forms of Government, and contained under the former . . . the onely way to make this a happy Government, is not onely to abolish all things that weare constituted under monarchy . . . But to sett upp a Government in all the parts of it sutable to our republike.[58]

This republican defence of change was one reason for the indespensability of Machiavelli, whose *Discourses* had insisted, 'Since . . . all human affairs are ever in a state of flux . . . either there will be improvement or decline.'[59] Nedham, Streater and Sidney all followed Machiavelli in turning this into a defence of a republic for expansion. In the words of Sidney, 'If it do not grow, it must pine and perish; for in this world nothing is permanent; that which does not grow better will grow worse.'[60] Thus one reason for accepting the inevitability of change was that 'in this world nothing is permanent'. This was, Sidney explained, because 'Nothing can or ought to be permanent but that which is perfect, and perfection is in God only, not in the things he has created.'[61] Streater agreed, pointing out that '*Gallen* in his fourteenth Book of the use of the parts of mans body, saith that nature would willingly have made her creature immortal, if by any means it might have been possible for her, the which cannot be, for that the Arteries, Veins, Sinews and Flesh could not be free from corruption.'[62] Yet in agreeing with Sidney that political bodies shared the corruptibility of their natural counterparts, so that 'perfection and true excellency is not to be attained to, neither is there any such . . . thing upon earth', Streater added: 'yet it is the duty of all to search after it'.[63] Thus when

Aristotle doth ascribe Perfection to . . . Civil Societie; the which I deny to be in any Citie, Empire, Government, or thing whatsoever . . . True it is, that some Cities do proceed some steps forwarder towards Perfection than others . . . If it were so that any thing could be perfect, it would be good; and there is not one thing good, but . . . *The onely Good*; meaning God . . . A Citie may grow towards Perfection, as *Rome* did to a very great Magnitude . . . yet . . . when it was at its greatest, it fell . . . I suppose that *Aristotle's* meaning was not, that Perfection consisteth in Greatness: I do also suppose them to be Fools, that do so esteem of Greatness . . . I suppose *Aristotle's* meaning is rather . . . in a Citie endeavouring to live well, and press towards Good, is the Perfection.[64]

[58] William Hickman, November 1650, quoted in Norbrook, *Writing the English Republic* pp. 270–1.
[59] Machiavelli, *Discourses* 1.6, p. 123.   [60] Sidney, *Discourses*, in *Sydney on Government* pp. 178–9.
[61] Ibid. p. 406.   [62] Streater, *Observations* no. 3, p. 13.   [63] Ibid. no. 5, p. 38.
[64] Ibid. no. 7, pp. 49–50.

For Harrington, by contrast,

> as man, seeing the world is perfect, can never commit any such sin as can render it imperfect or bring it unto a natural dissolution, so the citizen, where the commonwealth is perfect, can never commit any such crime as can render it imperfect or bring it unto a natural dissolution . . . a commonwealth rightly ordered may for any internal causes be as immortal, or long-lived, as the world.[65]

Moreover the natural body imitated by *Oceana*'s art (following Hobbes) was not simply 'that Rationall and most excellent worke of Nature, *Man*'.[66] To have followed *Leviathan* in imitating a single man would have been to repeat his error in making the resulting constitution a monarchy. More importantly, whereas a man was mortal, *Oceana* 'hath no principle of mortality'. That is because its political basis was not one person, but 'the universal commonwealth of mankind'. Its natural model was not a single being, but created nature as a whole ('the heavens that are in rotation'). 'But why should not this government be much rather capable of duration and steadiness by a motion? Than which God hath ordained no other unto the universal commonwealth of mankind, seeing one generation cometh and another goeth, but the earth remaineth firm forever.'[67]

It was in imitation of the heavens that 'the motions of *Oceana* are spherical'. Oceana's '*Councills upon their perpetuall Wheelings, Marches, and Counter-marches create her Armies*'. Its three 'Gallaxy[s]' elected magistrates to office for one, two and three years respectively, 'which Lists successively falling (like the signes or constellations of one Hemisphere, that setting cause those of the other to rise) cast the great Orbs of this *Common-wealth* into an Annual Triennial and Perpetual Revolution'.[68] It followed from the teaching of Hobbes ('if a thing is in motion, it will always be in motion, unless somewhat else stay it') that by transcending the mortality of particular creatures such a constitution might transcend mortality itself. Thus, although

> *we are the first that have shewn [this] unto the World . . . neither by Reason nor by her Experience is it impossible that a Common-wealth should be immortall; seeing the people being the materials never dyes, and the form which is motion must without opposition, be endlesse: The Bowl which is thrown from your hand, if there be no rub, no impediment, shall never cease: for which cause the glorious* Luminaries *that are the Bowles of* God *were once thrown for ever.*[69]

When the Lawgiver Olphaus Megaletor observed 'the rapture of [their] motion . . . without any matter of obstruction or interfering, but as it had

---

[65] Harrington, *Oceana*, in *Political Works* pp. 320–1.   [66] Hobbes, *Leviathan* p. 9.
[67] Harrington, *Oceana*, in *Political Works* p. 287.
[68] Harrington, *Oceana* (1656) p. 80.   [69] Ibid. p. 84.

been naturally . . . [he] abdicated the magistracy of Archon'.[70] 'Popular Government reaching the perfection of the kind, reacheth the perfection of Government . . . an *equal Commonwealth* is that onely which is without flaw, and containeth in it the full perfection of Government.'[71]

In a review of Zera Fink's *The Classical Republicans* in 1946, Leo Strauss rightly stressed the importance of this belief 'in the possibility of the immortal commonwealth'.

Fink finds 'a classical counterpart' to this belief . . . in Plato's *Laws* . . . however . . . certainly Plato and Aristotle did not believe in the immortality of any commonwealth, however perfect . . . Harrington could believe this because he held the belief that the perfect character of the commonwealth is independent of the moral qualities of the citizens. He thereby rejected the view of the classical thinkers, who defined the constitution not only in terms of institutions, but primarily in terms of the aims pursued by the community or its authoritative parts, and accepted the view advanced by Hobbes that man, as the 'maker' of commonwealths, can solve once and for all the problems inherent in man as the 'matter' of them.[72]

In claiming authorship of the first commonwealth to boast 'perfect equality', Harrington was certainly following a Platonic impulse. For Plato, too, 'Change . . . except in something evil, is extremely dangerous.'[73] Yet it was also a condition of the visible world. Although in that world God created 'the most perfect of created things', it was only the most perfect 'of visible things being made after a model in the Intelligible world'.[74] Thus when, in *The Timaeus*, in a passage invoked by Harrington,

the Father who had generated this saw here an image of the Eternal Gods, he rejoiced, and in his joy sought to make the world still more like to its model. And as the model is an Eternal Living Thing, he sought to make the universe like unto it, as far as may be. But the nature of that Living Model was eternal, and it was not possible to give this character fully to a generated thing. Therefore he devised a moving image of that fixed eternity: he made the heavens to be, by their structure . . . a likeness of that eternity which is fixed and one; and this we call *Time*.[75]

God, 'perceiving the visible universe in a state, not of rest, but of disorderly and irregular motion', did not abolish that motion but regulated it, 'reduc[ing] it out of disorder into order'.[76] When other writers assumed the imperfection of everything 'this side the sun', they were taking for granted

---

[70] Harrington, *Oceana*, in *Political Works* p. 342.
[71] Harrington, *Oceana* (1656) pp. 20, 22. Compare Neville, *Plato Redivivus* p. 100.
[72] Leo Strauss, Review of Zera Fink, *Classical Republicans*, *Social Research* 13, 3 (1946) pp. 394–5.
[73] Plato, *The Laws* p. 283.   [74] Plato, *The Timaeus* pp. 357, 366.
[75] Ibid. p. 367.   [76] Ibid. p. 356.

metaphysical assumptions shared by Platonism and Christianity. For the materialist Harrington, however, as God's handiwork would last forever, so correctly informed political anatomy could harness the durability not of a perishable creature, but of a timeless work of art.[77] As John Toland explained, he was 'convinc'd that no Government is of so accidental or arbitrary an Institution as people are wont to imagin: there being in Societys natural causes producing their necessary effects, as well as in the Earth or the Air'.[78]

It is accordingly correct, as noticed by Strauss and Hume, that by means of a perfect constitutional construct Harrington proposed to solve the problems inherent in the imperfection of man. In this his mentor was not Machiavelli, but Hobbes. It was from the standpoint of this natural philosophy that Harrington went on to contradict Machiavelli's belief in the inevitability of flux and change:

'If a commonwealth', saith [Machiavelli] . . . 'were so happy as to be provided often with men that when she is swerving from her principles, should reduce her unto her institution, she would be immortal'. But a commonwealth, as we have demonstrated, swerveth not from her principles, but by and through her institution . . . a commonwealth that is rightly instituted can never swerve . . . wherefore it is no less apparent . . . that Machiavel understood not a commonwealth as to the whole piece.[79]

This is not to deny that the constitutional model of *Oceana* ('The Model of the Commonwealth') is presented in the context of what was the first major historical analysis of the troubles ('The First and Second Preliminaries'). That history is, however, deductive rather than inductive, its purpose being to 'show . . . the Principles of Government'.[80] It was the opinion of Perez Zagorin that for Harrington those principles must 'come from history, and history alone'. Yet in Harrington's words, 'No man can be a politician except he be first a Historian *or a Traveller*' (my emphasis). 'Except he be', that is, an observer of nature, either in 'what has bin' or 'what is'.[81] 'Lycurgus, by being [only] a Traveller, became a legislator; but in times when prudence was another thing.'[82] In the ancient world prudence (a result of the successful observation of nature) was recorded in what is, not only (as in the Gothic world) in what had been. In the ancient world political instability resulted from the imperfect application of that prudence in the erection of 'equal

---

[77] Scott, 'The Rapture of Motion'.   [78] Toland, *Life of Harrington* p. xvii.
[79] Harrington, *Oceana*, in *Political Works* pp. 321–2.   [80] Harrington, *Political Works* p. 161.
[81] Perez Zagorin, *A History of Political Thought in the English Revolution* (1954) ch. 6; Harrington, *Oceana*, in *Political Works* p. 417.
[82] Ibid. p. 310.

commonwealths' incorporating an agrarian, the separation of dividing and choosing, and rotation. In the barbaric world of modern prudence, greater instability was an inevitable consequence of greater ignorance. In claiming to be the first writer to present to the world the prescription for a perfectly equal commonwealth, Harrington was attempting to engineer 'an exit' not 'from history', but from instability.[83] Thus at the point of turning from diagnosis of the malady to prescription of a cure, the text of *Oceana* was able to end a primarily historical mode of presentation.

After the Restoration Henry Neville repeated Harrington's material diagnosis of the problem, and his proffered cure, without the natural philosophy by which they had been informed. To this extent *Plato Redivivus* is like *Oceana* stripped of the latter's engagement with Hobbes, and to that extent also less emphatically Venetian. Thus the fall of 'the best and most glorious government that ever the sun saw' resulted from the Romans' 'having omitted in their institution to provide for the fixing of property . . . if they had kept their poverty, they had kept their government, and their virtue too'. This conclusion was 'backed by the judgement of . . . [the] incomparable Machiavel' who well observed Rome's fatal 'intermission of the Agrarian'. All 'changes' in government 'have turned upon this hinge of property', the fixing of which was 'the only way to make a commonwealth immortal'.[84]

By contrast it fell to Sidney to develop the Platonic assumptions of Milton, and to correct Machiavelli in the opposite direction. The problem was not that the Florentine had overstated the importance of change, but that he had not taken sufficient account of the need for it.

[S]uch is the condition of mankind, that nothing can be so perfectly framed as not to give some testimony of human imbecility, and frequently to stand in need of reparations and amendments . . . Some men observing this, have proposed a necessity of reducing every state, once in an age or two, to the integrity of its first principle: but they ought to have examined, whether that principle be good or evil, or so good that nothing can be added to it, which none ever was; and this being so, those who will admit of no change would . . . deprive[e] . . . mankind of the benefits of wisdom, industry, experience, and the right use of reason.[85]

In this way Sidney took a step beyond Machiavelli's classical cyclical view that the best that could be hoped for was the diligent 'imitation' of the most successful model in the past, toward the possibility of linear progress. Such progress was not, however, an inevitable condition of modernity,

---

[83] Cf. J. G. A. Pocock, 'A Discourse of Sovereignty', in Phillipson and Skinner *Political Discourse* pp. 403–6.

[84] Neville, *Plato Redivivus* pp. 91–2, 96–7, 99–100.   [85] Sidney, *Discourses*, ed. West pp. 461–2.

within which the decline of whole peoples into ignorance and poverty under tyranny was painfully evident. Rather it depended upon the 'right use of reason'. One context for this perception was the northern humanist relativism discussed in chapter 4.

> Changes therefore are unavoidable, and the wit of man can go no farther than to institute such, as in relation to the forces, manners, nature, religion or interests of a people and their neighbours, are suitable and adequate to what is seen, or apprehended to be seen: And he who would oblige all nations at all times to take the same course, would prove as foolish as a physician who should apply the same medicine to all distempers, or an architect that would build the same kind of house for all persons, without considering their estates, dignities . . . number . . . the time or climate in which they live, and many other circumstances.[86]

In Sidney's other key assumption that 'change or death', a condition of this world, 'is imperfection,'[87] it is possible to detect a correction of Harrington:

> [T]he wisdom of man is imperfect, and unable to forsee . . . an infinite variety of accidents, which according to emergencies, necessarily require new constitutions, to prevent or cure the mischiefs arising from them, or to advance a good that at the first was not thought on. And as the noblest work in which the wit of man can be exercised, were (if it could be done) to constitute a government that should last forever, the next to that is to suit laws to present exigencies, and so much as is in the power of man to forsee. And he that should resolve to persist obstinately in the way he first entered upon . . . does as far as in him lies, render the worst of errors perpetual.[88]

The role of political 'art' was not to construct a constitutional model capable of transcending human imperfection, but to work upon the imperfect matter of humankind itself. As God had given men reason to discriminate good from evil, with it came liberty to improve their lot by the accumulation of knowledge. Such education and experience necessarily had a political context. It was because progress or degeneration was thus determined by the nature of a people's government that Sidney 'thought a time of leisure might well be employed in examining . . . [the] doctrine [of Sir Robert Filmer] and the questions arising from it; which seem so far to concern all mankind, that, besides the influence upon our future life, they may be said to comprehend all that in this world deserves to be cared for'.[89]

The bestial barbarity in which many nations, especially of Africa, America and Asia, do now live, shews what human nature is, if it be not improved by art and discipline; and if the first errors, committed through ignorance, might not be

---

[86] Ibid. p. 173.   [87] Sidney, *Discourses*, in *Sydney on Government* p. 407.
[88] Sidney, *Discourses*, ed. West pp. 357–8.   [89] Ibid. p. 5.

corrected . . . we must return to the religion, manners and policy that were found in our country at Caesar's landing. To affirm this is no less than to destroy all that is commendable in the world, and to render the understanding given to men utterly useless . . . If men are not obliged to live in caves and hollow trees, to eat acorns, and to go naked, why should they be forever obliged to continue under the same form of government that their ancestors happened to set up in the time of their ignorance?[90]

Indeed 'whatever we enjoy, beyond the misery in which our barbarous ancestors lived, is due only to the liberty of correcting what was amiss in their practice, or inventing that which they did not know'.[91] In this pursuit of 'a perpetuall advance in all that is good' lay both the purpose of government and an explanation for the superior success of free states.

'Tis absurd to impute this to the change of times; for time changes nothing; and nothing was changed in those times but the government, and that changed all things. This is not accidental, but according to the rules given to nature by God, imposing on all things a necessity of perpetually following their causes . . . As a man begets a man, and a beast a beast, that society of men which constitutes a government upon the foundation of justice, virtue, and the common good, will always have men to promote those ends; and that which intends the advancement of one man's desires and vanity, will abound in those that will foment them.[92]

Thus the principal engine fuelling human progress (or decline) was the divinely authored struggle between good and evil. Not only were governments in the service of moral goodness well equipped to thrive by comparison with those devoted to self-interest; to seek this progress was a moral obligation. For good governments to abandon this ambition would give evil ones

a right of attacking us with all the advantages of the arms now in use, and the arts which by the practice of so many ages have been wonderfully refined, whilst we should be obliged to employ no others in our just defence, than such as were known to our naked ancestors when Caesar invaded them, or to the Indians when they fell under the dominion of the Spaniards. This would be a compendious way of placing uncontroll'd iniquity in all the kingdoms of the world, and to overthrow all that deserves the name of good.

In fact, however, it would be a great mistake 'to think that God has so far abandoned us into the hands of our enemies'.[93]

[90] Ibid. pp. 357–8. [91] Sidney, *Discourses*, in *Sydney on Government* p. 404.
[92] Sidney, *Discourses*, ed. West pp. 273–4. [93] Ibid. p. 358.

CHAPTER 10

Empire

Taking everything together then, I declare that our city is an education to Greece, and . . . each single one of our citizens, in all the manifold aspects of life, is able to show himself the rightful lord and owner of his own person . . . the power which our city possesses . . . has been won by those very qualities . . . Mighty indeed are the marks and monuments of our empire . . . Future ages will wonder at us, as the present age wonders at us now . . . you should fix your eyes every day on the greatness of Athens as she really is, and should fall in love with her . . . Make up your minds that happiness depends on being free, and freedom depends on being courageous.

Thucydides, Pericles' Funeral Oration, Athens 431 BC[1]

Let every man, with me, apply his mind seriously to consider, what their life and what their manners were; by what men and what measures, both in peace and war, their empire was gained and enlarged. When by degrees their discipline began to relax, let him attentively observe, first the declension of their manners, next their constant visible decay, and lastly their total degeneracy, till he comes to the present age, when we can neither bear our political distempers, nor endure a proper remedy.

Livy, *The Roman History*[2]

INTRODUCTION

The politics of war was a pressing question for English republicans. In chapter 5 we examined the application of theories of just war to the military defence of liberty (including liberty of protestant conscience). In this chapter we turn to the question of the military mission of the republic once founded. Must citizens also be soldiers, as Aristotle and Machiavelli insisted? If so, for what purpose? Should the republic be for preservation, or

[1] Thucydides, *The Peloponnesian War* pp. 147–8, 149–50.
[2] Livy, *The Roman History* Book 1, Preface (vol. 1 p. 4).

expansion? Was mere preservation possible, or safe? Was expansion morally justifiable? Was it an effect of liberty, resulting in a *grandezza* drawing upon, and comparable in value to, the virtues? Or was worldly glory, acquired by blood, the antithesis of a genuine moral virtue anchored in God? Could the liberty of one nation be sustained, or amplified, at the expense of that of others?

If these questions were posed by the republic's practical circumstances, they were also embedded in its classical and Christian sources. As Hume wrote of the ancient Greek cities, 'they were free states; they were small ones; and the age being martial, all their neighbours were continually in arms . . . A continual succession of wars makes every citizen a soldier.'[3] Military service was integral to Greek, as to Roman citizenship. Of the four cardinal virtues one was courage, acquired and exercised, as both Plato and Aristotle explained, by citizen-soldiers.[4] Athens's reward for its stunning military victory over the Persians at Salamis, much praised by English republicans, was an empire. One consequence of that empire, however, and both the fear it aroused among the Spartans and the errors of judgement to which it led among the Athenians, was the self-destructive catastrophe of the Peloponnesian war.[5]

In Rome came the most famous connection of political liberty to success in arms. As Sallust explained, in words quoted by both Nedham and Sidney, it was 'remarkable how the state grew once it had become free'.[6] For both Italian and English republicans it was a principal lesson drawn from Livy's *History* of the Roman republic that liberty furnished the basis for military greatness. Yet no less evidently, Roman history (as written by Sallust, Cicero, Livy and Tacitus) illustrated the dangers brought to the republic by such expansion. By the time of Sulla, and then Caesar, the state's military prowess and consequent material prosperity had become morally self-destructive. As a result virtue had given way to corruption, and then liberty itself to civil strife and tyranny. Following the restoration of English monarchy these analyses, too, would be influential.

Thereafter, some Christian moralists took an altogether different view of such imperial warmongering. Augustine's *City of God*, itself drawing upon Sallust, did not doubt that 'the Roman Empire extended far and wide, coming to greatness with so impressive a record of success . . . given lustre

[3] Quoted by Rahe, *Republics Ancient and Modern* vol. 1, p. 1.
[4] Plato, *The Republic*, trans. Lee, Books 2–4, pp. 107–12, 145–55, 174, 177.
[5] Thucydides, *The Peloponnesian War*.
[6] Sallust, *Bellum Catilinae*, VII.4, quoted by Armitage, 'John Milton: poet against empire' p. 209.

and glory by the heroic quality of its great men'.[7] Yet did not this pre-
eminent accomplishment among earthly cities come at a horrifying cost in
suffering and blood? And what was the precise worth of this 'earthly glory',
this 'glory of men in the immediate present'? Was it not 'puffed up with
empty conceit'? Certainly such 'temporal blessings' did not compare with
the 'eternal life and everlasting gifts' awarded for 'participation in that City
on high', that one true source of goodness and happiness.[8] Again, following
the Restoration this was a message, and a source, given serious attention by
Sidney as well as Milton. More generally English republicanism wrestled
with these issues, beginning with More's *Utopia*, which satirised the martial
pursuit of glory. Even the battle-hardened Sir Arthur Haselrig insisted in
1659, 'We ought not, for any fleshly advantage, to buy domination with
blood.'[9] Yet most Christians accepted war as a condition of this world,
and just war as a Christian duty. In addition, as we have seen, the English
republic drew upon an Elizabethan and early Stuart tradition of protestant,
anti-Spanish imperial and military ambition.

The most important English republican source on the subject of empire
was Machiavelli. Effectively reversing Augustine's analysis, his *Discourses*
contrasted the deep religiosity of the Romans, a key factor in their success,
with the modern political impact of a corrupt Roman Catholic church.[10]
At the same time he contrasted the military efficacy of the Roman religion
with the deleterious impact of other-wordly Christianity.[11] Now, amid the
ruins of Italy's liberty, the first step in the recovery of its political fortunes
must be reconstruction of its military capacities. To what exemplar state, in
this respect, should republican contemporaries look? Initially Machiavelli
appeared to consider this matter even-handedly, but the pretence was not
long maintained:

Should, then, anyone be about to set up a republic, he should first inquire whether
it is to expand, as Rome did, both in dominion and in power, or is to be confined
to narrow limits. In the first case it is essential to constitute it as Rome was constituted . . . because without a large population, and this well armed, such a republic
will never be able to grow, or to hold its own should it grow. In the second case it
might be constituted as Sparta and Venice were, but, since expansion is poison to
republics of this type, it should use every endeavour to prevent it from expanding,
for expansion, when based on a weak republic, simply means ruin. . . . [Thus]
Venice, having occupied a large part of Italy, most of it not by dint of arms, but of
money and astute diplomacy, when its strength was put to the test, lost everything
in a single battle.[12]

---

[7] Augustine, *City of God* p. 211.   [8] Ibid. pp. 211–19.   [9] *Diary of Thomas Burton* vol. III, p. 458.
[10] Machiavelli, *Discourses* Book I, ch. 12.   [11] Ibid. p. 98 (Preface to Book I).   [12] Ibid. p. 122.

Thus whereas Rome was powerful, Venice was weak. Moreover because 'all human affairs are ever in a state of flux and cannot stand still',

necessity will lead you to do many things which reason does not recommend. Hence if a commonwealth be constituted with a view to its maintaining the *status quo*, but not with a view to expansion, and by necessity it be led to expand, its basic principles will be subverted and it will soon be faced with ruin . . . Wherefore . . . one ought, in constituting a republic, to consider the possibility of its playing a more honourable role . . . Coming back then, to the first point we raised, I am convinced that the Roman type of constitution should be adopted, not that of any other republic, for to find a middle way between the two extremes I do not think possible. Squabbles between the populace and the senate should, therefore, be looked upon as an inconvenience which it is necessary to put up with in order to arrive at the greatness of Rome.[13]

The choice of relative safety, as well as glory, was to embrace the goddess of *fortuna*, rather than to attempt to wall the city off from her. The safety available was, in either case, highly uncertain. All the more reason to seek greatness rather than mere preservation, to seek to govern *fortuna* rather than to cower before her. If the expansionist city perished this would not be because of the choice it had made, but rather the fate awaiting 'all human affairs . . . in a state of flux'. It was thus not quite the case, as David Armitage has suggested, that Machiavelli followed Sallust in seeing liberty and expansion as 'ultimately irreconcileable.'[14] What ultimately doomed liberty was not expansion, but the wider flux of the political world. Meanwhile, the only adequate defence of liberty was a conquering army. The only adequate source of such an army was liberty itself given, in the manner of the Romans, but not the Venetians, to the people as a whole.

Most importantly the *Discourses* was not ultimately about the preservation of liberty. Its most revolutionary suggestion was that such preservation was not enough. It was from this preservation, Venice's accomplishment, that Machiavelli wished to shift the name of *grandezza*, in favour of 'the more honourable role' of expansion. Liberty was not the highest political value. Rather its value was instrumental, in that no city had ever been great except when it had been free.

It is easy to see how this affection of peoples for self-government comes about, for experience shows that cities have never increased either in dominion or wealth, unless they have been independent. It is truly remarkable to observe the greatness

---

[13] Ibid. pp. 123–4.
[14] Armitage, 'John Milton: Poet against Empire'; Scott, Review of Peltonen, *Classical Humanism* p. 950.

which Athens attained in the space of a hundred years after it had been liberated from the tyranny of Pisistratus. But most marvellous of all is to observe the greatness which Rome attained after freeing itself from its kings.[15]

This claim was able to draw upon a treasury of classical sources. The counter-case, however, no less classically sound, was put by the Venetian Paolo Paruta:

[W]ho can doubt but that the true end of a City is to have her Citizens live vertuously, not the inlarging of her Empire? . . . the perfection of Government lies in making a City vertuous, not in making her Mistress of many Countries. Nay the increasing of Territories, as it is commonly coupled with some injustice, so it is remote from the true end of good Laws . . . Governments which aim at Empire are usually short lived; which denotes their imperfection.[16]

At the end of the seventeenth century Charles Davenant agreed, concluding that 'Commonwealths well founded would be eternal if they could retain themselves within a reasonable extent of territory . . . while Commonwealths . . . extend their limits, they are working their own Bane, for all big Empires determine in a single Person.'[17] Yet the practical relevance of Machiavelli's analysis to the English republic's circumstances gave it an extraordinary impact.

MILTON AND THE EMPIRE OF THE SELF

The question of the relationship between political virtue and military vigour was an issue within English humanism well before the civil wars. This was so, first, when sympathy with the Dutch rebellion among Elizabethan protestants fused into a larger national military struggle against Spain. It was so, second, during the Thirty Years War, as the crushing of the Bohemian rebellion coincided with lamentable English military hesitation, and then failure.[18] In both cases, this confessional European military theatre had a vital imperial and global dimension. Within these contexts the writings and actions of such figures as Sir Philip Sidney, the first Earl of Essex, Sir Walter Ralegh, Francis Bacon and Thomas Scott established a tradition of militant protestant humanism upon which most English republican writers drew.

---

[15] Machiavelli, *Discourses* II.2, p. 275.

[16] Paolo Paruta, *Politick Discourses*, trans. Henry, Earl of Monmouth (1657), quoted in Armitage, *Ideological Origins* p. 131.

[17] Davenant, *An Essay upon Universal Monarchy* quoted in Pagden, *Lords of All the World* pp. 17, 103.

[18] Scott, *England's Troubles* chs. 3–4.

The same context helps to explain Bacon's deep interest in, and debt to, Machiavelli on the question of civic greatness. The pre-eminent qualification for such greatness, Bacon wrote, was 'the valour and military disposition of the people it breedeth: and . . . that they make profession of arms . . . No body can be healthfull without exercise, neither naturall body, nor politike; & to the politike body of a Kingdome or estate . . . an honourable forraine war is like the heat of exercise.'[19] For Bacon, as for Sir Philip Sidney, 'in a slothfull peace, both courages will effeminate, and manners corrupt'.[20] Most specifically, Bacon concurred with 'the authority of Machiavel . . . who scorneth the proverb . . . that Moneys are the sinews of wars; and saith there are no true sinews of wars but the very sinews of the arms of valiant men'.[21] In this, as we have seen, he was followed by Milton, who recorded the same passage with approval in his *Commonplace Book*.[22]

Of all the major republican writers, and in line with his Christian humanism, Milton was the most hesitant on the subject of war. Like others he was loud in his praise of the defensive achievement of the Dutch: 'What reason for waging war is more just than to drive off slavery? . . . Could it happen that you forgot the Dutch? Their republic, after the expulsion of the king of Spain, after wars that were lengthy but successfully waged, bravely and gloriously obtained its liberty.'[23] Moreover many of his writings exulted in the similar military accomplishment of the English, an effect of their virtue and the manifest blessing of God. From Guicciardini's *Historia*, Milton's *Commonplace Book* recorded that 'Tyrants attempt to destroy in the people an eagerness for arms. "Kings in the past, fearing an attack by the people, have kept them disarmed and estranged from military practice."'[24] From Machiavelli's *Art of War* it noted that author's opinion that 'A commonwealth is preferable to a monarchy: "because more excellent men come from a commonwealth than from a kingdom; because in the former virtue is honoured most of the time and is not feared as in a kingdom."'[25] The theme of the tyrant's 'feare . . . hatred and suspicion' of 'vertue' reappeared at the beginning of *The Tenure* (1649), and on the title page of *Eikonoklastes* (1650), in a passage from Sallust's *Bellum Catilinae*.[26]

---

[19] Bacon, 'Of the greatnesse of kingdomes', quoted in Peltonen, *Classical Humanism* pp. 201, 205.
[20] Peltonen, *Classical Humanism* p. 205; Worden, *The Sound of Virtue* p. 131.
[21] Bacon 'Of the true greatness of the kingdom of Britain', quoted in Peltonen, *Classical Humanism* p. 204.
[22] Milton, *Commonplace Book* pp. 414–15.
[23] Milton, *Defence* in Dzelzainis (ed.), *Political Writings* pp. 88, 155.
[24] Milton, *Commonplace Book* p. 471.   [25] Ibid. p. 421.
[26] Milton, *Tenure* p. 190; Milton, *Eikonoklastes*; see Armitage, 'John Milton: Poet against Empire' p. 210.

Yet in his notes from Machiavelli's *Discorsi*, made during the republic's own brief imperial heyday, there is a distinct note of caution. While recording a series of Machiavelli's injunctions concerning military tactics, his own most important opinion is that 'It is not the duty of every state to enlarge the boundaries of its power and to bring other nations under its rule. On the contrary Machiavelli wisely shows that it is dangerous to do so unless . . . the addition of that new realm is justly administered.'[27] In fact 'justice' is not a feature of Machiavelli's discussion. Rather this drew upon Livy and Juvenal's *Satires* to warn of the potentially corrupting influence of conquests upon 'even a well-ordered republic when the province or city it has acquired is given to luxurious habits which can be taken up by those who have intercourse with it'.[28] The concern with justice, which is Milton's own, conforms better to his other adage that 'Victory is based, not on strength or military experience, but on whether he who begins the war has God on his side.'[29] It is on this basis that he defended the regicide. Elsewhere, however, in *Eikonoklastes* and the *Defence of the English People*, Milton associates war as a condition with the divisive and wicked politics of tyrants and ecclesiastics. In the *Second Defence* his celebration of the republic's success in arms gives way to a brutal warning directed to its commander in chief: 'Unless your liberty is such as can neither be won or lost by arms, but is . . . sprung from piety, justice, temperance, in short, true virtue', it will soon be lost.

Many men has war made great whom peace makes small. If . . . the ability . . . of putting vast sums of money into the treasury, the power readily to equip land and sea forces, to deal shrewdly with ambassadors from abroad, and to contract judicious alliances and treaties has seemed to any of you greater, wiser, and more useful to the state than to administer incorrupt justice to the people, to help those cruelly harassed and oppressed, and to render to every man promptly his own deserts, too late will you discover how mistaken you have been.[30]

The *Second Defence* does not negate the value of the republic's military and diplomatic accomplishments (with which Milton worked closely as Secretary for Foreign Tongues). 'Honor too' it commands, 'what foreign nations think and say of us, the high hopes which they have for themselves as a result of our liberty, so bravely won, and our republic, so gloriously born'.[31] Yet it was the warning of the *Second Defence* that the value of these external conquests was predicated upon the internal substance of the virtues in the name of which war had been waged:

---

[27] Milton, *Commonplace Book* p. 499. [28] Machiavelli, *Discourses* II.19, p. 338.
[29] Milton, *Commonplace Book* p. 498. [30] Milton, *Second Defence* pp. 680–1. [31] Ibid. p. 673.

Unless you expel avarice, ambition, and luxury from your minds, yes, and extravagance from your families as well, you will find at home and within that tyrant who, you believed, was to be sought abroad and in the field . . . In fact, many tyrants, impossible to endure, will from day to day hatch out from your very vitals. Conquer them first. This is the warfare of peace, these are its victories, hard indeed, but bloodless, and far more noble than the gory victories of war.[32]

In the *Second Defence*, Milton's celebration of Cromwell's military achievement hinges upon this assumption. He who 'in one battle . . . broke the power of Hibernia' and 'in . . . one year . . . completely subdued and added to the wealth of England that realm [Scotland] which all our kings for eight hundred years had been unable to master' was 'Commander first over himself, victor over himself'.[33] In this Cromwell stood for an entire army, the superior moral integrity of which to the royalist 'mob' had attracted the patronage of God. Yet in this, of course, lay the danger for the future. It was no easy matter 'To rule with wisdom three powerful nations, to desire to lead their peoples from base customs to a better standard of morality and discipline than before'.[34] Yet for Cromwell, and for everybody engaged in the cause, the greatest danger of defeat lay within the parallel struggle for empire over the self. Thus

the loyalty of the armies and allies in whom you trust is fleeting, unless it be maintained by the power of justice alone. Wealth and honours, which most men pursue, easily change masters; they desert to the side which excels in virtue, industry, and endurance of toil, and they abandon the slothful. Thus nation presses upon nation, or the sounder part of a nation overthrows the more corrupt. Thus did you drive out the royalists. If you begin to slip into the same vices, to imitate those men, to seek the same goals, to clutch at the same vanities, you actually are royalists yourselves, at the mercy . . . of others . . . who, depending on the same prayers to God, the same patience, integrity, and shrewdness which were at first your strength, will justly subdue you.[35]

To be a Christian was to engage in the daily battle between good and evil. This internal struggle could also have a military dimension, in which justice would determine the outcome. This was, for Cromwell, a worrying perspective from which to contemplate the Commonwealth's subsequent military defeat at Hispaniola. Milton's ally Vane was not the only other republican to subject this to a Christian moral diagnosis. Thus *A Healing Question* distinguished between the old and still good 'Cause', in respect of which 'it pleased God (the righteous Judge, who was appealed to in the controversie) . . . to bless the Council, and Forces of the persons concerned',

---

[32] Ibid. pp. 680–1.　[33] Ibid. pp. 668, 670.　[34] Ibid. p. 674.　[35] Ibid. p. 681.

and more recently 'something rising up that seems accommodated to the private and selfish interest of a particular part . . . then truly adequate to the common good'.[36]

It may indeed be the case, as David Armitage has argued, that Milton came to see in the Protectorate an extinction of liberty partly attributable to the hazard of empire. Thus in England, as in Rome, victory on the battlefield, attributable to liberty, had produced overmighty generals by whom ultimately liberty had been destroyed. Yet for Milton, as for Vane, the primary problem was not empire itself. It was the detachment from that pursuit, externally, of the internal empire of reason. The true basis of liberty was not the military conquest of others, but the rational conquest of the self. What Milton opposed was an empire of power, in place of one of justice. Should such a thing emerge, this would suggest that the republican experiment had gone disastrously astray. What the defeat at Hispaniola signified was the much more worrying loss of this internal struggle. If this was exemplified by Cromwell his failure stood, in this respect, for a larger failure of those engaged in what had been the cause of God.

As several commentators have pointed out, Satan's tempting of Adam and Eve is depicted by Milton as a colonial venture. Earth, site of the garden of Eden, is a 'new World' created by God to be the home of 'some new race called Man'. In Pandemonium Satan's expedition is debated in Machiavellian terms, and once he has arrived in Eden he explains that

> Honour and empire with revenge enlarged,
> By conquering this new world, compels me now
> To do what else though damned I should abhor.
> So spake the fiend, and with necessity,
> The tyrant's plea, excused his devilish deeds.[37]

Yet it does not follow from such passages that Milton is a 'poet against empire', any more than it follows from Satan's wider deployment of the vocabulary of republicanism that Milton has turned against the republican cause. As we have seen, of that cause in general Satan's actions constitute a grotesque parody. The source of that moral deprivation is his separation from the only source of genuine virtue in God, 'Whom to obey is happiness entire.

> O sun, to tell thee how I hate thy beams
> That bring to my remembrance from what state
> I fell, how glorious once above thy sphere.[38]

---

[36] Vane, *A Healing Question* pp. 2–3.
[37] Armitage, John Milton: 'Poet against Empire' pp. 217–21 (including this quote).
[38] Milton, *Paradise Lost* Book IV, lines 37–41, p. 422.

Ruined by pride and ambition, it is Satan's fate to be plagued by precisely those 'many tyrants, impossible to endure', against which Milton's *Second Defence* had warned. Thus Satan is a Platonic and Augustinian study in tyranny, and as Milton noted from Augustine in his *Commonplace Book*, 'If in governmental rule there is any servitude, actually the one in authority is the slave.'[39] The sign of this slavery is not simply that he resorts to 'necessity, the tyrant's plea', but that he is 'compelled' by 'revenge' to do something against even the modest moral (that is, rational) scruples that he retains. Driven by his passions, this 'hell within him', Satan has surrendered the government of himself. His imperial mission is, therefore, a similar parody. It is achieved not by arms but by deception. As Sidney repeats in the *Court Maxims*, tyrants achieve their objectives 'by force or fraud, or both'.[40] When he sees the 'spotless innocence' of uncorrupted man Satan is tormented by 'ire, envy and despair . . . O hell! What do mine eyes with grief behold?' Even his physical stature is cringing, Gollum-like:

> Thence up he flew, and on the tree of life,
> The middle tree and highest there that grew,
> Sat like a cormorant; yet not true life
> Thereby regained, but sat devising death
> To them that lived; nor on the virtue thought
> Of that life-giving plant,
> But only used
> For prospect, what well used had been the pledge
> Of immortality. So little knows
> Any, but God alone, to value right
> The good before him, but perverts best things
> To worst abuse, or to their meanest use.[41]

Satan's resort to force had been against God himself, and he was spectacularly defeated. His crime was to seek, not empire, but 'Divided empire with heaven's king': empire severed from justice. What Milton opposes are 'acts of prowess eminent/And great exploits, but of true virtue void'. It is only subsequently in *Paradise Regained* that Milton abandons his faith that God rewards virtue on the battlefield by placing in the mouth of Jesus a more decisively Augustinian condemnation of conquest 'on earth',

> Where glory is false glory, attributed
> To things not glorious, men not worthy of fame.
> They err who glorious count it to subdue
> By conquest far and wide, to overrun

[39] Milton, *Commonplace Book* p. 474.   [40] Sidney, *Court Maxims* p. 13.
[41] Milton, *Paradise Lost* Book IV, lines 194–204, pp. 425–6.

Large countries, and in field great battles win,
Great cities by assault: what do these worthies,
But rob and spoil, burn, slaughter and enslave
Peaceable nations, neighbouring, or remote,
Made captive, yet deserving freedom more
Than those their conquerors, who leave behind,
Nothing but ruin wheresoe'er they rove.[42]

NEDHAM, STREATER, HARRINGTON

Machiavelli's interpretation of Livy finds its way far more directly into republican thought at this time through the writings of Milton's collegue Nedham. *Vox Plebis* (1646), heavily indebted to the *Discorsi*, identified Roman achievement as exemplary, as shown by the 'exceeding enlargement of their Common-wealth'.[43] It repeated Machiavelli's opinion that 'Common-wealths have never been much amplified, neither in dominion nor riches, *unlesse only during their Liberties.*'[44] In 1650 Nedham's *The Case of the Commonwealth* appeared with quotes on the title page from Sallust and Guicciardini which were developed in the final chapter by reference to Machiavelli.

'It is incredible to be told', saith Sallust, 'how exceedingly the Roman commonwealth increased in a short time after they had obtained their liberty' . . . It is wonderful to consider how mightily the Athenians were augmented both in wealth and power in the space of one hundred years after they had freed themselves from the tyranny of Pisistratus, but the Romans arrived to such a height as was beyond all imagination after the expulsion of their kings.[45]

These themes were expanded in *Mercurius Politicus*, in the context of the republic's military triumphs between 1651 and 1652, and then republished in *The Excellencie of a Free-State* (1656). Athens joined Rome as an exemplar state, to be contrasted to corrupt and tyrannical Venice. In an apparent criticism of the republic's continued reliance upon a professional army, Nedham invoked the authority of Aristotle to plead 'That the People be continually trained up in the exercise of Arms; and the Militia lodged only in the People's hands.'[46] The relationship asserted by Machiavelli between liberty and greatness was proved not simply by historical examples, but by 'the valiant Swisses, the Hollanders, and also our own Nation'.[47]

At the same time Nedham was also deploying another imperial language which drew upon, not Machiavelli, but the Bible. This was exploited in the

---

[42] Milton, *Paradise Regained* Book III, lines 69–79, p. 645. [43] [Nedham], *Vox Plebis* p. 3.
[44] Ibid. p. 66. [45] Nedham, *Case of the Commonwealth* pp. 116–17.
[46] *Mercurius Politicus* no. 103, 20–27 May 1652, p. 1. [47] Ibid. no. 85, 18–25 January 1652, pp. 1349–52.

service of, not the republic's land conquests, but its parallel campaign at sea, in part perhaps to appeal to opposition based within the New Model Army. It also connected to a wider imperial sensibility invoked since 1650 by a commonwealth newspaper with a keen interest in parallel revolutionary events elsewhere in Europe. According to this, if the outcome of the civil war registered the triumph of good over evil, and of justice over tyranny, to wish the resulting republic a successful imperial future was not to gratify selfish ambition. Of divine authorship, commonwealth principles applied universally. Thus Nedham informed the Dutch, one-time allies, that

> we of this Nation of *England*, do believe that there is such a Cause of God this day amongst us, that wil take off the *Burthen and the Yoak, and cause Justice to be administred equally to all, and establish Righteousnesse and Judgement in the Earth*: And that as it hath done much hereof in *England* already, so it will perfect it, and that God his will herein, will cause to be declared, and to proceed to other Nations, till the whole *Creation* that is now groaning under the exorbitant and wicked lusts of Kings and great ones . . . be delivered into freedom.[48]

This not only signified the re-emergence and intensification of a godly and protestant imperial language. By explaining the moral and religious, rather than simply politic, case for empire, it contextualised the imperial missions of not only Oliver Cromwell, but James Harrington.

Nedham's Machiavellian analysis was repeated by John Streater in 1654, on the grounds given in the *Discourses*: 'It behoveth those whose care it is . . . to defend a Commonwealth . . . to indeavour the increase thereof; for it is most certain that if a Commonwealth do not increase: it doth decrease, there is nothing under heaven that continueth one and the same thing always, there is nothing firm.'[49] For Streater, however, this propensity to increase was a principle of nature implanted by God, and noticed by Plato and Aristotle.

> Increase of Mankind is the blessing of God, *Jacob* told *Joseph* upon his comming into *Egypt*, my son saith he, *I thought one day, that I never should have seen thy face, but now I see thee, and God hath shewed me thy seed*; also it is not onely the blessing of God, but it is also the gift of God . . . *David* saith that children about a Table are as a pleasant Vine; the fruitfulnesse of the Womb hath been esteemed as a great blessing . . . where there hath been barrennesse.[50]

Thus

> Increase is natural and God gave Nature that stamp which cannot easily be done out, when he said to all things *Increase and multiply. Aristotle* . . . saith that there is

---

[48] Nedham, *The Case Stated* p. 53.   [49] Streater, *Observations* no. 3 19–26 April 1654, p. 18.
[50] Ibid. p. 19.

a natural desire in all things living, even of Plants, for to leave a like of their own kind behind them . . . *Plato* saith, that he which taketh not to him a wife doth deprive himself of Immortality: Therefore he saith it is requisit that every man do take a wife from thirty to five and thirty to preserve his memory and his being in his off spring.[51]

For Streater, therefore, the need for political expansion (increase in space) followed from a principle of numerical increase linked to the desire for conquest of time ('one dieth and of him liveth many . . . this is a kind of immortality on this side of the grave'). 'It is needful for a Common-wealth to increase that they may not decrease, and the way of increase is the society of man and wife. Therefore it is necessary that Adultery should be prevented, and too early joining of man and wife together . . . it is onely beneficial to a Commonwealth when . . . their Members are able to bear Armour.'[52]

Accordingly,

Many prudent States and Commonwealths have made great account of the sol-emnizing of Matrimony, accounted it a sacred thing, and a great prop to their Commonwealth, thereby to increase their number, and inlarge their Territories; the Romans did often by sending their Colonies abroad, as the Bee doth their young swarms; out of one stock many are raised, so out of one Commonwealth many may be erected.[53]

In providing territory for such increase, Streater outlined the 'hazard' attending

war with . . . neighbours near, to supplant them: the which would make room for their spare numbers, as well as adde to their greatnesse . . . Therefore it is safer to chuse some remote place or new Plantation, which no State claimeth, for by this means the Commonwealth . . . that doth do so, avoideth many wars . . . [though] what is won in pursuance of a defensive war: may be held with more justice then that which is onely made for inlarging the scope of their Territories, for conveniency of the Commonwealth, by providing for their overplus of people.[54]

For Harrington, too, conquest in space was linked to the conquest of time. Moreover, whereas for Streater, as 'Perfection in Civil Societies' was 'not to be attained to', for Harrington, as we have seen, it was indeed possi-ble. It was on the basis of this correction of the Florentine that Harrington had insisted, 'against the judgement of Machiavel', upon combining Vene-tian preservation with Roman expansion. Yet in contradicting Machiavelli's opinion that 'either there must be improvement or decline', Harrington

---

[51] Ibid. p. 21.   [52] Ibid. p. 20.   [53] Ibid. p. 18.   [54] Ibid. p. 21.

also removed the principal existing rationale for expansion. In its place, and significantly in its Protectoral context, the case is made in moral and scriptural terms. This is not only a development from the earlier godly and apocalyptic language deployed by Nedham. Among those to be persuaded by *Oceana* are, after all, those army officers by whom the country is governed, including the Lord Protector himself. Harrington's claims on behalf of *Oceana*'s mission to conquer in space are as extraordinary, and universal, as his claims for its conquest of time.

Having erected the world's first perfectly equal republic, there is a moral obligation to confer its blessings upon the world. Moreover if that which gives the commonwealth its stability in time is the material foundation of 'empire', God is also the author of moral laws of nature. What gives Oceana 'authority' is the moral content of Harrington's empire of laws: the social justice secured by the agrarian law; the institutional triumph of reason over 'the bondage of the passions'; the peace delivered to a country ravaged by civil war. As the product of divine authorship, these moral principles are, like their material foundation, of universal application. *Oceana* is erected upon the basis of that 'which God hath ordained . . . unto the universal commonwealth of mankind'.[55]

Thus the imperial mission enunciated by *Oceana* follows from the religious context of Harrington's natural (and moral) philosophy, and the religious content of his commitment to commonwealth principles:

> Hearken, I say; if thy brother cry unto thee in affliction, wilt thou not hear him? This is a commonwealth of the fabric that hath . . . a public concernment; she is not made for herself only, but given as a magistrate of God unto mankind, for the vindication of common right and the law of nature . . .
> Wherefore saith Cicero . . . of the Romans . . . we have rather undertaken the patronage than the empire of the world . . . A Commonwealth . . . of this make is a minister of God upon earth, to the end that the world may be governed with righteousness. For which cause . . . the orders last rehearsed are buds of empire, such as, with the blessing of God, may spread the arms of your commonwealth like an holy asylum unto the distressed world, and give the earth her sabbath of years or rest from her labours, under the shadow of your wings.[56]

Within this moral argument for empire, in the place of Machiavelli's *grandezza* is 'righteousness . . . the cause of God'. Thus

> to ask whether it be lawful for a commonwealth to aspire unto the empire of the world is to ask whether it be lawful for her to do her duty, or to put the world into a better condition than it was before . . . what can you think but if

---

[55] Harrington, *Oceana*, in *Political Works* p. 287.   [56] Ibid. p. 323.

the world should see the Roman eagle again, she would renew her age and her flight? Nor did she ever spread her wing with better omen than will be read in your ensigns . . . called in by an oppressed people . . . [to] interpose between them and their yoke . . . Wherefore . . . if the cause of mankind be the cause of God, the Lord of Hosts will be your captain, and you shall be a praise unto the earth.[57]

Thus informing Harrington's argument for empire is not a broader acceptance (as in Machiavelli, Nedham or Sidney) of the centrality of war to politics. It is a vision within which war is a temporary means to the realisation of a broader moral end. When the world is governed with universal righteousness, that peace which is the primary objective of Oceana's internal orders will become available (as 'holy asylum unto a distressed world') to all humankind.

SIDNEY AND NEVILLE

In Sidney's *Court Maxims* the subjects of conquest and empire are first raised by a claim from the courtier Philalethes concerning the foundation of monarchies in a 'right of conquest'. There follows a denial of any such right in general, as well as of the Norman 'conquest' in particular. Conquests, explains Eunomius, belong to nations, not persons (Sidney's examples are those of the Roman republic, of Alexander, of Ireland by England, of Naples and Milan by Spain). Philalethes then asserts that 'enlargement of dominion and increase of riches and power by conquests are ever beneficial to the nation that attains them'. Again Sidney denies this, instancing examples of 'many nations destroyed by their own conquests', notably Spain, 'weakened, dispeopled and ruined'.[58] Thus far the discussion conforms well enough to Sidney's later identification of the author of monarchical/tyrannical 'policy' as 'Machiavelli', praising the accomplishments of 'Cesare Borgia, Castruccio Castracani, Septimus Severus' (in *The Prince*).[59]

Yet in elaborating his case Sidney's own next source is Machiavelli's *Discourses*. From this he goes on to point out that the question of whether or not conquests are beneficial depends on 'the ends' for which 'a government be constituted'. Thus by contrast to Spain, Venice, Switzerland and Sparta, 'Rome was so constituted that the condition of citizens and city was bettered by conquests', at least until 'the prodigious power it arrived at brought in luxury and pride and destroyed discipline and virtue; for then ruin necessarily followed'. In addition (like Milton referring to Machiavelli's *Discourses* II.19) conquests must not be such as 'tend to corruption' of the

---

[57] Ibid. pp. 328–30.   [58] Sidney, *Court Maxims* pp. 13–16.   [59] Ibid. p. 24.

conqueror 'in discipline and manners'; they must be proportionate and well-absorbed, and they must furnish nourishment to the whole 'body' of a nation, not any 'disease' by which it may be 'discomposed', such as 'some one man or order of men too much prevailing'.[60] Finally, 'Rules of morality also are to be observed . . . States are to consider not only whether such conquests may be useful to them but whether they have a right of war.'[61]

These scruples may relate to Sidney's authorship of this tract for an English audience during the second Anglo-Dutch war. They are also in line with an explicit debt to Grotius and Augustine (and another perhaps to Milton). Nevertheless, Sidney goes on to spend the next several pages asserting the military superiority of republics. The pre-eminent example is that of Rome, which 'I think I may prefer . . . before all . . . the victories that have been gained by kings since the beginning of the world'. This is primarily because 'The nations over whom the Roman commonwealth triumphed were Italians, Greeks, Carthaginians, Gauls, Germans, and Spaniards, all of them in the height of their fierceness and valour, powerful in numbers, exercised in war, excelling in military discipline. No one of all these was ever conquered by any king.'[62] The same republican superiority in war was demonstrated by the United Provinces against Spain, Venice against the Ottomans, 'The commonwealths of Greece' against Persia, and finally 'the late Commonwealth of England', of which 'no man can say the power of a king subdued it'.[63] Yet the accomplishment of Rome also illustrated the finite nature of all 'worldly greatness'.

When this happy state had continued many hundreds of years, the fatal period came, which God seemed to have set to the highest worldly greatness and felicity: man could not pass it. The Roman virtue was the effect of their good laws and discipline. The world could not resist just and wise laws, exact discipline, and admirable virtue. Less glory might have been more permanent. The vastness, strength, and greatness that commonwealth had attained to, resembled that athletic complexion or habit mentioned by Hippocrates: when it comes to the highest pitch of strength, health, and activity that a human body is capable of, it must be diminished by letting blood, or purging, or it will break within itself.[64]

Indeed, as we will see, Sidney's analysis of the collapse of Roman liberty, echoing the experience of England, emphasised the self-destructive moral consequences of such 'success'. Meanwhile, accompanying these arguments, heavily indebted to Machiavelli, was another, indebted to Tacitus' *Annals* and *Agricola*. If the vitality of republics was demonstrated by their superiority in war, so that peace attributed to monarchs from Augustus Caesar

---

[60] Ibid. pp. 16–17.   [61] Ibid. p. 17.   [62] Ibid. p. 18.   [63] Ibid. p. 19.   [64] Ibid. p. 136.

onwards was created by the imposition of 'a desolation'. This was because 'all people grow proud when numerous and rich . . . The least injury puts them into a fury. But if poor, weak, miserable, and few they will be humble and obedient'.[65]

Sidney returned to both of these themes in the *Discourses*:

The Spaniards have established the like peace in the kingdoms of Naples and Sicily, the West-Indies, and other places . . . T'were an endless work to mention all the places where this peaceable solitude has been introduc'd by absolute monarchy; but popular and regular governments have always applied themselves to increase the number, strength, power, riches, and courage of their people.[66]

When the cities of Greece and Italy

were free, they loved their country, and were always ready to fight in its defence . . . They sometimes killed one another; but their enemies never got any thing but burying-places within their territories . . . Machiavelli [in the *History of Florence*] reports that in that time Florence alone, with the Val d'Arno, a small territory belonging to that city, could, in a few hours . . . bring together a hundred and thirty five thousand well arm'd men; wheras now that city, with all the others in that province, are brought to such despicable weakness, emptiness, poverty and baseness, that they can neither resist the oppressions of their own prince, nor defend him or themselves if . . . assaulted by a foreign enemy.[67]

In the *Discourses* these observations are associated not only with a more extensive proof of the military superiority of republics over monarchies, but with a broader defence of war:

'Tis ill, that men should kill one another in seditions, tumults and wars; but 'tis worse, to bring nations to such misery, weakness and baseness, as to have neither strength nor courage to contend for anything; to have left nothing worth defending, and to give the name of peace to desolation . . . Again, there is a way of killing worse than that of the sword . . . by taking from men the means of living, bring some to perish through want, drive others out of the country, and generally dissuade men from marriage, by taking from them all ways of subsisting their families.[68]

'That peace is only to be valued which is accompanied with justice.'[69] Peace simply might deserve praise 'if mankind were so framed, that a people intending hurt to none, could preserve themselves; but the world being so far of another temper, that no nation can be safe without valour and strength, those governments only deserve to be commended, which by discipline and exercise increase both, and the Roman above all, that excelled in both.'[70] Thus, 'experience teaching us that those only can be safe who are

---

[65] Ibid. p. 72.   [66] Sidney, *Discourses*, ed. West p. 262.   [67] Ibid. pp. 260–1.
[68] Ibid. pp. 259–61.   [69] Ibid. p. 160.   [70] Ibid. pp. 158–9.

strong; and that no people was ever well defended, but those who fought for themselves; the best judges of these matters have always given the preference to those constitutions that principally intend war . . . and think it better to aim at conquest, rather than simply to stand upon their own defence'.[71]

For Sidney, therefore, as for Machiavelli, expansion was the only reliable means of defence, and republics superior partly for this reason. Among several other reasons for this necessity, Sidney is led to 'principally insist upon one':

He that builds a city, and does not intend it should increase, commits as great an absurdity, as if he should desire his child might ever continue under the same weakness in which he is born. If it do not grow, it must pine and perish; for in this world nothing is permanent; that which does not grow better will grow worse. This increase also is useless, or perhaps hurtful, if it be not in strength, as well as in riches or number: for everyone is apt to seize upon ill guarded treasures.[72]

However, whereas for Streater increase was a divinely implanted biological law of nature, for Sidney it is a divinely implanted moral effect of good government: '[T]hat government is evidently the best, which, not relying upon what it does at first enjoy, seeks to increase the number, strength and riches of the people.' And it is principally because 'when a people multiplies, as they will always do in a good climate under a good government, such an enlargement of their territory, as is necessary for their subsistence, can only be acquired by war', that 'That is the best Government, which best provides for War.'[73]

Thus this argument rested not only upon Sidney's acceptance of Machiavelli's view that change was inevitable. It followed equally from his belief that the nature of a nation's government was the principal determinant of its 'improvement' or 'decline'. It was natural to a republic 'that the people being pleased with their present condition, may be filled with love to their country, encouraged to fight boldly for the publick cause, which is their own; and as men do willingly join with that which prospers, that strangers may be invited to fix their habitations in such a city, and to espouse the principles that reign in it'. This faith in the potential improvement, and expansion, of a state equipped with the appropriate political discipline was deeply indebted to Livy, whose account of the political development and military consequences of Roman manners permeates the *Discourses*.

Although from this discussion, at least, what scruples about expansion the *Court Maxims* had manifested had disappeared, Sidney's view remained strongly related to Milton's. According to this, prosperity or adversity were

[71] Ibid. p. 205.   [72] Ibid. p. 209.   [73] Sidney, *Discourses*, in *Sydney on Government* pp. 178–9.

God-given products of moral rectitude or depravity. Thus for Sidney, too, it was 'ridiculous to impute' the Romans' success 'to chance, or to think that fortune, which is of all things the most variable, could for so many ages continue the same course, unless supported by virtue':

'The secret counsels of God are impenetrable; but the ways by which he accomplishes his designs are often evident: When he intends to exalt a people, he fills both them and their leaders with the virtues suitable to the accomplishment of his end; and takes away all wisdom and virtue from those he resolves to destroy.'[74]

This did not mean that a people were mere ciphers for the divine will. The internal moral struggle (not simply public discipline, but self-discipline) was as important to Sidney's moral philosophy as to Milton's. Thus

commonwealths acknowledging no superior, except God alone, can reasonably hope to be protected by him only; and by him, if with industry and courage they make use of the means he has given them for their own defence. God helps those who help themselves; and men are by several reasons . . . induced to succour an industrious and brave people: But such as neglect the means of their own preservation are ever left to perish with shame.[75]

For Sidney, in an imperfect world this moral struggle had a necessary military dimension, both between nations and within a country. On the international stage, goodness and innocence which could not protect itself would be destroyed; internally, resistance to tyranny 'will be a hard work in those places where virtue is wholly abolished; but the difficulty will lie on the other side, if any sparks of that remain'.[76]

For Henry Neville, too, although he lacked Sidney's bellicosity, liberty remained the key to greatness. Thus in *Nicholas Machiavel's Letter* (1675) he had Machiavelli say that

under the happy and hopeful reign of our new Prince . . . we may say, that though our Common-wealth be not restored, our slavery is at an end, and . . . he coming in by our own choice, may . . . govern this State in great quietness, and with great clemency; so that our Posterity is like to enjoy ease and security, though not that greatness, wealth, and glory, by which our City hath for some years past (even in the most . . . tumultuous times of our Democracy) given Law to *Italy*, and bridled the ambition of foreign Princes.[77]

In *Plato Redivivus* the first question posed by the Noble Venetian concerning England's sick condition is 'for what reasons this nation, which has ever been

---

[74] Sidney, *Discourses*, ed. West p. 145.   [75] Ibid. p. 210.

[76] Sidney, *Discourses*, in *Sydney on Government* p. 262.

[77] [Neville], *Nicholas Machiavel's Letter* p. 2.

esteemed (and very justly) one of the most considerable people of the world; and made the best figure both in peace, treaties, war and trade; is now of so small regard, and signifies so little abroad'?[78] Like the discussion in Sidney's *Discourses* this has its context, not only in the concerns of Machiavelli and his English followers. It also addressed the anxieties animating a religious and political crisis largely caused by English impotence before the growing military menace of France.[79] For Neville, as for Sidney, because 'politic defects breed moral ones' such 'French Councels' were not causes but effects of 'the breech and ruin of our government'. Either 'the polity of England, must die of this disease; or in this delirium, must be governed from without and fall to the lot of some foreign power'.[80]

For Neville, as for Sidney, when even small states have 'stood upon right bottoms' the military results have been spectacular.[81] In Neville there is no argument that successful politics necessarily entails an increase of population, which will require an increase in territory. For him, however, the 'politic or moral ends of government' include not only 'quiet and peace' but 'plenty, prosperity and greatness'.[82]

---

[78] Neville, *Plato Redivivus* p. 79.
[79] Scott, *Algernon Sidney and the Restoration Crisis*, esp. chs. 2 and 6; Scott, *England's Troubles* chs. 7–8.
[80] Neville, *Plato Redivivus* p. 175.   [81] Ibid. pp. 81, 87, 98.   [82] Ibid. p. 111.

PART III
Chronology

CHAPTER II

Republicans and Levellers, 1603–1649

"[W]hat the greatest and choycest wits of *Athens, Rome,* or modern *Italy,* and those Hebrews of old did for their country, I in my proportion with this over and above of being a Christian, might doe for mine: not caring to be once nam'd abroad, though perhaps I could attaine to that, but content with these British Ilands as my world, whose fortune hath hitherto bin, that if the Athenians, as some say, made their small deeds great and renowned by their eloquent writers, *England* hath had her noble atchievements made small by the unskilfull handling of monks and mechanicks.'

John Milton, *Reason of Church-governement* (1641)[1]

1603–1641: COMMONWEALTH PRINCIPLES AND PRACTICE

Explicit advocacy of a republic was rare in England before 1648. Yet as the primary ingredients of republican moral philosophy were already in place, so the accusation of republicanism was frequently levelled by early Stuart kings and their supporters. The attribution to JPs and MPs of 'anti-monarchical' motives was a staple of Jacobean rhetoric: '[I]n every cause that concerns prerogative . . . [they] give a snatch against monarchy, through their puritanical itching after popularity.'[2] The 'imagined democracy' of Presbyterianism also derived from 'the turbulent humors of some that dream of nothing but a new hierarchy (directly opposite to the state of monarchy)'.[3] Charles I attributed his early problems to parliaments 'whose members wished to reduce his power to nothing'. These people were 'puritans', 'republicans' and 'enemies to monarchy'.[4] These were analyses

---

[1] Milton, *The Reason of Church-governement* p. 812.
[2] John Rushworth, *Historical Collections . . . beginning the Sixteenth Years of King James,* Anno 1618 (3 vols., 1659–82) vol. 1 p. 40; Johann Sommerville, 'James I and the Divine Right of Kings', in Linda Levy Peck (ed.), *The Mental World of the Jacobean Court* (Cambridge, 1991) pp. 65, 68.
[3] James I and Robert Cecil quoted by Kenneth Fincham and Peter Lake, 'The Ecclesiastical Policy of King James I', *Journal of British Studies* 24, 2 (1985) pp. 172, 176.
[4] Reeve, *Charles I and the Road to Personal Rule* p. 132.

supported both by the earlier identifiers of classical republicanism (Filmer, Hobbes) and by those Laudian clerics who found in 'Puritans' a 'Tribunitian . . . disaffection unto the soveraignty of princes'.[5] When disobedience among his English subjects gave way to armed resistance in Scotland, the king's public analysis was that 'the aim of these men is not Religion, as they falsly pretend and publish, but it is to shake all Monarchical Government, and to vilify our Regal Power'.[6]

These perceptions had both practical and intellectual contexts. A steady decline in the real military and fiscal power of the monarchy left early modern English kings and queens uncomfortably dependent upon the willing co-operation of their subjects, in the localities and in parliaments.[7] Simultaneously a royal minority (Edward VI) followed by two female monarchs (Mary, Elizabeth I) encouraged the development within the male political elite of a semi-autonomous aristocratic conciliar culture.[8] This became permeated by humanism and protestantism. Although there was nothing about either that was necessarily productive of disobedience to monarchy, when concern emerged about royal policy it was capable of being deeply informed by both.[9] Under Elizabeth such concerns expressed themselves primarily over the succession, the religious settlement and the European military situation of the 1580s. In the face of apparently dangerous negligence in all of these areas, a series of leading royal servants all stepped up to, and sometimes over, the limits of obedience.

Under these circumstances, according to James Harrington, the appearance of English monarchy was maintained only by the achievement of Elizabeth in 'converting her reign through the perpetual love tricks that passed between her and her people into a kind of romance'.[10] Having been the queen's only consort, thereafter the male political nation found itself in uncomfortable receipt of the news that the new Scots king considered it collectively to be his 'wife', and individually to comprise his children. Among the hallmarks of the new Stuart era were a series of claims for royal power ('God gives not Kings the stile of *Gods* in vaine, For on his Throne his Scepter doe they swey.'[11]) in conspicuously inverse proportion to its actual extent. This became dangerous only with the outbreak of the European

[5] Peter Heylyn, *A Briefe and Moderate Answer, to the seditious and scandalous challenges of Henry Burton* (1637) pp. 4, 5,7.

[6] Charles I, *Proclamation* (1639) in Rushworth, *Historical Collections* vol. II, p. 830.

[7] See chapter 3 above; and Scott, *England's Troubles* ch. 3.

[8] Alford, *The Early Elizabethan Polity*; Collinson, 'Monarchical Republic'.

[9] Scott, *England's Troubles* chs. 2–5; Worden, 'Classical Republicanism'; Peltonen, *Classical Humanism* chs. 4–5; Norbrook, *Writing the English Republic* ch. 1; Skinner, 'Classical Liberty'.

[10] Harrington, *Oceana*, in *Political Works* p. 198.   [11] James VI and I, *Basilikon Doron* p. 137.

war. It was against the backdrop of military inaction, followed by repeated failure, that rising public anxiety fed into escalating political crisis.

It was the concern of perhaps the most important author appealing to 'The Parliament' in this decade to educate 'a good and diligent man' to 'make . . . a good Citizen, a good Common-wealthsman'. Such a person was equipped with 'reason . . . the image of God . . . *to be wise*: For that is the end or scope of all'.[12] He had to overcome the 'vices' of (especially military)'sloth' and 'lethargy' in favour of '*diligence*, a vertue', accompanied by 'justice, charity, piety . . . prudence, study and counsell'. In these writings Thomas Scott's most important classical source was Aristotle. Concerning the claimed present 'contention . . . about the government of Common-weales' he contrasted the advice of Cato in favour of 'universall peace' to that of '*Scipio*' recommending 'action abroad'.[13] Like others in this decade he also used Lucan. At the same time his work was replete with biblical references. The 'generall grievances of the Church and State' were intertwined, for there was no difference between becoming 'a Galley-Slave . . . to . . . the Inquisition' and political 'slavery'.

Scott's broader target was a corrupt state where 'effeminate . . . Nobilitie be educated in an idle course of life . . . onely to hunt, to hawke, or daunce, or drinke, or court'. Of the same spirit was the 'Monopolist . . . racker of Rents . . . [and] taker of Bribes'. Such corruption was exemplified in the tyrant, 'Claudius . . . Nero . . . Caligula . . . Tiberius', whose policy it was 'To waste and impoverish . . . to sucke the life bloud out of the Commonwealth, thereby to deject the spirits of men . . . and so subjugate them under the yoke of slaverie'.[14] By contrast

to fill the veines of a decayed estate, to inrich a Commonwealth, to restore libertie, and to rule by vertuous Lawes: this requires wisdome . . . For the wealth of a State, stands not altogether in the wealth of one man: The Prince may be rich, and the State poore: but if the State be rich the Prince must needs be rich also.[15]

For the political exemplification of these commonwealth principles, Scott referred his 'Deare Countrimen' to the 'good Customes and Orders . . . established and practised amongst this diligent and happie people [the Dutch] . . . some of which I could wish translated into our Common-wealth'. Rejecting sloth they have chosen rather 'a safe Warre . . . then an unsafe peace'.[16] As their manners are frugal, their economic and fiscal government effective, and their society a genuine commonwealth, 'The Lawes

---

[12] Scott, *Belgicke Pismire* pp. 31, 36.   [13] Thomas Scott, *The Projector* (1623) pp. 1–2.
[14] Scott, *Belgicke Pismire* pp. 27, 30–2.   [15] Ibid. p. 37.   [16] Ibid. pp. 51 and 59–90 in general.

neede not limit them, whilst Reason is their Law.'[17] In addition to liberty of conscience, there

> I observe a generall freedome permitted and used, where generall actions which concerne all, and are maintained by all, are generally debated, argued, sifted and censured by all men without contradiction . . . And this is enough to make all wisemen . . . wish . . . that . . . our association might be firme, our imitation safe . . . Let us . . . flocke thither where all things abound, which wisemen and good men seeke: *Fidelity in bargaines and contracts, wisdome in counsell, strength in warre, brotherly love and assurance, modesty* and *frugalitie*; and that I may say all in a word, *Pietie*, and *Religion*.[18]

Even within England, in 'one place . . . the City of Norwiche' its 'wealth, people, beauty, order, and . . . quicke trading . . . The . . . good government of the Magistrates, the diligence of the Citizens', the thriving agriculture and industry were all 'principally occasioned by the example of . . . Dutch' settlers.[19] Well might Charles I's minister Sir Francis Cottington have attributed the refusal to pay tonnage and poundage in 1629 to an 'infection' from the United Provinces, 'whos kind of government pleaseth us much, and we would fayne be at it'.[20] Well might Thomas Hobbes have attributed the conduct of 'many men' in the subsequent 'troubles' to 'an imitation of the Low Countries: supposing there needed no more to grow rich than to change, as they had done, the forme of their Government'.[21] As we have seen, in entries in his *Commonplace Book* in the late 1630s or early 1640s Milton made a series of approving references to successful Dutch and Scots military resistance against popish tyranny. Alongside the assertion that 'England [is] a free nation not only at home but from all claim . . . from [the] pope',[22] he observed the 'zealous and excellent aid' given by 'The Dutch . . . to the English when the fleet of the Catholic Spaniards . . . prepared by Alva to confound the affairs of the English . . . [was] destroyed'.[23]

More broadly, as we have seen, the *Commonplace Book* entries of these years contain a series of observations about tyranny from Augustine, Guicciardini and others. According to Sir Thomas Smith, and his principal authority Aristotle, 'The tyrant seeks what benefits himself, the king what benefits his subjects.'[24] Note is made of the 'Tyrannicall practizes of Rich[ard]. 2. and his accomplices' and of Charles IX of France.[25] In observing that 'Tyrants pretend that they do not make war on anyone because

---

[17] Ibid. p. 81.   [18] Ibid. pp. 89–90.   [19] Ibid. pp. 95–6.
[20] State papers 16/530/36, quoted in Peter Salt's unpublished paper 'Charles I: a Bad King?'
[21] Hobbes, *Leviathan* p. 225.   [22] Milton, *Commonplace Book* p. 445.   [23] Ibid. p. 503.
[24] Ibid. pp. 442–3.   [25] Ibid. pp. 446, 453, 455.

of religion, but on certain ones who under that pretext are rebels against their rulers', Milton offered a sufficiently close commentary upon Charles I's public response to the Scots rebellion of 1639 to be able to re-use the point later in *Eikonoklastes*.[26] There was no explicit suggestion in Scott that the kingship of James I had become a tyranny. Rather it was, given the challenges facing the commonwealth, a failed and corrupt monarchy. By 1641, however, at least against the civil and ecclesiastical ministers of Charles I, the accusation of tyranny was explicit.[27]

Thus John Pym informed members of the Commons that the 'Arbitrary, and Tyrannical Power, which the *E. of Strafford* did exercise in his own person, and to which he did advise his Majesty . . . is destructive to Justice, the Mother of Peace; to Industry, the spring of Wealth; to Valour, which is the active vertue whereby the prosperity of a Nation can onely be procured, confirmed, and inlarged'.[28] Had this design been successful, to 'subvert the Fundamentall Lawes . . . [protecting] *Lives, Liberties,* and *Estates* . . . [as well as] *Religion* . . . we should within a short time have been brought into . . . *A servile condition . . . beget[ting] . . . a slavish temper and disposition* . . . so as to have been uselesse to our *friends*, contemptible to our *enemies*, and uncapable of undertaking any great *designe* either at home or abroad'.[29] In the early 1640s, as in the 1620s, the perception of political illness at home remained closely connected to that of ineffectuality abroad, especially in the protestant cause.

'TWO AND FIFTY DEGREES OF NORTHERN LATITUDE'

However, alongside their commonplace strictures against tyranny, the early entries in Milton's *Commonplace Book* display a more precocious character-istic. This is hostility to monarchy. '[T]he name of kings', we are told, 'has always been hateful to free peoples'.[30] 'A king, if he wishes to do his duty, is not truly a king but a steward of the people.'[31] 'Kings scarcely recognise themselves as mortals . . . except . . . on the day they die . . . [when] in the knowledge of their evil deeds, they confess . . . that they are wretched mortals.'[32] '[T]he life of princes . . . [is] wretched and constantly full of anxiety, even . . . those who . . . seem to be happy.' In the case of Milton, as

[26] Ibid. p. 501 and note 8; *Eikonoklastes* p. 85.
[27] John Morrill, 'Charles I and Tyranny', in Morrill, *The Nature of the English Revolution* (1993) discusses the reluctance of parliamentarians in 1641–2 to level this charge against the king himself.
[28] John Pym, *The Speech or Declaration of John Pym, Esquire . . . 12 April, 1641* (1641) p. 8.
[29] Ibid. pp. 2, 4, 8–10.   [30] Milton, *Commonplace Book* p. 440.
[31] Ibid. p. 439.   [32] Ibid. pp. 431–2.

of Sidney, a theoretical adherence to that Aristotelian distinction between
monarchy and tyranny was no barrier in practice to anti-monarchism.[33]
That monarchy was better than tyranny did not make it a good thing. In
particular, as Aristotle had explained, monarchy was 'fitting' only where
either (in Milton's later paraphrase) 'a king . . . far excels the rest' or (in
Sidney's) 'over those who are naturally beasts and slaves'.[34] From the evidence of his *Commonplace Book*, Milton decided at an early stage that
neither of these circumstances applied in the English situation. Accordingly, 'When many men are equal, as the majority are in every state, I think
that power should be granted on an equal basis and to all in turn: but who
does not think that it is quite unworthy for all to be slaves to their equal,
or to one who is quite often their inferior and very frequently a fool?'[35]

Thus in the *Commonplace Book* (leaving aside the Machiavellian entries
belonging to 1651–2) Milton related the suitability or otherwise of 'monarchy' to 'the people's disposition':

[A]s amoung the Romans who after thire infancy were ripe for a more free government then monarchy, beeing in a manner all fit to be ks. afterward growne
unruly, and impotent with overmuch prosperity . . . fit to be curb'd with a lordly
and dreadfull monarchy . . . Brutus and Cassius . . . felt themselves of a spirit to
free an nation . . . but consider'd not that the nation was not fit to be free, whilst
forgetting thire old justice and fortitude which was made to rule, they became
slaves to thire own ambition and luxurie.[36]

The question of England's fitness, or unfitness, for freedom dominated
Milton's reading of the revolution. In 1641, as he wrote against the tyranny
of prelacy, his public stance was one of optimism. From long years of study
and travel Milton had come upon the public stage in his own country
to celebrate and perhaps immortalise heroic deeds. In the winning of his
liberty '[T]he Englishman' had some advantages, being 'of many other
nations . . . least atheisticall . . . right pious, right honest, right hardy'.
Nevertheless '[I]f we look at his native towardliness in the roughcast without
breeding, some nation or other may haply be better compos'd to a naturall
civility.'[37] To the fundamental problem Milton alluded when he hoped that
he had benefited 'from the industry of a life wholly dedicated to studious
labours, and those naturall endowments haply not the worst for two and
fifty degrees of northern latitude'.[38] Like many English republicans here

[33] Scott, *England's Troubles* pp. 300–5.
[34] Milton, *Defence* pp. 53–4; Sidney, *Court Maxims* p. 65.
[35] Milton, *Defence*, in *Political Works* p. 99.   [36] Milton, *Commonplace Book* p. 420.
[37] Milton, *The Reason of Church-governement* pp. 796–7.
[38] Milton, *Areopagitica* pp. 489–90.

Milton was influenced not only by his own observations in France and Italy, but by the analysis of the effects of latitude and topography (determinants of climate) supplied in Book 5 of Jean Bodin's *Six Books of a Republic* (1572).[39] At 52 degrees (and above) of northern latitude Britain inhabited Bodin's frigid zone, diagnosed as gifted at the physical accomplishments of manufactury and war, but deficient in the prudent arts of politics and law (speciality of the temperate zone) and the intellectual culture of philosophy and pure sciences (speciality of the 'torrid' Mediterranean):

For the sunn, which we want ripens witts as well as fruits; and as wine and oyle are imported to us from abroad, so must ripe understanding and many civil vertues bee imported into our minds from forren writings and examples of be stages: wee shall else miscarry . . . and com short in the attempt of any great enterprise.[40]

Thus it fell to the English of the seventeenth century to secure 'their Countries liberty . . . from such a steepe disadvantage of tyranny and superstition grounded into our principles as was beyond the manhood of a *Roman* recovery'. If, by 1644, 'wee are already in good part arriv'd' at this objective, this could only 'bee attributed first . . . to the strong assistance of God our deliverer, next to your faithfull guidance and undaunted Wisdome, Lords and Commons of *England*'.[41] Nevertheless, winning this liberty would be one thing, keeping it another. This challenge emphasised the crucial importance on 'this Iland' of education.[42] It also underlined the importance of 'Books', the 'reason' in which was 'the Image of God' and the 'potencie of life' in which was well worth defending from a 'project of licencing crept out of the *Inquisition*'.[43] 'We can grow ignorant again, brutish, formall, and slavish, as ye found us; but you then must first become . . . oppressive, arbitrary, and tyrannous, as they were from whom ye have free'd us.'[44]

Thereafter Milton's hopes for England's liberty co-existed with his doubts. The hopes, naturally enough, were expressed in a rhetoric of encouragement and celebration which he took to constitute a key aspect of his public role and which were invested with a corresponding moral seriousness. Thus we hear in *Areopagitica* about 'a Nation not slow and dull, but of a quick, ingenious, and piercing spirit' preferred by 'that wise and civill Roman, *Julius Agricola*' to 'the labour'd . . . French'.[45] This 'Nation [was] chos'n before any other, that out of her . . . should be proclam'd . . . the first tidings . . . of Reformation to all *Europ*'.[46] 'Behold' London, 'this

---

[39] Bodin, *Six Bookes*, 'The Fift Booke' pp. 545–636; Zera S. Fink, 'Milton and the Theory of Climatic Influence', *Modern Language Quarterly* 2 (1949).
[40] Milton, MS Digression p. 451.   [41] Milton, *Areopagitica* p. 487.
[42] Milton, *Of Education* p. 363.   [43] Milton, *Areopagitica* pp. 492–3.
[44] Ibid. p. 559.   [45] Ibid. pp. 551–2.   [46] Ibid. p. 552.

vast City . . . the mansion house of liberty', compared to Rome under seige by Hannibal, 'the shop of warre hath not there more anvils and hammers waking, to fashion out the plates and instruments of armed Justice in defence of beleagur'd Truth, then there be pens and heads there, sitting by their studious lamps, musing, searching, revolving new notions and idea's [*sic*]'.[47] 'Methinks I see in my mind a noble and puissant Nation rousing herself like a strong man after sleep, and shaking her invincible locks.'[48] *The Tenure of Kings and Magistrates* (1649) celebrated the 'fortitude and Heroick vertue', 'fear[ing] nothing', of those 'Patriots' who had achieved 'the deliverance of thir Countrie'.[49] *A Defence of the People of England* (1651) accompanied fulsome praise of 'the noble liberators of my country' with the most nationalistic of Milton's references to the ancient constitution.

Yet as he demonstrated in *Areopagitica*, and more courageously in *The Readie and Easie Way* (1660), Milton also considered it his duty to warn. Thus even in the first months of the republic, as he publicly defended the regicide, in the manuscript Digression to his *History of Britain* Milton gave vent to his despair at the near-disastrous backsliding of the Presbyterian-dominated Long Parliament in the previous three years.[50] This had brought the nation 'after many labours, much blood-shed, & vast expence, to ridiculous frustration':

> For a parlament being calld and as was thought many things to redress, the people with great courage & expectation . . . chose . . . in parlament such as they thought best affected to the public good, & some indeed men of wisdome and integritie. The rest, and . . . the greatest part whom wealth and ample possessions or bold and active ambition rather then merit had commended to the same place, when onc[e] the superficial zeale and popular fumes that acted thir new magistracie were cool'd and spent in them, straite every one betooke himself, setting the common-wealth behinde and his private ends before . . . Then was justice delai'd & soone after deny'd, spite and favour determin'd all . . . ev'ry where wrong & oppression . . . maintain'd in secret or in op'n. Some who had bin called from shops & warehouses without other merit to sit in supreme councel[s] & committies, as thir breeding was, fell to hucster the commonwealth.[51]

This was commonwealth discourse directed against the tyranny of the few. Within this corrupt oligarchy,

> Thir votes and ordinances which men look'd should have contain'd the repealing of bad laws & the immediate constitution of better resounded with nothing els but new impositions, taxes, excises, yearlie, monthlie, weeklie [,] not to reck'n the

---

[47] Ibid. pp. 553–4.   [48] Ibid. pp. 557–8.   [49] Milton, *Tenure* p. 191.
[50] Nicholas von Maltzahn, 'Dating the Digression in Milton's *History of Britain*', *Historical Journal* 36, 4 (1993) pp. 945–56; see also Woolrych, 'Dating Milton's *History of Britain*'.
[51] Milton, *MS Digression* pp. 443, 445.

offices, gifts and preferments bestow'd and shar'd among themselves . . . [so that this] state . . . after infinite summs receiv'd & all the wealth of the church, not better imploy'd, but swallow'd up into a private gulfe . . . was not ere long asham'd to confess [itself] bankrupt.[52]

This attack culminated in a climatic analysis of northerly Britain's 'head-strong . . . intractab[ility] . . . to the industrie and vertue either of executing or understanding true civil government . . . Hence did thir victories prove as fruitless as thir losses dangerous.'[53] Milton's levelling of the republican accusation of private interestedness against the pre-Purge Long Parliament was notably bitter in tone but otherwise not unusual. The diatribe against Presbyterian 'hypocrisy' was consistent with Milton's other writings, and *The Tenure* in particular. More generally the *Digression* belonged to that literature of moral self-criticism that was a continuous feature of the revolution (and aspect of its integrity). As Edward Burrough put it: 'The principle of sincerity . . . of opposing oppression and pressing after reformation [was lost, and many] . . . became self-seekers [and] oppressors even as others before them.'[54] Specifically Milton's savage indictment echoed the Levellers. Like them he found the seeds of the revolution's failure in the moral failings, not of the 'rabble', but of those chosen in good faith to be their leaders. This emergence of republicanism from civil war radicalism, and that of the Levellers in particular, is more dramatically underlined by the career of Marchamont Nedham.

TRIBUNE OF THE PLEBS

It was by Nedham that the '*Tribunitian*' politics decried by defenders of the early Stuart monarchy came first to be explicitly advocated. Nedham appeared on the public stage as editor, from 1644, of the parliamentary newsletter *Mercurius Britanicus*. In this role he developed his own characteristically Machiavellian idiom of commonwealth discourse which was, like Milton's, precociously republican. Nedham's first move, in the context not only of a brutal civil war, but of that 'dimunition of majesty' by which it had been accompanied, was to bring into focus an image of monarchical absence. This challenged unexamined assumptions about the indespensability of monarchy. It was focused in part on the physical absence of the king from his capital city, and from his 'loyal'parliament. This was, however, a metaphor for the more fundamental absence of kingship as a form

---

[52] Ibid. p. 445.   [53] Ibid. p. 451.
[54] Quoted in Christopher Hill, *The Experience of Defeat: Milton and Some Contemporaries* (1984) p. 150; Scott, *England's Troubles* p. 267.

of government distinguishable from tyranny; of one person in the interest of his subjects. Thus as early as late 1644 Nedham announced 'my opinion of His *Majesties* death'.[55] In March 1645, reporting the failure of Charles to make serious concessions at Uxbridge, and the subsequent breakdown of the negotiations, he made a startling extrapolation from

The *Countries* cry . . . *help us O King*, yet he regards not, but sits *mopish* over the ruines of this too well-deserving *Nation*; I hope all is wel in the *Cranium*; and that he remembers who he is . . . Yet I see but small *Signes* of it; for was there ever such *adoe* . . . to get a *Prince* into his *Throne*? Which makes me beleeve, that he does absolutely intend to give it over, and never come neere it againe. Then how kindly should we take it, if Prince *Charles* [aged 14] would come to *London* . . . and fill up that *roome* in the *Monarchie*, which hath been too long *empty*: for that kind of *Government* cannot be continued without some body to supply it. Besides, the *Royall Robes* begin to wax *mouldy* for want of use; and if these chance to be spoyled, I doubt whether the exhausted, and oppressed *Kingdome*, will be at the *Charges* to make new ones.[56]

The first implication of this argument, in line with the analysis of Harrington but on a different basis, was that monarchy had lapsed, or was lapsing. In this respect Nedham's image of a vacant throne anticipated the argument of the 1689 Convention Commons. The second implication was that the absent monarchy had been replaced by a tyranny. Charles was 'in the way to undoe *Himself*, His *Posterity* and Kingdomes . . . *rambling abroad and ruining the People in such a manner, that no man would beleeve them to be His subjects.*' '[W]hat may we say when a *King* (whose private affections ought not to sway him in publique Affaires) shall forsake the *Great Councell* of his Kingdome, to be ruled wholly by his *Wife*?' This was a sovereign from whom it was impossible to 'wring one sigh or *Teare* . . . but on the contrary, [who] rejoyced in the *ruine* of his faithful *Subjects*.' 'It is a very wonder to me, that Princes cannot be weaned from that weak impolitique Paradox, judging themselves not Kings, unless their subjects be Slaves.' It was Charles's misfortune to attempt to follow '*Trick[s]of State* which *Machiavel* commends in his *Caesar Borgia*'.[57]

The third move in this process was to begin to invest with authority an alternative to monarchy. Nedham was proud to be 'writing for this Glorious *Parliament*'. It was one aspect of the dementia of royalism that 'these men . . . are not (or will not be) sensible of the Majesty and Dignity

[55] *Mercurius Britanicus* p. 541.   [56] Ibid. no. 72, 24 February–3 March 1645, pp. 575–6.
[57] Ibid. no. 86, 9–16 June 1645, p. 778; ibid. no. 91, 21–28 July 1645, p. 818; ibid. no. 92, 28 July–4 August 1645, p. 826; ibid. no. 99, 22–29 September 1645, p. 885; ibid. no. 119. 16–23 February 1646, pp. 1041–2.

of a Parliament'. In a significant linguistic move parliament was owed 'that *Reverence* due to so grave a Senate'. In an anticipation of the Anglo-Dutch interest argument of Sidney's *Court Maxims*, citizens of the Dutch republic were warned of attempts by the Prince of Orange to engage them 'in an irreligious, unprofitable, impolitick, destructive war against the *Parliament of England* . . . [in] *alliance* with a neighbour Monarch . . . absolutely Diametricall to the *Publick interest* of that *State*'.[58] It was, however, in December 1645 that Nedham lost control of what threadbare restraint he had ever possessed, anticipating in the process much of his own subsequent republican writing. Indeed the first sentence of the passage concerned ('This I know, that Kingdomes, *Commonwealths*, and *Governments*, have their *rises* and *fals*, their *Original, Acme*, and *Period*') was a précis of what would become chapter 1 of his *The Case of the Commonwealth of England, Stated* (1650) ('That Governments Have Their Revolutions and Fatal Periods').

History will tell you, that *Rome* once changed her *Kings* for *Consuls*, upon a petty occasion too, and under that *Consular authority* she arrived at her greatest glory, which was lost again in *Emperours*. Come down to the present times, and compare the Gallantry of *Venice*, as also of the other *Italian States*, and the thriving Liberty of *Holland*, with the *Slaves* of *Spain*, the *Peasants* of *France*, and the late encroaching *Prerogative* of *England*. So this being thoroughly weighed, every man will conceive that the *King* takes a most impolitique course, to give the People such large *provocations*, and so little hopes of his returne.[59]

Nedham's next, or rather parallel, move was to apply himself to the question of what form such '*Consular authority*' should take in England. *England's Miserie and Remedie* (1645), in which he may have had a hand, published on behalf of the perenially imprisoned 'Leiutenant Col. Lilburn', reminded 'the House of Commons that it was nothing lesse, then the representative body of the People, elected and set up, by the severall Shires and Burroughs . . . to make, alter, abrogate Lawes . . . to heare and relieve the Grievances of the people, and to reforme what is amisse in the Commonwealth'.[60] In support of this and related contentions against 'abuse of . . . power . . . [in] Princes, or what State soever', were brought the authority not only of Magna Carta,

---

[58] Ibid. no. 93, 11–18 August 1645, p. 834; ibid. no. 107, 24 November–1 December 1645, p. 946; ibid. no. 126, 13–20 April 1645, p. 1081.

[59] Ibid. no. 108, 1–8 December 1645, p. 954.

[60] *England's Miserie.* The possibility of Nedham's involvement is indicated by the content shared with *Vox Plebis* (as well as his later writings) including the passage concerning Caius Flaminius, probably taken from Ralegh's *History of The World*. See pp. 83–4 above. On Nedham's relationship to *Vox Plebis* see chapter 3 note 105.

and '*Buchannan* an Author without reproach', but 'before *Buchannan*, the Common-wealth of *Rome*.'[61] Thus when

> *C. Flaminius* . . . taught them to know and use their Power over himselfe, and his fellow Senators in reforming their disorders: For this the Commons highly esteemed him, and the Senators as deeply hated him . . . I hope the wisdome and Providence of the Parliament will prevent these extremities; yet I cannot but put them in remembrance, that small sparkles do oftentimes occasion great fires.[62]

The following year in *Vox Plebis* parliament was subjected to a much more developed version of this anti-senatorial Roman levelling. Once again '*Magna Charta*' was invoked and 'Lilburnes Sentence . . . refuted'. However extended sections of this much longer tract were filled with passages and paraphrases from Edward Dacre's English translation of Machiavelli's *Discorsi*.[63] Thus 'as hunger and poverty make men laborious; so Lawes duly adminstred, make them good; and good examples proceed from good education; and good education, from the due observance of . . . Lawes'. 'It is a most sure Rule in State policy, That all the Lawes that are made in favour of liberty, spring first from the disagreement of the people with their Governours.'[64] The most important example was the creation by the Roman people of '*Tribunes*, as *Guardians* of the publick liberty . . . which continued inviolable to them for the space of 800 yeares (after 300 yeares oppression of the Nobility) to the great honour and renown of their Nation, and exceding enlargement of their Common-wealth'.[65]

It was the job of this

> most honourable Commons, whom we have chosen & intrusted for us to sit at *Westm[inster]* as Guardians of our Birth-rights, and most powerful Tribunes of the people's liberties . . . who have made so many pious and feeling Declarations of their mindes now in print, concerning our by-past thraldome . . . *to maintain the lawes and liberties of the free-born Subjects of England*, and that SALUS POPULI shall be to them, their SUPREMA LEX.'[66]

Vox Plebis made use of many other passages from '*Machiavel* his discourses upon *Liv[y]*', plus Seneca, Livy and Guicciardini, and examples of the republican practice both of Rome and Athens. References to '*Manlius Capitolinus* . . . *Themistocles* . . . *[and] Alcibiades*' later reappeared in *The Case of The Commonwealth* (1650), *Mercurius Politicus* (1652) and *The Excellencie* (1656). It counselled against senatorial resistance to tribunitial politics in

---

[61] *England's Miserie* pp. 3–4.   [62] Ibid. p. 4.
[63] Raab, *Machiavelli* pp. 171–2; Glover, 'The Putney Debates'.
[64] [Nedham] *Vox Plebis* pp. 1, 3.   [65] Ibid. p. 3.   [66] Ibid. p. 58.

England by warning that 'Contentions . . . upon the *Agearian [sic] Law*' were one of the 'two . . . causes of that Republiques dissolution'.[67]

These were not the only Leveller tracts betraying possible signs of Nedham's authorship.[68] We may certainly date at least as early as 1646 the first public appearance of that radical Machiavellianism which was to be his most influential contribution to English republicanism. This material establishes that, while Nedham was a parliamentarian journalist, and before he became a royalist and then a republican journalist, he was a Lilburne-associated Leveller pamphleteer. This fact appears to shed light upon both of his subsequent dramatic moves. It was in September 1647 that Nedham began his new job as editor of the royalist *Mercurius Pragmaticus*. It is upon this transformation, followed in mid-1650 by the no less extraordinary assumption of editorship of the republic's *Mercurius Politicus*, that Nedham's fame as a chameleon is primarily founded. There is no need to downplay these reversals of allegiance, attended as they frequently were by abject personal circumstances, and accentuated by a tendency to attack precisely those positions Nedham had himself previously advanced. Nor, given Machiavelli's understanding of *virtu* as the capacity to do whatever was required by a particular situation, should they surprise us in the career of England's foremost Machiavellian. Nevertheless, Nedham's notoriety on point of allegiance, combined with insufficient attention to his Leveller credentials, has led to a neglect of the ideological context of this particular transformation.

As a Leveller Nedham had already by 1645 made the transition from supporting parliament's war effort to warning it against replacing the tyranny of one with another of the few. During late 1647 and 1648, following the breakdown of the attempted alliance with the army, many Levellers made the further transition of seeing the army grandees as the new would-be tyrants. Lilburne remembered that 'the [odious] word Leveller was framed and cast upon all those in the Army (or elsewhere) who are against any kind of Tyranny, whether in King, Parliament, Army, Council of State etc.'[69] From this standpoint, consistency of principle required alteration of allegiance. As the prospect of a military dictatorship loomed larger, Lilburne, Overton and others not only vigorously opposed these 'New Chaines', but also defended the king as one of the few remaining constitutional alternatives. One conclusion by Blair Worden concerning Nedham's chequered

---

[67] Ibid. p. 66   [68] See pp. 156–8 above, including notes 28, 35 and 36.
[69] John Lilburne, Richard Overton and Thomas Price, *The Second Part of England's New-Chaines* (1649) in W. Haller and G. Davies (eds.), *The Leveller Tracts 1647–1653* (Gloucester Mass., 1964) p. 1, note 1.

trajectory is that his real beliefs, if any, were probably consistently crypto-republican. The assumption follows both that Nedham's royalist ideological commitment, if any, was relatively superficial, and that the motivation for this phase of his public career was primarily personal, rather than political. Yet in 1647 defection to the king was not the most risk-free method of keeping body and soul together. On these grounds and others, Worden's analysis has been opposed by Jason Mc Elligott who points out that Nedham kept up his royalist writing until mid-1649 (and then escaped from custody), despite the draconian provisions of the new Commonwealth's Treason Act. For Mc Elligott, therefore, Nedham's 1647 'recantation' was genuine.[70] Yet what neither historian has pointed out is that Nedham's 'royalist' phase conforms closely, ideologically, to this broader Leveller trajectory.

Not only does *Mercurius Pragmaticus* continue to champion 'honest Joh[n] *Lilburne*', both for speaking the truth in 'plaine terms' and for promising to act upon it. His target in so doing is that conspiracy of the '*Military . . . Authority*' to erect a 'new *Commonwealth . . .* [of] 30,000 standing *Forces*' headed by 'his Soveraigne *Oliver . . .* Duke *Oliver . . .* King Nol . . . King *Cromwell* and his Son Prince *Ireton* (as Joh. Lilburne calls them)'.[71] In applauding Lilburne's vows on behalf of 'an inslaved *People*' to raise the common soldiery and '*all the Commons* of England' against this '*tyrannical*' conspiracy, and publishing a letter by him, Nedham associated himself personally with his comrade's fate ('since they have dealt thus rigorously with *John*, what then will become of me (poor *Pragmaticus?*)'[72]). When he reports 'the LEVELLERS . . . *Petition* to the *Generall*, by their Agents of *London*, to vindicate themselves from any Intent of *Killing the King*', Nedham remarks that 'all *honest* men may easily beleeve them'. The great danger of the time is rather 'this new tribe of LEVELLERS . . . far worse than the *old*; for, they mean[t] to have *even* dealing, but these intend . . . only to make a *step* for themselves that they mount into the Saddle'.[73] Nedham's campaign against '*Tyrannie*, by . . . their own *wills* and the *Sword*' culminated in his answer to the Army's *Remonstrance* of 20 November 1648. This suggested that all of this document's accusations against the king concerning

[70] Worden, '"Wit in a Roundhead"'; Gerard Jason Mc Elligott, 'Propaganda and Censorship: the Underground Royalist Newsbooks, 1647–1650', Ph.D. thesis, Cambridge University, 2001, pp. 62–5, 67–8, 72.

[71] Marchamont Nedham [editor], *Mercurius Pragmaticus* no. 4, 5–12 October 1647, pp. 2–4; ibid. no. 8, 2–9 November 1647, p. 58. Mc Elligott, 'Propaganda and Censorship', reversing Worden's location of ideological superficiality, describes this praise of the Leveller 'Champions of Liberty' as 'purely tactical' (p. 127).

[72] *Mercurius Pragmaticus* no. 4, p. 6.

[73] Ibid. no. 14, 14–21 December 1647; ibid. no. 20, 25 January–1 February 1648.

an attempt 'to advance his own *will and Interest . . . in an unlimited power over the lives, liberties, and goods of the People*' could more accurately be levelled at the army itself. It explained that the king had 'recovered the . . . Affections' of a 'People being tired out by the new *Tyrants* in Arms, and *Taxes*'. 'Give ear, and regard, O ye *Commons of England*, lest under a specious *pretence* for the *Liberty of the People* (which *Cromwell* himself once called a meer *Chimara*, and a thing not to be contended for) ye be drawne into *Parricide* and perpetuall *Slavery*.'[74]

Nedham was one of at least four prominent pro-parliamentary writers and printers who made the transition to royalist allegiance in 1647 and 1648. One of these, William Dugard, had become, like Nedham, a key participant in the propaganda machine of the new republic by the early 1650s. It was an aspect not only of Nedham's writing, but of royalist propaganda in 1647–9 more generally, to 'appeal to those citizens in London and the localities who had not previously supported the King, but had grown tired of the . . . high taxes occasioned by the maintenance of the army'.[75] Similarly, support for the Levellers and for Lilburne in particular was a feature of royalist periodicals like *Mercurius Pragmaticus* and *Mercurius Elenchitus* in 1649 as well as 1648, particularly after Lilburne's arrest for treason in the latter year.[76] This was not, however, a universal royalist position, and Nedham's own line, which was consistent across both of these years, was maintained against sometimes vigorous opposition.[77] The moment when he was finally required publically to repudiate the Leveller movement was when he accepted employment by the republic in 1650.[78] Even thereafter, however, as editor of *Mercurius Politicus* Nedham was to play a key role in the incorporation into republican ideology of Leveller ideas.

THE POLITICAL THEORY OF THE ENGLISH REVOLUTION

Thus in the climactic months between Pride's Purge and the establishment of a republic we find Milton and Nedham temporarily on opposite sides. Although deeply aware of the Rump's limitations, Milton was prepared to

---

[74] Marchamont Nedham, *A Plea for The King and Kingdome* (1648) Preface, pp. 6, 12, 22.

[75] Mc Elligott, 'Propaganda and Censorship' pp. 66–7, 69.

[76] Amos Tubb, 'The Ecstasy and the Agony: Royalist Newsbooks in the Aftermath of the Execution of Charles I', paper given at the National Conference on British Studies Annual Meeting, Baltimore, Maryland, 9 November 2002.

[77] Jason Peacey, '"The Counterfeit Silly Curr"': Money, Politics and the Forging of Royalist Newsbooks in the English Civil War', paper given at the National Conference on British Studies Annual Meeting, Baltimore, Maryland, 9 November 2002.

[78] Nedham, *Case of the Commonwealth* Part II, chapter 4: 'Concerning the Levellers'.

defend the army's intervention as necessary to purge and rescue the nation from the failure of its own representatives. For Nedham the moral integrity of the revolutionary leadership was less important than the constitutional integrity of the process by which it was selected and controlled. Yet it is a broader function of both Milton's and Nedham's writing during the 1640s to underline the close relationship between Leveller and republican ideas. This is easier to see now that we can acknowledge the classical content of Leveller, and the religious content of republican thought.[79] What was accordingly shared was not simply a religious commitment to liberty of conscience. It was also a political account of liberty, personal and public (as rational self-government, and freedom from oppression), anchored in a commitment to radical popular sovereignty.

Thus Overton and Walwyn's *Remonstrance of Many Thousand Citizens* (1646) acknowledged as the nation's 'soveraigne LORD' not a king, but 'the Universality of the People'.[80] Like Nedham later, Lilburne's *Regall Tyrannie discovered* (January 1647) collapsed the (Aristotelian) distinctions between tyranny and monarchy, subjection and slavery. The tract recounted 'The Tyrannie of the Kings of England, from the dayes of *William* the Invader . . . to this present *King Charles*'. The latter was the worst tyrant of all, deserving 'a more severe punishment' than either Edward II or Richard II. As guilty of the blood of thousands, there was a need to 'execute . . . justice upon him . . . in an exemplary manner . . . *For GOD is a just GOD, and will revenge innocent blood even upon Kings* (Judg 1, 6, 7 etc).' More generally '[T]his office of a King . . . is not in the least of God's institution, neither is it to be given to any man upon earth.'[81] 'God alone rules, and governs by his Will.' A king 'that is not God but a *meer man*, cannot make his *will*, a *rule*, and *law*, unto himself and others'. By 'the light of Nature and Reason, and the end wherefore God endowed Man with understanding . . . all lawfull . . . power . . . instituted amongst men, is by common agreement . . . exercised for the good, benefit and welfare of the Trusters'.[82] By the same 'Law of God, Nature and Reason . . . it is not lawfull for any man to subject himself, to be a slave . . . to be a slave, is to degenerate . . . into the habit of a Beast . . . [rather than a] creature . . . created in the *Image* of their *Creator* . . . And therefore, I am absolutely of Catoes mind . . . *no man can be an honest man, but he that is a free man.*'[83]

79 Glover, 'The Putney Debates'; Worden, 'Marchamont Nedham'; Scott, *England's Troubles* chs. 10, 13.
80 [Richard Overton and William Walwyn], *The Remonstrance of Many Thousand Citizens and other Free-Born People of England* title page.
81 John Lilburne, *Regall Tyrannie discovered* (January 1647) title page, pp. 14, 39, 57.
82 Ibid. title page, p. 9.   83 Ibid. title page, pp. 9, 11.

Other Leveller works complained to parliament that 'The continual oppressors of the nation have been Kings . . . and ye yourselves have told the King . . . "that his whole sixteen years' reign was one continued breach of the law" . . . And yet [you act] as if it were impossible for any nation to be happy without a King.'[84] The *Agreement of the People* (1647) set aside both monarchy and House of Lords, as impediments to the sovereign will of the people, and this was certainly a position which had broader support in the army. In the words of Mr Pettus at Putney:

itt hath pleased God to raise a companie of men that doe stand uppe for the power of the House of Commons, which is the Representative of the people, and deny the negative voice of King and Lords . . . For my parte I cannot butt thinke that both the power of Kinge and Lords was ever a branch of Tyranny, and if ever a people shall free themselves from Tyranny, certainly itt is after 7 yeares warre and fighting for their libertie.[85]

It was the accusation of John Wildman, among other supporters of the *Agreement*, that against these principles it was the objective of Cromwell, Ireton and other 'Grandees' to negotiate a moderated version of His Majesty's 'Restoration'.[86] It was another argument advanced by Wildman in favour of the *Agreement* that it subjected to the law not only 'the Kinge's Prerogative', but 'Parliament's priviledges'.[87] In the words of *The Charters of London* (of which Wildman may have been the author):

I say the people by themselves, or their legal Commissions chosen by them for that end, may make a Law or Lawes to govern themselves and to rule, regulate and guide all their Magistrates (whatsoever) Officers, Ministers, or Servants, and ought not in the least to receive a Law from them, or any of them, whom they have set over themselves, for no other end in the world, but for their better being and meerly with Justice, equity and righteousnesse, to execute the Lawes that they made themselves, and betrusted them with, as publique executors.[88]

Yet in fact, whatever the disagreements at Putney about the franchise, these key Leveller positions, in favour of popular self-government through representatives, and freedom 'from all pretence of negative voices, either in king or Lords', were both incorporated into Ireton's *Humble Remonstrance* of 16 November 1648.[89] At the same time in practice, even in relation to these principles, many writers agreed with Milton that means must be

---

[84] [Overton and Walwyn], *A remonstrance of many thousand citizens* p. 182.
[85] Firth (ed.), *The Clarke Papers* vol. 1, pp. 351–2.   [86] Ibid. p. 362.
[87] Ibid. p. 354.   [88] Lilburne, *The Charters of London* p. 4.
[89] See for instance *The humble petition of well-affected persons* clause 1, and *The Remonstrance of the Army* (16 November 1648), in Kenyon, *Stuart Constitution* pp. 278, 290.

subordinate to ends; that where the two diverged, the public good (a moral principle established by God) was not to be confused with the wishes of the public. Thus for Milton the cause was ultimately preserved by a few 'men of noblest temper' despite the 'sloth . . . inconstancie . . . weakness of spirit . . . or inbred falshood and wickednes' of the majority.[90] For John Goodwin, similarly, 'If a people be depraved and corrupt, so as to conferre . . . power . . . upon wicked men, they forfeit their power . . . unto those that are good, though but a few. So that nothing pretended from a non-concurrence of the people with the Army, will hold water.'[91] For others too, 'Now the common people . . . they onely regard the outward forme of Government, but the wiser people of the Nation they most minde the power of God in the forme.' Thus as 'The supreme power . . . is the *power of God* . . . so when the power of God leaves any forme of Government, we are not to stand by that forme.'[92]

> Now when it was . . . apparent, that the *King's* power was not God's power, but contrary to it, God . . . raises up *another power* in the Kingdome and breakes that in pieces: and then . . . *Parliament* . . . were mighty through . . . God's power . . . as long as they did cleave unto it: but now they not learning righteousnesse by God's judgements on the *King's* power . . . became as unjust, tyrannicall and oppressive as the former power, and much more . . . What ends have they prosecuted, but their owne? . . . I see none of the *power of God* left in the Kingdome . . . [but] in the Army: for certainly *the Power of God* . . . fought their battailes, and stormed their Cities and strong holds . . . and I have no where observed of late . . . any power that hath incouraged and protected . . . the *good*, and cashiered and punished . . . the *evill*, as they have done.[93]

Ireton's *Remonstrance* incorporated this protestant anti-formalism, opposing a 'blind Reverence of Persons and outward Things, fit for Popery and Slavery'. It also built upon this providentialism, following the progress of 'Those Contraries God hath . . . so separated viz. of Principles . . . of Liberty, with Principles of Tyranny . . . of Zeal and the Power of Godliness, with Principles of Formality and Superstition . . . we might say indeed, of Light with Darkness, of Good with Evil'.[94] In emphasising the irreconcilable 'Opposition' between 'Principles of Public Interest' and the 'Principles of Prerogative and particular Interest' characteristic of 'Kings' both the *Remonstrance* and other works invoked Machiavelli.[95] This interest

---

[90] Milton, *Tenure* p. 192.

[91] John Goodwin, *Right and might Well mett* (1 January 1649) pp. 10–11, 16.

[92] *A little Eye-Salve for the Kingdome and Armie, that they may see* (1647) pp. 2–3.

[93] Ibid. pp. 5–6.   [94] [Ireton], *The Humble Remonstrance* pp. 179–80, 187.

[95] Ibid. pp. 8–9, 187–90 (the guidance of the 'policy' of princes by 'force' and 'fraud'); J. Warr, *The Priviledges of the People* (5 February 1649) pp. 1, 5.

analysis was also capable of religious development, since the foundation of all monarchy lay, in the later words of Vane, in 'that great idol . . . self interest . . . a frame of spirit in direct contrareity to Christs . . . serving to promote and advance the great . . . interest of the Devill in the world'.[96]

Most early republican writing held, on the one hand, 'That no Nation is so strictly tied to any one form of civill Government or Law, but it is lawfull for the People to alter the same to another form or kind upon occasion', and yet on the other that 'experience shews . . . there is no kind of civil government more averse and opposite to the Kingdom of Christ and lesse helpful to it than Monarchie'.[97] Given the 'misery and mischief [that] ordinarily goes along with Monarchies, slaughtering and murdering the people', England's model lay in the achievement of 'commonwealths of Greece . . . the Switzers and . . . the *Venetian commonwealth*' in throwing it off. For 'Where the Government is a Free State, there men are encouraged to the study of wisdom, truth, justice, etc, because not titles there . . . or succession . . . but good parts make men capable of honor, authority, and place; neither is there a door open to them to come in by bribery and flattery, but chosen by their fitnesse, gifts and abilities.'[98]

Parliament built upon these claims in its *Declaration* of 22 March 1649, in which the long-standing anti-tyrannical discourse of a commonwealth took a fully fledged republican form. This was not, however, in March 1649, the dominant preoccupation of a populace traumatised by what a Dutch poet called 'This . . . Rubicon, crossed by none./Red with the Holy Blood poured forth from royal veins.'[99] In this context, it was one thing to extol the benefits of freedom, but another to persuade a sullen and hostile public to believe them. It was a recognition of the magnitude of this task that early the following year the regime released from prison the editor of a notorious Lilburne-friendly royalist newspaper. With the first issue of *Mercurius Politicus* in June 1650, Marchamont Nedham became 'the leading propagandist of the Commonwealth'.[100]

---

[96] Vane, *The Retired Man's Meditations* 'To the Reader' and p. 3.
[97] Eleutherius Philodemius *The Armies Vindication* (11 January 1649) title page, p. 15.
[98] Ibid. pp. 57, 62–3. [99] Quoted by Scherpbier, *Milton in Holland* p. 51.
[100] Worden, '"Wit in a Roundhead"' p. 326. An entry in Samuel Hartlib's 'Ephemerides' records: 'Needham the Pragmaticus or Mercurius Britannicus got 50.lb and is annually entertained by the State for Hue and Crie writing after the *king* etc. hee was disgraced in so much that hee could not obtain a Troopers-place. This neede made him so desperat.' Ephemerides 1650 Part 3 [May–October] 28/1/61B, in *The Hartlib Papers*, 2nd edn (Sheffield, HROnline, 2002).

CHAPTER 12

The English republic, 1649–1653

God hath . . . made you the happie Instruments of freeing us from the yoke of Kings . . . how nobly you asserted the Rights of England against Domestick Tyrannie, upon the neck of the late King . . . when Justice sat more gloriously inthroned than ever it did before on any earthly tribunal . . . *It is your honor, that God hath made you Founders of the most famous and potent Republick this day in the world, and your felicitie, that all your Enemies have no other Ground of quarrel, but that you are a Republick.*

Marchamont Nedham, Epistle Dedicatorie,
Of the Dominion . . . of the Sea (1652)

'A NEW ORDER IN THE STATE'?

In the early months of 1649, from the ashes of a tyranny, England erected its first 'Free State'. So, at least, ran the record of parliament's pronouncements. On 4 January the House of Commons voted 'That the people are, under God, the original of all just power.' On 7 February, little more than a week after the regicide, the resolution was carried without a division 'that it hath been found by experience . . . that the office of a king in this nation, and to have the power thereof in any single person, is unnecessary, burdensome, and dangerous to the liberty, safety, and public interests of the people'. On 22 February members of the newly established Council of State pledged themselves to 'the settling of the government of this nation for the future in way of a Republic, without King or House of Lords'.[1] On 22 March the government issued its *Declaration . . . Expressing the Grounds of their late Proceedings, And of Setling the present Government In the way of A Free State*, asserting the right of the people's representatives to make such a 'change', and drawing comfort from the superiority of other free states to monarchies.

---

[1] Woolrych, 'Dating Milton's *History of Britain*', p. 933; Blair Worden, *The Rump Parliament* (Cambridge, 1977) p. 181.

In practice, needless to say, the situation was more complicated. Although most of its members had at one time been elected by 'the people', 'the Rump parliament' as a government was created by the army. It consisted, first, of those MPs who had not been removed by Pride's Purge on 6 December 1648 for voting 'That the answers of the King . . . are a ground for the House to proceed upon for the settlement of the . . . Kingdom'.[2] Even among this minority many refused to be party to the king's trial and execution, absenting themselves from Westminster either because they disapproved of that procedure, or because they opposed the army intervention in civilian politics which had made it possible (this latter group included Vane and Sidney).[3] From February some of these members returned to take their seats, joined by others who had been purged but had retrospectively recanted.[4] No new elections to this body were ever held. Aside from the establishment of the Council of State, modelled on parliament's executive committees during the civil wars (the Derby House Committee, the Committee of Both Kingdoms) little overtly republican constitutional development took place. As Sir Arthur Haselrig later explained, disarmingly, 'force was much upon us. What should we do? We turned ourselves into a Commonwealth.'[5]

Publicly, this regime was vilified throughout the three kingdoms and the rest of Europe for its unprecedented 'parricide'. Nor did it ever outgrow the military shadow from which it had emerged, and by which it would ultimately be dissolved. Doubts arising from these circumstances affected not only the general public, but many members of the regime, including those who became its leading propagandists. In 1649 Nedham continued, in royalist guise, the Leveller attack upon England's 'new found [military] chaines'. Milton's animus in 1649 was not against those in 'the Parliament and Military Councel' who had found the 'wisdom, vertue and magnanimity' to wield the 'Sword of Justice' and 'avenge the effusion . . . [of] so great a deluge of innocent blood'.[6] It was directed, first, against those corrupt members of the Long Parliament who,

by so discharging thir trust . . . did not onely weak'n and unfitt themselves to be dispencers of what libertie they pretented, but unfitted also the people, now growne worse & more disordinate, to receave or to digest any libertie at all. ffor stories teach us that libertie sought out of season in a corrupt and degenrate age brought Rome it self into further slaverie.[7]

[2] David Underdown, *Pride's Purge: Politics in the Puritan Revolution* (1985) p. 138.
[3] Scott, *Algernon Sidney and the English Republic* pp. 92–3.
[4] Worden, *The Rump Parliament* pp. 61–7.
[5] Quoted in Sean Kelsey, *Inventing a Republic: The Political Culture of the English Commonwealth 1649–1653* (Manchester, 1997) p. 224.
[6] Milton, *Tenure* pp. 197, 237.   [7] Milton, MS Digression p. 449.

Although many of these had been weeded out in the Purge, some were now being readmitted upon conditions, and this 'great enterprise' would 'miscarry still' until leaders 'more then vulgar, bred up, as few of them were, in the knowledge of Antient and illustrious deeds, [and] invinceable against money, and vaine titles, impartial to friendships and relations had conducted their affaires'.[8]

Even if the republic should develop the leadership it needed, the braying royalism of the general public could not be ignored. Thus the *Defence* praised the regicides because 'with such firmness of heart as has scarcely been recorded before they fought and conquered not only their enemies in arms, but the inwardly hostile or superstitious beliefs of the mob as well, and each won for himself for the future the name of liberator in every land'.[9] The *Tenure*, to an even greater degree, contrasted the heroic accomplishment of a small minority ('in number less by many') with a larger public who, 'being slaves within doors . . . strive . . . to have the public State conformably govern'd to the inward vitious rule, by which they govern themselves'.[10] This identified the republic's greatest ideological challenge. It was one thing to kill the king. It would be another to kill kingship, and tyranny, in every English soul. In the unpromising diagnosis of Machiavelli, 'few men ever welcome new laws setting up a new order in the state unless necessity makes it clear to them that there is a need for such laws; and since such a necessity cannot arise without danger, the state may easily be ruined before the new order has been brought to completion'.[11]

To thus acknowledge, however, that England's first republican government was crooked in its birth, and that that birth was attended by manifold doubts and dangers, is not to question the existence of a 'new order in the state'. It has been suggested that this regime did not think of itself as a republic; that in a parliamentarian culture that word, like 'Leveller', was not one which people willingly applied to themselves; that its members never became in their own minds, let alone in external reality, anything other

---

[8] Ibid. pp. 431, 451; Worden, in 'Marchamont Nedham', appears to take Milton's Digression to be directed against the Rump itself (pp. 58–9). I have followed von Maltzahn ('Dating the Digression' p. 950; *Milton's History of Britain* pp. 23–4, 32) in seeing it as primarily directed against the pre-Purge parliament, though thereby warning against the readmission of 'secluded' MPs, and other forms of backsliding. In his subsequent description in February 1652 of the Council of State as dominated by 'mechanics, soldiers, home-grown, strong and bold enough, in public political affairs mostly inexperienced' there is continuity of content, but a reduction in bitterness, particularly given the plea that for the effects of this inexperience Mylius not blame 'the Commonwealth, nor the sounder men'. Quoted in Miller, *Oldenburg Safeguard* p. 172.
[9] Milton, *Defence* p. 336.   [10] Milton, *Tenure* p. 190.   [11] Machiavelli, *Discourses* I.2, pp. 105–6.

than the rump of an old regime.[12] Yet parliament's *Declaration* of March
1649 defended the decision 'to change the *Government* of this *Nation* from
the former *Monarchy* . . . into a *Republique*'. In this 'The *Representatives* of
the *People* now Assembled in *Parliament*'

received encouragement, by their observation of the *Blessing* of *God* upon other
States; The *Romans*, after their *Regifugium* of many hundred years together, *prospered* far more then under any of their *Kings* . . . The State of *Venice* hath flourished
for One thousand three hundred years: How much do the Commons in *Switzerland*, and other *Free States*, exceed those who are not so, in *Riches, Freedom, Peace*,
and all *Happiness?* Our *Neighbours* in the *United-Provinces*, since their *change* of
Government, have wonderfully increased in *Wealth, Freedom, Trade*, and *Strength*,
both by Sea and Land.[13]

The reason for this lay in the opposing principles informing monarchies
and republics. In the 'Times of our *Monarchs* . . . *Injustice, Oppression*
and *Slavery* were the [lot of] the *Common people*'. In '*Commonwealths*'
by contrast, 'they finde *Justice* duly administered . . . the seeds of *Civil
War* and Dissention, by particular *Ambition*, Claims of *Succession*, and the
like . . . wholly removed . . . a just *Freedom* of their *Consciences*, Persons and
Estates'.[14] In a subsequent *Declaration* the government confessed that its
members had been '*led* by several steps by the *providence* of God . . . *beyond*
what was either *first* propounded by us, or could reasonably have been
hoped to be brought to pass; the very discovery of so remote an end, in
the beginning of the Action, had been sufficient to have discouraged any
undertaking therein'.[15] Yet beyond the amazing consequent abolition of 'all
that Ecclesiastical *Hierarchy*, with all their *Tyrannical Courts* and *Attendants*,
the *Star-Chamber, High Commission Court, Ship-Money, Projects, Monopolies*
and *Purveyances*, the *Court of Wards* and *Tenures*, and all the dependencies
of it' it was clear about the revolution's fundamental achievement. This
lay in its having '*taken away* . . . the deepest *Root* and foundation of all
the People's *sufferings* . . . *Kingship* and *Tyranny* itself'.[16] In September 1651
Hermann Mylius, representative of Oldenburg, was advised by Sir Oliver
Fleming that the form of diplomtic address 'about a year ago unanimously
decided in Parliament once and for all time' was '*Parlamento Reipublicae*

---

[12] Blair Worden, 'Republicanism, Regicide and Republic: the English Experience', in Van Gelderen
   and Skinner, *Republicanism* vol. 1, pp. 317, 327: 'Rather than seeking to introduce a new form
   or category of government, the removers of kingship merely eliminated those features of the old
   constitution . . . which got in their way . . . It was principally the exploits of a parliament, not of a
   republic, of which members of the Rump would boast when remembering their rule.'
[13] *A Declaration of the Parliament* pp. 16, 20.   [14] Ibid. pp. 16–17.
[15] *A Declaration of the Parliament of England, In Vindication of their Proceedings* pp. 16–17.
[16] Ibid. p. 16.

Angliae'. In December 1652 an overture from the French ambassador was rejected, as lacking the word 'Reipublicae', and addressed merely to the 'Parlamento Populi Angliae'.[17]

Throughout this regime's life, the process continued of replacing the policies, machinery and iconography of monarchy.[18] These included the new 'GREAT SEALE OF ENGLAND', designed by Henry Marten, issued 'IN THE THIRD YEARE OF FREEDOME', and depicting the government of England and Ireland by an assembly.[19] In line with Hobbes's analysis of the ideological origins of the troubles, official defences of the regime deployed the history and ideology, not of English parliaments or of Europe's representative institutions, but of European and especially classical republics. At the same time, in what Nedham called 'good commonwealth's language' there existed a local rhetoric of continuity.[20]

Thereafter the extraordinary practical difficulties faced by the republic were the challenges in response to which its mature ideology was formed.[21] Of this development the first manifestation was the emergence within the government of republican self-belief.

THE STRUGGLE FOR SURVIVAL, 1649–1651

For members of the new regime the immediate need was to prevent a restoration of monarchy through Ireland or Scotland. Royalist naval forces were active not only in the Channel and North Sea, but in Ireland, the Mediterranean and the West Indies. In 1651 there was a royalist invasion of England from Scotland. On the continent the republic's first two ambassadors, Anthony Ascham in Spain and Isaac Dorislaus in the United Provinces, were murdered, leading George Wither to ask cavaliers why the regicide was such a crime if 'murder, and assassination be not'?[22] At the same

---

[17] *Calendar of State Papers . . . Venice* vol. XXVIII, 1647–1652, pp. 325–6. Fleming added: 'No republic since the beginning of the world [*Keine Republicq ab origine mundi*] ever rose up in so short a time without outside help by its own might except this one.' Miller, *Oldenburg Safeguard* p. 86.

[18] Norbrook, *Writing the English Republic* ch. 5; Kelsey, *Inventing a Republic*. In a letter to Samuel Hartlib in 1658, John Beale wrote of the continuing need to replace those 'Civil honor[s] . . . made a peageantry of Courte . . . & depreciated by vulgarity' with a 'Republican, legall, and regulated grant of honour . . . to them that have done eminent service abroad by Sea, or by Land'. *The Hartlib Papers*, Beale to Hartlib, 10 September 1658, Royal Society MSS, Boyle Letters 7.11 1A-2B.

[19] Scott, 'English Republican Imagination' p. 41; Norbrook, *Writing the English Republic* pp. 195–7.

[20] Kelsey, *Inventing a Republic* pp. 2, 202–3.   [21] Scott, 'English Republican Imagination'.

[22] G[eorge] W[ither], *Respublica Anglicana* p. 40. *A Declaration of the Parliament of England, Of their just Resentment of the Horrid Murther perpetrated on the Body of Isaac Dorislaus* (12 May 1649), blaming the act upon 'slaves to that Tyranny from which this Commonwealth hath happily . . . vindicated themselves', threatened to exact revenge 'upon such members of that party as . . . are at their mercy' (pp. 246–7).

time within England itself the government faced all the problems besetting a nation shattered by civil war, still oppressed by extraordinarily high
military taxation, and visited, in 1649, by harvest failure and starvation.
These challenges had to be addressed by an improvised post-monarchical
governmental apparatus with no precedent in the nation's history.

It is hardly surprising if the strain showed. On the first anniversary of
the regicide one MP committed suicide; another fell into depression and
died the following month; Bulstrode Whitelocke recorded that he was 'full
of melancholy and apprehensions of death'.[23] In April 1650 Henry Vane
wrote that they were 'now in a far worse state than ever yet they had been;
that all the world was and would be their enemies; that their own army
and General were not to be trusted; that the whole kingdom would rise
and cut their throats upon the first occasion; and that they knew not any
place to go unto to be safe'.[24] In this context, the co-option of Nedham
to put the republic's case was not accidental. To hostile 'Cavaliers', whose
predilections he knew so well, he offered republican opinion packaged in
royalist witty style ('Why Should not the *Commonwealth* have a Fool, as well
as the *King* had?') used to particularly good effect in mocking the progress
of 'that young Pretender' in Scotland.[25] To Levellers, still considered a
sufficient threat to command a chapter of Nedham's *Case*, he offered a
radical, populist account of republican ideology. To patriots of all stripes
he directed weekly news of the republic's military victories, its recognition
by foreign powers, and parallel struggles abroad. Thus Bordeaux 'once an
Appertenance of England . . . retains to this day an *English* spirit, being
resolved for a restauration of the Liberty of their Country'.[26] It was owing
in part to Nedham's capacity to supply a public appetite for information
and entertainment ('Since the *mad scabs* have such an Itch after *News*, Ile see
they shall not want *Mercury* to cure them'), and in part to the effectiveness
of the Printing Act of 20 September 1649 in securing *Mercurius* a near
monopoly, that the regime's journal 'flew every week to all parts of the
nation for more than ten years . . . 'tis incredible what influence it had'.[27]

[23] Worden, *The Rump Parliament* p. 224.
[24] Blair Worden, 'The Politics of Marvell's Horation Ode', *Historical Journal* 27, 3 (1984) p. 152.
[25] *Mercurius Politicus* no. 1, 6–13 June 1650, p. 1; no. 51, 22–29 May 1651, p. 815.
[26] Ibid. no. 1, 6–13 June 1650, p. 10; no. 14, 6–13 September 1950, p. 222; no. 29, 19–26 December 1650,
    p. 483.
[27] Ibid. no. 2, 14–21 June 1650, p. 27; Anthony Wood, quoted in Milton, *Complete Prose Works* vol. IV,
    pp. 53–6. Writing later to Samuel Hartlib, Moses Wall observed that concerning European news
    he was well informed, 'constantly having Needham's Mercurius, to whom I give credit for beyond-
    affairs, though his home-news I believe only the matters of fact which he relateth . . . knowing
    how court-relations and self-interest will wrest the writings of almost any man, though he hath

Nedham's explanation for the regime's present unpopularity co-opted a familiar source. It was 'the Florentine's subtile discourses upon Livy . . . [which] compare[d] such as have been educated under a monarchy or tyranny to those beasts which have been caged or cooped up all their lives in a den . . . and if they be let loose, yet they will return in again because they know not how to value or use their liberty. So strong an impression is made . . . by education and custom from the cradle.'[28] Milton's similar claim invoked Aristotle:

[If] after such a fair deliverance . . . with so much fortitude and valour shown against a Tyrant . . . people should seek a King . . . [they] would shew themselves to be by nature slaves, and arrant beasts; not fitt for that liberty which they cri'd out and bellow'd for, but fitter to be led back again into thir old servitude, like . . . clamouring and fighting brutes . . . that know not how to use or possess the liberty which they fought for.[29]

John Hall deployed a Platonic image to explain the phenomenon: 'He knows nothing that knows not how superstitiously the generality of Mankind is given to retain Traditions, and how pertinacious they are in the maintenance of their first Prejudices, insomuch that a Discovery or more refin'd Reason is as insupportable to them, as the Sun is to an Ey newly brought out of Darkness.'[30] Henry Parker too noted the key role of political education, in establishing the '*strong Byasses wisemen have, and obey*'. Thus 'Men born in popular States, think themselves bound to abhor all Kings, as being *De genere Bestiarum rapacium*: So *Rome* it self pronounced from the mouth of *Cato* the Censor. Others on the contrary, born under Monarchs, speak as odiously of Democracies.'[31] In fact,

Reading assures us, that *Rome* was not so just to other Nations, nor so constant to the Interest of her own Citizens, when she was under Kings and Emperors, as she was, when she chose her own Consuls, and limited Magistrates. Tis as apparent also at this day, that the people of *Venice*, the *German* Hans-Towns, *Switzerland*, the *United Provinces* etc do more flourish, and truly injoy the due benefits of Liberty, then the *French*, *Turkish*, or any Royalists Whatsoever. Tis further as visible by

better principles than Mr Needham hath'. *The Hartlib Papers*, Moses Wall to Hartlib, 9 January 1658/9, 34/4/20B. That it was also read abroad is the implication of an earlier letter from John Dury in Zurich, who prayed Hartlib 'salute Mr Needham for me, & intreat him in case any extracts bee communicated to him from Germanie . . . which have . . . contemptible expressions of German Princes that he would favour us so much who are abroad as not to insert them: in his last . . . these *"puffing Germane Princes"* . . . can do our cause no good; but may do harme'. Ibid. John Dury to Hartlib, 28 April 1655, 4/3/95A-B.

28 Nedham, *Case of the Commonwealth* pp. 111–12.
29 Milton, *Eikonoklastes* p. 581.   30 Hall, *The Grounds and Reasons of Monarchy* p. 3.
31 Henry Parker, Preface to *The True Portraiture of the Kings of England* (7 August 1650).

the publike banks of Treasure kept in Democracies, and the strange splendor which Traffick brings to them beyond Monarchies . . . The enemies of our present Government upbraide this our popular model, the rather because it exasperates all our neighbours against us; wheras this is a great argument for us, that our neighbours are troubled at the ejection of Monarchy.[32]

The focus of the government propaganda effort in 1650 was the solicitation of that public submission necessary for its immediate domestic security.[33] In the Engagement literature allegiance was demanded less because the republic was good than because it was a fact. Since 'all governments carry with them the Causes of their Corruption . . . we of the people must be contented with those governours into whose full possessions it is our destiny to fall'.[34] '[T]he Power of the Sword Is, and Ever Hath Been, the Foundation of All Titles to Government . . . [and] Nonsubmission to Government Justly Deprives Men of the Benefit of Its Protection.'[35] Further, however, Nedham argued that, however despised this regime, anything else would be worse. Indeed even in 1650 the last chapter of the *Case* summarised the positive arguments for 'the Excellency of a Free State above a Kingly Government'. It was at the beginning of the following year that Admiral Blake

remarked in the public square . . . at Cadiz . . . that with the example afforded by London all kingdoms will annihilate tyranny and become republics. England had done so already: France was following in her wake; and as the natural gravity of the Spaniards rendered them somewhat slower in their operations, he gave them ten years for the revolution in this country.[36]

Meanwhile the basis for a more generally positive ideological posture was being laid militarily. This effort was spearheaded by invasions of Ireland in 1649 and Scotland in 1650. These were accompanied by the aggressive construction and deployment of a navy not only to become the finest in Europe, but also a highly politicised republican force.[37] Naval administration was reformed under a new Admiralty Committee headed by Henry Vane. Officer's pay was substantially increased and shipboard discipline tightened. In the autumn of 1650, in what reads like an advertisement for

[32] Ibid.
[33] Quentin Skinner, 'Conquest and Consent: Thomas Hobbes and the Engagement Controversy', in G. E. Aylmer (ed.), *The Interregnum: the Quest for Settlement 1646–1660* (1974).
[34] Ascham, *Of the Confusions and Revolutions of Governments*, quoted in Scott, 'English Republican Imagination' p. 39.
[35] Nedham, *Case of the Commonwealth* Part I, chs. 2–3.
[36] Venetian Ambassador to Spain, 8 February 1651, in *Calendar of State Papers . . . Venice* vol. XXVIII, 1647–1652 (1927) p. 169.
[37] Capp, *Cromwell's Navy* pp. 2, 4–7.

republican morality (Platonic, puritan and Machiavellian), Mazarin was advised:

Not only are they powerful by sea and land, but they live without ostentation, without pomp, without emulation of one another. They are economical in their private expenses, and prodigal in their devotion to public affairs, for which each one toils as if for his private interests. They handle large sums of money, which they administer honestly, observing a severe discipline. They reward well, and punish severely.[38]

Sidney's comparable account of discipline in the New Model Army was seconded by Hermann Mylius who recorded in 1651,

Never has there been seen an army more modest and . . . scrupulously religious in external form of worship, which submits so willingly and obediently to such strict discipline. Depravity, blasphemy, swearing, profanation of the Sabbath or any wantonness, in word or deed, are neither heard not seen.[39]

Jean-Baptiste Lantin recorded in 1677:

le Comte de Sydney told me that . . . the English . . . Republic (*republique . . . des Anglois*) had three senior Magistrates (*Magistrats souverains*), the General of the land army, the Admiral of the Navy, and the Chancellor who administered justice; that each exercised their office for only one year; that there was a perpetual Council which supervised the entire government (*eu l'inspection sur tous*); that there were financial Officers who rendered exact accounts from time to time, reporting to Superior Officers, and that they also served for no more than one year; that they had an army of sixty thousand infantry and twenty thousand cavalry all ready to serve that Republic, and sixty warships well equipped and well paid.[40]

This account may shed less light upon this government's operation than upon its dissolution. Cromwell's concern could certainly be understood if from August 1652, when Sidney joined Vane as a member of the Council of State and manager of the naval war in progress, they really did regard that body as the highest authority, with subordinate power to be shared evenly between the army and the navy, the leaders of each entitled to serve for only one year. In August 1652 another observer reported on England's army of 50,000 men, 'all of English nationality entirely dependent on parliament, a sufficient explanation of the strength of the present government, which is the only power in the world with an army of this kind composed entirely of

---

[38] Quoted in Robert Brenner, *Merchants and Revolution: Commercial Change, Political Conflict, and London's Overseas Traders 1550–1653* (Princeton, 1993) p. 582.

[39] Quoted in Miller, *Oldenburg Safeguard* p. 40.

[40] 'Lantiniana' p. 100 (my translation). Lantin described Sidney (p. 99) as '[un] homme d'espirit, mais Republicain outré'.

its own countrymen'.[41] Nedham, too, dwelt upon the claimed conjunction of superior political and military management and 'strict . . . discipline'.

By September 1651, with the defeat of the King of Scots at Worcester, the war for the republic's immediate military security had been won. On 30 January 1652, the third anniversary of the regicide, Hermann Mylius began a letter to John Bradshaw with the flattering invocation 'This day in 1648 fatal to monarchs and monarchies'.[42] Between 1650 and 1652 royalist naval operations were destroyed, the rebellious colonies in the West Indies brought to heel, and Portugal, Spain and France forced to abandon their overt hostility. By late 1652 those powers which had been queueing to express their contempt were instead squabbling to secure an alliance. Between December 1652 and April 1653 Algernon Sidney met with the ambassadors of Portugal, Spain, France, Sweden, Hamburg, Tuscany, Holland and Austria.[43] During the winter of 1651–2 *Mercurius* reported that unlike a monarchy the government had decided to follow Roman example and grant Scotland the privileges of 'incorporation' with England, including representation at Westminster and free trade.[44] One year later England, Ireland and Scotland were united for the first time into a single commonwealth. By 1654 the republic had defeated the hitherto mightiest naval force in Europe (the United Provinces). As Sir Arthur Haselrig remembered in 1659 'You never had such a fleet as in the Long Parliament. All the powers in the world made addresses to him that sat in your chair.'[45]

Such accomplishments would have laid some basis for self-belief in any government. To understand their impact here, however, they must be set against the preceding record of monarchical military failure. The practical basis of this transformation lay in the fiscal, administrative and military experience and resources made available by parliamentary statebuilding between 1642 and 1649. It is perhaps not surprising, however, if to members of the new regime the military consequences were experienced as the effects, not of superior resources, but of superior government. Thus Sidney later remembered how

When Van Tromp set upon Blake in Foleston-Bay, the parliament had not above thirteen ships against threescore . . . to oppose the best captain in the world . . . Many other difficulties were observ'd in the unsettled state: Few ships, want of money, several factions, and some who to advance particular interests betray'd the publick. But such was the power of wisdom and integrity in those that sat at the helm, and

[41] *Calendar of State Papers . . . Venice* p. 266.   [42] Miller, *Oldenburg Safeguard* p. 157.
[43] Scott, *Algernon Sidney and the English Republic* p. 101.
[44] Worden, 'Marchamont Nedham' p. 73; see chapter 4 above.
[45] *Diary of Thomas Burton* vol. 1, p. 57 (3 February 1659).

their diligence in chusing men only for their merit was blessed with such success, that in two years our fleets grew to be as famous as our land armies; the reputation and power of our nation rose to a greater height, than when we possessed the better half of France . . . All the states, kings and potentates of Europe, most respectfully, not to say submissively, sought our friendship; and Rome was more afraid of Blake and his fleet, than they had been of the great king of Sweden, when he was ready to invade Italy with a hundred thousand men.[46]

A REPUBLIC FOR EXPANSION, 1651–1653

It was under the influence of this military transformation that English classical republicanism acquired its characteristic form.[47] Milton, a 'great crony' of Nedham's in this period, worked with him as state licenser of *Mercurius Politicus*.[48] It is thus significant that it was between November 1651 and February 1652 that Milton made in his *Commonplace Book* nineteen entries from Machiavelli's *Discourses* and *Art of War*.[49] From the latter Milton noted the Florentine's view that 'A commonwealth is preferable to a monarchy: "because more excellent men come from a commonwealth than from a kingdom; because in the former virtue is honoured most of the time and is not feared as in the kingdom".'[50] From the *Discourses* he recorded his claim that 'a republic makes fewer mistakes than a prince does in choosing its magistrates or councillors'; 'That a federation or league formed with a republic can be trusted more than one with a prince' (in the year of the proposed federation with the United Provinces); Machiavelli's arguments concerning the beneficial affects of tumults; and several observations concerning military strategy.[51] From Machiavelli's treatment of Roman history he observed the contrast between those who 'rule[d] by heredity', who had left 'off virtuous deeds' and were remarkable for nothing but 'luxury . . . and lust', and 'those who ruled by adoption . . . [who] were all good'.[52]

Some of these points were expanded upon by John Hall's *The Grounds and Reasons of Monarchy* (1651). Since its subjects 'languish in a brutish Servitude . . . Monarchy . . . [was] truly a Disease of Government'.

[S]o have the People bin never more fond of . . . Monarchs . . . than when Manners were at the highest corruption, which ever gave access of strength to them; nor have they more distasted them, than when their Spirits and Disciplin were the most

---

[46] Sidney, *Discourses*, ed. West pp. 278–9.

[47] Scott, 'The Rapture of Motion' pp. 143, 145. [48] Worden, 'Marchamont Nedham' p. 62.

[49] Maurice Kelley, 'Milton and Machiavelli's *Discorsi*' *SBUV* 4 (1951–2) pp. 123–7; Milton, *Commonplace Book* pp. 414–15.

[50] Ibid. p. 421. [51] Ibid. pp. 495, 496, 477, 504, 505. [52] Ibid. p. 475.

brave and healthful; so fatally disagreeing are true Liberty, which is the very source of Virtue and Generosity, and the impotent Domination of a single Tyrant.[53]

I could never be persuaded but it was more happy for a People to be dispos'd of by a number of Persons jointly interested and concern'd with them, than to be number'd as the Herd and Inheritance of One, to whose Lust and Madness they were absolutely subject; and that any Man of the weakest Reason and Generosity would not rather chuse for his Habitation that spot of Earth where there was access to Honor by Virtue, and no Worth could be excluded, rather than where all Advancement should procede from the Will of one scarcely hearing and seeing with his own Organs . . . amount[ing] to nothing else but . . . dangerous Slavery.[54]

In the same year the regime recorded an international triumph in *Joannis Miltoni Angli pro Populo Anglicano Defensio* (Milton's *Defence of the English People*). Replying to the French scholar Salmasius in tones of withering ridicule ('You dull, stupid, ranting, wrangling . . . empty windbag . . . You witless mortal')[55] this astonished Europe with the force of its denunciation of the slavish principles adhering to monarchy, as well as tyranny.[56] When the Dutch scholar Vossius received his copy in Stockholm, where Salmasius was also resident, he could only glance at the work before it was borrowed by Queen Christina, but remarked, 'I had expected nothing of such quality from an Englishman.'[57] More exuberantly than the *Tenure*, Milton's tract celebrated the demise of 'a king in all his power, ruling according to his lust . . . at length overcome in battle by his own people which had served a long term of slavery . . . condemned to capital punishment by the highest court of the realm and beheaded before the very gates of the palace'.[58] It lavished praise upon the regicides, 'those brave and upright men . . . whose deathless deeds now resound through the whole world . . . none ever undertook with loftier, or . . . with calmer heart a deed so excellent and so worthy of even the heroic days of old'. Could any man doubt, indeed, that 'these great and wonderful deeds [were] performed evidently by almighty God himself rather than by mortal men?'[59]

---

[53] Hall, *The Grounds and Reasons of Monarchy* pp. 13, 15.
[54] Ibid. p. 3.   [55] Milton, *Defence* pp. 324–5, 329.
[56] On kings see for instance pp. 354, 359, 367. Blair Worden has suggested that 'Milton's . . . political prose would have received far less attention from posterity but for the immortality of his poetry' ('Marchamont Nedham' p. 56). This may underestimate the attention attracted by that prose in his lifetime, an effect of both its content and political context. According to Aubrey, 'the only inducement of severall foreigners that came over into England, was chiefly to see Oliver Protector, and Mr John Milton . . . He was much more admired abrode then at home.' *Aubrey's Brief Lives* p. 202. Sidney's interlocutor Lantin showed similar curiosity about 'Jean Milton qui a ecrit contre Mr de Saumaise'. *Lantiniana* p. 108; see also p. 60.
[57] Quoted in Scherpbier, *Milton in Holland* p. 6.
[58] Milton, *Defence* pp. 302–3.   [59] Ibid. pp. 303, 307, 330.

Most importantly, quoting from Plato, Aristotle, Cicero, Sallust and Tacitus, as well as St Paul, Hotman, Buchanan and Philip de Comines, Milton celebrated the benefits of self-government under law. These were evidenced by the examples of Athens, Sparta, Rome (Milton described parliament as 'our Senate'), Israel and 'the great Dutch Republic'.[60] There were many references to Nero and Tiberius, as later in Streater's *Observations* and Sidney's *Discourses*. '[W]ho, in fact, is worthy of holding on earth power like that of God but some person who far surpasses all others and even resembles God in goodness and wisdom? The only such person, as I believe, is the son of God whose coming we look for.'[61] For the ancient pedigree of English liberty Milton quoted the usual medieval sources.[62]

With the survival of the republic militarily assured, some pamphlets also broached the question of the necessary consolidation of this freedom by the election of new representatives.[63] Unsurprisingly, given its Leveller ancestry, the most important publication pressing this issue was Nedham's *Mercurius Politicus*. At the same time, immediately following the victory at Worcester on 3 September 1651 *Mercurius* turned to the longer-term project of re-educating the English people. Given 'that in times past, the People of this Nation were bred up and instructed in the brutish Principles of *Monarchy*, by which means they have been the more averse from entertaining Notions of a more noble Form' a notorious '*Error* in Policy' was '*keeping of the People ignorant of those wayes and meanes that are essentially necessary for the preservation of their Liberty*'.[64] Thus in issue 68, of 18–25 September 1651, having noticed the previous week 'how mightily the Lord hath prospered this *Commonwealth* in a short time', Nedham's editorial began to set out the positive arguments for the 'Excellency of a Free State' broached in the last chapter of the *Case*.

How 'mightily' the Athenians and the Roman commonwealth had 'increased in a short time, after they had obtained Liberty'. As '*Cato* saith in *Plutarch*, even the greatest Kings or Tyrants, are farre inferior to those that are eminent in *Free-States*'. This was because republics were far more regarding of the 'Common good', and men under them 'more inflamed . . . to the

---

[60] Ibid. pp. 341, 344, 429–30, 533.   [61] Ibid. pp. 427–8.

[62] *Mirror of Justices*, *Modus Tenendi*, the 'Laws of Edward the Confessor', *Fleta*, Bracton, Fortescue, Holinshed, Matthew Paris. Ibid. pp. 490–5, 501–5, 526; Greenberg, *Radical Face*.

[63] 'Let us above all things keep up the *Parliaments* Supremacy above the Souldier or Divine.' *A New Remonstrance of the Freeborn People of England: Concerning This present Parliament, and a new Representative* (14 November 1651) p. 2; Isaac Pennington Jr, *The Fundamental Right, Safety and Liberty of the People . . . Briefly Asserted* (15 May 1651); *A Perswasive to Mutuall Compliance Under the Present Government* (18 February 1651); John Cooke, *Monarchy No Creature of God's Making* (26 February 1651); *The Tragedy of Marcus Tullius Cicero* (1651).

[64] *Mercurius Politicus* no. 92, p. 1457; ibid. no. 101 p. 1585.

love of glory and vertue'. As '*Cicero* saith in the first of his *Offices*, Man is a Noble Creature, born . . . to Rule rather then Obey'. Under government by '*Hereditary Succession*' men are 'deprived of the use of their Reason about choice of *Governors*, and forced to receive them blindly . . . whether it be Male, or Female, A Wise man, or a Fool, good or bad'. Such a form was fit only for 'beasts'.[65] The superiour morality, magnanimity and military valour of free states was illustrated by not only ancient but contemporary examples, above all that 'of our own Nation, whose high achievements may match any of the Ancients, since the extirpation of tyranny, and re-establishment of our Freedom in the hands of the People'.[66]

For the preservation of this liberty, the first step 'When Rome was once declared a *Free-State*' was 'not only to engage the People by an *Oath* against the Return of *Tarquin's* Family to the Kingdom, but also against the admission of any such Officer as *King* for ever; because . . . it was the especiall care of those worthy Patriots, to imprint . . . Principles in Mens minds . . . insomuch that the very name of *King* became odious to the *Roman* people'.[67] At that point 'the Government, was [still] retained within the hands . . . of the . . . *Senatorian* order of *Nobility*, the People not being admitted into any share', as in Venice today. Eventually, however, 'partly by Mutinies, and partly by Importunity, they compelled the *Senators* to grant them an Interest in *Offices of State*, and in the *Legislative power* . . . Hence arose those Officers called *Tribunes*, and those Conventions called *Assemblies* of the People.' This form was preferable, because 'as long as the *popular Interest* continued regular and more predominant than the other, so long the People were secure of their *Liberties* . . . Wheras, when the *Senate* afterwards worm'd the People out of Power . . . so *Rome* lost her Liberty' and the decline began towards the '*single Tyrannie*' of '*Caesar*'.[68]

Nedham identified one danger to such popular power in the '*projecting Grandees*' (including, presumably, 'King Nol') who had been the focus of his invective in *Pragmaticus*. He identified the other, following the earlier line of *Vox Plebis*, in the tendency of a parliament which should be securing the liberties of the people to act instead as 'a *standing Senate*'.[69] The solution in both cases, and indeed 'the Right, Liberty, Welfare, and Safety of a People [,] consists in a due succession of their *Supreme Assemblies*'. The 'right Constitution and orderly Motion of Them, is of the greatest consequence that can be, there being so much imbarqued in this Vessel, that if it should miscarry, all is irreperably lost'.[70] One reason for this – anticipating

---

[65] Ibid. no. 87 pp. 1381, 1383; see also Milton, *Tenure* pp. 198–9.
[66] *Mercurius Politicus* no. 85, p. 1352.   [67] Ibid. no. 70, p. 1109.
[68] Ibid. pp. 1110 (misnumbered 1100), 1111.   [69] Ibid. no. 72, p. 1142.   [70] Ibid. no. 74, p. 1173.

Harrington – was that 'because as *Motion* in bodies *natural*, so *Succession* in *Civil*, is the grand Preventive of Corruption'.[71] It was to be admitted 'that upon the close of a *Civill War*' such a settlement faced practical difficulties. Here Nedham accepted the view, later opposed by Harrington, that no one should be 'admitted into power' who had 'not been firm in their hearts to the *Interest of Liberty*'.[72] In the face of these problems 'a people ought with patience to acquiesce in the Justice and Wisdom of their *Trustees*'. On the other hand 'it concerns the *Trustees* themselves in no wise to tire out the patience . . . of the people', the defence of whose liberties is 'confessed by all, to consist *In a due and orderly succession of their Supreme Assemblies*'.[73] 'This is good *Common-wealth* Language, and without this . . . *due and orderly succession* of Power and Persons . . . it is impossible any Nation should long subsist in a State of Freedom.'[74]

Some issues of *Mercurius* (nos. 92–7) considered royalist objections to republican government, showing that every distemper feared (levelling, faction, tumults) was in fact worse under monarchy. Others considered notorious '*Errors* in Policy' juxtaposed to '*Rules* . . . essentially necessary to the preservation of a Commonwealth in a state of *Freedome*'. The importance of an army consisting only of citizens, '*and the Militia lodged only in the Peoples hands*', was illustrated from Aristotle and the practice of 'The *Romans* . . . after they had gained a plenary possession of Liberty in their *Tribuns* and *successive Assemblies*'.[75] Aristotle, Plutarch, Isocrates and Machiavelli explained how vital it was '*That Children should be educated and instructed in the Principles of Freedom*'.[76] No less important, again anticipating Harrington, was prevention of the same persons wielding both legislative and executive power, or (drawing upon Herodotus, Xenophon, Livy and Samuel Daniel) the '*Interests of the Publick*' being supplanted by the interest '*of a few particular Persons*'.[77] Nedham's last lesson, before putting 'a Period to this *Discourse*' in August 1652, concerned the folly of '*persecuting and punishing of men for their opinions in Religion*'.[78]

At the same time Nedham had become busy in another cause. During 1651 *Mercurius Politicus* had supported the Anglo-Dutch union project, agreeing that 'Those two great republics . . . formidable to kings . . . [and] equally hated by all monarchies in Europe . . . [should] become as one entire body.'[79] When by the following year proposed union had transmuted into

---

[71] Ibid. no. 78, p. 1237; no. 79, pp. 1255–6.
[72] Ibid. no. 106, p. 1659; no. 93, p. 1458.   [73] Ibid. no. 75, pp. 1189, 1191.
[74] Ibid. no. 79, p. 1257; no. 80.   [75] Ibid. no. 103, p. 1610.   [76] Ibid. no. 104, p. 1625.
[77] Ibid. nos. 109–110; no. 110, p. 1721.   [78] Ibid. no. 114, p. 1785.
[79] Quoted in Worden, 'Marchamont Nedham' p. 74; see also Worden, 'Classical Republicanism' p. 198.

war, we find Nedham prominently manning the ramparts. His translation of Selden's *Of the Dominion of the Sea* (1652) entailed an extravagant celebration of the republic's maritime power. His *The Case Stated Between England and the United Provinces* (1652) set the war in the context not only of the attempted '*strict League and Union*' but of the longer history of 'Amity and friendship . . . between the Commonwealth of *England* and the *United Provinces*' which the Dutch had betrayed.[80] The aggression of Van Tromp against Blake in Folkestone Bay had been caused in part by 'Malignant Spirits, to prevent that Union', and in part by Dutch resentment at the 'Act for *Navigation*'.[81] In all of these matters the Dutch now faced in England the government not of a monarchy but of 'a Commonwealth', as capable of identifying and zealously defending the public interest as they were themselves.

Throughout the tract it was not Nedham's strategy to deny the status of the United Provinces as a haven for religious and political liberty, and the highly effective pursuit of economic and political interest. He does not, that is to say, identify it as a false republic. Rather the complaint is that, despite crucial English assistance, these things have been enjoyed selfishly, indeed at the expense of others: 'If [it] . . . be that their sole businesse is to free themselves, and to have all the world their slaves, as they are able, as is manifest by the whole proceed of their affairs; and to shut up the commerce of the world from any but themselves . . . Then (I say) let *England* . . . take heed.'[82] Under these circumstances, and according to the rules of international interest theory, England's first duty was to defend itself, its own liberty and trade. Thereafter Nedham tied the present struggle to a universal 'Cause of God this day amongst us . . . to shake off the exorbitant and wicked lusts of Kings and great ones, whether in *Monarchies* or *States*'.[83] Informing this language was the threat, animated by the sting of rejection, that if the Dutch republic would not unite with the English peacefully, it might be made to do so by force.

This war effort seems to have attracted the support of more than one political faction. It is with republicans of an imperial turn of mind, and a more evident interest in trade than religion (including Henry Neville, Thomas Chaloner and Henry Marten), that Blair Worden has primarily associated Nedham.[84] However Neville was also linked to his relative Algernon Sidney, whose key ally was the religious Henry Vane.[85] The same was true of Milton, whose own association with Nedham at this time

[80] [Nedham], *The Case Stated* pp. 1–6. [81] Ibid. pp. 7, 9, 13. [82] Ibid. p. 52.
[83] Ibid. p. 53. [84] Worden, 'Classical Republicanism' pp. 184–9; Worden, '"Wit in a Roundhead"'.
[85] Scott, *Algernon Sidney and the English Republic* p. 96.

we have noted. As architect of the reformed navy, Vane had long worked
closely with Neville, Chaloner, Thomas Scot and others.[86] Having supported Neville's election to the House in 1649, Sidney sat with him and
Vane on the committees for the settlement of Ireland and Scotland, and
with Vane and Chaloner on one committee to supervise the finances of the
army and the treasurers at war and another to raise money for the navy.[87]
Most importantly, in the first elections held after the outbreak of the Anglo-
Dutch war Sidney was, with Vane, elected onto the Council of State (in
November 1652). There, in co-operation with Vane, his hectic schedule
was dominated by war management, including communications with the
Netherlands and the provision of naval supplies, and by membership of the
Committee for Trade and Foreign Affairs.[88] When Vane recovered control
of foreign policy in 1659 his first act was to send Sidney to the Baltic with
a fleet 'of good strength', to seek Anglo-Dutch naval co-operation.[89] It was
upon the crest of this imperial wave that the republic suddenly hit the very
rocks which Nedham had earlier identified.

DISSOLUTION

On 20 April 1653, in the first military coup since Pride's Purge, the last
fragment of the Long Parliament was ejected. Throughout the period since
Worcester relations between civilian republican leaders and the army had
been deteriorating.[90] The victorious army wished for a more obedient
enactment of its own ideological agenda, while some senior civilian MPs
wished to free the republic from its damaging, and limiting, military foundation. It had been one conclusion of Nedham's oft-repeated reading of the
history of Rome that it was the refusal of the Senate to share fairly with
the people at large the spoils of Roman military expansion which paved
the way for the military usurpations of Sulla and Caesar. More specifically,
his warnings about the need to 'keep any man, though he have deserved
never so well by good success or service, from being too great or popular'[91]
echoed growing concerns about Cromwell. Readers were reminded that in
Rome it was treason for a military commander to cross the Rubicon; that
the Roman sentence for '*Treason*' was to be either '*burnt alive, or hang'd upon
a Gibbet*'; about the Roman who, despite his 'extraordinary merits . . . by
greatening himself beyond the size of a good Citizen; and entertaining

---

[86] Brenner, *Merchants and Revolution* p. 582.
[87] Scott, *Algernon Sidney and the English Republic* pp. 99–100.   [88] Ibid. pp. 100–1.
[89] Ibid. ch. 8.   [90] Worden, 'Marchamont Nedham' p. 63.   [91] Quoted in ibid. p. 67.

thoughts and Counsels of surprizing the *publick Liberty*, was condemned to death'[92]; about the '*Catastrophe*' of the '*single Tyranny*' of '*Caesar*'. Since according to Machiavelli 'of all Beasts, a Prince should sometimes resemble the *Lyon*, and sometimes the *Fox*, then the People ought to observe *great ones* in both these disguises'.[93] Similarly, three weeks before the dissolution, John Streater informed readers that the Romans

never received such a stroak at their Libertie, as when *Caesar* was made perpetual Dictator: Therefore since we finde *Rome* strip'd of her liberty and glory, let *England* watch to hers: and to that end let us take notice of the wayes how persons that affect absolute Government endeavour the accomplishment thereof.[94]

It was the army's own explanation of the dissolution that, since mid-1652 in particular, on behalf of 'this Cause which the Lord hath so greatly blessed, and bore witness to . . . his Excellency and Officers of the Army . . . desired . . . the Parliament, to proceed vigorously in reforming what was amisse in Government, and to the settling of the Commonwealth upon a foundation of Justice and righteousnesse'. Instead, however, and in addition to 'an aversion' to reform, 'with much bitternesse and opposition to the people of God . . . a corrupt party' concentrated upon 'effecting the desire they had of perpetuating themselves in the Supream Government'.[95]

For which purpose, the said Party long opposed, and frequently declared themselves against having a new Representative: And when they saw themselves necessitated to take that Bill into consideration, they resolved to make use of it to recruite the House with Persons of the same Spirit and temper, thereby to perpetuate their own sitting.[96]

The long-standing committee 'to take into Consideration the settling of the Succession of future Parliaments' included Sidney, and was chaired by Vane.[97] One reason for its slow progress in the second half of 1652 may have been the priority given to management of the war. The decision to proceed with the Bill was taken in January 1653 and given impetus by the crucial and bloody victory of Blake off Portland on 20 February, which lifted the morale of the House.[98] Another possible basis for army opposition to Vane

---

[92] *Mercurius Politicus* no. 107, p. 1674.
[93] Ibid. no. 110, p. 1724; no. 113, p. 1773.   [94] Streater, *A Glympse* pp. 1–2.
[95] *A Declaration of the Lord Generall and His Councel of Officers Shewing the Grounds and Reasons for the dissolution of the late Parliament* (13 April 1653) pp. 2, 6.
[96] Ibid. p. 5.
[97] *Commons Journal* vol. 6, pp. 118, 132, 134, 307; Scott, *Algernon Sidney and the English Republic* pp. 96–7.
[98] Worden, *The Rump Parliament* p. 377; Capp, *Cromwell's Navy* pp. 80–1.

and his collegues at this point was that, as a successful naval conflict, the war constituted a locus of military achievement and prestige alternative to the army's own. This would imply, at the least, that God gave his support not to the army in particular, let alone to its individual leaders, but to a larger republican cause opposed to the interest of a single person. It was a matter of political as well as military significance that in 1652–3 for the first time expenditure on the navy (£1.4 million in 1653) outgrew customs revenue and absorbed part of the assessment usually reserved for the army.[99]

What is clear is that it was the 'Bill for a New Representative' that the House was feverishly attempting to pass, with Algernon Sidney sitting 'next to the Speaker on the right hand', on the very morning of the dissolution.[100] There is little evidence that the Bill was a recruiting measure. It is Blair Worden's judgement that, contrary to army apologias, this intervention was probably triggered by an attempt to open the door to genuine elections, even before the Commonwealth had 'taken root in the affections of men'.[101] If seen as an attempt to undo the effects of Pride's Purge, it is possible to understand the view that such 'preposterous haste' placed the republican settlement in danger. No doubt there were civilian members of the Rump prepared to risk a Restoration to liberate the government from military power. Yet bearing in mind his record as a whole, including the subsequent *Corrective* to Harrington concerning the importance of restricting participation to those faithful to the cause, it is hard to believe that Vane was one of these. Moreover the army had itself earlier been agitating for a dissolution.[102] Later John Streater reported that the morning before Cromwell

went to the House to act that Tragedy he made a *Speech* at the *Cock-Pit* to all the Officers . . . *That the hand of God had Eminently gone along with the Army in various and Improbable Successes . . . Therefore it did behove them to persevere in the work of Reformation; that Reformation could not be expected from the present Parliament: and that if they should put the People to Elect a New Parliament, it would but tempt God . . . that Five or Six men, or few more, setting themselves to the work, might do more in one day, then the Parliament had or would do in one hundred days.*[103]

Streater had also received

Credible Information . . . that the Parliament was at that time in Consultation about the putting a period to their sitting; and also providing for a Succession of Parliaments, with such qualifications as might be the best means to preserve the

---

[99] Ibid. p. 10.   [100] Worden, *The Rump Parliament* pp. 372–404.   [101] Ibid. p. 377.
[102] *A Declaration of the Armie . . . for The dissolving of this present Parliament* (10 August 1652).
[103] Streater, *Secret Reasons of State* pp. 2–3.

Interest of the Nation, by Governing it as a Commonwealth or Free-State; he did thereupon conclude, that Gen. *Cromwell* saw he should be thereby prevented to attempt the Supremacy, and also be reduced to a private capacity, unto the which he could not with safety Return: for it were not to be Imagined, that they would Dissolve, and leave the sole Command of the Arms of the *Common-wealth* in his hands; a Trust too great for any Mortal: This . . . was the principall Reason why he interrupted their Sitting.[104]

Sir Arthur Haselrig also later claimed that the dissolution

was resolved in a junto at the Cockpit . . . Next day, we were labouring . . . in the House on an act to put an end to that Parliament and to call another. I desired the passing of it with all my soul. The question was putting for it, when our General stood up, and stopped the question, and called in his Lieutenant, with two files of musqueteers.[105]

It is the (by no means uncontested) conclusion of the historian to write most recently on the subject that 'the Rump was dissolved . . . in order to prevent the successful transition to an electorally mandated free-state in which the commander-in-chief of the armed forces would remain little more than an important employee of the state'.[106] Whatever the reason, Cromwell paced

up and down the stage . . . in the middest of the House . . . chid[ing] them soundly, and pointing particularly upon somme persons, as . . . Sir Henry Vane to whome he gave very sharpe language . . . [when] Algernon Sydney . . . sayd he would not go out . . . Harrison and Wortley putt theyr hands upon Sydney's shoulders, as if they would force him to go out, then he rose and went towards the doore. The Generall went to the table where the mace lay . . . and sayd, 'Take away these baubles'; [and] sayd to young Sir Henry Vane . . . that he might have prevented this extraordinary course, but he was a Juggler, and had not so much as common honesty. All being gon out, the door of the House was locked.[107]

The dissolution divided republicans and the army. Initially the regime's most prominent apologists, Nedham and Milton, remained aboard a ship the republican credentials of which had now become controversial. By contrast, leading republican MPs, or 'commonwealthsmen', including Vane, Sidney, Haselrig and Scot, went into opposition. Between these two stances

---

[104] Ibid. pp. 3–4. [105] *Diary of Thomas Burton* vol. III, p. 99.

[106] Kelsey, *Inventing a Republic* p. 13; for an opposed analysis much more sympathetic to the army's predicament and possible motivations of principle see Woolrych, *Commonwealth to Protectorate* chs. 2–3.

[107] Account of the dissolution by the Earl of Leicester, as told by his son Algernon Sidney, in R. W. Blencowe (ed.), *Sidney Papers* (1823) pp. 140–1, quoted in Scott, *Algernon Sidney and the English Republic* p. 102.

may have been a third, which, while decrying a military intervention in which 'all laws, divine and human, seem to be transcendently violated', saw no solution in re-establishment of the Rump.[108] As it was not only the ambition of Cromwell, but also the flaws of the republic which had produced this disaster, the only long-term solution lay in the establishment of a new constitution proof against both factional division and individual moral failure.

It may have been partly from this latter perception, shared in 1653 by Henry Neville and James Harrington, that the latter's *Oceana* emerged. Yet the following chapter will consider in more detail the question of how Harrington arrived at his formula for settlement. It was argued by the commonwealthsmen that, along with the Rump, Cromwell had dissolved republicanism itself. This was not the view of apologists like Nedham, who claimed on behalf of the Protectorate that, far from negating republicanism, the *Instrument of Government* introduced in December 1653 had furnished it with a necessary element of separation of powers.[109] On this point and others Harrington's repackaging of English republicanism, with its own prescription for healing and settling, owed much more to the Protectorate's statement of its own case than has been acknowledged.

---

[108] Manuscript fragment attributed to Henry Neville, quoted and discussed by Worden in '*Oceana*: Origins and Aftermath' p. 117.

[109] For the *Instrument* see Kenyon, *Stuart Constitution* pp. 308–13.

CHAPTER 13

Healing and settling, 1653–1658

By shewing that a Commonwealth was a Government of Laws, and
not of the Sword, he could not but detect the violent administration of
the Protector by his Bashaws, Intendants, or Majors General . . . while
the Cavaliers on the other side tax'd him with Ingratitude to the
memory of the late King . . . To these he answer'd, that . . . the
Monarchy being now quite dissolv'd, and the Nation in a state of
Anarchy . . . he was . . . oblig'd as a good Citizen to . . . [shew]
his Countreymen . . . such a Model of Government as he thought
most conducing to their Tranquillity, Wealth, and Power: That the
Cavaliers ought of all People to be best pleas'd with him, since if
his Model succeeded, they were sure to injoy equal Privileges with
others, and to be deliver'd from their present Oppression; for in a well
constituted Commonwealth there can be no distinction of Partys, the
passage to Preferment is open to Merit in all persons.

John Toland, *Life of Harrington*[1]

REPUBLICAN COMPLIMENT

One theme of defences of the dissolution was not to dispute the genuineness
of the Bill for a New Representative, but to focus upon the danger which
would have been posed by genuinely free elections. 'The People . . . being
so divided and discompos'd . . . as the Sea after a storm . . . [to] permit
them to a choice of their own Governours' would have seen 'the Nation
turn'd wild into an irregular and dangerous Liberty . . . or reduc'd under
its former Tyranny'.[2] Another writer who praised the Rump for 'the wonderful alterations it hath brought in these Nations (not to mention what
influence . . . over all Europe) [so that] a man may truly say it was one of the
most famous, fortunate, wise Assemblies, amidst so many difficulties and

---

[1] Toland, *Life of Harrington* p. xviii–xix.
[2] *Sedition Scourg'd, or a view of that Rascally and Venemous Paper Entituled A Charge of High-Treason exhibited against Oliver Cromwell* (1653) p. 8.

complexities, as ever was', nevertheless insisted that 'the *Bill* which they had prepared, was circumstantiated so . . . the greatness of Liberty that was left in Election, could assure us of nothing else but hot confusion, and desperate revival of oppressed factions'. Army intervention had been necessary when 'They saw that the people (things so standing) were absolutely uncapable of that Power which was naturally theirs, and that it had been but to put a sword into a mad-man's hand.'[3]

In 1654, as in 1650, and in time for elections to the first Protectoral parliament, Marchamont Nedham published an agile defence of the new regime. *A True State of the Case of the Commonwealth* (1654), like the earlier *The Case of the Commonwealth* (1650), defended 'the necessity and Justness' of a 'great Change' (now one of 'several changes' and 'subsequent Alterations') which had troubled the consciences of many.[4] This was on the ground partly that particular political forms were transitory and of secondary importance ('being as the Shell to the Kernel'), and partly that the alternatives facing the nation were far worse. These still included either 'Anarchy and Confusion' or 'the *young Pretender* . . . almost a stranger to this Nation', fixed upon his 'private Interest'.[5] In addition, however, there were also now the disgruntled commonwealthsmen, still to 'awake out of their dreams of an imaginary Paradise . . . [who] make it their business by cunning insinuations to draw away the hearts of the Well-affected . . . as if we had turned our backs upon our former Principles, and introduced again that very thing, which was the great Bone of contention'.[6]

In 1650 Nedham's appointment as apologist, when he could otherwise have been convicted of treason, reflected the republic's view of the danger from popular royalism and Levellerism. Now we may take his commission to write *The State of the Case* as evidence of the Protectorate's felt need to propitiate republican opinion. Thus for 'the godly People of this Nation' the tract contained a powerful component of providential language.[7] Far from being a work of *de facto* theory, the *State* defended the regime on the basis of principle in general, and commonwealth principles in particular. 'That very thing' was of course monarchy. In this respect Nedham's most important claim was that it was the Rump which had been on the point of betraying the nation's hard-won liberty, leaving the army no choice but to intervene. '[S]tudious of Parties and private Interests, neglecting the publick', it had long delayed the '*Bill for a new Representative*', and only taken it up at the last minute, insincerely, to 'have had some . . . Pretext

[3] *Confusion Confounded; or, A firm way of Settlement settled and Confirmed* (1654) pp. 2–3.
[4] [Nedham], *A True State of the Case of the Commonwealth* p. 6.
[5] Ibid. pp. 14, 49.   [6] Ibid. p. 3.   [7] Ibid. p. 4

to thwart or scandalize that most necessary work of Dissolution'. Yet even 'admit that they had been real in their Intentions, for the putting a period to their own Authority (as was pretended)', constitutionally the Bill was fatally flawed,

intending that the Supream Authority should be lodged in *Biennial Parliaments*, and that they should have power to sit to make Laws, and Govern from two years to two years successively, (keeping by that means the Supream Legislative power alwaies in being) the evil consequences thereof. . . are discernable to every eye . . . For besides the infinite number of Laws which would have bin enacted . . . that in a few years no man could have told how to have behaved himself . . . the Supream Powers of making Laws, and of putting them in execution, were by that Bill to have been disposed in the same hands; which placing the *Legislative* and *executive Powers* in the same persons, is a marvellous In-let of Corruption and Tyranny: wheras the keeping of these two apart, flowing in distinct Channels, so that they may never meet in one . . . there lies a grand Secret of Liberty and good Government.[8]

As we saw in chapter 6, in *The Case* this was made into the basis of a defence of the *Instrument of Government* as a mixed constitution. The status of Nedham's new formulation as the regime's official position was underlined by the Protector himself when he explained to parliament,

I dare assert there is a just Liberty to the People of God, and the just Rights of the People in these Nations provided for, – I can put the issue thereof upon the clearest reason; whatsoever any go about to suggest to the contrary. But this not being the time and place for such an averment, 'I forbear at present'. For satisfaction's sake herein, enough is said in a Book entituled *A State of the Case of the Commonwealth*, published in January 1653[4].[9]

Cromwell wished to have his regime accepted as the nation's defence from ungodly royalism and 'men of Levelling Principles'. It was 'the great end . . . to wit, Healing and Settling' to bring together moderates of all camps, and thus reunite the nation, 'judging this most likely to avoid the extremes of Monarchy on the one hand, and Democracy on the other'.[10] When Harrington later also made separation of powers (in that case between proposing and resolving) fundamental to his own mixed constitution he explicitly defended it against the unicameralism of Hobbes on the one hand, and the Levellers and commonwealthsmen on the other.

---

[8] Ibid. pp. 9–10.
[9] Cromwell, speech of 22 January 1655, in *Oliver Cromwell's Letters and Speeches*, ed. Thomas Carlyle (3 vols., 1857) vol. III, p. 84.
[10] Cromwell, speech of 4 September 1654, in ibid. pp. 20–1.

Nor did Milton break immediately with Cromwell following the dissolution of the Rump. This was the less to be expected, given his warm support
for the military intervention of 1648–9, his greater pessimism concerning the personal qualities of parliamentarians and 'people', and the greater
weight he attached to religious objectives carried into the Protectorate.
Thus the *Second Defence* (1654) re-celebrated the achievement of those who
had 'followed . . . the Lord's manifest guidance' in 'heroically' ridding the
country of a 'grievous tyranny' backed by a 'venemous . . . mob'.[11] 'They
were not inflamed with the empty name of liberty by a false notion of virtue
and glory, or senseless emulation of the ancients. It was [with] their purity
of life and their blameless character . . . [and] the most righteous defence
of law and religion that . . . trusting completely to God . . . they put slavery
to flight.'[12] Reflecting the republic's imperial achievements, this message of
'Liberty' was conveyed 'from on high' to 'far flung regions and territories
across the sea . . . Here the manly strength of the Germans, hostile to slavery . . . there the lively and generous ardor of the . . . Franks . . . the . . . courage
of the Spaniards . . . the serene . . . magnanimity of the Italians . . . In short,
it is the renewed cultivation of freedom and civic life that I disseminate
throughout cities, kingdoms and nations.'[13]

While Nedham effected a constitutional compromise, the *Second Defence*
placed even more emphasis than usual upon the superior importance of
personal morality to institutions. Thus Milton defended and praised, not
the Protectorate, but Cromwell personally, drawing upon Aristotle's analysis of monarchy: 'there is nothing in human society more pleasing to
God . . . nothing in the state more just . . . than the rule of the man most
fit to rule'.[14] The dissolution of the Rump was justified in the same terms:
'When you saw delays being contrived and every man more attentive to his
private interest than to that of the state . . . you put an end to the domination of these few men, since they, although so often warned, had refused
to do so.'[15] Yet more broadly Milton's tract is not primarily a defence of
the new government. As the sequel to a work begun in 1651 (or 1649), its
political and emotional centres of gravity are in the past, a point underlined by its extended autobiography. When Milton praises the heroes of the
revolution, among the names invoked there are as many opponents of the
dissolution as supporters.[16] His eventual analysis of the present situation,
where liberty again hangs in the balance, returns to the familiar notes of

[11] Milton, *Second Defence* p. 549.   [12] Ibid. p. 552.   [13] Ibid. pp. 555–6.
[14] Ibid. pp. 668, 671–2.   [15] Ibid. p. 671.
[16] Blair Worden, 'John Milton and Oliver Cromwell', in Ian Gentles, John Morrill and Blair Worden
(eds.), *Soldiers, Writers and Statesmen of the English Revolution* (Cambridge, 1998) p. 258.

anxiety and admonition. Thus, presaging the role of Satan in *Paradise Lost*, Cromwell is warned to

Consider . . . how precious a thing is this liberty which you hold, committed to your care . . . Honour . . . what foreign nations . . . say of us, the high hopes which they have for themselves as a result of our liberty, so bravely won, and our republic, so gloriously born. If the republic should miscarry . . . and as quickly vanish, surely no greater shame and disgrace could befall this country. Finally, honor yourself, so that, having achieved that liberty in pursuit of which you endured so many hardships . . . you may not permit it to be violated by yourself . . . Certainly . . . he who attacks the liberty of others is himself the first of all to lose his own liberty and . . . the first of all to become a slave. And he deserves this fate. For if the very patron . . . of liberty . . . shall afterwards attack that liberty which he himself has defended, such an act must necessarily be . . . well nigh fatal not only to liberty itself but also to the cause of all virtue and piety.[17]

The present state of affairs may be temporarily necessary on the grounds that 'a people torn by so many factions (as after a storm, when the waves have not yet subsided) does not . . . permit that condition in public affairs which is ideal and perfect'. But 'If, having done with war, you neglect the arts of peace, if warfare is your peace and liberty, war your only virtue, your supreme glory, you will find, believe me, that peace itself is your greatest enemy . . . and what you thought liberty will prove to be your servitude.'[18] This is a warning not only to the Lord Protector, but to all those whose moral failings had made the Protectorate necessary. Thus frequently

it happens that a nation which cannot rule and govern itself, but has delivered itself into slavery to its own lusts, is enslaved also to other masters whom it does not choose, and serves not only voluntarily but also against its own will . . . You, therefore, who wish to remain free, either be wise at the outset or recover your senses as soon as possible. If to be a slave is hard, and you do not wish it, learn to obey right reason, to master yourselves.[19]

With this less than optimistic-sounding warning, Milton's public pen fell silent for four years. By December 1657, while continuing to draw his salary as Secretary for Foreign Tongues, he explained that 'I stay nearly always at home – and willingly.'[20] It was in early 1658, against the background of a broader republican attack upon the Humble Petition and Advice, that like Nedham two years earlier he chose to publish a revised edition of a first *Defence of the English People* written under very different circumstances.[21]

---

[17] Milton, *Second Defence* p. 673.   [18] Ibid. p. 680.   [19] Ibid. p. 684.
[20] Quoted in Woolrych, 'Historical Introduction' p. 2.
[21] Martin Dzelzainis, 'Milton and the Protectorate in 1658' in Armitage et al., *Milton*.

By the time of Oliver's death, his refusal of the crown notwithstanding, the Protectorate was no longer defensible in republican terms.

REPUBLICAN CRITICISM

In May 1653 members of the government of the City of London published a *Representation*, addressed to Cromwell, observing that 'this *Nation* . . . seemeth as in one day to be deprived of its *Antient* liberty . . . [of] being governed by Representatives, chosen by themselves', and entreating that 'some effectual means may be found . . . for the meeting of the Parliament again, that so in short time provision may be made for successive Representatives'.[22] A few months later *A Charge of High Treason* was published *against Oliver Cromwell Esq*, preferring the charge of establishing a 'mock Parliament . . . to take away the body of our Law . . . to the end . . . that thereby the Lords the people of *England* may be subject to the will, pleasures and intended Tirany of the said *Cromwell*', and calling upon

All the people of *England* . . . as one man, as well Masters, Sons, as Servants, repaire unto every County-Town . . . upon the 16th of *October* 1653 . . . and appear Armed . . . then and there to Elect and Chuse . . . so many persons as the people of the respective Counties, Cities, and Boroughs wont to chuse for to represent them in Parliament, the which may be Conducted to *London*.[23]

By John Streater England was cautioned, 'If the Common-wealth hath many Warrs . . . not [to] put the Conduct on one Members shoulders; but rather chuse severall Members for several Undertakings . . . never to let any of their members grow too great, nor continue too long in great Trusts.'[24] 'What miserable Wars, Murders, Burnings, Depopulations, Cruelties of all kindes were committed in the times of *Nero, Galba, Otho*, and *Vitellius*? which were personal quarrels of those, to grasp at the Empire . . . Likewise the Civil War between *Caesar* and *Pompey*.'[25]

In issue 10 of *Observations* there appeared a suspiciously topical account of the career of Nero, who first appeared on the public stage amid elaborate protestations of humility, professing himself a '*Laborious*, and *Painful Servant of the Commonwealth*', while courting the people and army alike (Cromwell: 'And for myself, I desire not to keep my place in this Government an hour longer than I may preserve England in its just rights').

---

[22] *To his Excellency, Oliver Cromwel . . . and to the honorable Councel of the Army . . . The humble Representation of severall Aldermen . . . and other Citizens of London* (20 May 1653).
[23] *A Charge of High-Treason exhibited against Oliver Cromwell Esq; for several Treasons by him committed* (1653).
[24] Streater, *A Glympse* (31 March 1653) p. 15.   [25] Ibid. p. 14.

However, once he had 'ascended the *Meridian*-line' and become 'unlim-
mitted . . . he shewed himself to be the worst of creatures', corrupting
the 'souldiery, 'making use of them to be the keepers of the peace, layeth
aside the people, he imprisons the commons', before embarking upon a
career of 'lust, pride and cruelty'.[26] It was characteristic of tyrants, Streater
explained, to forbid public speaking of the truth. However, this simply led
those 'being deprived of speaking, [to] take the greater liberty of thinking'.
'Another trick of pretenders to the Publike, is the levying of moneys for
common defence, which yet is oftentimes to defend only themselves, not
the Commonwealth.'[27]

These observations had a more precise political context. With the meeting of the first Protectoral parliament in prospect (September 1654), and
in contrast to those 'who flatter and lye, and call them vertuous and noble
Princes, which they know in their hearts to be no other than Tyrants, and
Enemies to their Country . . . Those that represent a People, ought not to
be daunted by the greatest Person or Forces under heaven. He is not fit to
represent his Country, that is not willing to lose his life.'[28] As Roman history showed, the only antidote to tyranny was 'to distinguish the common
profit from the private, and to prefer it before the private . . . Those who
are employed in the Supreme Councels of a Commonwealth, as they are
to arm themselves with wisdom and courage, so they are to lay aside all
partiality and private respect, and only mind that of the publike.'[29] Streater
reprinted in block capitals the oath taken by Roman senators to act only
'according to the Laws and Ordinances . . . of the Romans, by the which
our Commonwealth is governed . . . I shall not suffer that my judgement
or counsel shall be subject to favour, hatred, gifts or presents.'[30]

Other bitter attacks appeared upon the Protector's tyranny and apostasy,
not least by members of the army.[31] In the parliamentary elections of both
1654 and 1656 Cromwell faced vigorous republican opposition. In September 1656 a hundred members were '*violently kept out of the Parliament-house
by armed men hired by the Lord Protector*'. For 'assuming an absolute arbitrary sovereignty' the latter was named as 'the public capital enemy whom
every man ought to destroy' by a *Remonstrance, [and] Protestation* append-
ing ninety-eight signatures headed by those of Sir Arthur Haselrig and

---

[26] Streater, *Observations* no. 10, pp. 76–7; Cromwell, speech of 22 January 1655, in *Letters and Speeches*
vol. III, p. 84.
[27] Streater, *Observations* p. 68.   [28] Ibid. p. 58.   [29] Ibid. no. 9, pp. 67, 69.   [30] Ibid. p. 68.
[31] See for instance *The Protector, (So called,) In Part Unvailed: By whom the Mystery of Iniquity, is now
working . . . By a late member of the Army* (1655); I. S., *The PICTURE of a New COURTIER drawn
in a Conference, between Mr Timeserver, and Mr Plain-heart* (1656).

Thomas Scot.[32] Of Cromwell Algernon Sidney later said: 'he was a tyrant and a violent one (you need not wonder I call him a tyrant, I did so every day in his life, and acted against him too)'. Concerning another Rump leader, Sir Henry Vane jr, Sidney recorded:

There was a long and particular Friendship contracted between Cromwell and him, which he broke off as soon as he observ'd Cromwell to aim at the sole power, and attempt it by force. He . . . proposed to Cromwell no other way of renewing their Friendship, but that of quitting his Usurpation; and he alone unarm'd and imprisoned us'd severely to condemn him for his illegal power, for being puffd up and elevated with prosperity, and usurping the Command of the Army, by which reflexions he often disturbd and terrify'd him.[33]

Sidney's later colleague Slingsby Bethel, too, remembered that

Sir *Henry Vaine*, above any one Person, was the Author of *Oliver*'s Advancement, and did so long, and cordially Espouse his Interest, that he prejudiced himself (in the opinion of some) by it, yet so ungratefull was this Monster of Ingratitude, that he studied to destroy him . . . because he could not adhere to him in his Perjury and Falsenes . . . He appointing a Publick Day of Humiliation, and seeking of God for him, invited all Gods People in his Declaration, to offer him their advise in the weighty affairs then upon his shoulders: Sir *Henry* taking a rise from hence offered his Advise by a Treatise, called *The Healing Question*; But *Cromwell*, angry at being taken at his word, Seized, Imprisoned, and indeavoured to proceed further against him, for doing only, what he had invited him to do.[34]

The occasion of Cromwell's *Declaration*, issued on 14 March 1656, was the failure the previous year of the military expedition sent to take Hispaniola. Furnishing the Commonwealth's, and Cromwell's, first military defeat, this had a devastating effect on the Protector's confidence in the continued integrity of his providential mission.[35] Noting that 'The Lord hath been pleased in a wonderful manner to humble and rebuke us, in that expedition to the *West Indies*', the *Declaration* noted, with reference to the Book of Joshua ('keep yourselves from the accursed thing') that there was 'just reason to fear, that We may have either failed in the spirit and manner wherewith this business hath been undertaken, or that the Lord sees some abomination or accursed thing by which he is provoked thus to appear against Us'.[36]

[32] *To all the Worthy Gentlemen who are Duely Chosen . . . the 17 of September 1656. And to all the Good people of the Common-wealth of England* (1656); C. H. Firth, *The Last Years of The Protectorate 1656–1658* (2 vols., New York, 1964) *Volume I: 1656–1657*, pp. 21–3.

[33] Sidney, *Character of Henry Vane* pp. 279–80.

[34] Bethel, *The World's Mistake in Oliver Cromwell* p. 13.

[35] Blair Worden, 'Oliver Cromwell and the Sin of Aachan', in D. Beales and G. Best (eds.), *History, Society and the Churches* (1985).

[36] Quoted in Armitage, 'The Cromwellian Protectorate' pp. 543–4.

Vane's identification of this 'accursed thing' was not specific to this moment. Throughout his career his republican thought opposed the (monarchical) sin of 'Self-interest'. The focus of his massive *The Retired Man's Meditations*, published the previous year, had also been this 'great idol . . . a throne of iniquity . . . the Throne and seat of the beast'.[37] *A Healing Question* distinguished between the old and still good 'Cause', in respect of which 'it pleased God (the righteous Judge, who was appealed to in the controversie) . . . to bless the Council, and Forces of the persons concerned', and more recently 'something rising up that seems accommodated to the private and selfish interest of a particular part . . . then truly adequate to the common good'.[38] In the former, 'true freedom . . . in civils . . . [and] in spirituals', comprising 'the publique welfare and good of the nation', was consolidated 'under the rule and oversight of a Supreme Judicature; unto the wisdome of whose lawes and orders, the sword is to become most entirely subject and subservient'. This had its foundation 'in the whole Body of the people that have adhered to the cause, and by them derived unto their successive Representatives, as the most equal and impartial Judicature for the effecting hereof'.[39] If, by contrast, those people 'should come at last to be utterly denied the exercise of this right, upon pretence that they are not in capacity as yet to use it; which indeed hath some truth in it, if those that are now in power, and have the command of the Arms, doe not prepare all things requisite thereunto, as they may, and . . . ought', this would surely account for the 'great silence in Heaven . . . the three years last past'.[40]

Nay if in stead of favouring and promoting the peoples common good and welfare, self-interest and private gain should evidently appear to be the things we have aymed at all along; if these very Tyrannical principles and Antichristian reliques, which God by us hath punished in our predecessors, should again revive . . . If all those great advantages of serving the Lords will and design . . . shall at last be wrested and mis-improved to the enriching and greatning of our selves . . . shall we need to look any further for the accursed thing?[41]

Vane's tract ended by calling for a 'Convention of faithful, honest, and discerning men, chosen . . . by the free consent of the whole Body of adherents to this Cause . . . to debate freely' towards the establishment of a new 'fundamental Constitution'. By this 'shall be laid and inviolably observed . . . the conditions upon which the whole body so represented, doth consent to cast itself into a Civil and Politique incorporation'.[42]

---

[37] Vane, *The Retired Man's Meditations* 'To the Reader', p. 383.
[38] Vane, *A Healing Question* pp. 2–3.   [39] Ibid. pp. 8, 10, 15.
[40] Ibid. pp. 13, 22.   [41] Ibid. p. 14.   [42] Ibid. p. 20.

Three months later there appeared R. G.'s *A Copy of a Letter from an Officer of the Army in Ireland* which, anticipating both Harrington's historical analysis and his advocacy of an agrarian law, would later be accused by Toland of having tried 'to rob' the author of *Oceana* 'of the glory of his invention'.[43] To understand the collapse of English monarchy, the tract explained, it was necessary to go back to '*Henry the Seventh*', who when he

saw plainlie that he did owe his . . . Crown, more to the favour of those Lords who assisted him, then either to his own *Sword* or *Title*, he began to consider in how ticklish a posture he stood . . . [and] made it his whole aim and work to lessen and debase the nobilitie . . . by which he laid the foundation of *destroying his Posterity, not considering at all that the Lords could not be diminished, but by advancing and inriching the Commons*, whose desire of power must necessarilie increase accordinglie . . . [leading them to] strike not at this or that Prince, but at the verie *Root of Monarchy it self*, as being a thing useless . . . and indeed inconsistent with their Government and interest.[44]

In form and style *A Copy of a Letter* was quite different from *Oceana*. It was not a proposed model of government, but a prose polemic far more characteristic of republican writing of this period in general. In the style of Nedham earlier, and Sidney later, it was a work of Machiavellian interest theory extrapolating upon the *Discorsi*'s assertion that the interests of kings or tyrants (which are the same) and republics, are irreconcilably opposed. '[R]eason of state in Kings and Tyrants, is to keep mankind poore and ignorant . . . point blank contrary to the . . . maximes of a *Commonwealth*, which is the nursery of vertue, valor, and industrie.'[45] Most importantly *A Copy of a Letter* was characterised by a distinctive concentration upon the economic basis of these interests: 'The riches of the people in general, is the natural cause of destruction to all Regal States . . . *if all Kingdomes be neer their period and ruine, when the Subjects under them grow rich . . . contrariwise . . . Commonwealths do not decay, but when their people in general grow poore.*'[46] This was, as we have seen, a key aspect of the commonwealth genre, from More's *Utopia* to Sidney's *Maxims*, most particularly developed before Harrington by Nedham. It was in line with this tradition that *A Copy of a Letter* paid particular attention to the attempts by the ancients (Agis and Cleomenes in Sparta, and the Gracchi in Rome) 'to reduce those two excellent States to their first principles' by the introduction of agrarian laws.[47]

---

[43] See the discussions by Pocock, 'Historical Introduction', pp. 10–12, and Scott, *Algernon Sidney and the English Republic* pp. 115–16.
[44] R., G., *A Copy of a Letter* pp. 8–9.   [45] Ibid. p. 4.   [46] Ibid. p. 5.   [47] Ibid. p. 7.

By 1656 Harrington had links to Machiavellian republicans, inside and outside the army, as he did to royalists. One such was Streater, one-time army officer in Ireland (though not in 1654, when *A Copy of a Letter* claimed to have been written) and publisher of *Oceana*. Another was Henry Neville, believed to be the likely author of the *Letter* by contemporaries, later editor of Machiavelli, and the author of his own commonwealth discourse. When *Oceana* was published, Hobbes claimed that Neville 'had a finger in that pye'; Aubrey remarked 'tis like enough'; and Samuel Hartlib noted in his 'Ephemerides': 'Mr Nevil the witt commends it as one of the best books written in that kind.'[48] When Neville's own *Plato Redivivus* was published twenty-four years later its editor remarked that it was no fairer to accuse Neville of borrowing Harrington's ideas than to accuse Harrington of borrowing from *A Copy of a Letter*.[49]

The last important republican work of this year before *Oceana* was Marchamont Nedham's *Mercurius Politicus* editorials republished with amendments as *The Excellencie of a Free State* (1656). In its original contexts from 1645–6 and 1651–2 Nedham's Machiavellian populism had admonished the Long Parliament to secure the establishment of a genuinely free state. This had been under threat from tendencies both to senatorial oligarchy, and to tyranny among army grandees. As the Protectorate now came under increasing pressure from conservatives to complete the transition to monarchy, the republication of these editorials 'calling for an armed popular republic, with frequent parliaments and rotation of officers', constituted an act of radical opposition.[50] At this moment, accordingly, it is hard to deny Nedham the glory of being the regime's most important defender and opponent simultaneously. Nedham's purpose, a new introduction explained, was to open 'the Eyes of the People' in the face of advice being given to '*his Highness to lay aside Parliament . . . . and to lay a Foundation for absolute Tyranny, upon unbounded Monarchy*'. For 'a Free-State is much more excellent than a Government by Grandees or kings', the latter notorious for 'pleasing' the people 'onely with the name and shadow of Liberty in stead of the substance'.[51] 'How came it to pass . . . that *Julius Caesar* aspired, and in the end attained the Empire? . . . had not the Senate and People so long protracted the Power of *Pompey . . . in Asia*, and *Caesar . . . in Gallia, Rome* might have stood much longer in the possession of her Liberty.'[52]

---

[48] *Aubrey's Brief Lives* pp. 124–5; *Hartlib Papers*, 'Ephemerides' 1656 Part 4, 29/5/98A.
[49] Robbins (ed.), *Two English Republican Tracts* p. 68.
[50] Pocock, 'Historical Introduction' pp. 13, 34–7; Dzelzainis, 'Milton and the Protectorate', p. 203; Worden, 'Marchamont Nedham' pp. 77–81.
[51] Nedham, *Excellencie* p. 45.   [52] Ibid., 'The Right Constitution of a Commonwealth' p. 30.

Fortunately history showed that 'a People having once tasted the Sweets of Freedom, are so extreamly affected with it' that any such usurper must fear that 'upon the first opportunity' they will take their 'revenge'.[53] Even after '*Caesar*'s death' the Romans 'might have recovered their Liberty again, if they had taken care (as they might easily have done) to prevent the growing Greatness of *Augustus*, who gaining power first, by the courtesie and good will of the Senate and People, made use of it to establish himself in a Tyranny'.[54] To this the only antidote was 'a revolution of Government in the People's hands . . . the successive Revolution of Authority by their consent'.[55]

HARRINGTON'S 'MODEL' FOR HEALING AND SETTLING

Like Nedham's *Excellencie*, Harrington's *Oceana* appears to have been timed to coincide with the parliamentary elections of September 1656. However owing to printing problems, exacerbated or caused by inquiries by the government, the work did not appear until October or November.[56] Like the *Excellencie*, and as the work of 'England's premier civic humanist', *Oceana* has been interpreted as an exemplary work of republican opposition.[57] Thus it is the view of Blair Worden, building upon that of John Pocock, that 'Although . . . *Oceana* . . . distances itself from the program of the commonwealthmen, who want to restore the sovereign House of Commons, it is at one with them . . . in its detestation of Cromwell and of the expulsion of the Rump.'[58] This detestation manifests itself in Harrington's ironic representation of *Oceana*'s Lord Archon as a virtuous inversion of the real Lord Protector. In this role Lord Archon does everything for the effective establishment of the nation's liberty which the Lord Protector had often promised, but conspicuously failed to do. It is certainly true that Harrington's work sought to offer what the bungling Lord Protector had failed to deliver. First and foremost, however, this was not that 'liberty' so beloved of the commonwealthsmen, but peace and settlement: '*We are disputing whether we should have Peace, or War; For Peace, you cannot have without some Government, nor any Government without the proper Ballance: Wherefore if you will not fix this which you have, the rest is blood.*'[59]

[53] Ibid. pp. 46–9. Even an elective monarch was objectionable 'because their present Greatness gives them opportunity ever to practise such flights, that in a short time, the Government that they received onely for their own Lives, will be come entailed upon their Families . . . to mock the poor People, and adorn the triumphs of an aspiring Tyranny.' Ibid. p. 70.
[54] Ibid. p. 74.   [55] Ibid. pp. 77–80.   [56] Pocock, 'Historical Introduction' p. 14.
[57] Ibid. pp. 6–42; Worden, 'James Harrington' pp. 82–138.   [58] Ibid. p. 119.
[59] Harrington, *Oceana* (1656) pp. 113–14.

Moreover it is not easy to detect Harrington's 'detestation of the dissolution of the Rump' in an account of that body likening it (using Hobbes's
translation of Thucydides) to the Thirty Tyrants of Athens.[60] That this
tyranny of a few had now given way to a tyranny of one may have constituted another lost opportunity for settlement, but it was hardly a calamity
in its own right. Indeed for Harrington what gave unity to all of these
failures was their merely epiphenomenal status. No mere politicians could
solve the problem. To solve it, once and for all, it was necessary to see
beneath the surface of events to their material causes. This was the work of
a lawgiver, who must also be, in Harrington's view, a natural philosopher.
As for Hobbes, 'Policy is an art . . . [and] Art is the observation or imitation
of nature . . . Some . . . [have said] that I, being a private man, have been so
mad as to meddle with politics; what had a private man to do with government? My Lord, there is not any public person, not any magistrate, that has
written in the politics worth a button.'[61] Harrington's ambition to stand, to
this extent, outside the immediate political context, was not simply that of
a would-be political neutral. It was that of a philosopher, who wished like
Hobbes to elevate politics from polemic to the status of civil philosophy.

It is Worden's argument that, informed by a genuine hatred of Cromwell,
Harrington's dedication of *Oceana* to him is ironic (it is 'an anti-
dedication'), and his account of Lord Archon is an extended public joke at
the Lord Protector's expense.[62] It is certainly true that the text can be read
that way, and would have been by some readers. Yet presumably it was not
Harrington's intention that those readers should have included Cromwell
himself. When Harrington praises Lord Archon's 'lack of ambition in yourself' and 'virtues and merit', he is saying of Cromwell what Milton said of
him in 1654, and the opposite of what his republican opponents were saying
of him in 1656. By the latter date, these passages could have been read iron-
ically, in the mode of Streater's earlier account of the self-denying Nero. Yet
unlike Streater's *Observations*, *Oceana* is not directed only at republicans,
and moreover it is formally directed to the Lord Protector himself, praise
for whose 'incomparable patriot[ism]' contrasts strikingly with *Oceana*'s
criticism of the Rump. Moreover we know from the evidence of the text, as
well as the testimony of Toland, that it was published with a serious political
purpose, to be served most directly by enlisting Cromwell's support.[63]

---

[60] Ibid. p. 49.   [61] Harrington, *The Examination of James Harrington* p. 858.
[62] Worden, '*Oceana*: Origins and Aftermath' p. 122.
[63] On this point I agree with J. C. Davis that 'The dedication of *Oceana* to Cromwell is no mere
convention.' Davis, 'Equality in an Unequal Commonwealth: James Harrington's Republicanism
and the Meaning of Equality', in Gentles, Morrill and Worden, *Soldiers, Writers and Statesmen* p. 230.

This purpose was not, of course, to mock lost opportunities for settlement in the past. It was to achieve, in 1656, the settlement which had eluded the nation until that time. The broad strategy for the achievement of this objective was to show royalists, commonwealthsmen and supporters of the Protectorate, as *Oceana* attempts to do, that they have nothing to lose from such a settlement and everything to gain. As Toland recorded,

By shewing that a Commonwealth was a Government of Laws, and not of the Sword, he could not but detect the violent administration of the Protector by his Bashaws, Intendants, or Majors General . . . while the Cavaliers on the other side tax'd him with Ingratitude to the memory of the late King . . . To these he answer'd, that . . . the Monarchy being now quite dissolv'd . . . he was . . . oblig'd as a good Citizen to . . . shew his Countreymen . . . such a Model of Government as he thought most conducing to their Tranquillity, Wealth, and Power: That the Cavaliers ought of all People to be best pleas'd with him, since if his Model succeeded, they were sure to injoy equal Privileges with others, and to be deliver'd from their present Oppression; for in a well constituted Commonwealth there can be no distinction of Partys, the passage to Preferment is open to Merit in all persons.[64]

Within the resulting sustained exercise in multivocality, the voice to which least attention has been paid is its attempt systematically to address the Lord Protector's own agenda. In fact what *Oceana* has to say to (rather than simply about) England's government in 1656 is both highly specific and fundamental to its purpose. Yet this voice of *counsel* within the text has hardly been noticed.[65]

For instance, his heroic work done, Harrington's Lord Archon tore himself from a senate with 'tears in their eyes' and 'retired unto a country house of his, being remote and very private'. Recalling that in a speech to the first Protectoral parliament on 12 September 1654, Cromwell claimed to have begged, before the dissolution of the Rump, 'to have had leave to have retired to a private life', Blair Worden takes this to be another savagely ironic juxtaposition of Cromwell's profession to his (non-)practice.[66] Yet another, perhaps more straightforward reading is that Harrington's political intention in putting into the mouth of his Lord Archon the Lord Protector's own earlier words was to draw attention to *Oceana*'s claim to be furnishing Cromwell with the means for fulfilment of his own frequently stated ambitions. In relation to a work intended to appeal to many constituencies, and

---

[64] Toland, *Life of Harrington* p. xviii–xix.
[65] The most important exception is Norbrook's *Writing the English Republic* pp. 363–74. This emphasises Harrington's royalist as well as republican personal contacts and concludes that *Oceana* 'Virgilianized republicanism' for Protectoral consumption.
[66] Worden, '*Oceana*: Origins and Aftermath' pp. 122–3.

containing an element of counsel, even if Harrington believed Cromwell to be a hypocrite, all that such an interpretation assumes is that he did not believe that the Lord Protector took that view of himself.

In another more important part of the same speech Cromwell had said of the *Instrument of Government*: 'The Gentlemen that undertook to frame this Government did consult divers days together . . . How to frame somewhat that might give us settlement . . . I was not privy to their councils . . . [but] When they had finished their model in some measure . . . they became communicative.'[67] Not only is the *content* of *Oceana* unique among republican works, in sharing this primary ambition of 'settlement'. It is a no less singular feature of its *form* that it is a 'model'. Of the 'four parts' of which the text is composed, 'The Modell of the Commonwealth' accounts for over 80 per cent of the work.[68] In his 'Epistle to the Reader' Harrington claimed to have been 'not yet two years about it', that is to say, he began work shortly after promulgation of the *Instrument*. Partly for this reason, and partly because of problems during the printing process, he was deeply apologetic about the state of the text ('I am quite out of countenance at my worke'), which listed 159 errors. Yet while, therefore, 'the Discourses [that is, the other three parts of the work] be full of crudities', readers were assured that 'the Modell hath had perfect concoction'.[69]

In fact *Oceana*'s thirty numbered 'orders', dealing with similar electoral, political and military arrangements, are entirely explicable as a thought-through (and argued-through) replacement for the half-baked *Instrument*'s thirty-eight.[70] 'Shew me another intire Government consisting but of thirty orders . . . If you stir your hand, there go more nerves and bones into the motion; If you play, you have more Cards in the pack . . . [whereas] in a Commonwealth . . . where she is not perfect . . . every houre will produce a new Order.'[71] Yet such formal properties of the text, emphasised in the 1656 editions (of which there were two) by a table of contents in bold face, almost disappear in the modern *Political Works*. The contents pages of this, while listing the seven chapter titles of the editor's 'Historical Introduction', do not list the chapter titles of Harrington's own works. Within *Oceana*, Harrington's own wide-spaced, large-font table of contents is rendered as a continuation of the small-font, single-spaced text of his Introduction.[72] In addition to failing to communicate what Harrington himself considered crucial features of the work's *structure*, this also has the effect of making

[67] Cromwell, *Letters and Speeches* vol. III, p. 47. [68] Harrington, *Oceana* (1656) p. 1.
[69] James Harrington, *The Commonwealth of Oceana* (1656), printed for D. Pakeman, Epistle.
[70] Kenyon, *Stuart Constitution* pp. 308–13. [71] Harrington, *Oceana* (1656) pp. 180–1.
[72] Harrington, *Political Works*, ed. Pocock. pp. vii–viii, 160.

Oceana look much more like standard republican prose polemic than it was. Yet the formal features of Harrington's work, in addition to being unique, are inseparable from its claim to be, not polemic, but philosophy, and from the claim of 'The Modell' to offer, not simply settlement, but one the 'perfection' of which may render it 'immortal'.[73]

This is certainly the context into which Harrington later placed his intervention in *The Examination of James Harrington*:

> Oliver . . . having started up into the throne, his officers (as pretending to be for a commonwealth) kept a murmuring, at which he told them that he knew not what they meant, nor themselves; but let any of them show him what they meant by a commonwealth (or that there was any such thing) they should see that he sought not himself; the Lord knew he sought not himself, but to make good the cause. Upon this some sober men came to me and told me: if any man in England could show what a commonwealth was, it was myself. Upon this persuasion, I wrote; and after I had written, Oliver never answered his officers as he had done before.[74]

This suggests that Harrington's work was solicited by one or more officers, or 'some sober men' in contact with them, and that its first intended reader was the Lord Protector. In this context Harrington wrote not, like Vane, to claim that Cromwell sought himself, but rather to show him what a commonwealth was, and that there *was any such thing*. As a model of government *Oceana* contributed to a recent history of constitution-making associated with the army. Before the *Instrument* the most important such blueprint was the *Heads of Proposals* (1647). This was a rival to the victorious parliament's *Newcastle Propositions*, and it was followed in turn by the three Leveller *Agreements of the People*. We have encountered Harrington's view of the second *Agreement* in chapter 6 (and see chapter 14). Unlike the *Instrument*, his 'Modell' was not the work of a cabal of officers. Nor, however, did it expose the exact civil philosophy informing the constitution to the partisan opinion of Vane's republican convention. '[W]heras a book or a building hath not been known to attain perfection, if it had not had a sole author or architect, a commonwealth . . . is of the like nature.' Of this 'fabric' the sole author was, of course, Harrington himself. For political

---

[73] The discussion of 'the model qualities' of the text by T. R. W. Kubik ('How Far the Sword? Militia Tactics and Politics in the *Commonwealth of Oceana*', *History of Political Thought*, 19, 2 (1998) pp. 186–92) discerns a tension between 'philosophical' and 'practical' modelling. Yet it is an implication of Harrington's philosophy that constitutions must be precisely related to their practical circumstances. In the words of Charles Blitzer, *Oceana* was 'an elaborate attempt to translate abstract political principles into a workable governmental system. Every institution, device, and arrangement . . . is dictated by some theoretical consideration.' Blitzer, *Immortal Commonwealth* p. 208.

[74] Harrington, *The Examination of James Harrington* p. 859.

purposes, however, this lawgiver was the Lord Archon, and there followed a further apologia for the dissolution of the Rump:

My lord general, being clear in these points and the necessity of some other course than would be thought upon by the parliament, appointed a rendezvous of the army, where he spoke his sense agreeable to these preliminaries, with such success unto the soldiery that the parliament was soon after deposed; and himself . . . created, by the universal suffrage of the army, Lord Archon.[75]

In that 'art whereby my Lord Archon' subsequently 'framed the model of the commonwealth of Oceana', he was assisted by a Council of Legislators, who in addition to ransacking 'the mines of ancient prudence' engaged in what falsely appeared to be a process of public consultation. This persuaded 'the people, who were neither safely to be admitted unto, nor conveniently to be excluded from' such a process, to believe that the Model was 'no other than that whereof they themselves had been the makers'.[76] It was because English parliaments had been, for Harrington, part of the problem, rather than the solution, that *Oceana* is not addressed, like the works of Streater, Nedham and Vane, to the people, or to parliamentarians in particular. What was addressed to Cromwell was the formula for a 'perfectly equal commonwealth' to be enacted by a single lawgiver, but in a way capable of conferring upon it popular legitimacy.

While railing against those 'of Levelling principles' the Lord Protector had asserted 'As to the Authority of the Nation; to the Magistracy; to the Ranks and Orders of men . . . A nobleman, a gentleman, a yeoman; "the distinction of these:" that is a good interest of the Nation, and a great one!'[77] When *Oceana* described the 'mixture of . . . monarchy, aristocracy, and democracy' as 'the doctrine of the ancients', and insisted that that 'only is good', this was juxtaposed to the doctrine of Hobbes, who 'is positive that they all are deceived, and that there is no other government in nature than one of the three'. Whereas Nedham and Streater had accentuated the anti-aristocratic bias already to be found in Machiavelli, in elucidating his own 'principles of authority' Harrington agreed with the Lord Protector, insisting: 'There is something first in the making of a *Common-wealth*, then in the governing of her, and last of all in the leading of her Armies . . . peculiar unto the Genius of a Gentleman.'[78]

In addition to its constitutional formula, *Oceana* speaks to most of the government's other concerns. If Streater was correct that the dissolution

[75] Harrington, *Oceana*, in *Political Works* p. 207.   [76] Ibid. pp. 208–9.
[77] Cromwell, speech of 4 September 1654 in *Letters and Speeches* vol. III p. 21.
[78] Harrington, *Oceana*, in *Political Works* p. 162; Harrington, *Oceana* (1656) p. 25.

of the Rump was animated partly by concern about the army and its role in politics being cut down to size, *Oceana* addressed this anxiety. The commonwealth of Oceana is not simply a militarised polity, but a militarised society. Taking up a theme from Aristotle and Machiavelli, but amplifying it, for Oceana's citizen-soldiers (divided into 'horse' and 'foot') military and political participation are intertwined. That this is a genuine citizen militia entails another republican amendment to the existing constitution in the interests of stability and longevity. Here, however, a political issue which had informed the breakdown into military conflict in 1642 is addressed in the context of contemporary political developments (parliament having passed a Bill establishing a 'Select Militia' in October 1656).[79] At the same time, as befits the circumstances attending the generation of Harrington's work, Oceana's military mission is celebrated in the scriptural language characteristic of the Lord Protector's own army (and speeches). In the words of the Lord Archon,

My dear lords, Oceana *is as the rose of Sharon, and the lily of the valley . . . She is comely as the tents of Kedar, and terrible as an army with banners. Her neck is as the tower of David, builded for an armoury, whereon there hang a thousand bucklers and shields of mighty men . . . Arise, queen of the earth; arise, holy spouse of Jesus. For lo, the winter is past, the rain is over and gone.*[80]

In response to the recent military setback at Hispaniola, Oceana is a commonwealth for expansion. This expansionist mission is described in godly and apocalyptic language. More generally, *Oceana* makes extensive use of the Old Testament. It is neither Athens nor Rome which is Harrington's constitutional exemplar among the ancients (as Venice is among the moderns) but the commonwealth of Israel (and secondly Sparta). 'Now whether I have rightly transcribed these principles of a commonwealth out of nature, I shall appeal unto God and to the world. Unto God in the fabric of the commonwealth of Israel, and unto the world in the universal series of ancient prudence.'[81] Concerning matters of religious worship, breaking with the commonwealthsmen, Harrington opposes the attempt to separate civil and spiritual government. Rather he combines a national church, presided over by a state Council of Religion, with liberty for peaceful local 'gathered congregations' to meet separately from it. Again this was in conformity with existing arrangements under the Protectorate. As

---

[79] Kubik, 'How Far the Sword?' pp. 197–9.
[80] James Harrington, 'The Model of the Commonwealth', in *Oceana*, in *Political Works* p. 333.
[81] Harrington, 'The Preliminaries', in *Political Works* p. 174 (and pp. 174–86).

Mark Goldie put it, 'Cromwell's church was a judicious marriage of con-gregationalist Independency and Erastian centralism. So was Harrington's proposed church.'[82]

More broadly Harrington's agrarian law, with its associated rhetoric against covetousness, was his principal contribution towards interregnum (Christian humanist) social reform. At the same time 'The Modell' applied itself to the reshaping of not only central but local government. In his speech of 12 September 1654, Cromwell had claimed that his 'commission' and 'express approbation' came not only from 'Providence, in the sight of God', but from 'many Cities and Boroughs and Counties . . . from the County General-Assizes – the Grand Jury, in the name of the Noblemen, Gentlemen, Yeomen and Inhabitants . . . [by whom] all the Justice admin-istered in the nation hath been . . . all Justices of the Peace . . . All the Sheriffs in England are my witnesses'. In pursuit of its own 'ministry from God' it was from the units of local government ('orbs', 'galaxies', 'tribes', 'tropics', 'hundreds' and 'shires') and their officers (justices of the peace, jurymen, coroners, high constables, lords high sheriff, lieutenants, custos rotulorum, phylarchs, conductors) that Oceana's power was conveyed as 'sap from the root . . . unto [all] the branches of magistracy or sovereign power'.[83]

Finally the Harringtonian formula for healing and settling spoke directly to the government's security agenda, being proof against the sedition being fed both by royalists (seeking to reinstate Gothic prudence), and by Levellers/commonwealthsmen ('such sport was the destruction of Athens'). This had resulted most recently in the imposition of the Major Gener-als. Alone among republicans Harrington claimed to have extinguished the possibility of rebellion. This was, first, because political interest was a function of material interest, so that in a state with a popular superstruc-ture, reflecting a popular balance of dominion in the foundation, all parties would be admitted, and none would have an incentive to rebel. In addition, however, should any be so misguided as to oppose their own interest, the constitution with its many safeguards was proof against anything they could do. In this way an equal commonwealth, more effectively than Hobbes's *Leviathan*, deprived sedition of both its interest and its power:

---

[82] Goldie, 'The Civil Religion of James Harrington' p. 207; on the Cromwellian religious settlement see Woolrych, 'Historical Introduction' pp. 30–2.

[83] Harrington, *Oceana*, in *Political Works* p. 334; on this local government dimension see (in addition to chapter 3 above) J. C. Davis, 'Political Thought during the English Revolution', in Barry Coward (ed.), *A Companion to Stuart Britain* (Oxford, 2003) p. 391.

It is the government which, attaining unto perfect equality, hath such a libration in the frame of it, that no man living can show which way any man or men in or under it can contract any such interest or power as should be able to disturb the commonwealth with sedition; wherefore an equal commonwealth is that only which is without flaw and containeth in it the full perfection of government.[84]

In all of these ways *Oceana* identified the underlying causes of England's political instability and fixed them. The first of Harrington's two 'great discoveries' secured the foundation by preventing any further change in the balance of dominion by an agrarian law. The second secured the superstructure by separating debate from voting, and so ending that culture of democratic oratory the destructive consequences of which had been on show in English parliaments, as well as in ancient Athens.[85] The first was something the Protectorate had never even considered. The second involved a Venetian makeover of the Protectoral principle of separation of powers. In all of these respects Harrington rejected what he saw as the constitutional extremism, and political egotism, of Hobbes on the one hand and defenders of the Rump on the other. It is nevertheless crucial that *Oceana*'s model was republican in shape.[86] This was a matter of material necessity, determined by the balance of dominion. Amid the rip tide dragging the Protectorate back towards monarchy, *Oceana* sought to be the one viable republican alternative standing between the failing *Instrument* and the looming *Humble Petition and Advice*.

As the title of Vane's *A Healing Question* reminds us, *Oceana* was not the only republican act of Protectoral counsel. Yet it was the only one to make a systematic attempt to transcend party. Thus, like *A Healing Question*, *Oceana* spoke to the grievances of those alienated by the dissolution of the Rump, providing for an end to Protectoral government and the reinstitution of a republic. Unlike Vane, however, Harrington also spoke to the concerns animating the dissolution itself, subjecting the political process to constitutional controls, at once ferocious and irrevocable, making a restoration of monarchy, or any other effect of self-destructive popular folly, impossible. Under the circumstances Cromwell's response, as described by Toland, must have been more than a little galling:

---

[84] Harrington, *Oceana*, in *Political Works* p. 180; see Davis, 'Equality in an Unequal Commonwealth' pp. 238–9.

[85] Scott, 'Peace of Silence'.

[86] For a contrasting monarchical formula for settlement see *A Copy of a Letter Written to an Officer of the Army by A true Commonwealths-man, and no COURTIER, Concerning The Right and Settlement of our present Government and Governors* (19 March 1656/7).

[H]e did accordingly inscribe it to OLIVER CROMWEL, who, after the perusal of it, said . . . that what he got by the Sword he would not quit for a little paper Shot: adding . . . that he approv'd the Government of a single Person as little as any of 'em, but that he was forc'd to take upon him the Office of a High Constable, to preserve the Peace among the several Partys in the Nation, since he saw that being left to themselves, they would never agree to any certain form of Government, and would only spend their whole Power in defeating the Designs, or destroying the Persons of one another.[87]

[87] Toland, *Life of Harrington* p. xx.

CHAPTER 14

The good old cause, 1658–1660

Where is this goodly tower of a Commonwealth, which the English
boasted they would build to overshaddow kings, and be another *Rome*
in the west? The foundation indeed they laid gallantly; but fell into
a wors confusion, not of tongues, but of factions, then those at the
tower of *Babel*; and have left no memorial of thir work behinde them
remaining, but in the common laughter of *Europ*. Which must needs
redound the more to our shame, if we but look on our neighbours
the United Provinces, to us inferior in all outward advantages; who
notwithstanding, in the midst of greater difficulties, courageously,
wisely, constantly went through with the same work, and are setl'd in
all the happie enjoiments of a potent and flourishing Republic to this
day.

Milton, The Readie and Easie Way (2nd edn, 1660).[1]

What I have spoken, is the language of that which is not call'd amiss
the good Old Cause.

Ibid.[2]

THE REPUBLICAN MOMENT, 1659–1660

The failure in practice of Harrington's *Oceana* was not surprising. By comparison with the brief and prosaic working constitution it aspired to replace,
the self-conscious wit, baroque complexity and fantastic elaboration of
Oceana's 'orders' were hardly designed for ready absorption.[3] That this text
aspired to be not simply a constitution, but also both literature and civil

---

[1] Milton, *The Readie and Easie Way*, 2nd edn (1660) p. 423.   [2] Ibid. p. 462.
[3] A fact mocked by Nedham in the *Mercurius Politicus* satires on Utopian projects, nos. 352–4, 5–26
March 1657, although he included among the party seeking a cure for the 'many a Gudgeon . . . swim-
ming in the Brain' not only Harrington and Hobbes but 'the *High Notionall-Knight* . . . and
the wondrous wise Republican called *Mercurius Politicus* (who served up the Politicks in Sippets)'
(no. 352, p. 7644). Nedham's conclusion (no. 354, p. 7674) that 'there is a necessity of a settlement,
and . . . it matters not what the Form be, so we attain the ends of Government', could hardly have
been better contrived to infuriate the author of *Oceana*.

philosophy (in a word, 'art') substantially accounts for the contested history of its reception. Accordingly, demands were soon heard for a brief translation into English (*The Art of Lawgiving*, February 1659). In this Harrington was already to be found 'appealing' on behalf of his 'model . . . to the present or the next age'.[4]

In addition to its inaccessibility of form, there were also the challenges of *Oceana's* content. Contingency and faction furnished the texture of contemporary politics. Harrington invited the politically engaged to see themselves as the problem, and *Oceana* as the solution. A constitution proof against the sedition of any person or party entailed a radical reduction in the power of every group, in favour of that of the constitution itself. Thus the Protector, and supporters of the Protectorate, were invited to dissolve that constitution. Royalists were asked to renounce their dreams of restoration, and Rumpers like Haselrig and Scot the power both of a single chamber, and of their oratory within it. Similarly the ecclesiastical settlement of *Oceana* called for compromise from both independents and their opponents. The principal incentive offered by Harrington for such self-denial was permanent peace and settlement. Although these were universally valued, they were not the primary values animating the good old cause.

Nevertheless, *Oceana's* impact upon the terms of contemporary republican debate was immediate and enduring. Two ideas, in particular, became part of the arsenal of the commonwealthsmen. The first was Harrington's 'discovery' that a government's superstructure was determined by the 'balance of dominion in the foundation'. The second, more controversial, was his insistence that the only lasting solution to England's troubles was to be found in a reliance, not upon good men, but upon good orders. Thus was *Oceana* melted down from a 'model' to one or two key ideas, and from its ambition to transcend 'party' to furnishing ammunition for one of those parties, and especially one group within it. In this way it was absorbed by that culture of polemic which it had sought to replace. This was, moreover, a process which Harrington, and more importantly Henry Neville, to some extent assisted. This is why interpretations of *Oceana* from the standpoint of the 'Harringtonian moment' of 1659–60 tend to underestimate the independence of its original intention, and the interpretative significance of its formal structure. At the same time, however, *Oceana's* impact also owed a good deal to its philosophical pretensions. If these proved a barrier to the text's success in its own terms, which required its adoption as a whole, they

---

[4] Harrington, *The Art of Lawgiving* p. 692.

nevertheless lent new status to its key ideas, many developed from within the broader commonwealth tradition.

One measure of this status was that republican engagement with Harringtonian ideas in 1659–60 was general, rather than being confined to fellow-subscribers like Neville or Adam Baynes. That a figure like Vane, with his independent status and his ideological distance from Harrington, should nevertheless frame his *A Needful Corrective* (May 1659) as a letter to him, underlines his standing. Although outstanding studies exist, particularly of Harrington's impact, the republican writing of this year in general has not always been taken seriously.[5] Few of these ideas were new, and against a backdrop of intensifying intra-republican conflict, it is difficult for historians to avoid begging the main question by seeing the restoration of monarchy as inevitable. Yet here as in general institutional instability was a fruitful intellectual context. The death of Oliver Cromwell (September 1658), the calling of a new Protectoral parliament which failed to exclude republicans (January 1659), the fall of the Protectorate and restoration of the Rump (May 1659), and finally the collapse of the restored republic (October 1659–April 1660) all proved powerful stimuli to argument. Within this context what Colin Davis called this '*annus mirabilis* of Harringtonian expectation' was in fact the '*annus mirabilis*' of republican writing more generally.[6] In this last moment of hope, and then of despair, republican polemicists drew upon the full ideological heritage of 'the good old cause' to which Harrington himself had made the most ambitious contribution.

THE FALL OF THE PROTECTORATE, SEPTEMBER 1658–APRIL 1659

One consequence of the death of Oliver, in the inheritance of the Protectorship by his son, was a deepening of the monarchical profile of that institution. At the same time, in Richard Protectoral monarchy acquired a personal face ('an amiable countenance, so unlike his father's')[7] incapable of securing that succession. The first challenge faced by the regime came from republicanism within the army. Even the loyal address presented to Richard by Fleetwood and two hundred other officers on 21 September 1658

---

[5] For the politics of 1659–60 as a context for this writing see Woolrych, 'Historical Introduction' pp. 1–228; and Woolrych, *Britain in Revolution 1625–1660* (Oxford, 2002) Part 6. For Harrington's impact upon the political situation see Worden, '*Oceana*: Origins and Aftermath' pp. 126–38. For Harrington's ideological impact more generally, see Russell Smith, *Harrington* pp. 78–150; Pocock, 'Historical Introduction' pp. 100–27; Davis, *Utopia and the Ideal Society* pp. 242–276; Cotton, *Harrington* pp. 127–220.

[6] Davis, *Utopia and the Ideal Society* p. 243.　　[7] Woolrych, 'Historical Introduction', p. 8.

reminded him of the adherence professed by his father to 'that good old Cause and Interest of God and his People'.[8] During October and November republican agitation intensified, inside the army and outside it, and came to centre upon the London house of Sir Henry Vane. On 30 November Secretary Thurloe reported to Henry Cromwell,

The commonwealth's-men have their daily meetinges, disputeinge what kinde of comonwealth they shall have, takeinge it for granted, they may picke and choose; and they hope to prepare a part of the armye to fall in with them, wherein I hope they will be deceived; although I must needs say, I like not the aspect of things, and my feares are greater then my hopes.[9]

It was the decision taken to summon a parliament for late January 1659 that would move such discussions to centre stage. It also transposed them to a contested environment, since the republicans who to some extent dominated debate in Richard's parliament were in fact outnumbered more than two to one. Accordingly they could delay recognition of the governing constitution, with its single person and Other House, but they could not prevent it. In the meantime, however, republicans in the Commons, including the old Rumpers Haselrig, Scot, Vane and Neville, did succeed in publicly articulating the views of a republican opposition, and in providing an institutional focus for those petitioners and pamphleteers outside the House who were also doing so. In opposition, moreover, lay some unity, so that in some ways the months January to May 1659 constituted the republican revival's finest hour.

Thus on the eve of the session one pamphlet, published 'for the good and information of Parliament, Army and People', recounted *The Arguments Urged by the late Protector against the Government of this Nation by a King or a Single Person*.[10] Inside the House Haselrig responded to the introduction of 'An Act of Recognition of His Highnesses right and title' on 1 February with a history of England since the conquest, lasting several hours. Not one to underestimate the importance of his role, Haselrig explained:

It was a glorious work of our Saviour to die on the cross for our spirituals. This is as glorious a work for our civils, to put an end to the King and Lords. I appeal to all, if [under the Rump] the nation, that had been blasted and torn, began not exceedingly to flourish . . . Trade flourished; the City of London grew rich; we were the most potent by sea that ever was known in England.

[8] Ibid. p. 12.   [9] Quoted in ibid. p. 15.
[10] *A Brief Relation Containing an Abreviation of the Arguments Urged by the Late Protector* (January 1658).

Since the dissolution, however, 'We see what a confusion we are in. We have not prospered. Our army at Jamaica prospered not. The trade and glory of the nation are much diminished.'[11]

This praise of the Rump was echoed by Thomas Scot: 'We sat four or five years in the posture of a Commonwealth . . . We never bid fairer for being masters of the whole world . . . [T]ime well was, when two kingdoms were conquered, and the Dutch *tantum non*, by the counsels of a Parliament and some twenty of the Council.' These claims were accompanied by warm commendations, from Livy, of Roman anti-monarchism. If the English people were to renounce their proven capacity for self-government 'let us set up the Court of Wards again, not for our children but for our selves'.[12] Henry Vane added his own account of the 'taking away of kingship' and subsequent attempt 'to have resort to the foundation of all just power, and to create and establish a free state; to bring the people out of bondage'. He referred to the other successful contemporary example of Holland, as well as the counter-example of 'the impatience of the people of Israel: unless with the Israelites, we will return to Egypt, weary of our journey to Canaan'.[13] Vane praised the Rump's military successes and its scheme for Anglo-Scots union ('We conquered them, and gave them the fruit of our conquest in making them free denizens with us'). Above all he joined other republicans in opposing the 'thing called kingly power' in what guise soever, 'especially to serve a single person, or the interest of a few courtiers or flatterers . . . If the settlement be to settle tyranny and slavery, I hope you will not give money to maintain it.'[14]

Praise of the Rump was interrupted by Henry Neville ('Let us not return to the Government of the Long Parliament. It was an oligarchy, detested by all men that love a Commonwealth . . . it was not the Government contended for'). Neville redirected attention to the more general phenomenon of interregnum instability, caused by prior alteration of the balance of lands: 'The gentry do not . . . depend upon the peerage. The balance is in the gentry. They have all the lands.' Thus the only constitution which would end this instability was a mixture of 'a single person, senate, and popular assembly', though 'not King, Lords, and Commons': 'among popular assemblies in other commonwealths, there was an assembly to propound laws, and another to enact them, and a single person to put all in execution'.[15] In early May a pamphlet of which Neville was probably one author would use Scot's metaphor of wardship in an entirely different way. Far

---

[11] *Diary of Thomas Burton* vol. III, pp. 97, 99, 102.   [12] Ibid. pp. 111, 112, 473, 336.
[13] Ibid. pp. 173, 176–7.   [14] Ibid. pp. 318–19; vol. IV, pp. 178, 313.
[15] Ibid. vol. III, pp. 132–4, 229, 321; vol. IV, p. 322.

from seeing self-government as the alternative, for the authors of *The Armies Dutie* it was the function of a republican constitution to offer a political equivalent to wardship capable of saving the people from themselves:

> your Lordships dutie is no more then to contrive the best, most prudent form, and order, wherein the people may injoy their own, with the least hazard of being preyed upon by Tirants, or being disquieted by their own ignorant disorders and confusions. Your dutie to the people, is like that of a Guardian to an Heir, Not to give them an Estate, but to set down rules, how it shall be ordered for them, and they put in quiet Possession of it, to their most advantage and securitie.[16]

Neville's Harringtonian analysis was seconded by Adam Baynes ('The first thing is, to see the materials. All government is built on propriety . . . The Jewish commonwealth was founded in propriety . . . The Lacedaemonian Government was founded on propriety').[17] None of this impressed Mr Gott, who would 'not go back to times past, nor look forward to *Oceana*'s Platonical Commonwealth; things that are not, and that never shall be.'[18] Meanwhile, even Neville joined Vane in praising the Anglo-Scots union and the government responsible for it. And, despite these differences in theory, Haselrig, Neville, Vane and Scot co-operated in practice to oppose the *Humble Petition and Advice*, receive republican petitions, demand the release of republican prisoners, investigate the accusation of enslavement of free-born English persons, lament the decay of trade, and oppose Protectoral foreign policy.[19] The extended debates upon the situation in a Baltic sound crucial for English naval supplies frequently juxtaposed the military fortunes of 1649–53 with those of 1655. With the restoration of the Rump, in May 1659, Vane would superintend a revival of republican foreign and naval policy.[20]

On 16 February a pamphlet called *The Leveller* furnished a reminder of the pre-Harrington Machiavelli, and a more highly developed restatement of the one-time fusion of Leveller and republican principles.[21] In the process it exhibited a characteristic feature of the 1659 literature of the 'good old cause': its amalgamation of the classical republican idea of the government of laws, rather than of the will of men, with the parliamentary and subsequently Lockean language of 'life, liberties and estates'. *The Leveller*

---

[16] M[arten] and others, *The Armies Dutie* p. 13.

[17] *Diary of Thomas Burton* vol. III, pp. 147–8. [18] Ibid. p. 144.

[19] Ibid. pp. 369–403, 452–93, 578; vol. IV, pp. 152–7, 255–73 (and see chapter 4, above).

[20] Scott, *Algernon Sidney and the English Republic* pp. 124–42.

[21] Authorship of *The Leveller* is attributed to John Wildman by Maurice Ashley, *John Wildman* pp. 136–7, and Austin Woolrych, 'The Good Old Cause and the Fall of the Protectorate', *Cambridge Historical Journal* 13, 2 (1957), p. 158. See also Pocock, 'Historical Introduction' pp. 104–5.

compared those 'branded with the name of *Levellers*' by would-be tyrants
among 'some that were then Grandees, in the Parliament and Army', with
'the *Grachi* in *Rome* . . . to by such policy perish by the Peoples hands,
whose liberties they sought to vindicate'.[22] Among the blameless principles
animating these men was 'that the Government of *England* ought to be
by Laws, and not by Men . . . that *English* men ought to fear nothing
but God, and the breach of the Laws, not to depend upon the will of a
Court and their Council, for the security of themselves and their estates'.[23]
Further, all government ought to be in the hands of 'the people's deputies
in Parliament, to be chosen by them successively . . . 'tis the first principle
of a People's liberty, that they shall not be bound but by their own consent'.
There were, in this respect, 'two opposite interests, always at contention, in
the composing of laws . . . the interest of the Monarch and his family . . . to
over top the people . . . [and] the common and equal good of the whole
Nation'. Had the latter prevailed in recent years

then so many Fatherless and Widdows had not now been weeping for their lost
Husbands, and Fathers in *Jamaica*, and other forraign Countries, nor had so many
families been ruined, nor *England* impoverished by the loss of Trades occasioned by
the *Spanish* War, begun and prosecuted upon private interests or fancies, without
advice or consent of the People in Parliament.[24]

The third Leveller fundamental was equality before the law, and the fourth
an insistence upon a citizen army in 'a Constant Military posture, by and
under the commands of their Parliament', making unnecessary the 'hire
[of] Mercenary Souldiers'. It was shown by the history of Rome that it is
'prudent and safe for the People to be masters of their own Arms' because
'when the People which are owners of a Country, are disposed into a Military
form . . . they are sensible that they have more at stake than a daily stipend,
and are in no hopes to better their conditions . . . by betraying their
Country to Forraigners'.[25] The final Leveller fundamental was 'that all
God's People might enjoy their spiritual Christian Liberties, in worshiping
God according to their consciences . . . by whose dictates God commands
them to be guided . . . for the inward truth of mens Religion . . . is beyond
the Magistrates Power or Judgement'.[26]

Four days later, on 20 February, came the publication of Harrington's *The Art of Lawgiving*, plausibly seen by John Pocock as a deliberate
accompaniment to the Harringtonian speeches of Neville and others in

---

[22] *The Leveller: or, The Principles and Maxims concerning Government and Religion, Which are Asserted
by those that are commonly called, Levellers* (16 February 1659) p. 4.
[23] Ibid. p. 5.   [24] Ibid. pp. 6–7.   [25] Ibid. pp. 8–9.   [26] Ibid. pp. 9–10, 13.

the Commons.[27] This was divided into three books, the first recapitulating the principles informing *Oceana*'s Preliminaries, and the second devoting much more space than *Oceana* to the '*Commonwealth of the Hebrews*'. At the outset of the third, a summary of his 'Model of Popular Government', Harrington confessed his dilemma. The science of anatomy was so complex that 'the discourses of anatomists . . . are understood by so few that I may say they are not understood by any'. Yet 'Certain it is that the delivery of a model of government . . . is no less than political anatomy. If you come short of this, your discourse is altogether ineffectual; if you come home, you are not understood.'[28] In seeking upon this occasion to 'come home' more briefly Harrington again composed his discourse, in part, as a critique of the existing quasi-monarchical constitution. Once again his response was not simply that England must now be a commonwealth, but that it was, and had been for some time.

Because its foundation was the balance of dominion 'a commonwealth is not made by men but by God'. In this sense 'actually and positively England is a commonwealth . . . the question of the future state of it cometh not one whit upon the matter, which is already granted, but upon the form only. A commonwealth for the matter makes herself.'[29] Nevertheless, upon the capacity or otherwise of England's governors to grasp the form appropriate to this matter rested its hopes of ending 'a matter of a dozen years' of political instability comparable to 'The seditions under the commonwealth of Rome . . . from the time of the Gracchi'.[30] When, in his discussion of the context and causes of this instability, Harrington even had time to criticise *The Leveller*, published four days before his own work was completed, his perception of the distance between his own republicanism and Levellerism led him immodestly to ascribe its Machiavellianism to what the author 'had gathered out of *Oceana*'.[31] Yet as we have seen, some Leveller and most republican writing drew upon Machiavelli's *Discorsi* with far less amendment than did *Oceana* itself.

The only Leveller provision with which Harrington did not propose to argue was (in his doubtful summation) 'a national religion and liberty of conscience'. It was earlier in this same week that the long-silent Milton addressed 'to the Parlament of the Commonwealth of England' *A Treatise of Civil Power in Ecclesiastical Causes: Shewing That it is not lawfull for any power on earth to compell in matters of Religion.*[32] This was to take up an argument by which Levellers and most republicans were united, and for

---

[27] Pocock, 'Historical Introduction' pp. 101–4.   [28] Harrington, *The Art of Lawgiving* p. 656.
[29] Ibid. p. 704.   [30] Ibid. p. 692.   [31] Ibid. pp. 657–9.
[32] Milton, *Complete Prose Works* vol. VII, pp. 238–9.

which the principal spokesman in the House was Vane. Within a few days of
the Rump's restoration in May a committee had been established, including
Vane and Haselrig, to consider the cases of people who had been imprisoned
on grounds of conscience.[33] A day before the publication of Milton's tract,
a petition directed similarly 'To the Parliament of the Commonwealth of
England', with over twenty thousand signatures, called for the restoration to
that body of 'the supream Power and Trust, which the People (the Original
of all just Power) commit unto them'. Inside the House Haselrig, Scot,
Vane and Neville all called (unsuccessfully) for a vote of thanks.[34] Over
the following two months a series of pamphlets, republican and godly,
reminded parliamentarians and soldiers of the glorious history of the good
old cause. By the beginning of April Fleetwood and others of the General
Council of Officers were meeting with republicans such as Ludlow, with
the knowledge of Haselrig, Scot and Vane. In the words of Scot: 'there is a
good old cause, if their meetings be, to manage that, I shall not be against
them'.[35]

RESTORATION OF THE RUMP, MAY–SEPTEMBER 1659

The military coup which removed the Protectorate and its parliament came
on 21 April. Over the following two weeks, meetings continued between
the Council of Officers and republicans at Vane's house, leading to the
restoration of the Rump on 7 May. At the same time a flood of mainly
republican propaganda poured from the presses. One admonished the army
to '*remember from whence you are fallen . . . return and stand to, or fall with
the GOOD OLD CAUSE . . . [and] Recal (for the prosecution of what is
proposed) that Parliament who changed the Government from Kingly to a
Commonwealth, and whom the late Protector interrupted April 20, 1653*'.[36]
Another echoed this demand, both because this was 'the general Desire and
Expectation of most of the Officers and Souldiers of the *Army*, and of those
well-affected persons in the City and parts adjacent, who have adhered to
the parliaments Cause', and also because 'it is not sufficient (especially as
our Case stands) that those who . . . have the Management of publique
Matter, be pious and well-affected persons, but they should also be judicious
and prudent persons of great skill and experience in State affairs'.[37] A third,

---

[33] Woolrych, 'Historical Introduction' p. 74.   [34] Ibid. pp. 20–1.   [35] Ibid. pp. 59–64.

[36] *Twelve Plain Proposals Offered to the Honest and Faithful Officers and Souldiers* (28 April 1659); see also
Five Proposals Presented To the General Council of the Officers 'From many thousands Well-affected
to the Good Old Cause in and about the City of London'.

[37] *Some Reasons Humbly Proposed to the Officers of the Army, For the speedy Re-admission of the Long
Parliament Who Setled the Government In the way of a Free State* (28 April 1659) pp. 4–5.

'Directed to the surviving Members of that Parliament . . . the onely *Legal Parliament of England*', desired

That at your first *sitting down*, you may *ascertain* a *time* for your *ending*, and for the *Succession* and *Beginning* of a *new Representative*; and so settle the Foundations of our Government, as our Parliaments may be Successive, and of Course, with their certain times of their beginning and Ending; and with such Boundaries, Limitations and Powers, as all Arbitrariness in Government may be prevented, and the Rights and Freedoms of the People secured.[38]

Such appeals received the support of works like Streater's *The Continuation of this Session of Parliament Justified* (16 May 1659), the language of which also owed more to Leveller/republican commonwealth discourse, and its economic preoccupations, than to Harrington's adaptation of these. Streater's tract rehearsed the history of the '*Good Old Cause . . . viz.* Security of *Life, Liberty, and Estate*'. It celebrated the spectacular achievements of the Rump and recounted again the tyrannical motives underlying its dissolution. It was the Rump that had

settled as a Free State the most glorious Government under Heaven . . . Now . . . they begin to shew the Power, Vigour and Excellency of a *Councel* of a *Free People*: for at one and the same time they manage War with *Scotland* and *Ireland*, and passe that Act for Trade, that never to be forgotten Act, which occasioneth a Chargeable and Dangerous War with *Holland*: That Act was the Glory and Top of their great Advice; if it had been continued and duly Executed, *England* had been the most happy, and most rich People this day upon the face of the whole Earth: they had been the Ware-house of the World; the Exchange of *England* had over-ballanced all the Exchange of the World: it would have made Trading abound, and money as plentifull as dust.[39]

Against the grain of such reveries came *The Armies Dutie*. Its account of 'this righteous cause' was familiar enough. Before its apostacy the army had gloriously 'defended by arms' the principle that the English people 'ought to be governed only by the Laws: And their consciences, persons, or estates, to be at no mans will or mercy'. In pursuit of this end 'you caused the exercise of the chief Magistracie in *England* by a single person to be abolish'd, because it was dangerous . . . as well as uselesse and burdensome'.[40] However, to secure this cause for the future it was useless to trust to the government of 'good men'. It was because 'It's beyond the wisdome of man, to contrive an infallible provision, in the present age that the ruling power in the succeeding age, shall fall onlie into good mens hands' that the only

---

[38] *A Declaration of the Well-affected to The Good Old Cause* (2 May 1659).
[39] Streater, *The Continuation* pp. 11–12.   [40] M[arten] and others, *The Armies Dutie* p. 6.

'lasting bottom . . . to settle libertie and justice' lay in an 'order, or forme of Government'.[41] Secondly, the balance of property in England at the present time (a history of which was supplied) made it impossible to erect 'a Principalitie, or Monarchie'.[42] Thirdly, 'the order that hath alwaies been in effect amongst free people . . . hath been . . . They have ranked themselves into three orders, the people, the Senate, and the Magistrate, whereby they have made themselves partakers of all the benefit of the naturall Democracy, Aristocracy, and Monarchy . . . with controuls to every of their corrupt affections, unto which they were prone'.[43]

The Rump acknowledged its call: '*the Officers of the Army raised by this Parliament, calling to minde that the same Parliament, consisting of the Members which continued to sit until the 20th of April 1653. were assertors of the good old cause, and had a special presence of God with them, and were signally blessed in their work*'.[44] It pledged itself to dissolve by May the following year, and established a committee (which included Henry Neville and Henry Vane) to hear constitutional proposals.[45] The adoption of Harringtonian language had already been a minor feature of Vane's speeches in Richard's parliament.[46] In his *A Needful Corrective or Balance in Popular Government, Expressed in a Letter to James Harrington* it became the vehicle for a sympathetic critique of the Harringtonian position by an '*Advocate for the godly Man*'. Both Vane and Harrington believed in divinely authorised popular sovereignty, constituting a liberty, or 'state of free Citizens', to be juxtaposed to 'slavery and bondage'. Both agreed concerning its moral agency, 'right reason', and its constitutional expression in an 'Empire . . . of Laws, and not of Men'.[47] Yet as this reason had its origin in man's 'nature . . . as it was at first, holy and righteous', so since the fall, if we seek

that which is wanting to ballance and compleat the motion of mans will, in the exercise of its own freedome, that it is so little to be trusted and relyed on, in the pursuit of that which is the common Interest of mankind, and the publick good of humane Societies . . . we have it declared in that Scripture, which sayes, *It is not in man to order his own steps* . . . [there is] no Nation truly free that is in bondage to corruption, and alienated from the life of God by wicked works.[48]

This being the case, neither Harrington's agrarian in the foundation, nor 'the rotation and use of the Ballot' in the superstructure, was adequate

---

[41] Ibid. p. 14.   [42] Ibid. pp. 16–22.   [43] Ibid.

[44] *A Declaration of the Parliament Assembled at Westminster* (7 May 1659).

[45] Although the committee was not formally established until September, petitions were made to the House throughout the summer. Worden, '*Oceana*: Origins and Aftermath' pp. 134–5.

[46] *Diary of Thomas Burton* vol. III, p. 177: 'Though not perfect, yet . . . the foundations are laid, upon which we may build a superstructure of which we need not be ashamed.'

[47] Vane, *Needful Corrective* pp. 2–4.   [48] Ibid. pp. 6, 7.

compensation for the absence of the 'one chief Ingredient to quali-
fie . . . [people] to the exercise of the right of free Citizens . . . holiness in
principles, by way of spiritual birth'.[49] In 1659 it was more necessary than
ever to restrict citizenship to the morally and spiritually capable – adherents of the cause. In this respect the necessary lawgiver was none other than
'God and Christ himself'. Vane here agreed with many other writers who
recalled that 'The *Army* before their declension eminently declared for Jesus
Christ, and THIS THEN was the chief part of the *Good Old Cause*, viz. NO
KING BUT JESUS.' John Canne, too, urged the Rump to 'put . . . into
places . . . good men . . . such as will faithfully serve you and their Country',
avoiding 'servile mercenarie fellows . . . who (betraying their trust) sought
to betray the Commonwealth'.[50] By way of compromise, Vane proposed
that his 'Ruling Senate or Council of Elders, for the executive part of the
supreme Power', and 'Representative Body of the People', for 'the exercise of the Legislative Power', should be related as Harrington suggested,
with the former 'to propose' and the latter to 'assent or dissent'.[51] Such an
arrangement would resemble 'the practice of *Israels* Commonwealth . . . so
plainly of Divine Creation'.

Yet in *Pour Enclouer le Canon* (2 May 1659), as in *A Discourse upon
this saying*, Harrington warned against attempts to erect an oligarchy, 'not
elected by the people, but obtruded upon us under the notion of a senate or
a balance, or of religion; and it may be . . . a senate for life'. Such warnings
were echoed by the author of *Monarchy and Oligarchy prov'd parallel in
Tyranny*, who implored 'That Mr *Harrington*'s Writings be diligently and
seriously read and perused'.[52] Harrington rehearsed the unhappy history
of such arrangements in Israel, Sparta and Rome, and reiterated the need
for 'a senate . . . of three hundred, and a popular assembly of one thousand
and fifty, each for the term of three years, and to be annually changed in
one third part'.[53]

Other Harringtonian writings displayed varying levels of faithfulness to
the original model. The doctrine of the balance of dominion was used
to argue both that 'the form of Government in *England* must be new
and democratical',[54] and on the contrary, that the establishment of 'a Free-
State' in England was impossible.[55] The author of *A Model of a Democraticall*

---

[49] Ibid. p. 8. [50] John Canne, *A Seasonable Word to the Parliament-Men* (10 May 1659) pp. 3, 5.
[51] Vane, *Needful Corrective* pp. 9–10.
[52] *A Common-Wealth or Nothing; Or, Monarchy and Oligarchy prov'd parallel in Tyranny* (1659) p. 8.
[53] James Harrington, *Pour Enclouer le Canon*, in *Political Works* pp. 730–2.
[54] *A Letter from no far Countrey* (19 April 1660) pp. 13–14.
[55] *A Discourse for a King and Parliament* (1660).

Government drew heavily upon *Oceana* to separate 'the sole power of debating and proposing Lawes . . . in the Senate . . . [from] the sole Result in the Representative of the People'. All elected offices were to be subject to three-yearly rotation, including the executive 'Councell[s] of State . . . of War . . . and of Trade'.[56] On the other hand, participation in elections to 'An Assembly of a Representative of the People at *Westminster*, the 8th day of *May* next' was to be denied to 'Persons . . . that have Ayded, Abetted, or Assisted the late *King Charles* or his Son in their Warres against this *Parliament* or *Commonwealth*, unless they have given or shall give signal testimony of their good affections to the Government of these *Nations*, by way of a *Commonwealth*'.[57]

On the other side, in *An Essay in Defence of the Good Old Cause*, dated 4 July 1659, Henry Stubbe defended Vane's position against both Harrington and Richard Baxter, arguing for the separation of '*Civil*' and '*Spiritual Affairs*', a franchise limited to the 'honest party', and a Standing '*Coordinate Senate*' necessary both to control the militia and to defend liberty of conscience against that majority who opposed it.[58] In *A Letter to An Officer of the Army Concerning a Select Senate* Stubbe used Plato, Plutarch, Thucydides, Lucan, Bodin and Harrington himself to show from the histories of Sparta and Rome 'The *Necessity* and *Prudentialness* of such a *Senate*'.[59] Primarily at issue between Stubbe and Harrington was not the abstract desirability of Harrington's model, but its capacity to meet the extreme dangers posed by the present situation. This was, however, to dispute (or even fail to understand) the fundamental assumptions of Harrington's new institutional civil philosophy. Thus Stubbe, while praising Harrington's 'industry and learning' and the excellence of his '*equall Commonwealth*' in a nation morally fit for it, failed to see

how it can be imposed upon all, nor how a power can be erected over any men which is not derived from them . . . I think the *universality of this nation is not to be trusted with liberty at present*, that an *equall Common-wealth* is that whereunto we ought and may prudentially grow, but which we cannot at once fabrick, without running an extraordinary hazard of being again enslaved.[60]

---

[56] *A Model of a Democraticall government, humbly tendered to Consideration* (1659).

[57] Ibid. pp. 4–8; see Cotton, *Harrington* pp. 146–7.

[58] Stubbe, *An Essay in Defence of the Good Old Cause*, Preface p. 22; see also H[enry] S[tubbe], *The Commonwealth of Israel, or a Brief Account Of Mr Prynne's Anatomy of the Good Old Cause* (16 May 1659).

[59] Stubbe, *A Letter to An Officer of the Army Concerning a Select Senate mentioned by them in their Proposals to the late Parliament* (26 October 1659), title page, pp. 4–5.

[60] Ibid. p. 3.

'*Magistracy* . . . [being] the exercise of a *Morall power*', Stubbe picked up Harrington's metaphor of the mariner and the ship, pointing out that what was necessary for effective passage was not only 'a ship . . . well built, and ballasted, and fitted with tackling', but a crew 'vigorous . . . disciplined . . . [and] supplyed . . . by a gallantry of spirit'.[61]

With a majority of the nation favouring the return of monarchy and an end to liberty of conscience, one solution was to restrict participation in '*Mr Harrington's* modell . . . to the good people which have adhered to the *Good old cause*, and I suppose the *Common-wealth of Israel* may herein . . . become our pattern'. In fact the extent of danger posed by the present situation led Stubbe to follow Vane, and anticipate Milton's *Readie and Easie Way*, in concluding that 'I see no security but in some influencing *Senate*, who may so long continue as the necessity of the nation shall require it: for to determine them a *time of durance*, is . . . [to tell] the maligners of a *Commonwealth* . . . how long to cherish their hopes for.' Stubbe gave his reasons, from ancient history and elsewhere, for believing that such a '*Coordinate Senate*' would 'not degenerate into an *Oligarchy*'.[62] Meanwhile much literature concentrated upon that opposition to monarchy and tyranny, and religious persecution, upon which all republicans agreed.[63]

On 14 June 1659 parliament was petitioned 'to appoint a Committee to receive Mr *Harrington's* Propositions for setling the Government of this Commonwealth . . . This . . . is proposed with Mr. *Harrington's* consent.' For the committee the petition 'humbly proposed' a hundred named persons, including the Earl of Northumberland, Sir Anthony Ashley Cooper, Slingsby Bethel, Maximilian Petty, John Wildman, Richard Baxter, William Prynne and Matthew Wren.[64] Independently Harrington himself also petitioned the House.[65] At the same time there appeared perhaps the two most substantial Harringtonian works of the period. The first was *Chaos: or, A Discourse Wherein Is presented to the view of the Magistrate . . . a Frame of Government by way of a Republique, wherein is little or no danger of miscarriage, if prudently attempted, and throughly prosecuted by authority* (18 July 1659).[66] Although this model, created in 'Seven Days Work', did indeed register the impact of *Oceana*, not least in its agrarian law, it was a very independent development from that text.

[61] Ibid. pp. 4–5.   [62] Ibid. p. 7.

[63] See, for instance *A Publick Plea, Opposed to A Private Proposal* (18 May 1659); *No Return to Monarchy; and Liberty of Conscience Secured* (1659); Marchamont Nedham, *Interest Will not Lie* [Nedham], *News From Brussels* (1660).

[64] *A Proposition In Order to the Proposing of A Commonwealth or Democracie* (14 June 1659).

[65] James Harrington, *Valerius and Publicola* (1659), in *Political Works* p. 801.

[66] Discussed in Davis, *Utopia and the Ideal Society* pp. 244–54; Cotton, *Harrington* pp. 144–6.

Politically it abandoned the bicameralism of both Harrington and Vane in favour of a single-chamber parliament electing an executive Council of State.[67] More importantly, it was concerned primarily not with constitutional politics, but with economic and social government, and less with central than local government. As the basis of this effort a 'day's work' was employed establishing national, provincial, sub-provincial and parish statistical registries. To a greater degree than *Oceana*, *Chaos* applied 'herself' to the reformation and generation of local offices (including sheriffs, constables and churchwardens).[68] Private inheritance, land tenure and taxation were all reformed, and the broader consequences of economic change (including 'Pride, Tyranny and Oppression') addressed. Depopulation was diagnosed as a consequence of the dominance of London, and yet the social and economic importance of trade and manufactures (to be 'exported free from Customs and Impositions . . . for seven years') was emphasised.[69] Finally, *Chaos* was a blueprint not just for England, but for a united British commonwealth.

William Sprigge's *A Modest Plea for an Equal Common-wealth Against Monarchy* (18 September 1659) owed more to *Oceana*.[70] While Sprigge's tract did not itself 'presume . . . to Chalk out any particular modell, referring that to the wisdom of our Senators', it did commend Harrington by name, and repeat both his doctrine of 'the Ballance of lands' and the historical analysis to which it had given rise.[71] It shared Harrington's hostility to the legal and clerical professions, and his enthusiasm for an agrarian law and rotation of office. Like Harrington, though from a different perspective, it opposed what Sprigge argued was a false distinction between civil magistracy and religious ministry. As the commonwealth had witnessed the success of a godly army, so it would benefit no less from godly magistracy.[72] Politically, for Sprigge the pressing need was to keep out monarchy ('no other than a more gentle . . . expression of Tyranny'), 'Oligarchy, which is worse, nor yet . . . Anarchy, the worst of all three'.[73] Thereafter the attention of the tract, like that of *Chaos*, was directed less to the political superstructure than to its economic and social foundation. Sprigge's agrarian law was stricter than *Oceana*'s, and to a greater extent than Harrington he deplored the social consequences of economic inequality:

---

[67] *Chaos*, 'The Fourth Days Work' pp. 38–44.
[68] Ibid. pp. 5, 7–38 (The Second and Third Days Work).
[69] Ibid. pp. 1, 41–54 (The Fourth, Fifth and Sixth Days Work).
[70] Discussed by Davis, *Utopia and the Ideal Society* pp. 254–63.
[71] William Sprigge, *A Modest Plea for an Equal Common-wealth Against Monarchy* (1659) pp. 12–13, 16.
[72] Ibid. pp. 21–35. [73] Ibid. pp. 9, 18.

I know not of what temper other men may be that can relish the pleasures of their plentiful and luxuriant Estates, when so many of their own flesh lie stinking in the streets, and are clothed with rags and misery . . . Certainly the deafness of this uncharitable age to the cryes of the poor, is one of the crying sins of this Land.[74]

Sprigge developed Harrington's own hostility to primogeniture into 'An Apology for Younger Brothers, the Restitution of Gavil-kind, and relief of the Poor'.[75] In addition the tract attacked tithes, and contained Baconian proposals for the reform of the universities.[76]

Yet as proposals for reform became ever more ambitious, their practical prospects were diminishing. By September, within the Rump relations were deteriorating, as also between the House as a whole and the army. One commentator reported, 'the greatest heats that could be in words . . . between Sir [Arthur] Hazelrig and S[ir] H. Vayne, and that Mr Nevil and uthers was jeering at their division, and taking advantage of it'.[77] When in late September pressure was reapplied by army officers for consideration of the *Humble Petition* of 12 May, Haselrig reacted in an extreme way reminiscent of Denzil Holles in March 1647, branding some officers dangerous to the commonwealth. The result, on 12 October, was a stand-off between parliamentarians led by Haselrig and Scot, and army officers led by Lambert, settled to the advantage of the latter.

'ANARCHY', OCTOBER 1659–APRIL 1660

Haselrig's final political opportunity would come several months later, and would also be fumbled. As he explained to George Monck in April 1660, 'I have alwayes acted wth the authorety of parlmt and never against it and . . . have Hazarded my all to bringe the military power under the civill authorety'.[78] As a contemporary pamphlet put it, less kindly, 'Am not I Sir Arthur Haselrig the magnificent . . . more puissant than *Olphaus Megaletor*, Lord *Archon* of *Oceana*?'[79] The dissolution of October was the occasion for Milton's unpublished 'Letter to a Friend'. This expressed dismay at the second 'relapsing & so soon again backsliding' of an army that had already

---

[74] Ibid. pp. 54–6.
[75] See Joan Thirsk, 'Younger Sons in the Seventeenth Century', *History* 54 (1969) pp. 358–77. For this theme in the life as well as *Discourses* of Algernon Sidney see Scott, *Algernon Sidney and the English Republic* pp. 59–72.
[76] Sprigge, *Equal Common-wealth*, title page; Davis, *Utopia and the Ideal Society* pp. 262–3.
[77] Johnston of Wariston, *Diary*, quoted by Woolrych, 'Historical Introduction' p. 110.
[78] British Library, Egerton MS 2618, f. 71.
[79] *The Private Debates, Conferences and Resolutions of the late Rump* (1660) p. 4.

dissolved this 'old famous parlament' once 'without just autority' in 1653.[80]
It was 'scarce to be exampled among any Barbarians, that a paid army should
for . . . [such slight] cause, thus subdue the supreme power that sett them
up . . . to the sad dishonour of that army lately so renowned for the civilest
& best ordered in the world'.[81] 'Being now in Anarchy . . . The termes
to be stood on are Liberty of conscience to all professing Scripture . . .
And the Abjuracion of a single person.'[82] At this point 'whether the civill
government be an annual democracy or a perpetuall Aristocracy is too nice
a consideracion for the extremities wherein wee are & the hazard of our
safety from a common enemie, gapeing . . . to devour us'.[83] What was
necessery was some government, 'either the parlament readmitted to sitt,
or a councell of State, allowed of by the Army since they only now have
the power'.[84]

In fact the Committee of Safety, established a week later with twenty-
three members, did not claim to be any such government, but a body
charged (as ever) with establishing the basis for one. The members of the
Rump approached by Lambert and others to serve, including Vane, Ludlow
and Whitelocke, all made their excuses but remained in touch with the
committee, and in Vane's case came to play a central role in drawing up a
draft constitution excluding religion from the civil magistrate's authority.[85]
An alternative reaction to the Rump's second demise came with the establishment in October, and continuation until 'Febr[uary] 20 or 21' 1660,
of Harrington's Rota Club. Here at Miles's coffee-house in 'New Pallace-
yard' Harrington 'sate [with] his Disciples, and the Virtuosi', including
Henry Neville, John Wildman, Maximilian Petty, Sir William Petty, fellow
Royal Society member John Hoskins, Samuel Pepys and John Aubrey. We
hear from Pepys, who visited the club on 17 January, of Harrington's analysis of radical political instability by discussion of the 'state of the Roman
Government'.[86] Aubrey recorded:

The Discourses in this Kind were the most ingeniose, and smart, that ever I heard,
or expect to heare . . . the Arguments in the Parliament howse were but flatt to
it. Here we had (very formally) a *Balloting-box*, and balloted how things should
be caried . . . The room was every evening full as it could be cramm'd . . . The
Doctrine was very taking, and the more because, as to human foresight, there was

---

[80] Milton, 'A Letter to a Friend, Concerning the Ruptures of the Commonwealth', in *Complete Prose Works* vol. VII, pp. 324–5.
[81] Ibid. p. 327.   [82] Ibid. pp. 329–30.   [83] Ibid. p. 331.   [84] Ibid. p. 329.
[85] Woolrych, 'Historical Introduction' pp. 131–3.
[86] Samuel Pepys, *The Diary of Samuel Pepys*, ed. Robert Latham and William Matthews (1970), Volume I: 1660, pp. 20–1; see Russell Smith, *Harrington* pp. 100–8.

no possibility of the King's returne. But the greatest part of the Parliament-men perfectly hated this designe of *Rotation by Balloting*; for they were cursed Tyrants, and in love with their Power, and 'twas death to them, except 8 or 10, to admitt of this way, for H. Nevill proposed it in the Howse, and made it out to them, that except they embraced that Modell of Goverment [*sic*] they would be ruind.[87]

These disagreements were lost upon the author of *Twenty Three Decrees From the Committee of Safety of Oceana*, which depicted 'the Politick Casuists of the *Coffee Club*' liaising with 'the Committee of Safety at *Whitehall*' in pursuit of 'an Invention to escape *Tyburne*, if ever the Law be restored'. Other decrees provided 'That *Haringtons* Aphorismes and other Political slips be recommended to the *English* Plantation in *Jamaica*', that Johnston of Wariston and Hugh Peters 'Survey the *Government* of the *Moon*', and 'That if Sir *Arthur Haselrig* acquire his *Summum bonum*, which is to die with his *Arse* towards *Wallingford* House [headquarters of the Council of Officers], his Heirs may have the Liberty to wipe his breech with the Commission he gave himself.'[88] Yet the further deterioration of the political situation, between the march of General Monck from Scotland, re-establishment of the Rump (in December) and readmission of those members 'secluded' by Pride's Purge (on 21 February), stimulated one of Milton's finest prose works.

The first edition of *The Readie and Easie Way* was written in the last moment of republican hope, as the Rump raced to replenish its numbers before being forced to readmit the secluded members.[89] Publication of the second edition, following the dissolution of that assembly and the calling of the Convention, was courageous. '[I]n the midst of our Elections to a free Parlament', in defence of 'the best part of our libertie, which is our religion, and the civil part', Milton took square aim at 'this noxious humor of returning to bondage'.[90] In a tone continuous with the *Tenure* and the *Defences*, he recalled the 'just . . . and magnanimous . . . aboli[tion]' of kingship, 'turning regal bondage into a free Commonwealth, to the admiration and terrour of our emulous neighbours'.[91] Those who so acted were not 'bound by any statute of preceding Parlaments, but by the law of nature only . . . the beginning and the end of all Government . . . not to ecclesiastical canons, though never so ancient . . . which . . . are meer positive

---

[87] *Aubrey's Brief Lives* p. 125.
[88] *Twenty Three DECREES From the Committee of Safety in Oceana* (12 November 1659) pp. 3–7; see similarly Alazonamastix Philalethes, *Free Parliament Quares proposed to Tender Consciences* (1660) p. 2: 'Whether Hanging or Drowning be the best waies of Transportation of our late Republicans to the Common-wealths of *Utopia* or *Oceana*'.
[89] Woolrych, 'Historical Introduction' pp. 162–75, 343–9.
[90] Milton, *The Readie and Easie Way* pp. 407–9, 420.   [91] Ibid. p. 409.

laws'. As Milton had emphasised in the *Tenure*, 'The best affected . . . and best principl'd of the people, stood not numbring or computing on which side were most voices in Parlament, but on which side appeerd to them most reason . . . there being in number little vertue, but by weight and measure wisdom working all things.'[92] Now again 'is it just or reasonable, that most voices against the main end of government should enslave the less number that would be free? More just it is doubtless, if it com to force, that a less number compell a greater to retain, which can be no wrong to them, thir libertie'.[93]

Nor were thir actions less both at home and abroad then might become the hopes of a glorious rising Commonwealth: nor were the expressions both of armie and people . . . other then such as testifi'd a spirit in this nation no less noble and well fitted to the liberty of a Commonwealth, then in the ancient *Greeks* or *Romans*. Nor was the heroic cause . . . the constancie and fortitude that so nobly vindicated our liberty, our victory [against] . . . superstition and tyrannie unpraisd or uncelebrated in a written monument, likely to outlive detraction.[94]

After which,

for this extolld and magnifi'd nation, regardless both of honour wonn or deliver-ances voutsaf't from heaven . . . to creep back so poorly as it seems the multitude would to thir once abjur'd and detested thraldom of Kingship . . . argues a strange degenerate contagion suddenly spread among us fitted and prepar'd for new slaverie, but will render us a scorn and derision to all our neighbours . . . Besides this, if we returne to Kingship, and soon repent, as undoubtedly we shall, when we begin to find the old encroachments coming on . . . upon our consciences . . . we may be forc'd perhaps to fight over again all that we have fought, and spend over again all that we have spent, but are never like to attain thus far as we are now advanc'd to the recoverie of our freedom, never to have it in possession as we now have it, never to be voutsaf't heer after the like mercies and signal assistances from heaven in our cause, if by our ingratefull backsliding we make these fruitless . . . making vain and viler than dirt the blood of so many thousand faithfull and valiant *English* men, who left us in this libertie, bought with thir lives.[95]

Throughout the tract Milton juxtaposed the systems, and principles, of commonwealths and monarchies. The morality of the would-be court might be anticipated 'by the language of thir infernal pamphlets, the spue of every drunkard, every ribald . . . thir necks yok'd with these tigers of Bacchus, these new fanatics not of the preaching but the sweating-tub, inspir'd with nothing holier than the Venereal pox'.[96] Like Sidney's *Maxims,* Milton explained that 'of all governments a Commonwealth aims most to make the

---

[92] Ibid. pp. 414–16.   [93] Ibid. p. 455.   [94] Ibid. pp. 420–1.
[95] Ibid. pp. 422–4.   [96] Ibid. pp. 452–3.

people flourishing, vertuous, noble and high spirited', just as additionally 'trade flourishes no where more then in the free Commonwealths of *Italie, Germanie*, and the Low-Countries . . . at this day'.[97] By contrast it was the aim of 'Monarchs . . . to make the people . . . indeed . . . well fleec't, for thir own shearing and the supplie of regal prodigalitie; but otherwise softest, basest, vitiousest, servilest, easiest to be kept under; and not only in fleece, but in minde also sheepishest'.[98]

There remained only the question of how, in practice, the republic was to be preserved. Milton's deliberately uncomplicated blueprint was intended to be not only an antidote to the kind of Harringtonian constitution-mongering once mocked by Nedham, but also an escape from constitutional instability by cutting constitutional argument back down to size. When a pamphleteer composed a spoof *Censure of the Rota* upon Milton's work, it complained that

That which I disliked most in your Treatise was, That there is not one word of the balance of Propriety, nor the *Agrarian*, nor *Rotation*, in it, from the beginning to the end . . . a Commonwealth is like a great Top, that must be kept up by being whipt round and held in perpetuall circulation, for if you discontinue *the Rotation*, and suffer the Senate to settle, and stand still, down it falls immediately.[99]

This was a more effective satire upon Harrington's boffin-like technical preoccupations than upon Milton's more mainstream thought. Yet to say that for Milton ends governed means is also to notice that in his good old cause it was heroic deeds which gave occasion for words. Now, in this ultimate crisis 'few words will save us . . . few and easie things, now seasonably don'.[100] As the republican experiment collapsed in practice, Milton had a powerful reply to Harrington's talking-shop of 'ingeniose Discourse':

The way propounded is plane, easie and open before us; without intricacies, without the introducement of new or obsolete forms or terms, or exotic models; ideas that would effect nothing, but with a number of new injunctions, to manacle the native liberty of mankinde; turning all vertue into prescription, servitude and necessitie, to the great impairing and frustrating of Christian libertie.[101]

Foremost among such 'injunctions' was 'the hedge of an Agrarian law'.[102] As C. S. Lewis said of More's *Utopia*, 'From it, as from all other other imaginary states, liberty is more successfully banished than the real world,

---

[97] Ibid. pp. 460–2.   [98] Ibid. p. 460.
[99] *The Censure of the Rota upon Mr Milton's Book, Entituled, The Ready and Easie Way* (26 March 1659) pp. 14–15.
[100] Milton, *The Readie and Easie Way* p. 461.   [101] Ibid. p. 445.   [102] Ibid.

even at its worst, allows. The very charm of these paper citizens is that they cannot in any way resist their author: every man is dictator in his own book.'[103] Thus if the republican experiment ended, as it had begun, to the sound of argument, this was not only because of the 'faction' lamented by Milton as well as Harrington. It was because there were, even within the cause, issues in dispute, both religious and political, as important as the distinctions between anarchy and settlement, 'liberty and servitude . . . vertue and prescription'.

[103] C. S. Lewis, *English Literature in the Sixteenth Century, Excluding Drama* (Oxford, 1973) p. 168.

CHAPTER 15

Anatomies of tyranny, 1660–1683

If it be said, these and other nations after wearied with civil dissensions, have sought Monarchy as their port for rest I answer; few or none of them have sought Monarchy as their rest, but have fallen or bin driven into it as a ship upon a Rock: we may as well conclude death better then life because all men doing what they can to preserve life doe yet end in death. *That free states by divisions fall often into monarchy only shows Monarchy to be a state as death unto life. And as death is the greatest evil can befall a person, monarchy is the worst evil can befall a nation.*

Algernon Sidney, *Court Maxims* [1665][1]

But in the midst of judgement God . . . kept a lamp still burning in the house of David.

Ibid.[2]

INTRODUCTION

For adherents of the 'old cause' restoration of monarchy in 1660 was a calamity. As the Convention debated exceptions to the Act of Indemnity, the exact scale of the personal retribution to be exacted was initially unclear. Although only the twenty-nine regicides apprehended (including Thomas Scot) immediately suffered the ultimate penalty, as the Convention was replaced by the Cavalier parliament in 1661 the mood of reaction hardened.[3] Milton, after a period in hiding and following his arrest, successfully sued for pardon.[4] Nedham, too, remarkably survived to retire from politics and practise medicine.[5] In December 1661, however, Harrington was arrested, examined and imprisoned. Before his release he had contracted

---

[1] Sidney, 'Court Maxims' MS p. 17.   [2] Ibid. p. 200.
[3] *An Exact and most Impartial Accompt of the Indictment, Arraignment, Trial and Judgement (according to Law) of Twenty nine Regicides* (1660); see also Ludlow, *A Voyce from the Watch Tower* pp. 199–316.
[4] Worden, 'Milton, *Samson Agonistes*, and the Restoration' pp. 116–117.
[5] M. N. [Marchamont Nedham], *Medela Medicinae. A Plea For the Free Profession, and a Renovation of the Art of Physick* (1665), The Epistle Dedicatory.

the illness from which he would not recover before his death in 1677.[6] In 1662 Vane, though not a regicide, was arrested, tried and executed.[7] In 1663 Henry Neville, John Hutchinson and others were imprisoned, Hutchinson permanently.[8]

Abroad, Algernon Sidney, one of the restored Rump's plenipotentiaries to the Baltic Sound, wisely refrained from returning. After retirement in Rome he had, by 1663, made contact with regicides exiled in Switzerland, including Edmund Ludlow. The following year he joined others, including Slingsby Bethel, amid the more numerous exile community in the United Provinces.[9] Between 1662 and 1666 these exiles were hunted, and some killed, by royalist assassins. In 1662 three regicides were kidnapped in Delft by the king's ambassador George Downing, and returned to London where they were executed.[10] Between 1662 and 1665 parliament passed the Act of Uniformity, and other legislation comprising the so-called 'Clarendon Code'. By this the entire community of dissenting protestants (now 'fanatics') became subject to the penalties prescribed by that legal equation of religious dissent with political sedition which had faced Roman Catholics since Elizabethan times. This religious persecution became a key theme within early restoration republican writing.

Another was analysis of the republic's failure. One resource for this was biblical history, in particular the folly of the people of Israel in choosing a king, as recounted in the first book of *Samuel*. Another was classical history: as shown by Thucydides and Livy, the free cities of Athens and Rome had been overcome, not initially by any external military power, but by their own pride, corruption and divisions. This theme lent itself to futher Christian meditation upon the problem of human sinfulness. Most republican writing of this period took the form of an examination of tyranny, whether in the monarchical state or individual soul. None of this involved a fundamental break with earlier republican writing. Indeed in some ways, by reinforcing the customary condition of adversity, and adding to it the experience of religious persecution ('Bearing the Cross, Persecution, Self-Denial'), restoration gave this additional stimulus.[11] The return of monarchy/tyranny which had now come to pass was the same

---

[6] Toland, 'Life of Harrington' pp. xxx–xxxviii.
[7] Vane, *The Tryal of Sir Henry Vane, Kt, at the King's Bench, June 2nd and 6th 1662*; Ludlow, *A Voyce from the Watch Tower* pp. 311–15.
[8] Lucy Hutchinson, *Memoirs of the Life of Colonel Hutchinson*, ed. N. Keeble (1995) pp. 304, 310.
[9] Scott, *Algernon Sidney and the English Republic* chs. 9–11.
[10] *The Speeches, Discourses and Prayers, of Colonel John Barkstead, Col. John Okey, and Mr Miles Corbet, Upon the 19th of April, being the Day of their suffering at Tyburn, Together with an Account of the Occasion and Manner of their Taking in Holland* (1662); Scott, '"Good Night Amsterdam"' pp. 340–1.
[11] Keeble, *Literary Culture of Nonconformity* p. 23.

condition (whether in the military efforts of Charles Stuart in 1650–1, in the hearts of those charged with republican government, or in the Protectorate of the Cromwells) against which republican writing had always been directed.

In addition contemporaries lacked our retrospective knowledge that the return of monarchy would endure. A turn of events so sudden and miraculous ('for such a Restauration was never seene in the mention of any history, ancient or modern'[12]) could easily be undone. As the king explained to parliament in 1662 'He needed not to tell them, that there was a Republican Party still in the kingdom, which had the Courage still to promise themselves another Revolution.'[13] Moreover the prescription for restoration was disputed within the government itself (which contained, in the king, a determined opponent of the Act of Uniformity). Perhaps most importantly the restored monarchy never recovered the republic's one-time military power. As George Downing protested to the States General in 1662 'he observed that he was not received with the respect and observance now, that he was when he came from that Traitor and Rebell Cromwell'.[14] By 1667 the regime's first war against the Dutch had resulted in disaster.[15] By the 1670s England's military impotence had given rise to a relationship of clientage with France that appeared to threaten the country's religious and political independence.[16] With these political symptoms of military failure republicans associated the far from disguised moral failings of a notoriously dissolute court. To both, the claimed triumphs of the earlier republic offered an instructive contrast, augmented by the judgement of classical authorities (Livy and Tacitus), the Bible, and contemporary events (including the Great Plague and Great Fire).

Finally there was the question of what, precisely, was being restored. Despite the constitutional fiction of uninterrupted hereditary succession since 1649, in practice the settlement of 1660–5 kept open the possibility that the future of English monarchy would be decided by parliaments. As Sidney pointed out in the *Discourses*, although the parliamentary record during the 1660s was one of shameful reaction, if the principle could be established that parliaments were the arbiter, then opinion within them could change. Meanwhile, fiscally in particular, the crown restored in 1660 was not what it once had been. Not only was it now entirely dependent

---

[12] John Evelyn, *The Diary of John Evelyn*, ed. Esmond De Beer (Oxford, 1955), p. 244.
[13] Edward Hyde, Earl of Clarendon, *The Life of Edward Earl of Clarendon . . . Written by Himself*, vol. 1 (Oxford, 1760) p. 447.
[14] *Pepys Diary* vol. III, 1662, p. 45.
[15] Ibid. vol. VIII, p. 268.
[16] Scott, *Algernon Sidney and the Restoration Crisis*; Scott, *England's Troubles* chs. 8, 16.

upon customs revenues and parliamentary taxation, but the settlement of
1660–5 was heavily dependent upon the retention of recent republican
economic, fiscal and administrative innovations and personnel.[17] From
such circumstances, the significance of which only became fully clear in
the 1690s, arose an important question. Would the one-time early Stuart
'monarchical republic' be restored, or reformed?[18]

Thus in his *Advice to Charles II* the Marquess of Newcastle warned
against the confirmation of traditional corporate liberties on the grounds
that 'every corporation is a petty free state against monarchy'.[19] According
to Toland, it was an argument employed by Harrington to royalists in
1656 that 'if the Prince should happen to be restor'd, his Doctrin of the
Balance would be a light to shew him what and with whom he had to
do, and so . . . avoid the Miscarriages of his Father; since all that is said
of this doctrin may as well be accommodated to a Monarchy regulated by
Laws, as to a Democracy or more popular form of a Commonwealth'.[20] It
was precisely the purpose of Neville's *Plato Redivivus* (1680) to formulate
the substance of a Harringtonian republic in monarchical outward form.
Thus when Sidney said, in the *Discourses*, that 'absolute monarchy . . . is
all I dispute against, professing much veneration for that which is mixed,
regulated by law, and directed to the public good', this was not because
he had abandoned the unqualified anti-monarchism of both of his major
works.[21] Rather it was because as a first step he wished to achieve what
could be achieved of a 'government of laws and not of men'.

ANALYSES OF FAILURE

Before hope, however, there was despair and doubt, including self-doubt.
The first analyses of the republic's failure had been provided by Milton long
before, in the *Digression from the History of Britain*, the *Second Defence* and
The Readie and Easie Way. In the latter,

> That a nation should be so valorous and courageous to winn thir liberty in the
> field, and when they have wonn it . . . after ten or twelve years prosperous warr and
> contestation with tyrannie, basely and besottedly to run their necks again into the
> yoke which they have broken . . . will be an ignominie if it befall us, that never yet
> befell any nation possessd of thir libertie; worthie indeed themselves, whatsoever
> they be, to be for ever slaves.[22]

---

[17] Scott, '"Good Night Amsterdam"' pp. 350–6.
[18] For this as the fundamental tension besetting the restoration process see Scott, *England's Troubles* Part 3.
[19] Quoted in Halliday, *Dismembering the Body Politic* p. 54.   [20] Toland, 'Life of Harrington' p. xix.
[21] Sidney, *Discourses*, in *Sydney on Government* p. 106.   [22] Milton, *The Readie and Easie Way* p. 428.

In short, 'Shall we never grow old anough to be wise?' Given that, according to Aubrey, he began writing *Paradise Lost* 'about 2 yeares before the King came in',[23] it is no surprise that Milton's greatest anatomy of this moral failure took a very similar line. As we have seen, the exemplar of that failure is Satan, whose soul, driven by his 'disordered rage', is that both of the tyrant and of the slave. His disastrous prideful choice of self, before service to God, parallels that of the English people who had the opportunity, 'if we were aught els but sluggards or babies . . . [to] depend on none but God and our own counsels, our own active vertue and industrie'.[24] In leading his rebellious hordes to disaster, Satan learns 'too late/ How few sometimes may know, when thousands err'. Because he knows nothing, Satan makes the vulgar error of equating service to God with servitude, when it is the only basis of freedom.

> This is servitude,
> To serve the unwise, or him who hath rebelled
> Against his worthier, as thine now serve thee,
> Thyself not free, but to thyself enthralled.[25]

Yet in presenting Satan as a counterfeit republican ('Thus while he spake, each passion dimmed his face/Thrice changed with pale, ire, envy and despair/Which marred his borrowed visage, and betrayed/Him counterfeit, if any eye beheld'),[26] Milton does not content himself with casting the blame upon the monarch-doting rabble. It is one reason for the lust of the ignorant multitude after monarchy that they preferred the surface glitter of appearance over substance (especially of 'servile pomp' over the hard substance of liberty and virtue). Ludlow, too, lamented the English people's 'folly and madness in choosing a seeming good, instead of a reall one, and catching at shaddows and neglecting of ye substance'.[27] Yet for all its lofty pretensions the republican experiment, too, had fallen victim to a version of the same weakness. Had republicans remained true to God and to one another, had their virtue remained unspotted, had they adhered to the service of the public good, eschewing self-interest, then, however small their numbers, the republic would not have fallen. With the progressive failure to make that liberty won in the field a fact in peace, it became clear that what had been achieved was not the moral substance of an English republic but its mere outward appearance. Given his strictures in the *Second*

---

[23] *Aubrey's Brief Lives* p. 202.
[24] Milton, *The Readie and Easie Way* p. 427; Milton here quotes the scriptural passage ('*Go to the Ant, thou sluggard, saith Solomon; consider her waies, and be wise*') which inspired Scott's *Belgick Pismire* (1623).
[25] Milton, *Paradise Lost* Book 4, lines 147–8, 178–81.
[26] Ibid. lines 114–17.   [27] Ludlow, 'A Voyce from the Watchtower' f. 326.

Defence it is not surprising that for Milton, as for Ludlow, Vane and Sidney, a transcendent symbol of this moral apostacy was Oliver Cromwell.

More than anyone else, Satan is Cromwell, speaking the language of a noble cause, while hypocritically leading its followers to destruction. In this, too, there is an echo of Lucan's Caesar, who speaks the same language to the same effect.[28] Yet more broadly Satan stands not for any one person, let alone a single individual against whom all blame might be directed. The power of Milton's poem is anchored in the universality of its subject: the fallen moral condition of mankind. Thus some nineteenth-century commentators found Milton's depiction of God alienating, and in Satan the 'hero' of his poem. While this makes no sense of Milton's moral philosophy, it does register something crucial to his poetry, which is the reader's recognition in Satan's predicament of an element of themselves.

For Vane too, even before 1660, 'we are like the children of Israel in former times, rather hardened and made worse, for the most of us, by God's appearances and deliverances, than brought nearer to Him.'[29] All of these themes were to have echoes in the work of Sidney, who although a partisan of reason, was also a self-knowing creature of passion. Sidney's initial position in relation to restoration, writing from Copenhagen, was that 'Since the Parlmt hath aknowledged a king, I knowe and acknowledge I owe him the duty and service that belongs unto a subject and will pay it . . . If things are carried on in a legall and moderate way.'[30] Yet as he reminded his father 'I did not take the warre in which I was engaged to be a slight matter, nor to be done by halfes. I thought it undertaken upon good grounds, and that it was the part of an honest man to pursue them hartily.'[31] Accordingly, although he would render such duty, he would not 'submitte, recant, renounce, and ask pardon' or offer

congratulation or aknowledgement of our faults in having bin against this king or his father. The truth is, I could hope for noe good in a businesse that I should beginne with a lye . . . and I shall be the better contented with my fortune, when I see theare was noe way of avoiding it, that is not worse then ruine.[32]

As the prospects of his return to England receded, he ruminated:

I knowe the titles that are given me of fierce, violent, seditious, mutinous, turbulent . . . I knowe people will say I straine at knats and swallowe camells, that it is a strange conscience, that lets a man runne one violently till he is deepe in

---

[28] Norbrook, *Writing the English Republic* pp. 442–3.
[29] *Original Letters . . . to Oliver Cromwell* (1743) quoted in Judson, *Vane* p. 12.
[30] Algernon Sidney to the Earl of Leicester, Copenhagen, 28 May 1660, Sevenoaks Library, MS U1000/7 Z1/5. For Sidney's embassy see Scott, *Algernon Sidney and the English Republic* ch. 8.
[31] Sidney to the Earl of Leicester, Augsburg, 21 September 1660, Sevenoaks Library, MS U1000/7 Z1/7.
[32] Ibid. Augsburg, 26 September 1660, MS U1000/7 Z1/8.

civill blood, and then stops at a fewe words, and complements. That can earnestly endeavour to extirpate a long established monarchy, and cannot be brought to see his error, and perswaded to set one finger towards the setting together the broken pieces of it . . . I have enough to answeare all this in my own minde . . . I did not make my selfe, nor can I correct the defects of my creation. I walk in the light god hath given me, if it be dimme or uncertaine, I must beare the penalty of my errors.[33]

What replaced this introspection with anger and changed Sidney's mind about rendering the duty of a subject was the fate of his more resolute collegues, followed by the onset of religious persecution. Neither suggested a restoration 'legal' or 'moderate'. In particular, in the execution of his mentor and Kentish neighbour Henry Vane, like Sidney not a regicide, Algernon saw what could be his own fate. He could not know that it would become his own, after a trial for which he had prepared by studying 'the case of Henry Vane', but for which the crown also prepared with a 'Copy of ye prcepts or Rules of K[ing's] Bench in Sr Henry Vane's Case adapted to that of Algernoon Sidney'.[34]

Sidney's response to Vane's execution may be judged from the inscription left in the visitors' book at the Calvinist Academy at Geneva in 1663: '*Sit Sanguinis Ultor Justorum*' (Let there be revenge for the blood of the just).[35] He had passed through the city on his way to visit Ludlow (for whom Vane was also 'This choice Martyr of Christ, and Eminent Champion of his Countrey's Liberty') and other exiles at Vevey. This was, Ludlow recorded, 'in Expectation of an Opportunity wherein he might be more Active . . . expressing himself to us, w[i]th much affection and friendship; and to ye Publique w[i]th much honour and faithfulness not in ye least declining to owne us, and ye despised Cause for wch we suffred'.[36] In 1663–6, as in 1681–3, the most important practical context for Sidney's involvement in treasonous discussions was the renewed religious persecution of those years. As he later explained to his fellow prisoner in the Tower, John Hampden Jr, 'I am very much comforted by that which you say of the prayers of good people. If I know my self at all, I doe love them, and never enterd into any publike action, upon any other motive than a desire

---

[33] Ibid. Hamburg, 30 August 1660, MS U1000/7 Z1/4. These letters are published in Blencowe, *Sydney Papers*; see also Scott, *Algernon Sidney and the English Republic* ch. 9.

[34] Sidney, *The Trial of Algernon Sidney Esq* (1683), in *Sydney on Government* pp. 46, 53; Public Record Office, London, State Papers 44, no. 54, p. 228; Scott, *Algernon Sidney and the Restoration Crisis* chs. 13–14. 'Oh Vane', lamented the *Court Maxims*, as others would later for Sidney, 'thy condemnation was thy Glory, thy death gave thee a . . . never perishing Crown'. Quoted in Scott, *Algernon Sidney and the English Republic* p. 198.

[35] Charles Borgeaud, *Histoire de l'Universite de Geneve: l'Academie de Calvin 1559–1798*. vol. 1 (Geneva, 1900) pp. 442–3.

[36] Ludlow, 'A Voyce From the Watch Tower' f. 977.

of doing them good.'[37] In 1664 he wrote to Benjamin Furly in Rotterdam, 'I am certaine I can have noe peace in my owne spirite, if I doe not endeavour by all meanes possible, to advance the interest of gods people. Others may judge, from whence this temper doth proceed, better then I can. If it be from god, he will make it to prosper. If from the heat and violence of my owne disposition, I, and my designes, shall perish.'[38]

It is the assertion of the *Court Maxims* that 'As for the late Commonwealth of England . . . we had broken [the King's] armies, subdued his whole party in three nations, but God suffered divisions to arise amongst us for the punishment of our sins, and *so we came to be betrayed*.'[39] Of the Roman republic Cicero had lamented, 'we retain the name of a commonwealth, but we have lost the reality long ago'.[40] According to Augustine, the words given by Sallust to Cato to explain the fall of the republic were as follows:

Do not imagine that it was by force of arms that our ancestors made a great nation out of a small community . . . it was other causes that made them great, causes that with us have ceased to exist: energy in our own land, a rule of justice outside our borders; in forming policy, a mind that is free because not at the mercy of criminal passions. Instead of these we have self-indulgence and greed, public poverty and private opulence. We praise riches: we pursue a course of sloth. No distinction is made between good men and bad: the intrigues of ambition win the prizes due to merit. No wonder, when each of you thinks only of his own private interest; when at home you are slaves to your appetites, and to money and influence in your public life.[41]

It was surely of the contemporary relevance of this analysis that Sidney was thinking when he recalled, in 1665, that Rome's

valour had conquered their foreign enemies. Rival Carthage lay ignobly hid in its own ruin. The proudest kings had died under the weight of their chains . . . Many of the most powerful and warlike cities were buried in ashes. This success followed with a prodigious affluence of riches, introduced ambition and avarice, raising some citizens above the power of the law. Then did that victorious people turn its conquering hand into its own bowels, and fell by its own sword. That unequalled commonwealth which had sat like a queen ruling the nations, fell under the feet of one of her wicked sons. His impious successor destroyed all that excelled in valour, virtue, prudence, experience, or reputation. . . . The senate that had been

---

[37] East Sussex Record Office, Lewes, Glynde Place MSS no. 794, letter 1 p. 3.
[38] Beinecke Library, Yale University, New Haven, USA, Letter From Sidney to [Furly?], Undated MS letter in Sidney's hand, probably written in 1664, collected with other letters from Sidney, mainly to Furly. See Scott, *Algernon Sidney and the English Republic* p. 173.
[39] Sidney, *Court Maxims* p. 19.   [40] Ibid. pp. 73–4.
[41] Quoted by Augustine, *City of God* p. 200.

composed of men eminent in nobility, great in valour, admired in virtue, famous for victories, and, as its high honour, had Cato for their head and leader, was now full of unworthy wretches, depending wholly upon the will of a Caligula, Nero, Vitellius, or such like monsters.[42]

However, within the *Maxims* republican self-criticism takes a distant second place to fury at the 'shameful destructive folly' of the English people. 'What a weight of blood and guilt does England groan under on this account?' We 'recall from exile one of that detested race . . . suffering those to be sacrificed to his lust and rage, who had been the most worthy and successful instruments in our deliverance'.[43] The Stuart family

was most infamously polluted with blood. And though they have ever since added sin unto sin, and sold themselves to do all manner of evil, favouring superstition and idolatry and filling all the land with innocent blood, our madness has been such as to . . . add the crimes of faithlessness and ingratitude unto God, who, having through the abundance of his goodness broken the unworthy yoke laid on our necks, brought vengeance upon one impious head and . . . given us the opportunity of expelling and extirpating that wicked race. We could never be contented till we returned again into Egypt, the house of our bondage.[44]

This was the same rebellion against the monarchy of heaven described by Milton, with the same causes (child-like sinfulness and ignorance). But by Sidney this was placed in its contemporary context, as were its consequences. Those

bishops who lately altered the Common Prayer Book . . . should have said, the goodly and sacred fellowship of tyrants praise thee; the glorious army of thieves, murderers and blasphemers that uphold them magnify thee; the holy assembly of proud and cruel bishops, corrupt lawyers, false witnesses, and mercenary judges who persecute and endeavour to destroy thy church and people throughout the world, adorning the gates and towers of the city with the mangled limbs of thy choicest servants, to gratify the lusts and uphold the interest of their two masters, the king and the devil, do acknowledge thee.[45]

As in the late 1640s, this destruction of the innocent would not go unavenged:

We set up an idol and dance about it, though we know it to be most filthily polluted with innocent blood . . . Whilst the sword of the Lord hangs over our heads, we live carelessly and secure as the Canaanites when Joshua was ready to fall upon them. We promise ourselves peace, but there will be, can be, no true peace till by the blood of the wicked murderers a propitiation be made for the blood of the

[42] Sidney, *Court Maxims* pp. 136–7.
[43] Ibid. pp. 197–8.   [44] Ibid. p. 197.   [45] Ibid. p. 44.

righteous . . . I pray you, pardon this digression. I speak this in the anguish of my spirit, broken through the abundance of my sorrow, sighing for the iniquity of my people, praying to God that his wrath may not overflow the whole world.[46]

Like the Israelites the English had chosen 'to follow [other] nations in their beastly Idolatry . . . reject[ing] the Civil Government of God's own institution'. *'I look on those nations who voluntarily set up a king guilty of the same folly and sin as the Israelites were in asking for one.'* Even the Book of Samuel, however, described no such religious persecutions: 'I may even wish we had that only which was threatened by Samuel as a punishment to the Israelites. It would be a favour to us wee are fallen into such a condition.'[47] For Ludlow, too,

Thus is this poore nation, wherein the Lord had wrought such wounderfull thinges, now governed and disposed by the vilest and basest of the sonnes and daughters of men, whose deeds being altogether evill, and that continually, they therefore, hating the light, endeavour to suppress . . . those who hold forth this light, either in word or conversation.[48]

Yet these 'witnesses' to God's truth were also a part of 'that worke . . . ye Lord . . . hath on ye wheele'. According to John Carew, 'the way the Enemy tooke to suppress and destroy those who did not thinke ye Kings pson sacred, their blood would make many hundreds more to be pswaded of ye trueth of it, and that their blood would be of much advantage to ye Cause in forreigne ptes'.[49] In the analysis of Ludlow, 'The Lords day is coming . . . the wicked are like Spunges whom God fills, that he may squeeze, Like Leeches that shall vomit their blood.'[50] Concerning Sidney's design for an invasion of England, however,

I cannot promise my selfe a blessing from ye Lord upon [such] undertakings . . . till I observe a greater spirit of meekness and condescension amongst us then yet I doe . . . but when ye Lord hath humbled a people and fitted them for himselfe, making them willing to be abased for him he will certainly lift them up, and bring them to honour.[51]

Yet for Sidney God helped those who helped themselves. For good to triumph the godly would have to act.

---

[46] Ibid. p. 198 (transcription corrected by reference to the manuscript).

[47] Quoted in Scott, *Algernon Sidney and the English Republic* p. 198; Sidney, *Court Maxims* p. 43. Sidney's use of the Samuel text, a commonplace of republican writing, also echoes that of the Marian exiles Goodman (*How superior powers ought to be obeyed* . . . (1558) pp. 34–5, 140, 150) and Ponet (*A Short Treatise of politike Power* (1566) pp. 29–31, 44, 47).

[48] Ludlow, *A Voyce from the Watch Tower* p. 306.

[49] Ludlow, 'A Voyce from the Watch Tower' ff. 108–9, 327.

[50] Ibid. f. 323.   [51] Ibid. ff. 1057, 1082.

ANATOMIES OF TYRANNY

Like *Paradise Lost*, the *Court Maxims* is an anatomy of tyranny. In this case, however, the manifestation of that condition is not the disordered soul of Satan, but the political state of England. Sidney's depiction of the regime of Charles II as a tyranny, and so argument for armed resistance against it, is supported not only by proofs of the evil of that regime. The *Maxims* borrows from Machiavelli's *Discorsi*, and both English and Dutch republican interest theory, to insist that modern monarchy and tyranny are indistinguishable.[52] Monarchy was private interest government, republicanism government in the public interest. The two systems were thus founded in irreconcilably contrary principles, 'one in God, the other in the devil':

The greatest enmity is when . . . contrary principles lead into a contrary interest. It is men of . . . good principles which men of ill principles are afraid of. Good principles keep men steady and constant in the pursuit of a good interest, that of the community . . . The utmost contrariety unto all this . . . is, when, by the impulse . . . of the contrary principle, by one or more men the rule of justice is perverted and the administrators of it corrupted . . . [to] destroy all those who seek righteousness and would live innocently.[53]

This bears close comparison to Harrington's account of modern prudence, where 'some man, or some few men, subject a city or a nation, and rule it according to their private interest'. In Harrington, however, principles ('the Principles of Government') are a function of interest which has a material foundation.[54] For Sidney, interest is a function of principles. Thus Sidney's attack on the 'tyranny over consciences' found its focus in the same 'contrariety of principles' with the same root:

Tyrants and priests ever agree together against God and his anointed, as pagan idolators and Turks do. And the fanatics or true Christians follow the examples also of their forerunners, the prophets, apostles, and all the saints from the beginning of the world; continuing in faith, prayer, and exercise of the gifts God has given them, fearing nothing but sin . . . Here are Augustine's two cities of God and the world, or of God and the devil, still in uniform, fixed, constant opposition . . . The one vainly boasts and triumphs in a momentary perishing power, the other is steadfastly fixed upon the rock of Israel.[55]

Thus the Stuart court takes its 'maxims' from tyrants throughout the ages: Cesare Borgia, as described by Machiavelli; Nero, Caligula and Domitian, as described by Tacitus; the Stuarts themselves, described by Buchanan;

---

[52] Scott, 'Classical Republicanism' pp. 68–9.   [53] Sidney, *Court Maxims* pp. 148–9.
[54] Harrington, *Oceana*, in *Political Works* pp. 161, 171–2.   [55] Sidney, *Court Maxims* p. 106.

Charles IX of France, author of the Massacre of St Bartholmew's Eve; and Oliver Cromwell. Moreover it is guided not only by the self-interested principles of tyranny, but by the murderous practice of popery. The Stuarts' greatest triumph, in this respect, was authorship of the massacre of Irish protestants in 1641, a role recently acknowledged (Sidney claimed) by Charles II.

Nor can it be imagined our king had any other desire when he cut off Vane's head, than to destroy, as in its root, all virtue, wisdom, and godliness, since those, who were eminent in any of these qualities, looked on him as their master, and seemed to have learnt all they knew or practiced by his precepts or example. This was a stroke that showed how carefully he treads the steps of his ancestors.[56]

Sidney's interest analysis bridged domestic and foreign politics. Thus domestically the Stuarts subverted true religion, persecuting its faithful adherents, while learning 'from our divines . . . [to] say "*sacred Agathocles, Dionysius, Tiberius, Domitian, Diocletian . . . holy Caligula . . . holy Nero*"'.[57] These 'priests are not God's anointed . . . having nothing but exterior unction', and lacking 'spiritual unction . . . The like may be said of princes'.[58] Among such false ministers, 'we find it . . . [especially] important to keep up bishops in the height of their power and riches'.[59] Alongside the destruction of true religion, the other most important instrument of this tyranny is the corruption of lawyers and of the law, whereby 'spies, trepanners, false witnesses, counterfeiters of hands or seals, knights of the post, perjured jury-men, and those that corrupt them . . . are by that interest brought to depend upon the king . . . There never was a tyrant who did not govern by fraud.'[60] By such means, in place of England's once 'ancient, powerful, virtuous, warlike nobility . . . of all things most destructive to . . . absolute authority and power',[61] the court has erected an 'effeminate' titular nobility, 'creatures of the court, men of low birth and lower fortunes . . . great titles and blue ribands about their necks . . . raising them to the highest places who can pretend to no other merit than extreme obsequiousness to his majesty and absolute devotion to his interest'.[62] For the same reason, it is the policy of the court that 'the number, strength, and riches of the people of England must be abated':[63]

in all times seditions have begun in the richest and most populous cities. All the tumults in the Low Countries began in Antwerp, Ghent, Brussels . . . and all ours grew from the greatness and strength of London. Generally all people grow proud when numerous and rich . . . But . . . when the people are brought to be

---

[56] Ibid. pp. 185–6.   [57] Ibid. p. 44.   [58] Ibid. p. 52.   [59] Ibid. p. 87.
[60] Ibid. p. 115.   [61] Ibid. p. 68.   [62] Ibid. p. 66.   [63] Ibid. p. 72.

few, weak and poor, no such dangers are to be feared, everyone's thoughts will be confined to the seeking of necessaries and by extreme labour to get a pair of *canvas breeches, wooden shoes, coarse bread* . . . The opulency of the king of France proceeds principally from the peoples' poverty . . . We know how to take away dangerous persons with little noise and ruin London without burning it.[64]

As under the Roman emperors, 'says Tacitus (*Annals*, bk IV) . . . Former writers . . . might delight their readers with great and noble actions; we have nothing to relate but cruel commands, continual accusations, false friendships, and the destruction of the innocent'.[65]

Meanwhile, on the stage of Europe the Stuart court exhibits an identical enmity to the public interest. A 'strict friendship [is] to be held with the French that their customs may be introduced and the people by their example brought to beggary and slavery quietly'. This is because 'the government of France is the most absolute in these parts of the world, and we endeavour to bring ours to the same model'. This is despite the fact that the King of France poses the most serious danger of establishing a universal monarchy, so that it is in the rational interests of England to unite with weaker Spain to prevent this.[66] Instead, however, of looking to 'the general good and liberty of all Europe', the Stuart court looks for French protection of its 'private ends' against the hostility of its own people. Similarly, the advancement of true religion counts for nothing in Stuart foreign policy: 'We leave all those fine things that are for the public good, advancement of the cause of Christ in the world, and diminishing the power of antichrist, to the fanatics.' By the same token, the United Provinces are perceived as 'immortal, irreconcileable enemies, and by all imaginable ways we seek their ruin'.[67] Thus alongside the 'inseperable interests . . . of the Houses of Stuart and Orange', Sidney emphasises the parallel identity of interest between Dutch and English republicanism: 'The opposition between us and them, their concernments and ours, is universal and irreconcileable.'[68] This even involves a notably unconvincing attempt to explain away the earlier war between the two republics, which 'was not brought on by a contrariety of interests, nor . . . act of counsel; but both found themselves unaware involved in it by a fatality that none could understand. The effects of it were so pernicious to both, that they were endangered, and we destroyed by it.'[69]

---

[64] Ibid. pp. 71–2, 77.   [65] Ibid. p. 138.   [66] Ibid. pp. 152, 153, 157.
[67] Ibid. p. 161.   [68] Ibid. p. 176.
[69] Ibid. p. 171. Sidney's claim that the English republic was 'destroyed' by the first Anglo-Dutch war may be interpreted in support of the thesis that this was a key factor informing the Rump's dissolution.

Sidney's argument is apparently directed to the English godly, in the Netherlands exile community and at home, and to the Dutch government itself.[70] More broadly it is offered to everybody capable of recognising the truth that this is a government acting contrary to the public interest. Thus Sidney's account of the Stuart strategy for the destruction of England's trade is an attempt to detach the London-based merchant community from support of the Anglo-Dutch war in 1664–5. Predominantly, however, Sidney's language is godly. '[G]ood men' should not

despair of remedy. This evil is not incurable, since it may be cured *by the destruction of its authors*, as it often has been, both in Israel and other people, by the hand of God and man, the sword of the Lord and of Gideon. I may safely rely upon what history relates, reason dictates, Scripture denounces, and the spirit explains in this case for . . . whatsoever government is unjust, cannot be permanent, since God that did hate it, does hate it; he that has punished it, will punish it; because that is ever evil and he is ever good . . . The blood of the saints also cries aloud . . . and God will not long delay his appointed vengeance.[71]

Sidney's *Court Maxims* remained unpublished until the later twentieth century. Republican utterances published during the reign of Charles II had to be more circumspect. Thus the Anglo-Dutch interest theory of Sidney's *Maxims* was developed by his collegue Slingsby Bethel's *The World's Mistake in Oliver Cromwell* (1668) and *The Present Interest of England Stated* (1671), the latter republished in expanded form as *The Interest of Princes and States* (1680).[72] *The World's Mistake* does not overtly attack the restored monarchy. However it does join Milton, Sidney and Ludlow in attacking 'the Tyranny' of Cromwell for having destroyed the 'former Wealth and Prosperity' created by the policies of 'the Long Parliament'.[73] Moreover like the *Maxims* it takes as the present model of such successful civil, religious and economic government that 'Republick' called the United Provinces.

One of Bethel's concerns was to attack religious persecution as contrary to the 'Interest' of nations. Another was to defend the 'Protestant Interest' in Europe. His predominant mission, however, was to apply to English politics an economic interest analysis imported from Dutch republicanism. Thus 'The prosperity, or adversity, if not the life and death of a state, is bound up in the observing or neglecting its Interest.'[74] As in the *Court Maxims*

---

[70] For the political context of the *Court Maxims* see Scott, *Algernon Sidney and the English Republic* chs. 11–13.

[71] Sidney, *Court Maxims* pp. 150, 191.

[72] For Sidney's association with Bethel see Scott, *Algernon Sidney and the English Republic* pp. 214–16; Scott, *Algernon Sidney and the Restoration Crisis* pp. 162–71.

[73] Bethel, *The World's Mistake in Oliver Cromwell* pp. 14, 20.

[74] Bethel, *The Interest of Princes and States* 2nd edn (1681) pp. A3, A6.

and the work of a Dutch republican like Pieter De la Court, this interest had both domestic and foreign dimensions.[75] Domestically, the 'principal interest' of England, like that of the United Provinces, was 'Trade'. Abroad, as the *Court Maxims* had recommended, it lay in enmity with France and 'firm peace and amity with the Netherlands'.[76] Thus in 1671, on the eve of a third Anglo-Dutch war, Bethel warned:

yet having travelled their Countries, observed their Manners, and read their Disputes, and transactions with other Nations . . . in the generality of their Morals, they are a reproach to som Nations . . . [and] I cannot think their Trade or Wealth . . . to be a good or honest foundation for a quarrel; for their commerce [is] . . . alone the effect of Industry, and Ingenuity.[77]

Thus even in published writing, as evidenced also for instance in that of William Penn, the republic across the water served as an important alternative model, religious, political and economic.[78] Perhaps, as Sidney suggested, this helps to explain the Anglo-French attempt, inaugurated in 1670, to annihilate the United Provinces, by the repercussions of which English politics was to be so profoundly affected.[79]

An alternative locus for Restoration displacement of republican values occurred in colonial constitutional modelling. One example was the *Fundamental Constitutions of Carolina* (1669) drawn up by the Earl of Shaftesbury and John Locke, and described by Shaftesbury as 'a sort of republic'.[80] This provided for liberty of conscience, and a division of lands and political authority in which the influence of Harrington's *Oceana* has been detected. Another example was William Penn's own *Frame of the Government of . . . Pennsylvania* (1682), early drafts of which were read and criticised by Locke, Sidney and Benjamin Furly. This began by laying down a familiar doctrine of liberty: 'Any *Government* is **Free** . . . (what-ever be the Frame) **where the Laws Rule, and the People are a Party to those Laws**, and more than this is *Tyranny, Oligarchy* or *Confusion*.'[81]

---

[75] For the Dutch intellectual context for this writing see Scott, *Algernon Sidney and the English Republic* ch. 13.

[76] Bethel, *Interest of Princes* pp. 55–65.

[77] Bethel, *The Present Interest of England, Stated* (1671) p. 33.

[78] Penn, *England's Present Interest Considered* (1675); Penn, *An Essay Towards the present and Future Peace of Europe* (1693), both in Penn, *Political Writings* pp. 60, 418.

[79] Scott, *Algernon Sidney and the Restoration Crisis*; Scott, *England's Troubles* ch. 7.

[80] Locke, *Political Essays*, ed. Mark Goldie (Cambridge, 1997) pp. 160–81; Bliss, *Revolution and Empire* pp. 210–17; K. H. D. Haley, *The First Earl of Shaftesbury* (Oxford, 1968) pp. 242–8; Robert Weir, "'Shaftesbury's Darling'': British Settlement in the Carolinas at the Close of the Seventeenth Century', in Canny, *The Origins of Empire* pp. 381–2.

[81] Penn, *The Papers of William Penn*, ed. Mary Maples Dunn and Richard S. Dunn (2 vols., Philadelphia, Penn., 1981) vol. II, pp. 213.

It appears to have been Furly who introduced Sidney to Penn.[82] During 1679 and 1680 Penn worked hard on behalf of Sidney's attempts to enter the Commons.[83] Accompanying pamphlets called for not only liberty of conscience and 'Discovery and Punishment of the [Popish] *Plot*', but equally vigorous defence of 'our *Ancient Laws by New Ones . . .* such as relate to *Frequent Parliaments*, the only True Check upon *Arbitrary Ministers*'.[84] It was a long-standing theme of Penn's earlier writing 'That the People . . . may love and obey the Government . . . from the share they have in it'.[85] His understanding of this government of laws, rather than of men, was that of Milton and Sidney rather than Harrington. Thus, firstly, 'I do not find a Model in the World, that *Time, Place* and some singular Emergencies have not necessarily alter'd; nor is it easie to frame a *Civil Government*, that shall serve all places alike.' Similarly, should anyone say with Harrington '*Let us have* **good** **Laws**, and *no matter for the* **Men** *that Execute them*', Penn begged to disagree. For '*good Laws* may want *good Men*, and be abolished or evaded by *ill Men*; but *good Men* will never want *good Laws* nor suffer *Ill Ones*'. Thus his *Frame of Government* was not an immortal constitution, but rather a framework of law to be altered and amended by a '**General Assembly**, by whom all *Laws* shall be made'. Although it provided for fundamentals like liberty of conscience, it was because the progress of the colony would depend upon the moral qualities of its citizens that provision was made for (for instance) 'A *Committee* of **Manners, Education** and **Arts**'.[86]

Another striking public treatment of republicanism during this period, as a government of laws rather than of men, occurred in Nathaniel Lee's play *Lucius Junius Brutus* (performed briefly in 1680, and closed down by the authorities). Transposing the present 'troubled times' to ancient Rome, this told the story of the overthrow of the Tarquins and foundation of the republic ('For now's the time, To shake the Building of the Tyrant down').[87] It contrasted 'Justice' under 'A King', in respect of which 'You may be angry, and may be forgiven,/There's room for favor, and for benefit', with the 'Laws that are cruel, deaf, inexorable' by which a republic is governed. 'O, 'tis dangerous, To have all Actions judg'd by rigorous Law'. While Lee put

82 T. Forster (ed.), *Letters of Locke, Algernon Sidney, and Anthony Lord Shaftesbury* (1830) p. 88.
83 Scott, *Algernon Sidney and the Restoration Crisis* pp. 128–38, 155–62.
84 Penn, *England's Great Interest, in the Choice of this New Parliament Dedicated to all Her Free-Holders* (1679), in *Political Writings* pp. 384–5.
85 *Papers of William Penn* vol. II, pp. 147, 213. For Sidney's contribution see Scott, *Algernon Sidney and the Restoration Crisis* pp. 181–3.
86 *Papers of William Penn* vol. II, pp. 213, 217.
87 Nathaniel Lee, *Lucius Junius Brutus* (1680), in David Womersley (ed.), *Restoration Drama: an Anthology* (Oxford, 2000) p. 436 (Act I, lines 282–3).

empty rabble-rousing rhetoric in the mouth of Vinditius ('Sirs, I am a true
Commonwealths-man, and do not naturally love Kings'), true republican
virtue is exemplified by Brutus ('What? Dost thou kneel? Nay, stand up
now a Roman,/Shake from thy Lids that dew that hangs upon 'em/And
answer to th'austerity of my Vertue').

It is Brutus who reminds the Romans that 'You were once a free-born
People, fam'd/In his Forefathers days for Wars abroad,/The Conquerors
of the World; Oh *Rome*! Oh Glory!' It is Brutus who recalls the Tarquins' crimes, 'the horrid slaughter/Of all the Princes of the Roman Senate/
Invading Fundamental Right and Justice,/Breaking the ancient Customs,
Statutes, Laws,/With positive pow'r, and Arbitrary Lust'.[88] It is Brutus,
finally, who makes good the republican claim to terrifyingly impartial justice by the sacrifice of his sons.[89] This was, Lee tells us in the Dedication,
even 'Before I read Machivel's Notes [in the *Discourses*] upon the place, I
concluded . . . the greatest Action that was ever seen throughout all Ages on
the greatest Occasion.'[90] Although it draws forth, particularly from certain
emotionally involved females, its own accusation of tyranny ('Tyrannick
Brutus!'), the point of the play is to make clear that the quality of this
justice and Rome's greatness were indistinguishable.

> My Sons. No more: their Doom is past. Away.
> Thus shall we stop the mouth of loud Sedition,
> Thus show the difference betwixt the Sway
> Of partial Tyrants, and of a Free-born People,
> Where no man shall offend because he's great,
> Where none need doubt his Wives or Daughter's honor,
> Where all injoy their own without suspicion,
> Where there's no innovation of Religion,
> No change of Laws, nor breach of Priviledge,
> No desperate Factions gaping for Rebellion,
> No hopes of Pardon for Assassinates,
> No rash advancements of the Base or stranger,
> For Luxury, for Wit, or glorious Vice;
> But on the contrary, a Balanc'd Trade,
> Patriots incourag'd, Manufactors cherish'd,
> Vagabonds, Walkers, Drones, and Swarming Braves,
> The Froth of States, scum'd from the Commonwealth;
> Idleness banish'd all excess repress'd,

[88] Ibid. Act II, lines 13, 17, 20–1, 44–5, 200–4, 213–17.
[89] It is probably no coincidence that at the same time, for the defence of English protestantism, Charles
II was being asked to sacrifice his brother's claim to the succession.
[90] Ibid. p. 431.

And Riots check'd by Sumptuary Laws.
O, Conscript Fathers, 'tis on these Foundations
That *Rome* shall build her *Empire* to the Stars,
Send her Commanders with their Armies forth,
To Tame the World, and give the Nations Law,
Consuls, Proconsuls, who to the Capitol
Shall ride upon the Necks of Conquer'd Kings.[91]

Lee's play, informed like Sidney's *Maxims* by Livy and Tacitus as well as Machiavelli, interrogates an age devoid of both moral rigour and political or military greatness. England is, in 1680, a dissolute client state of Louis XIV's new *imperium*. The same context informs Neville's *Plato Redivivus*. By a series of prorogations between September 1679 and October 1680 the king kept his newly elected third parliament in being, but out of session.[92] In *Plato Redivivus* Neville agreed with Sidney, Penn and others that by 'adjourning, and proroguing, and dissolving them; contrary to the true meaning of the law', the court was frustrating the only 'true physician' capable of 'lay[ing] open the distemper' of the times and 'endeavour[ing] . . . a cure'.[93] Unlike some others, however, he set these policies in the context of not only similar measures pursued since 1672, but the crisis of parliaments which had existed for the best part of a century. Thus 'we are to this day tugging with the same difficulties . . . which our ancestors did before the year 1640; whilst the King has been forced to apply the same remedy of dissolution to his last parliaments, that his father used to his four first and king James to his three last'.[94] This was because such struggles were merely symptoms of a deeper structural problem: 'the breach and ruin of our government: which, having been decaying for near two hundred years, is in our age brought so near to expiration, that it lies agonizing; and can no longer perform the functions of a political life'. The same was true of all the other symptoms of the nation's malaise: 'the evil counselors, the pensioner-parliament, the thorough-paced judges, the flattering divines, the busy and designing papists, the French counsels'.[95] Like Sidney, Neville noted the present 'depravation of manners' which, however, he gave a political origin: 'corruption of . . . governments . . . must necessarily cause a depravation in manners; (as nothing is more certain than that politic defects breed moral ones, as our nation is a pregnant example)'.[96]

---

[91] Ibid. Act v, Scene ii, lines 41–65 (p. 461).
[92] Scott, *Algernon Sidney and the Restoration Crisis* pp. 57–60.
[93] Neville, *Plato Redivivus* p. 81.   [94] Ibid. p. 147.
[95] Ibid. p. 81.   [96] Ibid. p. 87; see also p. 131.

There followed a Harringtonian diagnosis both of government in general ('empire is founded in property') and of English government in particular. This concluded that in the present state of popular ownership of property, sovereign power lay, and had long lain, in parliaments.[97] Kings could either recognise this, allowing governments to function, or attempt to resist it, by resorting to the exercise of 'arbitrary power', as in France.[98] However such a tyranny, in which the king governed against not only the constitution, but the balance of property ('nature'), could not last.[99] It was the task of an English king almost without independent means to recognise his condition, and so repair 'the broken and ship-wrecked government of England'. Until this happened the country would be torn between a 'people and Parliament' fearing that 'the king intends to change the government and be arbitrary', and a 'king . . . fearing that his power will be so lessened by degrees, that . . . it will not be able to keep the crown upon his head'.[100]

In relation to parliaments, Neville argued, the crown's role was 'wholly ministerial'. The king could choose when parliament would assemble or dissolve, but not whether it would assemble; and when he used his negative voice to frustrate the wishes of his people, this was 'a violation of right, and infringement of the King's coronation-oath'.[101] By contrast, the king should consent to an abatement of the royal prerogative 'in those matters which concern our enjoyment of our . . . lives, liberties and estates'. There were, in particular, four royal prerogatives which should be exercised only in consultation with parliaments: the government of war and peace, control of the militia, nomination of civil and ecclesiastical offices, and disposal of revenues.[102]

Neville's proposals for control of these powers amounted to a more comprehensive substitute for an earlier royal offer of limitations on the powers of a popish successor. In this case, however, such limitations were to be unconditional and permanent.[103] These key powers ('or the protection of liberty, as Machiavel calls it') were to be placed in the hands of 'four several councils' nominated by, and accountable to, parliaments themselves.[104] These councils were subject, one-third at a time, to yearly rotation. The purpose was, said Neville, not only to secure due execution of the laws, but 'to make the law and the judges the only disposers of the liberties of

---

[97] Ibid. pp. 133–42.   [98] Ibid. pp. 119–20, 122.   [99] Ibid. p. 136.
[100] Ibid. p. 172.   [101] Ibid. p. 123, 128.   [102] Ibid. pp. 185–6.
[103] Thus the Duke of York considered the limitations scheme 'wors than exclusion', because a scheme to 'drop the Government more gently into a Commonwealth'. J. Clarke, *The Life of James II* (2 vols., 1816) vol. I, p. 635.
[104] Neville, *Plato Redivivus*, pp. 187, 190.

our persons'.[105] There needed to be, in addition, two entirely new laws: for fixed annual parliaments, and for peers to be appointed by parliament, not the king. Neville concluded by noting, in an echo of Milton, that he had not proposed the best form of government imaginable, but rather 'the best, that the people would or could receive'. Even so, he ended on a pessimistic note, not least because in the context of the present distemper, as Hobbes had observed in 1629,

> it is the nature of all popular councils (even the wisest that ever were, witness the people of Rome and Athens, which Machiavel so much extols) in turbulent times, to like discourses that heighten their passions and blow up their indignation; better than those that endeavour to rectify their judgements, and tend to provide for their safety.[106]

Neville's proposals were accompanied by much reassurance that the royal dignity would be enhanced rather than diminished by the kingdom's renewed political vigour. In this aspect of its purpose, as well as content, *Plato* was Harringtonian, a work of counsel not only to the court, but to parliamentarians. Similar arguments were offered by a Harringtonian pamphlet of the previous year, which foreshadowed some of Neville's proposals for parliamentary sovereignty and triennial rotation.[107]

The broadest aim of Sidney's *Discourses*, probably begun the following year, was to oppose the royal message, enunciated by Sir Robert Filmer's *Patriarcha* (1680), that government was a matter out of the people's hands: that they were 'subject[ed] . . . necessarily and universally to the will of one man'.[108] On the contrary, Sidney explained, humankind was naturally free, because equipped by God with reason. This reason authorised not only the defence of 'life, liberty and estate', but 'the choice of that society . . . we enter into . . . and the liberty of framing it according to our own wills, for our good'.[109]

If men were 'born under the necessity of perpetual slavery', their 'wisdom can be of no use to them'. If, on the contrary, 'men are naturally free, such as have wisdom and understanding will always frame good governments'.[110] Notwithstanding the assertion of Filmer to the contrary, God authorised no particular constitution, but government according to 'justice, mercy and truth'.[111] It was in this general sense that 'God, who disposes all things in wisdom and goodness . . . appoints a due place for all.'[112] To deprive people

---

[105] Ibid. p. 189.   [106] Ibid. p. 198; Scott, 'Peace of Silence'.

[107] *The Benefit of the Ballot: with the Nature and Use thereof. Particularly in the Republick of Venice* [1679?]

[108] Sidney, *Discourses*, ed. West p. 16.   [109] Ibid. p. 49.   [110] Ibid. p. 31.

[111] Ibid. p. 70.   [112] Ibid. p. 23.

of this rational choice was to turn humankind over to the government of 'tyrants with their slaves, and the instruments of their cruelties . . . the dregs of mankind', as 'Nero advised with none but musicians, players, chariot drivers, or the abominable ministers of his pleasures and cruelties'.[113] As Milton had observed of Salmasius, everything Filmer called the power of kings was actually a description of what Plato and Aristotle had called tyranny.[114] Not content with this, he sought also to deprive people of the right to 'restrain . . . such princes from doing evil, or punish[ing them] . . . if they will not be restrained'.[115] 'By this it will appear whose throne he seeks to advance, and whose servant he is, while he pretends to serve the king.'[116]

As with the *Maxims*, and by contrast with Neville's work, the *Discourses* offered no detailed constitutional prescription. Rather the imprint of the circumstances to which it was responding is most visible in its insurrectionary content. Yet as Neville had built his constitutional model around parliaments, so did Sidney his argument for armed self-defence. Whereas the *Court Maxims* had discussed parliaments only as authors of the nation's recent oppression, in the *Discourses* it is to them that Sidney turns for a solution.

---

[113] Ibid. pp. 14–15.   [114] Ibid. pp. 287–303.   [115] Ibid. pp. 10–11.   [116] Ibid. p. 7.

CHAPTER 16

Republicans and Whigs, 1680–1725

[I]t is to bee enquired, whether instead of an inclination . . . towards a Commonwealth there is not in England a generall dislike to it; If this is so . . . it will bee in vaine to dispute by *Reason* whilst *Humor* is against it . . . This maketh all the Republican Schemes, whether borrowed from the Ancient, or invented by the Moderne Doctors in Politiques, to bee no more than dreams . . . besides [which] . . . there are . . . some materials absolutely necessary for the carrying on such a fabrique, which are at present wanting amongst us; I mean Vertue, Morality, diligence, Religion . . . [so] that a Commonwealth is not *fit* for us, because *Wee* are not *fit* for a Commonwealth.

George Savile, Marquis of Halifax,
A Rough Draught of a New Modell at Sea (1687)[1]

THE QUESTION OF PARLIAMENTS, 1681–1683

By 1681, opponents of court policies perceived as popish, arbitrary and French faced even more severe problems than the 'late Prorogations and Dissolutions . . . strik[ing] at the very Root and being of Parliaments'. As Neville had predicted, a peaceful settlement of the crisis would prove elusive. One watershed was the dissolution of what turned out to be Charles II's last parliament in April 1681. Prorogations were one thing; government in the entire absence of parliaments was another.

This was the more so given the onset of a renewed and amplified religious persecution.[2] In the words of Sidney's *Apology*, written in late 1683,

God . . . Perhaps . . . will in mercy speedily visit his afflicted people. *I dye in the faith that he will doe it . . . and am soe much the more confident . . . [in] that his cause, and his people is more concerned now then it was in former time. The lust of one*

---

[1] Savile, *Rough Draught*, in *The Works of George Savile Marquis of Halifax* ed. Mark N. Brown (3 vols., Oxford, 1989) vol. 1, pp. 302–3.
[2] Mark Goldie, 'The Hilton Gang and the Purge of London in the 1680s', in Howard Nenner (ed.), *Politics and the Political Imagination in Later Stuart Britain* (Rochester, N.Y., 1997).

man and his favyrites was then only to be set up in the exercise of an arbitrary power over persons and [e]states; but now, the tyranny over consciences is principally affected, and the civill powers are stretched unto this exorbitant height, for the establishment of popery.[3]

One feature of the political literature confronting this situation was its (sometimes menacing) insistence on the need for a parliamentary solution. This echoed the claim once made by the Long Parliament that it was that body invested with the authority to act in an emergency for the kingdom's safety, even without, or if necessary against, the king himself.[4] One pamphlet referred to the 'Annual' parliaments provided for by 'Statutes made in the time of Edward the 3rd'.[5] Echoing Neville's analysis, *A Just and Modest Vindication of the Proceedings of the Two Last Parliaments* (1681) claimed that 'the court never did yet dissolve a parliament abruptly, and in a heat, but they found the next parliament more averse, and to insist upon the same things with greater eagerness than the former'.[6]

It is not to be denied, but that our kings have . . . been entrusted with the power of calling and declaring the Dissolutions of Parliaments. But, lest through defect of age, experience, or understanding, they should, at any time, forget, or mistake our constitution; or, by passion, private interest, or the influence of ill counselors, be so far misled as not to assemble parliaments, when the public affairs require it; or to declare them dissolved before the ends of their meeting were accomplished; the wisdom of our ancestors has provided by divers statutes, both for the holding of parliaments annually, and that they should not be prorogued or dissolved till all the petitions and bills before them were answered and redressed.[7]

England was like 'all other' civilised European nations in having a 'legal' government characterised by 'well proportioned distribution of powers, whereby the law doth at once provide for the greatness of the king, and the safety of the people'. As Bracton and Bodin both explained, 'it is from the law that [the king] hath his power, it is by the law that he is king, and for the good of the people by whose consent it is made'. Those around the king who opposed these true 'Common-wealth principles'

well know, that parliaments were ordained to prevent such mischiefs as they designed, and if they were suffered to pursue the ends of their institution, would endeavour to preserve all things in their due order. To unite the king unto his people, and the hearts of his people unto the king: to keep the regal authority within the bounds of law, and persuade his majesty to direct it to the public good

---

[3] Sidney, *Apology* pp. 196–7.   [4] Geoffrey Baldwin, 'The Self and the State' ch. 3.
[5] *A Dialogue at Oxford between a Tutor and a Gentleman, Formerly his Pupil, Concerning Government* (1681) p. 15; Pocock, *Virtue, Commerce and History* p. 226.
[6] Sidney [and Jones], *A Just and Modest Vindication* p. cxxxviii.   [7] Ibid. p. cxxxiv.

which the law intends. But as this is repugnant to the introduction of arbitrary power and popery, they who delight in both, cannot but hate it, and chuse rather to bring matters into such a state as may suit with their private interests . . . They can flatter the humor of a misguided prince, and increase their fortunes by the excesses of a wasteful prodigal. The phrenzy of an imperious woman is easily rendered propitious unto them, and they can turn the zeal of a violent bigot to their advantage.[8]

There was nothing explicitly republican about these 'principles', gratuitous insult though they offered to both the king's French Catholic mistress (the Duchess of Portsmouth) and his brother. However, as they had previously been central to the republican delegitimation of 'arbitrary' or tyrannical monarchy, now the revival of this rhetoric supplied a concept of legal government common to republicanism and Whiggism. 'Every English-Man that is not a knave or Fool . . . [is] no more for a Republick, than . . . the Laws make them . . . especially Queen *Elizabeth* having used the word *Commonwealth* in her speeches, and that it is the language of the Law.'[9] In the words of Sidney, 'oaths of allegiance [may be] taken' but 'Allegiance signifies no more (as the words, *ad legem* declare) than such an obedience as the law requires.' Locke similarly insisted: '*Oaths of Allegiance* . . . are taken . . . *Allegiance* being nothing but an *Obedience according to Law.*'[10]

Within this legal order the authority of parliaments, like that of any political institution, was instrumental. Thus Sidney did not 'insist upon the name of a parliament'; there was no 'charm' belonging to the name. Should better means be devised for the achievement of liberty and virtue these could, and should, 'be framed by the consent' of the nation. England, enjoying 'the natural liberty of nations', had always been governed by its own representatives, whether or not they had been been called a parliament, and whether or not they had authorised an executive office called monarchy. 'We may therefore change or take away kings . . . and in all the revolutions we have had in England, the people have been headed by the Parliament, or the nobility and gentry that composed it . . . when the kings failed of their duties.'[11]

Nor did Sidney hesitate to describe the powers of such representatives as 'arbitrary', since 'the establishment of government is an arbitrary act, wholly depending upon the will of men. The particular forms and constitutions, the whole series of magistracy, together with the measure of power given to everyone, and the rules by which they are to exercise their charge, are

[8] Ibid. p. clxx.   [9] [Slings by Bethel], *The Providences of God* (1694) p. 93.
[10] Sidney, *Discourses*, ed. West pp. 520–1; Locke, *Two Treatises* p. 386.
[11] Sidney, *Discourses*, read at Sidney's *Trial*, in *Discourses* (1763) pp. 126–7.

so also.'[12] On 7 January 1681 in the Commons, Sidney's friend Colonel Silius Titus had explained that 'mankind cannot consist together without a supreme Power, and that in our Government is the Legislative'.[13] These statements looked back to the claims of 'arbitrary' and 'absolute' power made for the civil war Long Parliament, particularly by Henry Parker.[14] This was not, however, because such institutions were infallible. On the contrary, it was because governments issued from 'the will of men' that they needed to be collective and bound by law. Even under such circumstances the record of restoration parliaments would not inspire over-confidence. On this point Sidney produced a reprise of Milton's attack on the Long Parliament (published by Roger L'Estrange in 1681):

Our kings had not wherewithal to corrupt many till these last twenty years, and the treachery of a few was not enough to pass a law . . . We are beholden to H[y]de, Cl[i]ff[o]rd and D[a]nby, for all that has been done of that kind. They found a parliament full of lewd young men chosen by a furious people in spite to the Puritans, whose severity had distasted them. The weakest of all ministers had wit enough to understand that such as these might be easily deluded, corrupted or bribed. Some were fond of their seats in parliament, and delighted to domineer over their neighbours by continuing in them. Others preferr'd the cajoleries of the court before the honour of performing their duty to the country that employ'd them. Some sought to relieve their ruined fortunes, and were most forward to give the king a vast revenue, that from thence they might receive pensions: others were glad of a temporary protection against their creditors. Many knew not what they did when they annulled the Triennial Act, voted the militia to be in the king, gave him the excise, customs and chimney-money, made the act for corporations, by which the greatest part of the nation was brought under the power of the worst men in it; drunk or sober pass'd the five mile act, and that for uniformity in the church.[15]

In 1647 the New Model Army had vowed to 'purge . . . such members as for their delinquency, or for corruptions, or abuse to the State, or undue exactions, ought not to sit there'.[16] Yet in the present context, whatever the risk,

'tis less than to put all into the hands of one man and his ministers: the hazard of being ruin'd by those who must perish with us, is not so much to be feared, as by one who may enrich and strengthen himself by our destruction. 'Tis better to

---

[12] Sidney, *Discourses*, ed. West p. 569.
[13] Anchitell Grey (ed.), *Debates in the House of Commons from the Year 1667 to the year 1694* (10 vols., 1763) vol. VIII, p. 278.
[14] Michael Mendle, *Henry Parker and the English Civil War* (Cambridge, 1995) pp. 86–8.
[15] Sidney, *Discourses*, ed. West p. 571.
[16] *A Declaration, or representation from His Excellency Sir Thomas Fairfax* (14 June 1647), in Kenyon (ed.), *Stuart Constitution* p. 265.

depend upon those who are under a possibility of being again corrupted, than upon one who applies himself to corrupt them, because he cannot otherwise accomplish his designs. It were to be wished that our security were more certain; but this being, under God, the best anchor we have, it deserves to be preserved with all care, till one of a more unquestionable strength be framed by the consent of the nation.[17]

Whereas a prince, pretending superiority to positive law, was a slave to his 'passions, interests, vices, or [the] malice and wickedness of [his] . . . ministers', an assembly regulated by that law was far preferable.[18]

These laws are either immemorial customs, or statutes. The first have their beginning and continuance from the universal consent of the nation. The latter receive their authority and force of laws from parliaments . . . These are under God the best defence of our lives, liberties and estates: they proceed not from the blind, corrupt and fluctuating humor of a man, but from the mature deliberation of the choicest persons of the nation, and such as have the greatest interest in it.[19]

In this respect,

The question is not, whether the parliament be impeccable or infallible, but whether an assembly of nobility, with a house of commons composed of those who are best esteemed by their neighbours in all the towns and counties of England, are more or less subject to error or corruption, than such a man, woman or child, as happens to be next in blood to the last king. Many men do usually see more than one . . . Such as are of mature age, good experience, and approved reputation for virtue and wisdom, will probably judge better than children or fools . . . If some counties or cities fail to chuse such men as are eminently capable, all will hardly be so mistaken as to chuse those who have no more of wisdom or virtue, than is usually entail'd upon families.[20]

The accusation of separation of (royal, private) interest from that of the public was equally common to Sidney's *Court Maxims* and *Discourses*, Marvell's *The Growth of Popery and Arbitrary Government* (1677), and Locke's *Two Treatises*. According to Locke, this was the condition of England when 'flattery prevailed with weak Princes to make use of [their] power for private ends . . . and not for the publick good . . . as if the Prince had a seperate Interest from the good of the Community . . . [this] tend[s] . . . to set up one part, or Party, with a distinction from . . . the rest'.[21] In this

---

[17] Sidney, *Discourses*, ed. West p. 572.   [18] Ibid. p. 534.   [19] Ibid. p. 558.

[20] Ibid. p. 532. As Sidney had explained in the *Maxims*, 'A senate or an assembly may . . . be deceived. But their passions are not so easily moved when composed of many men of the greatest experience and choicest parts.' Sidney, *Court Maxims* p. 30.

[21] Sidney, *Discourses*, in *Sydney on Government* pp. 188, 379–80; Locke, *Two Treatises* paras. 162–3.

respect the parliamentary nature of the Restoration settlement of 1660–5 could become the basis of an alternative kind of appeal:

> can his majesty believe that he doth duly repay unto his protestant subjects the kindness they shewed him, when they recalled him from a miserable, helpless banishment, and with so much dutiful affection placed him on the throne, enlarged his revenue above what any of his predecessors had enjoyed, and gave him vaster sums of money in twenty years, than had been bestowed upon all the kings since Wm I. should he, after all this, deliver them up to be ruined by his brother?[22]

This was an accusation of ingratitude to be repeatedly levelled by the *Discourses*, in terms reminiscent of the *Maxims*. In both works Sidney spoke not only, with Locke, of 'distinction' of interest, but 'irreconcileable contrariety'.

> When a magistrate . . . sets up an interest . . . in himself, repugnant to the good of the publick, for which he is made to be what he is . . . This creates a most fierce and irreconcileable enmity . . . The people think it the greatest of all crimes, to convert that power to their hurt, which was instituted for their good; and that the injustice is aggravated by perjury and ingratitude . . . and the magistrate gives the name of sedition or rebellion to whatsoever they do for the preservation of themselves and their own rights. When men's spirits are thus prepared, a small matter sets them on fire . . . and when any occasion whether foreign or domestick, arises, in which the magistrate stands in need of the people's assistance, they, whose affections are alienated, not only shew an unwillingness to serve him with their persons, and estates, but fear that by delivering him from his distress they strengthen their enemy, and enable him to oppress them.[23]

The last such occasion had been in 1640. In a conversation with his fellow conspirators in 1683, Sidney is reported to have explained, 'That he looked upon a rising in Scotland to be of infinite advantage and security to us . . . [and] he thought we must tell the world how the King had broken the laws and his own oath, and secure the settlement of the kingdom to a parliament, which if we were successful would know how to provide for the safety of themselves and the people.'[24] Locke's *Two Treatises* insisted that using 'force to hinder the *meeting* . . . *of the Legislative*, when the Original Constitution, or the publick Exigencies require it . . . [introduces] a state of War with the People, who have a right to *reinstate* their *Legislative in the Exercise* of their Power'.[25]

---

[22] Sidney [and Jones], *A Just and Modest Vindication* p. clviii.
[23] Sidney, *Discourses*, in *Sydney on Government* pp. 379–80.
[24] Ford, Lord Grey, *The Secret History of the Rye House Plot* pp. 51–3, 55. For Sidney's expectant commentary upon the Scots rising of 1679 see Scott, *Algernon Sidney and the Restoration Crisis* pp. 149–53.
[25] Locke, *Two Treatises* p. 388.

To Sidney it seemed clear from Roman history that it was one 'exercise of the natural liberty of nations' that 'If officers . . . neglected their duty of calling such assemblies when the publick affairs required, the people met by their own authority, and punished the person, or abrogated the magistracy.'[26]

> [Kings] may call parliaments, if there be occasion, at times when the law does not exact it; they are placed as sentinels, and ought vigilantly to observe the motions of the enemy . . . But if the sentinel fall asleep, neglect his duty, or maliciously endeavour to betray the city, those who are concern'd may make use of all other means to know their danger, and to preserve themselves . . . if that magistrate had been drunk, mad, or gained by the enemy, no wise man can think that formalities were to have been observed. In such cases every man is a magistrate; and he who best knows the danger, and the means of preventing it, has a right of calling the senate or people to an assembly.[27]

As it turned out, the invasion which did five years later confront a 'popish and arbitrary' prince deserted by his people, came not from Scotland but from the United Provinces. Among its public objectives was the summoning of a 'free' parliament. In the carefully chosen words of William's *Declaration*,

> It is . . . evident to all men, that the publick peace and happiness of any state cannot be preserved where the law, liberties and customs, established by the lawful authority in it, are openly transgressed and annulled; more especially, where the alteration of religion is endeavoured, and that a religion, which is contrary to law . . . those counselors, who have now the chief credit with the King, have overturned the religion, laws and liberties of these Realms, and subjected them . . . to arbitrary government.[28]

A MONARCHICAL REPUBLIC?

It was the most important actual objective of Dutch military intervention to bring the Stuart kingdoms into the European alliance against France. Within England, in turn, participation in this conflict furnished the decisive context for transformation of the English military-fiscal state. One consequence was to end the seventeenth-century crisis of monarchy by

---

[26] Sidney, *Discourses*, in *Sydney on Government* pp. 503, 505.
[27] Sidney, *Discourses*, ed. West pp. 528–9.
[28] William III [Caspar Fagel], *The Declaration of His Highness . . . for restoring the laws and liberties of England, Scotland and Ireland* (1688), in Robert Beddard (ed.), *A Kingdom Without a King* (Oxford, 1988) p. 125; Jonathan Israel, 'Introduction', in Israel, *The Anglo-Dutch Moment*; Scott, *England's Troubles* chs. 9, 20–21.

spectacularly refounding its fiscal and military effectiveness. In exchange for this power, however, the crown accepted a significant dimunition of its legal and constitutional autonomy. The result was a monarchy newly dependent upon parliaments; what some historians have called 'a crowned republic'.[29]

From 1689, in addition to its financial dependence upon annual parliaments, the crown reluctantly accepted a *Declaration of Rights*, the regulation by statute of the succession and the surrender (in 1694) of its sole prerogative to summon, prorogue and dissolve parliaments. In the first new coronation oath since 1308, William and Mary undertook to govern not only 'for the maintaining of the Protestant religion and the laws and liberties of this nation', but 'according to the statutes in Parliament agreed on, and the laws and customs of the same'. By 1698 parliaments had demonstrated political, as well as fiscal control of the nation's armed forces. The Act of Settlement of 1701, entitled 'An Act for the further limitation of the Crown, and better securing the rights and liberties of the subject', removed the power of royal pardon in relation to parliamentary impeachments, and subjected aspects of foreign policy, the king's dispensation of patronage, his relationship with his Privy Council and the whereabouts of his person to parliamentary approval.[30] In binding the crown to a protestant succession, it subordinated the hereditary and dynastic principle to the state's confessional security. This was to determine the outcome of a contest with its origins in the early Elizabethan succession crisis.

The effect of this was, in the words of John Somers, to secure after a century of strife what remained salvageable of a government 'legal, not arbitrary, and political, not absolute'. It was to preserve, that is to say, within a dramatically modernised military-fiscal infrastructure, these medieval, and in origin classical, political principles. This made it possible for some republican writers to claim the actual achievement of a government of laws rather than of men. The Act of Settlement specified that 'the laws of England are the birthright of the people'.[31] Yet this achievement was fragile, incomplete, and always in danger from domestic constitutional backsliding, to say nothing of the military contest with a foreign popish

---

[29] Jonathan Israel, *Conflicts of Empires: Spain, the Low Countries and the Struggle for World Supremacy 1585–1713* (1997) p. xix.

[30] Geoffrey Holmes, *The Making of a Great Power: Late Stuart and Early Georgian Britain 1660–1720* (1993) p. 216; Henry Horwitz, *Parliament, Policy and Politics in the Reign of William III* (Manchester, 1977) pp. 281–3; Julian Hoppit, *A Land of Liberty: England 1689–1727* (Oxford, 2000) p. 39.

[31] Hoppit, *Liberty* p. 40.

tyranny. At the same time a rapidly expanding political executive attracted growing opposition.[32]

It was a new Anglo-Dutch government, committed to the military contest against France, which completed the process of Anglo-Dutch statebuilding commenced during the 1640s and 1650s. The fortunes of Whiggism were bound up with those of a powerful modern fiscal-military state, heavily indebted to this legacy. Whereas the Levellers had emerged to challenge the Long Parliament's extraordinary new-found power, the English republic had inherited it. As, after 1649, the rhetoric of liberty from government had taken second place to that of puritan magistracy, so during the 1690s an emphasis upon parliamentary sovereignty would be accompanied by a renewed moral rhetoric of reformation of manners (to be defended against popery and corruption). These were combined with other ideological inheritances associated with the Levellers themselves, including an insistence upon liberty of conscience and other God-given natural rights, to be defended against arbitrary government or tyranny in whatever governmental form.

When, in 1665, the ex-republican George Downing tried to turn the royal exchequer into a bank, the Earl of Clarendon had complained that banks were republican institutions unfit for monarchy.[33] When in 1694 the Bank of England was actually founded, on the model of the Bank of Amsterdam, the same complaint ('that it would undermine royal authority for banks were only fit for republics') made little impression upon a militarily preoccupied Dutch king.[34] Five years later, in the *Dedication* of his edition of Harrington's *Oceana*, John Toland described the

BANK of *England*, which, like the Temple of SATURN among the *Romans*, is esteem'd so sacred a Repository, that even Foreners think their Treasure more safely lodg'd there than with themselves at home; and this not only don by the

---

[32] *Now is the Time: A Scheme for a Commonwealth* (1688); *Good Advice before it be too late* (1689); Mark Goldie, 'The Roots of True Whiggism 1688–1694', *History of Political Thought* 1, 2 (1980); Blair Worden, 'The Revolution'.

[33] 'Downing . . . told them . . . by making the Payment with Interest so certain and fixed, that . . . it should be out of any Man's Power to cause any Money that should be lent To-morrow to be paid before that which was lent Yesterday . . . he would make [the] Exchequer (which was now Bankrupt and without any Credit) the best and the greatest Bank in Europe . . . and all Nations would sooner send their Money into [it] . . . than into *Amsterdam* or *Genoa* or *Venice*. And it cannot be enough wondered at, that this Intoxication prevailed so far that no Argument would be heard against it . . . without weighing that the Security for Monies so deposited in Banks is the Republick itself, which must expire before that Security can fail; which can never be depended on in a Monarchy, where the Monarch's sole word can cancel all those formal Provisions . . . upon that and the like Acts of Parliament.' Edward Hyde, Earl of Clarendon, *The Continuation of the Life of Edward Earl of Clarendon*, vol. ii (Oxford, 1760) pp. 195–6.

[34] Quoted in Horwitz, *Parliament* p. 131.

Subjects of Absolute Princes, where there can be no room for any Public Credit, but likewise by the Inhabitants of those Commonwealths where alone such Banks were hitherto reputed secure. I am the more willing to make this Remark, because the constitution of our Bank is both preferable to that of all others, and coms nearest of any Government to HARRINGTON's Model.[35]

Thus by the 1690s legal and constitutional government was a fiscal, as well as political issue. No less important than, and closely tied to, parliamentary participation in the longer-term fiscal reconstruction of the British state, were the fiscal and administrative resources of London. This, too, built upon a deep mid-century involvement in republican politics and policy. When in 1679 the City faced a new period of crisis, it stressed the need for internal unity against the popish menace in the following terms:

Let it never be said of this Famous City (the present Envy of all her Neighbours) as once it was of old *Rome* (then the envy of the whole World) *Roma suis Viribus ruit*; Rome's Destruction was from her self . . . *Rome* indeed had many and powerful enemies Abroad; but had she not Divided within Her Self, and fallen into *Faction* at Home, those could not have hurt Her.[36]

In 1688 the author of this speech, Sir Robert Clayton, welcomed the Dutch invaders, and helped to put the financial resources of London at their disposal. As Toland recounted,

Whenever therefore the execrable design was hatcht to inslave the Inhabitants of this Country, the first Attemts were . . . made on the government of the City, as there also the strongest and most successful Efforts were first us'd to restore Freedom: for we may remember (to name one instance for all) when the late King was fled, and every thing in confusion, that then the chief Nobility and Gentry resorted to *Guildhall* for protection, and to concert proper methods for settling the Nation hereafter on a Basis of Liberty never to be shaken.[37]

Thus dedicating his edition of Harrington's *Oceana* 'to the Lord Mayor, Aldermen, Sherifs and Common Council of London', Toland went on to claim,

'Tis solely to its Government that *London* ows being universally acknowleg'd the largest, fairest, richest, and most populous City in the World . . . LIBERTY is the true Spring of its prodigious Trade and Commerce with all the known parts of the Universe, and is the original Planter of its many fruitful Colonys in *America*,

---

[35] John Toland, *To the Lord Mayor, Aldermen, Sherifs, and Common Council of London, The Dedication* of James Harrington, *Oceana*, ed. Toland (1700) p. iii.

[36] Sir Robert Clayton, *The Speech of Sir Robert Clayton Kt. Lord Mayor Select for the City of London* (29 September 1679) pp. 2–3.

[37] Toland, *The Dedication* p. iii; for the role of London in 1688–9 see Scott, *England's Troubles* pp. 218–25 and references there given.

with its numberless Factorys in *Europe, Asia*, and *Africa*: hence it is that every Sea is cover'd with our Ships, that the very Air is scarce exemted from our Inventions, and that all the Productions of Art or Nature are imported to this common Storehouse of Mankind . . . LIBERTY has elevated the native Citizens of *London* to so high a degree . . . she well deserves the name of a *New Rome in the West*, and, like the old one, to becom the Soverain Mistress of the Universe.[38]

In relation to the present war it was the optimistic view of Charles Davenant (a student of both Machiavelli and Sidney) that though 'great monarchies do easily overrun and swallow up the lesser tyrannies and principalities that are round them . . . they find much harder work, and another sort of opposition, when they come to invade commonwealths, or mixed governments, where people have an interest in the laws'.[39] However, in his *An Account of Denmark, As It was in the Year 1692* (1694), Robert Molesworth issued a warning: 'We all know how many grievous Tempests . . . this Vessel of our Commonwealth has undergone. The perpetual Contests between the Kings and the People (whilst those endeavour'd to acquire a greater Power then was legally due, and these to recover their just Liberties) have been the contending Billows that have kept it afloat'.[40] Although England might now have recovered its liberty, and increased European stature, the price of retaining these would be eternal vigilance. For it concerned every English person to know 'by what steps *Slavery* had within these last 200 years crept upon *Europe*, most of the Protestant, as well as Popish Countries having in a manner quite lost the Precious Jewel *Liberty*'.

To defend 'the legal Liberties of the *English Nation*' two things would be requisite. Since the first act of a '*Tyranny*' was 'the enslaving the Spirits of the People', the first was suitable education. For this the model came from 'The *Greeks* and *Romans*' who 'recommended above all things the Duty to their Country, the Preservation of the laws and Publick Liberty; subservient to which, they preach'd up Moral Vertues, such as Fortitude, Temperance, Justice, a Contempt of Death, etc'. Thus 'The Books that are left us of the *Ancients* . . . are full of Doctrines . . . and Examples exhorting to the Conservation or Recovery of the Publick *Liberty*, which was once valued above Life . . . and though *Brutus* be generally declaimed against by modern School-boys, He was then esteemed the true Pattern and Model of exact Vertue.'[41] Such education was the more necessary for

---

[38] Toland, *The Dedication* pp. i–ii, iv.
[39] Quoted in Kustaa Multamaki, *Towards Great Britain: Commerce and Conquest in the Thought of Algernon Sidney and Charles Davenant* (Helsinki, 1999) p. 155.
[40] Robert Molesworth, *An Account of Denmark, As it was in the year 1692* (1694), Preface.
[41] Ibid.

'the Gentlemen of *England* . . . since they make so considerable a part of
our Government in *Parliament*'. The second essential to the preservation
and improvement of recently secured liberty was not simply 'frequent free
Assemblies of the *States*', but their preparedness to improve the laws over
time. For 'nothing which even the Representative Body of the People does,
which shall afterwards tend to the detriment of the universality can then be
obligatory, because many things good and profitable at the time of making
those Laws may be quite contrary afterwards'. Such problems could only
be exacerbated if 'these Assemblies be hindred, or corrupted by sinister
practices'. Thus even 'the acts of one general *Parliament*, though a free
one, are not perpetually obliging . . . but [a part of] the acts of an eternal
Succession of *Parliaments*, who make, confirm, change, or repeal Laws at
their pleasure'.

Given these emphases it is no surprise to learn that Molesworth was
an admirer of Sidney, whose inscription in the Commonplace Book at the
University of Copenhagen he recalled.[42] Similarly the Scot Andrew Fletcher
insisted upon the need for political change. For Fletcher, as for Molesworth,
that modern European 'governments are changed from monarchies to
tyrannies' registered 'the alteration of government which happened in most
countries of Europe about the year 1500'. This was the republican historical
theory indebted to Hotman and De Comines (De Comines was quoted at
length).[43] Fletcher, however, related this transformation much more fully
to developments in modern European political economy. This reflected his
concern with the economic context for changes in public manners:

Thus the Italians began to come off from their frugal and military way of living,
and addicted themselves to the pursuit of refined and expensive pleasures . . . This
infection spread itself by degrees into the neighbouring nations. But these things
alone had not been sufficient to work so great a change in government, if a preceding
invention . . . had not produced more new and extraordinary effects than any had
ever done before . . . I mean, the invention of the needle, by the help of which
navigation was greatly improved, a passage opened by sea to the East Indies,
and a new world discovered. By this means the luxury of Asia and America was
added to that of the antients; and all ages, and all countries concurred to sink
Europe into an abyss of pleasures; which were rendered the more expensive by a

---

[42] '[M]anus haec inimica tyrannis/Ense petit placidam sub libertate quietem' ('this hand, enemy to
tyrants, seeks by the sword peace with liberty'). Molesworth does not record that before this emblem
Sidney signed himself 'PHILIPPUS SIDNEY'. Scott, *Algernon Sidney and the English Republic*
p. 133.

[43] Andrew Fletcher, *A Discourse of Government With relation to Militias* (Edinburgh, 1698), in Fletcher,
Political Works, ed. John Robertson (Cambridge, 1997) pp. 2, 4, 7–8.

perpetual change of the fashions in clothes, equipage and furniture of houses. These things brought a total alteration in the way of living, upon which all government depends.[44]

Amid these changes, "'Tis true knowledge being mightily increased, and a great curiosity and nicety in every thing introduced, men imagined themselves to be gainers in all points . . . But . . . they did not consider the unspeakable evils that are altogether inseperable from an expensive way of living.'[45] The question accordingly became, in a Europe dominated by absolute monarchies and modernising states dependent upon the new political economy of global commerce, how was liberty to be preserved? Within this context Fletcher's concern was specific, for like much of the most important republican writing of William's reign, his tract was a contribution to the debate in 1698 about a standing army.

The occasion for this was the cessation of the national military struggle with the Peace of Ryswick in 1697 (the first edition of Fletcher's *Discourse* was published in 1697). While the king wished, in the meantime at least, to maintain a substantial military establishment, many of his opponents wanted this fiscal burden rapidly dissolved. Fletcher was one of several writers to describe this issue as the crucial acid test of liberty: 'A good militia is of such importance to a nation, that it is the chief part of the constitution of any free government.'[46] This was not only because everywhere in Europe absolute monarchies and standing armies were inseparable. As authorities from Aristotle to Machiavelli had explained, so too were political liberty and citizen militias. 'That the whole free people of any nation ought to be exercised to arms, not only the example of our ancestors . . . [but] that of the wisest governments among the ancients' testified.

The militia of antient Rome, the best that ever was in any government, made her mistress of the world; but standing armies enslaved that great people . . . The Lacedemonians continued eight hundred years free, and in great honour, because they had a good militia. The Swisses at this day are the freest, happiest, and the people of all Europe who can best defend themselves, because they have the best militia.[47]

Accordingly for Fletcher, the most important aspect of that education of youth and formation of manners stressed by Molesworth concerned 'a severe discipline, and a right method of disposing the minds of men, as well as forming their bodies, for military and virtuous actions'.[48] Meanwhile, if commerce and money were the new motors of European politics, for what purpose was that money being deployed? What other than 'those

---

[44] Ibid. pp. 5–6.   [45] Ibid.   [46] Ibid. p. 21.   [47] Ibid. p. 22.   [48] Ibid. pp. 22, 24.

vast armies of mercenaries' condemned by Machiavelli had made possible 'this change . . . upon Europe to her affliction and ruin'? 'Let us then see if mercenary armies be not exactly calculated to enslave a nation.'[49]

[I]f a mercenary standing army be kept up, (the first of that kind, except those of the usurper Cromwel, and the late King James, that Britain has seen for thirteen hundred years) I desire to know where the security of the British liberties lies, unless in the good will and pleasure of the King. [Whereas] The subjects formerly had a real security for their liberty, by having the sword in their own hands . . . It must be a French fashion of monarchy, where the king has power to do what he pleases, and the people no security for anything they possess.[50]

It was important to understand, to avoid 'the fate of all the other kingdoms in Europe', that 'a government is not only a tyranny, when tyrannically exercised; but also when there is no sufficient caution in the constitution that it may not be exercised tyrannically'. Thus 'our forefathers had two securities for their liberties and properties, they had both the sword and the purse'.[51] In the newly dangerous context of modern political economy, the future of liberty in Britain would depend upon the capacity of parliaments to retain control of both.

Other pamphlets against a standing army included Toland's *The Militia Reformed* (1698) and Walter Moyle and John Trenchard's *An Argument, Shewing, that a Standing Army is inconsistent with A Free Government, and absolutely destructive to the Constitution of the English Monarchy* (Parts One and Two, 1697). According to the latter, whereas 'we see most Nations in *Europe* over-run with Oppression and Slavery, where the Lives, Estates and Liberties of the people are subject to the lawless Fancy and Ambition of the Prince', the case was otherwise in England. Within the outward form of monarchy lay the full constitutional achievement of liberty as earlier republicans had described it:

Our Constitution is a limited mix'd Monarchy, where the King enjoys all the Prerogatives necessary to the support of his Dignity, and Protection of his people, and is only abridged from the power of Injuring his own Subjects . . . and our Government may truly be called an Empire of Laws, and not of Men; for every Man has the same right to what he can acquire by his Labour and Industry, as the King hath to his Crown, and . . . No Man can be imprisoned, unless he has transgressed a Law of his own making . . . so that we enjoy a Liberty scarce known to the antient *Greeks* and *Romans*.[52]

---

[49] Ibid. p. 14.   [50] Ibid. pp. 12, 18.

[51] Andrew Fletcher, *Two Discourses Concerning the Affairs of Scotland* (Edinburgh, 1698) in Fletcher, *Political Works* p. 50.

[52] Walter Moyle and John Trenchard, *An Argument, Shewing* (1697) pp. 2–3.

Like Fletcher, and Machiavelli and Sidney before him, Moyle and Trenchard discussed

the *Israelites, Athenians, Corinthians, Achaians, Lacedemonians, Thebans, Samnites,* and *Romans* . . . [where] there was no difference between the Citizen, the Souldier, and the Husbandman, for all promiscuously took Arms when the publick Safety required it . . . that Nation is surest to live in Peace, that is most capable of making War . . . What is it that preserved the glorious Commonwealth of *Rome*, but Swords in the hands of its Citizens?[53]

They also made a conspicuous effort to adapt Harringtonian analysis to present circumstances.

[O]ur Constitution depending upon a due ballance between King, Lords and Commons . . . this Ballance can never be preserved but by an Union of the natural and artificial Strength of the Kingdom, that is, by making the Militia to consist of the same Persons as have the Property; or otherwise the Government is violent and against Nature, and cannot possibly continue.[54]

Thus it is no surprise that when the tract invokes 'the Authority of as great Men as the World hath produced' for the indespensability of 'a settled Militia', those named are Machiavelli, 'My Lord *Bacon*' and 'Mr. *Harrington*', who 'hath founded his whole *Oceana* upon a trained Militia'.[55] In the history of standing armies, by contrast, 'The first under *Cromwell*, expell'd that Parliament under which they had fought successfully for many Years; afterwards under General *Monk* they destroy'd the Government they before set up, and brought back *Charles* the Second.'[56] To this catalogue the *Second Part* added, 'the first Project we find for a Standing Army, in the Year 1629 . . . to bridle the Impertinence of Parliaments; to overaw the Parliament and Nation; to make Edicts to be Laws . . . in short, to overturn the whole Frame of this noble English Government'.[57] This was an example also revisited by Toland in his *A Defence of the Parliament of 1640. And the people of England, Against king Charles I . . . containing A short Account of some of . . . [his] many Illegal, Arbitrary, Popish and tyrannical Actions* (1698). The same author's version of Ludlow's *Memoirs* (1698–9) emphasised not only the dangers of corruption in general, but the Lord Protector's betrayal 'of the public cause' in particular: 'Certainly it can never be esteemed by a wise man to be worth the scratch of a finger to remove a single person acting by an arbitrary power, in order to set up another with the same unlimited authority.'[58] More broadly Toland was a key figure behind the creation, by

---

[53] Ibid. pp. 6–7, 12–13.   [54] Ibid. p. 4.   [55] Ibid. pp. 23–4.   [56] Ibid. p. 28.
[57] Moyle and Trenchard, *The Second Part of an Argument, Shewing* (1697) pp. 5–6.
[58] Quoted by Worden, *Roundhead Reputations* p. 74.

publication or republication, of what would become the English republican canon. In addition to Ludlow, and Harrington's *Oceana* (with 'Life', 1700), he was perhaps responsible for the first edition of Sidney's *Discourses* (1698) and republication of Neville's *Plato Redivivus* in the same year, and certainly for *The Life of John Milton* (1698), accompanied by Milton's *Historical and Political Works* (1698).

Given our knowledge of what Toland did to Ludlow's *Voyce* there is reason to pay attention to those features distinguishing Sidney's *Discourses* (for which no manuscript has survived) from his *Maxims*. These included drastic diminution of its religious content and elaboration of its sceptical Machiavellianism. Foremost among general developments in the moral discourse of this period, John Pocock identified 'politeness' as a Whig adaptation of classical republican virtue to meet the needs of commercial society.[59] If so this adaptation, which attempted to embrace passions like pride which had been the antithesis of Christian humanist virtue, involved significant discontinuity. Nor was the associated culture of civility peculiar to Whiggism, or indeed to the early eighteenth century.[60] Nevertheless under the premiership of Sir Robert Walpole, John Trenchard and Thomas Gordon's *Catos Letters* listed 'all civil virtue, and happiness, every moral excellency, all politeness, all good arts and sciences' as among 'the necessary effects . . . of liberty'.[61] Foremost among authorities enlisted in defence of this liberty were Harrington and Sidney.

From Machiavelli, readers were reminded that 'as a tyranny cannot be established but by destroying Brutus; so a free government is not to be preserved but by destroying Brutus's sons'.[62] For the detection of public corruption ('the iniquity of the times, or the iniquities of particular men') the lessons of ancient and modern histories were brought to bear. That Sidney was 'an author who can never be too much valued and read' derived from his account of the impact of tyranny, of the relationship between civil liberty and military virtue,[63] of the distinction between liberty and slavery,[64] and more generally of the relationship between government and manners. 'Liberty cannot be preserved', Sidney was quoted as saying,

---

[59] Pocock, *Machiavellian Moment* pp. 462–505; see also Lawrence Klein, *Shaftesbury and the Culture of Politeness: Moral Discourse and Cultural Politics in Early Eighteenth Century England* (Cambridge, 1994).

[60] Markku Peltonen, 'Politeness and Whiggism, 1688–1732', unpublished draft article; Peltonen, *The Duel in Early Modern England: Civility, Politeness and Honour* (Cambridge, 2003). See also Iain Hampsher-Monk, 'From Virtue to Politeness', in van Gelderen and Skinner, *Republicanism* vol. II.

[61] Quoted in Peltonen, 'Politeness' p. 21.

[62] Trenchard and Gordon, *Cato's Letters* vol. I, no. 16. II February 1720.

[63] Ibid. 10 February 1721, pp. 450–71.   [64] Ibid. 27 January 1721, pp. 426–42.

if the manners of the people are corrupted; nor absolute monarchy introduced, where they are sincere . . . Man naturally follows that which is good, or seems to him to be so. Hence it is, that in well-governed states, where a value is put upon virtue, and no one honoured unless for such qualities as are beneficial to the publick; men are from the tenderest years brought up in a belief, that nothing in this world deserves to be sought after, but such honours as are acquired by virtuous actions; By this means virtue itself becomes popular, as in Sparta, Rome, and other places, where riches (which, with the vanity that follows them, and the honours men give to them, are the root of all evil) were either totally banished, or little regarded.[65]

This warning about riches did not here, any more than in Sidney himself, stand in the way of another disquisition concerning the superiority of republican cities to 'single rulers' in matters of commerce and naval power.[66] Here, as in Sidney's *Discourses*, England took its cue from a succession of free states including Athens, Venice and the Netherlands. All this despite the fact that England was not a republic, at least in Harringtonian terms.

It proceeds from a consummate ignorance in politicks, to think that a number of men agreeing together can make and hold a commonwealth, before nature has prepared the way; for she alone must do it. An equality of estate will give an equality of power; and an equality of power is a commonwealth, or democracy: An agrarian law, or something equivalent to it, must make or find a suitable disposition of property . . . and without all this it is impossible to settle a commonwealth here.[67]

Yet in a world where the 'immense majority of the whole race of men crouch under the yoke of tyrants', England was 'a free state', both popular and legal, its 'parliaments . . . the keepers and barriers of our liberty'. Indeed 'our government is a thousand degrees nearer a-kin to a commonwealth . . . than it is to absolute monarchy'. This made 'Mr Sidney's book' not only 'eternally true', but 'agreeable to our own constitution, which is the best republick in the world, with a prince at the head of it'. Nor were the passages quoted from Sidney 'republican passages, unless virtue and truth be republican'.[68] In short, the form of the nation's consititution was only important in general terms, in subjecting magistracy to the rule of law. The survival of the Dutch republic ('the most virtuous and flourishing state which ever yet appeared in the world') owed far more to the moral qualities of its citizens and public life, than to the manifest fragilities of its constitution.[69]

This rhetorical continuity was the more striking in that the moral philosophy actually expounded by *Catos Letters* frequently departed from Sidney's

[65] Ibid. 15 April 1721, pp. 180–5; 22 April 1721, pp. 189, 190.
[66] Ibid. 13 February 1721, pp. 442–50. [67] Ibid. vol. II, 14 July 1722, p. 614.
[68] Ibid. vol. I no. 37, 15 July 1721, p. 262. [69] Ibid. vol. II, 14 July 1722, pp. 617–18.

own. In its sceptical insistence upon the primary importance of the passions, this owed far more to Hobbes than to Milton.⁷⁰ This was particularly obvious in the discussion of the natural 'Equality . . . of Men', in which passages in explicit agreement with Hobbes not only stood in sharp contrast to Sidney's account of natural inequality, but took issue with passages from Aristotle's *Politics* which he had quoted in his support.⁷¹ Similarly, *Cato* emphasised, in a manner comparable to Locke, that liberty was an absolute and inalienable property of all men, by virtue of their God-given reason.⁷² Although Sidney agreed with this as a statement about rights derived from nature, in practice like Milton he had emphasised the unequal capacity of different persons, and nations, to give this liberty political expression. Yet none of this impeded the relevance to *Cato*'s political purposes of Sidney's relentless juxtaposition of liberty and virtue to tyranny and corruption. Following the accession of George III in 1760, Sidney's standing as a 'patriot hero' was further augmented, resulting in a series of republications of his works (six in English between 1750 and 1805) and thereafter biographies (in addition to those prefacing his works, five between 1813 and 1885).⁷³

CONCLUSION: THE ANGLO-DUTCH ACHIEVEMENT

The eighteenth-century impact of English republican writing was at least as powerful outside the country as within it. This was particularly so on the European continent (the Netherlands, Germany and France) and in the American colonies.⁷⁴ Sidney's *Discourses* was published not only in England and Scotland, but in France, the Netherlands, Germany and America. By 1734 Rousseau and Montesquieu, who both praised him, owned copies.⁷⁵

---

⁷⁰ Ibid. vol. 1, 29 July and 5 August 1721, pp. 273–82; a point noted by Pocock, *Machiavellian Moment* pp. 470–1. See also the discussion in Rahe, *Republics Ancient and Modern*, volume II, pp. 203–5.
⁷¹ Ibid. 16 September 1721, pp. 306–8.
⁷² Ibid. 30 December 1721, pp. 405–13.
⁷³ For details see Scott, *Algernon Sidney and the English Republic* pp. 1–2; Scott, *Algernon Sidney and the Restoration Crisis* p. 361. See also Worden, *Roundhead Reputations* pp. 172–4.
⁷⁴ R. C. Winthrop, *Addresses and Speeches 1852–1867* (1867) pp. 154–6; Robbins, 'Algernon Sidney's *Discourses*' p. 276; Robbins, *The Eighteenth Century Commonwealthman*; Scott, *Algernon Sidney and the English Republic* ch. 1; Peter Karsten, *Patriot-Heroes in England and America* (Madison, Wisc., 1978); Russell Smith, *Harrington*; Bailyn, *Ideological Origins*; G. P. Gooch, *Germany and the French Revolution* (1920) pp. 62, 117.
⁷⁵ Karsten, *Patriot-Heroes* pp. 215–16; R. Shackleton, 'Montesquieu and Machiavelli: a Reappraisal', *Comparative Literature Studies* 1 (1964) pp. 8–10; Bertrand Russell, *History of Western Philosophy* (1946) p. 749; Jean-Jacques Rousseau, *The Social Contract and Discourses*, ed. G. D. H. Cole (1973) pp. 93, 120; Rousseau, *Political Writings* ed. C. E. Vaughan (2 vols., Oxford, 1962) vol. 1, p. 240; vol. II pp. 205–6.

During the French revolution the writings of Nedham, Milton, Harrington and Sidney were all translated and adapted.[76] In America John Adams wrote to Jefferson in 1823 calling for 'As splendid an edition of . . . [the *Discourses*] as the art of printing can produce – as well for the intrinsic merit of the work, as for the proof it brings of the bitter sufferings of the advocates of liberty from that time to this.'[77] Rousseau, Adams and Jefferson all associated Sidney and Locke as pre-eminent political authorities, Jefferson adding to the list Aristotle and Cicero, and Adams Plato and Aristotle, Cicero, Livy and Harrington.[78] According to the analysis by H. Trevor Colbourn, by far the predominant political texts held by eighteenth-century American libraries, public and private, were *Catos Letters*, Locke's *Two Treatises* and Sidney's *Discourses*.[79]

This is to remind us that for French, American, Dutch and German political writers, English republicans were key sources for Enlightenment.[80] According to Jonathan Israel this was a Europe-wide phenomenon 'that most emphatically was not inspired by any single nation, be it France, England, or the Netherlands, but rather had its centre of gravity in north-western Europe and particularly in the inner circuit linking Amsterdam, the other main Dutch cities, Paris, London, Hamburg and Berlin'.[81] By contrast to it, 'the Renaissance and the Reformation . . . are really only adjustments . . . to what was still a theologically conceived and ordered regional society, based on hierarchy and ecclesiastical authority'. Yet the Enlightenment,

European and global – not only attacked and severed the roots of traditional European culture in the sacred, magic, kingship, and hierarchy, secularizing all institutions and ideas, but . . . effectively demolished all legitimation of monarchy, aristocracy, woman's subordination to man, ecclesiastical authority, and slavery,

---

[76] Aulard, *The French Revolution* vol. 1, p. 111; H. T. Parker, *The Cult of Antiquity and the French Revolutionaries* (Chicago, 1937) pp. 172–3, 175–7; *Lettre de felicitation de Milord Sidney*; Hammersley, 'Camille Desmoulins's *Le Vieux Cordelier*' pp. 115–32; Baker, 'Transformations of Classical Republicanism'.

[77] *The Adams-Jefferson Letters* quoted by Thomas West, 'Foreword', in Sidney, *Discourses*, ed. West p. xv. See also Robbins, 'Algernon Sidney's *Discourses*'; Bailyn, *Ideological Origins* pp. 34–5, 40, 45, 132.

[78] Thomas Jefferson, *Political Writings*, ed. J. Appleby and T. Ball, 2nd edn (Cambridge, 1999) pp. 148, 273–4; Patterson, *Early Modern Liberalism* p. 279.

[79] H. Trevor Colbourn, *The Lamp of Experience* (Chapel Hill, 1965) pp. 199–232, discussed by Karsten, *Patriot-Heroes* p. 35.

[80] J. G. A. Pocock, *Barbarism and Religion: the Enlightenments of Edward Gibbon* (2 vols., Cambridge, 1998); Porter, *The Creation of the Modern World*; Israel, *The Radical Enlightenment*. See chapter 4 above.

[81] Israel, *The Radical Enlightenment* p. 141.

replacing these with the principles of universality, equality, and democracy. This implies the Enlightenment was of a different order of importance for understanding the rise of the modern world than the Reformation and Renaissance.[82]

This is in some ways a surprising claim from the author of a masterly study of the Dutch republic, one achievement of which is to show how deeply its Renaissance, Reformation and Enlightenment were intertwined. One outcome of the Dutch revolt was the creation within *ancien régime* Europe of a 'new world' to rival that of the Americas – a transformed society, economic, social, technological, intellectual, political.[83] Yet the intellectual origins of the revolt, and subsequent Dutch 'miracle', lay in that same combination of Renaissance and Reformation (including Christian humanism, and radical reformation) that we have seen at work in an English revolution inspired by Dutch example. Not only the Enlightenment, but northern humanism and the Reformation had 'their centres of gravity in North-western Europe', and especially its major cities.

We have not found in English republican writing evidence of the relentless progress of 'secular and rational' at the expense of biblical and ecclesiastical authority, but rather a Christian reason deriving from Plato and Erasmus. This did not stand in the way of more 'secular' influences, including that of Machiavelli, or more contemporary ones like natural philosophy, and it was itself a contributor to Enlightenment philosophy, in England as in the United Provinces. It is not easy to see the thought of Machiavelli as 'theologically conceived', or to imagine that of Rousseau without Machiavelli, who placed as little emphasis upon human rationality as he did. Meanwhile, Europe did not have to wait for the French revolution to witness a bloody assault upon 'ecclesiastical authority, monarchy, aristocracy, and slavery'. This was accomplished during the 1640s by the radical protestant New Model Army. Nor were the 'newly invented channels of communication, ranging from newspapers, magazines, and the salon to the coffee-shop'[84] products only of the later seventeenth century. Rather they were developments from a culture of international news and public

---

[82] Ibid. pp. vi–vii.

[83] 'Early modern observers were especially struck by the innumerable "novelties" and innovations which one encountered there in virtually every field of activity. Visitors continually marvelled at the prodigious extent of Dutch shipping and commerce, the technical sophistication of industry and finance, the beauty and orderliness, as well as cleanliness, of the cities, the degree of religious and intellectual toleration to be found there, the excellence of the orphanages and hospitals, the limited character of ecclesiatical power, the subordination of military to civilian authority, and the remarkable achievements of Dutch art, philosophy and science.' Israel, *Dutch Republic* p. 1 (and Introduction in general); for Enlightenment, including its 'radical' strain, see chs. 34 and 39.

[84] Israel, *The Radical Enlightenment* p. vi.

opinion, especially religious opinion, visible from the 1620s (or perhaps 1580s) exhibiting a direct Dutch influence upon English affairs.

Not only were the causes, and course, of the Dutch and English troubles deeply intertwined. So were the wider processes by which, first, the republic of the United Provinces, and subsequently the United Kingdom of Great Britain, were modernised. These transformations drew upon linkages of geography, economy and culture with their own larger regional, European and global contexts. They embraced agriculture, trade, religion, print culture, military affairs, political economy and state administration. Within this context the most important fact about British geography was not its archipelagic character. It was the location of the Thames estuary opposite those of the Scheldt, the Maas and the Rhine, creating a regional zone of cultural, economic and religious-military interaction. The United Provinces was a modern fiscal-military state, the building of which, a century earlier than England's, had incorporated religious and political pluralism, and involved the evolution of new, and specifically republican, political structures.[85] Yet England's late development was correspondingly spectacular. From the ashes of the troubles, still on view in 1688 with the collapse, in the face of Dutch invasion, of James II's army, there had arisen within three decades the world's pre-eminent military and imperial power.

As Sidney had put it, in 1665, 'if those [United] provinces encompassed with such difficulties oppugned with the vast power of Spain . . . have with small helps attained so great prosperity, England, if so governed, may promise itself incomparably more, abounding in all they want, and being free from all inconveniences they suffered or feared, apprehending no opposition but that of the Stuart family'.[86] After 1689, England became 'so governed' fiscally (the 'Financial Revolution'), militarily (Dutch-led military reconstruction), religiously (protestant liberty of conscience) and politically (Britain becoming the only major power other than the United Provinces to be governed by Estates).[87] By then England had been learning from the Dutch for over a century, in fishing, agriculture and textiles; in the long-distance trades in slaves and spices; in colonial activity more generally in East Asia and the Americas; in domestic political and religious conduct and ideology; from the military revolution which had enabled the Dutch republic to withstand the might of Spain; and from the new Dutch modes of indirect taxation and public credit. It was under the Anglo-Dutch government of 1689–1702 that all the elements of this established apprenticeship

---

[85] Jan de Vries and A. van der Woude, *The First Modern Economy* (Cambridge, 1997); Israel, *Dutch Republic* chs. 11–14.
[86] Sidney, *Court Maxims* p 162.   [87] Scott, *England's Troubles* ch. 21.

came together to respond with state-moulding success to an unprecedented demand for resources for war.[88]

It was in this context that, in 1707, there came into being the United Kingdom of Great Britain, and it was during successive military struggles, particularly against France, that inhabitants of England, Scotland, Wales and Ireland began to think of themselves as British for the first time. It was this military power, and the Anglo-Dutch political-fiscal revolution by which it was supported, which made possible the superimposition over three kingdoms of a supranational state. Moreover, from the moment of its creation the power and resources commanded by this state were not simply local, or European, but imperial and global. If by the 1730s Britain ruled an empire understood to be 'Protestant, commercial, maritime and free', this followed earlier Dutch, as well as English example.[89] And if by 1730 Dutch maritime and mercantile supremacy had itself been eclipsed by that of Great Britain, this was a development partly financed by Dutch and Huguenot immigrants to south-eastern England.[90]

In all principal respects these developments had been anticipated by the republican experiment of mid-century, not least the abortive attempt at Anglo-Dutch political union. Thus, if there is reason for scepticism concerning Israel's claims for the superior importance of Enlightenment over Reformation and Renaissance, it is because this abstracts one part of a complex historical problem. If the three processes were deeply intertwined, so in their experience of them were England and the Netherlands, with other European societies. Yet concerning the importance of the Anglo-Dutch achievement there seems much less doubt. By the consequences of this the world would genuinely be transformed.

---

[88] Scott, 'What the Dutch Taught Us'.   [89] Armitage, *Ideological Origins* p. 173.

[90] Peter Spufford, 'Access to Credit and Capital in the Commercial Centres of Europe', in Karel Davids and Jan Lucassen (eds.), *A Miracle Mirrored: the Dutch Republic in European Perspective* (Cambridge, 1995) p. 328; Charles Wilson, *Anglo-Dutch Commerce*.

Appendix: 'a pretty story of horses' (May 1654)

[A]s . . . the Oxe laboureth for the man, and the man directeth the Oxe how to work for the best advantage of both, as also the man laboureth in his directing of the Oxe . . . as to build a Staul . . . to shelter him from the sharp piercing cold of the winter, and in giving him fodder to eat and cleansing of his staul, there be many creatures that God by nature hath made usefull and helpfull to the society of man-kind, and gave them a kind of sociable nature . . . The Elephants drive the Triumphant Chariot of *Pompey* the great, they were very usefull to the Carthagenians in their wars with the Romans, Lions may be usefull, Oxen, Horses, Asses, and Mules are, the Dog is also a very serviceable and sociable creature . . . What benefit do the Citizens of *Alepo* receive by their Pigeons or carrying Doves, as they call them . . .

These and many others plainly demonstrate the Dominion of man . . . God made man Lord, and gave him Dominion over all creatures, the which he may rule and govern for his advantage, and not make such slaves of those creatures that are more sociable then other as they are: the horse that noble creature that God himselfe in *Job* presents a description of, in whom is comprehended many excellent qualities, saith God to *Job* hast thou given the horse strength, hast thou cloathed his neck with Thunder, canst thou make him afraid as a Grashopper, the glory of his Nostrils is terrible, he paweth in the valley, and rejoyceth in his strength, he goeth on to meet the armed men, he mocketh at fear and is not affrighted, neither turneth he back from the sword, the Quiver ratleth against him, he swalloweth the ground with fiercenesse and rage, he saith amongst the Trumpets, Ha, ha, and he smelleth the battel a far off, the Thunder of the Captains and the shouting &c. See what a degeneration is in this excellent creature that now is indeed another thing then . . . is here described, instead of his being, not afraid as the Grashopper, they generally are afraid of Grashoppers, Frogs, or the like inferior Creatures, the reason is, for that they are not imployed in such services that are not sutable to their Spetie: the horse should be the Theater on whose back heroick men should act the part of their valour, to defend their liberty and country.

Indeed on the contrary through the neglect of those who have governed they have been suffered to slight the keeping of horse fit for the wars, probably it hath been done out of a politick consideration, they fearing horses and arms in the hands of the people might be imployed against them, those that cannot trust a people their Dominion is not long lived. *Machiavil* after a great deal of pro and

358

con, ingeniously confesseth that a people are the best guard of those in power, and the best guardians of their own liberty . . . but this by the way. I shall present thee with a pretty story of horses, to shew how conformable to the government of man the horse is above all other creatures.

Politian a Greek Author *lib*.1.ch.15 saith that the Sybarites did give themselves to all manner of delights and sports, amongst the rest they would bring into their places of feasts horses taught to stand upright upon their hinder feet: and at the sound of Flutes would dance and move their forefeet very nimbly, like as a Morris dancer moveth his hands, and in this dancing would keep compasse and measure: now it happened that a certain Flute player, had received some disgrace among the Sybarites, about the time that they were drawn into the field against the Crotaniats, with whom they had war the Flute player run to the Crotaniats, and promised them that if they would trust to his fidelity, he would take a course that all the horsemen of the Sybarites army should be taken prisoners by them with ease, the Crotaniats thereupon made him a Collonel, he taketh certain minstrels of *Croton*, and taught them on the Flute to play such a jygge, so at the drawing forth of the battel, placed them on the wings of the Battalians to be opposite to the Sybarites horse, and upon the joining of battel, these Fluters began to sound with their Flutes the jygge, upon the hearing of which the horses fell a dancing and cast their Riders, instead of preparing for the battle, by which means they lost the day: but indeed most of the horses of this age are more fit for the servile works of the Mule, Dromadary and Asse then for the wars, there is a perfect degeneration in their kind.

For the prevention of which it was once in *England* provided in the 27 of H.8. that he that had inclosure of a mile compasse should keep two breeding Mares of 13 hand high, and he who had or farmed 4 miles compasse of inclosure, should keep 4 of like height, and that these Mares should not be covered by any stoned horses under 14 hand in height, each hand to be 4 inches, if the like care were as is here provided, it would raise the horse to be somewhat near the description of him in *Job*, it is requisite that every thing should be imployed in that which is most sutable to its nature: nature hath appointed every thing for a several end and purpose . . . the Oxe for the plough, *Aristotle* speaketh but of one Oxe, the ploughing by one Oxe we are strangers to in our days: perhaps they put them to plough single, with their yoaks to reach a good distance from his shoulders, so that the traces might not wring or gaul the sides of the Oxe . . . it is probable they did not plough with so heavy Ploughs, nor plough deep in many parts their ploughing is but a scratching of the ground, to our ploughing here in *England*, the which cannot be so good husbandry, for the more the ground is opened the better it contributes of it[s] strength, seed is of an attractive nature, and when it is cast in a proper soyl it draweth unto it the strength of the earth, to assist it in perfecting its work of production of increase, the earth indeed is the mother, God took of the dust of the earth, and made man, &c, it giveth suck all that it beareth, of the fatnesse of the earth man is fed, so of other creatures, the earth produceth Trees, the Trees leaves, the leaves worms, on which the smaller Birds feed; the Ravens young of which Christ speaketh of, is fed the most miraculously of all other creatures, they are left in a forlorn condition by the old, so soon as they are hatched, but God feedeth them, he hath caused nature to produce of the dung (which they make) a little worm, which is the sooner perfected by the heat of their bodies, the which they eat from day to day until they are feathered to flie abroad.

Reader, *if I lead thee at any time out of the way of the method of a discourse in hand it shall be but to shew thee some pleasant prospect, or the various Lanskips, that nature, time, and history presents us with.*

John Streater, *Observations* no. 5, 2–9 May 1654, pp. 33–6.

Bibliography

Note: place of publication is London unless otherwise specified.

1. MANUSCRIPTS

Beinecke Library, Yale University, New Haven, USA, Letters from Algernon Sidney to Benjamin Furly, 1664–1680.

Bodleian Library, Oxford, MS Eng. Hist c.487, Edmund Ludlow, 'A Voyce from the Watch Tower'.

British Library, London, Add MS 63,057, Gilbert Burnet, manuscript transcript of 'History of My Own Time' (2 vols.).

British Library, London, Egerton MS 2618.

East Sussex Record Office, Lewes, Glynde Place Archives MSS no. 794, Letter from Algernon Sidney, probably to John Hampden, 6 October 1683.

The Hartlib Papers, 2nd edn (Sheffield, HROnline, 2002)

  Beale, John, to Samuel Hartlib, 10 September 1658, Royal Society MSS, Boyle Letters 7.11 1A-2B.

  Dury, John, to Hartlib, 28 April 1655, 4/3/95 A-B.

  Dury, John, 'Memo on Protestant Exiles and Commonwealth Trade', 53/6A.

  Hartlib, Samuel, 'Ephemerides' 1650 Part 3 [May–October] 28/1/61B; 1656 Part 4, 29/5/98A.

  Wall, Moses, to Hartlib, 9 January 1658/9, 34/4/20B.

Kent Archives Office, Maidstone, De Lisle MSS, U1475 Z1/9, Commonplace Book of Robert Sidney, 2nd Earl of Leicester; U1475 C97/1; C124/2.

Paris, Bibliothèque Nationale, Fr. MS 23254, Jean-Baptiste Lantin, 'Lantiniana', Jean-Baptiste Lantin's record of conversations with Algernon Sidney, Paris, 1677.

Public Record Office, London, State Papers 44, no. 54.

Sevenoaks Library, MS U1000/7 Z1/4-8, Letters from Algernon Sidney to the Earl of Leicester, 1660.

Warwickshire Record Office, MS CR 1886 Algernon Sidney, 'Court Maxims, Discussed and refelled'.

2. PRINTED PRIMARY SOURCES

The Agreement of the People (1647), in Kenyon, *Stuart Constitution.*

Allen, William [i.e. Edward Sexby], *Killing Noe Murder. Briefly Discourst in Three Quaestions* (1657), in David Wootton (ed.), *Divine Right and Democracy: an Anthology of Political Writing in Stuart England* (Harmondsworth, 1986).

Aristotle, *Ethics*, ed. Jonathan Barnes (Harmondsworth, 1984).

The Politics, ed. Stephen Everson (Cambridge, 1988).

Ascham, Anthony, *Of the Confusions and Revolutions of Governments* (1649).

Aubrey, John, *Aubrey's Brief Lives*, ed. Oliver Lawson Dick (1958).

Augustine, *City of God*, ed. David Knowles (Harmondsworth, 1981).

Bacon, Francis, 'Of the True Greatness of Kingdoms and Estates', in *Bacon's Essays*, ed. Edwin A. Abbott (2 vols., 1889) vol. 1.

Bacon, Nathaniel, *A historical and political discourse of the laws and government of England* (1682).

Ball, William, of Barkham, Esquire, *Constitutio Liberi Populi. OR, The Rule of a Free-born People* (1646).

Baxter, Richard, *Reliquiae Baxterianae: or, Mr Richard Baxter's Narrative of the most Memorable Passages of his Life and Times* (1696).

Baylor, Michael (ed.), *The Radical Reformation* (Cambridge, 1991).

The Benefit of the Ballot: with the Nature and Use thereof. Particularly in the Republick of Venice [1679?].

Bethel, Slingsby, *The Interest of Princes and States*, 2nd edn (1681).

The Present Interest of England, Stated (1671).

The World's Mistake in Oliver Cromwell; or, A short Political Discourse, shewing, That Cromwell's Mal-administration, (during his Four Years, and Nine Moneths pretended Protectorship,) layed the Foundation of Our present Condition, in the Decay of Trade (1668).

[Bethel, Slingsby] *The Providences of God* (1694).

[Bethel, Slingsby] *The Right of Chusing Sheriffs* (1689).

Blencowe, R. W. (ed.), *Sydney Papers* (1823).

Bodin, Jean, *Six Bookes of a Commonweale*, a facsimile reprint of the English translation of 1606, ed. K. D. McRae (Cambridge, Mass., 1962).

Borgeaud, Charles, *Histoire de l'Universite de Geneve: l'Academie de Calvin 1559–1798*, vol. 1 (Geneva, 1900).

A Brief Relation Containing an Abreviation of the Arguments Urged by the Late Protector (January 1658).

Buchanan, George, *De Jure Regni apud Scotos*, trans. 'Philalethes' (1680).

Burton, Thomas, *Diary of Thomas Burton*, ed. J. T. Rutt (4 vols., 1828).

Calendar of State Papers and Manuscripts relating to the English Affairs existing in the archives and collections of Venice, vol. XXVIII, 1647–1652 (1927)

Canne, John, *A Seasonable Word to the Parliament-Men* (10 May 1659).

The Censure of the Rota upon Mr Milton's Book, Entituled, The Ready and Easie Way (26 March 1659).

Chaos: Or, A Discourse Wherin is presented to the view of the Magistrate . . . a Frame of Government by way of a Republique (1659).

The Character of Mercurius Politicus (14 August 1650).

A Charge of High-Treason exhibited against Oliver Cromwell Esq; for several Treasons by him committed (1653).

Cicero, *On the Commonwealth*, in *On the Commonwealth and On the Laws*, ed. James Zetzel (Cambridge, 1999).

Clarke, J., *The Life of James II* (2 vols., 1816).

Clayton, Sir Robert, *The Speech of Sir Robert Clayton Kt. Lord Mayor Select for the City of London* (29 September 1679).

Commons Journal vols. 6 and 7.

A Commonwealth, and Commonwealths-men, Asserted and Vindicated (1659).

A Common-Wealth or Nothing; Or, Monarchy and oligarchy prov'd parallel in Tyranny (1659).

Confusion Confounded; or, A firm way of Settlement settled and Confirmed (1654).

Cook, John, *Monarchy No Creature of God's Making* (26 February 1651).

Coppe, Abiezer, *A Remonstrance of the Sincere and Zealous Protestation of Abiezer Coppe Against the Blasphemous and Execrable Opinions recited in the Act of Aug. 10 1650* (1650), in Nigel Smith (ed.), *A Collection of Ranter Writings* (1983).

A Copy of a Letter Written to an Officer of the Army by A true Commonwealths-man, and no COURTIER, Concerning The Right and Settlement of our present Government and Governors (19 March 1656/7).

Cromwell, Oliver, *Oliver Cromwell's Letters and Speeches*, ed. Thomas Carlyle (3 vols., 1857).

Daillé, Jean, *A Treatise Concerning the Right Use of the Fathers* (1651).

[de la Court, Pieter], 'De Witt and other Great Men in Holland', *The True Interest and Political Maxims of the Republic of Holland* (1702).

A Declaration of the Armie . . . for The dissolving of this present Parliament (10 August 1652).

A Declaration of the Lord Generall and His Councel of Officers Shewing the Grounds and Reasons for the dissolution of the late Parliament (13 April 1653).

A Declaration of the Parliament Assembled at Westminster (7 May 1659).

A Declaration of the Parliament of England, Expressing the Grounds of their late Proceedings, And of Setling the present Government In the way of A Free State (22 March 1648 [1649]).

A Declaration of the Parliament of England, Of their just Resentment of the Horrid Murther perpetrated on the Body of Isaac Dorislaus (12 May 1649).

A Declaration of the Parliament of England, In Vindication of their Proceedings, And Discovering the Dangerous Practices of several Interests, Against the Present Government (27 September 1649).

A Declaration, or representation from His Excellency Sir Thomas Fairfax (14 June 1647), in Kenyon (ed.), *Stuart Constitution*.

A Declaration of the Well-affected to The Good Old Cause (2 May 1659).

A Dialogue at Oxford between a Tutor and a Gentleman, Formerly his Pupil, Concerning Government (1681).

A Discourse for a King and Parliament (1660).

Dryden, John, *Absalom and Achitophel*, 5th edn, revised (1682).

England's Memorable Accidents (24–31 October 1642).

Erasmus, *The Education of a Christian Prince*, ed. Lisa Jardine (Cambridge, 1997).

Evelyn, John, *The Diary of John Evelyn*, ed. Esmond De Beer (Oxford, 1955).

An Exact and most Impartial Accompt of the Indictment, Arraignment, Trial and Judgement (according to Law) of Twenty nine Regicides (1660).

Filmer, Sir Robert, *Patriarcha*, in Johann Sommerville (ed.), *Sir Robert Filmer: Patriarcha and Other Writings* (Cambridge, 1991).

[Finch, Henry], *An Exact and most Impartial Accompt of the Indictment, Arraignment, Trial, and Judgement (according to Law) of nine and twenty Regicides* (1660).

Firth, C. H. (ed.), *The Clarke Papers* (4 vols., 1899–1965).

Five Proposals Presented To the General Council of the Officers (1659).

Fletcher, Andrew, *A Discourse of Government With relation to Militias* (Edinburgh, 1698), in Fletcher, *Political Works*, ed. John Robertson (Cambridge, 1997).

  Two Discourses Concerning the Affairs of Scotland (Edinburgh, 1698), in *Fletcher, Political Works*.

Forster, T. (ed.), *Letters of Locke, Algernon Sidney, and Anthony Lord Shaftesbury* (1830).

Foundations of Freedom; or an Agreement of the People: Proposed as a Rule for future Government in the Establishment of a firm and lasting Peace (1648).

Good Advice before it be too late (1689).

Goodman, C., *How superior powers ought to be obeyed of their subjects and wherein they may lawfully by God's word be disobeyed and resisted* (Geneva, 1558; facsimile Amsterdam, 1972).

Goodwin, John, *Right and might Well mett* (1 January 1649).

Grevil[le], Sir Fulke, Lord Brooke, *The Life of the Renowned Sir Philip Sidney* (1652).

Grey, Anchitell, (ed.), *Debates in the House of Commons, from the Year 1667 to the Year 1694* (10 vols., 1763).

Grey, Ford, Lord, *The Secret History of the Rye House Plot* (1754).

Grotius, Hugo, *De Jure Belli ac Pacis Libri Tres*, vol. II, trans. F. W. Kelsey (Oxford, 1925) The Translation, Book I.

Hakluyt, Richard, *Discourse of Western Planting* (1584), in E. G. R. Taylor (ed.), *The Original Writings and Correspondence of the Two Richard Hakluyts* vol. II (1935).

Hall, John, *The Grounds and Reasons of Monarchy Considered* (1651).

Hammond, Henry, *A Defence of the Learned Hugo Grotius From the Accusations of Inward Socinianism and Outward Popery* (1655).

  The Workes of the Reverend and Learned Henry Hammond, ed. John Fell (1674).

Harrington, James, *Aphorisms Political*, in *Political Works*.

  The Art of Lawgiving (1659), in *Political Works*.

  The Commonwealth of Oceana (1656), printed for D. Pakeman.

  The Common-wealth of Oceana (1656), printed by J. Streater, for Livewell Chapman.

The Commonwealth of Oceana and A System of Politics, ed. J. G. A. Pocock (Cambridge, 1992).

The Commonwealth of Oceana (1656) in *Political Works*.

A Discourse Showing that the Spirit of Parliaments, With a Council in the Intervals, Is not to be trusted for a Settlement (21 July 1659) in *Political Works*.

A Discourse upon this Saying: The Spirit of the Nation is not yet to be trusted with Liberty; lest it introduce Monarchy, or invade the Liberty of Conscience (1659), in *Political Works*.

The Examination of James Harrington, in *Political Works*.

The Political Works of James Harrington, ed. J. G. A. Pocock (Cambridge, 1977).

Pour Enclouer le Canon (1659), in *Political Works*.

The Prerogative of Popular Government (1658), in *Political Works*.

Valerius and Publicola (1659), in *Political Works*.

Heylyn, Peter, *A Briefe and Moderate Answer, to the seditious and scandalous challenges of Henry Burton* (1637).

Historical Manuscripts Commission Report, De Lisle and Dudley MSS (6 vols.) vol. 6.

Hobbes, Thomas, *Behemoth; or, The Long Parliament*, ed. Ferdinand Tonnies (Chicago, 1990).

Leviathan, ed. R. Tuck (Cambridge, 1996).

Of Liberty and Necessity: A Treatise (1654), in Sir William Molesworth (ed.), *The English Works of Thomas Hobbes*, volume VI (1840).

'On the Life and History of Thucydides' and 'To the Readers', in R. B. Schlatter (ed.), *Hobbes' Thucydides* (New Brunswick, N.J., 1975).

Hotman, Francois, *Francogallia*, ed. R. E. Giesey, trans. J. H. M. Salmon (Cambridge, 1972).

The humble petition of well-affected persons (11 September 1648), in Kenyon, *Stuart Constitution*.

Hume, David, *Political Essays*, ed. Knud Haakonssen (Cambridge, 1994).

Hutchinson, Lucy, *Memoirs of the Life of Colonel Hutchinson*, ed. N. Keeble (1995).

Hyde, Edward Earl of Clarendon, *A Brief View and Survey of the Dangerous and pernicious Errors to Church and State, in Mr Hobbes' Book, Entitled Leviathan* (1676).

The Continuation of the Life of Edward Earl of Clarendon, vol. II (Oxford, 1760).

The History of the Rebellion and Civil Wars in England, ed. W. D. Macray (6 vols., Oxford, 1888; repr. 1958).

The Life of Edward Earl of Clarendon . . . Written by Himself, volume I (Oxford, 1760).

I. S., *The PICTURE of a New COURTIER drawn in a Conference, between Mr Timeserver, and Mr Plain-heart* (1656).

An Impartial Account of the Proceedings of the Common Hall of the City of London at Guildhal (24 June 1682).

[Ireton, Henry], *The Humble Remonstrance of his Excellency Thomas Lord Fairfax* (16 November 1648).

[Ireton, Henry], *The Remonstrance of the Army* (16 November 1648), in Kenyon, *Stuart Constitution*.

James VI and I, *Basilikon Doron. Or His Majesties Instructions to His Dearest Sonne, Henry The Prince*, in *The Workes of the Most High and Mighty Prince, James* (1616).

James II, 'Life of James II 1660–1698, Written by Himself', in J. MacPherson (ed.), *Original Papers* (2 vols., 1775).

Jefferson, Thomas, *Political Writings*, ed. J. Appleby and T. Ball (Cambridge, 1999).

Kenyon, J. P. (ed.), *The Stuart Constitution: Documents and Commentary* 2nd edn (Cambridge, 1986).

Lee, Nathaniel, *Lucius Junius Brutus* (1680), in David Womersley (ed.), *Restoration Drama: an Anthology* (Oxford, 2000).

A Letter from no far Countrey (19 April 1660).

Lettre de felicitation de Milord Sidney aux Parisiens et a la Nation Francoise, ou resurrection de Milord Sidney (Paris, 1789).

The Leveller: or, The Principles and Maxims concerning Government and Religion, Which are Asserted by those that are commonly called, Levellers (16 February 1659).

Lilburne, John, *The Charters of London: The Second Part of London's Liberties in Chaines Discovered* (18 December 1646).

London's Liberty In Chains discovered. And, Published by Lieutenant Colonell John Lilburn, Prisoner in the Tower. Octob. 1646.

Regall Tyrannie discovered (January 1647).

Liburne, John and Richard Overton, *The out-cryes of oppressed commons* (1647).

Lilburne, John, Richard Overton and Thomas Prince, *The Second Part of England's New-Chaines Discovered* (1649).

A little Eye-Salve for the Kingdome and Armie, that they may see (1647).

Livy, *The History of Rome by Titus Livius*, volume II (1926).

The Roman History by Titus Livius of Padua with the Entire Supplement of John Freinsheim, volume III (1744).

Locke, John, *A Letter on Toleration*, trans. J. W. Gough (Oxford, 1968).

Political Essays, ed. Mark Goldie (Cambridge, 1997).

Two Treatises of Government, ed. Peter Laslett, 2nd edn (Cambridge, 1967).

London's Liberties (1682).

London's Liberties; or a Learned Argument of Law and Reason Upon Saturday, December 14 1650. Before the Lord Mayor, Court of Aldermen, and Common Councell at Guild Hall, LONDON, Between Mr Maynard Mr Hales and Mr Wilde Of Councell for the Companies of London And Major John Wildman and Mr John Price Of Councell for the Freemen of London (1650).

Ludlow, Edmund, *A Voyce From the Watch Tower Part Five 1660–1662*, ed. A. B. Worden (1978).

Machiavelli, Niccolò, *The Discourses*, ed. Bernard Crick (Harmondsworth, 1985).

Machiavels Discourses. upon the first Decade of T. Livius translated out of the Italian by E. D., 2nd edn (1636).

M[arten], H., H. N[eville], I. L., I. W[ildman], I. I. and S. M., *The Armies Dutie* (May 1659).

Mene Tekel; or, The Downfal of Tyranny (1663).

Milton, John, *An Apology Against a Pamphlet Call'd A Modest Confutation of the Animadversions upon the Remonstrant against Smectymnuus* (1642), in *Complete Prose Works*, vol. I.

Areopagitica; A Speech of Mr John Milton For the Liberty of Unlicenc'd Printing (1644), in *Complete Prose Works*, vol. II.

Commonplace Book, in *Complete Prose Works* vol. I.

Complete Prose Works, gen. ed., D. M. Wolfe (8 vols., New Haven, Conn., 1953–82).

A Defence of the People of England (1651), in *Complete Prose Works* vol. IV.

Of Education (1644), in *Complete Prose Works* vol. I.

Eikonoklastes (1649), in *Complete Prose Works* vol. III.

History of Britain, in *Complete Prose Works* vol. VI.

'A Letter to a Friend, Concerning the Ruptures of the Commonwealth', in *Complete Prose Works* vol. VII.

MS Digression to the *History of Britain*, in *Complete Prose Works* vol. VI.

Observations upon the Articles of Peace (1649), in *Complete Prose Works* vol. III.

Paradise Lost (1666), in *John Milton: a Critical Edition of the Major Works*, ed. Stephen Orgel and Jonathan Goldberg (Oxford, 1991).

Political Writings, ed. Martin Dzelzainis (Cambridge, 1991).

The Readie and Easie Way to Establish a Free Commonwealth, 2nd edn (1660), in *Complete Prose Works* vol. VII.

The Reason of Church-governement Urg'd against Prelaty (1641), in *Complete Prose Works* vol. I.

Of Reformation Touching Church-Discipline in England (1641), in *Complete Prose Works* vol. I.

Samson Agonistes (1671), in *John Milton: a Critical Edition*.

Second Defence of the English People (1654), in *Complete Prose Works* vol. IV.

The Tenure of Kings and Magistrates (1649), in *Complete Prose Works* vol. III.

Two Books of Investigations into Christian Doctrine Drawn From the Sacred Scriptures Alone, in *Complete Prose Works* vol. VI.

A Model of a Democraticall government, humbly tendered to Consideration (1659).

Molesworth, Robert, *An Account of Denmark, As it was in the Year 1692* (1694).

More, Thomas, *Utopia*, ed. George M. Logan and Robert M. Adams (Cambridge, 1989).

Moyle, Walter, and John Trenchard, *An Argument, Shewing, that a Standing Army is inconsistent with A Free Government, and absolutely destructive to the Constitution of the English Monarchy* (Parts I and II, 1697).

Nedham, Marchamont, *The Case of the Commonwealth of England Stated* (1650), ed. P. A. Knachel (Charlottesville, Va., 1969).

Epistle Dedicatorie, in John Selden, *Of the Dominion, Or, Ownership of the Sea* (1652).

The Excellencie of a Free-State (1656).

Interest will not Lie: Or, A View of England's True Interest (12 August 1659).

[editor] *Mercurius Britanicus* no. 72, 24 February–3 March 1645; no. 86, 9–16 June 1645; no. 91, 21–28 July 1645; no. 92, 28 July–4 August 1645; no. 93,

11–18 August 1645; no. 99, 22–29 September 1645; no. 107, 24 November–1 December 1645; no. 108, 1–8 December 1645; no. 119, 16–23 February 1646; no. 126, 13–20 April 1646.

[editor] *Mercurius Politicus. Comprising the summe of all Intelligence, with the Affairs and Designs now on foot in the three Nations of England, Ireland, and Scotland* nos. 1–120, 1650–3; nos. 352–4, 5–26 March 1657.

[editor] *Mercurius Pragmaticus* no. 4, 5 – 12 October 1647; no. 8, 2–9 November 1647; no. 14, 14–21 December 1647; no. 20, 25 January–1 February 1648.

A Plea for The King and Kingdome (1648).

[Nedham, Marchamont], *The Case Stated Between England and the United Provinces, In this present Juncture* (1652).

[Nedham, Marchamont], *England's Miserie and Remedie in a Judicious Letter . . . concerning Leiutenant Col. Lilburn's Imprisonment in Newgate* (14 September 1645).

[Nedham, Marchamont], *News From Brussels* (1660).

[Nedham, Marchamont], *A True State of the Case of the Commonwealth* (1654).

[Nedham, Marchamont], *Vox Plebis, or, The Peoples Out-cry Against Oppression, Injustice, and Tyranny* (1646).

[Nedham, Marchamont], M. N., *Medela Medicinae. A Plea For the Free Profession, and a Renovation of the Art of Physick* (1665).

Neville, Henry, *Plato Redivivus: or, A Dialogue Concerning Government* (1680), in Robbins, *Two English Republican Tracts*.

[Neville, Henry], *Nicholas Machiavel's Letter to Zanobius Buondelmontius in Vindication of Himself and His Writings* (1675), in *The Works of the Famous Nicholas Machiavel* (1675).

A New Remonstrance of the Freeborn People of England: Concerning This present Parliament, and a new Representative (14 November 1651).

No Return to Monarchy; and Liberty of Conscience Secured (1659).

Now is the Time: A Scheme for a Commonwealth (1688).

Overton, Richard, *An Appeal from the Degenerate House of Commons* (1647), in Woodhouse, *Puritanism and Liberty*.

An Appeale from the Degenerate House of Commons (1647), in D. M. Wolfe (ed.), *Leveller Manifestoes of the Puritan Revolution* (New York, 1967).

The Commoners Complaint [n.d.].

[Overton, Richard and William Walwyn], *A remonstrance of many thousand citizens . . . to their House of Commons* (1646), in Andrew Sharp (ed.), *Political Ideas of the English Civil Wars 1641–1649* (1983).

[Overton, Richard and William Walwyn], *The Remonstrance of Many Thousand Citizens, and Other Free-Born People of England* (1646).

Parker, Henry, Preface to *The True Portraiture of the Kings of England* (7 August 1650).

Penn, William, *England's Great Interest, in the Choice of this New Parliament Dedicated to all Her Free-Holders* (1679), in *Political Writings*.

England's Present Interest Considered (1675), in *The Works of William Penn* (2 vols., 1756).

An Essay Towards the present and Future Peace of Europe (1693), in *Political Writings*.

One Project for the Good of England (1679), in *The Works of William Penn* (2 vols., 1756).

The Papers of William Penn, ed. Mary Maples Dunn and Richard S. Dunn (2 vols., Philadelphia, Penn., 1981).

The Political Writings of William Penn, ed. Andrew Murphy (Indianapolis, Ind., 2002).

Pennington, Isaac, Jr, *The Fundamental Right, Safety and Liberty of the People . . . Briefly Asserted* (15 May 1651).

The People's Right Briefly Asserted. Printed for the Information of the Commonality of England, France, and all other neighbour Nations, that groan under the oppression of Tyrannical Government (1649).

Pepys, Samuel, *The Diary of Samuel Pepys*, ed. Robert Latham and William Matthews (8 vols., 1970).

A Perswasive to Mutuall Compliance Under the Present Government. Together with A Plea for a Free State Compared with Monarchy (18 February 1651)

The Petition of January 1648, in D. M. Wolfe (ed.), *Leveller Manifestoes of the Puritan Revolution* (New York, 1967).

Petition of 11 September 1648, in D. M. Wolfe (ed.), *Leveller Manifestoes of the Puritan Revolution* (New York, 1967).

Philalethes, Alazonamastix, *Free Parliament Quares proposed to Tender Consciences* (1660).

Philodemius, Eleutherius, *The Armies Vindication* (11 January 1649).

Plato, *The Laws*, trans. Trevor J. Saunders (Harmondsworth, 1975).

The Portable Plato, ed. Scott Buchanan (Harmondsworth, 1982).

The Republic, trans. H. D. P. Lee (Harmondsworth, 1959).

The Republic of Plato, ed. F. M. Cornford (Oxford, 1941).

The Timaeus, in William Whewell, *The Platonic Dialogues For English Readers* (Cambridge, 1861) vol. III.

[Plattes, Gabriel], *A Description of the Famous Kingdome of Macaria* (1641).

Ponet, John, *A Short Treatise of politike Power* (1566).

The Private Debates, Conferences and Resolutions of the late Rump (1660).

A Proposition In Order to the Proposing of A Commonwealth or Democracie (14 June 1659).

The Protector, (So called,) In Part Unvailed: By whom the Mystery of Iniquity, is now working . . . By a late member of the Army (1655).

A Publick Plea, Opposed to A Private Proposal (18 May 1659).

Puffendorf, Samuel von, *The Law of Nature and Nations* (1749).

Pym, John, *The Speech or Declaration of John Pym, Esquire . . . 12 April, 1641* (1641).

R. G., *A Copy of a Letter from an Officer of the Army In Ireland, to His Highness the Lord Protector* (1656).

Ralegh, Sir Walter, *The History of The World. In Five Bookes* (London, 1621).

The Remonstrance of Many Thousand Citizens, and other Free-Born People of England (1646).

Rivers, Marcellus, and Oxenbridge Foyle, *England's Slavery or Barbados Merchandize; Represented In a Petition to the High and Honourable Court of Parliament* (1659).

Robbins, Caroline (ed.), *Two English Republican Tracts* (Cambridge, 1969).

Rousseau, Jean-Jacques, *Political Writings*, ed. C. E. Vaughan (2 vols. Oxford, 1962).

The Social Contract and Discourses, ed. G. D. H. Cole (1973).

Rushworth, John, *Historical Collections . . . beginning the Sixteenth Year of King James, Anno 1618* (3 vols., 1659–82).

Savile, George, Marquis of Halifax, *The Works of George Savile Marquis of Halifax*, ed. Mark N. Brown (3 vols., Oxford, 1989).

Scott, Thomas, *The Belgicke Pismire* (1623).

The Projector (1623).

Vox Populi. Or News from Spayne (1622).

Vox Regis (1625).

Scripture and reason pleaded for defensive arms (1643), quoted in Andrew Sharp (ed.), *Political Ideas of the English Civil Wars 1641–1649* (1983).

Sedition Scourg'd, or a view of that Rascally and Venemous Paper Entituled A Charge of High-Treason exhibited against Oliver Cromwell (1653).

A Short Discourse between Monarchical and Aristocratical Government (1649).

Sidney, Algernon, *The Apology of Algernon Sydney, in the Day of his Death*, in *Sydney on Government*.

The Character of Henry Vane Jnr. in V. Rowe, *Sir Henry Vane the Younger* (1970) Appendix F.

Court Maxims, ed. Hans Blom, Eco Haitsma Mulier and Ronald Janse (Cambridge, 1996).

Discourses Concerning Government, ed. T. West (Indianapolis, Ind., 1990).

Discourses Concerning Government . . . with His Letters Trial Apology and Some Memoirs of His Life (1763)

Discourses Concerning Government, in *Sydney on Government*.

Sydney on Government: the Works of Algernon Sydney, ed. J. Robertson (1772).

The Trial of Algernon Sidney Esq (1683), in *Sydney on Government*.

The Very Copy of a Paper Delivered to the Sherriffs (1683), in 'Memoir of Algernon Sidney', *Sydney on Government*.

[Sidney, Algernon, and Sir William Jones], *A Just and Modest Vindication of the Proceedings of the Two last Parliaments* (1681), in *State Tracts of the Reign of Charles II* (1689) vol. IV, Appendix 15, pp. clxviii–clxix.

Sidney, Sir Philip, *The Defence of Poesy*, in *Sir Philip Sidney: Selected Writings*, ed. Richard Dutton (1987).

Smith, Sir Thomas, *A Discourse of the Commonweal of This Realm of England*, ed. Mary Dewar (Charlottesville, Va., 1969).

De Republica Anglorum, ed. Mary Dewar (Cambridge, 1982).

Some Reasons Humbly Proposed to the Officers of the Army, For the speedy Re-admission of the Long Parliament Who Setled the Government In the way of a Free State (28 April 1659).

The Speeches, Discourses and Prayers, of Colonel John Barkstead, Col. John Okey, and Mr Miles Corbet, Upon the 19th of April, being the Day of their suffering at Tyburn, Together with an Account of the Occasion and Manner of their Taking in Holland (1662).

Spinoza, Benedict de (Baruch), *The Political Works of Spinoza*, ed. A. G. Wernham (Oxford, 1958).

Sprigge, William, *A Modest Plea for an Equal Common-wealth Against Monarchy* (1659).

Starkey, Thomas, *A Dialogue between Pole and Lupset*, ed. T. F. Mayer (1989).

Streater, John, *The Continuation of this Session of Parliament Justified; and the Action of the Army Touching that Affair Defended* (1659).

A Glympse of that Jewel, Judicial, Just, Preserving Libertie (1653).

Observations Historical, Political and Philosophical, Upon Aristotles first Book of Political Government : Together, With a Narrative of State-Affaires in England, Scotland, and Ireland: As also from other Parts beyond the Seas nos. 1–11, April– July 1654.

Secret Reasons of State In Reference To the Affairs of these Nations, At the Interruption of this present Parliament Anno 1653 (23 May 1659).

Stubbe, Henry, *An Essay in Defence of the Good Old Cause, or A Discourse concerning the Rise and Extent of the power of the Civil Magistrate in reference to Spiritual Affairs* (1659).

A Further Justification of the Present War Against the United Netherlands (1673).

A Letter to An Officer of the Army Concerning a Select Senate mentioned by them in their Proposals to the late Parliament (26 October 1659).

S[tubbe], H[enry], *The Commonwealth of Israel, or a Brief Account Of Mr Prynne's Anatomy of the Good Old Cause* (16 May 1659).

Temple, William, *Observations Upon the United Provinces of the Netherlands* (1673).

Thucydides, *History of the Peloponnesian War*, ed. M. I. Finley, trans. Rex Warner (Harmondsworth, 1975).

To all the Worthy Gentlemen who are Duely Chosen . . . the 17 of September 1656. And to all the Good people of the Common-wealth of England (1656).

To his Excellency, Oliver Cromwel . . . and to the honorable Councel of the Army . . . The humble Representation of severall Aldermen . . . and other Citizens of London (20 May 1653).

Toland, John, *A Defence of the Parliament of 1640. And the people of England, Against king Charles I . . . containing A short Account of some of . . . [his] many Illegal, Arbitrary, Popish and tyrannical Actions* (1698).

'The Life of James Harrington', in *The Oceana of James Harrington . . . with An Exact Account of his Life* (1700).

The Life of John Milton (1698).

To the Lord Mayor, Aldermen, Sherifs, and Common Council of London, The Dedication to, James Harrington, *Oceana*, ed. Toland (1700).

[Toland, John], *Christianity not Mysterious* (1696).

The Tragedy of Marcus Tullius Cicero (1651).

A Treatise of the Execution of Justice, wherein it is clearly proved, that the Execution of Judgement and Justice, is as well the Peoples as the Magistrates Duty (1660).

Trenchard, John and Thomas Gordon *Cato's Letters*, ed. Ronald Hamowy (2 vols., Indianapolis, Ind., 1995).

Twelve Plain Proposals Offered to the Honest and Faithful Officers and Souldiers (28 April 1659).

Twenty Three DECREES From the Committee of Safety in Oceana (12 November 1659).

[Tyrell, James], *Patriarcha Non Monarcha* (1681).

Vane, Henry, *An Epistle General to the Mystical Body of Christ on Earth, the Church Universal in Babylon* (1662).

   A Healing Question propounded and resolved (1656).

   A Needful Corrective or Ballance in Popular Government, Expressed in a Letter to James Harrington, Esquire (1659).

   The Retired Man's Meditations (1655).

   The Tryal of Sir Henry Vane, Kt, at the King's Bench, June 2nd and 6th 1662.

Walwyn, William, *The Bloody Project* (1648), in Jack R. McMichael and Barbara Taft (eds.), *The Writings of William Walwyn* (Athens, Ga., 1989).

   The Power of Love (1643), in Jack R. McMichael and Barbara Taft (eds.), *The Writings of William Walwyn* (Athens, Ga., 1989).

Warr, J., *The Priviledges of the People* (5 February 1649).

William III [Caspar Fagel], *The Declaration of His Highness . . . for restoring the laws and liberties of England, Scotland and Ireland* (1688), in Robert Beddard (ed.), *A Kingdom Without a King* (Oxford, 1988).

Winstanley, Gerrard, *The Law of Freedom in a Platform* (1651), in Christopher Hill (ed.), *Winstanley: The Law of Freedom and Other Writings* (Harmondsworth, 1973).

Winthrop, R. C., *Addresses and Speeches 1852–1867* (1867).

W[ither], G[eorge], *Respublica Anglicana or the Historie of the Parliament* (1650).

Woodhouse, A. S. P. (ed.), *Puritanism and Liberty: Being the Army Debates (1647–9) from the Clarke Manuscripts with Supplementary Documents* (1951).

Wren, Matthew, *Considerations upon Mr Harrington's Oceana* (1657).

   Monarchy Asserted, or The State of Monarchicall and Popular Government, 2nd edn (1660).

3. SECONDARY SOURCES

Alford, Stephen, *The Early Elizabethan Polity: William Cecil and the British Succession Crisis, 1558–1569* (Cambridge, 1998).

Armitage, David, 'The Cromwellian Protectorate and the Languages of Empire', *Historical Journal* 35, 3 (1992).

   The Ideological Origins of the British Empire (Cambridge, 2000).

   'John Milton: Poet against Empire', in Armitage et al., *Milton*.

Armitage, David, Armand Himy and Quentin Skinner (eds.), *Milton and Republicanism* (Cambridge, 1995).

Ashcraft, Richard, *Revolutionary Politics and John Locke's Two Treatises of Government* (Princeton, 1986).

Ashley, Maurice, *John Wildman: Plotter and Postmaster* (1947).

Aulard, A., *The French Revolution 1789–1804* (2 vols., 1910).

Bailyn, Bernard, *The Ideological Origins of the American Revolution* (Cambridge, Mass, 1971).

Baker, Keith Michael, 'Transformations of Classical Republicanism in Eighteenth Century France', *The Journal of Modern History* 73 (March 2001).

Baldwin, Geoffrey, 'The Self and the State 1580–1651', PhD. thesis, Cambridge University, 1998.

Baron, Hans, *The Crisis of the Early Italian Renaissance* (2 vols., Princeton, 1955).

Beckles, Hilary, 'The "Hub of Empire": the Caribbean and Britain in the Seventeenth Century', in Canny, *The Origins of Empire*.

Birmingham, Robert, 'Continental Resonances in Mid-Seventeenth Century English Radical Religious Ideas', M.Phil. thesis, Cambridge University, 1998.

Bliss, Robert, *Revolution and Empire: English Politics and the American Colonies in the Seventeenth Century* (Manchester, 1990).

Blitzer, Charles, *An Immortal Commonwealth: the Political Thought of James Harrington* (New Haven, Conn., 1970).

Bonney, Richard, *The European Dynastic States 1494–1660* (Oxford, 1991).

Braddick, Michael, *The Nerves of State: Taxation and the Financing of the English State, 1558–1714* (Manchester, 1996).

State Formation in Early Modern England c.1550–1700 (Cambridge, 2000).

Bradshaw, Brendan, 'More on Utopia', *The Historical Journal* 24, 1 (1981).

Braudel, Fernand, *The Mediterranean and the Mediterranean World in the Age of Philip II* (Berkeley and Los Angeles, 1996).

Breen, T. H., *The Character of the Good Ruler: a Study of Puritan Political Ideas in New England 1630–1730* (New Haven, Conn., 1970).

Brenner, Robert, *Merchants and Revolution: Commercial Change, Political Conflict, and London's Overseas Traders 1550–1653* (Princeton, 1993).

Brett, A. S., *Liberty, Right and Nature: Individual Rights in Later Scholastic Thought* (Cambridge, 1997).

'Natural Right and Civil Community: the Civil Philosophy of Hugo Grotius', *Historical Journal* 45, 1. (2002).

Brewer, John, *Sinews of Power: War, Money and the English State 1688–1783* (1989).

Brigden, Susan, *New Worlds, Lost Worlds: the Rule of the Tudors, 1485–1603* (Harmondsworth, 2000).

Brown, A. L., *The Governance of Late Medieval England 1272–1461* (1989).

Burgess, Glenn, *The Politics of the Ancient Constitution* (Basingstoke, 1992).

'Repacifying the Polity: the Responses of Hobbes and Harrington to the "Crisis of the Common Law"', in Ian Gentles, John Morrill and Blair Worden (eds.), *Soldiers, Writers and Statesmen of the English Revolution* (Cambridge, 1998).

Burke, Peter, 'Tacitism', in T. A. Dorey (ed.), *Tacitus* (1969).

Burns, J. H. and Goldie, Mark (eds.), *The Cambridge History of Political Thought 1450–1700* (Cambridge, 1991).

Cameron, W. J., *New Light on Aphra Behn* (Auckland, 1961).

Campos Boralevi, Lea, 'Classical Foundational Myths of European Republicanism: the Jewish Commonwealth', in van Gelderen and Skinner, *Republicanism* vol. I.

Canny, Nicholas (ed.), *The Oxford History of the British Empire*, Volume I: *The Origins of Empire: British Overseas Enterprise to the Close of the Seventeenth Century* (Oxford, 1998).

Capp, Bernard, *Cromwell's Navy: the Fleet and the English Revolution 1648–1660* (Oxford, 1989).

Carrive, Paulette, *La pensée politique d'Algernon Sidney 1622–1683. La querelle de l'absolutisme* (Paris, 1989).

Cassirer, Ernst, *The Platonic Renaissance in England* (1953).

Cave, A. A., 'Thomas More and the New World', *Albion* 23 (1991).

Champion, J. A. I., *The Pillars of Priestcraft Shaken: the Church of England and its Enemies, 1660–1730* (Cambridge, 1992).

Coffey, John, *Politics, Religion and the British Revolutions: the Mind of Samuel Rutherford* (Cambridge, 1997).

Collinson, Patrick, 'The Monarchical Republic of Elizabeth I', *Bulletin of the John Rylands Library* 69 (1987).

De Republica Anglorum: Or, History with the Politics Put Back (Cambridge, 1990).

'Conclusion', in Collinson (ed.), *The Sixteenth Century* (Oxford, 2002).

'"The State as Monarchical Commonwealth": "Tudor" England', *Journal of Historical Sociology* 15, 1 (2002).

Condren, Conal, *The Language of Politics in Seventeenth Century England* (Basingstoke, 1994).

Cotton, James, 'James Harrington and Thomas Hobbes', *Journal of the History of Ideas* 42 (1981).

James Harrington's Political Thought and its Context (1991).

Cromartie, Alan, 'Harringtonian Virtue: Harrington, Machiavelli, and the Method of the *Moment*', *Historical Journal* 41, 4 (1988).

Davis, J. C., 'Against Formality: One Aspect of the English Revolution', *Transactions of the Royal Historical Society*, 6th ser., 3 (1993).

'Equality in an Unequal Commonwealth: James Harrington's Republicanism and the Meaning of Equality', in Ian Gentles, John Morrill and Blair Worden (eds.), *Soldiers, Writers and Statesmen of the English Revolution* (Cambridge, 1998).

Fear, Myth and History: the Ranters and the Historians (Cambridge, 1986).

'Gerrard Winstanley and the Restoration of True Magistracy', *Past and Present* 70 (1976).

'The Levellers and Democracy', *Past and Present* 40 (1968).

'Political Thought during the English Revolution', in Barry Coward (ed.), *A Companion to Stuart Britain* (Oxford, 2003).

'Religion and the Struggle for Freedom in the English Revolution', *Historical Journal* 35, 3 (1992).

Utopia and the Ideal Society: a Study of English Utopian Writing 1516–1700 (Cambridge, 1981).

De Krey, Gary, 'Revolution *Redivivus*: 1688–1689 and the Radical Tradition in Seventeenth-Century London Politics', in L. Schwoerer (ed.), *The Revolution of 1688–1689* (Cambridge, 1992).

De Sola Pinto, V., *Peter Sterry, Platonist and Puritan 1613–1672* (Cambridge, 1934).

de Vries, Jan, and A. van der Woude, *The First Modern Economy* (Cambridge, 1997).

Diamond, Craig, 'Natural Philosophy in Harrington's Political Thought', *Journal of the History of Philosophy* 16, 4 (1978).

Donoghue, John, '"Soldiers in the Army of the Lord": Thomas Venner, Impressment, and Radical Republicanism in the Atlantic World 1636–1657', unpublished essay, University of Pittsburgh, 2003.

Dzelzainis, Martin, 'Milton and the Protectorate in 1658', in Armitage et al., *Milton*.

'Milton's Classical Republicanism', in Armitage et al., *Milton*.

Elliott, J. H., *The Old World and the New 1492–1650* (Cambridge, 1992).

Fenlon, D. B., 'England and Europe: *Utopia* and its Aftermath', *Transactions of the Royal Historical Society* (1974).

Fincham, Kenneth, and Lake, Peter, 'The Ecclesiastical Policy of King James I', *Journal of British Studies* 24, 2 (1985).

Fink, Zera S., *The Classical Republicans: an Essay in the Recovery of a Pattern of Thought in Seventeenth Century England* (Evanston, Ill., 1945).

'Milton and the Theory of Climatic Influence', *Modern Language Quarterly* 2 (1949).

Firth, C. H., *The Last Years of The Protectorate 1656–1658* (2 vols., New York, 1964).

Fitzmaurice, Andrew, 'The Civic Solution to the Crisis of English Colonization', *Historical Journal* 42, 1 (1999).

Humanism and America: an Intellectual History of English Colonisation 1500–1625 (Cambridge, 2003).

Fox, Alistair, 'Facts and Fallacies: Interpreting English Humanism', in Alistair Fox and John Guy (eds.), *Reassessing the Henrician Age: Humanism, Politics and Reform 1500–1550* (Oxford, 1986).

Fukuda, Arihiro, *Sovereignty and the Sword: Harrington, Hobbes, and Mixed Government in the English Civil Wars* (Oxford, 1997).

Gardiner, S. R., *History of England from the Accession of James I to the Outbreak of the Civil War 1603–1642* (10 vols., 1895).

Glover, Samuel Dennis, 'The Putney Debates: Popular versus Elitist Republicanism', *Past and Present* 164 (1999).

Goldie, Mark, 'The Civil Religion of James Harrington', in Anthony Pagden (ed.), *The Languages of Political Theory in Early-Modern Europe* (Cambridge, 1987).

'The Hilton Gang and the Purge of London in the 1680s', in Howard Nenner (ed.), *Politics and the Political Imagination in Later Stuart Britain* (Rochester, N.Y., 1997).

'The Roots of True Whiggism 1688–1694', *History of Political Thought* I, 2 (1980).

'The Unacknowledged Republic: Officeholding in Early Modern England', in Tim Harris (ed.), *The Politics of the Excluded, c.1500–1850* (2001).

Gooch, G. P., *Germany and the French Revolution* (1920).

Gough, J. W., 'Harrington and Contemporary Thought', *Political Science Quarterly* 45, 3 (1930).

Grafton, Anthony, 'Humanism and Political Theory', in Burns and Goldie, *The Cambridge History of Political Thought*.

New Worlds, Ancient Texts: the Power of Tradition and the Shock of Discovery (Cambridge, Mass., 1992).

'Spinoza and the Dutch Roots of the Enlightenment', Review of Jonathan Israel, *Radical Enlightenment* in *Times Literary Supplement* (9 November 2001).

Greenberg, Janelle, *The Radical Face of the Ancient Constitution: St Edward's 'Laws' in Early Modern Political Thought* (Cambridge, 2001).

Greengrass, Mark, Michael Leslie and Timothy Raylor (eds.), *Samuel Hartlib and Universal Reformation: Studies in Intellectual Communication* (Cambridge, 1994).

Grell, O., J. Israel and N. Tyacke (eds.), *From Persecution to Toleration: the Glorious Revolution and Religion in England* (1991).

Grell, Ole Peter, *Calvinist Exiles in Tudor and Stuart England* (Aldershot, 1996).

Guy, John, *Thomas More* (2000).

Haakonssen, Knud, 'Republicanism', in Robert Goodin and Philip Pettit (eds.), *A Companion to Contemporary Political Philosophy* (Oxford, 1993).

Haitsma Mulier, Eco O. G., *The Myth of Venice and Dutch Republican Thought in the Seventeenth Century* (Assen, 1980).

Haley, K. H. D., *The British and the Dutch: Political and Cultural Relations through the Ages* (1988).

The First Earl of Shaftesbury (Oxford, 1968).

Halliday, Paul, *Dismembering the Body Politic: Partisan Politics in England's Towns 1650–1730* (Cambridge, 1998).

Hammersley, Rachel, 'Camille Desmoulins's *Le Vieux Cordelier*: a Link between English and French Republicanism', *History of European Ideas* 27 (2001).

Hampsher-Monk, Iain, 'From Virtue to Politeness', in van Gelderen and Skinner, *Republicanism* vol. II.

Hankins, James, *Plato in the Italian Renaissance* (2 vols., Leiden and New York, 1990).

(ed.), *Renaissance Civic Humanism: Reappraisals and Reflections* (Cambridge, 2000).

Harris Sacks, David, 'Discourses of Western Planting: Richard Hakluyt, European Wars of Religion and the Beginnings of the British Empire', seminar paper given at Trinity Hall, Cambridge, 21 November 2001.

'The Prudence of Thrasymachus: Sir Thomas Smith and the Commonwealth of England', in Anthony Grafton and J. H. M. Salmon (eds.), *Historians and Ideologues* (Rochester, N.Y., 2001).

Hexter, J. H., 'Introduction', in *The Complete Works of St Thomas More* vol. IV, ed. S. J. Edward Surtz and J. H. Hexter (New Haven, Conn., 1965).

'Thomas More: On the Margins of Modernity', *Journal of British Studies* 1, 1 (1961).

Hill, Christopher, *The Experience of Defeat: Milton and Some Contemporaries* (1984).
Intellectual Origins of the English Revolution (Oxford, 1965).
Milton and the English Revolution (1977).
'Science, Religion and Society in the Sixteenth and Seventeenth Centuries', a debate with Hugh Kearney and Theodore Rabb, *Past and Present* 31 (1965).
The World Turned Upside Down: Radical Ideas during the English Revolution (1991).

Hindle, Steve, *The State and Social Change in Early Modern England, c.1550–1640* (Basingstoke, 2000).

Hirst, Derek, *England in Conflict* (1999).
'Locating the 1650s in England's Seventeenth Century', *History* 81, 3 (1996).
The Representative of the People? Voters and Voting in England under the Early Stuarts (Cambridge, 1975).

Holmes, Geoffrey, *The Making of a Great Power: Late Stuart and Early Georgian Britain 1660–1722* (1993).

Hoppit, Julian, *A Land of Liberty?: England 1689–1727* (Oxford, 2000).

Horst, Irvin, *The Radical Brethren: Anabaptism and the English Reformation to 1558* (Nieuwkoop, 1972).

Horwitz, Henry, *Parliament, Policy and Politics in the Reign of William III* (Manchester, 1977).

Houston, Alan Craig, *Algernon Sidney and the Republican Heritage in England and America* (Princeton, 1991).

Houston, Alan Craig, and Steven Pincus (eds.), *A Nation Transformed?* (Cambridge, 2001).

Hughes, Anne, *The Causes of the English Civil War*, 2nd edn (Basingstoke, 1998).

Hunter, Michael, 'Science and Heterodoxy: an Early Modern Problem Reconsidered', in Hunter, *Science and the Shape of Orthodoxy: Intellectual Change in Late Seventeenth-Century Britain* (Woodbridge, 1995).

Hunter, Michael, *Science and Society in Restoration England* (Cambridge, 1981).

Hutton, Ronald, Review of Houston and Pincus, *A Nation Transformed?* in *English Historical Review* 117, 472 (2001).

Innes, Stephen, *Creating the Commonwealth: the Economic Culture of Puritan New England* (1995).

Israel, Jonathan (ed.), *The Anglo-Dutch Moment: Essays on the Glorious Revolution and its World Impact* (Cambridge, 1991).
Conflicts of Empires: Spain, the Low Countries and the Struggle for World Supremacy 1585–1713 (1997).
The Dutch Republic: Its Rise, Greatness and Fall 1477–1806 (Oxford, 1995).
'The Emerging Empire: the Continental Perspective 1650–1713', in Canny, *The Origins of Empire*.
'England, the Dutch Republic, and Europe in the Seventeenth Century', *The Historical Journal* 40, 4 (1997).
Radical Enlightenment: Philosophy and the Making of Modernity, 1650–1750 (Oxford, 2001).

'Toleration in Seventeenth-Century Dutch and English Thought', in Simon Groenveld and Michael Wintle (eds.), *Britain and the Netherlands* xi: *Religion, Scholarship and Art in Anglo-Dutch Relations in the Seventeenth Century* (Zutphen, 1994).

Jacob, J. R., *Robert Boyle and the English Revolution* (New York, 1977).

Jacob, Margaret C., *The Radical Enlightenment: Pantheists, Freemasons and Republicans* (1981).

Johns, Adrian, *The Nature of the Book: Print and Knowledge in the Making* (Chicago, 1998).

Johnston, David *The Rhetoric of Leviathan* (Princeton, 1996).

Jones, J. R., *The Anglo-Dutch Wars of the Seventeenth Century* (1996).

Jones, Whitney R. D., *The Tudor Commonwealth 1529–1559: a Study of the Impact of the Social and Economic Developments of Mid-Tudor England upon Contemporary Concepts of the Nature and Duties of the Commonwealth* (1970).

Judson, Margaret, *The Political Thought of Henry Vane the Younger* (Philadelphia, 1969).

Jurdjevic, Mark, 'Virtue, Commerce, and the Enduring Florentine Republican Moment: Reintegrating Italy into the Atlantic Republican Debate', *Journal of the History of Ideas* 62, 4 (2001).

Karsten, Peter, *Patriot-Heroes in England and America* (Madison, Wisc., 1978).

Keeble, N. H., *The Literary Culture of Nonconformity in Later Seventeenth-Century England* (Athens, Ga., 1987).

Kelley, Maurice, 'Milton and Machiavelli's *Discorsi*', *SBUV* 4 (1951–2).

Kelsey, Sean, *Inventing a Republic: the Political Culture of the English Commonwealth 1649–1653* (Manchester, 1997).

Kidd, Colin, *British Identities before Nationalism: Ethnicity and Nationhood in the Atlantic World, 1600–1800* (Cambridge, 1999).

Kishlansky, Mark, *Parliamentary Selection: Social and Political Choice in Early Modern England* (Cambridge, 1986).

Klassen, P. S. *The Economics of Anabaptism 1525–1560* (The Hague, 1964).

Klein, Lawrence, *Shaftesbury and the Culture of Politeness: Moral Discourse and Cultural Politics in Early Eighteenth Century England* (Cambridge, 1994).

Koenigsberger, H. G., 'Dominium Regale or Dominium Politicum et Regale', in Koenigsberger (ed.), *Politicians and Virtuosi* (1986).

Kristeller, Paul, 'Humanism', in Charles B. Schmitt, Quentin Skinner and Eckhard Kessler (eds.), *The Cambridge History of Renaissance Philosophy* (Cambridge, 1988).

Kubik, T. R. W., 'How Far the Sword? Militia Tactics and Politics in the *Commonwealth of Oceana*', *History of Political Thought* 19, 2 (1998).

Lacey, W. K., and B. W. J. G. Wilson, *Res Publica: Roman Politics and Society According to Cicero* (Oxford, 1970).

Laydon, John Patrick, 'The Kingdom of Christ and the Princes of the Earth: the Political Uses of Apocalyptic and Millenarian Ideas in England 1648–1653', PhD. thesis, Cambridge University, 1976.

Lesses, G., 'Virtue and the Goods of Fortune in Stoic Moral Theory', *Oxford Studies in Ancient Philosophy* 7 (1989).

Levine, Joseph, *The Battle of the Books: History and Literature in the Augustan Age* (Ithaca, N.Y., 1991).

Between the Ancients and the Moderns: Baroque Culture in Restoration England (New Haven, Conn., 1999).

Lewis, C. S., *English Literature in the Sixteenth Century, Excluding Drama* (Oxford, 1973).

A Preface to Paradise Lost (Oxford, 1942).

Lichtenstein, A., *Henry More* (Cambridge, 1962).

Loach, Jennifer, *Parliament under the Tudors* (Oxford, 1991).

Loewenstein, David, *Representing Revolution in Milton and his Contemporaries* (Cambridge, 1991).

McRae, Andrew, *God Speed the Plough: the Representation of Agrarian England, 1500–1660* (Cambridge, 1996).

Mc Elligott, Gerard Jason, 'Propaganda and Censorship: the Underground Royalist Newsbooks, 1647–1650', Ph.D. thesis, Cambridge University, 2001.

Maitland, F. W., *The Collected Papers of Frederic William Maitland* vol. I, ed. H. A. L. Fisher (Cambridge, 1911).

Marshall, John, *John Locke: Resistance, Religion and Responsibility* (Cambridge, 1994).

Mayer, Thomas, *Thomas Starkey and the Commonweal: Humanist Politics and Religion in the Reign of Henry VIII* (Cambridge, 1988).

Mendle, Michael, *Dangerous Positions: Mixed Government, the Estates of the Realm, and the Making of the Answer to the XIX Propositions* (Birmingham, Ala., 1985).

Henry Parker and the English Civil War (Cambridge, 1995).

Miller, Leo, *John Milton and the Oldenburg Safeguard* (New York, 1985).

Morgan, Hiram, 'The Colonial Venture of Sir Thomas Smith in Ulster, 1571–1575', *The Historical Journal* 28 (1985).

Morrill, John, 'The Army Revolt of 1647', in Morrill, *The Nature of the English Revolution* (1993).

'Charles I and Tyranny', in Morrill, *The Nature of the English Revolution* (1993).

Morrow, John, 'Introduction', in William Godwin, *History of the Commonwealth of England*, ed. Morrow (2003).

Muldrew, Craig, *The Economy of Obligation: the Culture of Credit and Social Relations in Early Modern England* (Basingstoke, 1998).

Multamaki, Kustaa, *Towards Great Britain: Commerce and Conquest in the Thought of Algernon Sidney and Charles Davenant* (Helsinki, 1999).

Nelson, Eric, 'Greek Nonsense in More's *Utopia*', *Historical Journal* 44, 4 (2001).

'The Greek Tradition in Republican Thought', Fellowship dissertation submitted to Trinity College, Cambridge, August 2000.

Nelson, Scott, *The Discourses of Algernon Sidney* (1993).

Norbrook, David, *Writing the English Republic: Poetry, Rhetoric and Politics 1627–1660* (Cambridge, 1999).

Oestreich, G., *Neostoicism and the Early Modern State* (Cambridge, 1982).

Ormrod, David, *The Rise of Commercial Empires: England and the Netherlands in the Age of Mercantilism, 1650–1770* (Cambridge, 2003).

Packer, J. W., *The Transformation of Anglicanism* (1969).

Pagden, Anthony, *Lords of All the World: Ideologies of Empire in Spain, Britain and France c.1500–c.1800* (New Haven, Conn., 1995).

Pangle, Thomas, *The Spirit of Modern Republicanism* (Chicago, 1988).

Parker, Geoffrey, *The Military Revolution: Military Innovation and the Rise of the West 1500–1850*, 2nd edn (Cambridge, 1996).

Parker, H. T., *The Cult of Antiquity and the French Revolutionaries* (Chicago, 1937).

Parker, W. R., *Milton*, vol. 1 (Oxford, 1968).

Parnham, David, *Sir Henry Vane, Theologian: a Study in Seventeenth-Century Religious and Political Discourse* (1997).

Patterson, Annabel, *Early Modern Liberalism* (Cambridge, 1997).

Peacey, Jason, '"The Counterfeit Silly Curr": Money, Politics and the Forging of Royalist Newsbooks in the English Civil War', paper given at the National Conference on British Studies Annual Meeting, Baltimore Maryland, 9 November 2002.

Peltonen, Markku, 'Citizenship and Republicanism in Elizabethan England', in van Gelderen and Skinner, *Republicanism* vol. 1.

Classical Humanism and Republicanism in English Political Thought 1570–1640 (Cambridge, 1995).

The Duel in Early Modern England: Civility, Politeness and Honour (Cambridge, 2003).

'Politeness and Whiggism, 1688–1732', unpublished draft article.

Phillipson, Nicholas and Quentin Skinner (eds.), *Political Discourse in Early Modern Britain* (Cambridge, 1993).

Pincus, Steven, 'Neither Machiavellian Moment nor Possessive Individualism: Commercial Society and the Defenders of the English Commonwealth', *American Historical Review* (June 1998).

Protestantism and Patriotism: Ideologies and the Making of English Foreign Policy 1650–1668 (Cambridge, 1996).

Pocock, J. G. A., *The Ancient Constitution and the Feudal Law: a Study of English Historical Thought in the Seventeenth Century* (Cambridge, 1958).

The Ancient Constitution and the Feudal Law . . . A Reissue with a Retrospect (Cambridge, 1987).

Barbarism and Religion: the Enlightenments of Edward Gibbon (2 vols., Cambridge, 1998).

'A Discourse of Sovereignty', in Phillipson and Skinner, *Political Discourse.*

'England's Cato: the Virtues and Fortunes of Algernon Sidney', *Historical Journal* 37, 4 (1994).

'Historical Introduction', in *The Political Works of James Harrington*, ed. Pocock (Cambridge, 1977).

'Introduction', in James Harrington, *The Commonwealth of Oceana and A System of Politics*, ed. Pocock (Cambridge, 1992).

The Machiavellian Moment: Florentine Political Thought and the Atlantic Republican Tradition (Princeton, 1975).

Politics, Language and Time: Essays in Political Thought and History (New York, 1971).

'Spinoza and Harrington: an Exercise in Comparison', *Bijdragen en Mededelingen Betreffende de Geschiedenis der Nederlanden* 102, 3 (1987).

Virtue, Commerce and History: Essays on Political Thought and History, Chiefly in the Eighteenth Century (Cambridge, 1985).

Porter, Roy, *The Creation of the Modern World: the Untold Story of the British Enlightenment* (New York, 2000).

Powicke, F. J., *The Cambridge Platonists* (1926).

Raab, Felix, *The English Face of Machiavelli: a Changing Interpretation* (1964).

Rahe, Paul, 'Antiquity Surpassed: the Repudiation of Classical Republicanism', in Wootton, *Republicanism*.

Rahe, Paul, 'Marchamont Nedham and the Origins of Liberal Republicanism', paper given at the Annual Meeting of the American Political Science Association, Philadelphia, 31 August 2003.

Republics Ancient and Modern (3 vols., Chapel Hill, N.C., 1994): *Volume I: The Ancien Regime in Classical Greece; Volume II: New Modes and Orders in Early Modern Political Thought*.

'Situating Machiavelli', in Hankins, ed. *Ranaissance Civic Humanism*.

Ranke, Leopold von, *A History of England Principally in the Seventeenth Century* (6 vols., Oxford, 1875).

Reeve, John, *Charles I and the Road to Personal Rule* (Cambridge, 1989).

Reinhard, Wolfgang (ed.), *Power Elites and State Building* (Oxford, 1996).

Richards, Jennifer, *Rhetoric and Courtliness in Early Modern Literature* (Cambridge, 2003)

Robbins, Caroline, 'Algernon Sidney's *Discourses Concerning Government*: Textbook of Revolution', *William and Mary Quarterly*, 3rd ser., 4 (1947).

The Eighteenth Century Commonwealthsman (New Haven, Conn., 1959).

'Henry Neville, 1620–94', in Robbins, *Two English Republican Tracts*.

Robinson, F. G., *The Shape of Things Known* (Cambridge, Mass., 1922).

Rodger, N. A. M., *The Safeguard of the Sea* (New York, 1997).

Rodgers, Daniel, 'Republicanism: the Career of a Concept', *Journal of American History* 79 (June 1992).

Roseveare, Henry, 'Prejudice and Policy: Sir George Downing as Parliamentary Entrepreneur', in D. C. Coleman and Peter Mathias (eds.), *Enterprise and History: Essays in Honour of Charles Wilson* (Cambridge, 1986).

Rubenstein, Nicolai, 'Italian Political Thought 1450–1530', in Burns and Goldie, *The Cambridge History of Political Thought*.

Russell, Bertrand, *History of Western Philosophy* (1946).

Russell, Conrad, *Parliaments and English Politics 1621–1629* (Oxford, 1979).

'Parliaments and the English State at the End of the Sixteenth Century', first Trevelyan Lecture given at the University of Cambridge, 1995.

Russell Smith, H. F., *Harrington and his Oceana: a Study of a Seventeenth Century Utopia and its Influence in America* (New York, 1971).

Salmon, J. H. M., *The French Religious Wars in English Political Thought* (Cambridge, 1959; repr. Westport, Conn., 1981).

Renaissance and Revolt (Cambridge, 1987).

Salt, Peter, 'Charles I: a Bad King?', unpublished paper.

Samuel, Irene, *Plato and Milton* (Ithaca, N.Y., 1947).

Sanderson, John, *"But the People's Creatures": the Philosophical Basis of the English Civil War* (Manchester, 1989).

Savonius, Sami-Juhani, 'Jean Le Clerc's and John Locke's *Kulturkampf* against Authoritarianism, 1688–1702', seminar paper given at Trinity Hall, Cambridge, 27 February 2002.

'John Locke and the Civil Philosophy of the *Bibliothecaires* circa 1688–circa 1702', Ph.D. thesis, Cambridge University, 2002.

Schenck, W., *The Concern for Social Justice in the Puritan Revolution* (1948).

Scherpbier, H., *Milton in Holland: a Study in the Literary Relations of England and Holland before 1730* (Amsterdam, 1969).

Scott, Jonathan, *Algernon Sidney and the English Republic 1623–1677* (Cambridge, 1998).

Algernon Sidney and the Restoration Crisis 1677–1683 (Cambridge, 1991).

'Classical Republicanism in Seventeenth-Century England and the Netherlands', in van Gelderen and Skinner, *Republicanism*, vol. I.

England's Troubles: Seventeenth-Century English Political Instability in European Context (Cambridge, 2000).

'England's Troubles: Exhuming the Popish Plot', in Tim Harris, Paul Seaward and Mark Goldie (eds.), *The Politics of Religion in Restoration England* (Oxford, 1990).

'The English Republican Imagination', in J. S. Morrill (ed.), *Revolution and Restoration: England in the 1650s* (1992).

'"Good Night Amsterdam." Sir George Downing and Anglo-Dutch Statebuilding', *English Historical Review* 118, 476 (2003).

'The Law of War: Grotius, Sidney, Locke and the Political Theory of Rebellion', *History of Political Thought* 13, 4 (1992).

'The Peace of Silence: Thucydides and the English Civil War', in Miles Fairburn and W. H. Oliver (eds.), *The Certainty of Doubt: Tributes to Peter Munz* (Wellington, 1996).

'The Peace of Silence: Thucydides and the English Civil War', amended version, in G. A. J. Rogers and Tom Sorell (eds.), *Hobbes and History* (2000).

'Radicalism and Restoration: the Shape of the Stuart Experience', *Historical Journal* 31, 2 (1988).

'The Rapture of Motion: James Harrington's Republicanism', in Phillipson and Skinner, *Political Discourse*.

Review of Fukuda, *Sovereignty and the Sword*, in *English Historical Review*, 115, 462 (2000).

Review of Hindle, *The State and Social Change* and Braddick, *State Formation*, in *English Historical Review*, 116, 469 (2001).

Review of Peltonen, *Classical Humanism*, Armitage et al., *Milton*, and Sidney, *Court Maxims*, in *English Historical Review* 112, 448 (1997).

Review of Wootton, *Republicanism*, in *Parliamentary History* 16, 2 (1997).

'What the Dutch Taught Us: the Late Emergence of the Modern British State', *Times Literary Supplement* (16 March 2001) pp. 4–6.

Seaberg, R. B., 'The Norman Conquest and the Common Law: the Levellers and the Argument from Continuity', *Historical Journal* 24, 4 (1981).

Shackleton, R., 'Montesquieu and Machiavelli: a Reappraisal', *Comparative Literature Studies* 1 (1964).

Sharpe, Kevin, *The Personal Rule of Charles I* (New Haven, Conn., 1992).

Skinner, Quentin, 'Classical Liberty, Renaissance Translation and the English Civil War', in Skinner, *Visions of Politics, Volume II: Renaissance Virtues* (Cambridge, 2002).

'Conquest and Consent: Thomas Hobbes and the Engagement Controversy', in G. E. Aylmer (ed.), *The Interregnum: the Quest for Settlement 1646–1660* (1974).

The Foundations of Modern Political Thought (2 vols., Cambridge, 1978).

'Introduction: the Reality of the Renaissance', in Skinner, *Visions of Politics, Volume II: Renaissance Virtues* (Cambridge, 2002).

Liberty before Liberalism (Cambridge, 1998).

Reason and Rhetoric in the Philosophy of Hobbes (Cambridge, 1996).

'A Reply to My Critics', in James Tully (ed.), *Meaning and Context: Quentin Skinner and his Critics* (Princeton, 1988).

'The Republican Ideal of Political Liberty', in Gisela Bock, Quentin Skinner and Maurizio Viroli (eds.), *Machiavelli and Republicanism* (Cambridge, 1990).

'Sir Thomas More's *Utopia* and the Language of Renaissance Humanism', in A. Pagden (ed.), *The Languages of Political Theory in Early Modern Europe* (Cambridge, 1987).

'A Third Concept of Liberty', *London Review of Books* (4 April 2002).

Visions of Politics, Volume I: Regarding Method (Cambridge, 2002).

Smith, Nigel, *Literature and Revolution in England 1640–1660* (New Haven, Conn., 1994).

'*Paradise Lost* from Civil War to Restoration', in N. H. Keeble (ed.), *Writing of the English Revolution* (Cambridge, 2001).

'Popular Republicanism in the 1650s: John Streater's "Heroick Mechanicks"', in Armitage et al. *Milton*.

Sommerville, Johann, 'James I and the Divine Right of Kings', in Linda Levy Peck (ed.), *The Mental World of the Jacobean Court* (Cambridge, 1991).

Spufford, Peter, 'Access to Credit and Capital in the Commercial Centres of Europe', in Karel Davids and Jan Lucassen (eds.), *A Miracle Mirrored: the Dutch Republic in European Perspective* (Cambridge, 1995).

Stayer, James, *The German Peasants War and Anabaptist Community of Goods* (Montreal, 1991).

Stein, Arnold, *Heroic Knowledge* (Minneapolis, Minn., 1957).

Strauss, Leo, *The Political Philosophy of Hobbes* (Chicago, 1952).

Review of Fink, *Classical Republicans, Social Research* 13, 3 (1946).

Sullivan, Vickie, 'Algernon Sidney: Machiavellian Republican and Ambivalent Liberal', paper given at the Annual Meeting of the American Political Science Association, Philadelphia, 31 August 2003.

'The Civic Humanist Portrait of Machiavelli's English Successors', *History of Political Thought* 15, 1 (1994).

Taft, Barbara, 'That Lusty Puss, the Good Old Cause', *History of Political Thought* 5, 3 (1984).

'T Hart, Marjolein, '"The Devil or the Dutch": Holland's Impact on the Financial Revolution in England, 1643–1694', *Parliaments, Estates and Representation* 11, 1 (1991).

Tawney, R. H., 'Harrington's Interpretation of his Age', *Proceedings of the British Academy* 27 (1941).

Thirsk, Joan, 'Younger Sons in the Seventeenth Century', *History* 54 (1969).

Thomas, Keith, 'The Levellers and the Franchise', in G. E. Aylmer (ed.), *The Interregnum: the Quest for Settlement 1646–1660* (1972).

Tilly, Charles (ed.), *The Formation of Nation States in Western Europe* (Princeton, 1975).

Todd, Margo, *Christian Humanism and the Puritan Social Order* (Cambridge, 1987).

Trevor-Roper, H. R., 'The Gentry 1540–1640', *Economic History Review Supplements* no. 1 (Cambridge, 1953).

Tubb, Amos, 'The Ecstasy and the Agony: Royalist Newsbooks in the Aftermath of the Execution of Charles I', paper given at the National Conference on British Studies Annual Meeting, Baltimore, Maryland 9 November 2002.

Tuck, Richard, 'The Civil Religion of Thomas Hobbes', in Phillipson and Skinner, *Political Discourse*.

'Grotius and Selden', in Burns and Goldie, *The Cambridge History of Political Thought*.

Natural Rights Theories (Cambridge, 1979).

Philosophy and Government 1572–1651 (Cambridge, 1993).

Tyacke, Nicholas (ed.), *England's Long Reformation 1500–1800* (1998).

Underdown, David, 'The Harringtonian Moment', *Journal of British Studies* 18, 2 1979.

Pride's Purge: Politics in the Puritan Revolution (1985).

van Gelderen, Martin, 'The Machiavellian Moment and the Dutch Revolt: the Rise of Neostoicism and Dutch Republicanism', in Gisela Bock, Quentin Skinner and Maurizio Viroli (eds.), *Machiavelli and Republicanism* (Cambridge, 1990).

The Political Thought of the Dutch Revolt 1555–1590 (Cambridge, 1993).

van Gelderen, Martin, and Quentin Skinner (eds.), *Republicanism: a Shared European Heritage* (2 vols., Cambridge, 2002).

Viroli, Maurizio, *From Politics to Reason of State: the Acquisition and Transformation of a Language of Politics 1250–1600* (Cambridge, 1992).

von Maltzahn, Nicholas, 'Dating the Digression in Milton's *History of Britain*', *Historical Journal* 36, 4 (1993).

Milton's History of Britain (Oxford, 1991).

'The Whig Milton, 1667–1700', in Armitage et al., *Milton*.

Walker, William, '*Paradise Lost* and the Forms of Government', *History of Political Thought* 22, 2 (2001).

Webster, Samuel, *The Great Instauration: Science, Medicine and Reform, 1626–1660* (1975).

Wedgwood, C. V., *The Trial of Charles I* (1964).

Weir, Robert, '"Shaftesbury's Darling": British Settlement in the Carolinas at the Close of the Seventeenth Century', in Canny, *The Origins of Empire*.

West, Thomas, 'Foreword', in Sidney, *Discourses* ed. West.

White, Thomas, 'Pride and the Public Good: Thomas More's Use of Plato in *Utopia*', *Journal of the History of Philosophy* 20, 4 (1982).

Williams, G. H., *The Radical Reformation* (1962).

Wilson, Charles, *Anglo-Dutch Commerce and Finance in the Eighteenth Century* (Cambridge, 1941 repr. 1966).

Profit and Power: a Study of England and the Dutch Wars (1957).

Woolf, D. R., T*he Idea of History in Early Stuart England* (Toronto, 1990).

'In Praise of Older Things: Notions of Age and Antiquity in Early Modern England', in Anthony Grafton and J. H. M Salmon (eds.), *Historians and Ideologues* (Rochester, N.Y., 2001).

Woolrych, Austin, *Britain in Revolution 1625–1660* (Oxford, 2002).

Commonwealth to Protectorate (Oxford, 1982).

'Dating Milton's *History of Britain*', *Historical Journal* 36, 4 (1993).

'The Good Old Cause and the Fall of the Protectorate', *Cambridge Historical Journal* 13, 2 (1957).

'Historical Introduction', John Milton, *Complete Prose Works, Volume VII: 1659–1660*, rev. edn (New Haven, Conn., 1980).

Wootton, David (ed.), *Republicanism, Liberty and Commercial Society 1649–1776* (Stanford, 1994).

'"Ulysses Bound": Venice and the Idea of Liberty from Howell to Hume', in Wootton, *Republicanism*.

Worden, Blair, 'Ben Jonson among the Historians', in Peter Lake and Kevin Sharpe (eds.), *Culture and Politics in Early Stuart England* (Basingstoke, 1994).

'Classical Republicanism and the Puritan Revolution', in V. Pearl, H. Lloyd-Jones and B. Worden (eds.), *History and Imagination* (Oxford, 1981).

'The Commonwealth Kidney of Algernon Sidney', *Journal of British Studies* 24 (January 1985).

'English Republicanism', in Burns and Goldie, *The Cambridge History of Political Thought*.

'Introduction', in Edmund Ludlow, *A Voyce From the Watch Tower Part Five 1660–1662*, ed. Worden (1978).

'James Harrington and *The Commonwealth of Oceana*, 1656', in Wootton, *Republicanism*.

'John Milton and Oliver Cromwell', in Ian Gentles, John Morrill and Blair Worden (eds.), *Soldiers, Writers and Statesmen of the English Revolution* (Cambridge, 1998).

'Marchamont Nedham and the Beginnings of English Republicanism, 1649–1656', in Wootton, *Republicanism*.

'Milton, *Samson Agonistes*, and the Restoration', in Gerald MacLean (ed.), *Culture and Society in the Stuart Restoration* (Cambridge, 1995).

'Milton's Republicanism and the Tyranny of Heaven', in Gisela Bock, Quentin Skinner and Maurizio Viroli (eds.), *Machiavelli and Republicanism* (Cambridge, 1990).

'*Oceana*: Origins and Aftermath', in Wootton, *Republicanism*.

'Oliver Cromwell and the Sin of Aachan', in D. Beales and G. Best (eds.), *History, Society and the Churches* (1985).

'The Politics of Marvell's Horation Ode', *Historical Journal* 27, 3 (1984).

'The Question of Secularization', in Houston and Pincus, *A Nation Transformed?*

'Republicanism, Regicide and Republic: the English Experience', in van Gelderen and Skinner, *Republicanism* vol. 1.

'Republicanism and the Restoration, 1660–1683', in Wootton, *Republicanism*.

Review of Skinner, *Liberty before Liberalism*, in *London Review of Books* (5 February 1998).

'The Revolution of 1688–9 and the English Republican Tradition', in Israel, *The Anglo-Dutch Moment*.

Roundhead Reputations: the English Civil Wars and the Passions of Posterity (2001).

The Rump Parliament (Cambridge, 1977).

The Sound of Virtue: Philip Sidney's Arcadia and Elizabethan Politics (New Haven, Conn., 1996).

'"Wit in a Roundhead": the Dilemma of Marchamont Nedham', in Susan Amussen and Mark Kishlansky (eds.), *Political Culture and Cultural Politics in Early Modern England* (Manchester, 1995).

Wrightson, Keith, *Earthly Necessities: Economic Lives in Early Modern Britain* (New Haven, Conn., 2000).

Zagorin, Perez, *A History of Political Thought in the English Revolution* (1954).

Milton: Aristocrat and Rebel: the Poet and his Politics (Rochester, N.Y., 1992).

Zetzel, James, 'Introduction', in Cicero, *On the Commonwealth and On the Laws*, ed. Zetzel (Cambridge, 1999).

Index